INVENTORY 1985

SEVEN PLAYS
by
BERTOLT BRECHT

SEVEN PLAYS BY BERTOLT BRECHT

Edited and with an introduction by
Eric Bentley

GROVE PRESS, INC.
NEW YORK

CONTENTS

ACKNOWLEDGMENTS

Mr. Charles Laughton and Mr. Frank Jones kindly gave permission for the use of their work.

The following made helpful suggestions on particular points of translation: Mr. W. H. Auden, Mr. Martin Esslin, Mr. Theodore Hoffman, Mr. Frank Jones, and Mr. Louis Simpson.

Dr. Evert Sprinchorn kindly supplied a summary of two books by J. V. Jensen.

A special word of thanks is due to Dr. Hugo Schmidt for his systematic criticism of my own translations of *Mann ist Mann* and *Im Dickicht der Städte* (*In the Swamp*).

The present adaptation of *Mother Courage* was commissioned by the Broadway producers, Lee Paton and Robert Welber. Suggestions for it were made not only by them but also by their stage director, David Brooks, their composer, Darius Milhaud, their musical director, Samuel Matlowski, their star, Katina Paxinou, and their designers, Teo Otto and Mordecai Gorelik.

The present adaptation of *The Good Woman of Setzuan* was commissioned for production at the Royal Court Theatre in London and the Phoenix Theatre in New York. Thanks are due to both managements. Of the many persons who made valuable suggestions, I cannot but mention George Devine and Uta Hagen.

Mr. Leo Kerz gave me encouragement without which I might never have completed my translations of either *Mother Courage* or *A Man's a Man*.

Mr. R. P. Blackmur invited me to give six lectures on Brecht, as part of the Christian Gauss Seminars at Princeton University, in the spring of 1960. I think this was the first "course" on Brecht to be given in any institution, East or West. It enabled me to rough out a book on the subject. The present *Homage to B. B.* represents my work in progress.

Finally, I wish to thank Mr. Barney Rosset. There's a lot of prattle in America about enterprise. Barney Rosset, so far as my personal acquaintance goes, is one of the few enterprising Americans.

E. B.

A NOTE ON
THE PRESENT ENGLISH VERSIONS
AND THE MUSIC FOR THE PLAYS

Though there is no agreement among professionals as to the right way of bringing a play over from one language to another — in fact, *because* there is no such agreement — the public should be told, in each particular case, what it is getting. Above all: is it getting what purports to be a very close rendering of the original or what is admittedly a very free rendering?

Four of the versions in this book are close renderings. Three (*Galileo, The Good Woman of Setzuan,* and *Mother Courage*) are not.

I am myself uncertain what is the best approach to the translating of Brecht. A good play can be translated in more ways than one—and should be translated more than once, as some of Brecht's plays already have been. The reader will probably be glad that more than one approach is exhibited in this volume.

Anyone wishing to check the English against the original should be warned that a Brecht translator often has his choice of several alternative readings, corresponding to different German *mss.* and editions. Except in the case of the three freer renderings, a note before each play in the present book indicates what German text has been followed.

On the title page of each play is recorded the date when the original play was written. These dates, naturally, are different from the dates of first publication and first performance.

Every play in this volume calls for some degree of singing, though not even the words are indicated for the song mentioned in *In the Swamp* (opening of Scene 3).

A Man's a Man once had music by Kurt Weill, which now seems to have disappeared. A revised German version of the play has music by Paul Dessau. In the present English text, the song "A

Man's a Man" goes with the anonymous music printed in the first German edition (Arcadia Verlag, 1926).

There is as yet no score for the English text of *Saint Joan of the Stockyards*.

Hanns Eisler's score for *Galileo* was originally made for the English version, not the German original. It has been published, however, with the German words only (in Eisler's *Lieder und Kantaten*).

The score Paul Dessau made for the German *Good Woman of Setzuan* was also used in the London and New York productions. But a score specially composed for the English lyrics by Stefan Wolpe is now generally used by English-language producers.

The Dessau music for the German *Mother Courage* has been used up to now in the various English-language productions, but the lyrics of the present adaptation were written for a score by Darius Milhaud.

The English lyrics to *The Caucasian Chalk Circle* do not fit the score which Dessau made for the German lyrics. There have been several American scores, however, which were specially composed for the English words. The one most widely used is by Myron Fink.

E. B.

INTRODUCTION: HOMAGE TO B. B.
BY ERIC BENTLEY

Those great poets, for example, men like Byron, Musset, Poe, Leopardi, Kleist, Gogol . . . are and must be men of the moment, sensual, absurd, fivefold, irresponsible, and sudden in mistrust and trust; with souls in which they must usually conceal some fracture; often taking revenge with their works for some inner contamination, often seeking with their high flights to escape into forgetfulness from an all-too-faithful memory; idealists from the vicinity of *swamps*. . . .

— NIETZSCHE
translated by Walter Kaufmann

Art, life, and politics are inseparable and at the same time in conflict.

— BLOK
translated by I. Freiman

PRELIMINARY

Brecht, 1960. A writer, as Aristotle might say, is either fashionable or unfashionable. Neither condition is desirable. To be fashionable is to be celebrated for the wrong reasons, and to be unfashionable is not to be celebrated at all.

In the past ten years, Bertolt Brecht has passed from the depths of unrecognition to the heights of a chic celebrity. Such a change is not without interest to the gossip columnist or even the social historian. To the serious reader — and to the serious theatregoer if he exists — it is a bore. And in the history of the drama it is just a bad thing: Brecht has died, and what we have chosen to inherit is a cult, an *ism.*

Is it so long since the same thing happened to Ibsen? For half a century, a foggy phenomenon called Ibsenism, and many plays distinguished only for their Ibsenism, have stood in the way of Henrik Ibsen. Only after many years was any favorable change discernible, and by 1960 it was possible for Raymond Williams to write: "Ibsenism is dead, and Ibsen is very much alive."

Alas, poor Brecht! He stands where Ibsen stood in 1910: he is dead, and Brechtism is very much alive. But history need not repeat itself. War can be waged on Brechtism in the name of Brecht. More shrewdly: the cult of Brecht might be exploited to arouse a deeper interest in the work of Brecht. The coming of the cult has this to be said for it, that the old air of secrecy has gone. Brecht's works are at least there to be read. There is even such a thing as Brecht scholarship. And a real discussion of Brecht could and did begin when Martin Esslin and Ernest Borneman broke through the taboos by which the priests of the cult hoped to keep their idol holy, if unreal.

The errors that have been promoted by the cultists (and the dilettantes) will be exposed gradually as genuine criticism proceeds. But one error needs pointing out in advance, as it is shared by the enemies of the cultists, particularly by the critic whom the cult has most infuriated, Herbert Luethy. This is the notion that there are two Brechts, who correspond to the period before his conversion to Marxism (1928) and the period after. To Mr.

Luethy, the early Brecht is a good thing, the later a bad, just as to many Communists and fellow-travelers, the early Brecht is a bad thing, the later a good.

It would be strange indeed if a poet could cut his creative life so neatly in half. I believe that one can only get the impression that Brecht did so if one is blinded by political prejudice. If Brecht had a divided nature, it was — as the word *nature* implies — divided all his life long. Such a division is discernible in every major play. Otherwise, the lifework of Brecht has a most impressive unity: what is found in the late plays is found in the early ones, and *vice versa*. This is not to say that there is no development, nor is it to deny that Brecht *attempted* something like the total change which the doctrinaires on both sides attribute to him. One might say he providentially failed in this attempt. More probably, he surely if dimly knew what he was doing. Behind the attempt to change was the knowledge that one cannot — and a wily, conniving refusal to go to all lengths in attempting the impossible. This is speculation about the fact of unity in Brecht's work. About the fact itself there can be little doubt.

Necessary to the appreciation of this fact is the discovery or rediscovery of the early plays, particularly *Baal* and *In the Swamp*.

IN THE SWAMP

Emotional Dynamics. Brecht's later plays were so unconventionally constructed that the dramatic critics, being the men they are, were bound to think them badly constructed. *In the Swamp* is well-constructed and, for all the absence of act divisions, is constructed in a fairly conventional way. Brecht's originality shows less in the over-arching main structure than in the details of his rendering of the emotions and their dynamics.

The word *dynamics* may at first seem inapplicable because the subject is passivity. But human passivity has its own negative dynamics — as has a donkey that refuses to budge, a possum that pretends to be dead, or a poodle that begs to be whipped. It would be arbitrary to assume that there is less drama in cessation than in initiation, in refusal than acceptance, in surrender than resistance. Nor is the passive man consistently passive. He is passive so much that occasionally he has to be the opposite. He overcompensates for inaction by action that is rash, sudden, and extreme. No lack of dynamics here! Combining the negative dynamics of refusal with the insane lunges of passivity interrupted, the young Brecht makes a drama out of apparently undramatic materials. Very modern materials. Critics have not been slow to see the connection between the Brecht of 1920 and the plays of Beckett in the fifties. If only Beckett had a quarter of Brecht's constructive power! It seems to me that the later author, for all his true theatricality, could not find the emotional dynamics to animate a full-length play. . . .

Speaking of the aggressions of the passive type of person, the works of Brecht embody aggressions of colossal proportions, and make a special appeal to persons who harbor such aggressions of their own. I have known many Brechtians intimately: one and all persons positively possessed by aggression. This is something to think about when you read some of the current French and British Brechtians, who can give their writing a coolness of tone that accords with the theories of the Meister. Those theories came into being to create such a rational coolness of tone — and conceal the heat and irrationality of the aggressive impulse.

The Menagerie of Bertolt Brecht. Between the art of Bertolt Brecht and the discussion of that art, a great gulf has been fixed. Maybe it was Brecht who fixed it by becoming a Marxist and letting us know about his art, even his early art, only in Marxist terms. Hence, for example, if you read about Mackie the Knife in Brecht's Notes, you would expect anything but the Mackie the Knife of Brecht's own play. The Notes are about capitalism and the world around us. The play shows . . . well, what? If this type of figure must be characterized in one word, that word will have to be *grotesque*. Yes, a grotesque figure may *represent* capitalism and the world around us, but here we are changing the subject to the author's intentions. What has he *done*? He has created a group of grotesques. This creation in no way results from Marxism; it antedates Brecht's reading of Marx. What one should rather observe is the way in which Brecht, when he joins the Left, brings his menagerie with him. All he has to do is rename his jackals Capitalists.

By this time (1960), there are many people who approve of Brecht on the ground that he was a Communist. But is that why they are attracted to his work? Rather, he is approved for one reason and enjoyed for another. Some of the enjoyment may indeed be rather improper, almost illicit. An unbeatable combination!

Amerika. The menagerie is all complete in *In the Swamp.* In Garga and Shlink we already hear the sentiments and accents of Peachum. Worm and Baboon are our first Brechtian henchmen. The nickelodeon plays *Ave Maria,* a Salvation Army officer shoots himself after uttering the last words of Frederick the Great, and a lynch gang goes into action at the bidding of the police! It is the Amerika that was discovered not by C. C. but by B. B. It is the Amerika of *Mahagonny* and *The Seven Deadly Sins.*

Homosexuality. The modern subject *par excellence?* Yet still an unusual subject for a play when Brecht wrote *In the Swamp;* and it seems that people can read this play and miss it. They miss a lot. If homosexuality is not talked about, it is as fully implicit as in Genet's *Deathwatch.*

There is candor and candor. If homosexuality is now a standard subject of sentimental commercial literature, that literature can be trusted to impose its own limitations on the subject as it did on previous "daring" subjects. For example, Broadway plays on the theme only permit us to *discover* that the hero is homosexual just as older plays let us discover that the unmarried heroine was pregnant.

Homosexuality can appear in commercial culture only by way of pathetic romance. A homosexual disposition is accepted as arbitrarily *there.* Society is "arraigned" for its failure to see this. Here, as it were, is a group of people who prefer strawberries to raspberries, and society has made the eating of strawberries illegal: pathos! Brecht on the other hand, while he doesn't tag characters with clinical labels, reaches what clinicians will recognize as the big facts.

One reason the treatment of homosexuality seems not very

explicit in *In the Swamp* is that the author clearly puts sex in its place — the place for this kind of sex being entitled Masochism. As in Genet, eros is subordinated to the struggle for power; in which struggle Brecht's characters tend to wish to lose.

Nihilism: a Query. Discussions of Brecht's philosophy — of this period *or later* — would gain from an understanding of his emotions and attitudes. His philosophy as of this period is always described as Nihilism. But is Nihilism a philosophy? Is it not rather an emotional attitude in a philosophically-minded person? The philosophy is pessimistic, but pessimism becomes nihilist only when espoused with resentment and rage. Nihilists are destroyers, though to study particular nihilists is often to find that they were very passive men. Are they men who become active only in destruction? And when they are converted to Causes which make high moral claims, can their Nihilism be discarded as a mere opinion?

A MAN'S A MAN

A New Brecht. The protagonists of the earlier plays — Baal, Kragler, and Garga — were mouthpieces for Brecht's own yearnings and agonies. We are still not as far as he liked to think from the agonized-ecstatic dramas of the Expressionists. With *A Man's a Man* emerges the Brecht the world knows. The transition is rather an abrupt one, and I wonder that more has not been made of it. Formally speaking, it could be taken as a switch from tragedy to comedy. Brecht's final attitude would be vehemently anti-tragic. The new-fangled notion of Epic Theatre can be construed as a synonym for traditional Comedy.

Influences. None, luckily, are as marked as those of Rimbaud and Büchner on *Baal* and *In the Swamp*. Yet surely Charlie Chaplin runs these pretty close. It would be hard to prove this, of course, though Brecht's admiration of Chaplin is a matter of record, and the latter's influence is obvious enough in such later plays as *Puntila* and *Schweyk in World War II*. As far as *A Man's a Man* is concerned, one needn't stress Chaplin individually: I would judge the influence to be that of American silent movie comedy in general. It was this influence (among others) that enabled Brecht to write, as he already wished to, much more impersonally. He was able to dispel the Expressionistic penumbra, and draw his own creatures on white paper, as it were, in hard black lines. Georg Grosz may have been as valuable to him as Chaplin.

Later Revisions. He succeeded so well that later he was able to believe that *A Man's a Man* was Marxist before the fact: all it needed was a few extra touches, and it would be the model anti-capitalist and anti-war play. The extra touches involved the omission of the superb final scenes (10, 11), and hence the blurring of the crucial Bloody Five-Galy Gay relationship. It was perhaps the puritanism of his Communist friends that made Brecht omit the castration episode (as it certainly made him tone down or omit the racier jokes). Brecht's famous revisions were usually doctrinaire and were seldom improvements.

Structure. The first version of *A Man's a Man* has a very clear structure. The accident to Jip provides only the point of departure. At the center of the action is Uriah. It is Uriah who decides that, since men are all interchangeable, Jip can be replaced: it is just a matter of picking out Galy Gay, making sure that Jesse and Polly go along, and then keeping at it. While Uriah conducts his experiment on Galy Gay, Bloody Five conducts one on himself. What's in a name? — the phrase would make a good title for the play. Bloody Five changes into a civilian at the bidding of Widow Begbick. His humiliations in the role persuade him to change back again and cling to the name Bloody Five at any cost. "It is not important that I eat; it is important that I am Bloody Five." Well, Bloody is successful by his own standard, but Galy Gay is even more successful by drawing the opposite conclusion: one shouldn't make a "fuss about a name" and "it is very important that I eat." Final Curtain.

Pirandello. Within this clear structure, there are some less clear, but no less fascinating, things, such as the one piece of spoken verse in the play (Scene 9, Sixth Number), in which Brecht goes far beyond a sociological statement and enters the depths of personal confusion. Indeed, the whole of the Fourth and Sixth Numbers bears witness to a very intimate kind of distress concerning lack of identity, and the vehicle that Brecht finds to carry the sense is singularly Pirandellian:

URIAH: Fire!
    GALY GAY *falls in a faint.*
POLLY: Stop! He fell all by himself!
URIAH: Shoot! So he'll hear he's dead!
    They shoot.

Is A Man's a Man *Topical?* In some ways, not. As of 1960, our Galy Gays wouldn't be so easily persuaded that war is pleasant. In some ways, too, this play was old-fashioned even in 1925. The imperialism envisaged seems to be that of the nineties ("We're soldiers of the Queen, my lads"), of jingoism, and the days when swords still had glamour, and Orientals seemed to some a lesser breed without the law.

The play belongs to the era of Georg Kaiser's critique of the Machine Age — man dwarfed by his machinery and caught in it — whereas in 1960 Professor Galbraith tells us that the machine is on the decline and that in the Affluent Society persons will be important. This last argument, however, is not really damaging to *A Man's a Man*, for *in what way* are our new managers and executives important? As organization men — as interchangeable ciphers. In their world, Bertolt Brecht's message is still pertinent: a man is most definitely a man.

Martin Esslin has remarked that the play is a prophecy of brainwashing. A good point, but the fable of brainwashing is combined, at least in the first and best version, with one that contradicts it: a fable of a sorcerer's apprentice or Frankenstein's monster. Uriah's brainwashing of Galy Gay can hardly be deemed successful if then Galy Gay eats Uriah's rations! Perhaps the right conclusion is that Brecht's fable happily transcends the topical applications that will crop up from time to time. Of the latter, here is one from *The Nation,* June 11, 1960:

Rockefeller, the most intellectual advocate of strong Civil Defense, detailed his argument in the April, 1960, issue of

Foreign Affairs . . . Rockefeller's words harmonize with the ponderous theorizing of other *Foreign Affairs* contributors who talk in terms of numbers and percentages instead of horror and anguish, as if war were a chess game. . . . When we concentrate on numbers, survival, and victory, as Rockefeller does, and drive from our minds visions of writhing bodies and screaming flesh, then war becomes thinkable. . . .

Cruelty. It would be hasty to imagine that, in finding his own genre, Brecht could change his emotional system. The emotional patterns of *In the Swamp* are found in the later plays in this or that disguise.

The Brechtian world revolves about an axis which has sadism and masochism as its north and south poles. In one play after another, Brecht saw the humaneness in human nature swamped out by inhumanity, by the cruelty of what he at first thought of as the universe and later as capitalist society. The standard ending of Brecht plays is the total victory of this cruelty. If, near the end of *Days of the Commune*, he indicates in a song that the workers may do better later on, the fact remains that he chose as his subject a classic defeat. *In Brecht's world, badness is active, while goodness is usually passive*. That antithesis is well rendered in *A Man's a Man* in Uriah and Galy Gay. It will be the making of the split good-and-bad ladies of *The Seven Deadly Sins* and *The Good Woman of Setzuan*. And, as Ernest Borneman has added, the passivity is not simply good, it has its perverse aspect — Galy Gay relishes his humiliations.

At the end of *King Lear*, Kent sees the world as a rack on which human beings are stretched. That's Brechtian. People talk of the lack of emotion in his plays. Perhaps they mean in his theory of his plays, or perhaps they mean the lack of pleasant emotions. Being tortured is a violent emotional experience, and Brecht's characters, from the earliest plays on, live (it is his own metaphor, taken from Rimbaud) in an inferno. Shlink is lynched, Bloody Five castrates himself, Galy Gay is brainwashed. . . . What of the later plays written (we are told) in the spirit of rationalistic positivism and permitting the audience to keep cool? Self-castration occurs again in *The Private Tutor*. *The Good Woman* is the story of the rending asunder, all but literally, of a young woman. In *Courage*, we watch a mother lose all three children by the deliberate brutality of men. In *Galileo* (as not in actual history), everything hinges on the threat of physical torture. Though torture cannot very well (*pace* Shakespeare) be shown on stage, Brecht devised scenes which suggest great physical violence without showing it and push mental torment to the limits of the bearable.

Are we to take plays like *A Man's a Man* and *Mahagonny* as forecasts of the Nazi regime or even as comment on the already active Nazi movement? If so, we shall have to characterize as "Nazis" certain characters in the very earliest Brecht plays. The fact is that if the Nazis had never existed, Brecht would have invented them.

The scene in which Mother Courage is asked to identify the corpse of her son is thought by some to derive straight from such incidents in recent history — one of which is shown directly by Brecht in "The Zinc Box" (*The Private Life of the Master Race*). But is not the essence of the matter already present in that scene in *A Man's a Man* where the corpse of Galy Gay is supposed to be in a crate and the actual (or former) Galy Gay makes a tormented speech about it?

Brecht the stage director was always insisting that the perpetrators of cruelty not be presented demonstratively. Instead of gesticulating and declaiming, they were to be businesslike, "sachlich." The actors usually found the reason for this in "the Brecht style," "the alienation-effect and all that," but what Brecht chiefly wanted was to make the cruelty real instead of stagey. And he had in mind a different sort of cruelty from that which the average actor would tend to think of — the cruelty of men who live by cruelty and by little else, men who can order tortures as matter-of-factly as an actor orders a cocktail. Here Brecht pierces through into the pathological — the pathology of a Himmler or an Eichmann.

Whatever else is said of cruelty in Brecht's plays, the nature and quantity of it defeat any attempt on the spectator's part to remain detached in the manner recommended in Brecht's theoretical writings. Brecht's theatre is a theatre of *more than usually violent* emotion. It is a theatre for sadists, masochists, sado-masochists, and all others with any slight tendency in these directions — certainly, then, a theatre for everybody.

SAINT JOAN OF THE STOCKYARDS

Here Bernard Shaw's Joan enters the menagerie of Bertolt Brecht, Chicago being its location in no less than three Brecht plays — *In the Swamp* and *Arturo Ui* are the others.

Parody. Parody is more important to modern than to any previous school of comedy. Already in Shaw, parody had become very serious — a way of calling attention to dangerous fallacies.

It has been said that good parody parodies good authors and does not decrease your respect for them. The authors parodied in this play are Shakespeare, Goethe, and Schiller, and certainly they are not the target. One could begin to explain what the target is by mentioning that many supporters of Hitler could and did quote all three of these authors a great deal.

To Shaw, Bertolt Brecht's attitude was ambivalent. Already in a tribute he paid the older author in 1926, Brecht had said in passing that the most treasured possessions of Shaw characters were opinions. What Brecht thought of the right to your own opinions had already been indicated in certain speeches of Shlink and Uriah. Hence he is at pains to ensure that *his* Joan is entangled in circumstances, not besieged by epigrams.

Whether Brecht had understood Shaw is another matter. It is by circumstances — those of the capitalist system, as interpreted by a Marx or a Brecht — that Shaw's Major Barbara is trapped. Nor are the opinions of Brecht's Joan Dark held to be immaterial. It is to an opinion (atheism) that she is finally won over, and Brecht tips the audience the wink that, had she lived any longer, she would have accepted that last word in opinions: Communism.

Now as to Brecht's use of works by Goethe and Schiller, Shakespeare and Shaw in this play, the first two had better be ignored by readers of an English translation, for even the reader who spots the allusions to *Faust II* and *The Maid of Orleans* is still in the dark.

The "light" is the reverent acceptance by the German philistine public of their classics, a reverence that precludes any positive critical interpretation. To the English-speaking audience, the Shakespearean blank verse should, on the other hand, have something to say. For we know the emptiness of our Anglo-Saxon acceptance of Shakespeare, and we can see how serious Brecht's verse has to be to express the utter falsity of the mode of life depicted. In the Brechtian parody, this falsity is quite the reverse of self-proclaimed. The speeches of Mauler and Cridle and the rest are a good deal more dignified, intelligent, plausible than many speeches in the Congressional Record.

Shavianism. As for Shaw, as I said, ambivalence reigns. He is parodied and he is plagiarized. The borrowings are less from *Saint Joan* than from *Major Barbara.* The essence of Brecht's tale, like Shaw's, is that a girl of superior caliber joins the Salvation Army but is later disenchanted by discovering that the Army is involved in "the contradictions of the capitalist system." (Shaw and Brecht were the only good "Marxist playwrights" — partly, no doubt, because they regarded the dialectic as dramatic and not just as valid.) More interesting still is the adoption by both playwrights, in their maturer vein, of fine young women with shining eyes, and a limited or non-existent interest in men, as the bearers of the banner of the ideal.

Communism. On the Communist question this play is discreet but clear. The Communists are very seldom mentioned by name — but every mention is also a genuflection.

Yet the Communist critic Schumacher observes that Brecht's treatment of the masses is "abstract" — for him a very dirty word. The Communist critic Kurella observed that such bourgeois converts to leftism as Brecht were obsessed with the conversion of bourgeois to leftism. It was a Communist critic who shows no knowledge of Brecht's work, Christopher Caudwell, who wrote the classic denunciation of such converts in the last chapter of his *Illusion and Reality* (1937). Though today the fellow-travelers are shocked to hear Brecht accused of "unconscious dishonesty," that formula was applied by Caudwell to the whole class that Brecht belonged to — bourgeois writers with Communist leanings.

Official, or semi-official, Party writers never had much of a liking for Brecht's attempts to deal with working-class life. It is true that he got it all out of books, out of brief slumming expeditions, out of his imagination. *The menagerie would do very well as Capitalists, but how to render the Proletariat?* Generally, we get those incarnations of sterling simplicity that many believe in and few have met with — I paraphrase one of the few great proletarian artists, D. H. Lawrence. The mother in Brecht's adaptation of Gorky's novel is an example. Another tack is that of Agit-Prop: treat the workers as a group and present them on stage as a singing or verse-speaking choir. *Saint Joan of the Stockyards* belongs to Brecht's Agit-Prop phase.

GALILEO

History. The historical understanding played no part in the writing of *Galileo*, nor did Brecht pay his respects to historical accuracy except in the broad outline and in certain details. True, not a great deal is known. But quite enough is known for us to be sure that the historical Galileo was nothing like this; nor were his problems of this type; nor did his opponents resemble those whom Brecht invents for him.

Galileo is not a Marxist play either. What Marxist historian would accept the unhistorical major premise: namely, that if an Italian scientist had refused to renounce Copernicus in 1633 "an age of reason would have begun," and hence our age of unreason would have been avoided? What Marxist historian could accept the notion that a Catholic scientist of the seventeenth century, whose best friends were priests, who placed both his daughters in a convent as young girls, was halfway a Marxist, resented convents and churchgoing, doubted the existence of God, and regarded his tenets in physics as socially revolutionary?

But it is one of the open secrets of dramatic criticism that historical plays are unhistorical. They depend for their life on relevance to the playwright's own time — and, if he is lucky, all future times — not on their historicity.

It might, of course, be asked, why a playwright would choose historical material at all, and pretend to be limited by it. There are reasons. For one, he relies on the public's ignorance of the secrets, closed or open, of dramatic criticism. Audiences assume that most of what they see in a history play did happen, and it may be that most of the "history" in the popular mind comes from such sources. By popular, I don't mean proletarian. I met a Hollywood director at the premiere of *Galileo* and asked him what he thought of it. "As a play? I don't know," he answered, "but it is always thrilling to hear the truth, to see what actually happened!" Well, the joke was not on Brecht, and this incident helps to explain why historical plays are still written.

The Character of Brecht's Galileo. It is a play — not fact but fiction — and one of the criteria by which playwrights are judged is their ability to create characters who can, as it were, "take up their bed and walk" — who can assume the frightening autonomy of the six who once stood in the path of Pirandello. This play lives, to a large extent, by the character of the protagonist, a character which Brecht cut out of whole cloth — that is to say, created out of his own resources. What makes this Galileo a fascinating figure is that his goodness and badness, strength and weakness, have the same source: a big appetite and a Wildean disposition to give way to it. His appetite for knowledge is of a piece with his appetite for food, and so the same quality can appear, in different circumstances, as magnificent or as mean. I don't see how the theory of epic theatre could do justice to the ambiguity here. It calls for a theory of tragedy. The problem is not social and conditioned but personal and inherent.

Whatever the theorist makes of it, that particular ambiguity is very satisfyingly presented — is perhaps the play's chief exhibit. There is another ambiguity, equally fascinating, if not equally well defined. In this work, the self-denunciatory impulse in Brecht — not to speak again of masochism — has a field day. His Galileo denounces himself twice, and the two denunciations are designed to be the twin pillars upon which the whole edifice rests. The first of them, the historic abjuration of Copernicanism, was, we may be sure, what suggested the play in the beginning. The second was Brecht's invention.

One can hardly hear either for the crackle of dialectics. The first is immediately condemned by Andrea ("Unhappy is the land that breeds no hero"), and defended in a very Brechtian proverb by Galileo ("Unhappy is the land that *needs* a hero"). Then Galileo changes his mind, and in the last scene (as performed), the argument is reversed. Andrea takes the line that the abjuration had been justified because "Science has only one commandment: contribution," Galileo having by now contributed the *Discorsi*. Thereupon Galileo whips himself up into a self-lacerating fury: "Any man who does what I have done must not be tolerated in the ranks of science!" He who had made the great False Confession, which according to Brecht destroyed him in the eyes of the good and just, now makes the great True Confession, *which is his destruction in his own eyes — and before the eyes of the only person in the story with whom he has an emotional relationship.*

It is theatre on the grandest scale, and I call the conception fascinating because it is an attempt to bring together the most widely divided sections of Brecht's own divided nature: on the one hand, the hedonist and "coward," on the other the "hero" — and masochist. It is hardly necessary to say that "no masochism was intended." Any element of masochism destroys, of course, the Marxist intention of this finale. But, once again, *Brecht is not Marxism.* Brecht is Brecht — and Galileo is *his,* not Marx's, prophet.

Here the conscious and the unconscious motives are so directly in conflict that complete clarity cannot result. What we get is an impression of improbability. We recognize that the final self-denunciation is all very moral, but we are not convinced that the old reprobate would actually make it. Such a person naturally believes, "Unhappy is the land that needs a hero." What changed his mind? There would be a drama in such a change, and one wouldn't like to miss it. When Brecht simply *announces* the change, Galileo seems only his master's voice — a very different thing from being, as he was till then, his master's embodiment.

The matter is even less clear than I make it out. It is almost possible to believe that Galileo is only scolding himself (for which we give him credit) and in general is the same man as before. In giving his *ms.* to Andrea he pretends he is, as usual, giving way to weakness, succumbing to temptation. The incident, particularly in the 1938–9 version, is very endearing. In this respect the man is true to character to the end, and one has to admit his character has its points. *It is possible, in the main, to stay pro-Galileo to the end.* A familiar Brechtian feature! Moral disapproval goes one way, but human sympathy goes the same way! On stage the apparatus of alienation is called into action *as a fire brigade.* The whole effort of the Berlin Ensemble production is to counteract the natural flow of sympathy to Galileo. These actors know this particular job well. They have performed it for *Puntila;* as I write, they are performing it for a *Threepenny Opera* in which Mackie is not to be allowed any charm; and they try in vain to perform it for *Mother Courage.*

Galileo as a Portrait of the Artist. The term "portrait of the artist" — for novelists and dramatists at least — is a relative one. A character may be three quarters self-portrait and one quarter a portrait of someone else or sheer invention. The proportion of self-portrayal may indeed be anything from zero to a hundred per cent. There is sense in speaking of a portrait of the artist only when the relation to the artist is very marked and of special significance. In the present case, it is.

As already noted, there is a lot of Brecht in Baal, Kragler, and Garga. Then Brecht did not sit to himself for a long time. Which presumably means that he split himself up into *all* his characters. He often put the idealistic part of himself inside one of the young ladies with the shining eyes. He was likely to let the non-idealistic part of himself into the rogue of any play. . . .

Why Galileo Galilei? Auden says the poet cannot portray the poet, and points to Shaw's Marchbanks as an awful example. But the poet can portray the poet by pretending he is something else such as an architect (Solness) or a philosopher (Jack Tanner) — or a scientist (Galileo). Marxism considers itself scientific, which is one reason why it appealed to Brecht. Then there is the matter of History again. Whether or not the playwright is scrupulous about the historical record, a historical play carries the Idea of Fact. . . .

Getting rid of one's personality, Brecht had written at the time he gave himself to social causes, was an amusing business. If only the subjective did not exist! If only one *were* history! And science! And by the time one *is* history and science — in this play, *Galileo* — it is interesting that one still has the same human constitution as before: one is a genius, one would like to be committed to a cause, but one is a rogue.

Rogues and Knaves. Rogues are different from Knaves — at least in plays. Uriah is a knave. He is the Enemy, the Cruel World, Capitalism, etc. So, I think, is Peachum. They are nothing if not active, while your rogue, though applying himself busily to this or that, is fundamentally passive. Widow Begbick is a rogue, and in a late version of the script sings a song celebrating her passivity — she calls it not resisting the current of the river. Macheath is more rogue than knave, and it is passivity, in the form of "sexual submissiveness," that defeats him, as the story indicates and two long songs emphasize. Brecht in fact created a long line of rogues of whom Mother Courage and Puntila are only the most conspicuous. They differ from the knaves in being likable, even charming. Whatever disapproval we might feel is cancelled by the fact that their roguery is unsuccessful and was predestined to be so. Or it is successful in a very small and unimportant area. Brecht will make sure we understand that our hatred, if given primarily to them, is misdirected.

Or will he? The problem is complicated by the extent to which the rogue is always Brecht himself. His enjoyment of himself was qualified by an unusually large quota of self-hatred. The former would show itself in first drafts; the latter would be given full play in later revisions, not to mention notes and other outside comments. (The first drafts of *Puntila* and *Galileo* are particularly revealing.)

Heroism, Martyrdom, Masochism. It has been pointed out that the passive sufferers of Brechtian drama are offset by the heroic resisters. It has also been pointed out that what the heroes do is as passive as what the sufferers do: they obey, consent, submit. Galileo, then, is given his choice of two kinds of passivity: submit to fear or submit to torture. The passive characters of the early plays (Galy Gay, Shlink) had submitted to torture — masochistically. Galileo submits to fear and later denounces himself — most masochistically, as we have seen — before Andrea. Had he submitted to torture, that would have certified him a hero and therefore no masochist. Such would be Brecht's alibi. But he didn't use it. And it is not a valid alibi because writer and character are distinct in this: that the portrayal of non-masochistic heroism can itself be a highly masochistic act.

In any event, it is not really heroism, but martyrdom, that is in question, and it is well known that only a thin line divides masochistic submission from true martyrdom. If Galileo were tortured, you wouldn't get a tragedy, but, from Brecht's viewpoint, a happy ending, with Galileo a martyr of science. Here, however, we use the term martyr in a debased way. In Brecht's view, Galileo should have been willing to die because the news of his refusal to recant could have been exploited by the right side. This is the kind of thing we have in mind in modern politics when we say: let's not ruin such and such a man or we'll provide our opponents with a martyr. Anything further from the original idea of martyrdom could hardly be imagined.

Gluttony: a Deadly Sin. The most famous line Brecht wrote is: "Erst kommt das Fressen, dann kommt die Moral" — eating comes first, morality second. It is one of his passive and charming rogues speaking (or rather, singing): Macheath. The sentiment is one that the passive and charming Brecht would endorse, but that the active and activ*ist* Brecht would denounce. He denounces it in *Puntila* where a tale is told, in tones of awe, of a young man named Athi whose heroic deed it was to starve rather than eat food that came from his capitalist foe. In this context — again it is the context of Brecht's own mind and work that matters — Galileo's love of food takes on more meaning. I rather think Laughton got the part because Brecht had seen the ravenous eating he did in the *Henry VIII* film. (In *Galileo*, Laughton tore a chicken apart in exactly the same way.) Galy Gay's superiority to Bloody Five in *A Man's a Man* consists in his knowing that "it is very important that I eat," and his transformation in the final scene is shown mainly in his wolfing the rations of the three others. *In the Swamp* culminates in a conclusion written in a similar form of words, though containing no reference to food. "It is not important," says this particular passive protagonist (Garga), "to be the stronger one, but to be the living one." He is providing the reason for all that gluttony —

as well as the provocation for Athi's hunger strike. Such, by the way, are the kind of details through which the unity of Brecht's work is discovered.

It will be recalled that Brecht's word both for commercial entertainment and for the sensuous, thought-inhibiting, action-inhibiting high art of our era was: culinary.

THE GOOD WOMAN OF SETZUAN

Anna-Anna. Already in *The Seven Deadly Sins*, Brecht had made of his usual antithesis — kind *vs.* cruel, humane *vs.* inhumane, natural *vs.* unnatural, idealistic *vs.* realistic — a division within the same person. The world being bad, the good person requires a bad "half" if he is to survive. In this proposition, there is no contradiction between Brecht's natural constitution and Marxism, provided the negative side be identified with capitalism. Even the key role of the economic motive was something Brecht had worked out on his own: in *A Man's a Man*, written before the conversion to Marxism, we find Uriah only able to hold on to Galy Gay by the lure of a "deal."

Drama Schematic and Abstract. Brecht did not like the word *abstract*. He made a personal motto of the phrase "truth is concrete." And in this, most of the literary world, on both the sides of the Iron Curtain, agrees with him. But what are they all agreeing to? The word *concrete* is an abstraction, and all art is abstracted from life, with considerable subtraction and distortion along the way — just think of the Brecht menagerie!

But I would not try to empty the antithesis concrete/abstract of all meaning. It makes sense to say *The Three Sisters* presents life more concretely than does the *Oresteia;* and it is a fact that writers today emulate this concreteness rather than that abstractness. Even so, most non-modern drama was more abstract, and modern drama continually reverts to relative abstractness. After Ibsen (concrete), Expressionism (abstract).

Brecht believed that he reinstated the concrete. But did he? On the contrary, beginning with *A Man's a Man,* he created a dramaturgy as schematic and abstract as any workable dramaturgy well could be. With its numbering, its blackboard demonstrations, its many unashamedly two-dimensional characters, it is surely the abstractest thing in drama since the Spanish *autos* of the seventeenth century. Nor am I speaking merely of the *Lehrstücke*. Beginning with *A Man's a Man*, and not least in *The Good Woman of Setzuan*, Brecht's drama is all schematic and abstract — more so perhaps than is acceptable to the larger theatre public of many countries today.

A Man's a Man has the form of a scientific demonstration. One draft actually ends with the words "Quod erat demonstrandum." *The Good Woman* is similar. As in the earlier play, the first sequence of action presents a premise or hypothesis. Then comes the action, which is divided into clearly demarcated sections, each proving its own point. As Shen Te puts it at the end, she had only tried:

1. to help her neighbor
2. to love her lover, and
3. to keep her little son from want.

These are the three main sections and "actions" of the play. When Shen Te has failed in all three respects, even with increased help each time from her alter ego Shui Ta, she makes her appeal to the gods. There is nothing they can do. Q.E.D.

It sounds dismal! And what could have been a worse fate for the theatre than the theories and "schemes" of Brecht without his talent, which so often works, not hand in hand with the theories and "schemes," but at daggers drawn with them? This much must be conceded to those who abhor the schematic and the abstract: the schematic and the abstract never amount to theatre, drama, literature, art, *by themselves*. Yet, if what is added is not the "concrete" characterization and milieu that we are used to, what is it? In other words:

What is Epic Theatre Actually? In the first instance, a misnomer. And this Brecht, in effect, has admitted. The word *epic* suggests too many things or the wrong things. In England and America, there is the added trouble that our schools don't make much use of the old triple division of literature: epic, lyric, dramatic. There is a lot to be said for *not* using it, as the dramatic is not a separate genre running parallel to the others without touching them. The dramatic has traditionally embraced epic and lyric elements.

But "epic" does make a good antithesis to "lyric." In *Illusion and Reality*, Caudwell makes them so different it would be hard to conceive of the same person excelling at both, harder still to find him combining the two in one work. Caudwell's theory, over-simplified, is that the lyric writer writes himself while the epic writer writes the world. Even my oversimplification helps in explaining Brecht, who was originally a "lyric" poet, but who, when he discovered the world, tried to do without the self altogether and create a wholly "epic" drama.

Brecht never really succeeded in writing a novel — i.e., never became a fully epic writer. He remained the Poet as Playwright, and if we speak not of intentions but attainments, we should call his theatre a lyric theatre. The name would certainly bring out his qualities, rather than his defects.

There are defects — or perhaps deficiencies would be the word — in the area where the novelist or epic writer excels, namely, in the full presentation of individual character. Brecht would show at his worst in a comparison with Ibsen. But Ibsen — the "modern" Ibsen, that is — would show at his worst in a comparison with Brecht: for he has cut out the lyric element by the roots.

Lyric theatre would also prove a misleading term. There would be confusion with opera — or with decorative drama written in verse like, say, Christopher Fry's plays. Caudwell's formula guides us to a deeper interpretation of the lyric: the writer's relation to all of life is always at stake in it. The "lyricism" of *The Good Woman of Setzuan* is not isolated in the songs or bits of spoken verse. Rather, these are emanations of the spirit in which the whole play is composed. The prose, too, is poetry — not decorative, but of the essence.

Epic Theatre is Lyric Theatre. The twentieth century has seen a series of attempts to reinstate poetry in the theatre. Brecht made the most successful of these attempts. How? If it was not because he was a better poet — and one can scarcely maintain that he was a better poet than Yeats or Eliot — why was it? Cocteau's phrase "poetry of the theatre" as distinct from "poetry *in* the theatre" helps us toward the answer. As early as 1920, Eliot had completely debunked the kind of drama that is poetic chiefly in consisting of mellifluous or even exquisite lines. Nonetheless, his own interest continued to be in the poetic line and the way it was written: the free verse of *The Cocktail Party* is offered as an alternative to the blank verse and stanzas of the Victorians. Now, though Brecht too had his alternative forms of dialogue to offer, they are but a part of a Grand Design to replace the Victorian drama in all departments. And it is the design as a whole that provides the answer to the question: what kind of lyric theatre? The poetry *of* the theatre is not a poetry of dialogue alone, but of stage design, of lighting, of acting, and directing. Nor is it enough that these be "imaginative" — to use Robert Edmond Jones' word for his vision of a poetry of the theatre — they must also be called to order — subordinated to the statement which is being made. For this theatre is no fireworks display. It is not there to show off the theatre arts, together or individually, but to show off the world around us and the world within us — to make a statement about that world. Hence, while Jones' designs often look better in a book than on the stage, photographs of the Brechtian stage, thrilling as they are, fall short of doing justice to the phenomenon itself. There is this difference too. Jones was adding his own vision to that of an author: two inevitably somewhat disparate contributions were made toward what would be at best a happy combination. In the Brecht theatre, though others made contributions, he himself laid the foundation in every department: he was the stage designer, the composer, and the director. The production as a whole, not just the words, was the poem. It was in essence, and often in detail, *his* poem.

Collaboration. It has not escaped attention that, following the title page of a Brecht play, there is a page headed: *Mitarbeiter* — Collaborators. It has only escaped attention that these names are in small type and do not appear on the title page of the book or, presumably, on the publisher's royalty statements.

All the collaborators, and many who have witnessed the work of collaboration, have testified to Brecht's penchant for collaborating. We learn that at one period he didn't like to write alone and sitting down but only pacing the floor and talking with several "collaborators." We hear of his willingness to snap up a phrase or notion supplied by an onlooker.

Yet Brecht had no talent at all for collaboration if the word carries any connotation of equality, of give and take. His talent was for domination and exploitation, though the ethics of the procedure were in this sense satisfactory, that his collaborators were always people who wanted and needed to be dominated and exploited. That this should be true of friends and mistresses who never wrote anything notable of their own goes without saying. It is true also of the Big Names, including the biggest name of all — that of Kurt Weill. Weill has no more enthusiastic and enthralled listener than myself: the success of his music for *Mahagonny* and the other Brecht works is not in question. But how was that success achieved? Brecht sometimes intimated that he himself contributed some or all of the tunes of *The Threepenny Opera*. For years I considered this a boast. Later I came to believe it. For I saw the way Brecht worked with composers, and I listened to the music Weill wrote before and after his collaboration with Brecht. Weill took on the artistic personality of any writer he happened to work with. He had no (artistic) personality of his own. For a theatrical composer this is conceivably an advantage. I am not arguing that point. I would only mention in passing that what is true of Weill, is true of Eisler. The music of both is parasitic. When parasitic upon Brecht, it is nearly always superb. Parasitic upon second-raters, it is second-rate. And when they attempt music that is not parasitic at all, music that is bolstered by no writer, music that is not imitative of any composer, or even music that is not in some sense, serious or flippant, a parody of other music, they court disaster.

What kind of stage designs has Caspar Neher made for other playwrights? Often, very good ones, but in what way? Either in his Brecht style or in some established mode that would not mark off his work from that of any other eminent modernist. The "originality" of Neher is concentrated in the work he did for Brecht. Since that work was inspired *by* Brecht, it is clear that the word originality is in need of redefinition.

Brecht dominated not only the collaborators who were present in the flesh but also the dead or absent writers whose works he adapted. *The Threepenny Opera* is not a "steal" but a new work and just as "original" as John Gay's *Beggar's Opera*. In no case can the success or the character of a Brecht work be attributed to the writer or writers whom he drew upon. Though you might, for example, believe that Brecht "ruined" *The Private Tutor*, by that very token you can hardly attribute the proven effectiveness of the new play to Lenz.

Hence, what is interesting is not the legal issue of plagiarism — a hare started by Alfred Kerr long ago — but a critical problem: how was it that Brecht arrived at his results in this particular way? Perhaps the burden of proof is on those who regard the opposite procedure as normal, since it is only in recent times that "life" and not literature has come to be regarded as the usual source for a dramatist's plots and characters. The most "original" playwright of all, Shakespeare, is also the one who keeps scholars busiest studying his literary sources. Molière said he took his material wherever he found it — and the place he meant was literature or the theatre, not "life." Why did Brecht return to the earlier method? The question can hardly be answered *en passant*, but one thing is clear: that in exploring the whole range of dramatic art Brecht rediscovered the many-sided significance of collaboration.

The heart of the matter is, perhaps, that the individual artist contributes less to his art than is commonly supposed. A large contribution is always made by collaborators, visible and invisible. Drama, being narrative in a concentrated form, relies even more on the collaboration of others than does fiction. The dramatist draws, for example, on more "conventions" as a welcome shortcut — conventions being unwritten agreements with the audience. Similarly, he is inclined to use, not the raw material of life, but material that has already been "worked" by another artist. In fine, it takes all sorts of collaboration to make dramatic art, the final collaborative act being that which unites performer and spectator.

The book from which most comments on this last subject are — directly or indirectly — taken is *The Crowd* by Gustave LeBon. There is a fatal equivocation in it. LeBon fails to distinguish between the crowd in the concrete (say, 1000 people of any kind in a theatre) and the crowd in the abstract (the proletariat, the masses, etc.). Slurring over this simple difference, he enjoys himself reaching unwarranted conclusions.

In English we would call the first phenomenon the audience, and the second the public; and it occurs to me that English is unusual in having these two words. In French the audience is called *le public*, in German, *das Publikum*. Language seems to put English-speaking persons in immediate possession of a useful distinction.

We have heard much, too much, of the contribution the audience makes to a show. The audience laughs or cries, is attentive or fidgety, creates an atmosphere, sets up a current of psychic electricity between itself and the players. . . . All of which is to speak of the problems that arise at the end of the whole process of writing and rehearsing. No essential problem can be solved at that late point, as has a hundred times been shown in the history of American "out-of-town try-outs," without, of course, anyone's learning the lesson.

The audience's collaboration is one thing, the public's is another. There comes to mind Synge's historic statement that all art is a collaboration between the artist and his people. Synge correctly observed that something had gone terribly wrong in modern times. In my terms: the problem of the modern theatre is the problem, not of the audience only, but of the public.

One sign of this is that your audience problem can often be solved, while the problem of the public remains where it was. The problem of the audience has been that it has lacked homogeneity, common purpose, warmth. You can get these things by picking an audience of people united in a common faith. I would say T. S. Eliot solved the audience problem when he put on *Murder in the Cathedral* in the cathedral at Canterbury. Here is a theatrical "experiment" that succeeded. But that audience did not help Mr. Eliot to write his play. The public was not only not collaborating, it was absent, indifferent, even hostile.

Bertolt Brecht's radical reconsideration of theatre and drama includes a reconsideration of both audience and public. The trade unions and other large groups who would buy out the house once a week in the Germany of the Twenties obviously represented a new audience and might also suggest the idea of a new public that corresponds to a new working-class culture. Seen in this connection, Brecht's Communism will not appear as unplausible as it does to many of his readers in America today. Such readers would do well to remember that an artist will accept almost anything if it seems to offer a future for his art.* Brecht accepted Communism as Pascal advised accepting supernatural religion: as a bet according to which you have everything to gain and very little to lose. Concerned for the integrity of the theatre art, Brecht looked to proletarianism as the only way in which the artist could regain the kind of collaboration which Synge in 1900 thought was barely available any more.

Now, in his estimates of power and political success, Brecht showed shrewdness. At a time when the Soviet Union was considered weak, and the huge social-democratic movement in Western Europe tended to be anti-Communist, Brecht put his money on Moscow. There is little need, in 1960, to explain what a sound investment that was — if political success is the criterion. What if we apply other criteria — especially the very simple one of an audience and a public for Brecht?

As far as the public goes, one normally considers it as collaborating with the artist while he is planning and writing. Brecht, however, believed that he belonged with the public of the future. Only socialism could give his works a home. He once told me in so many words that if world socialism did not come about he did not expect his works to have any future at all.

The Soviet Union gave Brecht the Stalin Peace Prize. East Germany gave him a place to live and a large subsidy for a theatre. Does this amount to a public? Did Brecht's plays find their proper habitat? Did Epic Theatre establish itself as the theatre of the Communist countries?

There was a small production of *Threepenny Opera* in Russia some thirty years ago! Despite the visit of the Berlin Ensemble in 1957, the Russians are still (1960) not doing any Brecht plays. Nor are most of the East German theatres. The failure to find a public

* "Only by crawling on his belly can an unpopular and troublesome man get a job that leaves him enough free time." Thus spake (Brecht's) Galileo.

is total. On the other hand, Brecht has found an enthusiastic audience. But it consists of just the sort of people he ostensibly didn't want — chiefly the liberal intelligentsia of "decadent" Paris and London.

As for what Brecht really wanted, we find the same ambivalence in this field as in others. When in America, he was brave about being ignored on Broadway. "Why expect them to pay for their own liquidation?" he once said to me. But he fretted about it too, and made a few stabs at crass commercial success. His attitude to the avant-garde theatre was similar. The "so-called avant garde" was not important, but, "under certain conditions," it would take up his plays. "What conditions?" I once asked him. "Well," he replied, "if I were a Frenchman — or if I became the rage in Paris." And to be the rage in Paris — "intellectual," "advanced," almost "revolutionary" Paris — is, as far as worldly success goes, the highest achievement of Brecht to date.

Even aside from politics, it is questionable whether Brecht could have had what he wanted. There comes to mind George Lukacs' statement that, in the great ages, the drama flowed "naturally" from the existing theatre, while, from Goethe on, the poet-dramatist rejects the theatre, writes plays which are "too good for it," and then calls for the creation of the kind of theatre which will be good enough for the plays. Brecht saw the weakness of the post-Goethe position — without being able to escape it. If there is any theatre you cannot see a man's plays naturally flowing from it is a theatre that doesn't yet exist! If there is any public that is not a collaborator it is a public that isn't yet there! We all applaud the work of the Berlin Ensemble, but that institution is not the product of a new proletarian society. Its audience is the bourgeois avant garde. Its leaders — Herr Engel and Frau Weigel — are noble relics of the culture of the despised Weimar Republic. As for Bertolt Brecht, the point is not so much that he didn't succeed in getting any plays written about the doings in East Germany, as that, if he had, they would inescapably have been the product of the mind and sensibility that made *In the Swamp*. Has it escaped notice that the East German critics have been happier with Thomas Mann, who made no bones about being bourgeois, than with this uncomfortable Bavarian rogue?

Has The Good Woman of Setzuan *Dated?* This query is not as easy as it sounds, because all plays "date" in many respects, even though some go on being played and read forever. In this case, the question is, does the play belong irretrievably to the Depression Era? It does presuppose general unemployment on the one hand, and, on the other, slave-driver capitalists, like those of the factory system in the classic era of capitalism as described by Marx and Engels. An audience which does not presuppose these things will not cry "How true!" as often as the author would like. Today's audience knows, for example, that the composer who in the thirties predicted the swift demise of American capitalism in *The Cradle Will Rock* is now writing another revolutionary opera with the help of money from Henry Ford.

But such changes in background are negative factors: they only explain why a play will not receive an artificial "lift" from the audience. To the extent that *The Good Woman* is a good play and not absolutely confined in relevance to the Depression, it can command an audience. I see no reason to try to limit the interpretation of Brecht's plays to what is known to be his own understanding of them. As Shaw would put it, he was only the author. He was neither the audience nor the arbiter. During the Stalinist era, *The Good Woman* presented a good picture of current tendencies in Soviet society, with Shui Ta as the necessary "realistic" correction of the earlier idealism, and Yang Sun as eventually a high Party functionary, rising by the path of Stakhanovism. More permanently, the two sides of Shen Te, as they arise from the divided nature of Brecht, express such a division for all of us — and the tendency thereto which exists *in* all of us.

MOTHER COURAGE

Beyond Place and Time. It would be rash to expect this play to be any more historical than *Galileo* is. The vein of cynicism in which Mother Courage sings and speaks of war is the tone of the twentieth century, more particularly of Bertolt Brecht, and not that of seventeenth-century peasant women. Like Brecht's Galileo, she has all the negative side of Marxism under her belt, lacking only the positive belief in social progress.

Indications of place mean no more than indications of time. You can tell that from the way Brecht would change both. "The Song of the Great Souls" in *Mother Courage* (Sweden, Germany, etc., the seventeenth century) is taken bodily from *The Threepenny Opera* (England, nineteenth-twentieth centuries). "The Song of the Fishwife and the Soldier" seems, from its setting in *Mother Courage,* to tell a German tale. The omission of the one word Volga conceals the fact that an earlier rendering had set it in Russia. An action can be transported thousands of miles by the changing of a single word! In short, there is no concrete locality in Brecht's drama. Place, like time, is abstract. This feature represents an inheritance from Expressionism. Brecht's work is continuous with that of the Expressionists to the extent that he tried to construct abstract models of his subject. *Mahagonny* and *The Threepenny Opera* provide, not a socialist-realist report on capitalism, but, as it were, the Platonic idea of it.

But Brecht sank his roots much deeper in human history than the Expressionists did — and in the history of the abstract in drama. Obsessed with religion — a subject he could not keep away from for more than a few pages at a time — he often thought in terms of traditional religious abstractions. He wrote a *Seven Deadly Sins* and talked of writing a *Dance of Death.* His first and best book of poems had the form of a breviary. Converted to Communism, his mind ran, not forward to some Artwork of the Future, but back to the cantata and the oratorio. His "invention," the *Lehrstück,* is a sort of Catholic morality play revised by a Marxist reader of Luther's Bible.

The Deadly Sins and the Christian Virtues. We have seen that *The Good Woman* is a schematic and abstract study of the three parts of Shen Te's goodness: love of her neighbor, love of her man, and love of her offspring. *Mother Courage* is equally schematic, and is also tripartite. The action divides into three sections at the end of each of which a child is killed. Each child represents one of the virtues. Eilif is called The Brave Son. Swiss Cheese is called The Honest Son. Kattrin is characterized by Kindness in the little charade of the black cross. In that charade, the whole action is seen in advance. In "The Song of the Wise and Good," near the end, it is summed up retrospectively and abstractly — that is, in terms of the virtues themselves. Caesar, too, was brave and got killed. Socrates was honest and got killed. St. Martin was kind and died of cold. As it was demonstrated in *The Seven Deadly Sins* that natural and healthy impulses become "sins" which society will not tolerate, so it is demonstrated in *Mother Courage* that the cardinal virtues are not for this world. In other words, *Mother Courage* is quite close, in what it says, to *The Good Woman*. For that matter, it is close to *The Threepenny Opera*, where also "The Song of the Great Souls" — under the name of "The Song of Solomon" — can be taken as a summary of the whole play. Brecht is one of those artists — Ibsen and Conrad are others — who do not really change their subject from one work to the next but, all their life long, worry the same point.

Such an artist soon becomes a bore unless that point is of great moment and unless he can present it in various aspects. How can the principle of variety be applied to the notion of the Virtues? One way is by irony. Eilif's bravery turns out in the end to be only what is wrongly called bravery: like Galy Gay he is transformed into a foolhardy bandit. Another way to variety is by parallelism and contrast in character and narrative. Not only is one brother offset by a second, the daughter is offset by another kind of daughter (a daughter of joy). Yvette's career yields the one success story in the play. This has its own irony. Yvette's success is doubly ambiguous: it is accompanied by physical and moral deterioration, and it is exhibited with (the author's) disapproval. Kattrin, by contrast, is a failure at the start and becomes more of a failure all the time. But just as Brecht (in the full text) had drawn an analogy between Swiss Cheese and Christ, so he makes of Kattrin his own type of hero — the activist — and confers upon her a kind of glory.

The Positive Hero. At this point, the virtue which Kattrin represents comes within range of the virtue of the Positive Hero in Soviet literature. But that was not the kind of abstractness to which Brecht was naturally drawn. He is careful not to make Kattrin an

idealist. It is not for an idea that she dies but, on the contrary, because, on the subject of children, she is not rational: she is a
Kindernarr, crazy for little ones. If Brecht moves toward the abstract in this characterization, the abstraction is not Philanthropy
but Mother Love, an instinct which is celebrated in a whole series
of his plays. Another touch that belongs very much to this poet,
rather than to a school of thought, is that Kattrin cannot speak. In
the world here depicted, Virtue has no voice, or at least, if she
has, even the poet cannot find it. And yet there is rebellion. "The
stones begin to speak," says the scene-heading. And Mother Courage had called Kattrin "a stone in Dalarna." (Symbolism with a
vengeance! Though symbolism, in Brecht circles, was as nasty a
word as abstraction, like abstraction it will prove a necessary word
to true critics of Brecht.)

Brecht chose to be the voice of the voiceless. Such was the positive side of his impulse toward radicalism, a side sometimes obscured by his readiness to excuse Stalinist brutality.

> Und die Einen sind im Dunkeln
> Und die Anderen sind im Licht.
> Und man siehet die im Lichte
> Die im Dunkeln sieht man nicht.*

Precisely to *bring* light into this darkness was the mission of
Bertolt Brecht, who had all the makings of a popular, though not
of a proletarian, poet.

The "drum" scene is possibly the most powerful scene, emo-
tionally, in twentieth-century drama. Any actress playing Courage
might be hard put to it to hold her own, and, if one "sovietized"
the play, Kattrin would be the protagonist. To put her mother
center stage was to invite the complaint that the play was not
truly Communist but pacifist, defeatist, and bourgeois. But Brecht
did put her mother center stage, and did not entitle his play *Dumb
Kattrin.*

That Brecht should have proved the leading Communist writer

---

* "And these are in the dark, and those are in the light, and you can see
the ones in the light: those in the dark you can't see." From *The Threepenny Film.*

of the Stalin era is perhaps the most striking of all the Brechtian contradictions. The Positive Hero is one of the few ideas which Stalin and Zhdanov contributed to literary discussion, and Brecht stood for nothing if not the opposite. His protagonists from Baal through Azdak are nothing if not *negative* heroes. Brecht got angry when actresses made Courage noble and even — supreme error! — courageous. For this writer's first weapon — and here again he stands in direct contrast to Stalin's writers — is irony. Nicknamed Courage by a fluke, as she readily explains, the lady represents, in the first instance, the diametric opposite of courage, namely, cowardice, and the diametric opposite of active virtue, namely, passivity. That she keeps herself busy — works her hands to the bone, in fact — is an added irony. Such are the "ridiculous superhuman efforts" which Brecht's Galileo attributes to the peasantry in general: they are passive in the class struggle, which is to say, in history. As in her previous incarnation as Widow Begbick, Mother Courage is content to flow with the tide — even though her own song (of the Fishwife) tells where the tide inexorably leads, namely, to death.

Critics of *Mother Courage* could hardly fail to observe that people in it die, but they don't seem to have noticed that dying is implicit in the play from the first scene on — a scene which begins with the song, "Let your men drink before they die!" and ends with the prophecy of the death of all three children. The vision of death and the prospect of death is what is most vivid about the play. The spirit it is shot through with is, in fact, that of the death-wishing Brecht of the early plays: Mother Courage is a new spokesman for the old disenchantment. If Brecht put some of himself into Kattrin and she sums up Brecht the activist and lover of mankind, he put even more into his passive and negative heroine, Mother Courage the coward.

The final touch — which I think only one critic (Esslin) has spotted — is that, in the last instance, Mother Courage does have courage, not the kind that Brecht officially favored, not the kind he could have admitted, perhaps, to be there at all, but surely the kind he must have covertly respected since he makes it command respect in the play. This is, to borrow a phrase from Brecht's friend Paul Tillich,* "the courage to be" — in this case, the courage to exist in the face of a world that so powerfully recommends non-existence.

Critics who confront *Mother Courage* may need to speak not only of abstraction and symbolism but of the tragic. But this we have already found to be true of *Galileo*. We shall find it true of *The Caucasian Chalk Circle* as well.

Why the Thirty Year's War? Because in German history it is the *locus classicus* of death — the death, not of individuals, but of cities and populations. Brecht had seen World War I, and could foresee World War II. Even if the play did not find a permanent place in the repertoire, it would always remain a great literary document of our age of world wars, as Grimmelshausen's *Simplicissimus* is a great literary document of the seventeenth century.

To some extent Grimmelshausen was the inspirer of *Mother Courage*. His work certainly brought to Brecht a sense of death, decay, and disaster, corresponding rather closely to his own. Yet insofar as the sources — or provocations — of the play are literary, there is an author who has an even better claim to be considered the main source. If the Thirty Years War had been lived through by Grimmelshausen, it had been seen in perspective by a much better-known German writer who also happens to be Germany's most widely admired dramatist, Friedrich Schiller.

The left-wing intelligentsia of the twenties had it in for Schiller. Piscator de-glamorized *The Robbers* by making it a picture of the class struggle à la Marx. Brecht was strongly anti-Schiller. There were times when he seemed to see himself as *The* Anti-Schiller, a sort of German equivalent of The Anti-Christ. If Schiller gave the heroic view of the war — classical in its dignity, romantic in its presentation of women — Brecht would give the anti-heroic, anti-classical, anti-romantic worm's eye view. *Mother Courage* stands to *Wallenstein* as *Saint Joan of the Stockyards* to *The Maid of Orleans*. This is, of course, a two-sided statement, for, as I said above, Brecht did not merely parody the classics. His procedure in his *Saint Joan* contrasts with that of modernizers in

* I do not know how much of a friend, but it happens that the only time I have seen Dr. Tillich was in Brecht's apartment on East 56th Street in New York. E. B.

general who take an old theme and vulgarize it. No work of Brecht's is so resolutely stately. He was trying to find an equivalent for Schiller's sublimity. As for *Mother Courage*, it might well have been suggested by the first part of the *Wallenstein* trilogy.

THE CAUCASIAN CHALK CIRCLE

Charm and Naiveté. How is this play built? The incident of the chalk circle takes up only one scene. What is the rest of the play there for? So that we can get to know the Judge? But he doesn't appear till the second half. What is the first half of the play there for? It would be hard, I think, to find a satisfying reason in the doctrinaire terms in which Brecht and his colleagues discussed plays. Why couldn't a reason be found along traditional artistic lines? Not all the play is didactic. Was not Brecht capable of relaxing a little, telling a touching story, and filling it out with a poem and a song?

He was. Not the least of the many disservices of his theorizing to his cause was to obscure the presence in his work of the primary attributes of good theatre. Take such a thing as *charm*. The word has been pre-empted, latterly, by advertisers of clothing and cosmetics. That isn't the word's fault. Only the most egregious art-snob or the blindest art-theorist can overlook the role of charm in art. In the theatre, which directs itself to the eyes and ears, it is primary. Goethe himself speaks of going to the theatre to gaze at beautiful bodies. What beauty is to the body, charm is to the word, to the person. How vacuous to discuss the "thought patterns" in *As You Like It* and not allow for the charm of Rosalind's personality! How portentous to deal with Shaw as Marxist, Wagnerian, vegetarian, anti-vivisectionist, and pass over the fact that his characters woo us and win us — not with their philosophy but with their charm! Another of the open secrets of Brecht was that while he attacked other forms of charm he had his own. Being a dramatist, he passed it on to his characters, particularly to those with whom he was strongly identified — Galy Gay, Macheath, Galileo, Mother Courage, Azdak.

Something similar needs to be said of *naiveté*. The word has been used more and more in our century because more and more people have come to regard themselves as *not* naive — as subtle fellows. It is now the usual word with which to strike down an argument you cannot answer, an opponent whose weak spot you cannot find. It is pleasant, therefore, to find Brecht, in his last years, saying a good word for naiveté. He described it (I believe) as a sort of ultimate goal for any stylist.

In question here, then, is not the kind of simplicity an artist starts out with at the age of nineteen; for that matter, his style may well be at its most "complex" at that age. In question is the simplicity that is achieved when much complexity has been worked through and worn down. To the truly naive reader, such not-really-naive art is "deceptively" simple. The late lyrics of Brecht are a case in point. They are positively cryptic. The sense is between the lines. It is doubtful if Brecht is really simpler than poets who parade their "difficulty."

Of the charm of *The Caucasian Chalk Circle* there is no doubt. As to whether the presentation is naive, that is a matter of definition. In any case, naiveté of style would be no guarantee of unambiguousness of import. Like many another wily Bavarian peasant, Bertolt Brecht could be devious in very simple words. And in case the word devious gives offense, I hasten to add that what we call deviousness in behavior becomes, in literature of genius, richness of texture and fullness of significance.

Chinese Boxes. Friedrich Luft has said that while the younger Brecht wished to use theatre to alter the world, the later Brecht took a step back when he said the theatre should only show the world to be alterable. I'm not so sure that even the earlier Brecht theatre had such direct designs on the world as had the theatre of Piscator or Odets, but I agree that some sort of withdrawal took place later. I would place it in the late thirties. And the right explanation is the simple one: that Brecht was forced by Hitler into a withdrawal from political life in his own country. Living among foreigners who did not know him or his language, he could not be the kind of writer he had recently decided to become: the Party activist. He was forced into that very withdrawal which most artists crave — and which the activist seeks to avoid. Those of us who knew Brecht in exile can testify to the extent of the withdrawal. It is to Hitler, then, that we owe the big plays of these years, plays which were more deeply meditated, drawn from sources deeper inside as well as more remote in time, than those of the preceding years.

I mean chiefly *Galileo*, *Mother Courage*, and *The Caucasian Chalk Circle*, the last of which marks an end point. I have read most of what Brecht is known to have written afterwards, and I find him taking no new steps — only retracing old ones. In the sense here suggested, *The Caucasian Chalk Circle* is his last play. It is certainly the play of deepest withdrawal. The form, puzzling at first, can be seen as Chinese boxes, one inside the other, Azdak's story being a box within the Grusha story, the innermost box (to my mind) being the narrative of Azdak's two big songs.

The first of these songs is a description from the time of Azdak's grandfather of the miserable state of the people and the appalling conduct of the ruling caste. The second of the songs describes a popular revolution. It is based on an ancient document which Brecht had already quoted in his essay on five ways of telling the truth. The further back we go in time the closer we come to what Brecht regards as present and future. The flashback is used, as it were, in order to flash forwards. The urgent and the ultimate are presented in a dream within a dream, a memory within a memory. All of which is stressed precisely when the socialist moral is stated at the end: Azdak "disappeared and was never seen again," and his time became a legend of a "brief golden age."

The Prologue. And we are not surprised when we read that West German theatres put the play on as a "charming fantasy," or that the dialecticians of the East rise up in wrath to explain the Prologue. The Prologue is not set in prehistoric times but at a date later than the year when Brecht started work on the play. If the rest of the play, without the prologue, might be taken to be "unreal," the prologue is set in what for a Communist is the most real of all real places, Soviet Russia. It might also be assumed that, once the Prologue is played, you can't forget it, and so everything that happens all evening is seen in direct relation to it.

Now it seems to me quite likely that this was what Brecht intended, and certainly the prologue was not added after Brecht got to East Berlin — it was present in the first manuscript I saw of the play (1946). The question is whether we can take the will for the deed. If the little Prologue cannot function as some of Brecht's Marxist friends would wish it to, it is not for lack of good intentions but for lack of weight. It does not, in fact, stay in the mind and compel us to refer back to it later. To the *Intendanten* of the West who omitted it, I would say: put it back in and relax, it will make no difference.

Everything of course depends on the political views you bring to the play — which is to admit that the play exerts persuasive power on none. The Prologue itself, in the eyes of all except the converted, presents yet another fantasy: the non-Russian Stalinist's view of Stalin's Russia. One can see that this fantasy was meant to be the largest of all the Chinese boxes — and was not meant to be a fantasy. For that matter, set in Georgia, the play is without doubt intended as a bouquet to the most stalwart Georgian of them all, Joseph Stalin, from a future winner of the Stalin Peace Prize. The quotation from Mayakovsky, Stalin's favorite poet, is "a word to the wise. . . ."

Brecht and Tragedy. The last time I saw Bertolt Brecht (June, 1956) we spoke of Ernst Busch's performance as Azdak, and Brecht said the actor had missed the "whole tragic side of the role." I think the comment has the highest interest for Brecht criticism because Brecht usually talked *against* tragedy, and those who have found "a tragic side" in his work have assumed that he was unconscious of it. What *is* tragic about Azdak? On the surface, the part is all racy and ironic comedy. But, aside from anything he says, Azdak performs an action near the beginning of his part of the play which casts a good deal of light on the whole: *having let the Grand Duke escape, he denounces himself to the authorities for so doing.* It is a very bizarre incident, in itself hard to believe, and, as acted by Busch, flatly incredible. What is its moral and psychological content? First, self-denunciation, as often in Brecht and Communist culture generally, is seen as good. Azdak is doing what Galileo abysmally failed to do: taking his punishment. Second, the "goodness" is cancelled by the fact that the authorities surrendered to are bad. The tragedy of Azdak, as found in this incident, is that his effort at heroism is reduced to absurdity by the circumstances. "Doch die Verhältnisse, sie sind nicht so," to quote Mr. Peachum, "that isn't how things are." *The tragedy of Azdak is that his life is a comedy*.

The incident has a third aspect. It carries a note of personal poignancy to the degree — the very considerable degree — that Azdak represents his author. There is nothing tragic, of course, in Brecht's willingness to denounce himself. What is tragic is his suspicion that the authorities he might denounce himself to were no better than those he had rebelled against. If *The Caucasian Chalk Circle* is implicitly dedicated to Stalin, also implicit is the question: what if Stalin should prove a Grand Duke — or a mad Czar? One can hardly forget that *Galileo* and *The Caucasian Chalk Circle* followed in the wake of the self-denunciations of Radek and Bukharin.

I am not concerned here with manuscripts that have been coming to light showing that, in the fifties, Brecht was more than worried about Communism in East Germany. My point is rather that this more-than-worry — this haunting suspicion — antedates "East Germany." Disenchantment was burnt deep into Brecht's personality, and it would be naive to think that it affected only his thoughts about capitalism. Stalin's pact with Hitler in 1939 was a baffling blow, and Brecht (as he once told me) had not been able to say, with Nexö and others, "Well, Hitler is a socialist too." He was full of doubt, dread, and guilt, as some of his poems testify — and as some of his conversation testified. And what makes most credible Wolfgang Harich's claim in 1956 that Brecht belonged to the anti-Ulbricht, anti-Stalin "rebellion" is that Brecht had for a long time kept ajar that door to non-Stalinist thoughts which better Communists kept tightly shut. I have heard him defend Silone in company that was horrified, and in June, 1956, the book I saw open on his desk in East Berlin was the American edition of Koestler's *The Invisible Writing*. . . . The dark lining to Azdak's comic coat of many colors is the tragedy of the disenchanted revolutionary.

Azdak, oddly enough, has much in common with Galileo — Brecht's Galileo. Not only are they both of them rogues in the sense defined above, they both embody the same contradictions: for instance, of talking, particularly about sex, like men about town, but behaving more like hermits. They are essentially solitary. Azdak comes out of solitude and returns to it. Galileo is progressively detached from the world and his friends. Both characters reflect the isolation of Brecht.

I recall exchanging letters with Brecht about certain rather elementary and even banal problems of Communism and literature. I was brought up sharp by his remarking that *I was the only person with whom he discussed such things.** Now I was not a member of what was regarded as his circle of intimates. As a non-Communist, I was, in a sense, not even *persona grata*. I suddenly realized that Bertolt Brecht, surrounded by disciples and "comrades," lived, intellectually at least, in a state of total isolation. Behind that Iron Curtain, it is not only the Pasternaks who have lived alone! Nor, perhaps, was it only behind the Iron Curtain that Brecht lived lonely amid the crowd. Things were no doubt quite similar in California, where *The Caucasian Chalk Circle* was written.

Why labor a commonplace? However anti-tragic a poet's philosophy, if he is truly a poet, the tragedy of his life will find some echoes in his work. To the question: was this what Brecht meant when he spoke of the tragic side of Azdak, one must answer, in

---

* Letter from Bertolt Brecht to Eric Bentley, dated November 12, 1949. The first part of the letter contains a defense of Brecht's interpretation of *Hamlet* against what I had called "inaccuracies" in it. The next topic is his play *Days of the Commune*. I had said one had to be a Marxist to accept it. Brecht comments: "[That] is probably correct. But, to take a classical example, must one not accept the viewpoints of Montaigne or Bacon before one can accept *Hamlet* or *Troilus and Cressida?*" It is after adding that his play offered no deliberate parallel between the Paris of the Commune and the Berlin of the days of the air-lift that Brecht made the statement paraphrased in my text. Here it is translated literally: "For the rest, you are more or less (*ziemlich*) the only one with whom I discuss such things (*derlei*) and to whom I write about them — if not enough! After all that you have done for me, no estrangement can result on my side from sharp criticism that you may make of this play or that: you are thoroughly entitled to it." In a final paragraph urging me to come and practise stage direction with him in Berlin before directing his plays at home, Brecht refers to my "defense of his theory, the only defense actually that has been made" (*die wirklich einzig dastehend ist*), and adds: "we are trying to bring out your studies in the *Neue Rundschau* or in *Sinn und Form*. They are first class." E. B.

the first place, "obviously not," but, in the second place, "yes."

"Theater ist einfältig, wenn es nicht vielfältig ist." This punning dictum of Brecht's can be freely translated: Theatre is simple-minded unless it is open-minded, or: the dramatic poet has a one-track mind unless his mind runs on several tracks. One sometimes has to quarrel with Brecht's "contradictions." But *to quarrel with* can be *to pay homage to*. In any event, there are authors who *must* be quarrelled with — not because (or not only because) they are wrong and you are right, but because this is the only way they can be encountered. Was anyone ever able to read Nietzsche without fighting him? There are philosophers whose views you just mem-orize: Nietzsche makes you fight. He is "wrong" — but he is hard to answer! He is "wrong" — but unlike those who are right he is hard to ignore or forget! What is a philosopher for, finally? And even if you decide that a philosopher is there to provide you with correct opinions, is that what an artist is for? There is another view, namely, that the artist is there to experience and express the contradictions, whether or not he can resolve them. If this view is valid, a critic is not captious when he points out what those contradictions are. Nor is he accusing the artist of stupidity or deceitfulness if he remarks that some contradictions were less conscious than others. The criticism that is unworthy of Brecht (here I return to my starting point) is the criticism that ignores or denies the contradictions. Precisely *this* criticism is either dis-ingenuous or simple-minded — and makes Brecht so.

If there is a tendency now, in Paris or East Berlin, to put Brecht on a pedestal, one should recall that the older German poets are already on such pedestals, and that Bertolt Brecht spent quite a lot of energy trying to pull them down.

IN THE SWAMP

A Boxing Match Between Two Men
in the Giant City of Chicago

(1921–1923)

English Version by
Eric Bentley

AUTHOR'S NOTE (1927)

The present text is a re-working of the play *Im Dickicht* which was produced in Munich, 1922, and in Berlin, 1924. It is dedicated to my wife Marianne Brecht.

TRANSLATOR'S NOTE

In the 1927 edition Brecht lengthened the title to *Im Dickicht der Städte*. This could be translated *In the Thicket of the Cities* except that the term *Dickicht* is not limited to undergrowth and has connotations of vastness and waste. Where the word occurs in the text that follows I have translated it by *thicket* or *jungle* according to context. The word *forest* I reserved to translate *Wald* with. Neither *thicket* nor *jungle* makes a title that corresponds to the German, so I have drawn upon a passage in the dialogue where the word Swamp is used. I realize that Upton Sinclair's *The Jungle* may have been in the back of Brecht's mind, and that the Sinclair novel is set in Chicago. Nevertheless, to American ears, the associations of the word *jungle* are oriental and heroic. To German ears, the associations of *Dickicht* are not.

Otherwise I have tried to stick faithfully to the 1927 edition, published by Propyläen Verlag, Berlin, preserving even the anomalies, such as the confusion of British and American money, and Brecht's possibly not serious belief that you can sail from Chicago to Tahiti. Every indication that this is a mythic, not an actual, America has its value, all the more so in a rendering which is couched in American speech.

It is arguable that the fight of the two men was seen by Brecht as wrestling rather than boxing. I tend to think that the image shifted from time to time in Brecht's mind. I have stuck to boxing or used the noncommittal word *fight*. Shlink does call Garga a fist-fighter, and Brecht does speak both of boxing and shadow-boxing in the essay, *On Reading Through My Early Plays*.

In the German editions, the quotations with which the text is studded are not identified. I have identified the ones I could track down.

AUTHOR'S FOREWORD

You find yourself in the year 1912 in the city of Chicago. You observe the inexplicable boxing match between two men, and you are present at the downfall of a family which has come from the savannas into the jungle of the big city. Do not rack your brains over the motives for this fight but note the human stakes, judge without prejudice the style of each contestant, and direct your interest to the finish.

CHARACTERS

SHLINK, *lumber dealer, a Malay*
GEORGE GARGA
JOHN GARGA ⎱ *his parents*
MAE GARGA ⎰
MARIE GARGA, *his sister*
JANE LARRY, *his girl friend*
SKINNY, *Chinese,* SHLINK'S *secretary*
COLLIE COUCH, *called The Baboon, a pimp*
J. FINNAY, *called The Worm, hotel owner*
PAT MANKYBODDLE, *called Manky, a coxswain*
A MAN *from the Salvation Army*
SNUB NOSE
A saloon keeper named KEN SI
C. MAYNES, *owner of a rental library*
WAITER
A YOUNG SECRETARY
AN EMPLOYEE
MEN

1

C. MAYNES' RENTAL LIBRARY IN CHICAGO

Morning of August 8, 1912.
GARGA behind the counter. A bell rings.
SHLINK and SKINNY enter.

SKINNY: If we've read rightly, this is a rental library. We'd like to take a book out.

GARGA: What sort of book?

SKINNY: A thick one.

GARGA: For yourself?

SKINNY (*who looks at* SHLINK *before each answer*): No, not me. It's this gentleman.

GARGA: Your name?

SKINNY: Shlink, lumber dealer, 6 Mulberry Street.

GARGA (*writes the name down*): A penny per week per book. Pick one.

SKINNY: No, you should pick one.

GARGA: This is a mystery story, not a good book. That's a better one, a travel book.

SKINNY: You say it so simply: not a good book?

SHLINK (*comes closer*): Is that one of your opinions? I'd like to buy it from you. Is ten dollars too little?

GARGA: I'll make you a present of it.

SHLINK: Does that mean you'll change your opinion and call it a good book?

GARGA: No.

SKINNY: You could buy some clean linen with the money.

GARGA: My job here is just to wrap books.

SKINNY: This drives the customers away.

4

GARGA: What do you want from me? I don't know you. I've never seen you.

SHLINK: I'm offering you forty dollars for your opinion of this book, a book I don't know and that doesn't make any difference.

GARGA: I'll sell you the opinions of Mr. J. V. Jensen and Mr. Arthur Rimbaud but I won't sell you *my* opinion.*

SHLINK: *Your* opinion doesn't make any difference either. Only, I want to buy it.

GARGA: But I can afford opinions.

SKINNY: You come from a family of transatlantic millionaires?

GARGA: My family lives on stinking fish.

SHLINK (*cheering up*): A fighting man! One would expect the words which would give me pleasure, and help to rescue your family from fish, to leap to your lips.

SKINNY: Forty dollars! That's a lot of clean linen for you and your family.

* Brecht wrote this play under the influence of J. V. Jensen's *The Wheel* and Arthur Rimbaud's *A Season in Hell.* The former (1905) is the sequel to the same author's *Madam D'Ora* (1904), and a friend who reads Danish has supplied the following summary of both books: "The protagonist is a lay preacher named Evanston who, though an insignificant person at the beginning of the story, assumes monstrous proportions before the end. He represents animal energy, is a homosexual, and something of the amoral Superman. In *Madame D'Ora* Evanston, who has killed a woman in London, manages to place the blame for the crime on a famous scientist. In *The Wheel,* set in Chicago, Evanston becomes a successful revivalist under the name Cancer. The substance of the novel is the conflict between Cancer and Lee, a journalist who aspires to be a poet and who dreams of making America into the kind of civilization Europe might have been if the Gothic instead of the Gallic influence had prevailed. Cancer wants Lee to write the Bible of the new religion, and in the long, central dialogue of the novel, confesses he has been in love with Lee ever since Lee cut him to pieces in a boxing match. The conflict between these two, says Jensen, is 'relentless and can end only with the extermination of one of them, because one is fighting blind but with all the strength of the savage, while to the other it was simply a matter of life or death.' Lee kills Evanston, gives up his dreams of Gothic splendor, and realizes that salvation lies in the work of creating a new civilization." Even a summary convinces one that the relationship of Rimbaud and Verlaine contributed less to *In the Swamp* than the relationship of Cancer and Lee. E. B.

GARGA: I'm not a prostitute.

SHLINK (*humorously*): I hardly think my fifty dollars would make a dent in your soul.

GARGA: To raise your offer is a renewed insult, and you know it.

SHLINK (*naively*): You ought to know which is better: a pound of fish or an opinion, and for that matter: two pounds of fish or this opinion.

SKINNY: My dear sir, don't get any deeper into this.

GARGA: I'll have you thrown out.

SKINNY: That you go on having opinions stems from your failure to understand life.

SHLINK: Miss Jane Larry says you wanted to go to Tahiti?

GARGA: And how do you happen to know Jane Larry?

SHLINK: Since she's not getting paid for the shirts she takes care of, she's starving. It's three weeks now since you let her catch a glimpse of you.

GARGA *drops a pile of books.*

SKINNY: Careful! You're an employee.

GARGA: I am helpless in the face of your aggressions.

SHLINK: You are poor.

GARGA: I live on rice and fish, that's no secret.

SHLINK: Sell!

SKINNY: Are you the Oil King?

SHLINK: People on your street feel sorry for you?

GARGA: I cannot shoot up a whole street.

SHLINK: Your family, which came up from the plains . . .

GARGA: Sleeps three in a bed beside a burst drainpipe. I smoke at night so I can sleep. The windows are shut, for Chicago is cold, in case it amuses you to know.

SHLINK: Surely, your girl friend . . .

GARGA: Sews shirts at two dollars apiece. Net profit sixpence. I recommend her to you. We spend Sundays together. Our bottle of whiskey costs forty cents, no more, no less, forty cents, if this entertains you.

SHLINK: You're not putting your real thoughts on the table.

GARGA: No.

SHLINK: Since one can't live on sixpence net profit.

GARGA: As for entertainment, one follows one's own taste. One loves Tahiti. I hope you don't object.

SHLINK: You are well-informed. It's the simple life. Along Cape Hay storms still occur. Farther south are the tobacco islands, rustling green fields. One can live like a lizard.

GARGA (*looking out of the window, dryly*): Ninety-five in the shade. Noise from the Milwaukee Bridge. Traffic. Morning. As ever.

SHLINK: And this morning, which is not as ever, I begin my boxing match with you. I'll start by rocking the ring. (*He rings.* MAYNES *enters.*) Your man is on strike.

MAYNES: Why aren't you taking care of these gentlemen, George?

SKINNY (*sharply*): He's being rude to us!

MAYNES: How do you mean?

SKINNY: We cannot stomach his greasy linen.

MAYNES: How do you dress for this job, Garga? Think this is a lunch counter? It will not happen again, gentlemen.

SKINNY: He's saying something. He's cursing up his sleeve. Why don't you use the voice God gave you?

GARGA: I'd like to ask you for different linen, Mr. Maynes. On twenty dollars a week I can hardly open a whorehouse.

SHLINK: Go to Tahiti. The people don't wash there.

GARGA: Thank you. Your solicitude is touching. I'll have my sister pray for you in church.

SHLINK: I hope you will. She has nothing to do.

GARGA: You'll need some incense.

SHLINK: Manky's a suitable man for your sister. He's crazy about her. And your sister doesn't bat an eyelash when her parents are starving.

GARGA: Are you running a detective bureau? Your concern for us is flattering — I hope.

SHLINK: You are simply shutting your eyes. As to your family, catastrophe is inevitable. You're the only one earning a living, and you can afford opinions! Better go to Tahiti right away. (*Shows him a navigation chart he has brought.*)

GARGA: I've never seen you in my life before.

SHLINK: There are two steamship lines.

GARGA: You just bought this chart, huh? It's new.

SKINNY: Just think — the Pacific Ocean!

GARGA (*to* C. MAYNES): Won't you show these gentlemen out? They're buying nothing. They're driving away the customers. They've been spying on me. I don't know them.

> J. FINNAY, *called The Worm, enters.* SHLINK *and* SKINNY *step back, without a sign of recognition.*

THE WORM: Is this C. Maynes' rental library?

MAYNES: In person.

THE WORM: A damnably dark sort of place.

MAYNES: Do you wish books, magazines, stamps?

THE WORM: So those are books? A filthy business. And what for? There are enough lies. "The sky was black, the clouds ran towards the east." Why not towards the south? What people will swallow!

MAYNES: Let me wrap this book for you, sir.

SKINNY: Why won't you let him catch his breath? And does this gentleman look like a bookworm? I ask you.

GARGA: It's a plot.

THE WORM: Indeed! She says: "When you kiss me, I always see your lovely teeth." How can you *see* when you're kissing? But that's the way she is. Future generations will know of it. Lascivious creature! (*He treads on books with the heel of his shoes.*)

MAYNES: Oho, sir, you'll have to pay for the destroyed copies!

THE WORM: Books! What good are they? Did libraries stop the San Francisco earthquake?

MAYNES: Get the sheriff, George.

THE WORM: I have a brandy shop — that is honorable work.

GARGA: He isn't drunk.

THE WORM: I tremble all over like an aspen-leaf when I see such loafers.

GARGA: It's clear as daylight. It's me they are after.

COUCH, *called* The Baboon, *enters with* JANE LARRY. THE WORM *steps back without giving a sign of recognition.*

THE BABOON: Come on in, my little white hen. This is C. Maynes' rental library.

GARGA: Shut the store, Maynes. Strange creatures are crawling into your papers. You're getting moths in your magazines.

THE WORM: I always say: let's see the whites of life's eyes!

THE BABOON: Remove your face. I can't stand paper. Especially not *news*paper.

GARGA: Get your gun!

SHLINK (*steps forward*): Please sell!

GARGA (*notices* JANE): No!

JANE: George, is this your store? What are you staring for? I just went for a walk with this gentleman.

GARGA: Go for a walk then.

THE BABOON: Oho, he is prickly! Maybe you don't believe her? In my excitement I am tearing this book to bits. You still don't believe her?

MAYNES: I'll fire you if you don't believe her. My books are going to hell.

GARGA: Go home, Jane, please. You are drunk.

JANE: I don't know what's wrong with you, George. The gentlemen are nice to me. (*She drinks out of* THE BABOON's *bottle.*) They bought me cocktails. It's hot today, ninety-five degrees. It goes through your body like a thunderbolt, George.

GARGA: Go home now. I'll come tonight.

JANE: You haven't come home in three weeks. I'm not going home any more. I am fed up with sitting among the shirts.

THE BABOON (*pulls her into his lap*): You won't have to any more, either.

JANE: Oh, you're tickling. Let go of me! George doesn't like it.

THE BABOON: In short: she has a body that's worth a few dollars.

Can you pay it, sir? It's a matter of love. It's a matter of cocktails.

THE WORM: Maybe you want the little Miss to stay pure? She should be scrubbing stairs maybe? She'll be a washerwoman?

SKINNY: You expect a nice white grouse to turn out an angel?

GARGA (*to* SHLINK): Do you want to make a prairie of this place? Knives? Guns? Cocktails?

THE WORM: Stop! You won't leave your place here. It's possible someone will go overboard. Sell!

GARGA: Strange. Everybody seems to be in on this but me. — Jane!

THE BABOON: Tell him!

JANE: Don't look at me like that, George! Maybe this is my only chance. Can *you* buy me cocktails? Oh, it's not for the cocktails! It's just this: I look in the mirror in the morning, George. For the last two years. You would go away and work for four weeks. When you got sick of it and needed to drink a while, it was my turn. I can't stand it any longer. The nights, George! This doesn't mean I'm bad. I'm not. It's wrong of you to look at me like that.

THE BABOON: You're wise. Here, take a drink, you'll get wiser fast.

GARGA: That whiskey wrecked your brain. Do you hear what I'm saying? I'm saying: Let's go away! Together! To Frisco! Wherever you want. I don't know if a man's love can last, but listen: I promise to stay with you.

JANE: You can't, little Georgie.

GARGA: I can do anything. I can even make money, if that's it. I have a feeling for you. Words can't say it. But we'll see eye to eye again. I'll come tonight. Yes, tonight.

JANE: I hear all you say, you needn't shout so, and you needn't tell these gentlemen you never loved me. You speak out of the bitterest bitterness of your heart. I have to listen, of course. I know it, and you know it.

THE WORM: Monkey business! Just tell him you were in bed with this gentleman from nine to half past ten this morning.

JANE: It wouldn't be good, maybe. But it's good you know it's not the whiskey or the heat.

SHLINK: Sell! I'll double the price again. Don't be unfriendly.

GARGA: That doesn't count. What's from nine to eleven as against two years?

SHLINK: I assure you, two hundred dollars is a trifle to me. I hardly dare to offer it to you.

GARGA: Maybe you'd be so kind as to send your friends away.

SHLINK: As you wish. But please observe the way things are on this planet, and sell.

MAYNES: You're a fool and a ninny and a phlegmatic coolie. Just think . . .

SKINNY: Your innocent parents bent with care!

THE WORM: Your sister!

THE BABOON: Your girl friend. This lovely young creature!

GARGA: No! No! No!

SHLINK: Tahiti!

GARGA: I'm turning it down.

MAYNES: You are fired!

SHLINK: Your economic security! Watch the boxing ring! It's shaking!

GARGA: This is freedom. Here, take my coat! (*Takes it off.*) Divide it! (*Takes a book* from the shelf, reads:*) "Idolatry! Lies! Lechery! I am an animal, a Negro, but maybe I'm saved. You are fake Negroes, madmen, savages, misers! Merchant, you are a Negro, General, you are a Negro. Emperor, you old leper, you are a Negro, you drank untaxed liquor from Satan's factory. Oh, this people, in raptures about fever and cancer!

* Rimbaud's *A Season in Hell*. But I translate here from the German because Brecht did not know French and relied on a German version by the same Ammer who translated Villon, much to the benefit of *The Threepenny Opera*. Also, Brecht has done some editing of the Rimbaud text both here and in the extract in Scene 10. The French original reads: "Je suis une bête, un nègre. Mais je puis être sauvé. Vous êtes de faux nègres, vous, maniaques, féroces, avares. Marchand, tu es nègre; magistrat, tu es nègre; général, tu es nègre; empereur, vieille démangeaison, tu es nègre; tu as bu d'une liqueur non taxée, de la fabrique de Satan. — Ce peuple est inspiré par la fièvre et le cancer." E. B.

(*Drinks.*) I am unschooled in metaphysics, do not understand the laws, have no morals. I'm a wild man. You are wrong."

SHLINK, SKINNY, THE WORM, *and* THE BABOON *have gathered around* GARGA *and clap their hands in applause as at a performance.*

SHLINK (*smoking*): How you work yourself up! Nothing'll happen to you.

JANE (*on his neck*): It's as bad as all that, George?

GARGA: Here are my shoes! Are you smoking your little black cigar, sir? The slobber might run down your jaw. Here's my handkerchief. Yes, I will auction off this woman! I will throw these papers around your ears! I ask for the tobacco fields of Virginia and for a ticket to the Islands. I ask, I beg you for my freedom! (*Runs out in shirt and trousers.*)

SHLINK (*calling after him*): I am Shlink! Shlink the lumber dealer! Six Mulberry Street!

SKINNY: He's on the march. What is this paper worth?

THE WORM: You really want to pay?

MAYNES: Ten dollars' worth of books.

SKINNY: Here's twenty.

THE BABOON (*to* JANE, *who is crying*): Aha! Now comes the awakening! You can cry in the gutter.

THE WORM: One must look into the whites of life's eyes.

SHLINK: What is this stuff worth?

MAYNES: The clothes? Jacket? Tie? Shoes? They're not really for sale. Ten dollars.

SKINNY: We finally got under his skin. Let's take his clothes along. SHLINK *has slowly gone out at the back.* SKINNY *follows with the bundle of clothes.*

2

OFFICE OF THE LUMBER DEALER C. SHLINK
CHICAGO

Evening of August 22 before seven.

SHLINK *at a little table.*

SKINNY'S VOICE (*left, at the back*): Seven wagon-loads Kentucky

THE WORM (*at the back*): Arrived.

SKINNY: Two wagon-loads boards.

THE WORM: There's someone here who wants to talk to Mr. Shlink.

SHLINK: Have him come in.

THE WORM: This is Mr. Shlink!

GARGA *enters.*

SHLINK (*happy now*): Well, there you are. Here are your clothes. Put them back on.

GARGA: You expected me? Brought my clothes? Filthy rags. (*Kicks the bundle of clothes away.*)

SHLINK *strikes a small gong.*

MARIE (*enters*): George!

GARGA: You here, Marie?

MARIE: Where've you been, George? They were worried about you. And how you do look!

GARGA: What are you doing here?

MARIE: I take care of the laundry. We can live on it. Why do you look at me like that? You look like you've not had it so good. I'm doing all right here. They said you'd been fired.

GARGA: Marie! Pack your things and be off home! (*Walks around.*) I don't know what they want with me. They've harpooned me. And pulled me to them. With ropes, it seemed. "I'll stick to you, sir." But leave my sister out of this!

13

SHLINK: As you like. (*To* MARIE:) But get him some clean linen first and a suit, if it's all the same to you.

MARIE: My brother, whom I cannot understand, says I should leave you.

SHLINK: And please go home afterwards. I am no expert at laundry.

   MARIE *leaves.*

SHLINK: Have you had anything to drink?

GARGA: Please let me know if this is not exactly what you intended.

SHLINK: I only have rice brandy. I will order the kind you prefer. You prefer cocktails?

GARGA: I get everything done at one and the same time. I spend a few weeks drinking, making love, and smoking all at once.

SHLINK: And thumbing through the encyclopedia?

GARGA: . . . You know everything.

SHLINK: When I heard of your habits, I thought: a good fighter.

GARGA: That linen is taking a long time.

SHLINK: Excuse me! . . . (*Stands up and strikes the gong.*)

MARIE (*enters*): Here is your linen, George, and the other clothes.

GARGA: You can wait till we go away together. (*Changes clothes behind a screen.*)

MARIE: I must say good-bye, Mr. Shlink. I didn't get to finish the laundry. Many thanks for your hospitality here.

GARGA (*from behind*): The suit has no pockets.

   SHLINK *whistles.*

GARGA (*comes out*): Who are you whistling for? I request that you quit whistling for people in these your last weeks on earth.

SHLINK: I await your orders!

GARGA: You wanted prairie life. You can have it. You've taken the skin off my back for your own amusement. A new skin compensates for nothing. I'll make a clean sweep of you. (*A gun in his hand.*) An eye for an eye, a tooth for a tooth.

SHLINK: You'll fight?

GARGA: Yes! Of course, without obligations.

SHLINK: And without asking for a reason?

GARGA: Without asking for a reason. I don't want to know why you need a fight. The reason would certainly be a dirty one. It is enough for me that you think yourself the better man.

SHLINK: Well then, let us consider the matter. My house and my lumber business, for example, put me in a position to sick the dogs on you. Money is everything. Good. But my house is yours, this lumber business belongs to you. From today on, Mr. Garga, I place my fate in your hands. I don't even know you. From today on I am your creature. Every glance from your eyes will disturb me. Each one of your wishes, even those I don't know, will find me willing. Your cares are my cares, my strength will be your strength. My feelings will be dedicated to you alone, and you will be angry.

GARGA: I accept the engagement. I hope you won't have anything to laugh about.

Noiselessly THE BABOON, SKINNY, *and* THE WORM *enter.* GARGA *grins, seeing that their suits are like his.*

SHLINK: This house and this lumber business, entered in the files of Chicago under the name of Shlink, are transferred today to Mr. George Garga of Chicago.

GARGA (*to* SHLINK): That's me. Good. You have some stripped tree-trunks in stock? How many?

SHLINK: Offhand: four hundred. I don't know.

SKINNY: They belong to Broost & Co., Virginia.

GARGA: Who sold these tree trunks?

THE WORM: I, The Worm, owner of the Chinese Hotel in the coal district.

GARGA: Sell this lumber again.

THE WORM: Sell twice? That's fraud.

GARGA: Yes.

THE WORM: Who'll be responsible for this order?

GARGA: Shove this lumber off to Frisco under the name of Mr. Shlink's firm and hand the money over to Mr. Shlink who'll

take care of it till I request him to give it to me. Any objec-
tion, Mr. Shlink?

SHLINK *shakes his head.*

THE WORM: This is barefaced profiteering! It'll bring the sheriff
down on your neck!

GARGA: When?

SHLINK: Within six months at most. (*He brings the master ledger
to* GARGA.)

THE BABOON: The swamp!

GARGA: Storks live off the swamp.

THE BABOON: Better go to work with a razor than with crooked
papers. Can one forget that Chicago is cold?

GARGA: You meant your real lumber business, Shlink? The house,
the tree trunks, the inventory?

SHLINK: Yes. Here is the master ledger.

GARGA: Pour ink over the ledger, you!

SKINNY: Me?!

SHLINK *hands him a bottle of ink.*

SKINNY (*leaning over the ledger*): All the entries! All the deals!

GARGA: Pour ink over them.

SKINNY *pours cautiously.*

THE BABOON: Enjoy your dinner!

THE WORM: Twenty years and more, poof! What a lark! I can
make nothing of it. This was once a lumber business.

GARGA: Now shut off the saw, and this lumber business is finished!

THE BABOON: As you say, boss! (*Exit.*)

*The saw noise outside stops. The staff put on their coats and
stand against the wall.* GARGA *gives a resounding laugh.*

MARIE: What are you doing, George?

GARGA: Quiet! Fire that fellow, Mr. Shlink!

SHLINK: You can go.

SKINNY: Go? I'll have been here twenty years in April.

SHLINK: You are fired.

MARIE: I don't believe it's good, what you're doing, George!

GARGA: Please go home, Marie.

MARIE: And please come with me. This only means trouble. Let him alone, Mr. Shlink!

SHLINK: Give me your orders, Garga!

GARGA: Certainly. Now, with nothing left for you to do here, I'll ask you to arrange a little game of poker with your former foremen, Shlink.

SHLINK *and the staff sit down at the poker table.*

MARIE: But you're coming home with me, George. This may be a "lark" but you don't understand it.

GARGA: We grew up on the plains, M. Here we're up for auction.

MARIE: Us? What do they want from us?

GARGA: Listen, you are not the target. They just want to drag you in. There's a fellow who spat a small cherrystone into my eye two weeks ago. I'm here to look him over. I have a gun in my pocket. I encounter a bow — a retreating bow. He offers me his lumber business. I understand nothing, but I take it. I'm alone in the prairie, I can do nothing for you, M.

THE WORM (*from the back to them*): He plays like a cardboard god. I'll swear he plays false.

GARGA (*to* SHLINK): I understand nothing, sir. I'm the Negro in this. I came with a white flag, and now I unfurl it for an attack. Hand over the papers which are your securities and your private means, and I'll put them in my pocket.

SHLINK: Please don't be too disgusted to find how modest they are!

SHLINK *and* GARGA *leave.*

SKINNY: Even though things here have been bad, and it rained in on one's coat, being fired is an injustice.

THE WORM: Don't gab. (*Mocks him.*) So it rained in, and he still thinks it's just a matter of rotten floorboards!

SKINNY: I love you, lady. You have a way of stretching out your hand to. . . .

THE WORM: Oho! He has no bed now, and he wants to take a woman into it.

SKINNY: Come with me. I will work for you. Come with me.

THE BABOON (*also comes forward*): Pitiful! All kinds: black, golden yellow, and white as the skin of an apple! Negro women! From hip to foot, made to measure! Round thighs, damn it, not poultry-shears like this one here! The Papuan girl! Forty bucks for that Papuan girl!

SHLINK (*in the doorway, calls back*): Yes, that is all.

THE WORM: No, you are barbaric. Ungrateful! The lady is innocent, and she smokes a pipe? She never sang this tune, but who can say that she has no fire in her? Forty dollars, and all for the lady.

SKINNY: Whatever your heart desires!

THE BABOON: Without powder, of course. Uncooked, naked flesh. What latitude! Seventy dollars for *toi cha!**

MARIE: Protect me, Mr. Shlink!

SHLINK: I am ready to protect you.

MARIE: Tell me: shall I listen to him?

SHLINK: No one here loves you. He loves you.

GARGA (*has entered*): You like it at the market? There's a lot of lumber here, and now a few pounds of flesh are up for auction! And Jiu Jitsu is known as the happy and carefree art, isn't it?

SHLINK (*goes up to him, ruffled*): Aren't you making things too easy for yourself?

MARIE (*to* GARGA): You should have helped me. You must leave with me right away, George, something terrible has occurred. Maybe even, if I go now, this *won't* be the end. I think you're blind: don't you see you are losing?

At the back the sound of two guitars and a drum is heard. Chorus of girls: "Jesus takes the sinners to Himself."

GARGA: I see you are ready to give yourself up. This is the swamp which will swallow you. Here's something for you, Marie, here's the Salvation Army, marching towards you, Marie!

* A friend who knows both Cantonese and the ways of the world suggests that this means "for the privilege of being the first to have her." E. B.

(*Gets up from the little table, goes toward the back.*) Hey! Hello! Salvation Army!

THE WORM (*to* MARIE): A river is drained off here. At night the place is haunted by the ghosts of drowned rats. Go home to your parents!

GARGA: Clean up! Take the whiskey away! (SHLINK *does so,* MARIE *helps him.*) Come in, fellows!

SHLINK *has opened the wooden gate bowing low. A young man from the Salvation Army enters. Behind him, two girls with guitars and an old sinner with a drum.*

MAN: You're calling me?

THE WORM: Hallelujah! The Salvation Army!

GARGA: I think nothing of your activities. If you need a house, you can have this.

MAN: The Lord will bless you.

GARGA: Maybe. (*To* SHLINK:) Did you inherit this house and the papers?

SHLINK: No.

GARGA: You worked forty years?

SHLINK: With tooth and nail. I only took off four hours for sleep.

GARGA: You came here poor?

SHLINK: I was seven. I have worked ever since.

GARGA: You have nothing but this?

SHLINK: Nothing.

GARGA (*to the* MAN): I'm giving you this man's property on condition that, on behalf of the orphans and drunks whose shelter this will be, you will let me spit in your intolerable face.

MAN: I am a minister.

GARGA: Get set!

MAN: I mustn't.

GARGA: Snow is falling on orphans. Drunkards are dying like flies. And you protect your face.

MAN: I am ready. I have kept my face clean. I am twenty-one; you must have your reasons. Please understand me, and ask the lady to turn around.

MARIE: I'll despise you if you do it.

MAN: I expect you to. There are better faces than mine; none are too good for this.

GARGA: Spit in his face, Shlink, if you don't mind.

MARIE: This isn't good, George. I really don't care for it.

GARGA: A tooth for a tooth, if you don't mind.

SHLINK *steps coolly up to the* MAN, *spits right into his face.* THE WORM *bleats. The reformed sinner beats the drum.*

MAN (*shakes his fists, weeps*): Forgive me.

GARGA (*throws the papers at him*): That is the donation contract. It's for the Salvation Army. And this is for you. (*Gives him the gun.*) Now get out. You are a pig.

MAN: Thank you in the name of the mission. (*Bowing awkwardly, he leaves. The hymns die away remarkably fast.*)

GARGA: You have ruined the joke for me. Your crudity is incomparable. I will keep some of your paper money. I won't stay here. Because this is the point, Mr. Shlink from Yokohama: I'm going to Tahiti.

MARIE: You're a coward, George. When the minister just went out, you squinted, I saw you. How desperate you are!

GARGA: When I came here, I'd been skinned — right down to the bone. I'm trembling from two weeks of spiritual debauchery. I spit in his face: many times. He swallows it. I despise him. It is over.

MARIE: Pfui!

GARGA: You left me in the lurch. A tooth for a tooth.

MARIE: Are you continuing your fight with me? You never knew any limit. God will punish you. I want nothing from you but my own peace.

GARGA: And to seek bread for your parents in a whore's bed. And to sell the stink of horses and to say: this isn't me! That you may do well in bed and live long in the land. (*Exit with the others.*)

MARIE: I don't quite understand you, Mr. Shlink. But you can go in four directions, where others only have one, huh? A man has many possibilities, hasn't he? I see that: a man has many possibilities.

SHLINK *shrugs his shoulders, turns, and leaves at the back.* MARIE *follows him.*

3

LIVING ROOM OF THE GARGA FAMILY

Evening of August 22, after seven.
A dirty attic. In the back of the room, a curtain in front of a balcony from the roof.

JOHN GARGA, MAE. MANKY *sings a song.*

JOHN: Something happened here that is hard to talk about.

MANKY: They say your son George is mixed up in a deal of the kind that never ends. They say he's been having something to do with a yellow man. A yellow man seems to have done something with him.

MAE: One mustn't stick one's nose in.

JOHN: If he is fired, we can eat mold.

MAE: Since early childhood he couldn't stand having anything hanging over him.

MANKY: They say you shouldn't have rented your daughter Marie to that yellow man.

MAE: Yes. M has been gone two weeks, too.

MANKY: Everyone must notice how it all hangs together.

MAE: When our daughter left, she said they made her an offer in a meat store. She was to get twenty dollars a week, and only had to do the wash.

MANKY: A yellow man and laundry!

JOHN: In such cities you can't see from this house to the next. You don't know what it means to read a particular newspaper.

MANKY: Or to have to buy a ticket.

JOHN: When people have to take these electric streetcars, they perhaps get . . .

MANKY: Stomach cancer.

JOHN: Without knowing it. Wheat in America grows summer and winter.

MANKY: But all of a sudden, without anyone telling you, you have no lunch. You walk the streets with your children, who observe the fifth commandment to the letter, and suddenly you're only holding the hand of your son or daughter in yours, while your son and daughter themselves have sunk over their heads in quicksand.

JOHN: Hello! Who is it?

GARGA *stands in the doorway.*

GARGA: Gabbing again?

JOHN: Finally bringing the money for these two weeks?

GARGA: Yes.

JOHN: Do you still have your job or not? A new coat, eh? You must have been well paid for something? This is your mother, George. (*To* MAE:) What are you standing around for like Lot's wife? Your son's arrived. Our son has come to invite us for dinner in the Metropolitan Bar. Is he pale, your dear son? Somewhat drunk, eh? Come on, Manky, let's go. We can smoke our pipes on the stairs! (*Both leave.*)

MAE: Tell me, George, are you mixed up with someone?

GARGA: Was someone here?

MAE: No.

GARGA: I have to go.

MAE: Where to?

GARGA: Some place. You always get scared.

MAE: Don't go.

GARGA: I have to. A certain man insults another. That is unpleasant for the latter. But a certain man under certain circumstances will pay a whole lumber business to insult another. That is, of course, even more unpleasant. In such cases, the insulted man ought to leave town, but since it might be too pleasant, maybe even that is no longer possible for him. Anyhow, he must be free.

MAE: Aren't you?

GARGA: No. (*Pause.*) We are not free. It starts with coffee in the mornings, and with whippings if one acts like a fool, and the tears of the mother salt the soup of the children, her sweat washes their shirts, and one is secure until the ice-age sets in, and the root sits in the heart. And when a man is grown, and wants to do something and give it everything, he finds he is already paid for, initiated, certified, sold at a high price. And he is not free to go under.

MAE: Tell me what makes you sick.

GARGA: You cannot help me.

MAE: I can help you. Do not run away from your father. How are we to live?

GARGA (*gives her money*): I've been fired. But here is money for six months.

MAE: We're worried because we've heard nothing from your sister. But we hope she still has her job.

GARGA: I don't know. I advised her to leave that yellow fellow.

MAE: I know that I cannot tell you things, like other mothers.

GARGA: Oh, all the many other people, all the many good people, all the many other and good people, who stand at their lathes and earn their bread and turn out many good tables for the many good bread-eaters, all the many good table-makers and bread-eaters with their good families, who are so many they're crowds already, and nobody spits in their soup, and no one despatches them with a good kick into the good old Beyond, and no deluge breaks over them with a "Stormy the night and the sea mounts high."*

MAE: Oh George!

GARGA: No, don't say: oh George! I can't stand it. I don't wish to hear it.

MAE: *You* don't wish to? What about me? How am I to live? The walls are so dirty, and the stove won't last out the winter.

GARGA: Ah, Mother, it's plain as your hand, all this can't last, your stove can't, nor can your walls.

MAE: That's your opinion. Are you blind?

* Such a song appears in a later Brecht work, *Mahagonny*. E. B.

GARGA: Not the bread in the box, not the dress on your back, not your daughter, nothing can last.

MAE: Yes, shout! Say it so that all can hear. How everything is for nothing, how all trouble is too much to bear, and one is the smaller for it. But how am I to live? I still have a long time to live.

GARGA: Well then, if it is so bad, you tell me the cause.

MAE: You know.

GARGA: That's just it.

MAE: But how do you mean that? What do you think I said? I will not have you look down on me this way, I bore you, and gave you my milk, and then bread, I beat you, and you should look on me differently. A man is what he wants to be, I'll tell him nothing, he worked for us.

GARGA: I'd like you to come with me.

MAE: What did you say?

GARGA: I'm asking you to come south with me. I'll work there. I can fell trees. We'll build a log cabin, and you'll cook for me. You're necessary to me.

MAE: Who are you talking to? The wind? But when you return, then you can look and see where we were when time gave out. (*Pause.*) When are you going?

GARGA: Now.

MAE: Tell them nothing. I'll put your things together and put the bundle under the stairs.

GARGA: Thank you.

MAE: It's all right.

Both leave. THE WORM *enters cautiously and sniffs around the room.*

MANKY: Hello, who's here? (*Enters with* JOHN.)

THE WORM: I am a gentleman. Mr. Garga, Mr. John Garga, I suppose?

MANKY: What do you want here?

THE WORM: I? Nothing! May I speak to your good son, I mean if he's taken his bath?

JOHN: What is it about?

THE WORM (*shaking his head sadly*): How inhospitable! But where is your worthy son resting, if it isn't asking too much?

JOHN: He's out. And you go to hell! This is not an information bureau.

MAE *enters.*

THE WORM: Oh too bad! too bad! We miss your dear son uncommonly, sir. It's also a matter of your daughter, if you are really interested.

MAE: Where is she?

THE WORM: In a Chinese hotel, milady, in a Chinese hotel.

JOHN: What?

MAE: Mother of God!

MANKY: What does this mean? What's she doing there, man?

THE WORM: Nothing. Eating. Mr. Shlink wishes to tell you and your son, he should come get her, she's too expensive, it runs into money, the lady has a healthy appetite. She doesn't make a move. She pursues us with immoral propositions, she's even demoralizing the hotel, she has the police at our throats, sir.

MAE: John!

THE WORM (*shouts*): In short: she's hanging round our necks.

MAE: Jesus!

MANKY: Where is she? I'll fetch her.

THE WORM: Yes, fetch her. Are you a dachshund? How would you know where the hotel is? A young chap like you? It's not so simple. You should have looked after the lady. It's all your son's fault. He should come for this bitch, take care of this himself, if you please. Tomorrow night we'll set the police in motion.

MAE: Good God! Just tell us where she is. I don't know where my son is. He's gone away. Don't be hardhearted! Oh Marie! Oh John! Plead with him! What's happened to M? What's happening to me? George! What sort of a city is this, John, what sort of men are these? (*Exit.*)

SHLINK *steps into the doorway.*

THE WORM (*scared, mumbling*): Yes, I . . . the house has two entrances . . . (*Sneaks out.*)

SHLINK (*humbly*): I am Shlink. I was a lumber dealer and now I catch flies. I have nothing to do. I am fifty-four. Can I help you? I saw downstairs on the enamel plate the name of a man I know.

MANKY: You are Shlink? You are keeping the daughter of these people under guard.

SHLINK: Who is that?

JOHN: Marie Garga, sir, my daughter, Marie Garga.

SHLINK: Don't know her. I don't know your daughter.

JOHN: The man who was just here . . .

MANKY: Presumably on your orders . . .

JOHN: Who just sneaked out when you came in!

SHLINK: I don't know him.

JOHN: But my son and you . . .

SHLINK (*laughs*): You are making fun of a poor man. I'm not much. I gambled away my wealth. You often can't tell how things happen. I offer you my arms.

MANKY: I know where bottom is when I bring the brig into harbor.

JOHN: Look before you leap.

SHLINK: Lonely from stiffness of the joints at an age when the ground must close up so the snow won't fall into the cracks, I see you deserted by your breadwinner. I'm not without pity. Then, too, my work would have purpose.

JOHN: Reasons don't fill the belly. We are not beggars. You can't eat herrings' heads. Your loneliness doesn't meet here with a heart of stone. You wish to put your elbows on the table with some family. We are poor people.

SHLINK: I relish all things, my stomach can digest stones.

JOHN: The bedroom is small. We sleep like shellfish.

SHLINK: I would live here with pleasure. I sleep on the floor and only need half as much space as I am long. I am cheerful as a child once I've shielded my back from the wind.

JOHN: Good, I understand. You don't want to wait outside in the wind. Come in under the roof.

MAE (*enters*): I must run into town before night.

JOHN: You're always away when I need you. I have given this man shelter. He is lonely. Since your son has gone, one place is free. Shake hands.

MAE: We come from the plains.

SHLINK: I know.

JOHN: What are you doing in the corner?

MAE: I am fixing myself a bed under the stairs.

JOHN: Where is your bundle?

SHLINK: I have nothing. I'll sleep on the stairs, ma'am. I'm not forcing myself on you. I'll not shake hands. There is yellow skin on mine.

MAE (*coldly*): I will.

SHLINK: I don't deserve it. I meant what I said. You don't mean my skin, forgive me.

MAE: I open the window over the stairway at night. (*Exits.*)

JOHN: She has a good soul under the skin.

SHLINK: The Lord bless her! I am a simple man, ask no words from my mouth, there's nothing in it but teeth.

4

CHINESE HOTEL

Morning of August 24.

SKINNY. THE BABOON. JANE.

SKINNY (*in the doorway*): Don't you ever think of opening a new business?

THE BABOON (*in a hammock, shakes his head*): The Chief is taking a walk along the pier, checking the passengers of all ships to Tahiti. Some fellow there has run off with his whole soul and his whole fortune, maybe to Tahiti. It's him he's looking for. He has collected and saved everything that was left over, down to the last cigar butt. (*About* JANE:) That girl there — he's fed her for three weeks gratis. And that fellow's sister too, a respectable person, he takes care of her too. His intentions in that regard are impenetrable. Often he talks with her all night long.

SKINNY: You people let him throw you out on the street, and then start paying his bills? And not just his!

THE BABOON: The few dollars he earns carrying coal he turns over to this fellow's family. He's living with them. But he can't stay there, they can't bear the sight of him. The fellow simply "took" him. Bought an excursion ticket to Tahiti, and left a tree trunk hanging over the Chief's neck that may fall now at any minute. In five months at the latest there'll be a little courtroom discussion about selling lumber twice.

SKINNY: And you subsidize such a wreck?

THE BABOON: He needed some fun. You give credit to a man like that. If the other fellow stays lost, the Chief will be top man again in the lumber business in three months.

JANE (*half-dressed, powders herself*): I always thought I would end up this way: in a Chinese house of ill fame.

THE BABOON: You still haven't the remotest idea what they have in mind for you.

Two voices are heard behind a screen.

MARIE: Why don't you ever touch me then? Why do you always wear this tobacco-smelling sack? I have a suit for you like the other men wear. I can't sleep. I love you.

JANE: Sh! Listen! Now you can hear them again!

SHLINK: I'm not worthy. I don't understand virgins. Then, too, I've been aware of the smell of my race for years.

MARIE: Yes, it's bad, bad, yes, it's that.

SHLINK: You shouldn't get so cut up about it. See: my body is numb. The skin is affected. Human skin is by nature too thin for this world, that's why man takes such pains to make it grow thicker. The procedure would be unexceptionable if one could only stop it growing. A piece of tanned leather, for instance, stays the same, but skin grows. Gets thicker and thicker.

MARIE: Is that because you cannot find an opponent?

SHLINK: In the first stage, the table, for example, still has edges. Afterwards, and that is what's disagreeable, the table is rubber. But at the stage of thick skin, there's neither table nor rubber left.

MARIE: Since when have you had this disease?

SHLINK: Since my youth on the rowboats of the Yangtse-kiang. The Yangtse tortured the junks. The junks tortured us. There was a man who'd make his way through the ranks of the oarsmen by treading on their faces. At night we were too lazy to move our faces out of the way. Oddly enough, he was never too lazy to walk on them. For our part, we had a cat to torture; she drowned learning to swim, though she'd eaten the rats off our bodies. Such people all had this disease.

MARIE: When were you on the Yangtse-kiang?

SHLINK: We lay in the rushes in the early morning and felt the disease grow on us.

THE WORM (*enters*): The wind has eaten the fellow up. In all Chicago, neither hide nor hair of him.

SHLINK: You'd do well to sleep a little. Again nothing?

SHLINK *leaves. Through the open door is heard the noise of Chicago waking up: cries of milkmen, rolling of meat wagons.*

MARIE: Chicago wakes amid the cries of milkmen and the loud rolling of meat wagons. Time of newspapers and fresh morning air. To go away would be good, and to wash with water is good, and the savanna and the asphalt road have something to offer. Now, for instance, a cool wind blows in the savanna, where we were once. I am sure it does.

THE BABOON: You still know the short catechism, Jane?

JANE (*rattling it off*): It'll get worse, it'll get worse, it'll get worse. *They start to clean things up, pull up the blinds, air the mattresses.*

MARIE: As far as I'm concerned, I'm somewhat out of breath. I want to sleep with a man and I don't know how to. Some women are like dogs, yellow and black, and yet I can't do it. I'm torn to bits. The walls are like paper, you can't breathe, you've got to set fire to everything. Where are the matches, a black box, that the flood might come! Oh, when I swim away, there are two parts, swimming in two directions. That's the end.

JANE: Where's he gone?

THE BABOON: He's inspecting the faces of those who are going away, those for whom Chicago is too cruel.

JANE: There's an east wind. The Tahiti ships are lifting anchor.

5

SAME HOTEL

One month later, September 19 or 20.
A dirty bedroom. A hallway. A glass-enclosed whiskey bar.
THE WORM. GEORGE GARGA. MANKY. THE BABOON.

THE WORM (*speaks from the hallway into the bar*): He did *not* sail away. The harpoon is deeper in than we supposed. We thought the earth had swallowed the fellow. But he's in Shlink's room licking his wounds.

GARGA (*in the bedroom*): "In my dreams I call him my hellish husband — that dog, Shlink. We are parted from bed and board, he hasn't got a room. His little bride smokes Virginia cigars and earns something to put in her stockings." That's me. (*Laughs.*)

MANKY (*in the bar behind the glass*): Life is peculiar. I, for my part, for instance, knew a man, a thoroughly first-rate man, but he loved a woman. Her family was starving to death. He had two thousand dollars, but he looked on while they starved. He made love to the woman with his two thousand dollars, because otherwise he couldn't get her. A nasty business, but he can't be held responsible.

GARGA: "Look, I am a sinner. I loved the desert, scorched orchards, dilapidated shops, tepid drinks.* You're mistaken. I am a little man." I have nothing to do with Mr. Shlink from Yokohama!

THE BABOON: Yes, the lumber dealer, for example. He never showed a sign of having a heart. But one day, through passion, his

---

* Of the passages in quotation marks in the first part of this scene, I have found a source only for this one sentence: "J'aimai le désert, les vergers brûlés, les boutiques fanées, les boissons tièdies" — Rimbaud's *A Season in Hell*. Garga's "Someday I shall be his widow" may have been suggested by Rimbaud's "Je suis veuve . . . — J'étais veuve . . ." E. B.

whole business went to hell. And now he carries coal down there. His hand was once at the throat of the whole quarter!

THE WORM: We took him in here like a worn-out race hound. But if he still can't get away from his little bone, which by chance has turned up again, our patience, too, will be at an end.

GARGA: "Some day I shall be his widow. Surely the day has already been marked in the calendar. And I shall walk in clean under-wear behind his corpse, my legs spread good and wide in the warm sun."

MARIE (*enters with a lunch basket*): George!

GARGA: Who is that? (*Recognizes her.*) The way you look! Like a soiled rag!

MARIE: Yes.

THE WORM (*into the bar*): He's blotto. And now his sister's come to see him. He's telling her she's soiled. Where's the old man?

THE BABOON: Coming today. I've brought Jane here. Another fish hook, I suppose. Everything's staked on this boxing match.

JANE (*shakes her head*): I don't understand you. Give me a drink. Gin.

MARIE: I'm glad you had a better opinion of me. That's why you're surprised to find me here. I, too, remind you of the days when you were the pride of the fair sex in Shimmy and Ragtime, with a crease in your trousers on a Saturday night, and your only vices were tobacco, whiskey, and love of woman, which are all right for men. I'd like you to think of all this, George. (*Pause.*) How do you live?

GARGA (*lightly*): At night it gets cold here. Would you like something? Are you hungry?

MARIE (*lightly, shakes her head, looks at him*): Oh George, for some time there have been vultures overhead.

GARGA (*lightly*): When were you home last?

MARIE *silent.*

GARGA: I heard you keep company here.

MARIE: Oh. Who takes care of them at home?

GARGA (*cold-blooded*): I can set your mind at rest. I heard someone takes care of them. I know what you're doing too. And I know something about a Chinese hotel.

MARIE: Is it pleasant to be so cold-blooded, George?

GARGA *looks at her.*

MARIE: Don't look me in the face. I know you're a Catholic.

GARGA: Go ahead.

MARIE: I love him. Why don't you say something?

GARGA: Love him! It will weaken him!

MARIE: Please don't look up at the ceiling all the time — I can't get him.

GARGA: That's a disgrace!

MARIE: I know — Oh, George, I'm cut in half. Because I can't get him. I tremble inside my clothes when I see him. Then I say the wrong thing.

GARGA: I can't tell you the right thing. A woman who gets herself rejected! I had one girl, she wasn't worth a bottle of rum, but she knew how to lead men on! She paid her way. She knew what she could do.

MARIE: You say such sharp things. They swim into my head like alcohol. Are they any good? You should know if they're any good. But I understand you now.

SHLINK *enters the hallway.*

THE WORM: Speaking from experience, let me tell you that all humanity, with its horse hair and rhinoceros hide, is a prey to paper dreams. And nothing is as much like paper as real life.

MARIE GARGA *turns around and bumps into* SHLINK.

SHLINK: You here, Miss Garga?

MARIE: A woman who tells a man she loves him offends propriety. I want to tell you my love for you proves nothing. I want nothing from you. It is not easy for me to tell you this. And maybe it's obvious anyway.

GARGA (*comes out of the bedroom*): Stay here, Marie. We were driven to the big city but we have the faces of the plains.

You mustn't let yourself be pushed around. You needn't do anything you don't want to do.

MARIE: No, George.

GARGA: It's like this: he works like a horse and I wallow in my pool of absinthe.

SHLINK: The conquerors of the world like to lie on their backs.

GARGA: The owners of the world work.

SHLINK: You have worries?

GARGA (*to* SHLINK): You're forever sizing me up — every time I look at your face. Have you been thinking you bet on the wrong horse? Your face has aged.

SHLINK: Thank you for not forgetting me. I almost thought you were in the South. I ask your forgiveness. I took the liberty of supporting your unhappy family with the work of my hands.

GARGA: Is that true, M? I really didn't know. So you're worming your way in? Does your royal lowness enjoy providing for my family? You make me laugh. (*Goes to the bedroom at left, lies down, laughs.*)

SHLINK (*follows him eagerly*): Laugh! I love your laughter. Your laughter is my sunshine, it was miserable here before. What grief not to see you! It's been three weeks, Garga.

GARGA: I was satisfied, all in all.

SHLINK: Yes, you're bathing in milk.

GARGA: Only my back wears thin as a fishbone from lying down.

SHLINK: How miserable life is! You bathe in milk, and the milk is bad milk.

GARGA: I want more from life than to rip off the heels of my shoes on you.

SHLINK: I must beg you to leave my humble self and my intentions out of account. But I am here. If you have to give up, you can't leave the ring innocent.

GARGA: But I am giving up. I'm going on strike. I'm throwing in the towel. Are you sunk so deep into me? You're a small, hard betel-nut, one should spit you out, one knows it is harder than teeth, it is all shell.

SHLINK (*cheered*): I make every effort to provide the target you need. I place myself under every light, Mr. Garga. (*Steps into the light.*)

GARGA: Do you want to auction off your pock-marked soul here? Are you hardened against all sufferings? . . . Hard?! . . .

SHLINK: Bite through the nut.

GARGA: You are withdrawing to my position. You start a meta-physical boxing match and you leave behind a shambles.

SHLINK: You mean this matter of your sister? I slaughtered noth-ing that you put a protecting hand over.

GARGA: I only have two hands. What is human for me, you swallow it like so much meat. You open my eyes to some new source of supply precisely by stopping it up. You make my own family into a source of supply. *You* live on *my* resources! And I grow thinner and thinner. Now I am getting into metaphysics! And yet you dare to vomit all this up in my face!

MARIE: Please, George, can't I go? (*She withdrews to the back.*)

GARGA (*brings her forward*): On the contrary! We've just begun talking about you. You have just come into my field of vision.

SHLINK: I have the misfortune to step on soft spots. I yield. You realize the value of your inclinations only when the object of them is lying in the morgue, and I feel the need to point out to you what your inclinations are. But please continue. I understand you completely.

GARGA: But I do make the sacrifice. Am I refusing?

MARIE: You should let me go. I am afraid here.

GARGA: Come, you! (*Runs into the hallway.*) Let's found a family!

MARIE: George!

GARGA: Stay here! (*Calls to* SHLINK:) Take part in this as a human being, sir!

SHLINK: I don't for a second refuse.

GARGA: You love this man? He remains passive?

MARIE *weeps*.

SHLINK: I hope you won't overstrain yourself. (*Runs back into the bedroom.*)

GARGA: Don't worry. It will be a step forward. It's Thursday evening, isn't it? This is the Chinese hotel. And that is my sister Marie Garga, isn't it? (*Runs out.*) Come here, my sister! Here's Mr. Shlink from Yokohama. He has something to say to you.

MARIE: George!

GARGA (*goes off for drinks*): I fled into the precincts of the city where women with big crooked orange mouths are cowering, oh so white, in the glowing thornbushes.

MARIE: It's night already in the window, and today I want to go home.

SHLINK: I'll go with you if you like.

GARGA: Their hair was black-lacquered scales, very thin, their eyes were wiped by the winds of the debauchery of the drunken night and the victims in the fields.

MARIE (*softly*): Please don't ask it of me.

GARGA: Their thin dresses, like iridescent snake-skins, as if soaked through by everlasting rains, slapped against their ever-excited limbs.

SHLINK: I really did ask you. I have no secrets from anyone.

GARGA: These completely cover them down to their toe nails, which are inlaid with copper. Whereupon the Madonna in the clouds turns pale at the thought of her sisters. (*Returns, gives* SHLINK *a glass.*) Don't you want to drink? I find it necessary.

SHLINK: Why do you drink? Drinkers lie.

GARGA: It is fun to talk to you. When I drink, half my thoughts swim downwards. I guide them to the bottom, and they don't feel so heavy. Drink!

SHLINK: I'd rather not. If that's all right with you.

GARGA: I invite you, and you refuse . . .

SHLINK: I don't refuse. But my brains are all I've got.

GARGA (*after a moment*): I beg your pardon, let's go halves: you

cut down on brains. When you have drunk, you will make
love.

SHLINK (*drinks, making a ceremony of it*): When I've drunk, I
shall make love.

GARGA (*shouts into the bedroom*): Do you want a glass, M? No?
Why don't you take a chair?

THE BABOON: Shut your trap! I've heard you talk till now. Now be
quiet.

GARGA (*to* MARIE): This is the black hole. Now forty years will
go by. I don't say no. The bottoms are dropping out. The
scum shows itself, but its desires are too weak. I was at sea
and for four hundred years I used to dream I had the salt
wind in my eyes. How smooth the sea was! (*He drinks.*)

SHLINK (*submissive*): May I take your hand, Miss Garga? Shall
I throw myself submissively at your feet? Please come with
me. I love you.

MARIE (*runs into the bar*): Help! They're selling me!

MANKY: Here I am, baby.

MARIE: I knew you'd be where I was.

GARGA: As at the opera, a breath of wind opens up cracks in the
partitions!

SHLINK (*roars*): Get out of this bar, Miss Garga, if you please!
MARIE *gets out of the bar.*

SHLINK: Please don't throw yourself away, Miss Garga.

MARIE: I want to find a room where there's nothing. I don't want
much any more, I promise you I never will again, Pat.

GARGA: Fight for your chance, Shlink.

SHLINK: Think of the years that are passing, Miss Garga. You can
sleep now.

MANKY: Come with me, I have four hundred pounds. That means
a roof in the winter, and there'll be no phantoms except in
peep-shows.

SHLINK: Please, Miss Garga, go with me, I beg you! I'll treat you
like my wife and serve you and hang myself without a fuss if
I hurt you even once.

GARGA: He isn't lying. He definitely isn't lying. That's what you'll
get when you're with him — a penny at a time. (*Goes into
the bar.*)

MARIE: Now, Pat, if I don't love you, do you love me?

MANKY: I think so. And nowhere between heaven and earth is it
written that you don't love me, baby.

GARGA: So it's you, Jane. Killing some cocktails? You hardly look
like yourself. Sold everything already?

JANE: Take him away, Baboon. I don't like his face. He bothers
me. I may not live in the land of milk and honey, but I don't
need to make myself a laughing stock, Bab.

THE BABOON: I'll break anyone's nose who calls you an old shoe!

GARGA: Did they feed you with the others? Your face has been
licked up like lemon ice cream. Damnation, you went around
in fine rags like in an opera, but now it's as if someone had
poured black powder over you. But I give you credit for not
coming here first of your own accord because the flies had
done it on you, my pie-eyed hen.

MARIE: Let's go. I'd have liked to do you the favor, Shlink, but I
can't. It isn't pride.

SHLINK: Stay, if you like! I won't repeat my offer if it doesn't
appeal to you, but don't let the Hole swallow you! There
are many vacant seats that are not next to a man.

GARGA: Not for a woman. Let her be, Shlink! Don't you see what
she's after? If you'd preferred a roof in the winter, Jane, you'd
still be sitting with your shirts, Jane.

SHLINK: Drink before making love, Marie Garga!

MARIE: Come, Pat, this is not a good place. Is she your woman,
George? Is she? I'm glad I got to see her. (*Off with* MANKY.)

SHLINK (*calls after them*): I won't give you up. Come back when
you're reduced to misery.

THE BABOON: An old shoe, sir, which is rather far gone! (*Laughs.*)

GARGA (*lights up* SHLINK *with a candle*): Your face is in good shape.
I'm put off by your good intentions.

SHLINK: The sacrifices on both sides are considerable. How many
ships do you need for Tahiti? Shall I hoist my shirt for a sail —

or your sister's? I burden you with your sister's fate. You have opened her eyes to what she'll be among men forever and forever: an object. I hope I haven't frustrated you. I'd almost won her as a virgin, but you'd decided I should get what was left over. Don't forget the family which you are abandoning in its need. You have now seen what you are sacrificing.

GARGA: I want to slaughter them all now. I know it. — I'm ready to get a jump ahead of you. I understand, too, why you've stuffed them with what you earned carrying coal till they are good and fat. But I can't allow the price of our joke to be beaten down. And now I'll also take this little animal you've been saving for me in my arms.

JANE: I won't be insulted. I stand alone in the world. I take care of myself.

GARGA: I now request that you turn over the money from the lumber which was sold twice and which I hope you have saved for me. For the time has come.

SHLINK *pulls the money out and turns it over to him.*

GARGA: I am completely drunk. But even though I am drunk, I still have a good idea, Shlink, a first-class idea. (*Off with* JANE.)

THE BABOON: That was the last of your money, sir. And where did you get it? You'll be questioned about it yet. Broost & Co. have asked for the lumber they paid for.

SHLINK (*without listening to him*): A chair. (*They have occupied all the chairs and don't make a move to stand up.*) My rice and water!

THE WORM: There's no rice for you any more, sir. Your account is overdrawn.

6

LAKE MICHIGAN

End of September.
Woodland. SHLINK. MARIE.

MARIE: The trees seem draped with human dung, the sky near enough to touch, how indifferent it leaves me! I'm freezing. I'm like a half-frozen quail. I can't help myself.

SHLINK: If this will help you: I love you.

MARIE: I threw myself away. Oh, my love has become such a bitter fruit. Others have their good season when they love, but I wither here, I fret my life away. My body is defiled.

SHLINK: Tell me it's all over with you, it will relieve your feelings.

MARIE: I went to bed with a man who is like an animal. I gave myself to him many times, though my whole body was numb, and I couldn't get warm. He smoked Virginias in between, a sailor! I loved you every hour I spent inside those walls, and I got so worked up that he thought it was love and tried to finish me. I slept a black sleep. I owe you nothing, yet my conscience cries out to me that I have defiled my body which belongs to you though you rejected it.

SHLINK: I'm sorry you're freezing. I mean: the air is warm and dark. I don't know how the men of this country speak to their mistresses. If this will help you: I love you.

MARIE: I am such a coward. My courage is gone with my innocence.

SHLINK: You will wash yourself clean.

MARIE: Maybe I should go down to the water, but I can't. I'm not ready. Oh, this despair! The heart which can't be stilled! In everything I'm only half. And I don't love, it's just vanity. I hear what you say, for I'm not deaf, I have ears, but what does it mean? Maybe I'm sleeping, someone will wake me, and maybe I'm the kind that act shamefully just to have a roof over their heads. And maybe I deceive myself and shut my eyes.

SHLINK: Come, it's getting cold here.

MARIE: But the leaves are warm and good against the sky, which is too close.

They leave.

MANKY (*comes in*): Her tracks point this way. You need a sense of humor this September. The lobsters are mating, the love-cry of the red deer is heard in the thicket, and the badger can be hunted. But my fins are cold and I wrap my black stockings in old newspapers. Where she's living, that's the worst. If she lies around in the slimy brandy bar like a fish-bone, she'll never herself get a clean shirt. Nothing but stains! Oh, Pat Mankyboddle, I proclaim martial law over you! Too weak to defend myself, I go over to the attack. The bitch will be swallowed with her skin of feathers, digestion will be accelerated by prayers, vultures will be shot according to martial law, and hung up in Mankyboddle's Museums. Brrr! Words! Truth without a tooth! (*He pulls a gun out of his pocket.*) This is the coldest answer. Sniffing around in this thicket for a female, you old pig? On all fours with you! Damn, but this is Suicide Wood! Watch it there, Paddy! Where should the woman go when it's all over with her from top to toe? Drop it, Paddy, smoke a little, eat a bite, put that thing in your pocket! March! (*Off.*)

MARIE (*returns with* SHLINK): It is repugnant to God and man. I'll not go with you.

SHLINK: What a decadent attitude! Your insides need an airing.

MARIE: I can't. You're sacrificing me.

SHLINK: You'll always have to put your head in *some* man's armpit, what matter whose?

MARIE: I'm nothing to you.

SKLINK: You can't live alone.

MARIE: How quickly you took me — as if I were going to run away. And how like a sacrifice!

SHLINK: You ran into the bushes like a mad bitch, and like a mad bitch you run out again.

MARIE: Am I as you say? I'm always as you say. I love you. Make no mistake about that, I love you. I love you like a mad bitch. You say it. But now pay me. Yes, I'd enjoy being paid. Give me your bills, I want to live on the money. I'm a whore.

SHLINK: There's moisture all over your face. You are a whore!

MARIE: Give me the money without mocking me. Don't look at me. The moisture isn't tears, it's just the fog.

SHLINK *gives her bills.*

MARIE: I will not say thank you, Mr. Shlink from Yokohama. It was an even bargain: no one has to say thank you.

SHLINK: Get out of this business! You'll earn nothing. (*Off.*)

7

LIVING ROOM OF THE GARGA FAMILY

September 29, 1912.

JOHN GARGA, MAE, GEORGE, JANE, MANKY, *all in new clothes at a wedding breakfast.*

JOHN: Since the man whom no one around here likes to mention, whose skin is different but who goes down to the coal district for the sake of a certain family of his acquaintance, yes, to work for them night and day, yes, since this man with the different skin holds his protective hand over us in the coal district, things are better with us every day in every respect. Today, without knowing there *was* a wedding, he has made it possible for our son George to have a wedding fit for the head man of a great firm. Brand new ties, black business suits, a slight odor of whiskey between our teeth — among new furniture!

MAE: Isn't it strange that this man of the coal district should earn so much just by carrying coal?

GARGA: I am the one who earns the money.

MAE: You got married overnight. Wasn't it a little hasty, Jane?

JANE: Snow also melts, then where is it? And the wrong person is chosen, that often happens.

MAE: It isn't a matter of the right man or the wrong, it's just that people won't leave him alone.

JOHN: Rot! Eat your steak and shake hands with the bride!

They kiss.

GARGA (*takes her by the wrist*): It's a good hand. I feel quite well here. Let the wallpaper peel off, I put on a new suit, I eat steaks, I taste plaster here, I am covered with cement, finger-thick, I see a piano. Hang a wreath around the photograph of our sister Marie Garga, born twenty-one years ago on the

44

plains. Put some immortelles under glass. It is good to sit here, good to lie here. The black wind can't come here.

JANE (*stands up*): What's wrong, George? Have you a fever?

GARGA: Fever feels good to me, Jane.

JANE: I always wonder what you want with me, George.

GARGA: Why are you so pale, Mother? I should think the prodigal son must be lurking beneath your roof again. Why stand around like plaster pictures on the wall?

MAE: I think it's the boxing match you are talking about.

GARGA: There are flies in my brain, aren't there? I can brush them off, can't I? (SHLINK *enters.*) Oh, Mother, take a steak and a glass of whiskey and offer them to our guest, who is welcome! For I was married this morning. My dear wife, tell the tale!

JANE: I and my husband, we went to the Sheriff, right out of bed in the morning, and we said: Can you get married here? He said: I know you, Jane — will you always stay with your husband? But I could see he was a good man with a beard, and he had nothing against me, and so I said: Life isn't exactly what you think.

SHLINK: I congratulate you, Garga. You seek revenge.

GARGA: There's a horrible fear in your smile. Rightly. Don't eat so fast! You have time! Where is Marie? I hope she's taken care of. Her satisfaction must be complete. Unfortunately there isn't a chair empty for you right now, Shlink. There's one chair too few. Outside of that, these furnishings are new and complete. Observe the piano! It is pleasant. I wish to spend my evenings here with the family. I've entered upon a new phase of life. Tomorrow I return to C. Maynes in the lending library.

MAE: Oh George, aren't you talking too much?

GARGA: You hear? My family doesn't wish me to keep up relations with you. Our acquaintanceship is over, Mr. Shlink. It brought us great profit. The furniture speaks for itself. The new suits of my whole family make a clear statement. Ready cash is not lacking. Thank you.

Silence.

SHLINK: May I ask one more favor in a personal matter? I have here a letter from Broost & Co. I see on it, moreover, the judicial seal of the State of Virginia. I note that I have not opened it yet. You would oblige me if you would do so. Whatever it may be, in your mouth any revelation, even the worst, will sound more pleasant. (GARGA *reads*.) A pointer from you in this, my very own affair, would make things easier for me.

MAE: Why do you say nothing, George? What are you planning, George? Again your face looks as if you had a new plan. I fear nothing so much. You sit behind your unknown thoughts as behind smoke. We wait like cattle in the stockyards. You say: wait a little. You go away, you come back, and we can't recognize you, and we don't know what you've done to yourself. Tell me your plan, and if you don't have one, admit it, so I can act accordingly. I, too, must plan for the time ahead. Four years in this city of iron and dirt! Oh George!

GARGA: The bad years were the best years, you see, and now they are over. Don't say anything to me. You, my parents, and you, Jane, my wife, I have decided to go to jail.

JOHN: What are you saying? Is this where your money came from? That you would end in jail was written on your forehead when you were five. I didn't ask what happened between you two. I was always sure it was filthy. You lost track of the ground under your feet. Buying pianos and going to jail, dragging in whole baskets of steak and depriving a family of its means of support, that's one and the same thing to you. Where is Marie, your sister? (*He tears off his coat, and throws it down.*) There's my coat back, I didn't want to put it on. But I'm used to suffering whatever humiliations this city may have in store for me.

JANE: How long will it be, George?

SHLINK (*to* JOHN): Some lumber was sold twice. Naturally, that means jail, since the Sheriff won't bother about the circumstances. I, your friend, could explain many things to the Sheriff as niftily as Standard Oil could explain its tax declaration. I am willing to listen to your son, Mrs. Garga.

JANE: Don't let them talk you into anything, George, do what you think necessary, regardless. I'm your wife, I'll take care of the house while you're away.

JOHN (*with a resounding laugh*): She'll take care of the house! A girl picked off the streets only yesterday! We're to be supported by the income on sin!

SHLINK (*to* GARGA): You have indicated that your heart is still with your family. You wish to spend your evenings with this furniture. Many thoughts center on me, your friend, and I am busy removing the stones from your path. I am ready to keep you in the bosom of your family.

MAE: You mustn't go to jail, George.

GARGA: I know, Mother, you don't understand. How hard it is to injure a man! And to destroy him, quite impossible! The world is too poor. We have to work ourselves to the bone to find missiles to throw at her.

JANE (*to* GARGA): You're philosophizing while the roof rots off over our heads.

GARGA (*to* SHLINK): Graze up and down this world of ours. You will find ten bad people but not one bad deed. Man is destroyed by trivial causes alone. No, now I'll liquidate all: I'll draw a line under our account, and then go.

SHLINK: Your family wishes to know if they mean anything to you. Whoever you do not support falls down. One more word, Garga!

GARGA: I make you all a present of freedom.

SHLINK: They will rot on your account. They aren't many now, they might get pleasure, as you do, from making a clean sweep, cutting up the dirty tablecloth, shaking the cigar butts out of their clothes. They could all try to imitate you — in order to be free, in order to be indecent in sloppy underclothes.

MAE: Be quiet, George, it's all true, what he says.

GARGA: At last I see something, if I half shut my eyes, in a cold light. Not your face, Mr. Shlink. Perhaps you have none.

SHLINK: Forty years are now found to have been filthy, but there will be a great freedom.

GARGA: That's the way it is. The snow tried to fall, but it was too cold. Again left-overs will be eaten, again they will go hungry, and I, I am slaying my enemy.

JOHN: I see only weakness. Nothing else. Ever since I first saw you. Go. Leave us. Why shouldn't they take the furniture away?

GARGA: I have read that soft waters are a match for whole mountains. And I'd still like to see your real face, Shlink, your milk-white, damned invisible face.

SHLINK: I don't care to talk with you any more! Three years! For a young man it's no more than opening a door! But for me! I have not made a profit on you, if that is any consolation. But you leave no traces of regret in me, now that I shall mix again in this noisy city and carry on my business as I did before your time. (*Off.*)

GARGA: I only have to phone the police. (*Off.*)

JANE: I'll be in the Chinese bar. I don't like to see police. (*Off.*)

MAE: I sometimes think Marie too will never come back.

JOHN: She has only herself to blame. Why should one help them when they are vicious?

MAE: When else should one help them?

JOHN: Don't talk so much!

MAE (*sits down by him*): I wanted to ask what your plans are.

JOHN: My . . . ? None at all. An era has just ended.

MAE: You understood what George intends to do?

JOHN: More or less. The worse for us.

MAE: And what will you live on?

JOHN: On the money that is left, and on the piano that will be sold.

MAE: It will all be taken away from us because it was dishonestly come by.

JOHN: Maybe we'll go back to Ohio. We'll do something or other.

MAE (*gets up*): I wanted to tell you something else, John, but I can't. I didn't believe a man could suddenly be damned. But it's decided in heaven. On just an ordinary day, nothing unusual about it. From that day on, someone is damned.

JOHN: What are you going to do?

MAE: I'm going to do something quite definite, John, I take a lot of pleasure in it. Don't think it's for this or that reason. I'll put a little more coal on, I'll put your supper in the kitchen. (*Off.*)

JOHN: Take care the ghost of a shark doesn't gobble you up on the stairs.

WAITER (*enters*): Mrs. Garga has ordered a grog for you downstairs. Do you wish to drink in the dark or shall I light up?

JOHN: Light up — of course.

WAITER *off*.

MARIE (*enters*): Don't make a speech. I have money on me.

JOHN: You dare come in? This is a fine family! How do you look?

MARIE: I look good. But where did you get all this new furniture? Did you take in a lot of money? I've taken in a lot too.

JOHN: Where did you get it?

MARIE: You want to know?

JOHN: Give it to me. You let me go hungry: I'm not the same man any more.

MARIE: You'll take the money then. Despite the new furniture. Where is Mother?

JOHN: Deserters are stood up against the wall.

MARIE: Did you send her out on the streets?

JOHN: Be cynical, all of you, roll in the gutter, drink grog. But I'm your father, you can't let me starve to death.

MARIE: Where's she gone?

JOHN: You can go too. I'm used to being left behind.

MARIE: When did she go?

JOHN: My life is over, and I'm condemned to be poor and lick the spittle of my own children. But I want nothing to do with vice. I cannot but chase you away.

MARIE: Give me the money back. It wasn't for you anyhow.

JOHN: I won't think of it. You can sew me up in a sack. And now let me ask you for a pound of tobacco.

MARIE: Good-bye. (*Off.*)

JOHN: They have no more to tell a man than can be told in five minutes. No more lies than that. (*Pause.*) Yes, in two minutes everything there is to say could be kept quiet.

GARGA (*returning*): Where is Mother? Has she gone? Did she think I'd never come back? (*He runs out, comes back again.*) She's taken her other dress along. She'll not come back. (*He sits down at the table and writes a letter.*) "To the Police. I wish to direct your attention to the Malayan lumber dealer C. Shlink. This man has pursued my wife Jane Garga and seduced* my sister Marie Garga, who was in his service. George Garga." Of my mother I say nothing.

JOHN: That is the liquidation of our family.

GARGA: I write this letter, and I put this document in my pocket, so I can forget everything. And after three years — for that's how long they'll lock me up — eight days before my release, I shall turn this document over to the police, so that this man will be driven from the city and be absent from my eyes when I see the place again. For him the day of my release will be marked by the howling of the lynch gang.

* Brecht was later to change this to "raped." E. B.

8

THE PRIVATE OFFICE OF C. SHLINK

Afternoon of October 20, 1915, about one P.M.

SHLINK. A YOUNG (MALE) SECRETARY.

SHLINK (*dictating*): Write Miss Marie Garga, who is seeking a secretarial job here, that I don't care to have anything to do with her, or any member of her family, ever again. — To Standard Real Estate. Dear Sirs: Today, since not a single share remains in the hands of outside companies and our financial situation is a stable one, nothing stands in the way of your offer of a five-year contract.

AN EMPLOYEE (*brings a man in*): This is Mr. Shlink.

MAN: I have three minutes to give you an important message. You have two minutes to grasp the situation. Half an hour ago a letter arrived at the police commissioner's office from one of the state prisons. It is signed by a certain Garga, who pins various crimes on you. The police car will be here in five minutes.* You owe me one thousand dollars.

SHLINK *gives him the money; the* MAN *leaves.*

SHLINK (*while he carefully packs a bag*): Keep the business going as long as you can. Send those letters off. I'll be back. (*Exit quickly.*)

---

* Brecht was later to change this passage. It is the newspapers, not the police, who are informed, and it is the reporters who are expected in five minutes. E. B.

9

BAR IN THE CHINESE QUARTER

October 28, 1915.

THE WORM, THE BABOON, SNUB NOSE, THE MAN FROM THE
SALVATION ARMY, JANE, MARIE GARGA. *Noise from outside.*

THE BABOON: Do you hear the howling of the lynch gang? Dangerous days for China Town! Eight days ago the crimes of a
Malayan lumber dealer were uncovered. Three years ago he
got a man sent to jail, three years this man kept it to himself,
but eight days before his release he sent a letter to the police
and uncovered all.

SNUB NOSE: The human heart!

THE BABOON: The Malayan himself has fled, naturally. But he's
finished.

THE WORM: You can't say that about any man. Observe this planet
of ours! A man is not finished all at once but at least a hundred
times over. Each man has all too many possibilities. Just listen,
for instance, to the story of G. Wishu the human bulldog. I
have to have nickelodeon music with this. (*Nickelodeon.*)
This is the life story of the dog George Wishu. George Wishu
was born on the green isle of Ireland. After a year and a half,
in the company of a fat man, he came to the great city of
London. His own country let him go like a stranger. In London
he soon fell into the hands of a cruel woman, who subjected
him to gruesome tortures. After enduring much suffering, he
ran away to a spot where they hunted him between green
hedges. He was shot at with big, dangerous guns, and foreign
dogs chased him many times. So he lost a leg, and from then
on had quite a limp. After several of his undertakings had
failed, tired of life and half-starved, he found refuge with an
old man who shared his bread with him. There he died, relaxed

and calm, after a life full of disappointments and adventures,
at the age of seven and one half years. His grave is in Wales.
— I'd like to know how you'll get all this under one hat, sir.

SNUB NOSE: Who is that on the Wanted sign?

THE WORM: That is the Malayan they're looking for. He was
bankrupt once before. But in three years he brought the entire
lumber trade back into his own hands, for which he was
much hated in the district. He would be one of the mighty in
Chicago if the man in jail had not dragged his crimes into the
light of day. (*To* JANE:) When will your husband be out of
jail?

JANE: Yes, that's it. I knew it before. Don't think, gentlemen, I don't
know it. It's the twenty-eighth, whenever that may be.

THE BABOON: Cut the cackle, Jane.

SNUB NOSE: And what sort is *she* — with her indecent dress?

THE BABOON: That is the victim, the sister of the man in jail.

JANE: Yes, that's my sister-in-law. She acts as if she didn't know
me. After I married her brother, she didn't come home one
single night.

THE BABOON: The Malayan ruined her.

SNUB NOSE: What is she putting in the pail?

THE WOMAN: I can't see it. She's saying something too. Quiet, Jane!

MARIE (*lets a bill float into the water-pail*): When I had the bills
in my hands, I saw God's eyes on me. I said: I did it all for him.
God turned away. It was as if the tobacco fields sighed. What
bitter poverty it all turned into! One bill! Another! Watch
me fall apart! Watch me throw away my purity! Now the
money's gone! But I don't feel easier . . .

GARGA (*enters with* C. MAYNES *and three other men*): I have asked
you to come and see with your own eyes that an injustice has
been done me. I have brought you along, Mr. Maynes, so I
have a witness that, when I returned after three years, I found
my wife in a place like this. (*He leads the men to the table
where* JANE *is sitting*.) Hello, Jane. How are you?

JANE: George! Is today the twenty-eighth? I didn't know. I'd have been home. Did you notice how cold it was there? Did you realize I would come here to get warm?

GARGA: This is Mr. Maynes. You know him. I'll be working for him again. And these are gentlemen from our street who are interested in my situation.

JANE: How do you do, gentlemen? Oh George! This is terrible of me! To miss your day! What will you think of me, gentlemen? Ken Si, take care of these gentlemen!

SALOON KEEPER (*to* SNUB NOSE): That's the man from jail who denounced him.

GARGA: Hello, Marie. Did you wait for me? — My sister is here, too, as you see.

MARIE: Hello, George. Everything fine?

GARGA: Let's go home, Jane.

JANE: Oh George, you say that. But if I go home with you, you'll only scold me, and I'd rather tell you straight out: the place hasn't been cleaned up.

GARGA: I know.

JANE: That's nasty of you.

GARGA: I won't scold you, Jane. We'll start afresh. The boxing match is over. You can tell that by the fact that I've driven my opponent out of town.

JANE: No, George, everything always gets worse. People say it'll get better but it always gets worse because it always *can* get worse. I hope you like it here, gentlemen? We could go some place else, of course . . .

GARGA: But what's wrong with you, Jane? Aren't you pleased I've come to get you?

JANE: You know, George. If you don't know, I can't tell you.

GARGA: What do you mean?

JANE: Don't you see, George, a human being is different from what you think, even if he *is* almost finished. Why did you bring these gentlemen along? I always knew I'd end up this way. When they told me in communion class what would happen to the weak, I thought right away: "That will happen to me. You don't have to prove it to anybody."

GARGA: Then you don't want to go home?

JANE: Don't ask, George.

GARGA: But I am asking, my love.

JANE: Then I must say it this way. Look, I have slept with this gentleman. (*Points to* THE BABOON.) I confess it, gentlemen, what difference does it make, nothing'll ever get better.

THE BABOON: The devil's in her.

MAYNES: Horrible.

GARGA: Listen, Jane. Now comes your last chance in this city. I'm ready to forget all this. You have these men as witnesses. Come home with me.

JANE: That's nice of you, George. It's certainly my last chance. But I don't want it. Things are not right between us, you know that. I'm going now, George. (*To* THE BABOON:) Come!

THE BABOON: Enjoy your dinner!

Both leave.

ONE OF THE MEN: This man has nothing to laugh about.

GARGA: I'll leave the apartment open, Jane. You can ring the bell at night.

THE WORM (*walks up to the table*): Maybe you've noticed it: there is a family among us that is surviving only in bits and pieces. This family, which, so to speak, the moths have got into, would joyfully sacrifice its last penny if someone could tell them where their mother, the mainstay of the household, is to be found. I did see her one morning at seven, a woman of some forty years, cleaning up a fruit cellar. She'd opened a new business. Her old face was in good shape.

GARGA: But you, sir, weren't you employed in the lumber business of the man for whom they are now searching Chicago from top to bottom?

THE WORM: I? I never saw the man. (*Off.*)

THE WORM *throws a coin into the nickelodeon on leaving. It plays Gounod's "Ave Maria."*

MAN FROM THE SALVATION ARMY (*at a corner table, reading the liquor list in a hard voice, "tasting" every word*): Cherry

Flip, Cherry Brandy, Gin Fizz, Whiskey Sour, Golden Slipper, Manhattan Cocktail, Curaçao extra sec Orange, Maraschino Cusinier and the specialty of this bar: Egg Nog. This drink alone has in it: Egg, raw egg, sugar, cognac, Jamaica rum, milk.

SNUB NOSE: Do you know about drinks, sir?

MAN: No!

Laughter.

GARGA (*to his companions*): You will understand that the exposure of my shattered family, though necessary, is humiliating for me. But you will also have understood that this yellow weed must never be allowed to grow in our city again. My sister Marie was, as you know, in the service of this man Shlink for some time. I have to proceed as cautiously as possible when I talk with her now, you understand, for my sister has preserved a certain vestige of fine feeling even in her deepest misery. (*Sits down by* MARIE.) May I see your face?

MARIE: It isn't one. This is not me.

GARGA: Yes. But I recall you once said in church, you were nine at the time, "from tomorrow on he will come unto me." And we supposed you meant God. Yes.

MARIE: Did I say that?

GARGA: I love you still, no matter how neglected and how defiled. But even if you know you can do anything you like with me when I tell you: "I'll always love you," I still want to tell you.

MARIE: And you look at me now? Right in my face?

GARGA: Right in your face. A person stays what she is even if her face falls apart.

MARIE (*stands up*): But I don't want that. I don't want you to love me like that. I love myself as I used to be so don't say I was never different.

GARGA (*loudly*): Are you earning any money? Do you live only off the men who pay you?

MARIE: Did you bring people along to let them know this? Can you buy whiskey here? With a lot of ice? Well, let it be made public. I threw myself away, but then I asked a price for it right after they began to notice what I was and that I could make a living that way. Now it goes smoothly. I have a good body, I won't allow smoking in my presence, but I'm no longer a virgin, I know how to make love. Here's my money. But I earn more, I want to spend it, that is exactly what I want. When I've earned it, I don't want to have to save it, here it is, I throw it in the pail over there. That's me.

MAYNES: Frightful.

ANOTHER MAN: One daren't laugh.

MAN FROM THE SALVATION ARMY: Man lasts much too long. That is his chief fault. He can start too much up with himself. He's too hard to wreck. (*Off.*)

MAYNES (*and the other three men stand up*): We have seen, George Garga, that an injustice has been done you.

SNUB NOSE (*approaches* MARIE): Whores! (*He neighs.*) Vice is the perfume of the ladies.

MARIE: We whores! With powder on our faces so you can't see our eyes, which were blue once. Men who make deals with crooks make love with us. We sell our sleep. We live off maltreatment.

A shot is heard.

SALOON KEEPER: The man shot himself in the neck.

Several men drag in the body of the MAN FROM THE SALVATION ARMY, *and lay him on the table among the glasses.*

FIRST MAN: Don't touch him. Hands off!

SECOND MAN: He's saying something.

FIRST MAN (*bent over him, loudly*): Have you any wishes? Have you relatives? Where shall we take you to?

MAN FROM THE SALVATION ARMY (*mumbling*): La montagne est passée: nous irons mieux.*

GARGA (*over him, laughing*): He has misfired in more ways than one. He thought those were his last words but they are the

---

* "We've passed the mountain, we'll do better now." The "famous last words" of Frederick the Great. That the Prussian king died, as he had lived, in French has comic point for the German audience, and I presume that is why Brecht left the remark untranslated. E. B.

last words of another man. Secondly, those were not his last words because he shot wide and there is only a slight flesh wound.

FIRST MAN: Indeed! Too bad! He did it in the dark. He should have done it in the light.

MARIE: His head is hanging back. Put something under it. How thin he is! Now I recognize him too, it's the one whose face he spat in.

All, except MARIE *and* GARGA, *leave with the wounded man.*

GARGA: He has too thick a skin. It bends the point of anything you stick into it. There aren't that many kinds of spikes.

MARIE: You're thinking of *him* all the time?

GARGA: I admit it.

MARIE: How low they bring you, love and hate!

GARGA: How low! — Do you still love him?

MARIE: Yes. — Yes.

GARGA: And no prospects for better winds?

MARIE: Yes, at times.

GARGA: I wanted to help you. (*Silence.*) This fight was such a debauch that today I need all Chicago to stop me continuing it. Of course, it's possible he himself didn't plan to continue it. He indicated that at his age three years could be equivalent to thirty. In consideration of all these circumstances, without actually being present, I have destroyed him by a very crude device. Besides which, I make it simply impossible for him to see me. This last blow will not be discussed between us any more: I won't let him speak to me. In the city, on each street corner, the taxi drivers are watching to make sure he won't show up in the ring at the moment when the knock-out that was preceded by no fight is accepted as a matter of course. Chicago throws in the towel for him. I don't know where he's hiding; but he knows.

SALOON KEEPER: Lumber yards are burning in Mulberry Street.

MARIE: It's good if you've shaken him off. But now I'm going.

GARGA: I'll stay at the center of this lynching operation. But in the evening I shall come home. We shall live together. (MARIE *off*.) I shall once more drink hot, black coffee in the morning, wash my face with cold water, put on fresh clothes, the shirt first. I will comb things out of my brain in the morning, the city will seem a happy, eventful noise all around me, now that I'm no longer eaten by this passion within that only dragged me down and down. But I still have many things to do. (*Opens the door all the way and listens, laughing, to the howling of the lynch gang, now louder.*)

SHLINK (*enters, wearing an American suit*): You are alone? It was hard to get here. I knew you were released today, I've been looking for you at your house. They're on my heels. Quick now, Garga, come with me!

GARGA: Are you out of your mind? I denounced you to be rid of you!

SHLINK: I am not a brave man. I died three times over on my way here.

GARGA: Yes, I hear they're hanging yellow men from the Milwaukee Bridge like so much bright-colored washing.

SHLINK: We must be all the quicker about it. You know you *have* to come. We are not through.

GARGA (*all the more slowly since he realizes* SHLINK *is pressed for time*): Unfortunately you make this request at a bad time. I have company. My sister Marie Garga, ruined in September three years ago, taken unawares. My wife, Jane Garga, wrecked at the same time. Finally, a man from the Salvation Army, name unknown, spat on and finished, though of no consequence. And above all, my mother, Mae Garga, born in 1872 in the south. She vanished three years ago in October, vanished even from memory, she has no face now, it fell from her like a yellow leaf. (*Listens.*) What screams!

SHLINK (*also listening intently*): Yes. But it isn't the right kind of screaming yet, the white screaming. Then they'll be on us. Then we'll have one minute. Listen: now! Now! There it is — the white screaming! Come with me!
GARGA *leaves quickly with* SHLINK.

10

ABANDONED RAILROAD WORKERS' TENT ALONG
THE GRAVEL PITS OF LAKE MICHIGAN

November 19, 1915, about two A.M.

SHLINK. GARGA.

SHLINK: The everlasting clamor of Chicago has stopped. Seven times three days the heavens have been pale, the air has turned blue-grey like grog. Now there is silence, which hides nothing.

GARGA (*smoking*): You fight light-heartedly. What metabolism! I still had my childhood before me. The oil fields with their little blue rape seeds. The polecat in the glens, the carefree rapids.

SHLINK: Truc. It was written all over your face! Now it is hard as amber with here and there a carcass embedded in it, a transparent carcass.

GARGA: You went on being lonely?

SHLINK: Forty years.

GARGA: Now, at the end, you fall victim to the black mania of this planet — the mania for contact.

SHLINK (*smiling*): Through enmity?

GARGA: Through enmity.

SHLINK: You have understood, then, that we are comrades, comrades in a metaphysical action. Our acquaintance was short. For a time, however, it was predominant. The time flew by. The stages of life are not those of memory. The end is not the goal, the last episode is not more important than any other. I have twice owned a lumber business. Two weeks ago it was again registered under your name.

GARGA: Have you premonitions of death?

SHLINK: Here is the master ledger of your lumber business. It begins where ink was spilled over the figures.

GARGA: You have kept it on you? Open it yourself. It must certainly be dirty. (*He reads.*) A clean account. Nothing but withdrawals. On the seventeenth: Lumber business, twenty-five thousand dollars for Garga. Before that: another ten dollars for clothes. After that, once: twenty-two dollars for Marie Garga, "our" sister. At the very end: the whole business burned to the ground. — I can't sleep any more, I'll be glad when you have quicklime over you.

SHLINK: Don't deny what was, Garga! Don't look just at the accounts. Remember the question as we originally put it. Pull yourself together: I love you.

GARGA: (*observes him*): But how revolting of you! You are horribly unappetizing, an old man like you!

SHLINK: Possibly I won't get an answer, but if you get the answer, think of me, even if by that time I have mud in my mouth. What are you listening for?

GARGA (*lazily*): You have a heart — or traces of one. You are old.

SHLINK: Is it good to show one's teeth?

GARGA: When they are good teeth.

SHLINK: The endless isolation of man makes even of enmity an unattainable goal. Even with animals it is impossible to come to an understanding.

GARGA: Nor does speech help all that much.

SHLINK: I have watched animals. Love — warmth from bodily proximity — is our only grace in all the darkness. But the union of the organs is the only union,* and it can never bridge the gap of speech. Still, they come together to beget new beings who can stand at their side in their inconsolable isolation. And the generations look coldly into each other's eyes. If you stuff a ship with human bodies till it bursts, there will still be such loneliness in it that one and all will freeze. Are you listening, Garga? Yes, so terrible is the isolation that there

* "The only thing that is real in this world is the pleasure of the senses. . . . The only proof that I exist is that I am ecstatic with lust." — J. V. Jensen's Evanston. E. B.

isn't even a fight. The forest! That's where mankind comes from. Hairy, with the teeth of an ape, good beasts who knew how to live, everything was so easy, they simply tore each other to bits. I can see them clearly, how, their flanks trembling, they stared into the whites of each other's eyes, sunk their teeth into each other's throats, and rolled down the slopes. The one that bled to death among the roots was conquered. The one that trampled down most young trees was the victor. You have your ears cocked for something, Garga?

GARGA: Shlink, I have listened to you now for three weeks. And all the time I expected to be seized with rage on any provocation, however petty. But now as I look at you, I notice that your babbling irritates me and that your voice nauseates me. Isn't it Thursday evening? How far is it to New York? Why do I sit here wasting my time? Haven't we been lying here three weeks? We thought the planet would change its course on that account! But what happened? Three times it rained, and once there was a wind at night. (*Stands up.*) I think it is time for you to pull off your shoes, Shlink. Pull off your shoes, Shlink, and give them to me. You probably haven't much money left now. Shlink, I am putting an end to the boxing match, which is now in its third year, here in the woods of Lake Michigan, because the raw material is used up. The fight ends — now. I cannot finish it off with a knife. I have no big words for it. My shoes are full of holes, and your speeches won't keep my toes warm. It is very clear, Shlink: the younger man wins.

SHLINK: Today at times one could hear the spades of the railroad workers, even out here. You listened closely, I noticed. You are getting up, Garga? You are going, Garga? You are betraying me?

GARGA (*lies down lazily*): Yes. That's just what I'm going to do, Shlink.

SHLINK: And never, George Garga, never any resolution to this fight? Never any understanding?

GARGA: No.

SHLINK: But you'll come out of it with your naked life in your pocket?

GARGA: A naked life is better than any other life.

SHLINK: Tahiti?

GARGA: New York. (*Laughs ironically*.) "I will go there and I will return with iron limbs, dark skin, and rage in my eye. On seeing my face, men will think I come of a strong race. I'll have gold, I'll be idle and brutal. Women love to nurse such wild invalids on their return from the hot countries. I'll swim, trample grass, hunt, and above all, smoke. Imbibe drinks like boiling metal. I'll mingle with life, and be saved!"* — What nonsense! Words, on a planet which is not in the middle! When you've been covered with quicklime a long time — for the old yields to the young, such is natural selection — I shall choose what entertains me.

SHLINK: What kind of attitude is that? Please take your pipe out of your big mouth! If you're trying to say you've become impotent, say it in some other tone of voice.

GARGA: As you please.

SHLINK: That gesture shows you are unworthy to be my opponent.

GARGA: I simply complained that I am bored.

SHLINK: You said you complained? You! A hired boxer! A drunken salesman! Whom I bought for ten dollars! An idealist who couldn't tell his legs apart, a nothing!

* "Nager, broyer l'herbe, chasser, fumer surtout; boire des liqueurs fortes comme du métal bouillant, — comme faisaient ces chers ancêtres autour des feux. Je reviendrai, avec des membres de fer, la peau sombre, l'oeil furieux; sur mon masque, on me jugera d'une race forte. J'aurai de l'or: je serai oisif et brutal. Les femmes soignent ces féroces infirmes retour des pays chauds. Je serai mêlé aux affaires politiques. Sauvé. Maintenant je suis maudit, j'ai horreur de la patrie . . . Ne pas porter au monde mes dégoûts et mes trahisons . . . A qui me louer? Quelle bête faut-il adorer? . . . Quels coeurs briserai-je? Quel mensonge dois-je tenir? — Dans quel sang marcher?" I am quoting much more from this passage than Garga recites. After all, he breaks off, shouting: "What nonsense!" And he has just *mis*quoted: he says, "I'll mingle with life," where Rimbaud has, "I'll mingle with (get mixed up in) political affairs." Brecht put a lot of himself into Garga, and in this passage we can discern where, in the experience of Brecht, nihilism leaves off and communism begins. E. B.

GARGA (*laughing*): A young man! Be honest with yourself.

SHLINK: A white man, hired to grind me to dust, to stuff a bit of disgust or decay in my mouth so I'd have the taste of death on my tongue. Five hundred feet away in these woods you will find a crowd of lynchers.

GARGA: Yes, maybe I am a leper, but what does it matter? You are a suicide. What do you offer me now? You hired me, but you did not pay me.

SHLINK: You received what men like you need. I bought you some furniture.

GARGA: Yes, it was a piano that I got out of you, a piano that had to be sold. I ate meat for once. I bought one suit but I sacrificed my sleep to your love of gabbing.

SHLINK: Your sleep, your mother, your sister, and your wife. Three years of your stupid life. But how annoying! Now it has a low ending. You didn't understand what it was about. You wanted my end; I wanted the boxing match. Not the physical contest but the spiritual.

GARGA: And the spiritual, too, is nothing.* It is not important to be the stronger one, but to be the living one. I cannot conquer you, I can only trample you into the ground. I shall carry my raw flesh into the icy rains. Chicago is cold. I shall go there. It is possible that I am doing the wrong thing. But I still have a lot of time. (*Off.*)

SHLINK *falls to the floor.*

SHLINK (*rises*): Since the last dagger thrusts have been exchanged, also the last words, those at any rate that we happened to think of, I thank you for the interest you have shown my person. We have lost much. Little but our naked bodies remains. In four minutes the moon will rise, and your lynch gang may well be here. (*He notices that* GARGA *is gone and runs after him.*) Do not leave, George Garga! Do not quit because you are young! The forests are cut down, the vultures

* "Le combat spirituel est aussi brutal que la bataille d'hommes; mais la vision de la justice est le plaisir de Dieu seul." — From the last page of Rimbaud's *A Season in Hell.* E. B.

satiated, and the golden answer will be buried in the earth! (*Turns around. A milky light rises in the thicket.*) November nineteenth. Three miles south of Chicago. West wind. Four minutes before moonrise: drowned, catching fish.

MARIE (*enters*): Please don't drive me away. I'm an unhappy girl. *The woods grow lighter all the time.*

SHLINK: It piles up. Fish that swim into your mouth . . . What crazy light is that? I'm very busy.

MARIE (*taking off her hat*): I don't look good any more. Don't look: the rats have nibbled at me. I bring you what is left.

SHLINK: What a milky light! Ah yes! *Haut goût!* Huh?

MARIE: Do you find my face bloated?

SHLINK: Do you know you'll be lynched if the mob catches you here?

MARIE: It's all the same to me.

SHLINK: Please let me spend my last minute alone.

MARIE: Come, hide yourself in the bushes. There's a hideout in the quarry.

SHLINK: Damnation! Are you out of your mind? Don't you see that I must look this thicket over one more time? To that end the moon is rising. (*Goes to the entrance.*)

MARIE: I see only that you have lost your way. Have pity on yourself!

SHLINK: Can't you do me this last favor?

MARIE: I only want to look at you. I realize that I belong here.

SHLINK: Maybe so. Stay. (*In the distance sirens are heard.*) Two o'clock. I must get to safety.

MARIE: Where is George?

SHLINK: George? Ran away. What a miscalculation! To get to safety. (*He tears his scarf off.*) The barrels stink already. Good, fat fish, caught by myself! Well dried, nailed up in boxes. Salted! First placed in ponds, then purchased, counted, richly stuffed! Death-seeking, suicidal fish that swallow the hooks as if they were holy wafers. Pah! (*He spits.*) Quick now! (*He goes to the table, sits down, drinks from a little bottle.*) I, Wang Yen, called Shlink, begotten in Yokohama in northern Peiho beneath the constellation of the tortoise, I have owned a lumber business, I have eaten rice, I have dealt with many kinds of people, I, Wang Yen, called Shlink, fifty-four years old, ended three miles south of Chicago, without issue.

MARIE: What's wrong with you?

SHLINK (*sitting*): Are you here? My legs are growing cold. Throw a cloth over my face. Have pity! (*He collapses.*)

Groans in the bushes, steps, hoarse curses from the back.

MARIE: What are you keeping your ears open for? Answer! Are you asleep? Are you still cold? I am with you! What do you want with a cloth?

At this moment openings are being slashed into the tent with knives. Into these openings, without a sound, slip the lynchers.

MARIE (*goes over to them*): Go away! He is dead. He doesn't want anyone to look at him.

11

PRIVATE OFFICE OF THE LATE C. SHLINK

Eight days later.

The lumber business lies in ashes. Signs are hanging around: "This business for sale."

GARGA. JOHN GARGA. MARIE GARGA.

JOHN: It was stupid of you to let this business burn down. Now you can sit between charred beams. Who is going to buy them?

GARGA (*laughs*): They're cheap. But what will you do?

JOHN: I thought we could stay together.

GARGA (*laughs*): I'm leaving. Are you going to work?

MARIE: I'll work. But I won't scrub stairs like my mother.

JOHN: I'm a soldier. We slept in troughs. The rats on our faces never weighed less than seven pounds. When they took my gun away, and it was over, I said: "From now on each of us will sleep with his cap on his head."

GARGA: In short: everyone sleeps.

MARIE: Let's go now, Father. Evening's coming on, and I still don't have a room.

JOHN: Yes, let's go. (*Looks around.*) Let's go. A soldier by your side. Forward against the jungle of the city!

GARGA: I have it behind me. Hey!

MANKY (*enters beaming, his hands in his pockets*): It's me. I read your ad in the paper. If your lumber yard isn't too expensive, I'll buy it.

GARGA: What's your offer?

MANKY: Why are you selling?

GARGA: I'm going to New York.

MANKY: And I'm moving here.

GARGA: How much can you pay?

MANKY: I've got to have some cash left for the lumber business.

GARGA: Six thousand. If you take the girl with it.

MANKY: All right.

MARIE: I have my father with me.

MANKY: And your mother?

MARIE: She isn't around now.

MANKY (*after a time*): All right.

MARIE: Get your contract ready!

The men sign it.

MANKY: We'd like to get a bite to eat. Like to come along, George?

GARGA: No.

MANKY: Will you still be here when we get back?

GARGA: No.

JOHN: Good-bye, George! Take a good look at New York. You can come back to Chicago when they're at your throat.

The three leave.

GARGA (*holding on to the money*): To be alone is a good thing. The chaos is used up now. It was the best time.

A MAN'S A MAN

The metamorphosis of the porter
Galy Gay in the army barracks at
Kilkoa in the year nineteen hundred
and twenty-five

A Comedy

(1924–1925)

English Version by
Eric Bentley

TRANSLATOR'S NOTE

British soldiers would normally speak some British dialect. But this isn't a normal play. It presents an India in which the temples are Chinese. And for that matter it presents a British army, as of 1925, which takes its orders from a queen. It presents an Irishman who has no Irish characteristics whatever. To normalize the language would be equivalent to correcting the geography and the social structure. In the original, the soldiers do not even speak like Germans. The lingo is a special and complex one, invented by Brecht: no one ever talked that way. In German this language has its own effectiveness. It is for the reader or spectator to judge whether the language of this translation has its own effectiveness. It cannot but be marked by some peculiarities not to be found in the original. Most notably, there are Americanisms in the dialogue. When on my high horse, I would claim that this is the most significant "alienation effect" of the present rendering. More modestly, let me say that this version was made with American actors in mind. And I would add that Brecht also must surely have had American actors in mind when he wrote the play — he remembered what he had seen on the silent screen in those days of the Keystone Cops and Mack Sennett and Chaplin.

The present version is based on the 1926 edition, published by Arcadia Verlag, Berlin.

CHARACTERS

URIAH SHELLEY

JESSE MAHONEY ⎱ *four soldiers of a machine gun*

POLLY BAKER ⎰ *unit in the British army in India*

JERAIAH JIP

CHARLES FAIRCHILD, *called Bloody Five, a sergeant*

GALY GAY, *an Irish porter**

MRS. GAY

MISTER WANG, *in charge of a Tibetan Pagoda*

HIS SEXTON

WIDOW LEOCADIA BEGBICK, *canteen owner*

JOBIA

BESSIE ⎱ *her daughters, halfbreeds who*

ANN ⎰ *constitute a jazz band*

SOLDIERS

Topographical note: Some actual places are referred to — such as Calcutta and Cooch Behar. But one does not find in the Columbia Lippincott Gazetteer such names as Kilkoa, Sir el Dchowr, Daguth, Bourabay. E. B.

* Described in the German as a packer, Galy Gay doesn't pack anything, he carries — for whoever wants something carried. Hence he is not a stevedore or longshoreman. When asked if he is of Irish descent, he replies: I think so. Pronounced by a German, his name sounds like: Gahli Guy, and so might seem reminiscent of Bali Hai and other Oriental names. I do not suggest that his name be pronounced this way in an English-language production. I only wonder if he is Irish. He sounds like a coolie, and might be a Malay, like Shlink of *In the Swamp*. E. B.

1

KILKOA

GALY GAY *and* MRS. GAY.

GALY GAY: My dear wife, I have made a decision: today, for after all it suits our budget, I shall purchase a fish. Such an act is not beyond the means of a porter who doesn't drink, smokes very little, and has almost no passions. D'you think I should purchase a large fish, or would you require a little one?

MRS. GAY: A little one.

GALY GAY: What kind of fish should it be, that you require?

MRS. GAY: I was thinking of a good flounder. But beware of the fishwives, my friend, for they are lewd and on the lookout for men, and you have a soft heart, Galy Gay.

GALY GAY: That is true. But a waterfront porter has nothing. I can expect them to leave me in peace.

MRS. GAY: You're like an elephant, the most cumbersome beast in the world of beasts, but, when it comes to running, he runs like a passenger train. Then there are these soldiers, the worst men in the world, and already, so I hear, arriving in untold numbers at the railway station. They must be standing around in the market place already, and we can consider ourselves lucky if they aren't committing burglary and murder. It isn't safe to be alone any more, they go around in fours.

GALY GAY: They won't do anything to an ordinary waterfront porter.

MRS. GAY: You never know.

GALY GAY: Well, put the water on for the fish, I'm working up an appetite. I'll be back in a minute.

MRS. GAY: Please don't wander around. I'll lock myself in the kitchen, so you'll have no worries about any stray soldiers.

72

2

STREET BESIDE THE OLD PAGODA OF THE YELLOW MONKS

FOUR SOLDIERS: URIAH SHELLEY, JESSE MAHONEY, POLLY BAKER, JERAIAH JIP, *with a machine gun, on their way to camp. They have been drinking whiskey and singing "A Man's a Man."*

JESSE: Everybody, halt! Kilkoa! Just as the mighty tanks of our queen must be filled with gasoline, so they can be seen rolling along the goddamned roads of this all-too-endless Eldorado, even so indispensable, to the soldier, is the drinking of whiskey.

JIP: How much whiskey have we got left?

POLLY: We are four. We have five bottles. That means we've got to get eleven more bottles.

JESSE: That takes money.

URIAH: There are people who have something against soldiers, but a single one of these pagodas contains more copper than it takes to send a regiment from Calcutta to London.

POLLY: The hint our dear friend Uriah has given us concerning a pagoda which is dilapidated and covered with fly-shit but which may also be stuffed full of copper certainly merits our most serious attention.

JIP: For my part, I've *got* to have more to drink, Polly.

URIAH: Patience, my friend. This Asia has a hole: one can crawl through it.

JIP: Uriah, Uriah, you know what my mother used to tell me? "Do anything you like, dearly beloved Jeraiah, but beware of pitch." And around here it smells of pitch.

POLLY: The door's not shut.

JESSE: Careful, Uriah, there's sure to be deviltry behind it.

URIAH: What are these windows for? Make a line out of your

73

belts, and let's fish for poor-boxes. This way. (*He leans through the window and lowers the line on the inside.*)

POLLY: Got something?

URIAH: No: my helmet fell in.

POLLY: Hell, you can't go back to camp without your helmet!

URIAH: Oho, the things I'm fishing up! What an establishment! Just look! Rat traps! Man traps!

JESSE: Let's give up. This is no ordinary temple. This is a trap.

URIAH: A temple's a temple. I've got to get my helmet back. What about this bamboo bell pole, for instance?

POLLY: Yes, that should do it.

URIAH *climbs the pole. It bends.*

URIAH: It's bending over the balconies, you see, but not enough by a long shot. I'm not heavy enough, you climb the pole, Polly.

POLLY *clambers up, the bell pole bends enormously; also the bell starts to ring enormously.*

URIAH: Shut its mouth, Jesse!

POLLY: Are you a sharpshooter or not? Shoot!

JESSE *shoots the bell down.* POLLY *lets out a great cry.*

JESSE: What's eating you? You're making more noise than five bells!

URIAH: It fell on his foot. Now I jump! (*He jumps, and goes right through, as the balcony floor gives way.*) Ow!

POLLY: Has the balcony fallen apart? My God, I can't hold on much longer.

JESSE: That's not playing fair.

URIAH: Down, you coward!

POLLY: Easy for you to talk.

URIAH: For me? How so? I practically jumped my leg off.

POLLY *slithers down — into the rat traps.*

POLLY: Ow!

JESSE: Right into the rat traps!

POLLY: It hurts terribly.

JIP: Found any money?

JESSE: We have drunk too much, don't you all agree, to be fully equal to such a special problem as this extremely active temple evidently presents?

URIAH: Very well. I'm not going to stop at this point. Look at Polly! The matter is entering the serious stage. Give me your identity cards. "Military identity cards must in no way be damaged." A man can be replaced any time, but nothing is sacred any more unless it's identity cards.

They surrender their papers to him.

POLLY: Polly Baker.

JIP: Jeraiah Jip.

JESSE: Jesse Mahoney.

URIAH: Uriah Shelley. All of the eighth regiment, quartered at Kankerdan, machine gun unit. Forward march!

They clamber up a fire ladder on to the roof and crawl into the pagoda. At a small window above appears the yellow face of MISTER WANG.

JIP: Good morning, sir. Are you the owner? Lovely neighborhood.

URIAH (*inside*): Now pass me the bread-knife, Jesse, so I can break these poor-boxes open.

MISTER WANG *smiles, as does* JIP.

JIP: Frightful to belong to such a pack of hippopotami! Come out, all of you! There's a man on the second floor!

Inside, electric chimes at intervals.

URIAH: Mind where you're treading! What's wrong, Jip?

JIP: A man on the second floor.

URIAH: A man? Then out of here right away! Hey!

A lot of shouting and cursing.

Your foot's in my way! Let's go! Now I can't move my foot any more! The shoe's gone too! Polly, don't quit on us *now!* Never! The jacket too, Uriah? But what's a jacket? The whole temple must go! What, what? Hell, my pants are sticking! That's what comes of rushing things. That oaf Jip!

JIP: Found something by this time? Whiskey? Rum? Gin? Brandy? Ale?

JESSE: Uriah has ripped his pants on a bamboo hook, and the shoe on Polly's good foot is stuck in a trap.

POLLY: Jesse himself is hanging on the electric wire.

JIP: Just as I thought.

He goes in through the door. The THREE *come out above, pale, in rags, bleeding.*

POLLY: This calls for revenge.

URIAH: This temple has no conception of fair play. What animals!

POLLY: Blood must flow.

JIP (*from inside*): Hey!

POLLY (*advances along the roof; his shoe gets caught*): Now my other shoe's gone!

URIAH: Now I shoot up the whole caboodle.

The THREE *climb down and aim the machine gun at the pagoda.*

POLLY: Fire!

They fire.

JIP: Ow! What are you all doing?

POLLY: Where are you hiding out?

JIP: Here. First a pole fell on my head, and then you shot me through the finger.

JESSE: What are you doing in that rat trap anyway?

JIP: I came for the money. Here it is.

URIAH: The biggest drunk among us finds it, first go. (*Loudly:*) Come right out — through this door.

JIP (*sticks out his head above*): Where?

URIAH: Through this door.

JIP: Ouch! What's this?

POLLY: What's wrong with him?

JIP: Just look!

URIAH: Something else?

JIP: My hair! Ow! My hair! I can't move forwards! And I can't move backwards! Ow! My hair! It's fastened to something! Uriah, find out what my hair's stuck to! Ow! Uriah, cut me loose! I'm hanging by the hair!

URIAH: Jesse, your bread-knife to cut him loose!

This is done.

POLLY: And now he has a bald patch. Everyone will recognize him.

JESSE: A Wanted sign in human form.

URIAH: A bald patch will betray us. Lay him in that leather chest. We'll return this evening and shave the whole of his head so there's no bald patch to be seen.

They stuff him into a palanquin that is standing among the trees, and hurriedly depart.

3

HIGHWAY BETWEEN KILKOA AND THE CAMP

BLOODY FIVE, *a Sergeant, steps out from behind a tree and nails a Wanted sign to the tree.*

BLOODY FIVE: Nothing in a very long time has struck me as so strange, me, Bloody Five, Sergeant of the British Army, also called the Tiger of Kilkoa! (*He points to the sign with one finger.*) Burglary at the Pagoda of the Yellow Monks. Bullet holes in the pagoda roof. Clue to the mystery: a quarter pound of hair embedded in pitch. Bullet holes in the roof? There must be a machine gun unit behind that. A quarter pound of hair on the scene of the crime? Somewhere there must be a man with a quarter pound of hair missing. Should there be a man with a bald patch in a machine gun unit, that would be the guilty party. Simple! But who comes here?

He steps back behind the tree. The THREE SOLDIERS *enter and are appalled to see the sign.*

BLOODY FIVE (*stepping forward*): Haven't you seen a man with a bald patch?

POLLY: No.

BLOODY FIVE: Your appearance! You look like you'd just had breakfast in an ant heap. How about taking your helmets off? And where's your fourth man?

URIAH: Answering a call of nature, Sergeant.

BLOODY FIVE: Then let's wait and ask him if he hasn't seen a man with a bald patch. (*They wait.*) Quite a long call of nature.

JESSE: Maybe he's gone back another way.

BLOODY FIVE: It were better, let me tell you, to have declared a state of siege and to have mutually shot yourselves in your mother's womb, than to come to roll-call today without your fourth man! (*Exit.*)

URIAH: Before the drum sounds for roll-call, we've got to have a fourth man.

POLLY: I hope this isn't *our* sergeant. If this rattlesnake is taking roll-call, we might as well stand with our backs to the wall right now, Uriah.

POLLY: Here comes a man. Let's secretly observe him.

> *They hide. Enter* GALY GAY, *in the wake of* WIDOW BEGBICK. *He carries her basket of cucumbers.*

BEGBICK: This road is very little frequented. A woman might have a hard time of it here — vis à vis any man who might wish to embrace her.

GALY GAY: As the owner of a canteen, you have to deal with soldiers every day of the week. They're the worst sort of men in the world, so you cannot but have learned how to wrestle with them.

BEGBICK: Oh, sir, you should never say things like that to a woman. There are certain words, my dear sir, that bring women to the point where their blood starts to tingle.

GALY GAY: I'm just an ordinary waterfront porter.

BEGBICK: Roll-call for the new recruits is due in a few minutes. The drums are rolling already, as you can hear. There'll be no one on the road.

GALY GAY: If it's really so late, I must hurry back to Kilkoa: I still have a fish to buy.

BEGBICK: Permit me one question, Mister, if I heard your name right, Galy Gay. Is great strength needed in the porter's profession?

GALY GAY: I wouldn't have believed I could be held up nearly ten hours by unforeseen interruptions from quickly buying a fish and going home. But once I get rolling I'm like a passenger train!

BEGBICK: It is, of course, one thing to buy a fish to fill your belly with, and quite another to help a lady carry her basket. But

the lady might know how to show her gratitude in a manner
that outweighs the pleasure of eating fish.

GALY GAY: Frankly, what I want is to go and buy a fish.

BEGBICK: I quite understand, sir. But don't you think it's been
getting late? The shops are shut, and all the fish are sold.

GALY GAY: I have an imagination, let me tell you. For example, I've
often had enough of a fish before I've even seen it. But some
people have their fish many times over. They go to buy it,
then they do buy it, their fish, that is, then they carry it home,
then they cook it to a turn, their fish, that is, then they wolf it
down, and even then, when they're in bed at night, and think
they have written Finish to the chapter entitled Digestion,
that sad little fish is still keeping them busy. All because they
have no imagination.

BEGBICK: I have a suggestion to make. For the money you were
going to buy a fish with, buy this cucumber. To oblige you,
I'll lower the price.

GALY GAY: But I don't need a cucumber.

BEGBICK: Well, I certainly didn't think you'd shame me like this!

GALY GAY: It's just that the water's on for the fish.

BEGBICK: I see. Just as you wish. Just as you wish.

GALY GAY: Please believe me when I say I should very much like to
oblige you.

BEGBICK: It's clear that when you open your mouth, you only put
your foot in it.

GALY GAY: I certainly mustn't disappoint you. If you still want to
let the cucumber go for less, the money will be found.

URIAH (*to* JESSE *and* POLLY): This is a man who can't say no.

GALY GAY: Careful. There are soldiers around.

BEGBICK: Heaven knows what they're after: it's just before roll-
call. Give me my basket quick. There would seem to be little
point in my gossiping the time away with you a moment
longer. (*Exit.*)

URIAH: This is our man.

JESSE: One who can't say no.

POLLY: He even has red hair like good old Jip. (*He steps forward.*)

JESSE: Never look a gift horse in the mouth, it may be an ass.

POLLY: Nice evening, this evening.

GALY GAY: Yes, sir, it is.

POLLY: Look, it's very remarkable, sir, but I can't get the idea out of my head that you must be from Kilkoa.

GALY GAY: Kilkoa? Of course. There stands my little hut, so to speak.

POLLY: I'm very, very happy to hear it, Mister . . .

GALY GAY: Galy Gay.

POLLY: Yes, you have a little hut there, haven't you?

GALY GAY: And that's how you happen to know me? Or maybe you know my wife?

POLLY: Your name, yes, your name is, just a moment, Galy Gay.

GALY GAY: Quite right. That *is* my name.

POLLY: I knew it. That's me all over. For instance, I'll take a bet you're married. But why are we just standing around, Mister Galy Gay? These are my friends Jesse and Uriah. Come over to the canteen and smoke a pipe with us!

GALY GAY: Thank you. But my wife is expecting me in Kilkoa. And silly as it may seem, I haven't got a pipe.

POLLY: A cigar then. You can't beg off now, can you, it's such a lovely evening?

GALY GAY: No, that's right, now I can't say no.

POLLY: And you'll get your cigar into the bargain.

All FOUR *leave.*

4

CANTEEN OF WIDOW LEOCADIA BEGBICK

SOLDIERS *sing*. WIDOW BEGBICK'S THREE DAUGHTERS *play the accompaniment.*

THE SONG OF WIDOW BEGBICK'S TRAVELLING BAR

In Widow Begbick's travelling bar
You can smoke and sleep and drink for years on end.
From Singapore to Cooch Behar
Begbick's beer wagon's your friend.
    From Kamakura to Bengal
    When someone can't be seen at all
    They say: He's down the Widow's Well!
    "With toddy, gum, and hi hi hi
    On the road past heaven, on the rim of hell,
    Keep your trap shut, Tommy, keep your hat on, Tommy,
    From the Soda Mountain to the Whiskey Dell!"

In Widow Begbick's travelling bar
You get just what you want, by gum.
It rolled through good old Indi*ah*
When the drink you drank came from your mum.
    From Kamakura to Bengal
    When someone can't be seen at all
    They say: He's down the Widow's Well!
    "With toddy, gum, and hi hi hi
    On the road past heaven, on the rim of hell,
    Keep your trap shut, Tommy, keep your hat on, Tommy,
    From the Soda Mountain to the Whiskey Dell!"

And if battle roars in the Punjab Vale
In Begbick's Bar we join the hunt

And smoke and sleep and drink her darkest ale
In full view of the nigger front.
    From Kamakura to Bengal
    When someone can't be seen at all
    They say: He's down the Widow's Well!
    "With toddy, gum, and hi hi hi
    On the road past heaven, on the rim of hell,
    Keep your trap shut, Tommy, keep your hat on, Tommy,
    From the Soda Mountain to the Whiskey Dell!"
Enter WIDOW BEGBICK.

BEGBICK: Good evening, soldiers all! I am Widow Begbick, and this is my beer wagon, which, when hooked up to the big military transport trains, rolls over every railway track in India. And because you can drink as you ride — yes, both at the same time! — and because you can also sleep as you ride, it is called Widow Begbick's Travelling Bar, and from Hyderabad to Rangoon everyone knows how many soldiers have found refuge in it when they weren't being treated right. Jobia, get those pennies from the soldiers for the lovely song just played by Widow Begbick's Jazz Band, otherwise the pigs will wriggle out of it. But do it politely, O flower on the soldier's dusty path.

JOBIA: Why?

She takes up the collection. Enter the THREE SOLDIERS *and* GALY GAY.

THE THREE: Is this the canteen of the eighth regiment?

SOLDIERS: It is. Are there only three of you? Where's your fourth man?

URIAH: What sort of man is the sergeant?

SOLDIERS: Not nice.

POLLY: Very disagreeable — that the sergeant is not nice.

JOBIA: Name: Bloody Five, the Tiger of Kilkoa. Description: the human typhoon. Battle cry when he sees a man who's ripe for the Johnny-are-your-pants-dry-Wall: "Pack your bag now, Johnny!" He has an unnatural olfactory sense: he can smell crimes. And when he smells a crime, he sings out: "Pack your bag now, Johnny!"

JESSE: Really.

SOLDIER: Yes, you'll soon see what the score is in Kilkoa.

POLLY (*to* GALY GAY): My dear sir, you are in a position to do a small favor to three poor soldiers in their hour of need, and without going to any special trouble either. Our fourth man, what with saying good-bye to his wife, is late, and if there aren't four of us at roll-call, we shall be thrown into the black dungeons of Kilkoa. It would therefore be a help if you would put on one of our uniforms, stand by when they number off the new recruits, and call out his name. That would be all. Don't let a cigar more or less that you may possibly be smoking at our expense influence your decision.

GALY GAY: It isn't that I wouldn't very much like to oblige you but unfortunately I must rush home. I cannot act as I might wish to.

POLLY: Our heartfelt thanks. I freely admit that I expected it of you. Yes. You cannot do what you'd like to do. You'd like to go home but you cannot go home. Our heartfelt thanks, sir: the confidence we placed in you at first sight was fully merited.

JESSE: Your hand, sir.

URIAH: To this end, allow us to robe you in the honored vestments of the venerable British Army.

He rings. BEGBICK *comes in.*

POLLY: Are we addressing the owner of the camp canteen, the world-famous Widow Begbick? We are a machine gun unit of the eighth company. May I be open with you, Widow Begbick? (*He whispers something in her ear.*)

BEGBICK: I see. You've lost a complete set of regimentals?

POLLY: Yes, while our friend Jip was in the bathhouse, some Chinese made off with his uniform.

BEGBICK: I see. In the bathhouse?

JESSE: To be open, wide open, with you, Widow Begbick, it has to do with a little joke.

BEGBICK: I see. A little joke?

POLLY: Isn't that about it, dear sir? It has to do with a little joke?

GALY GAY: Yes, yes, it has to do, so to speak, with — a cigar.

He laughs. THE THREE *laugh too.*

BEGBICK: How helpless a weak woman is beside three such strong men! No one shall ever say of Widow Begbick that she wouldn't let a man change his trousers.

GALY GAY (*quickly*): What goes on? Actually?

JESSE: Actually — nothing at all.

All FOUR *laugh.*

GALY GAY: Isn't it dangerous — when they find out?

POLLY: Not a bit. Anyhow, in your case just once is the same as not at all.

GALY GAY: That's true. They do say just once is the same as not at all.

SOLDIER: This is the famous machine gun unit that decided the outcome of the battle of Hyderabad and which is named The Scum. And now it's ours. Their crimes shall follow them like their shadows!

A SOLDIER *brings on the Wanted sign and nails it down.*

SOLDIERS: And right behind them, another of those signs.

All leave. Re-enter BEGBICK *with the regimentals.*

POLLY: This is the honored vestment we are buying for you. Try it on, Brother Galy Gay.

POLLY *and* URIAH *put it on* GALY GAY.

BEGBICK: It'll cost you ten shillings, I'm giving it away.

POLLY: Ten shillings!

URIAH: Bloodsucker! We'll pay three at the most. It's much too small, too.

JESSE (*at the window*): Rain clouds all of a sudden! If it rains now, the palanquin will be wet, and if the palanquin is wet, it will be taken into the pagoda, and if it is taken into the pagoda, Jip will be discovered, and if Jip is discovered, it's all up with us.

GALY GAY: Too small. I'll never get into it.

POLLY: Hear that? He'll never get into it.

GALY GAY: And the shoes pinch terribly.

URIAH: Everything's too small — not usable! Two shillings!

POLLY: Quiet, Uriah. Seven shillings, because everything's too small, and the shoes in particular pinch badly, isn't that so?

GALY GAY: Out of the ordinary. They pinch extremely.

URIAH: The gentleman is not so easygoing as you, Polly.

BEGBICK: Good! Eight shillings. Otherwise, the Company would get wind of the crime that's described on that sign, you shit-pots!

JESSE: Think it's going to rain, Widow Begbick?

BEGBICK: Well now, I must take a look at Sergeant Bloody Five. It's well known in army circles that in time of rainfall he succumbs to terrible attacks of sensuality. He's completely changed, inside and out.

JESSE: It mustn't rain on any account — because of our joke.

BEGBICK: On the contrary. It need only start raining, and Bloody Five, the most dangerous man in the Indian Army, is as un-dangerous as a milk-tooth, for, when it rains, Bloody Five is transformed into The Bloody Gent, and The Bloody Gent concentrates on girls for three days on end.

A SOLDIER (*entering to make an announcement*): Everybody re-port for roll-call because of that Pagoda story. They say a man is missing, so they're going to call the roll, and examine identity cards. (*Exit.*)

JESSE (*to* GALY GAY): All you have to do is call out our comrade's name. As loud as possible and very distinct. It's nothing!

POLLY: And our lost comrade's name is Jeraiah Jip.

GALY GAY (*politely*): Jeraiah Jip.

POLLY: It is pleasant to meet cultured gentlemen who know how to behave in every situation.

THE FOUR *leave at the back, each of them bowing.*

JESSE (*leaving*): If only it doesn't rain!

BEGBICK: And now there stands up in the ranks, before the very eyes of Bloody Five, a man who isn't a soldier of any kind! And the porter Galy Gay is a very special sort of man. Here comes Bloody Five.

JOBIA: The sergeant looks like a walking bayonet stand, why is that?

Enter BLOODY FIVE, *frightfully changed.*

BEGBICK (*looks at him*): Hey, Jobia, quick: put the roof up over the canteen, it's going to rain!

BLOODY FIVE (*while the* EIGHTH COMPANY *call their names*): You laugh, but I tell you I'd like to see the whole thing go up in flames, this Sodom of the rocking-chair and whiskey bar, and you with it, for you're a Gomorrah in yourself, you gobble me up when you look at me like that, you whitewashed Babylon!

BEGBICK: You know, Charlie, a woman enjoys seeing a man in such a passionate mood!

BLOODY FIVE: The human race began to disintegrate when the first muttonhead failed to button up. Keep your trap shut! As a book, the army field manual has its shortcomings, but it's the only one a man can depend on, if he *is* a man, because it gives him a backbone, and accepts full responsibility before God. Actually, one should dig a hole in the ground, and put dynamite in it, and blow the whole earth to smithereens. Then maybe they'd realize we mean business!

OFFICER'S VOICE (*outside, giving orders*): Machine gunners! Call! Names!

BLOODY FIVE (*humming*): "Pack your bag now, Johnny!" (*Now he hears* THE THREE *call their names.*) Yes, and now: a little gap.

GALY GAY'S VOICE: Jeraiah Jip.

BLOODY FIVE (*let down*): They've cooked something up.

BEGBICK: I tell you, Sergeant, before the black rain of Nepal has been falling for two nights on end, you will be more gently disposed to the misdeeds of mankind. For you are perhaps the sexiest man beneath the sun. And you will sit down at table with insubordination, and the desecrators of the temple will look you straight in the eye, for your crimes will be as numberless as the sands of the sea.

BLOODY FIVE: Yes, but then we'd see a little action. Make no mis-

take, my love, we would then take action against little old
Bloody Five, and no half measures about it. It's as simple as
that. (*Exit* BLOODY FIVE. *Outside:*) Eight men up to the navel
in hot sand for not having regulation haircuts!

Enter THE THREE *with* GALY GAY, *to the bar*.

POLLY: A glass of whiskey to your health, sir!

GALY GAY: Oh, a little favor — man to man, so to speak — can never
hurt. Look, I'm drinking whiskey just like it was water and
saying to myself: I did these gentlemen a good turn. Isn't that
what really matters in this world? You send up a little balloon
— saying "Jeraiah Jip" is no harder to say than "Good evening" — and you're just the man people wish you to be — it's
not difficult at all.

POLLY: Unhappily we're in a hurry. A dangerous rain wind has
blown up. And, you see, we must shave someone's head.

GALY GAY: Couldn't I help with that too?

URIAH: There are people who have to stick their noses into everything. Give such people your little finger, and they grab your
whole hand.

POLLY: Drink several cocktails at our expense. (*Leaving:*) When
we've gone to work on Jip's head with these scissors, he won't
have any bald patch any more. Only it mustn't rain, that's all.
It mustn't rain.

Exeunt THE THREE.

BEGBICK (*brings a cocktail for* GALY GAY): Haven't we met before
this evening? (GALY GAY *shakes his head.*) Isn't your name
Galy Gay? (GALY GAY *shakes his head.*) Aren't you the man
who carried my cucumber basket?

GALY GAY: No. I am not.

BEGBICK (*at the window*): It's started to rain.

5

INSIDE THE PAGODA OF THE YELLOW MONKS

MISTER WANG *and his* CHINESE SEXTON.

SEXTON: It's raining.

WANG: Bring our leather palanquin in where it's dry. (*Exit* SEXTON.) And now our last source of income has been stolen. And it's raining on my head through those bullet holes. (THE SEXTON *drags in the palanquin. Groans from inside it.*) What's that? (*He looks in.*) I knew it. I knew it would be a white man when I saw how filthy the palanquin was. Oh dear, he's in soldier's uniform. And he has a bald patch, the thief. They simply cut his hair off. What shall we do with him? He's a soldier, so he won't have any sense. A soldier of the queen, covered with vomited liquor, helpless as a barnyard chick, and so drunk his own mother wouldn't know him! One could make a present of him to the police. But what good is that? When the money's all gone, what good is justice? And all he can do is grunt. (*Furiously, to the* SEXTON:) Pick him up and stuff him in the prayer box, you hole in a Swiss cheese! And see that his head sticks out at the top. The best thing we can do is make a god out of him. (*The* SEXTON *puts* JIP *in the prayer box.*) Bring me paper! We must hang out paper banners in front of the house without delay! We must set to and paint some posters! I want this to be on the grand scale! No false economies! These must be posters no one can overlook! What good is a god if he doesn't get talked about? (*A knock.*) Who's that at my door so late?

POLLY: Three soldiers.

WANG: His comrades. (*He lets* THE THREE *in.*)

POLLY: We're looking for a man — a soldier, I should say — who is fast asleep in a leather chest which was right in front of this rich and noble temple.

WANG: May his awakening be a pleasant one!

POLLY: But, you see, this chest has vanished.

WANG: I understand your impatience: it proceeds from uncertainty. I myself am looking for several people — in all about three people — soldiers, I should rather say — and I cannot find them.

URIAH: It'll be hard. I think you may as well give up. But we thought you might know something about the leather chest.

WANG: Alas, no. The unpleasant fact is that all you soldiers of the queen wear the same clothes.

JESSE: It isn't unpleasant. There's a man in the aforementioned leather chest who is very sick.

POLLY: Having also lost some hair through this illness, he urgently needs help.

URIAH: Would you have seen some such man?

WANG: Alas, no. But I have found some such hair. However, a sergeant from your army took it. To return it to its rightful soldier.

JIP *groans in the prayer box.*

POLLY: What is that, sir?

WANG: A milch cow. Fast asleep.

URIAH: A milch cow that sleeps badly, it seems.

POLLY: This is the palanquin that we stuffed Jip into. Permit us to examine it.

WANG: It is best if I tell you the whole truth. That, you see, is another palanquin.

POLLY: It's as full of vomit as a spittoon on the third day of Christmas. Jesse, it's clear that Jip was in there.

WANG: Not so. He cannot have been. No one would sit in such a dirty palanquin.

JIP *in the prayer box groans loudly.*

URIAH: We must have our fourth man if we have to slaughter our grandmothers to get him.

WANG: The man you are looking for is not here. But that you may see that the man who you say is here — and who I do not know to be here — is not your man, permit me to explain it all to you with the aid of a drawing. Allow your unworthy servant to draw four criminals with chalk. (*He draws them on the door of the prayer box.*) One of them has a face, so that one sees who he is, but three of them have no faces. They cannot be recognized. Yet the one with the face has no money, therefore he is no thief. But the ones with the money have no faces, therefore they cannot be recognized. That's how it is as long as they are not together. But when they are together, the three headless men grow faces, and other people's money will be found in their pockets. I would never be able to believe you if you said that a man who might be found here was your man.

THE THREE *threaten him with their weapons, but at a sign from* WANG *the* SEXTON *appears with* CHINESE VISITORS *to the temple.*

JESSE: We wouldn't wish to disturb your rest any longer, sir. Also, your tea does not agree with us. On the other hand, your drawing is a work of art. Let's go!

WANG: It hurts me to see you leave.

URIAH: Ten horses won't be able to stop our comrade coming back to us — wherever he may be when he wakes. Or don't you agree?

WANG: Perhaps ten horses won't. But perhaps one small part of one horse will. Who knows?

URIAH: As soon as he's got the whiskey out of his head, he'll come.

THE THREE *leave. Much bowing low.*

WANG: When the old whiskey has been drunk, maybe the new will be drunk.

JIP (*in the box*): Hey!

WANG *calls the attention of his* VISITORS *to his god.*

6

CANTEEN

Late at night. GALY GAY *is seated on a wooden chair, sleeping. The* THREE SOLDIERS *appear at the window.*

POLLY: He's still sitting there. Looks like an Irish mammoth, huh?

URIAH: Maybe he didn't want to leave because it was raining.

JESSE: Hard to tell. But now we're going to need him again.

POLLY: You don't think Jip's coming back?

JESSE: Uriah, I know Jip's not coming back.

POLLY: We can hardly tell that to this porter again.

JESSE: What do *you* think, Uriah?

URIAH: I think I'll go and hit the hay.

POLLY: But if this porter gets up now and goes through that door, our heads will be hanging by a hair.

JESSE: True. But I'm going to sleep too. You mustn't ask too much of a man.

POLLY: Maybe it's all to the good if we do hit the hay. It's too depressing! And it's all the rain's fault.

THE THREE *leave.*

7

INSIDE THE PAGODA OF THE YELLOW MONKS

Toward morning. Large posters everywhere. Sound of an old phonograph and a drum. In the background rather large-scale religious ceremonies seem to be taking place.

WANG (*goes up to the prayer box, to the* SEXTON): Roll those camel-dung balls faster, you piece of manure. (*At the box:*) Still asleep, Mister Soldier?

JIP'S VOICE: Do we get out soon, Jesse? This carriage rocks terribly, and it's as narrow as a latrine.

WANG: Now don't imagine you're in a railway carriage, Mister Soldier. It's only the whiskey in your honorable head that shakes.

JIP: Rubbish! What kind of voice is that on the phonograph? How about stopping it?

WANG: Come out, Mister Soldier, eat a piece of the meat from a cow!

JIP: Can I have a piece of meat, Polly? (*He bangs on the box.*)

WANG (*runs toward the back*): Quiet, miserable creatures! The god whom you hear knocking on the boards of the prayer box wants five taels. Divine grace is being showered on you! Sexton, take up the collection.

JIP: Uriah, Uriah, where am I?

WANG: Knock a little more, Mister Soldier. On the other side, Mister General. With both feet and with considerable vim.

JIP: Hey! What *is* this? Where am I? Where are you — Uriah, Jesse, Polly?

WANG: Your humble servant desires to know what you would like in the way of food and strong drink, Mister Soldier.

JIP: Hey! Who is it?

WANG (*in the voice of a fat rat*): This moderately fat rat is your friend Wang from Tientsin, Colonel.

JIP: The city I'm in — what's it like?

WANG: A miserable one, honored patron, a hole named Kilkoa.

JIP: Let me out!

WANG (*toward the rear*): When you have rolled the camel dung into balls, lay out the balls on a bowl, beat the drum, and light them. (*To* JIP:) I'll let you out at once if you promise not to run away, Mister Soldier.

JIP: Open up, voice of a muskrat, open up, d'you hear me?

WANG: Stop! Believers all, stop! Remain where you are one minute! The god is speaking to you — in three claps of thunder. Count the claps carefully! Four. No, five. Too bad: it's five taels you are to sacrifice to him. (*Knocks at the prayer box. In a kind voice:*) Here's a steak, Mister Soldier, to feed your honorable face with.

JIP: Now I catch on: my guts are eaten away. I must have poured pure alcohol in there. Yes, it is possible I have drunk very much. Now I must eat equally much.

WANG: You can eat a whole cow, Mister Soldier, and one steak is already prepared. But I'm afraid you will run away, Mister Soldier. Will you promise me not to run away?

JIP: I want to see things first. (WANG *lets him out.*) How did I get in?

WANG: Through the air, Mister General, you got in through the air.

JIP: Where was I when you found me?

WANG: Deigning to rest your limbs in an old palanquin, sublime one.

JIP: And where are my comrades? Where is the eighth regiment? Where is the machine gun unit? Where are the twelve railway trains and the four elephant parks? Where is the British Army? Where are they all gone, you yellow, grinning spittoon?

WANG: Beyond the Punjab Mountains. They left last month. But here's your steak.

JIP: What? How about me? Where was I? What was I doing while they marched off?

WANG: Whiskey, much whiskey, one thousand bottles. You earned some money too.

JIP: Didn't any of them ask for me?

WANG: Alas, no.

JIP: That's very disagreeable.

WANG: If they should come now — looking for a man in a white soldier's uniform — shall I bring them to see you, Mister Minister of War?

JIP: You needn't bother.

WANG: If you don't wish to be disturbed, Johnny, just step inside this box, Johnny, when people turn up who offend your honorable eye.

JIP: Where's that steak? (*Sits and eats.*) It's too small! What's that terrible noise?

Drumming. Smoke from the camel-dung balls rises toward the ceiling.

WANG: Those are the prayers of the faithful who are on their knees over there.

JIP: It comes from a very tough part of the cow. Who're they praying to?

WANG: That is their secret.

JIP (*eating faster*): This is a good steak, but I have no right to be sitting here. Polly and Jesse must certainly have waited for me. Maybe they're still waiting. It tastes like butter. It's bad of me to be eating it. Listen, Polly's just saying to Jesse: Jip will certainly turn up — when he's sober, Jip will turn up. Maybe Uriah won't wait so manfully, because of course Uriah is a bad man, but Jesse and Polly will say: Jip'll turn up. There can be no doubt this is a suitable meal for me after all those drinks. If only Jesse didn't rely so implicitly on good old Jip. But he'll surely be saying: Jip won't betray us. And naturally, that's hard for me to bear. It's all wrong for me to be sitting here, but the meat is good meat.

8

CANTEEN

Early morning. GALY GAY *is asleep on a wooden chair.* THE THREE *are playing billiards.*

POLLY: Jip will turn up.

JESSE: Jip won't betray us.

POLLY: When he's sober, Jip will turn up.

URIAH: Hard to tell. Anyhow, we won't let this porter go, with Jip still walking the tiles.

JESSE: He didn't leave.

POLLY: He must be frozen. Spent the night on that chair.

URIAH: Anyhow, we got a good night's sleep. Now we're on the up and up again.

POLLY: And Jip will turn up. With the good sense of a well-rested soldier, I see it quite clearly. That yellow bullfrog took advantage of our tiredness. When Jip's whiskey is done, Jip will turn up.

Enter MISTER WANG. *Goes to the bar and rings.* BEGBICK *comes in.*

BEGBICK: No liquor for native stinkers! Not even yellow ones!

WANG: For a white one: seven bottles of good old Victoria Whiskey.

BEGBICK: Seven bottles Victoria for a white one? (*She gives him seven bottles.*)

WANG: For a white one, yes.

Bows to THE FOUR *and leaves.* JESSE, POLLY, *and* URIAH *look at each other.*

URIAH: Seven bottles of Victoria Whiskey? Now Jip will NOT

96

turn up. And therefore this porter Galy Gay from Kilkoa must become Jeraiah Jip, our comrade.

THE THREE *look the sleeping* GALY GAY *over.*

POLLY: How can we get away with it, Uriah? We have nothing but Jip's papers.

JESSE: They're enough. There's got to be a new Jip. Why all the fuss about people? One's as good as none at all. It's impossible to speak of less than two hundred at a time. Each can have an opinion of his own, of course. What difference does that make? A quiet man can quietly appropriate two or three opinions-of-his-own. Men of character? Kiss my ass.

POLLY: But what will he say when we turn him into the soldier Jeraiah Jip?

JESSE: A man like that does the turning all on his own. Throw him into a puddle and he'll grow webs between his fingers in two days.

URIAH: Whatever happens to him, we've got to have a fourth man. Wake him up!

POLLY (*wakes* GALY GAY *up*): A lucky thing you didn't go away, dear sir. Circumstances have arisen to prevent our comrade Jip from making a punctual appearance.

URIAH: You are of Irish descent?

GALY GAY: I think so.

URIAH: That's an advantage. Mister Galy Gay, you're not more than forty, I trust?

GALY GAY: No. Less.

URIAH: That's splendid. Don't tell me you have flat feet?

GALY GAY: Somewhat.

URIAH: That decides it. Your happiness is assured. For the time being, you may stay.

GALY GAY: I'm afraid my wife's waiting for me. Because of a fish.

POLLY: We understand and respect your solicitude. It's worthy of an Irishman. But your presence here is very welcome. What's more, it fits. The opportunity is perhaps at hand for you to become a soldier. (GALY GAY *is silent.*) A soldier's life is most pleasant. Every week we receive a handful of money exclusively for tramping up and down India and keeping an eye on these streets and pagodas. Be so good as to observe the comfortable leather sleeping bags which are delivered free to every soldier. Take a look at this gun which bears the stamp of the firm Everett and Co. Most of the time we amuse ourselves fishing. And Mamma — as we have christened the army in jest — Mamma buys the fishing tackle. As we fish, several military bands play in alternation. You spend the rest of the day smoking in your bungalow or lazily observing the golden palace of some Rajah, whom, moreover, you may shoot, should it take your fancy. The ladies expect many things of us soldiers, but never money. As you will admit, this is a further convenience.

GALY GAY: I see that a soldier's life is a pleasant one.

URIAH: Surely. So without more ado you can hold on to that uniform with its pretty brass buttons, and you have the right at all times to be addressed as Mister. Mister Jip.

GALY GAY: You wouldn't wish to make a poor porter unhappy?

URIAH: So you want to leave?

GALY GAY: Yes, I must be leaving.

JESSE: Polly, bring him his clothes.

POLLY (*with his clothes*): Why don't you want to be Jip, actually?

BLOODY FIVE *pops up in the window.*

GALY GAY: Because I'm Galy Gay. (*Goes to the door.* THE THREE *look at each other.*)

URIAH: Wait just a minute.

POLLY: Maybe you know the saying: Make haste slowly.

URIAH: You're dealing with men who do not lightly incur obligations to strangers.

JESSE: Whatever your name might be, you should certainly be rewarded for your kindness.

URIAH: It's a matter of — yes, just stay there with the doorknob in your hand — a deal.

GALY GAY *stays there.*

JESSE: The best deal that Kilkoa has to offer, isn't it, Polly? You know we only have to catch —

URIAH: It is our duty to offer you a chance to participate in this really tremendous deal.

GALY GAY: Deal? Did you say deal?

URIAH: Maybe I did. But then you have no time.

GALY GAY: There's time and time.

POLLY: Ah, so you *might* have time. If you knew about this deal, you *would* have time. Lord Kitchener had time to conquer Egypt.

GALY GAY: I believe you. Is it a big deal?

POLLY: Maybe it would be — for the Maharajah of Peshawar. For such a great man as yourself, maybe it wouldn't be.

GALY GAY: I can always turn around and go home. (*He sits.* BLOODY FIVE *disappears from the window.*)

POLLY: What an elephant!

GALY GAY (*overhearing him*): An elephant? Of course, an elephant *would* be a gold mine. If you have an elephant, you won't end up in the poorhouse.

URIAH: Elephant?! And how we have an elephant!

GALY GAY: On hand? I mean: is this elephant on hand?

POLLY: An elephant! How he insists on an elephant!

GALY GAY: Do you have your elephant on hand?

POLLY: Has it ever been recorded that a deal was made with an elephant which was not on hand?

GALY GAY: Good. If that's settled, I'd just like to carve out my own piece of meat, Mister Polly.

URIAH (*hesitating*): It's just — well, the Devil of Kilkoa!

GALY GAY: What's that — the Devil of Kilkoa?

POLLY: Speak lower. You are speaking the name of the human typhoon, Bloody Five, our sergeant.

GALY GAY: What has he done to get a name like that?

POLLY: Oh, nothing. Once in a while he takes someone who gives the wrong name at roll-call, wraps him in six square feet of canvas, and rolls him under the feet of his elephants.

GALY GAY: So you'd need a man with a head on his shoulders.

URIAH: Comrade, you have a big head.

POLLY: There must be something in it — a big head like that.

GALY GAY: Don't mention it. Though I do know a riddle that might interest cultured gentlemen such as you.

JESSE: You see before you three powerful solvers of riddles.

GALY GAY: It goes this way. White; a mammal; sees behind as good as in front.

JESSE: It's very difficult.

GALY GAY: You won't get anywhere with this riddle. I myself didn't get anywhere with this riddle. A mammal; white; sees behind as good as in front. A blind white horse.

URIAH: That riddle is terrific.

POLLY: And you carry all this in your head?

GALY GAY: Mostly, because I don't write very well. But for almost any deal, I'm the man.

BLOODY FIVE (*enters*): One small moment. There's a woman outside looking for a man named Galy Gray.

GALY GAY: Galy Gay! He's called Galy Gay, the chap she's looking for!

BLOODY FIVE: Step inside, Mrs. Gray, here's someone that knows your husband.

URIAH *lets out a frightful oath.* THE THREE *quickly go and stand against the wall.*

GALY GAY: Leave it all to me. Galy Gay has tasted blood.

BLOODY FIVE, *humming his "Johnny" refrain, re-enters with* MRS. GAY.

MRS. GAY: Excuse a humble little woman, good sirs, also her dress, I was in such a hurry. Ah, so there you are, Galy Gay! But can it really be you — in uniform!

GALY GAY: No.

MRS. GAY: I don't understand you. How do you come to be in uniform? You look good in it too, everyone will have to hand it to you. You are a very peculiar man, Galy Gay.

URIAH: Her brain's affected.

MRS. GAY: It isn't easy to have a husband who can't say no. So big and fat on the outside, you'd never guess he had an inside like a raw egg.

URIAH: I'd like to know who she's talking to. These are insults.

BLOODY FIVE: Mrs. Gray's brain is in the best of form. Please go on talking, Mrs. Gray. Your voice is sweeter than sweet music to me.

MRS. GAY: I don't know what you're after this time with your famous self-conceit. But you'll come to a bad end. Now come along with me. But say something. Has your voice gone?

GALY GAY: I think you must be saying all this to me. You're confusing me with someone else, I tell you. And what you're saying about him is stupid and not right.

MRS. GAY: What do you say? Confusing? Have you been drinking? He can't hold his liquor, you know.

GALY GAY: I'm as much your Galy Gay as I am Commandant of this camp.

MRS. GAY: It was just this time yesterday that I put the water in the pot. But you never brought the fish.

GALY GAY: And what sort of a fish would that be now? You talk like someone with no sense at all — and before all these gentlemen!

BLOODY FIVE: A remarkable case. Such terrible thoughts come flooding into my mind, I almost turn to ice. Do you know this woman? (THE THREE *shake their heads*.) What about you?

GALY GAY: In my lifetime, between Ireland and Kilkoa, I have seen much. But I never set eyes on this woman before.

BLOODY FIVE: Tell the lady what your name is.

GALY GAY: Jeraiah Jip.

MRS. GAY: This is outrageous. Though when I look at him, Sergeant, it's almost as if he was not my husband Galy Gay the porter but something quite different, I couldn't exactly say what.

BLOODY FIVE: Well, we shall see!

Bewildered, MRS. GAY *leaves with* BLOODY FIVE.

GALY GAY (*goes beaming over to* JESSE): It's always been said of all the Galy Gays in Ireland: they hit the nail on the head!

URIAH (*to* POLLY): Before the sun has set seven more times, this man must be another man.

POLLY: But will it work, Uriah? Turning a man into another man?

URIAH: Yes. One man is just like all the others. A man's a man.

POLLY: But the army might break camp any minute, Uriah.

URIAH: Of course it might break camp any minute. But isn't this canteen still here? Don't you know the artillery has arranged for horse racing to take place here? I tell you God will not suffer the least of us to perish — by letting the army march today. He will think it over at least three times.

POLLY: Listen.

Trumpet sounds breaking of camp. Drums.

BLOODY FIVE (*enters*): The army is setting out for Tibet!

Exit, humming "Johnny." GALY GAY *takes his bundle of clothes and tries to slip quickly out.* THE THREE *seize him and throw him on to the chair.*

METAMORPHOSIS OF A LIVING HUMAN BEING IN THE ARMY BARRACKS AT KILKOA IN THE YEAR NINETEEN HUNDRED AND TWENTY-FIVE

INTERJECTION

Spoken by the WIDOW LEOCADIA BEGBICK *beside a portrait of Mister Bertolt Brecht.*

A Man's a Man is Mister Bertolt Brecht's contention.
However, that's something anyone might mention.
Mister Brecht appends this item to the bill:
You can do with a human being what you will.
Take him apart like a car, rebuild him bit by bit —
As you will see, he has nothing to lose by it.
We come to this chap — like one man to another —
And with emphasis, but no fuss, persuade our brother
To adjust to this world as it is and just let rot
The fish he planned to boil in his private pot.
Now Mister Brecht hopes you will see the ground beneath
    your feet
Melt away like sleet.
And he hopes you won't miss the moral of Galy Gay's case:
That this world is a dangerous place.

WIDOW BEGBICK'S CANTEEN

Noise of a camp breaking up. A big voice shouts from the rear: "The war that was planned has now broken out. The army is setting out for Tibet. The queen orders her soldiers, with all their elephants and cannon, to board the trains. She orders the trains to proceed to Tibet. Your general therefore commands you to be seated in the trains before the moon rises."

BEGBICK (*runs through the canteen, driving her* DAUGHTERS *before her*): The army's pulling out. If no one gives us a hand, we'll find ourselves stuck here. (*Exit with* DAUGHTERS.)

THE THREE SOLDIERS (*rush in*): Now he'll have to be reconstructed on the double. For which we need an elephant. For if this Galy Gay makes a deal with an elephant, and there's something wrong about this deal, he will prefer being Jeraiah Jip to being Galy Gay the Crook. So the important thing is for us to make an elephant.

URIAH: Jesse, stick this pole in the elephant's head from that wall there, and, Polly, you take a whiskey bottle, and I'll spread this map over you both.

Behind a wall they build an artificial elephant.

BEGBICK: What are you doing with my elephant head?

POLLY: Making an elephant. And if you care to help us, we'll pack your canteen for you.

BEGBICK: What do you want me to do?

JESSE: Go to the man you will find walking up and down outside and tell him you're in the market for an elephant.

BEGBICK: Good. But then you machine gunners must pack my canteen. (*Exit.*)

SOLDIERS (*have come on; they watch* THE THREE, *who are building a small elephant around* JESSE *and* POLLY): Tell us: what's this about your fourth man?

JESSE: Our fourth man, who is called Jeraiah Jip, has a touch of sunstroke and thinks he's —

URIAH: — a porter from foreign parts. Name of Galy Gay.

POLLY: So we think we are —

JESSE: An army elephant, name of Billy Humph.

GALY GAY (*at the window*): Is the elephant there?

POLLY: It will be. Wait outside.

URIAH: Polly, take the whiskey bottle, so the elephant can make water and, when Galy Gay's looking, pour away. (*To the* SOLDIERS:) Listen. We're going to make him a present of the elephant and tell him to sell it. Then, when he sells it, we arrest him.

SOLDIERS (*laughing*): D'you think he'll take that for an elephant?

POLLY: Is it such a bad job?

URIAH (*angry*): He *will* take that for an elephant. He's interested in buying and selling. I tell you he'd take this whiskey bottle for an elephant if someone pointed at it and said: sell me that elephant!

SOLDIERS: We don't believe you.

URIAH (*looking out the window*): Come in, Mister Galy Gay. The deal is in full swing.

GALY GAY (*enters*): And what's it all about?

URIAH: This deal concerns the surplus and non-registered army elephant Billy Humph. Our battle-cry is: to each his elephant.

GALY GAY: Very enlightening. Who's auctioning him off?

URIAH: Anyone who can sign his name as the owner.

GALY GAY: But who is going to sign his name as the owner?

URIAH: Would *you* like to?

GALY GAY: Yes. But then my name must be kept out of it.

URIAH: Care for a cigar?

GALY GAY: Why?

URIAH: So you can preserve your equanimity. The elephant has a bit of a cold.

GALY GAY: Do we have a buyer?

BEGBICK (*goes to* GALY GAY): Oh, Mr. Galy Gay! I want an elephant. Do you happen to have one? It isn't important whether it's large or small. But I've wanted to buy one ever since I was a child.

GALY GAY: Widow Begbick, it is possible I have just the one for you.

BEGBICK: Take the wall away. The cannon will follow.

SOLDIERS: Right you are, Widow Begbick.

BEGBICK: Now daughters o' mine, come out and make music, so the soldiers can dismantle our canteen and like it.

The THREE DAUGHTERS *come and play on jazz instruments.*

URIAH: And while you're all at it, I'll be thinking over what to do with him.

He sits down on a chair. During the singing of the first strophe of the song "A Man's a Man" one wall of the Canteen is taken down. The elephant can now be dimly seen.

A MAN'S A MAN: 1

So you're in the army as well, Danny Boy?
For I'm in the army as well, Danny Boy!
And when I see old pals like you
I'm glad I'm in the army too!
Had you never seen me here before?
I had never seen you here before!
   That's all right, Dan.
   For a man is a man.
   You needn't shout.
   Really, Dan, my dear man,
   What is there to shout about?
   For men are men.
   Let us say that again:
   A man's a man.
   So it's all right, Dan.
   Kilkoa's sun shines down upon
   Six thousand soldiers and their doom.

A MAN'S A MAN

So you're in the arm—y as well, Dan—ny boy? For I'm in the arm—y as well, Danny boy! And when I see old pals like—

you, I'm glad I'm in the arm—y——

too! Had you never seen me— here— be—

fore? I had never seen you— here— be—

—fore! That's all right, Dan!

For a man is a man!

— You needn't shout! Really, Dan, my dear

man, what is there to shout about?

For men are men!

Let us say that a — gain:

A man's a man!

So it's all right, Dan!

Kil — ko — a's sun shines down up —

— on   six   thousand soldiers and their

doom.   When they are   dead

no tears are   shed.   None on the list is

ever missed. —

And so we sing: — who cares on

whom — the ruddy sun of

old Kil—ko—a shone? —

2. So, Dan, you had rice for your dinner today?
   For, Dan, I had rice for my dinner today!
   Without a chicken in the pot
   A soldier's life is not so hot.
   And, Dan, after dinner did you throw up?
   After dinner, Dan, I too threw up!

3. You saw Jenny Smith as well, Danny Boy?
   I saw Jenny Smith as well, Danny Boy!
   And Jenny Smith, that dear old hen,
   Makes army life look good again!
   And, Dan, did you sleep with Miss Smith as well?
   Danny Boy, I slept with Miss Smith as well!

4. So, Dan, are you packing your kitbag as well?
   For, Dan, I am packing my kitbag as well!
   And when I see you pack and go
   My soldier's breast is full of woe!
   And, Dan, have you nothing to put in your bag?
   I have nothing, either, to put in my bag!

5. So, Dan, are you off on your travels tonight?
   For, Dan, I am off on my travels tonight!
   When you depart, such is my pride,
   I must be marching at your side!
   But, Dan, do you know where you're traveling to?
   For I do not know where I'm traveling to!

(When they are dead no tears are shed.
None on the list is ever missed.)
And so we sing: who cares on whom
The ruddy sun of old Kilkoa shone?

FIRST NUMBER

URIAH (*whistles*): First Number: the Elephant Deal. The machine gun unit hands over an elephant to the man who wishes to have his name kept out of it. (*He leads the elephant forward by a rope.*) Billy Humph, Champion of Bengal, Elephant in the service of the British Army, etc.

GALY GAY (*catches sight of the elephant and is terrified*): Is that the army elephant?

SOLDIER: He has a bad cold, as you can see from his blanket.

GALY GAY: The blanket isn't the worst of it. (*He walks round in some consternation.*)

BEGBICK: I'm in the market for that elephant. When I was a child I wanted an elephant as big as the Hindu Kush Range, but now that one will do.

GALY GAY: Well, Widow Begbick, if you really want this elephant, I'm its owner.

BLOODY FIVE (*voice backstage*): "Pack your bag now, Johnny!"

THE SOLDIERS: The Devil of Kilkoa! (*They seem to flee.*)

BEGBICK: Everyone stay here. I won't have this elephant taken away from me. (*Exit.*)

URIAH (*to* GALY GAY): You hold the elephant for a minute.

GALY GAY, *alone, holds the elephant by the very end of the rope.*

SOLDIERS (*watch over him from behind a wall*): Now really! He doesn't dare look at it. He holds it as far away from him as he can.

GALY GAY: My mother used to tell me one knows nothing for certain. But you, Galy Gay, you know nothing, either for certain or otherwise. You went out this morning to purchase a fish; you now have an elephant; and who knows what tomorrow may bring? But it's all one so long as you get paid.

SOLDIERS (*at back*): Has he gone?

URIAH (*ditto*): The tiger of Kilkoa was only passing by. Widow Begbick gave him a good hard look.

SECOND NUMBER

URIAH (*downstage of the door, whistles*): Now comes the Second Number: The elephant at auction. The man who wants his name kept out of it sells the elephant.

SOLDIERS (*come in with* URIAH): You still have your doubts about this elephant?

GALY GAY: Now he's being bought, I have no doubts.

URIAH: Of course not. If he's being bought, he's all right, huh?

GALY GAY: I can't say no to that. An elephant's an elephant, especially when bought.

URIAH: And here comes Widow Begbick with the check.

BEGBICK: Does the elephant belong to you?

GALY GAY: Like my own foot. (*He stands near the elephant.*) He weighs three hundredweight. And when it comes to chopping wood, a whole forest is no more to him than a blade of grass in the wind. Just as you see him, Billy Humph represents a small fortune to whoever might own him.

BEGBICK: Three hundred rupees.

GALY GAY: Three hundred rupees! Going, going, gone. Widow Begbick, you may now take over Billy Humph from his former owner, myself, and pay for him with a check.

BEGBICK: Your name?

GALY GAY: I want my name kept out of it.

BEGBICK: Now give me a pencil so I can make out the check — to the gentleman who wants his name kept out of it.

URIAH (*aside to the others*): When he takes the check, grab him.

BEGBICK (*with a roar of laughter*): Here it is, O man who wants his name kept out of it! Your check!

SOLDIER (*lays a hand on his shoulder*): In the name of the Indian Army, what are you up to?

GALY GAY: Me? Nothing. (*He laughs foolishly.*)

SOLDIER: What elephant is this you've got?

GALY GAY: Which elephant is that?

SOLDIER: Chiefly the one behind you. And don't try to get out of it, see!

GALY GAY: I don't know the elephant.

OTHER SOLDIERS: Oho! We can testify this man said the elephant was his.

BEGBICK: Like his own foot, he said.

GALY GAY (*tries to leave*): I'm afraid I must go home. My wife is waiting, it's urgent. I'll come back and talk it over later. Goodbye. (*To* BILLY *who follows hard on his heels:*) Stay there, Billy, don't be so wilful! Your sugar cane grows there!

URIAH: Stop! (*To the Men:*) Take your pistols. Cover this crook. For that's what he is.

POLLY, *inside* BILLY HUMPH, *laughs loudly.* URIAH *hits him.*

URIAH: Polly, shut your trap.

The top side of the tent slides down. POLLY *is now visible.*

POLLY: Damn!

GALY GAY, *now completely confused, looks at* POLLY, *then from one to the other. The elephant runs off.*

BEGBICK (*walks over to* GALY GAY): What's this? (*Pointing toward* BILLY:) That isn't an elephant at all. It's a tent and some men. All fake! A fake elephant for my real gold!

SOLDIERS: Arrest him! Galy Gay the Crook, arrest him!

THE SOLDIERS *tie up* GALY GAY.

BLOODY FIVE (*stands in the doorway*): "Pack your bag now, Johnny!"

BEGBICK (*puts a cloth over* GALY GAY'S *head*): How are you, Sergeant? (*To the* SOLDIERS:) Pack up the canteen and sing "A Man's a Man."

BLOODY FIVE: What's that you're covering up with a cloth?

BEGBICK: Oh, nothing. (*Roaring, to the* SOLDIERS:) Sing!

*The canteen is further dismantled during the singing of the
second strophe of "A Man's a Man."* URIAH *sits thinking in
his rocking chair.*

A MAN'S A MAN: 2

So, Dan, you had rice for your dinner today?
For, Dan, I had rice for my dinner today!
Without a chicken in the pot
A soldier's life is not so hot.
And, Dan, after dinner did you throw up?
After dinner, Dan, I too threw up!
  That's all right, Dan.
  For a man is a man.
  You needn't shout.
  Really, Dan, my dear man,
  What is there to shout about?
  For men are men.
  Let us say that again:
  A man's a man.
  So it's all right, Dan.
  Kilkoa's sun shines down upon
  Six thousand soldiers and their doom.
  (When they are dead no tears are shed.
  None on the list is ever missed.)
  And so we sing: who cares on whom
  The ruddy sun of old Kilkoa shone?

BLOODY FIVE: What's that you were covering up?

BEGBICK: Are you trying to stir up trouble in my canteen? Fingers
to your trouser seams when you speak to me, you old bone!
Isn't it shameful that a lady should be forced to resort to such
language, you snot-nose? Never enter my canteen again in that
sergeant's dress!

BLOODY FIVE: What?

BEGBICK: If you come to Widow Begbick's Bar, I require tails and a bowler hat.

BLOODY FIVE: Today, Bloody Five, your blood is again as stormy as the Ganges. You can never survive this rainy night without the daughters of this old cloaca. Widow Begbick, I must see your daughters.

BEGBICK: Sergeant, I must see your bowler hat.

BLOODY FIVE: Never, never, never. (*As he goes:*) If you do this, Bloody Five, you'll have succumbed to the sensual side of your nature, hook, line, and sinker. (*Exit.*)

THIRD NUMBER

URIAH (*whistles. The* SOLDIERS *uncover* GALY GAY): Right. Now comes the Third Number: the trial against the man who wants his name kept out of it. Make a circle round the crook and cross-examine him and don't stop till you know the naked truth.

GALY GAY: I beg leave to say something.

URIAH: You've said plenty this evening, pal. Who knows what the man was called who put the elephant up for sale?

A SOLDIER: He was called Galy Gay.

URIAH: Who can testify to that?

SOLDIERS: We can.

URIAH: What does the accused have to say about it?

GALY GAY: It was someone who wanted his name kept out of it.

SOLDIERS *murmur*.

A SOLDIER: I heard him say he was Galy Gay.

URIAH: Aren't you?

GALY GAY (*slyly*): Well, if I *were* Galy Gay, maybe I'd be the man you're looking for.

URIAH: So you are *not* Galy Gay?

GALY GAY: No. I am not. (*In a whisper.*)

URIAH: And you were not present maybe when Billy Humph was put up to auction?

GALY GAY: No. I wasn't present.

URIAH: But you saw that it was someone called Galy Gay who made the sale?

GALY GAY (*lifting his hand as witness, just as the* SOLDIERS *had done*): Yes. I can testify to that.

URIAH: Then you *will* have it that you were there?

GALY GAY: I can testify to that.

URIAH: Did you all hear? Do you all see the moon? The moon is high in the sky, and he is deep in this dirty elephant deal. In the Billy Humph business, he wasn't altogether straightforward.

SOLDIERS: No. He certainly was not. The fellow said it was an elephant. But it wasn't. It was made of paper.

URIAH: Then he sold a fake elephant. That would mean the death penalty, of course. What do you say to that?

GALY GAY: At first, it was a regular elephant, later it was a fake, and it's very hard to sort everything out, High Court of Justice.

URIAH: It's certainly quite involved, but even so I think you'll have to be shot, you've brought yourself under such grave suspicion. Now listen, I've heard of a soldier, who was called Jip, and admitted it at various roll-calls, and he wanted people to believe he was called Galy Gay. Are you this Jip maybe?

GALY GAY: No. Certainly not.

URIAH: So you're not called Jip? What *are* you called? (GALY GAY *is silent.*) No answer? Then you are someone who wants his name kept out of it? (GALY GAY *is silent.*) Are you the man, maybe, who wanted his name kept out of it when the elephant was sold? Silent again? That is tremendously suspicious, almost enough to convict you. Well, now we must confer. (*They go off to confer except for* TWO. URIAH, *leaving:*) He's willing not to be Galy Gay now, but I think we'll need to threaten him with the death penalty a little more.

GALY GAY: Can you hear what they are saying?

TWO SOLDIERS: No.

GALY GAY: Are they saying I am this Galy Gay?

TWO SOLDIERS: They're saying it's no longer certain.

GALY GAY: Yes, it's no longer certain, is it?

BEGBICK (*enters; to* GALY GAY): Note this, pal: one man is no man. (*Exit.*)

JESSE (*enters*): Isn't that Galy Gay sitting there all tied up?

SOLDIERS: Hey, you! Answer!

GALY GAY: I think you're confusing me with someone else, Jesse. Take a closer look.

JESSE: Oh, then you're not Galy Gay? (GALY GAY *shakes his head.*) Go away for a minute. I have to talk to him: he has just been sentenced to death.

GALY GAY: Has it gone that far? Oh, Jesse, help me. You are a great soldier.

JESSE: How did it all come about?

GALY GAY: Well, you see, Jesse, I don't know. We were smoking and drinking, and I jabbered my soul away.

JESSE: What they're saying is that it's one Galy Gay who's to be killed.

GALY GAY: That can't be me.

JESSE: Well, then you're not Galy Gay? Look me in the eye. I'm Jesse, your friend. Aren't you Galy Gay from Kilkoa?

GALY GAY: No. You're making a mistake.

JESSE: There were four of us when we left Kankerdan. Were you there?

GALY GAY: Yes. In Kankerdan. I was there.

JESSE: I agree.

URIAH (*back with the* SOLDIERS; *to* GALY GAY): Stand up, man without a name, and give ear. The military court of Kilkoa has condemned you to be shot by eight riflemen.

GALY GAY: That cannot happen.

URIAH: It is happening. And pay attention, pal, because, firstly, you stole and sold an army elephant, which is larceny, because, secondly, you sold an elephant which was not an elephant, which is fraud, and because, thirdly, you have neither a name nor an identity card and may be a spy or even a swindler who gave the wrong name at roll-call.

GALY GAY: Oh, Uriah, why are you like this to me?

URIAH: Now come. And handle yourself like a good soldier as you learnt to in the army. March!

SOLDIERS: Go with him and be shot.

GALY GAY (*throws himself on the ground*): Oh, not so fast! I'm not the man you're looking for. I don't even know him. My name is Jip, I swear it. What is an elephant compared to a man? And I don't even know the creature. I didn't see the elephant. Only the rope that I was holding. Please go away! I'm someone else. At most I bear that man some very slight resemblance, and you confuse me with him. I am not Galy Gay. I am not.

SOLDIERS: Yes, you are. And no one else is. Under Kilkoa's three rubber trees, Galy Gay will see his blood flow. Come on!

GALY GAY: Oh dear, surely there must be formalities, the charges must be written up, and it'll be found that it wasn't me, and I'm not called Galy Gay? A considered judgment must be arrived at. You don't do such a job between noon and midday, when someone's to be sent to the slaughter!

SOLDIERS: March!

GALY GAY: What do you mean, march? I am not your man. What I wanted was to buy a fish, are there any fish here? What are those cannon rolling in the distance? What's that battle music roaring outside? I'm not going to budge. I'll hold on to this grass, yes, even if it's fake. This must all stop, I insist! But why is no one here, if a man is to be butchered? Uriah, Jesse, Polly, help me!

URIAH (*to* BEGBICK): The moon is up, all the way up, and now he consents to be Jip. I'm glad the cannon haven't gone by yet.

The cannon are heard rolling past.

BEGBICK: The cannon! We must be climbing on that train. Get all the canteen things together!

SOLDIERS: At your service, Widow Begbick.

URIAH *sits in his chair. The canteen is being further dismantled during the singing of the third strophe of "A Man's a Man."*

A MAN'S A MAN: 3

You saw Jenny Smith as well, Danny Boy?
I saw Jenny Smith as well, Danny Boy!
And Jenny Smith, that dear old hen,
Makes army life look good again!
And, Dan, did you sleep with Miss Smith as well?
Danny Boy, I slept with Miss Smith as well!
  That's all right, Dan.
  For a man is a man.
  You needn't shout.
  Really, Dan, my dear man,
  What is there to shout about?
  For men are men.
  Let us say that again:
  A man's a man.
  So it's all right, Dan.
  Kilkoa's sun shines down upon
  Six thousand soldiers and their doom.
  (When they are dead no tears are shed.
  None on the list is ever missed.)
  And so we sing: who cares on whom
  The ruddy sun of old Kilkoa shone?

FOURTH NUMBER

URIAH (*whistles*): Now comes the Fourth Number: the shooting of Galy Gay in the army barracks at Kilkoa.

BEGBICK: When they load the elephants and you're not finished, that'll be the end of your story, my men! (GALY GAY *is led back and then forwards again. He walks like the protagonist of a tragedy*.) Room there for a malefactor condemned to death by the military tribunal!

SOLDIERS: Now, look, this is a man who's going to be shot. That may be a pity, he certainly isn't very old. Why, he doesn't even know how he got into this.

URIAH: Halt! Would you like to relieve yourself for the last time?

GALY GAY: Yes.

URIAH: Guard him.

GALY GAY: I heard someone say the soldiers must leave when the elephants arrive so I've got to be slow.

SOLDIERS: You've got to be quick.

GALY GAY: I can't. Is that the moon?

SOLDIERS: Yes, it's getting late.

GALY GAY: Isn't that Widow Begbick's Bar where we always used to drink?

URIAH: No, buddy, it's the rifle range, and that's the Johnny-are-your-pants-dry-Wall. Hey! Stand in line there, and load those guns. There should be eight of them.

SOLDIERS: The light's bad. You can hardly see.

URIAH: Yes, the light's bad.

GALY GAY: Listen, this will never do. When you shoot, you've got to be able to see.

URIAH (*to* JESSE): Take this paper lantern over there, and hold it up near him. (*He blindfolds* GALY GAY. *Loudly:*) Load all guns! (*Quietly:*) What are you doing there, Polly? You're *really* putting a bullet in! Take that bullet out!

POLLY: Oh, excuse me. I almost *really* loaded my gun. We nearly had a *real* misfortune on our hands!

The elephants are heard passing at the back. Everyone stands for a moment petrified.

BEGBICK: The elephants!

URIAH: All that makes no difference. He must be shot. I'm going to count up to three. One!

GALY GAY: That will be enough, Uriah. The elephants have arrived, haven't they? Am I to stay on now, Uriah? Why are you all so terribly quiet?

URIAH: Two!

GALY GAY (*laughs*): You're funny, Uriah. I can't see you because I'm blindfolded. But your voice sounds dead serious.

URIAH: And one more makes —

GALY GAY: Stop! Don't say three, or you'll be sorry. If you shoot now, you're bound to hit me. Stop! Wait a while. Listen! I confess. I confess I don't know what happened to me. Believe me, I'm a man — now don't laugh — who doesn't know who he is. But I'm not Galy Gay, that I do know. The man that's to be shot, I'm not him. But who am I? I've forgotten. Last night, when it was raining, I knew. But was it raining last night? And if you please, when you look toward the spot where this voice comes from, over here or over there, that's me, if you please. Address yourselves to that spot. Say to it: "Galy Gay" or something. Say: "Have pity." Say: "Give me a piece of meat." The place where it disappears is Galy Gay, also the place where it pops up again. Remember this at least: when you find someone who's forgotten who he is, that's me. Please let him go — please — one more time.

URIAH *has said something in* POLLY's *ear. Now* POLLY *runs behind* GALY GAY *and flourishes a great big club.*

URIAH: "One more time" equals "no more time." Three! (GALY GAY *lets out a shriek.*) Fire!! (GALY GAY *falls in a faint.*)

POLLY: Halt! He fell all by himself!

URIAH (*shouts*): Shoot! So he'll hear he's dead! (*They shoot.*) Throw him over there under the tree.

VOICE OF BLOODY FIVE: "Pack your bag now, Johnny!"

BEGBICK: Pack up! Pack up!

BLOODY FIVE (*enters in tails and bowler hat*): Who's shooting around here? Everybody stand still!

URIAH (*smashes his hat down on his head from behind*): Shut your mouth, civilian!

A burst of laughter.

BEGBICK: Pack up! Pack up!

She takes BLOODY FIVE *over to her* DAUGHTERS *who are making music. The canteen is further dismantled during the singing of the fourth strophe of "A Man's a Man."*

A MAN'S A MAN: 4

So, Dan, are you packing your kitbag as well?
For, Dan, I am packing my kitbag as well!
And when I see you pack and go
My soldier's breast is full of woe!
But, Dan, have you nothing to put in your bag?
I have nothing, either, to put in my bag!
    That's all right, Dan.
    For a man is a man.
    You needn't shout.
    Really, Dan, my dear man,
    What is there to shout about?
    For men are men.
    Let us say that again:
    A man's a man.
    So it's all right, Dan.
Kilkoa's sun shines down upon
Six thousand soldiers and their doom.
(When they are dead no tears are shed.
None on the list is ever missed.)
And so we sing: who cares on whom
The ruddy sun of old Kilkoa shone?

FIFTH NUMBER

URIAH: Well then, the man who insists on sticking his nose into everything must be razed to the ground. This Number is a slight digression.

BEGBICK: It's nearly eleven o'clock. Soon now you'll hear the train whistle!

The THREE, BEGBICK, BLOODY FIVE, *and the* THREE DAUGHTERS *sit round a table.*

BLOODY FIVE: First of all, ladies, it is my intention to lay before you a few items from my photographic collection. Rarities in their way. I have certain items that the British Museum hasn't got.

BEGBICK: If they can drink your health in seven glasses of liquor, they'll enjoy looking at your photographs, Mister Fairchild.

BLOODY FIVE: Oh, Miss Jobia, this little man has a head of his own. Look, Widow, she's on her third glass already. (*Pointing to* GALY GAY:) What species of deathwatch beetle is that?

URIAH: Why don't you show us how you can shoot, my dear Fairchild?

BEGBICK: There's hardly one woman in ten can resist such a sharpshooter as the sergeant!

BLOODY FIVE: No!

SOLDIERS: Oh, go on, shoot, Bloody Five!

BLOODY FIVE: Will you put the lights out if I do?

They laugh. He staggers to the bar.

JOBIA: Oh, Bloody, do it for my sake, you really should. I'll put out the lights, too, whenever you wish.

BLOODY FIVE: I place an egg here. How many paces?

SOLDIER: Four.

BLOODY FIVE (*goes to a considerable distance*): Here's a plain ordinary army pistol. (*He shoots.*)

JOBIA: The egg's untouched.

BLOODY FIVE: Untouched?

SOLDIERS: Completely. It even got twice as big.

BLOODY FIVE: That's strange. I thought I could hit it. Couldn't someone put a few lights out now? I want to unmask this deathwatch beetle!

BEGBICK: You can have the lights out now, my Fairbaby!

SOLDIER: I for one never heard such bragging. It's a fiasco.

BLOODY FIVE: Yes, yes, you're a lot of pigs.

SOLDIERS: Bravo, bravo!

BLOODY FIVE: Urine tanks! (*He laughs. They all laugh.*) If I should tell you, for instance, you should eat your own unsalted shit, that would be only reasonable. (*Laughter.*) If I should tell you to do that, you'd wonder how I could be so mild. And maybe I *won't* be able to much longer! (*Laughter.*) Are you putting the lights out now? What kind of deathwatch beetle *is* this?

URIAH: Three cheers for good old Bloody! Give him a glass of whiskey. (*They roar the cheers, and he drinks.*) How did you get the name Bloody Five, actually?

SOLDIERS: Show us!

BLOODY FIVE (*to* JOBIA): Shall I tell the story, ladies?

JOBIA: Oh, Bloody!

BLOODY FIVE: Then will you put the lights out right away? This is the Lake Chad River.

SOLDIERS: Widow Begbick, you are the Lake Chad River!

BLOODY FIVE: You are five Sikhs.* Their hands are tied behind their backs. I arrive with a plain ordinary army pistol. I wave it about a bit for them to see. Then I say: this pistol has misfired a number of times, it's got to be tried out. Like so. And I shoot — fall down, you there, bang! — then four times more. That was all, gentlemen. (*General applause.*) Lights out!

SOLDIERS: What a great soldier you are, Bloody! You give off sparks! Thrilling! The strength of those loins must be terrific too! What? And such a nice man at the same time! At bottom, so good natured!

SOLDIER (*enters*): Is Sergeant Charles Fairchild here? The general's orders are these: run and get your company lined up in the freight station.

* Lake Chad is in Africa, which may explain why in later editions Brecht omitted the word for *lake*. But the solecism is surely in keeping with others in this play, with those in *In the Swamp*, and with things like Turnbridge and Highgate Moors in *The Threepenny Opera*. Incidentally, *Sikhs* is written *Shiks* in the German: I was tempted to translate it as *sheiks*. Later German editions have *Hindus*. One of the few oddities I have not reproduced is *Blody* Five for *Bloody* Five. E. B.

BLOODY FIVE: Don't say it's me!

SOLDIER: There's no sergeant here of that name. (SOLDIER *leaves*.)

POLLY: Lanterns out! Jip's waking up!

BEGBICK: To hell with the lanterns! Girls, get out of here fast!

BLOODY FIVE: Don't you want to try a little two-step? (*He sings and dances.*)
Two dark eyes,
A purple mouth ...

BEGBICK: Finish packing up my canteen. I'll take care of Bloody. (*To* JOBIA:) Get the wagon ready and get gone.

BLOODY FIVE: Jobia! Jobia! Where is little Jobia? I've got to have her — or I'll be raping this damned deathwatch beetle!

BEGBICK: Come, my lad, I'll take care of you. The wagons are under way.

BLOODY FIVE: Good. Over here. A woman's a woman.

BEGBICK (*exiting*): The wall down, the roof in the box, leave the counter and the urinal to the last. And if you're not finished with this little job by the time the train whistle blows, you can have yourselves buried alive.

They both leave.

SIXTH NUMBER

URIAH (*whistles*): Now comes the last Number. In the year 1925, funeral procession and graveside oration of Galy Gay, the last man of character! Get the nickelodeon crate and put a nice funeral procession together for us!

SOLDIERS (*carry the nickelodeon crate on their shoulders and sing to the tune of Chopin's funeral march*): And now he drinks his whiskey no more!

GALY GAY (*wakes up*): Who is that they're carrying?

JESSE: One who, at his final hour, was shot.

GALY GAY: What was his name?

JESSE: Just a moment. If I'm not mistaken, his name was Galy Gay.

GALY GAY: And what's happening to him?

JESSE: To who?

GALY GAY: To this Galy Gay.

JESSE: Oh, now he's being buried.

POLLY: Isn't that Jip? Jip, you must get up at once, and make the oration at the burial of the deceased Galy Gay. For you knew him — better than we did, maybe.

GALY GAY: Yes.

JESSE: Then pace the ground between the rubber trees, and prepare the Galy Gay funeral oration!

GALY GAY *walks among the rubber trees. Next to him, never leaving his side,* JESSE *and* POLLY.

POLLY: Remember losing your tobacco pouch at Hyderabad? You said: "One time is no time."

GALY GAY *shakes his head.*

JESSE: And the episode with the tip?

POLLY: The time you stole the lady's fish and tricked her into thinking you were her husband?

GALY GAY *shakes his head.*

BEGBICK (*coming out*): Need anything? For all illnesses, even including cholera, the army uses nothing but castor oil. Illnesses not cured by castor oil don't happen to soldiers. Want some castor oil?

GALY GAY (*shakes his head*): The day I came out, my mother marked it in her calendar, and the one who yammered, it was me. This bundle of flesh, hair, and nails. Mc. Mc.

JESSE: Yes, Jeraiah Jip, Jeraiah Jip from Tipperary.

GALY GAY: One who carried fish for tips. An elephant betrayed him. One who had to catch a nap on a wooden chair for lack of time, for, in the hut he lived in, the fish water was on the boil. And the machine gun hadn't got cleaned yet, because someone had given him a cigar and eight rifles, of which one was missing. What was his name?

URIAH: Jip. Jeraiah Jip!

GALY GAY: No baggage for me to carry, sir?

BEGBICK (*coming out*): You know where it all leads? To death. This army is marching toward the fire-spewing guns of Tibet! Sixty thousand men will be marching tonight, all in the same direction. This direction is from Kilkoa to Tibet and not the other way round. When a man finds himself in that particular river, he looks around for two others, one on the right, and one on the left, and his gun and his knapsack and a dogtag round his neck and a number on the dogtag, so it'll be known who he belonged to, when they find him, and he'll have his very own place in the grave of the many!

BLOODY FIVE (*beckoning*): Begbick!

Exit BEGBICK. *The train whistle is heard.*

SOLDIERS: The whistle! Now each man for himself! We must get our knapsacks! (*They run off.*)

GALY GAY: Is that the crate he's lying inside of?

URIAH: Yes.

POLLY (*to* JESSE): If he opens it up, we're done for.

GALY GAY (*to* POLLY): Was he a good man or a bad?

POLLY: Oh, he was quite a dangerous fellow!

GALY GAY (*goes to the crate*): And he got shot too, after all. And I was there.

POLLY: And if he looks inside, we're done for.

URIAH: Listen, Polly, and you, Jesse. Comrades, the three of us have survived. Now that the hair by which we three hang over the abyss is breaking, listen to what I have to tell you before the last wall of Kilkoa toward eleven at night. The man we need must have a short time for reflection because he's changing himself for such a long time. And so I, Uriah Shelley, draw my army pistol, and threaten you both with instant death if you so much as move.

JESSE: But if he looks in the crate, the jig is up.

They sit and wait.

GALY GAY:

I could not look without dropping dead on the spot
At a face emptied out in a crate
Face of a certain person known to me once

From the shimmering surface of the water into which
Someone looked and then
As I should know
Perished.
And so I cannot open up this crate
Because of this fear that is in both of me.
For perhaps
I am a Both that once
The changing surface of the earth produced
Tied to a navel, formed like a bat, and hanging
Between rubber trees and hut by night,
A Thing that would like to be gay.
One man is no man: someone must call him something.
And so
I would gladly have looked in this trough
Because the heart is tied to the parent's heart, but
If the difference between yes and no is not so great
And if I did not look at the elephant
I close one eye in what concerns myself and shed
What's not acceptable in me and so become
A nice man.

He stands up and goes to the rubber trees at the back.

And I (the first I and the second)
We inspect the rain and the wind
That wets us and that dries us, and
We build our strength by eating.
(*To the* THREE:) You there, can you see me at all? Where am
I? (POLLY *points to him.*) Yes. Correct. Now what am I doing?

POLLY: Bending your arm.

GALY GAY: Right. So I bend my arm. Am I doing it again now?

POLLY: Yes. A second time.

GALY GAY: I have bent my arm twice. And now?

POLLY: Now you're walking like a soldier.

GALY GAY: You walk like that?

POLLY: Just like that.

GALY GAY: What do you say, when you want something from me?

POLLY: Jip.

GALY GAY: Then say: walk around, Jip.

POLLY: Walk around, Jip.

SOLDIERS (*enter with knapsacks*): All aboard!

URIAH: Your funeral oration, Friend Jip, your funeral oration.

GALY GAY: Then lift Widow Begbick's nickelodeon crate with the mysterious body inside, lift it two feet in the air, then lower it six feet in Kilkoa's earth, and hear his burial oration, presented by Jeraiah Jip from Tipperary, which is no easy thing to do, as I am not prepared. But anyway, here lies Galy Gay, a man who was shot. He went off in the morning to buy a little fish, by evening had an elephant, and that same night was shot. Do not believe, my friends, that he was less than the best of men during his time on earth. He even had a straw hut on the edge of town and other things besides, about which it might be best to be silent. It was a great crime that he committed, this very good man. Well, people can say what they want, but actually it was only an oversight, and I was far too drunk, gentlemen, but a man's a man, and so he had to be shot. And now the wind is considerably cooler, as always toward morning, and I think we'll be going a long way from here, and it's not any too comfortable. (SOLDIERS *applaud*.) Why have you all packed up?

POLLY: Why, we've got to leave tonight for Tibet.

GALY GAY: Well, why haven't *I* packed?

POLLY: Here, Cap'n. Here are your things, Cap'n.

GALY GAY: What? Am I to tie that dirty old bag on my back? It's an outrage.

SOLDIERS (*laugh*): You can't give him *that* knapsack. The Cap'n is a man who knows what kind of knapsack is his due.

GALY GAY: What's that? Give me that junk. I need two knapsacks anyway. This is really the end. I'll show you what Jeraiah Jip of Tipperary is made of!

POLLY: Here's my best repeating rifle for the Cap'n.

JESSE: Here's my knapsack.

POLLY: Three cheers for our Cap'n.

BEGBICK: And don't forget my bamboo poles, my lads!

GALY GAY: Well then! Each man take a bamboo pole with him to Tibet so we can get going.

SOLDIERS *carry a large package into the wagons.*

BEGBICK: That was the human typhoon.

During the singing of the last strophe of "A Man's a Man," all disappear toward the back. Only the rubber trees remain.

A MAN'S A MAN: 5

So, Dan, are you off on your travels tonight?
For, Dan, I am off on my travels tonight!
When you depart, such is my pride,
I must be marching at your side!
But, Dan, do you know where you're travelling to?
For I do not know where we're travelling to!
    That's all right, Dan.
For a man is a man.
You needn't shout.
Really, Dan, my dear man,
What is there to shout about?
For men are men.
Let us say that again:
A man's a man.
So it's all right, Dan.
Kilkoa's sun shines down upon
Six thousand soldiers and their doom.
(When they are dead no tears are shed.
None on the list is ever missed.)
And so we sing: who cares on whom
The ruddy sun of old Kilkoa shone?

10

ON THE MOVING TRAIN. NIGHT:
TOWARD MORNING

The COMPANY *is asleep on hammocks.* JESSE, URIAH, *and* POLLY *sit and keep guard.* GALY GAY *sleeps.*

JESSE: The world is frightful. You can't rely on people.

POLLY: The meanest creature alive, and the weakest, is man.

JESSE: We've tramped all the roads of this all-too-endless country in dust and rain, from the Hindu Kush Range to the great plains of the southern Punjab, but from Benares to Calcutta by sun or moon, all we have seen is treachery. This man whom we took up, and who now has taken our blankets off our beds so that we miss our sleep, is like an oil can with a hole in it. Yes and No are the same to him: he says this today and that tomorrow. Oh, Uriah, we've exhausted all our wisdom. Let us go to Leocadia Begbick — she's keeping watch over the sergeant, to see he doesn't fall off — and let's ask her to lie down with this man so he'll feel good and not ask questions. For though she's old, she still has warm blood, and a man feels fine when he's in bed with a woman. Stand up, Polly! (*They go to* WIDOW BEGBICK.) Come in, Widow Begbick, we don't know if we're standing on our head or our heels, and we're afraid of going to sleep on the job, and there's this man who is sick. Lie down with him, will you, and act like you'd slept with him, help to make him feel good.

BEGBICK (*enters, sleepy*): I'll do it — for seven pay envelopes.

URIAH: You can have all we earn in seven weeks.

    BEGBICK *lies down next to* GALY GAY.

JESSE: She'll be Mrs. Jip. What more can he ask?

    JESSE *covers the couple with newspapers.*

GALY GAY (*wakes up*): What's that, shaking so?

URIAH (*to the others*): It's the elephant, nibbling at your hut, you grumbler.

GALY GAY: What's that, hissing so?

URIAH (*to the others*): It's the fish, boiling in the water, you nice man.

GALY GAY (*stands wearily up and looks through the window*): A woman. Sleeping bags. Telegraph poles. It's a train.

JESSE: Act asleep. (THE THREE *do so*.)

GALY GAY (*approaching a sleeping bag*): Hey you!

SOLDIER: Whatja want?

GALY GAY: Where are you people heading for?

SOLDIER (*opening one eye*): The front. (*He goes on sleeping.*)

GALY GAY: They're soldiers. (*Wakes another after looking out through the window.*) Hey soldier, what time is it? (*Gets no answer.*) Toward morning. What day of the week is it?

SOLDIER: Between Thursday and Friday.

GALY GAY: I must get off. Hey you, the train's got to stop!

SOLDIER: The train won't stop.

GALY GAY: If the train won't stop, and everybody's asleep, I'll lie down and sleep till it does stop. (*Sees* BEGBICK.) There's a woman lying next to me. What woman would it be, that's been lying here all the night?

JESSE: Hello, comrade! Good morning!

GALY GAY: Oh, I'm very glad to see you, Mister Jesse.

JESSE: Quite a man of the world, I see! Taking your ease here with a woman in full view of everyone!

GALY GAY: Yes, isn't it remarkable? Almost improper, eh? But you know: a man is a man. He isn't his own master. I wake up and, look, a woman right next to me!

JESSE: Yes, look!

GALY GAY: And would you believe it, I often don't even know the woman I find there in the morning? To come right out with it, man to man, I don't know her. And, Mister Jesse, between us men, could you tell me who she is?

JESSE: Oh, you show-off! This time it's Widow Leocadia Begbick — obviously. You'd know who your friend was all right, if you dipped your head in cold water. Then again, do you even know your own name?

GALY GAY: Oh yes.

JESSE: What is it? (GALY GAY *is silent*.) You do know your name.

GALY GAY: Yes.

JESSE: That's good. A man must know who he is when he goes to war.

GALY GAY: There's a war on?

JESSE: The Tibetan War.

GALY GAY: Tibetan War. But if a fellow didn't know for a moment who he was, it'd be funny, wouldn't it? When he's going to war!

BEGBICK: Jippy, where are you?

GALY GAY: Who does she mean?

JESSE: I think she means you.

GALY GAY: Here!

BEGBICK: Come on, give me a kiss, Jippy!

GALY GAY: Gladly. But I think you're confusing me with someone.

BEGBICK: Jippy!

JESSE: This gentleman claims his head is none too clear. He says he doesn't know you.

BEGBICK: Oh! You'd put me to shame before this gentleman!

GALY GAY: If I dip my head in cold water, I'll recognize you at once. (*He sticks his head in water*.)

BEGBICK: You know me now?

GALY GAY (*lies*): Yes.

POLLY: Then you know who *you* are, too?

GALY GAY (*slyly*): Didn't I know before?

POLLY: No. You went haywire and wanted to be someone else.

GALY GAY: Who?

JESSE: And things still haven't improved, I see. I think you're still a public danger, because when people called you by your name last night, you became as dangerous as a murderer.

GALY GAY: All I know is that my name is Galy Gay.

JESSE: Here we go again, everybody! Call him Galy Gay, as he says, or he'll go haywire.

URIAH: Well, well, you can play the wild man, Mister Jip from Ireland, till they tie you to the post outside the canteen and it rains at night. We've been your comrades since the Battle of the Lake Chad River, and we'd sell the shirts off our backs to be of service to you.

GALY GAY: Oh, as for your shirts, that won't be necessary.

URIAH: Talk to him just the way he wants.

JESSE: Don't worry, Uriah. Would you like a glass of water, Galy Gay?

GALY GAY: Yes, that's my name.

JESSE: Galy Gay, of course. What else? But be calm. Lie down for a while. Tomorrow — the hospital, a lovely bed, and castor oil, and you'll feel better, Galy Gay. Rubber-soled shoes only, everyone, our comrade Jip — Galy Gay, I mean — is sick.

GALY GAY: Now, gentlemen, I don't quite see the situation yet. But, though one may have a bag to carry, that bag, however heavy, may have, as they say, a soft spot.

POLLY (*supposedly in secret to* JESSE): Don't let him look in his wallet or he'll read his actual name in his papers and go right off his head.

JESSE: Identity cards are such a good thing. The best of us has an imperfect memory. That's why we soldiers, who can hardly be expected to carry everything in our heads, have a wallet hanging by a string round our necks, and, in this wallet, an identity card! One's name! If a man were to think of his name too often, that wouldn't be good.

GALY GAY (*goes to the back, looks gloomily into his papers, and goes into his corner*): I just won't think about it any more. I'll simply sit on my behind and count telegraph poles.

VOICE OF BLOODY FIVE: What shame has come over me? Where is my name that was a byword from Calcutta to Cooch Behar?

Where is the yesterday that is gone forever? Even my coat is gone, the coat I wore! They dumped me in a train as if I were destined for the stockyards! I have a gag in my mouth like a condom at the wrong end, and throughout the length and breadth of the train they say I'm Bloody Five no longer! I must go and fix things so that this train can be thrown on a junkheap like a bit of twisted stovepipe. I'll crush them like vermin, those who've done this to me, as sure as my name's Bloody Five. It is not important that I eat: it is important that I am Bloody Five. It's as simple as that.

JESSE: Bloody! Wake up, Widow Begbick!

BLOODY FIVE *enters in messed-up civvies.*

GALY GAY: Has something happened to your name, maybe?

BLOODY FIVE: You're the most miserable of the lot, and I'll crush you first. Tomorrow you'll all be tin cans! (*He sees* BEGBICK *take a seat. She smiles.*) Damnation! There you sit, Gomorrah! I'm Bloody Five no more — what did you do to me? Go away! (BEGBICK *laughs.*) What are these clothes I have on? Are they suitable? What kind of head is this on my shoulders? Is it nice? Am I to sleep with you once again, Sodom?

BEGBICK: If you'd like to, go ahead.

BLOODY FIVE: I would NOT like to! Go away! The eyes of the whole country are upon me. I was a big wheel. A cannon wheel. My name is Bloody Five. A name that is to be found three times over all through the pages of history!

BEGBICK: Then don't go ahead, if you *wouldn't* like to.

BLOODY FIVE: Don't you know what happens to my manhood when you sit there like that?

BEGBICK: "If thy manhood offend thee, pluck it out!"

BLOODY FIVE: You don't have to tell me twice! (*Exit.*)

GALY GAY (*calling after him*): Stop! Don't take action because of a name! A name is an uncertain thing, you can't count on it!

BLOODY FIVE'S VOICE: It's as simple as that. This is the answer. Here's a rope. Here's an army pistol. What do you know? Rebels are always shot. It's as simple as that! "Pack your bag now, Johnny!" No girl in the world will ever cost me a penny again!

That's it. It's as simple as that. I needn't even take my pipe out of my mouth. I hereby assume my responsibilities. I must do it — to remain Bloody Five. Fire!

A shot.

GALY GAY (*who has been standing at the door for some time, laughs*): Fire!

SOLDIERS (*in coaches behind and in front*): Did you hear that scream? Who screamed? Someone must have got hit! They've stopped singing right to the front of the train. Listen!

GALY GAY: I know who screamed and I know why. On account of his name, this gentleman did something very bloody to himself. He shot his sex away. I was very fortunate to see it, for now I see where pigheadedness leads, and what a bloody thing it is for a man to be dissatisfied with himself and make such a fuss about his name! (*He runs to* BEGBICK.) Don't think I don't know you. I know you very well. And it is also a matter of complete indifference. But tell me, quick, how far are we from the city where we met?

BEGBICK: Many days' march. Further every minute.

GALY GAY: How many days' march?

BEGBICK: At the moment when you asked the question, it must have been a hundred days' march.

GALY GAY: And how many men are there in this train for Tibet?

BEGBICK: A hundred thousand.

GALY GAY: Yes! A hundred thousand! And what do they eat?

BEGBICK: Rice and dried fish.

GALY GAY: They all eat the same?

BEGBICK: All eat the same.

GALY GAY: Yes. All eat the same.

BEGBICK: They all have hammocks to sleep in, each man his own. And cotton uniforms in summer.

GALY GAY: How about the winter?

BEGBICK: Khaki uniforms.

GALY GAY: Women?

JESSE: The same.

GALY GAY: Winter and summer?

JESSE: The same women.

BEGBICK: And now you do know who you are?

GALY GAY: Jeraiah Jip is my name. (*He runs over to* THE THREE *and shows his name in his papers.*)

JESSE (*and the others smile*): Correct. You know when to bring your name in, friend Jip.

GALY GAY: How about dinner? (POLLY *brings him a plate of rice.*) Yes, it is very important that I eat. (*He eats.*) How many marching days does the train cover every minute?

BEGBICK: Ten.

POLLY: How happily he curls up in his seat! How he stares at everything, counts telegraph poles, and enjoys the speed of the train!

JESSE: I can't look at him. It's disgusting that a mammoth prefers to turn into a louse rather than be called to his fathers, just because a couple of guns are held under his nose.

URIAH: No. It's a proof of vitality. So long as the real Jip doesn't turn up in the rear singing "A Man's a Man," I think our troubles are over.

A SOLDIER: What's that noise in the air?

URIAH (*smiling wickedly*): The thunder of cannon. We are approaching the hills of Tibet.

GALY GAY: No more rice for me?

11

DEEP IN FAR TIBET LIES THE SIR EL DCHOWR MOUNTAIN FORTRESS

And, on a hill, amid the thunder of cannon, JERAIAH JIP *sits waiting. Meanwhile: the marching of military columns, the singing of "A Man's a Man."*

VOICES (*from below*): Thus far and no farther. This is the Sir el Dchowr Mountain Fortress which commands the narrow pass to Tibet.*

GALY GAY'S VOICE (*behind the hill*): Run! Run! Or we'll be too late! (*He bobs up with a cannon minus its barrel on his back.*) Out of the train, and into the battle; I like this. A cannon is something to live up to.

JIP: Have you seen a machine gun unit with only three men in it?

GALY GAY (*irresistible as a war elephant*): There's no such thing, soldier. Our unit, for instance, consists of four men. One to your right, one left, one behind, and one in front, and it's in that formation that we get through every pass, however narrow.

BEGBICK (*bobs up; she carries a barrel on her back*): Don't run so fast, Jippy! You only do it because you have the heart of a lion!

THE THREE *turn up. Groaning, they drag their machine gun.*

JIP: Hello, Uriah. Hello, Jesse. Hello, Polly. I'm back.

THE THREE *pretend not to see him.*

JESSE: We must fix up the machine gun right away.

URIAH: The noise of the cannon is so loud already, you can't hear yourself speak.

POLLY: We must keep an eagle eye on the Sir el Dchowr Fortress.

* This contradicts the scene heading but so it is. E. B.

GALY GAY: I'll shoot first. One of you carries the cannon, one throws it down to the ground, one aims it at the enemy, everybody gets cracking, and everything's all right.

BLOODY FIVE (*enters*): "Pack your bag now, Johnny!" Well, there's that scum of a Galy Gay. Come here, you! What kind of a man are you?

GALY GAY (*smiles in his face*): A man's a man. And no man is no man. But I won't tell anyone.

BLOODY FIVE: He's the saddest sack of the lot. I'll annihilate all four of them. It's as simple as that. But first I must get this battle going. The Sir el Dchowr Fortress bothers me. I don't seem able to take it. Well then, everybody start shooting! Except you.

GALY GAY: No, no, no, Sergeant, that's wrong. Not what ONE man wishes, but what they ALL wish. Something in our way? Then it must come down. One can't keep all these gentlemen waiting. One must simply shoot in this direction. The mountain won't collapse under its own weight. And I know quite well what these men all wish. Never to see the damn thing again, and straight ahead!

BLOODY FIVE: But when I've taken the Sir el Dchowr Fortress, when I've heard my name Bloody Five shouted from a thousand throats to fill me with strength, I'll confront this chap again and ask him who he is. (*Exit.*)

JIP: Hello, Jesse. Hello, Uriah. Hello, Polly. How are you? I haven't seen you for quite a time. I was held up, you know. I hope you weren't inconvenienced on my account. I couldn't easily get away any quicker. I'm happy to be with you again. Better late than never. Why don't you speak?

POLLY: What can we do for you, sir? (POLLY *places a plate of rice on the machine gun for* GALY GAY.) Wouldn't you like to eat your rice ration, the battle is about to begin?

GALY GAY: Give it here. (*He eats.*) So, first I eat my rice ration, then I get the amount of whiskey that falls to my lot, and while I eat and drink, I observe this mountain fortress, to the end of finding its soft spot. Then it'll be an easy matter.

JIP: Your voice is quite different, Polly. But your sense of humor is the same. For my part, I was busy with a rather successful project of my own. Then I had to drop it. For your sake, naturally. You're not angry with me?

URIAH: I'm afraid we shall have to let you know that you have evidently come to the wrong door.

POLLY: We don't know you.

JESSE: It's always possible we've met. But there's a lot of human material in the army, sir.

GALY GAY: I'd like another rice ration. You haven't given me *yours*, Uriah.

JIP: You're all very different, you know that?

URIAH: Very possibly. Such is life in the army!

JIP: But I'm your old comrade Jip!

THE THREE *laugh. Then* GALY GAY *starts laughing; and they stop.*

GALY GAY: Another ration! There's a battle today, I have an appetite. I like this mountain fortress better all the time.

POLLY *gives him his third plate.*

JIP: Who's this who eats your rations for you?

URIAH: That is no one's business but our own.

JESSE: Look, you can never be good old Jip. Good old Jip would never have betrayed and abandoned us. Good old Jip wouldn't have got held up. And so you cannot be good old Jip.

JIP: But I am.

URIAH: Prove it.

JIP: Will none of you admit he knows me? Then let me tell you this, and don't you forget it: you are very hard. And it takes no prophet to know you'll come to a bad end. Give me my papers.

GALY GAY (*going over to* JIP, *plate in hand*): You're making some mistake. (*Back to the entrance.*) He's a bit cracked. (*To* JIP:) Maybe you haven't eaten for days? Would you like a glass of water? (*Back.*) We mustn't irritate him. (*To himself:*) You don't know where you belong? That doesn't matter. Just sit down over here till we've won the battle. Please don't get

too near the noise of the cannon, or you'll need great strength
of soul. (*To* THE THREE:) He doesn't know his way around.
(*To* JIP:) It's true you need papers. Who'll let you run
around without? Polly, run to the box on the cannon, the
one with the little megaphone in it, and get the papers of
that Galy Gay, the fellow you used to tease me about. (POLLY
runs.) A man who has dwelt in the lowlands where the tiger
asks the jaguar about his teeth knows how good it is to have
something on him in black and white. For today, on every
side, they try to steal your name from you. I know what a
name is worth. Oh, children, why did you call me Galy Gay
that time and not just Mister Nobody? Those are dangerous
games. They could easily have had consequences. But I say:
Let bygones be bygones. (*He gives* JIP *the identity card.*)
Here's your identity card. Take it. Anything else you'd like?

JIP: You're the best of the bunch. You at least have a heart. As for
you others, I curse you!

GALY GAY: So you men won't have to hear too much of this curse
I'll make a noise with the cannon. How does it work, Widow
Begbick, show me!

JIP: May the icy wind of Tibet suck the marrow from your bones!
Never will you hear the bell in the harbor of Kilkoa, you
devils. You shall march to the end of the world, and then
march back again, and that several times! Your teacher the
devil won't want you around when you're old, so you'll have
to go on marching — across the Gobi Desert by day, and by
night across the green waving rye fields of Wales. All this
will befall you because you betrayed a comrade in his need.
(*Exit.* THE THREE *are silent.*)

GALY GAY: You see, Widow Begbick, even if the fortress is made of
solid bronze, if its time is come, it will fall over. Someone
need only pass by and spit on it, and it will just plain disappear.
Well then, now I know the fortress, and I know the cannon.
I shall make it with five shots.

First shot.

BEGBICK (*smoking a cigar*): You belong to that breed of great
soldiers who in former times made the army a terror to the

world. Five such fellows would be a threat even to a woman. (*Second shot.*) I can prove that in the battle of the Lake Chad River it wasn't the worst men in the company who thought of my kisses. A night with Widow Begbick was something men would give up their whiskey for, something they'd save two weeks' pay for. They had names like Genghis Khan, known from Calcutta to Cooch Behar. (*Third shot.*) One embrace of the beloved Irish colleen would calm their manly blood. You can read in *The Times* how tranquilly they entered the fight at Bourabay, Kamakura, and Daguth. (*Fourth shot.*)

GALY GAY: What once was a mountain fortress will now fall down!

The Sir el Dchowr Mountain Fortress starts to fall.

POLLY: For heaven's sake, what are you doing?

Enter BLOODY FIVE.

GALY GAY: This is terrific. Leave me alone. I've tasted blood.

BLOODY FIVE: What are you doing? Just look over there! Well, I'm going to stick you in the antheap up to your head, or you'll be shooting the Hindu Kush Range into the sea. My hand is quite steady. (*He aims his pistol at* GALY GAY.) It's not trembling in the least. You are now looking your last upon the world.

GALY GAY (*letting off the fifth shot vehemently*): One more shot. Just one. The fifth!

From the abyss there goes up a cry of joy: "The Sir el Dchowr Mountain Fortress, which blocked the pass to Tibet, has now fallen! The army marches into Tibet!"

BLOODY FIVE: So. Now I can hear what I'm used to: the army on the march. And now I can confront this man. (*He confronts* GALY GAY.) Who are you?

SOLDIERS' VOICES (*from below*): Who is the man who has taken the Sir el Dchowr Fortress?

GALY GAY: One moment. Polly, get me that little megaphone, so I can tell them. (*He shouts through the megaphone:*) It's me! One of yourselves! Jeraiah Jip!

VOICES (*from below*): What did you do to free the pass?

GALY GAY (*through the megaphone*): Practically nothing! My position is: A Man's a Man!

VOICES (*from below*): Then you're the greatest man the army has, Jeraiah Jip! The human fighting machine!

GALY GAY (*puts down the megaphone*): Now step forward, and give me your papers. We are now passing the frontier of icebound Tibet.

They give him their papers.

POLLY: Polly Baker.

JESSE: Jesse Mahoney.

URIAH. Uriah Shelley.

GALY GAY: Jeraiah Jip. Quick march!

THE FOUR *march off singing "A Man's a Man."*

POLLY (*over his shoulder*): He'll have our heads yet.

SAINT JOAN
OF THE STOCKYARDS

(1929–1930)

English Version by
Frank Jones

CHARACTERS

PIERPONT MAULER
CRIDLE
LENNOX } *Meat Kings*
GRAHAM
SLIFT

JOAN DARK
MARTHA } *Black Straw Hats*
MAJOR PAULUS SNYDER
JACKSON

MULBERRY, *a landlord*
MRS. LUCKERNIDDLE, *a worker's wife*
GLOOMB, *a worker*
MRS. SWINGURN, *a worker's wife*
A WAITER
AN OLD MAN
A BROKER
AN APPRENTICE
TWO DETECTIVES
FIVE LABOR LEADERS
TWO POLICEMEN

And, as groups: WHOLESALERS, STOCKBREEDERS, SMALL SPECULATORS, WORKERS, NEWSBOYS, PASSERS-BY, JOURNALISTS, VOICES, MUSICIANS, SOLDIERS, POOR FOLK

1

THE MEAT KING PIERPONT MAULER GETS A LETTER FROM HIS FRIENDS IN NEW YORK

Chicago stockyards.

MAULER (*reading a letter*): "As we can plainly see, dear Pierpont, the stock market has been badly constipated for some little time. Also tariff walls to the south of us are resisting all our attacks. In view of this it seems advisable, dear Pierpont, to let the packing business go." I have this hint today from my dear friends in New York. Here comes my partner. (*Hides letter.*)

CRIDLE: Well, my dear Pierpont! Why so gloomy?

MAULER:

Remember, Cridle, how some days ago —
We were walking through the stockyards, it was evening —
We stood beside our brand-new packing machine.
Remember, Cridle, the ox that took the blow,
Standing there blond, huge, dumbly gazing up
Toward Heaven: I feel the stroke was meant for me.
Oh, Cridle! Oh, our business is bloody.

CRIDLE:

So — the old weakness, Pierpont!
Almost incredible: you, giant of packers,
Lord of the stockyards, quaking at the kill,
Fainting with pain, all for a fair-haired ox!
Don't tell a soul of this but me, I beg you.

MAULER:

O loyal Cridle!
I oughtn't to have visited the stockyards!
Since I went into this business — that's seven
Years — I'd avoided them; and now — oh, Cridle,
I cannot bear it any longer! I'm giving up today.
You take this bloody business, with my share!

I'll let you have it cheap: you above all,
For no one else belongs to it like you.

CRIDLE: How cheap?

MAULER:

No long palaver can be held
On such things by old friends like you and me.
Let's say ten million.

CRIDLE:

That would not be expensive but for Lennox,
Who fights with us for every case of meat
And ruins our market with his cutthroat prices
And will break us all if he does not go broke.
Before he falls, and only you can fell him,
I shall not take your offer. Until then
Your cunning brain must be in constant practice.

MAULER:

No, Cridle! That poor ox's outcry
Will nevermore go mute within me. Therefore
This Lennox must fall fast, for I myself
Have willed to be a decent man henceforth
And not a butcher. Cridle, come with me,
And I will tell you what to do to make
Lennox fall fast. But then you must
Relieve me of this business, which hurts me.

CRIDLE:

If Lennox falls.
Exeunt.

2

THE COLLAPSE OF THE GREAT PACKING PLANTS

In front of the Lennox Plant.

THE WORKERS:

    We are seventy thousand workers in Lennox's packing plant
        and we
    Cannot live a day longer on such low wages.
    Yesterday our pay was slashed again
    And today the notice is up once more:
    ANYONE NOT SATISFIED
    WITH OUR WAGES CAN GO.
    All right then, let's all go and
    Shit on the wages that get skinnier every day.

    A silence.

THE WORKERS:

    For a long time now this work has made us sick
    The factory our hell and nothing
    But cold Chicago's terrors could
    Keep us here. But now
    By twelve hours' work a man can't even
    Earn a stale loaf and
    The cheapest pair of pants. Now
    A man might just as well go off and
    Die like a beast.

    A silence.

THE WORKERS:

    What do they take us for? Do they think
    We are going to stand here like steers, ready
    For anything? Are we

153

Their chumps? Better lie and rot!
Let's go right now.

A silence.

THE WORKERS:
It must be six o'clock by now!
Why don't you open up, you sweatshop bosses? Here
Are your steers, you butchers, open up!

They knock.

Maybe they've forgotten us?

Laughter.

THE WORKERS:
Open the gates! We
Want to get into your
Dirt-holes and lousy kitchens
To cook stuffed meat
For the eaters who possess.

A silence.

We demand at least
Our former wages, even though they were too low, at least
A ten-hour day and at least ——

A MAN (*crossing stage*):
What are you waiting for? Don't you know
That Lennox has shut down?

NEWSBOYS *run across stage.*

THE NEWSBOYS: Meat king Lennox forced to shut down his plants!
Seventy thousand workers without food or shelter! M. L.
Lennox a victim of bitter competitive struggle with Pierpont
Mauler, well-known meat baron and philanthropist.

THE WORKERS:
Alas!
Hell itself
Shuts its gate in our faces!
We are doomed. Bloody Mauler grips
Our exploiter by the throat and
We are the ones who choke!

P. MAULER

A street.

THE NEWSBOYS: Chicago Tribune, noon edition! P. Mauler, meat
baron and philanthropist, to attend opening of the P. Mauler
Hospitals, largest and most expensive in the world! (P. MAULER
passes, with two men.)

A PASSER-BY (*to another*): That's P. Mauler. Who are the men walking with him?

THE OTHER: Detectives. They guard him so that he won't be
knocked down.

TO COMFORT THE MISERY OF THE STOCKYARDS, THE BLACK STRAW HATS
LEAVE THEIR MISSION-HOUSE. JOAN'S FIRST DESCENT INTO THE DEPTHS

In front of a Black Straw Hats Mission.

JOAN (*at the head of the Black Straw Hat shock troop*):
In gloomy times of bloody confusion
Ordered disorder
Planful wilfulness
Dehumanized humanity
When there is no end to the unrest in our cities:
Into such a world, a world like a slaughterhouse —
Summoned by rumors of threatening deeds of violence
To prevent the brute strength of the short-sighted people
From shattering its own tools and
Trampling its own bread-basket to pieces —
We wish to reintroduce
God.
A figure of little glory,
Almost of ill repute,
No longer admitted
To the sphere of actual life:
But, for the humblest, the one salvation!
Therefore we have decided
To beat the drum for Him
That He may gain a foothold in the regions of misery

And His voice may ring out clearly among the slaughterhouses.
To THE BLACK STRAW HATS:
And this undertaking of ours is surely
The last of its kind. A last attempt
To set Him upright again in a crumbling world, and that
By means of the lowest.
They march on, drums beating.

FROM DAWN TO DARK THE BLACK STRAW HATS WORKED IN THE STOCK-
YARDS, BUT WHEN EVENING CAME THEY HAD ACCOMPLISHED JUST
ABOUT NOTHING

In front of the Lennox Plant.

A WORKER: They say there's another spell of dirty dealing going
on at the livestock market. Till it's over we'll have to bide
our time, I guess, and live on air.

A WORKER: Lights are on in the offices. They're counting up the
profits.

THE BLACK STRAW HATS *arrive. They put up a sign: "Room
for a Night, 20 cents; With Coffee, 30 cents; Hot dogs, 15
cents."*

THE BLACK STRAW HATS (*singing*):
Attention, your attention!
We see you, man that's falling
We hear your cry for help
We see you, woman calling.
Halt the autos, stop the traffic!
Courage, sinking people, we're coming, look our way!
You who are going under,
See us, oh, see us, brother, before you say you're beat!
We bring you something to eat,
We are still aware
That you are standing out there.
Don't say it can't be helped, for things are changing
The injustice of this world cannot remain
If all the people come and join us marching

And leave their cares behind and help with might and main.
We'll bring up tanks and cannon too
And airplanes there shall be
And battleships over the sea
All to conquer a plate of soup, brother, just for you.
For you, yes, you, poor folk,
Are an army vast and grand,
So even in times like these
We've all got to lend you a hand!
Forward march! Eyes right! Rifles ready to fire!
Courage, you sinking people, we're coming, look our way!

During the singing the BLACK STRAW HATS *have been distributing their leaflet, "The Battle Cry," spoons, plates and soup. The* WORKERS *say "Thank you" and listen to Joan's speech.*

JOAN: We are the Soldiers of the Lord. On account of our hats we are also called the Black Straw Hats. We march with drums and flags wherever unrest prevails and acts of violence threaten, to remind men of the Lord whom they have all forgotten, and to bring back their souls to Him. We call ourselves soldiers because we are an army and when we are on the march we have to fight crime and misery, those forces that want to drag us down. (*She begins to ladle out the soup herself.*) That's it, just eat some hot soup and then everything will look real different, but please give a little thought to Him who bestows it upon you. And when you think that way you will see that this is really the complete solution: Strive upward, not downward. Work for a good position up above, not here below. Want to be the first man up, not the first man down. Surely you realize now what sort of trust you can place in the fortunes of this world. None at all. Misfortune comes like the rain, that nobody makes, and still it comes. Tell me, where does all your misfortune come from?

AN EATER: From Lennox & Co.

JOAN: Maybe Mr. Lennox has more worries right now than you have. After all, what are you losing? His losses run into millions!

A WORKER: There's not much fat floating in this soup, but it contains plenty of wholesome water and there's no lack of warmth.

ANOTHER WORKER: Shut up, revellers! Listen to the heavenly text, or they'll take away your soup!

JOAN: Quiet! Tell me, dear friends, why are you poor?

WORKER: Aw, *you* tell *us*.

JOAN: All right, I will tell you: it is not because you aren't blest with worldly goods — that is not for all of us — but because you have no sense of higher things. That is why you are poor. These low pleasures for which you work so hard, a bite to eat, nice homes, the movies, they are just coarse sensual enjoyments, but God's word is a far finer, more inward, more exquisite pleasure, maybe you can't think of anything sweeter than whipped cream, but God's word, I tell you, is still sweeter, honestly it is, oh, how sweet God's word is! It's like milk and honey, and in it you dwell as in a palace of gold and alabaster. O ye of little faith, the birds of the air have no *Help Wanted* ads and the lilies of the field have no jobs, and yet He feeds them, because they sing His praises. You all want to get to the top, but what kind of top, and how do you propose to get there? And so it's we Straw Hats who ask you, quite practically: What does a man need to rise?

WORKER: A starched collar.

JOAN: No, not a starched collar. Maybe you need a starched collar to get ahead on earth, but in God's eyes you need much more than that around you, a quite different sort of splendor, but before Him you don't even have a rubber collar on, because you have utterly neglected your entire inner natures. But how are you going to get to the top — whatever, in your ignorance, you call the top — by brute force? As if force ever caused anything but destruction! You believe that if you rear up on your hind legs there'll be heaven on earth. But I say to you: that way not paradise but chaos is created.

WORKER (*enters, running*):
A position has just opened up!
It pays, and it's calling you over
To Plant Number Five!

It looks like a urinal on the outside.
Run!

THREE WORKERS *put down full plates of soup and run.*

JOAN: Hey, you, where are you off to? Talk to you about God, *that*
you don't want to hear, eh?

A BLACK STRAW HAT GIRL: The soup's all gone.

THE WORKERS:
The soup's all gone.
Fatless it was and scant,
But better than nothing.

All turn away and stand up.

JOAN: Oh, keep your seats, no harm's done, the grand soup of heaven
never gives out, you know.

THE WORKERS:
When will you finally
Open your roachy cellars,
You butchers of men?

Groups form.

A MAN:
How am I to pay for my little house now, the cute damp thing
With twelve of us in it? Seventeen
Installments I've paid and now the last is due:
They'll throw us onto the street and never again
Will we see the trampled ground with the yellowish grass
And never breathe again
The accustomed pestilent air.

A SECOND MAN (*in a circle*):
Here we stand with hands like shovels
And necks like trucks wanting to sell
Our hands and necks
And no one will buy them.

THE WORKERS:
And our tool, a gigantic pile
Of steam hammers and cranes,
Barred in behind walls!

JOAN: What's up? Now they're simply leaving! Finished eating, have you? Hope you enjoyed it? Thanks. Why have you listened till now?

A WORKER: For the soup.

JOAN: We're moving on. Sing!

THE BLACK STRAW HATS (*singing*):
Go straight to the thick of the fight
Where there's the toughest work to do.
Sing with all your might! It may still be night,
But already the morning is coming in might!
Soon the Lord Jesus will come to you, too.

A VOICE FROM THE REAR: There's still work to be had at Mauler's!

Exeunt WORKERS, *all but a few women.*

JOAN (*gloomily*):
Pack up the instruments. Did you see how they hurried
Away as soon as the soup was gone?
This thing gets no higher up
Than the rim of a dish. It believes
In nothing that it does not
Hold in its hand — if it believes in hands.
Living from minute to minute, uncertainly,
They can no longer raise themselves
From the lowest ground. Only hunger
Is a match for them. They are touched
By no song, no word
Penetrates their depths.

To the bystanders:

We Black Straw Hats feel as though we were expected to satisfy a hungry continent with our spoons.

The WORKERS *return. Shouting in distance.*

THE WORKERS (*in front*): What's that yelling? A huge stream of people from the packing houses!

A VOICE (*in back*):
Mauler and Cridle are shutting down too!
The Mauler works are locking us out!

THE RETURNING WORKERS:
> Running for jobs, we met halfway
> A stream of desperate men
> Who had lost their jobs and
> Asked us for jobs.

THE WORKERS (*in front*):
> Alas! From over there, too, a troop of men!
> You can't see the end of it! Mauler
> Has shut down too! What's to become of us?

THE BLACK STRAW HATS (*to* JOAN): Come along with us now. We're freezing and wet and we have to eat.

JOAN: But now I want to know who's to blame for all this.

THE BLACK STRAW HATS:
> Stop! Don't get mixed up in that! They're sure
> To give you an earful. Their minds are stuffed
> With low ideas! They're lazybones!
> Gluttonous, shirkers, from birth onward
> Void of all higher impulse!

JOAN: No, I want to know. (*To the* WORKERS:) Tell me now: why are you running around here without any work?

THE WORKERS:
> Bloody Mauler's locked in battle
> With stingy Lennox; so we go hungry.

JOAN: Where does Mauler live?

THE WORKERS:
> Over there where livestock is bought and sold,
> In a big building, the livestock market.

JOAN:
> There I will go, for
> I have to know this.

MARTHA (*one of the Black Straw Hats*):
> Don't get mixed up in that! Ask many questions
> And you'll get lots of answers.

JOAN: No, I want to see this Mauler, who causes such misery.

THE BLACK STRAW HATS:
> Then, Joan, we take a dark view of your further fate.

Do not mix in the quarrels of this world!
He who meddles in a quarrel becomes its victim!
His purity swiftly perishes. Soon
His small warmth perishes in the cold
That reigns over everything. Goodness abandons him
Who flees the protective hearth.
Striving downward
From level to level toward the answer you never will get,
You will disappear in dirt!
For only dirt is stuffed into the mouths
Of those who ask without caution.

JOAN: I want to know.

Exeunt BLACK STRAW HATS.

3

PIERPONT MAULER FEELS A BREATH
FROM ANOTHER WORLD

In front of the livestock market. Lower level, JOAN *and*
MARTHA *waiting; upper level, the meat packers* LENNOX *and*
GRAHAM, *conversing.* LENNOX *is white as chalk.*

GRAHAM:
How you have felt the blows of brutal Mauler,
My good friend Lennox! There's no hindering
The rise of this monstrosity: to him
Nature is goods, even the air's for sale.
What we have inside our stomachs he resells to us.
He can squeeze rent from ruined houses, money
From rotten meat; throw stones at him,
He's sure to turn the stones to money; so
Unruly is his money-lust, so natural
To him this lack of nature that he himself
Cannot deny its driving force within him
For I tell you: himself, he's soft, does not love money,
Cannot bear squalor, cannot sleep at night.
Therefore you must approach him as though you could hardly
    speak,
And say: "Oh, Mauler, look at me and take
Your hand off my throat — think of your old age — "
That will frighten him, for sure. Maybe he'll cry . . .

JOAN (*to* MARTHA):
Only you, Martha, have followed me this far.
All the others left me with warnings
As if I were bound for the end of the world.
Strange warning from their lips.
I thank you, Martha.

MARTHA: I warned you too, Joan.

JOAN: And went with me.

MARTHA: But will you really recognize him, Joan?

JOAN: I shall know him!

CRIDLE (*coming out of building*):
Well, Lennox, now the underbidding's over.
You're finished now and I'll close up and wait
Until the market recovers. I'll clean my yards
And give the knives a thorough oiling and order some
Of those new packing machines that give a fellow
A chance to save a tidy sum in wages.

LENNOX:
Damnable times!
Waste lies the market, flooded out by goods.
Trade, that was once so flourishing, lies fallow.
Scuffling over a market that's long been costive,
You wrecked your own prices by underbidding one another: thus
Do buffaloes, fighting for grass, trample to shreds the grass they fight for.

MAULER *comes out, with his broker,* SLIFT, *among a crowd of* PACKERS, TWO DETECTIVES *behind him.*

THE MEAT PACKERS: Now everything's a matter of holding out!

MAULER:
Lennox is down. (*To* LENNOX): Admit it, you are out.
And now I ask you, Cridle, to take over
The packing plant as stated in our contract,
Presuming Lennox finished.

CRIDLE:
Agreed, Lennox is out. But also finished
Are good times on the market; therefore, Mauler,
You must come down from ten million for your stock!

MAULER:
What? The price stands
Here in the contract! Here, Lennox, see if this
Is not a contract, with a price right on it!

CRIDLE:

Yes, but a contract made in better times!
Are bad times also mentioned in the contract?
What can I do alone with a stockyard now
When not a soul will buy a can of meat?
Now I know why you couldn't bear to watch
More oxen dying: it was because their flesh
Cannot be sold!

MAULER:

No, it's my heart
That swells, affected by the creature's shrieks!

GRAHAM:

Oh, mighty Mauler, now I realize
The greatness of your actions: even your heart
Sees far ahead!

LENNOX: Mauler, I wanted to talk with you . . . again . . .

GRAHAM:

Straight to his heart, Lennox! Straight to his heart!
It's a sensitive garbage pit!

He hits MAULER *in the pit of the stomach.*

MAULER: Ouch!

GRAHAM: You see, he has a heart!

MAULER:

Well, Freddy, now I'll make a settlement with Cridle
So he can't buy a single can from you,
Because you hit me.

GRAHAM:

You can't do that, Pierpy! That's mixing
Personal matters with business.

CRIDLE: O.K., Pierpy, with pleasure. Just as you please.

GRAHAM: I have two thousand workers, Mauler!

CRIDLE: Send them to the movies! But really, Pierpy, our agreement isn't valid. (*Figuring in a notebook.*) When we contracted for your withdrawal from the business, the shares — of which you hold one-third, as I do — stood at 390. You gave them to me for 320; that was cheap. It's expensive today; they're at a hundred now, because the market's blocked. If I'm to pay you off I'll have to throw the shares onto the market. If I do that they'll go down to 70, and what can I use to pay you then? Then I'll be done for.

MAULER:
If that's your situation, Cridle, I must certainly
Get my money out of you right away,
Before you're done for.
I tell you, Cridle, I am so afraid
I'm all of a sweat, the most I can let you have
Is six days! What am I saying? Five days
If that's your situation.

LENNOX: Mauler, look at me.

MAULER: Lennox, you tell me if the contract says anything about bad times.

LENNOX: No.
Exit.

MAULER (*watching him go*):
Some worry seems to be oppressing him,
And I, on business bent (would I were not!)
Did not perceive it! Oh, repulsive business!
Cridle, it sickens me.

Exit CRIDLE. *Meanwhile* JOAN *has called one of the* DETECTIVES *over to her and said something to him.*

THE DETECTIVE: Mr. Mauler, there are some persons here who want to talk to you.

MAULER:
Unmannerly lot, eh? With an envious look, eh?
And violent, no doubt? I
Cannot see anyone.

THE DETECTIVE: They're a pair from the Black Straw Hat Organization.

MAULER: What kind of an organization is that?

THE DETECTIVE: They have many branches and are numerous and respected among the lower classes, where they are called the Good Lord's Soldiers.

MAULER:

> I've heard of them. Curious name:
> The Good Lord's Soldiers . . . but
> What do they want of me?

THE DETECTIVE: They say they have something to discuss with you.

> *During this the market uproar has resumed: Steers 43, Hogs*
> *55, Heifers 59, etc.*

MAULER:

> All right, tell them I will see them.
> But tell them also they may say nothing that I
> Do not ask about first. Nor must they break out
> Into tears or songs, especially sentimental ones.
> And tell them it would be most profitable to them
> For me to get the impression
> That they are well-meaning people, with nothing to their
> discredit,
> Who want nothing from me that I do not have.
> Another thing: do not tell them I am Mauler.

THE DETECTIVE (*going over to* JOAN):

> He consents to see you, but
> You must ask no questions, only answer
> When he asks you.

JOAN (*walking up to* MAULER): You are Mauler!

MAULER. No, I'm not. (*Points to* SLIFT.) That's him.

JOAN (*pointing to* MAULER): You are Mauler.

MAULER: No, he is.

JOAN: You are.

MAULER: How do you know me?

JOAN: Because you have the bloodiest face.

> SLIFT *laughs.*

MAULER: You laugh, Slift?

> *Meanwhile* GRAHAM *has hurried off.*

MAULER (*to* JOAN): How much do you earn in a day?

JOAN: Twenty cents, but food and clothing are supplied.

MAULER:

>Thin clothes, Slift, and thin soup too, I guess!
>Yes, those clothes are probably thin and the soup not rich.

JOAN: Mauler, why do you lock the workers out?

MAULER (*to* SLIFT):

>The fact that they work without pay
>Is remarkable, isn't it? I never heard
>Of such a thing before — a person working
>For nothing and none the worse. And in their eyes
>I see no fear
>Of being down and out.

>*To* JOAN:

>Extraordinary folk, you Black Straw Hats.
>I shall not ask you what particularly
>You want of me. I know the fool mob calls me
>Mauler the Bloody, saying it was I
>Who ruined Lennox or caused unpleasantness
>For Cridle — who, between ourselves, is one
>Of little merit. I can say to you:
>Those are just business matters, and they won't
>Be interesting to you. But there's something else, on which
>I would like to hear your views. I am thinking of giving up
>This bloodstained business, as soon as possible; once for all.
>For recently — this *will* interest you — I saw
>A steer die and it upset me so
>That I want to get rid of everything, and have even sold
>My interest in the plant, worth twelve million dollars. I gave it
>>to that man
>For ten. Don't you feel
>That this is right, and to your liking?

SLIFT:

>He saw the steer die and made up his mind
>To butcher wealthy Cridle
>Instead of the poor steer.
>Was that right?

>*The* PACKERS *laugh.*

MAULER: Go on, laugh. Your laughter's nothing to me. Some day
    I'll see you weep.

JOAN:
    Mr. Mauler, why have you shut down the stockyards?
    This I must know.

MAULER:
    Was it not an extraordinary act to take my hand
    Out of a might concern, simply because it is bloody?
    Say this is right, and to your liking.
    All right then, don't say it, I know, I admit, some people
    Did poorly out of it, they lost their jobs,
    I know. Unhappily, that was unavoidable.
    A bad lot anyway, a tough mob, better not go near them, but
        tell me:
    My act in withdrawing my hand from the business,
    Surely that is right?

JOAN: I don't know whether you ask in earnest.

MAULER:
    That's because my damned voice is used to faking,
    And for that reason too I know: you
    Do not like me. Say nothing.

    To the others:

    I seem to feel a breath from another world wafted toward me.

    He takes everybody's money from them and gives it to JOAN.

    Out with your money, you cattle butchers, give it here!

    He takes it out of their pockets, gives it to JOAN.

    Take it to give to the poor folk, Joan!
    But be assured that I feel no obligation in any way
    And sleep extremely well. Why am I helping here? Perhaps
    Just because I like your face, because it is so unknowing,
        although
    You have lived for twenty years.

MARTHA (*to* JOAN):
    I don't believe in his sincerity.
    Forgive me, Joan, for going away now too:

It seems to me you also
Should really drop all this!

Exit MARTHA.

JOAN: Mr. Mauler, you know this is only a drop in the bucket. Can
you not give them real help?

MAULER:

Tell the world I warmly commend your activities and
Wish there were more like you. But
You mustn't take this thing about the poor this way.
They are wicked people. Human beings do not affect me:
They are not guiltless, and they're butchers themselves.
However, let's drop the matter.

JOAN: Mr. Mauler, they are saying in the stockyards that you are to
blame for their misery.

MAULER:

On oxen I have pity; man is evil.
Mankind's not ripe for what you have in mind:
Before the world can change, humanity
Must change its nature.
Wait just one more moment.

In a low tone, to SLIFT:

Give her more money away from here, when she's alone.
Say "for the poor folk," so that she can take it
Without blushing, but then see what she buys for herself.
If that's no help — I'd rather it were not —
Then take her with you
To the stockyards and show her
Those poor of hers, how wicked and gross they are, full of
    treachery and cowardice
And how they themselves are to blame.
Maybe that will help.

To JOAN:

Here is Sullivan Slift, my broker; he will show you something.

To SLIFT:

I tell you, it's almost intolerable in my eyes
That there should be people like this girl, owning nothing

But a black hat and twenty cents a day, and fearless.

Exit MAULER.

SLIFT:

I would not care to know what you want to know;
Still, if you wish to know it, come here tomorrow.

JOAN (*watching* MAULER *go*):

That's not a wicked man, he is the first
To be scared from the tanglewoods of meanness by our drums,
The first to hear the call.

SLIFT (*departing*):

I give you fair warning: do not take up with those people
Down in the yards, they're a lowdown lot, really
The scum of the earth.

JOAN: I want to see it.

4

THE BROKER SULLIVAN SLIFT SHOWS JOAN DARK THE WICKEDNESS OF THE POOR: JOAN'S SECOND DESCENT INTO THE DEPTHS

The stockyards district.

SLIFT:
> Now, Joan, I will show you
> The wickedness of those
> For whom you feel pity and
> How out of place the feeling is.

> *They are walking alongside a factory wall inscribed "Mauler and Cridle, Meat Packing Company." The name Cridle has been painted out in crosswise strokes.* TWO MEN *come through a small gate.* SLIFT *and* JOAN *hear their conversation.*

FOREMAN (*to a young apprentice*): Four days ago a man named Luckerniddle fell into our boiler, we couldn't stop the machinery in time so he got caught in the bacon-maker, a horrible thing to happen; this is his coat and this is his cap, take them and get rid of them, all they do is take up a hook in the cloakroom and make a bad impression. It's a good plan to burn them, right away would be best. I entrust the things to you because I know you're a reliable man. I'd lose my job if the stuff were found anywhere. Of course as soon as the plant opens again you can have Luckerniddle's job.

THE APPRENTICE: You can count on me, Mr. Smith. (*The* FOREMAN *goes back in through the gate.*) Too bad about the fellow that has to go out into the world as bacon, but I feel bad about his coat too, it's still in good shape. Old Man Bacon has his can to wear now and won't need this any more, but I could use it very well. Shit, I'll take it. (*Puts it on and wraps his own coat and cap in newspaper.*)

JOAN: I feel sick.

SLIFT: That's the world as it is. (*Stopping the young man.*) Wherever did you get that coat and cap? Didn't they belong to Luckerniddle, the man that had the accident?

YOUNG WORKER: Please don't let it get around, sir. I'll take the things off right away. I'm pretty nearly down and out. That extra twenty cents you get in the fertilizer-cellars fooled me into working at the bone-grinding machine last year. There I got it bad in the lungs, and a troublesome eye inflammation too. Since then my working capacity has gone down and since February I've only been employed twice.

SLIFT: Keep the things on. And come to Canteen No. Seven at noon today. You'll get a free lunch and a dollar there if you tell Luckerniddle's wife where your cap and coat came from.

YOUNG WORKER: But, sir, isn't that sort of raw?

SLIFT: Well, if you don't need the money . . . !

YOUNG WORKER: You can rely on me, sir.

JOAN *and* SLIFT *walk on.*

MRS. LUCKERNIDDLE (*sitting in front of the factory gate, lamenting*):
You in there, what are you doing with my husband?
Four days ago he went to work, he said:
"Warm up some soup for me tonight!" And to this
Day he hasn't got back! What have you done with him
You butchers! Four days I have been standing here
In the cold, nights too, waiting, but nobody tells me
Anything, and my husband doesn't come out! But I tell
You, I'm going to stand right here until I get to see him!
You'll rue the day if you've done him any harm!

SLIFT (*walking up to the woman*): Your husband has left town, Mrs. Luckerniddle.

MRS. LUCKERNIDDLE: Oh, don't give me that again.

SLIFT: I'll tell you something, Mrs. Luckerniddle, he is out of town, and it's very embarrassing to the factory to have you sitting around here talking foolishness. So we'll make you an offer which could not be required of us by law. If you give up your search for your husband, you may eat dinner in our canteen every noon for three weeks, free.

MRS. LUCKERNIDDLE: I want to know what's become of my husband.

SLIFT: We're telling you, he's gone to Frisco.

MRS. LUCKERNIDDLE: He has not gone to Frisco, he's had some accident because of you, and you're trying to hide it.

SLIFT: If that's what you think, Mrs. Luckerniddle, you cannot accept any meals from the factory, but you will have to bring suit against the factory. But think it over thoroughly. I shall be at your disposal in the canteen tomorrow. (SLIFT *goes back to* JOAN.)

MRS. LUCKERNIDDLE: I must have my husband back. I have nobody but him to support me.

JOAN:

She will never come.
Twenty dinners may mean much
To one who is hungry, but
There is more for him.

JOAN *and* SLIFT *walk on. They stop in front of a factory canteen and see* TWO MEN *looking in through a window.*

GLOOMB: There sits the overseer who's to blame for my getting my hand in the tin-cutting machine — stuffing his belly full. We must see to it that this is the last time the swine gorges at our expense. You'd better give me your club, mine will probably splinter right off.

SLIFT: Stay here. I want to talk to him. And if he approaches you, say you're looking for work. Then you'll see what kind of people these are. (*Going up to* GLOOMB.) Before you get carried away into doing something — that's the way it looks to me — I'd like to make you a profitable proposition.

GLOOMB: I have no time right now, sir.

SLIFT: That's too bad, because there would have been something in it for you.

GLOOMB: Make it short. We cannot afford to let that swine go. He's got to get his reward today for that inhuman system he plays overseer to.

SLIFT: I have a suggestion to make for your own benefit. I am an inspector in the factory. Much inconvenience has been caused by your place remaining vacant. Most people think it too dangerous, just because you have made all this to-do about your fingers. Now it would be just fine if we had someone to fill that post again. If you, for example, could find somebody for it, we would be ready to take you on again right away — in fact, to give you an easier and better-paid job than you've had up to now. Perhaps even a foreman's position. You seem a clever man to me. And the one who has it now happens to have got himself disliked lately. You understand. You would also have to take charge of production speed, of course, and above all, as I say, find somebody for that place at the tin-cutting machine, which, I admit, is not safe at all. Over there, for instance, there's a girl looking for work.

GLOOMB: Can a man rely on what you say?

SLIFT: Yes.

GLOOMB: That one over there? She looks weak. It's no job for anyone who tires easily. (*To the others:*) I've thought it over, we'll do the job tomorrow night. Night's a better time for that kind of fun. So long. (*Goes over to* JOAN.) Looking for a job?

JOAN: Yes.

GLOOMB: Eyesight good?

JOAN: No. Last year I worked at a bone-grinding machine in the fertilizer cellars. I got it bad in the lungs there and a troublesome eye inflammation too. Since then my work-capacity has gone down badly. I've been out of a job since February. Is this a good place?

GLOOMB: The place is good. It's work that even weaker people, like yourself, can do.

JOAN: Are you sure there's no other place to be had? I've heard that working at that machine is dangerous for people who tire easily. Their hands get unsteady and then they grab at the blades.

GLOOMB: That isn't true at all. You'll be surprised to see how pleasant the work is. You'll fan your brow and ask yourself how people could ever tell such silly stories about that machine.

SLIFT *laughs and draws* JOAN *away*.

JOAN: Now I'm almost afraid to go on — what will I see next! *They go into the canteen and see* MRS. LUCKERNIDDLE, *who is talking to the* WAITER.

MRS. LUCKERNIDDLE (*figuring*): Twenty dinners ... then I could ... then I'd go and then I'd have . . . (*She sits down at a table*.)

WAITER: If you're not eating you'll have to leave.

MRS. LUCKERNIDDLE: I'm waiting for somebody who was going to come in here today or tomorrow. What's for dinner today?

WAITER: Peas.

JOAN:
There she sits.
I though she was firmly resolved, and feared
That still she might come tomorrow, and now she has run here
     faster than we
And is here already, waiting for us.

SLIFT: Go and take her the food yourself — maybe she'll think again.

JOAN *fetches a plate of food and brings it to* MRS. LUCKERNIDDLE.

JOAN: Here so soon?

MRS. LUCKERNIDDLE: It's because I've had nothing to eat for two days.

JOAN: You didn't know we were coming in today, did you?

MRS. LUCKERNIDDLE: That's right.

JOAN: On the way over here I heard someone say that something happened to your husband in the factory and the factory is responsible.

MRS. LUCKERNIDDLE: Oh, so you've reconsidered your offer? So I don't get my twenty meals?

JOAN: But you got along with your husband very well, didn't you? People told me you have nobody except him.

MRS. LUCKERNIDDLE: Well, I've had nothing to eat for two days.

JOAN: Won't you wait till tomorrow? If you give up your husband now, no one will ask after him any more.

MRS. LUCKERNIDDLE *is silent*.

Don't take it.

MRS. LUCKERNIDDLE *snatches the food from her hands and begins to eat greedily.*

MRS. LUCKERNIDDLE: He's gone to Frisco.

JOAN:
And basements and storerooms are full of meat
That cannot be sold and is going rotten
Because no one will take it away.

The WORKER *with the cap and coat enters, rear.*

WORKER: Good morning, is this where I eat?

SLIFT: Just take a seat beside that woman over there.

The man sits down.

That's a good-looking cap you have there.

The WORKER *hides it.*

Where did you get it?

WORKER: Bought it.

SLIFT: Well, where did you buy it?

WORKER: Not in any store.

SLIFT: Then where did you get it?

WORKER: I got it off a man that fell into a boiling vat.

MRS. LUCKERNIDDLE *feels sick. She gets up and goes out. On the way out she says to the* WAITER:

MRS. LUCKERNIDDLE: Leave the plate where it is. I'm coming back. I'm coming here for dinner every day. Just ask that gentleman.
Exit.

SLIFT: For three whole weeks she will come and feed, without looking up, like an animal. Have you seen, Joan, that their wickedness is beyond measure?

JOAN:
But what mastery you have
Over their wickedness! How you thrive on it!
Do you not see that it rains on their wickedness?
Certainly she would have liked
To be true to her husband, as others are,

And to ask after the man who supported her
For some time longer, as is proper.
But the price was too high: it amounted to twenty meals.
And would that young man on whom
Any scoundrel can rely
Have shown the coat to the dead man's wife
If things had gone as he would like?
But the price appeared too high to him.
And why would the man with only one arm
Have failed to warn me? if the price
Of so small a scruple were not so high for him?
Why, instead, did he sell his wrath, which is righteous, but too
    dear?
If their wickedness is beyond measure, then
So is their poverty. Not the wickedness of the poor
Have you shown me, but
The poverty of the poor.
You've shown the evil of the poor to me:
Now see the woes of evil poverty.
O thoughtless rumor, that the poor are base:
You shall be silenced by their stricken face!

5

JOAN INTRODUCES THE POOR TO THE LIVESTOCK EXCHANGE

The Livestock Exchange.

THE PACKERS:
We have canned meat for sale!
Wholesalers, buy canned meat!
Fresh, juicy, canned meat!
Mauler and Cridle's bacon!
Graham's sirloins, soft as butter!
Wilde's Kentucky lard, a bargain!

THE WHOLESALERS:
And silence fell upon the waters and
Bankruptcy among the wholesalers!

THE PACKERS.
Due to tremendous technical advances
Engineers' hard work and entrepreneurs' farsightedness
We have now succeeded
In lowering prices for
Mauler and Cridle's bacon
Graham's sirloins, soft as butter
Wilde's Kentucky lard, a bargain
BY ONE-THIRD!
Wholesalers, buy canned meat!
Seize your opportunity!

THE WHOLESALERS:
And silence fell upon the mountaintops
And hotel kitchens covered their heads
And stores looked away in horror
And middlemen turned pale!
We wholesalers vomit if we so much as

See a can of meat. This country's stomach
Has eaten too much meat from cans
And is fighting back.

SLIFT: What news from your friends in New York?

MAULER:

Theories. If they had their way
The meat ring would be lying in the gutter
And stay there for weeks till there wasn't a peep left in it
And I'd have all that meat around my neck!
Madness!

SLIFT:

I'd have to laugh if those men in New York really had
Tariffs lowered now, opened up the South
And started a bull-market — just supposing! — and we
Were to miss the bus!

MAULER:

What if they did? Would you be harsh enough
To hack your pound of flesh from misery
Like this? Look at them, watching for a move,
As lynxes do! I couldn't be so harsh.

WHOLESALERS:

Here we stand, wholesalers with mountains of cans
And cellars full of frozen steers
Wanting to sell the steers in cans
And no one will buy them!
And our customers, the kitchens and stores,
Are stuffed to the ceiling with frozen meat!
Screaming for buyers and eaters!
No more buying for us!

PACKERS:

Here we stand, packers with slaughterhouses and packing space
And stables full of steers; day and night the machines
Run on under steam; brine, tubs and boiling vats
Wanting to turn the lowing ravenous herds
Into canned meat and nobody wants canned meat.
We're ruined.

STOCKBREEDERS:
> And what about us, the stockbreeders?
> Who'll buy livestock now? In our stables stand
> Steers and hogs eating expensive corn
> And they ride to town in trains and while they ride
> They eat and eat and at stations
> They wait in rent-devouring boxcars, forever eating.

MAULER:
> And now the knives motion them back,
> Death, giving livestock the cold shoulder,
> Closes his shop.

PACKERS (*shouting at* MAULER, *who is reading a newspaper*):
> Traitorous Mauler, nest-befouler!
> Do you think we don't know who's selling livestock here —
> Oh so secretly — and knocking the bottom out of prices?
> You've been offering meat for days and days!

MAULER:
> Insolent butchers, cry in your mothers' laps
> Because the hunted creature's outcry ceases!
> Go home and say that one of all your number
> Could not hear oxen bellow any longer
> And would rather hear your bellow than their bellow!
> I want my cash and quiet for my conscience!

A BROKER (*bellowing from the Exchange entrance, rear*):
> Terrific drop in stock exchange quotations!
> Colossal sales of stocks. Cridle, formerly Mauler,
> Whirl the whole meat ring's rates down with them
> Into the abyss.

> *Uproar arises among the meat-packers. They rush at* CRIDLE, *who is white as chalk.*

PACKERS:
> What's the meaning of this, Cridle? Look us in the eye!
> Dumping stocks, with the market the way it is?

BROKERS: At 115!

PACKERS:
> Are your brains made of dung?

It's not yourself alone you're ruining!
You big shit! You criminal!

CRIDLE (*pointing to* MAULER): There's your man!

GRAHAM (*standing in front of* CRIDLE):
This isn't Cridle's doing, someone else
Is fishing these waters and we're supposed to be the fish!
There are people who want to take care of the meat-ring, now,
And do a final job! Defend yourself, Mauler!

PACKERS (*to* MAULER):
The story is, Mauler, that you're squeezing your money
Out of Cridle, who, we hear, is groggy already, and Cridle
Himself says nothing and points to you.

MAULER:
If I leave my money in this Cridle's hands an hour longer —
A man who's confessed to me personally that he's lazy — who
     among you
Would still take me seriously as a businessman? And I want
     nothing
So much as for *you* to take me seriously.

CRIDLE (*to the bystanders*): Just four weeks ago I made a contract
with Mauler. He wanted to sell me his shares — one-third of
the total — for ten million dollars. From that time on, as I've
just found out, he has been secretly selling quantities of livestock, cheap, to make a still worse mess of prices that are sag-
ging already. He could ask for his money whenever he wanted
to. I intended to pay him by disposing of part of his shares on
the market — they were high then — and reinvesting part.
Then the drop came. Today Mauler's shares are worth not
ten but three million. The whole plant is worth ten million
instead of thirty. That's exactly the ten million I owe Mauler,
and that's what he wants overnight.

PACKERS:
If you're doing this, making things hard for Cridle,
Whose in-laws we are not, then you're well aware
That this concerns us too. You're stripping
All business bare: the fault is yours

If our cans of meat are as cheap as sand,
Because you ruined Lennox with cheap cans!

MAULER:

You shouldn't have gone and slaughtered so many cattle,
You raving butchers! Now I want my money;
Though you should all go begging, I must have
My money! I have other plans.

STOCKBREEDERS:

Lennox smashed! And Cridle groggy! And Mauler
Pulls all his money out!

SMALL SPECULATORS:

Oh, as for us, the little speculators,
Nobody cares. They scream when they see
The colossus topple, but don't see where it falls,
Whom it strikes down. Mauler! Our money!

PACKERS: Eighty thousand cans at 50, but fast!

WHOLESALERS: Not a single one!

Silence.

The drumming of the BLACK STRAW HATS *and* JOAN's *voice are heard.*

JOAN: Pierpont Mauler! Where is Mauler?

MAULER:

What's that drumming? Who
Is calling my name?
Here, where every man
Shows his bare chops all smeared with blood!

The BLACK STRAW HATS *march in. They sing their war-chant.*

BLACK STRAW HATS (*singing*):

Attention, pay attention!
There is a man who's falling!
There is a cry for help!
There is a woman calling!
Halt the autos, stop all traffic!
Men falling all around us and no one looks their way!
Is there no sight in your eye?

Say hello to your brother, not just any guy!
Get up from where you've dined —
Is there no thought in your mind
For the starving folk nearby?
I hear you say: it will always be the same,
The injustice of the world will still remain.
But we say this to you: You've got to march
And leave your cares and help with might and main
And bring up tanks and cannon too
And airplanes there shall be
And battleships over the sea
To conquer a plate of soup, poor brother, just for you.
You've all got to lend us a hand
And it must be today
For the army of the good
Is not a vast array.
Forward march! Eyes right! Rifles ready to fire!
Men falling all around us and no one looks their way!

*Meanwhile the Exchange battle has continued. But laughter,
prompted by exclamations, is spreading toward the front of
the scene.*

PACKERS: Eighty thousand cans at half price, but fast!

WHOLESALERS: Not a single one!

PACKERS: Then we're finished, Mauler!

JOAN: Where is Mauler?

MAULER:

Don't go, Slift! Graham, Meyers,
Stay there in front of me.
I don't want to be seen here.

STOCKBREEDERS:

Not a steer to be sold in Chicago any more
This day spells ruin for all of Illinois
With mounting prices you prodded us on into raising steers
And here we stand with steers
And no one will buy them.
Mauler, you dog, you are to blame for this disaster.

MAULER:

    Enough of business. Graham! My hat. I've got to go.

    A hundred dollars for my hat.

CRIDLE: Oh, damn you to hell.

    Exit CRIDLE.

JOAN: Now, you stay here, Mr. Mauler, and listen to what I have
to say to you. It is something you all may hear. Quiet! Yes, indeed, you hardly think it right for us Black Straw Hats to turn
up like this in the dark hidden places where you do your business! I've been told about the kind of things you do here, how
you make meat more and more expensive by your carryings-
on and subtle trickery. But if you ever supposed you could
keep it all concealed, then you're on the wrong track, now and
on the Day of Judgment, for then it will be revealed, and how
will you look then, when our Lord and Savior has you walk
up in a row and asks with His big eyes, "Well, where are my
steers? What have you done with them? Did you make them
available to the people at prices within their reach? What has
become of them, then?" And when you stand there embarrassed, groping for excuses, the way you do in your newspapers, which don't always stick to the truth, then the steers
will bellow at your backs in all the barns where you keep them
tucked away to make prices go sky-high, and by their bellowing they will bear witness against you before Almighty God!
Laughter.

STOCKBREEDERS:

    We stockbreeders see nothing funny in that!

    Dependent on weather, summer and winter, we stand

    Considerably nearer the Lord of old.

JOAN: And now an example. If a man builds a dam against the un-
reasonable water, and a thousand people help him with the
labor of their hands, and he gets a million for it, but the dam
breaks as soon as the water rises and everybody working on it
and many more are drowned — what kind of man is he who
builds a dam like that? You may call him a businessman or a
rascal, depending on your views, but we tell you he's a num-
skull. And all you men who make bread dear and life a hell

for human beings, so that they all become devils, you are
numskulls, wretched, stingy numskulls and nothing else!

WHOLESALERS (*shouting*):

Because of your irresponsible
Juggling with prices and filthy lust for profit
You're bringing on your own ruin!
Numskulls!

PACKERS (*shouting back*):

Numskulls yourselves!
Nothing can be done about crises!
Unshakable above our heads
Stands economic law, the not-to-be-known.
Terrible is the cyclic recurrence
Of natural catastrophes!

STOCKBREEDERS:

Nothing to be done about your hold on our throats?
That's wickedness, barefaced lying wickedness!

JOAN: And why does this wickedness exist in the world? Well, how
could it be otherwise? Naturally, if a man has to smash his
neighbor's head for a ham sandwich so that he can satisfy his
elementary needs, brother striving with brother for the bare
necessities of life, how can the sense of higher things help being stifled in the human heart? Why not think of helping your
neighbor simply as serving a customer? Then you'll understand the New Testament in a flash, and see how fundamentally
modern it is, even today. Service! Why, what does service
mean if not charity — in the true meaning of the word, that
is! Gentlemen, I keep hearing that the poor haven't enough
morals, and it's true, too. Immorality makes its nest down there
in the slums, with revolution itself for company. I simply ask
you: Where are they to get morals from, if they have nothing
else? Where can they get anything without stealing it? Gentlemen, there is such a thing as moral purchasing-power. Raise
moral purchasing-power, and there's your morality. And I
mean by purchasing-power a very simple and natural thing —
that is, money, wages. And this brings me back to the practical
point: if you go on like this you'll end by eating your own

meat, because the people outside haven't got any purchasing power.

STOCKBREEDERS (*reproachfully*):

Here we stand with steers

And nobody can afford them.

JOAN: But you sit here, you great and mighty men, thinking that no one will ever catch on to your tricks, and refusing to know anything about the misery in the world outside. Well then, just take a look at them, the people whom your treatment has brought to this condition, the people you will not admit to be your brothers! Come out now, you weary and heavy-laden, into the light of day. Don't be ashamed!

JOAN *shows to the Exchange crowd the poor people she has brought along with her.*

MAULER (*shouting*): Take them away! (*He faints.*)

A VOICE (*rear*): Pierpont Mauler has fainted!

THE POOR PEOPLE: He's the one to blame for everything!

The PACKERS *attend to* MAULER.

PACKERS:

Water for Pierpont Mauler!

A doctor for Mauler!

JOAN:

If you, Mauler, showed me the wickedness

Of the poor, now I show you

The poverty of the poor, for they live far away from you

And that puts beyond their reach goods they cannot do

without —

The people out of sight, whom you

Hold down in poverty like this, so weakened and so urgently

In need of unobtainable food and warmth that they

Can be just as far away from any claim

To higher things than the lowest gluttony, the beastliest habits.

MAULER *comes to.*

MAULER: Are they still here? I implore you, send them away.

PACKERS: The Black Straw Hats? You want them sent away?

MAULER: No, those others, behind them.

SLIFT: He won't open his eyes before they get out.

GRAHAM:
Can't bring yourself to look at them, eh? But it was you
Who brought them to this state.
Shutting your eyes won't rid you of them,
Far from it.

MAULER:
I beseech you, send them away! I'll buy!
Listen, all of you: Pierpont Mauler's buying!
So that these people may get work and go.
Eight weeks' production in cans of meat —
I'll buy it!

PACKERS: He's bought! Mauler has bought!

MAULER: At today's prices!

GRAHAM (*holding him up*): And what about back stocks?

MAULER (*lying on the floor*): I'll buy 'em.

GRAHAM: At 50?

MAULER: At 50!

GRAHAM: He's bought! You heard it, he has bought!

BROKERS (*shouting through megaphones, rear*): Pierpont Mauler
keeps the meat market going. According to contract, he's
taking over the meat-ring's entire stock, at 50, as of today, besides two months' production, starting today, also at 50. The
meat-ring will deliver at least four hundred tons of canned
meat to Pierpont Mauler on November 15.

MAULER: But now, my friends, I beg you, take me away.

MAULER *is carried out.*

JOAN:
That's fine, now have yourself carried out!
We work at our mission jobs like plough-horses
And this is the kind of thing you do up here!
You had your man tell me I shouldn't say a thing.
Who are you, I'd like to know,
To try to muzzle the Lord in His goodness? You shouldn't even
Muzzle the ox that's yoked to the thresher!
And speak I will.

To the poor people:

You'll have work again on Monday.

POOR PEOPLE: We've never seen such people anywhere. But we'd prefer them to the two that were standing beside him. They have a far worse look than he does.

JOAN: Now sing, as a farewell song, *Who Ever Feels the Lack of Bread.*

BLACK STRAW HATS (*singing*):
Who ever feels the lack of bread
Once he's given the Lord his bond?
A man will never be in need
If he stays within God's grace.
For how shall snow fall on him there?
And how shall hunger find that place?

WHOLESALERS:
The fellow's sick in his head. This country's stomach
Has eaten too much meat from cans and it's fighting back.
And he has meat put into cans
That no one will buy. Cross out his name!

STOCKBREEDERS:
Come on, up with those prices, you lousy butchers!
Until you double livestock prices
Not an ounce will be delivered, for you need it.

PACKERS:
Keep your filth to yourselves! We will not buy.
For the contract which you saw agreed on here
Is a mere scrap of paper. The man who made it
Was not in his right mind. He couldn't raise
A cent from Frisco to New York
For that kind of business.

Exeunt PACKERS.

JOAN: Well, anyone who is really interested in God's word and what He says and not just in what the ticker tape says — and there must be some people here that are respectable and conduct their business in a God-fearing way, we have nothing against that — well, he's welcome to visit our Divine Service

Sunday afternoon in Lincoln Street at two P.M. Music from
three o'clock, no entrance charge.

SLIFT (*to the* STOCKBREEDERS):

What Pierpont Mauler promises he fulfills.
Breathe freely now! The market's getting well!
You who give bread and you to whom it's given,
At last the doldrums have been overcome!
They menaced confidence, and even concord.
You who give work, and you to whom it's given,
You're moving in and opening wide the gates!
Sensible counsel, sensibly adopted,
Has got the upper hand of foolishness.
The gates are opening! The chimney's smoking!
It's work you've both been needing all the time.

STOCKBREEDERS (*placing* JOAN *up on the steps*):

Your speech and presence made a great impression
On us stockbreeders and many a man
Was deeply moved, for we
Have terrible sufferings too.

JOAN:

You know, I have my eye
On Mauler, he has woken up, and you,
If there's something you need to help you out,
Then come with me, that he may aid you also,
For from now on he shall not rest
Till everyone is helped.
For he's in a position to help: so
Let's go after him.

Exeunt JOAN *and* BLACK STRAW HATS, *followed by the* STOCK-
BREEDERS.

6

THE CRICKET CAUGHT

The City. The broker SULLIVAN SLIFT'S *house, a small one with two entrances.*

MAULER (*inside the house, talking to* SLIFT): Lock the door, turn on all the lights there are — then take a good look at my face, Slift, and see if it's true that anybody could tell by it.

SLIFT: Tell what by it?

MAULER: My business!

SLIFT: A butcher's? Mauler, why did you fall down when she talked?

MAULER:
What did she say? I did not hear it,
For behind her there stood such people with such ghastly faces
Of misery — misery that comes
Before a wrath that will sweep us all away —
That I saw nothing more. Slift,
I will tell you what I really think
About this business of ours.
It can't go on this way, nothing but buying and selling
And one man coldly stripping off another's skin:
There are too many people howling with pain
And they are on the increase.
That which falls into our bloody cellars
Is past all consolation:
When they get hold of us they'll slap us against the pavement
Like rotten fish. All of us here,
We're not going to die in our beds. Before
We get that far they will stand us up against walls
In throngs, and cleanse the world of us and
Our hangers-on.

SLIFT: They have upset you! (*Aside:*) I'll make him eat a rare steak. His old weakness has come over him again. Maybe he'll come to his senses after enjoying some raw meat. (*He goes and broils* MAULER *a steak on a gas stove.*)

MAULER:
I often ask myself why
I'm moved by that fool talk, worlds away,
The cheap, flat chitter-chatter they study up . . .
Of course, it's because they do it for nothing, eighteen hours
      a day and
In rain and hunger.

SLIFT:
In cities which are burning down below
And freezing up on top, there are always people
Who'll talk of this and that — details that aren't
In perfect order.

MAULER:
But what is it they're saying? In these cities, incessantly
On fire, in the downward rush
Of howling humanity,
Surging toward hell without respite
For years on end, if I hear a voice like that —
Foolish, of course, but quite unlike a beast's —
I feel as if I'd been cracked on the backbone with a stick
Like a leaping fish.
But even this has only been evasion until now, Slift,
For what I fear is something other than God.

SLIFT: What is it?

MAULER:
Not what is above me
But what is below me! What stands in the stockyards and
      cannot
Last through the night and will still — I know —
Rise up in the morning.

SLIFT: Won't you eat a little meat, my dear Pierpont? Think, now you can do it with a clear conscience again, for from this day onward you won't have anything to do with cattle-slaughtering.

MAULER:

Do you think I should? Perhaps I could.

I ought to be able to eat now, oughtn't I?

SLIFT: Have a bite to eat and think over your situation. It's not very satisfactory. Do you realize that today you bought up everything there is in cans? Mauler, I see you engrossed in the contemplation of your noble nature, allow me to give you a concise account of your situation, the external, the unimportant one. The main point is that you've taken one hundred and fifty tons of stocks away from the meat-ring. You'll have to get rid of these in the next few weeks on a market that can't swallow one more can even today. You've paid 50 for them, but the price will go down at least to 30. On November 15, when the price is 30 or 25, the meat-ring will deliver four hundred tons to you at 50.

MAULER:

Slift! I'm done for!

I'm finished. I've gone and bought up meat.

Oh, Slift, what have I done!

Slift, I've loaded myself with all the meat in the world.

Like Atlas I stumble, cans by the ton on my shoulders,

All the way down to join the people who sleep

Under bridges. Only this morning

Many men were about to fall, and I

Went to see them fall and laugh at them

And tell them not a soul

Would be fool enough to buy meat in cans now

And while I stand there I hear my own voice saying:

I'll buy it all.

Slift, I've gone and bought meat, I'm done for.

SLIFT: Well, what do you hear from your friends in New York?

MAULER: That I ought to buy meat.

SLIFT: You ought to do what?

MAULER: Buy meat.

SLIFT: Then why are you yammering because you have bought it?

MAULER: Yes, they told me I ought to buy meat.

SLIFT: But you have bought meat!

MAULER:

Yes, that is so, I did buy meat, but I bought it
Not because of the letter that said I should
(That's all wrong anyhow, just armchair theory)
Not from any low motives, but because
That person gave me such a shock, I swear
I barely riffled through the letter, it only came this morning.
Here it is. "Dear Pierpont——

SLIFT (*reads on*): —— today we are able to inform you that our money
is beginning to bear fruit. Many Congressmen are going to vote
against tariffs, so it seems advisable to buy meat, dear Pierpont.
We shall write you again tomorrow."

MAULER:

This bribery, too, is something
That shouldn't happen. How easily a war
Might start from a thing like that, and thousands bleed
For filthy lucre. Oh, my dear Slift, I feel
That nothing good can come of news like this.

SLIFT:

That would depend on who had written the letters.
Bribing, abolishing tariffs, making wars —
Not everybody can do that. Are these people all right?

MAULER: They're solvent.

SLIFT: But who are they?

MAULER *smiles*.

Then prices might go even higher still?
Then we'd be sitting pretty after all.
That might be a prospect if it wasn't for the farmers —
By offering all their meat, only too eagerly,
They'd bring prices crashing down again. No, Mauler,
I don't understand that letter.

MAULER:

Think of it this way: a man has committed theft

And is caught by a man.
Now if he doesn't knock the other man down
He's done for; if he does, he's out of the woods.
The letter (which is wrong) demands (so as to be right)
A misdeed like that.

SLIFT: What misdeed?

MAULER:
The kind I could never commit. For from now on
I wish to live in peace. If they want to profit
By their misdeeds — and they will profit —
They need only buy up meat wherever they see it,
Beat into the stockbreeders' heads the fact
That there's too much meat around and mention
The flattening of Lennox and take
Their meat away from them. This above all:
Take the stockbreeders' meat from them . . . but then
They'll be duped all over again . . . no, I'll have nothing
To do with that.

SLIFT: You shouldn't have bought meat, Pierpont.

MAULER:
Yes, it's a bad business, Slift.
I'm not going to buy so much as a hat or a shoe
Until I get out of this mess, and I'll be happy
If I have a hundred dollars when I do.

Sound of drums. JOAN *approaches, with the* STOCKBREEDERS.

JOAN: We'll lure him out of his building the way you catch a cricket. You stand over there, because if he hears us singing he'll try to get out the other way, to avoid meeting me again: I'm a person he doesn't care to see. (*She laughs.*) And so are the people who are with me.

The STOCKBREEDERS *take up a position in front of door, right.*

JOAN (*in front of door, left*): Please come out, Mr. Mauler, I must talk to you about the terrible condition of the stockbreeders of Illinois. I also have several workers with me — they want to ask you when you're going to reopen your factory.

MAULER: Slift, where's the other exit? I don't want to run into her

again, still less the people she has with her. I'm not opening
any factories now, either.

SLIFT: Come out this way.

They go through the interior to door, right.

STOCKBREEDERS (*in front of door, left*): Come on out, Mauler, our
troubles are all your fault, and we are more than ten thousand
Illinois stockbreeders who don't know whether they're coming or going. So buy our livestock from us!

MAULER:

Shut the door, Slift! I'm not buying.

With the whole world's canned meat around my neck,

Now should I buy the cattle on the dog-star?

It's as if a man should go to Atlas when

He can barely drag the world along, and say:

"They need another carrier on Saturn."

Who's going to buy the livestock back from me?

SLIFT: The Grahams, most likely — they need it!

JOAN (*in front of door, left*): We're not leaving the place until the
stockbreeders get some help.

MAULER: Most likely the Grahams, yes, they need livestock. Slift,
go out and tell them to let me have two minutes to think things
over.

SLIFT *goes.*

SLIFT (*to the* STOCKBREEDERS): Pierpont Mauler wishes to give careful consideration to your request. He asks for two minutes'
thinking time.

SLIFT *re-enters the house.*

MAULER: I'm not buying. (*He starts figuring.*) Slift, I'm buying.
Slift, bring me anything that looks like a hog or a steer, I'll
buy it, whatever smells of lard, I'll buy it, bring every speck of
fat, I'm the buyer for it, and at today's price too, at 50.

SLIFT:

Not a hat will you buy, Mauler, but

All the cattle in Illinois.

MAULER: Yes, I'll still buy that. Now it's decided, Slift. Take A.

He draws an A on the closet door.

A man does something wrong, let that be A,
He did it because his feelings overcame him,
And now he goes on to do B, and B's wrong too
And now the sum of A and B is right.
Ask the stockbreeders in, they're very nice people,
Badly in need and decently clothed and not
The sort of folk that scare you when you see them.

SLIFT (*stepping out in front of the house; to the* STOCKBREEDERS): To save Illinois and avert ruin from its farmers and stockbreeders, Pierpont Mauler has decided to buy up all the livestock on the market.

STOCKBREEDERS: Long live Pierpont Mauler! He's saved the livestock trade!

They enter the house.

JOAN (*calling after them*): Tell Mr. Mauler that we, the Black Straw Hats, thank him for this in the name of the Lord. (*To the workers:*) If the people who buy cattle and the people who sell cattle are satisfied, then there'll be bread once more for you too.

7

THE EXPULSION OF THE MONEY-CHANGERS
FROM THE TEMPLE

The Black Straw Hats' Mission. The BLACK STRAW HATS, *sitting at a long table, are counting out from their tin boxes the widows' and orphans' mites they have collected.*

BLACK STRAW HATS (*singing*):
Gather the pennies of widows and orphans with song!
Great is the need
They have no roof or bread
But Almighty God
Won't let them go hungry long.

PAULUS SNYDER (*Major of the Black Straw Hats, getting up*): Very little, very little. (*To some poor folk in the background, among them* MRS. LUCKERNIDDLE *and* GLOOMB:) You here again? Don't you ever leave this place? There's work at the stockyards again, you know!

MRS. LUCKERNIDDLE: Where? The yards are shut down.

GLOOMB: We were told they would open up again, but they haven't.

SNYDER: Well, don't go too near the cash-box. (*He motions them still further back.*)

MULBERRY, *the landlord, enters.*

MULBERRY: Say, what about my rent?

SNYDER: My dear Black Straw Hats, my dear Mulberry, my honored listeners! As to this troublesome problem of financing our operations — anything that's good speaks for itself, and needs propaganda more than anything — hitherto we have aimed our appeals at the poor, indeed the poorest, on the assumption that they, being most in need of God's help, were the people most likely to have a bit left over for Him, and that their sheer numbers would produce the desired effect. To our regret, it has been borne in upon us that these very classes manifest an attitude of reserve toward God that is quite beyond explanation. Of course, this may be due to the fact that they have nothing. Therefore, I, Paulus Snyder, have issued an invitation in your name to Chicago's wealthy and prosperous citizens, to help us launch a major offensive next Sunday against the unbelief and materialism of the city of Chicago, primarily among the lower orders. Out of the proceeds we shall also pay our dear landlord, Mr. Mulberry, the rent he is so kindly deferring for us.

MULBERRY: It would certainly be very welcome, but please don't worry about it.

Exit.

SNYDER: Well, now go happily about your work and be sure to clean the front steps.

Exeunt BLACK STRAW HATS.

SNYDER: Tell me, are the locked-out workers in the stockyards still standing there patiently, or have they begun to talk like rebels?

MRS. LUCKERNIDDLE: They've been squawking pretty loud since yesterday, because they know the factories are getting orders.

GLOOMB: Many are saying already that they won't get any more work at all if they don't use force.

SNYDER (*to himself*): A good sign. The meat kings will be more likely to come and listen to our appeal if they're driven in by stones. (*To the* POOR PEOPLE:) Couldn't you split our wood, at least?

POOR PEOPLE: There isn't any more, Major.

Enter the packers CRIDLE, GRAHAM, SLIFT, MEYERS.

MEYERS: You know, Graham, I keep asking myself where that livestock can be hiding out.

GRAHAM: That's what I'm asking too, where can that livestock be hiding out?

SLIFT: So am I.

GRAHAM: Oh, you too? And I guess Mauler is too, eh?

SLIFT: I guess he is.

MEYERS:
> Somewhere some swine is buying everything up.
> Someone who knows quite well that we're committed
> By contract to deliver meat in cans
> And so need livestock.

SLIFT: Who can it be?

GRAHAM (*hitting him in the stomach*):
> You cur, you!
> Don't play any tricks on us there, and tell Pierpy not to either!
> That's a vital spot!

SLIFT (*to* SNYDER): What do you want of us?

GRAHAM (*hitting him again*): What do you think they want, Slift? (SLIFT, *with exaggerated mockery, makes the gesture of handing out money.*) You said it, Slift!

MEYERS (*to* SNYDER): Fire away.

They sit down on the prayer benches.

SNYDER (*in the pulpit*): We Black Straw Hats have heard that fifty thousand men are standing around in the stockyards without work. And that some are beginning to grumble and say: "We'll have to help ourselves." Aren't your names beginning to be called as the ones to blame for fifty thousand men being out of work and standing idly in front of the factories? They'll end by taking the factories away from you and saying: "We'll act the way the Bolsheviks did and take the factories into our own hands so that everybody can work and eat." For the story is getting around that unhappiness doesn't just come like the rain but is made by certain persons who get profit out of it. But we Black Straw Hats try to tell them that unhappiness does come down like the rain, no one knows where from, and that they are destined to suffering and there's a reward for it shining at the end of the road.

PACKERS: Why mention rewards?

SNYDER: The reward we speak of is paid out after death.

PACKERS: How much will it cost?

SNYDER: Eight hundred dollars a month, because we need hot soup and loud music. We also want to promise them that the rich will be punished — when they're dead, of course. (*The* PACKERS *laugh noisily*.) All that for a mere eight hundred a month!

GRAHAM: You don't need that much, man. Five hundred.

SNYDER: Well, we could get along with seven hundred and fifty, but then ——

MEYERS: Seven hundred and fifty. That's better. Let's make it five hundred.

GRAHAM: You do need five hundred, certainly. (*To the others:*) They've got to get that.

MEYERS: Out with it, Slift, you fellows have that livestock.

SLIFT: Mauler and I have not bought one cent's worth of livestock, as true as I'm sitting here. The Lord's my witness.

MEYERS (*to* SNYDER): Five hundred dollars, eh? That's a lot of money. Who's going to pay it?

SLIFT: Yes, you'll have to find someone who will give it to you.

SNYDER: Yes, yes.

MEYERS: That won't be easy.

GRAHAM: Come on, Slift, cough it up, Pierpy has the livestock.

SLIFT (*laughing*): A bunch of crooks, Mr. Snyder.

All laugh except SNYDER.

GRAHAM (*to* MEYER): The man has no sense of humor. Don't like him.

SLIFT: The main point is, man, where do you stand? On this side of the barricades, or the other?

SNYDER: The Black Straw Hats stand above the battle, Mr. Slift. This side.

Enter JOAN.

SLIFT: Why, here's our sainted Joan of the Livestock Exchange!

THE FOUR (*shouting at* JOAN): We're not satisfied with you, can't you tell Mauler something from us? You're supposed to have some influence with him. They say he eats out of your hand. Well, the market is so short of livestock that we have to keep an eye on him. They say you can bring him round to doing whatever you want. Have him get that livestock out. Listen, if you'll do this for us we're willing to pay the Black Straw Hats' rent for the next four years.

JOAN *has seen the poor people and is shocked.*

JOAN: Why, what are you doing here?

MRS. LUCKERNIDDLE (*coming forward*):
The twenty dinners are all eaten now.
Please don't get angry because I'm here again.
It's a sight I would be glad enough to spare you.
That's the awful thing about hunger: no sooner
Is it satisfied than back it comes again.

GLOOMB (*coming forward*):
I know you, it was you I tried to talk
Into working on that slicer that tore my arm off.
I could do worse things than that today.

JOAN: Why aren't you working? I did get work for you.

MRS. LUCKERNIDDLE: Where? The stockyards are closed.

GLOOMB: We were told they would open up again, but they haven't.

JOAN (*to the* PACKERS): So they're still waiting, are they?

The PACKERS *say nothing.*

And I thought they had been provided for!
It's been snowing on them now for seven days
And the very snow that kills them cuts them off
From every human eye. How easily
I forgot what everyone likes to forget for the peace of his
    mind!
If one man says things are all right again, no one looks into
    them.

To the PACKERS:

But surely Mauler bought meat from you? He did it at my request! And now you still refuse to open up your factories?

CRIDLE, GRAHAM, MEYERS: That's quite right, we wanted to open up.

SLIFT: But first of all you wanted to leap at the farmers' throats!

CRIDLE, GRAHAM, MEYERS: How are we to do any slaughtering when there's no livestock?

SLIFT: When Mauler and I bought meat from you we took it for granted you would start employment going again so that the workers would be able to buy meat. Now who will eat the meat we got from you? For whom did we buy meat if consumers can't pay for it?

JOAN: Look, if you people have control of all the equipment your employees use in your all-powerful factories and plants, then the least you could do would be to let them in, if they're kept out it's all up with them, because there is a sort of exploitation about the whole thing, and if a poor human creature is tormented till the blood comes, and can think of no way out but to take a club and bash his tormentor's head in, then it scares the daylights out of you, I've noticed that, and then you think religion's fine and it's supposed to pour oil on the troubled waters, but the Lord has His pride too, and He won't pitch in and clean your pigsties for you all over again. And I run around from pillar to post, thinking: "If I help you people on top, the people under you will also be helped. It's all one in a way, and the same strings pull it," but I was a prize fool there. If a man wants to help folks that are poor it seems he'd better help them get away from you. Is there no respect left in you for anything that wears a human face? Some day, maybe, you won't rate as human beings either, but as wild animals that will simply have to be slaughtered in the interest of public order and safety! And still you have the confidence to enter the house of God, just because you own that filthy Mammon, everybody knows where you got it and how, it wasn't come by honestly. But this time, by God, you've come to the wrong people, we'll have to drive you out, that's all, yes, drive you out with a stick. Come on, don't stand there looking so stupid, I know human beings shouldn't be treated like steers, but you aren't human beings, get out of here, and fast, or I'll lay violent hands on you, don't hold me back, I know what I'm doing, it's high time I found out. (JOAN *drives them out, using as a stick a flag held upside down. The* BLACK STRAW HATS *appear in the doorways.*) Get out! Are you trying to turn the house of God into a stable? Another Livestock Exchange? Get out! There's nothing for you here. We don't want to see such faces here. You're unworthy and I'm showing you the door. For all your money!

THE FOUR: Very well. But forty months' rent goes with us — simply, modestly, irretrievably. We need every cent of it anyway: we're facing times as terrible as the livestock market has ever seen. (*Exeunt.*)

SNYDER (*running after them*): Please stay, gentlemen! Don't go, she has no authority at all! A crazy female! She'll be fired! She'll do whatever you want her to do.

JOAN (*to the* BLACK STRAW HATS): Well, that certainly wasn't very smart at a time like this, what with the rent and all. But we can't think about that now. (*To* LUCKERNIDDLE *and* GLOOMB:) Sit down back there, I'll bring you some soup.

SNYDER (*returning*):

Go on, make the poor your guests
And regale them with rainwater and fine speeches
When there's really no pity for them up above,
Nothing but snow!
You followed your very first impulses,
Utterly without humility! It is so much easier
Simply to drive the unclean out with arrogance.
You're squeamish about the bread we have to eat,
Much too curious how it's made, and still
You want to eat it! Now, woman above the world,
Get out in the rain and face the snowstorm in righteousness!

JOAN: Does that mean I'm to take off my uniform?

SNYDER: Take off your uniform and pack your bags! Get out of this house and take along the riff-raff you brought us. Nothing but riff-raff and scum followed you in here. Now you'll be in that class yourself. Go and get your things.

JOAN *goes out and comes back dressed like a country servant, carrying a little suitcase.*

JOAN:

I'll go find rich man Mauler, he is not

Without fear or good will, and ask his help.
I won't put on this coat or black straw hat
Ever again or come back to this dear house
Of songs and awakenings till
I bring in rich man Mauler as one of us,
Converted from the ground up.
What if their money has eaten away
Their ears and human faces like a cancer
Making them sit apart but loftily
Beyond the reach of any cry for help!
Poor cripples!
There must be *one* just man among them!
Exit.

SNYDER:

Poor simpleton!
You're blind to this: set up in huge formations
The givers and the takers of work
Confront one another:
Warring fronts: irreconcilable.
Run to and fro between them, little peacemaker, little
    mediator —
Be useful to neither and go to your doom.

MULBERRY (*entering*): Have you the money now?

SNYDER: God will still be able to pay for the definitely scanty shelter
He has found on earth, I said scanty, Mr. Mulberry.

MULBERRY: Yes, pay, that's the ticket, that's the problem! You said
the right word then, Snyder! If the Lord in His goodness pays,
good. But if He doesn't pay, not so good. If the Lord in His
goodness doesn't pay His rent, He'll have to get out, and
what's more, He'll have to go on Saturday night, eh, Snyder?
Exit.

8

PIERPONT MAULER'S SPEECH ON THE INDISPENSABILITY OF CAPITALISM AND RELIGION

MAULER:

> Well, Slift, today's the day
> When our good friend Graham and all his crew
> Who wanted to wait for the lowest livestock prices
> Will have to buy the meat they owe us.

SLIFT:

> It will cost them more, because anything
> The Chicago market can show in the way of lowing cattle
> Is ours now.
> Every hog they owe us
> They'll have to buy from us, and that's expensive.

MAULER:

> Now, Slift, let loose all your wholesalers!
> Let them torment the livestock market with demands
> For everything that looks like hogs and cattle
> And so make prices go up and up.

SLIFT:

> What news of your Joan? There's a rumor
> Around the Livestock Exchange that you slept with her.
> I did my best to scotch it. She hasn't been heard of
> Since that day she threw us all out of the temple:
> It's as though black roaring Chicago had swallowed her up.

MAULER:

> I liked her action very much,
> Throwing you all out like that. Yes, that girl's afraid of nothing.
> And if I'd been along on that occasion

She'd have thrown me out with the rest and that's
What I like about her and that house of hers,
The fact that people like me are impossible there.
Force the price up to 80, Slift. That will make those Grahams
Rather like mud you stick your foot into
Merely to see its shape again.
I won't let an ounce of meat go by:
This time I'll rip their skins off for good and all,
In accordance with my nature.

SLIFT:

I'm overjoyed that you've shaken off
Your weakness of the past few days. And now
I'll go and watch them buy up livestock.

MAULER:

It's high time this damn town had its skin ripped off
And those fellows taught a thing or two
About the meat market: what if they do yell "Crime!"

Enter JOAN, *carrying a suitcase.*

JOAN: Good morning, Mr. Mauler. You're a hard man to find. I'll
just leave my things over there for the time being. You see,
I'm not with the Black Straw Hats any more. We had an
argument. So I thought, well, I'll go and look after Mr.
Mauler. Having no more of that wearing mission work to
do, I can pay more attention to the individual. So, to begin
with, I'm going to occupy myself with you a little, that is,
if you'll let me. You know, I've noticed that you are much
more approachable than many other people. That's a fine
old mohair sofa you have there, but why do you have a sheet
on it? — and it isn't made up properly, either. So you sleep
in your office? I thought surely you would have one of those
great big palaces. (MAULER *says nothing.*) But you're quite
right, Mr. Mauler, to be a good manager in little things too,
being a meat king. I don't know why, but when I see you I
always think of the story about the Lord when He visited
Adam in the Garden of Eden and called out, "Adam, where
are you?" Do you remember? (*Laughs.*) Adam is standing
behind a bush with his arms up to the elbows in a doe, and he

hears the voice of God just like that, with blood all over him.
And so he acts as if he wasn't there. But God doesn't give up,
and calls out again, "Adam, where are you?" And then Adam
says, faintly and blushing crimson: "This is the time you
pick to visit me, right after I've killed a doe. Oh, don't say a
word, I know I shouldn't have done it." But your conscience is
clear, Mr. Mauler, I hope.

MAULER: So you're not with the Black Straw Hats any more?

JOAN: No, Mr. Mauler, and I don't belong there either.

MAULER: Then what have you been living on? (JOAN SAYS *nothing*.)
I see. Nothing. How long ago did you leave the Black Straw
Hats?

JOAN: Eight days ago.

MAULER (*turns away and weeps*):
So greatly changed, and in a mere eight days!
Where has she been? To whom has she been talking? What
was it
That drew those lines around her mouth?
The city she has come from
Is a thing I do not yet know.
He brings her food on a tray.
I see you very much changed. Here's something to eat, if you
like. I'm not hungry myself.

JOAN (*looking at the food*): Mr. Mauler, after we drove the rich
people out of our house —

MAULER: Which amused me very much, and seemed the right
thing to do —

JOAN: The landlord, who lives on the rent we pay, gave us notice
to get out next Sunday.

MAULER: Indeed! So the Black Straw Hats are poorly off finan-
cially?

JOAN: Yes, and that's why I thought I'd go and see Mr. Mauler.
(*She begins to eat hungrily*.)

MAULER: Don't you fret. I'll go into the market and get you the
money you need. Yes, I'll do that, I'll get hold of it whatever
it costs me, even if I have to slice it right out of the city's

skin. I'll do it for you. Money's expensive, of course, but I'll produce it. That will be to your liking.

JOAN: Yes, Mr. Mauler.

MAULER: So you go and tell them: "The money is on the way. It will be there by Saturday. Mauler will get hold of it. He just left for the livestock market to dig it up." That matter of the fifty thousand didn't go so well, not exactly as I wanted it. I was unable to get them work immediately. But for you I'll make an exception, and your Black Straw Hats shall be spared, I'll get the money for you. Run and tell them.

JOAN: Yes, Mr. Mauler!

MAULER:
There, I've put it in writing. Take it.
I too am sorry that the men are waiting for work
In the stockyards and not very good work at that.
Fifty thousand men
Standing around in the stockyards, not even leaving at night.

    JOAN *stops eating*.

But that's the way this business goes:
It's to be or not to be — a question whether
I am to be the best man in my class or go
The dark and dreary way to the stockyards myself.
Also, the scum is filling up the yards again
And making trouble.
And now — I'll tell you the simple truth — I would have liked
To hear you say that what I do is right
And my business is natural: so
Tell me for sure that it was on your advice
I ordered meat from the meat-ring and from
The stockbreeders too, thus doing good; then,
Because I know well that you are poor and right now
They're trying to take away the very roof over your heads,
I'll give you something in return, as token
Of my goodwill.

JOAN: So the workers are still waiting in front of the slaughter-houses?

MAULER:

Why are you set against money? and yet look
So very different when you haven't any?
What do you think about money? Tell me,
I want to know; and don't get wrong ideas,
The way a fool will think of money as
Something to be doubted. Consider the reality,
The plain truth, not pleasant maybe, but still
True for all that: everything is unsteady and the human
    race
Is exposed to luck, you might say, to the state of the weather,
But money's a means of making some improvement — even
    if only
For certain people — apart from that, what a structure!
Built up from time immemorial, over and over again
Because it keeps collapsing, but still tremendous: demanding
    sacrifice,
Very hard to set up, continually set up
With many a groan, but still inescapably
Wresting the possible from a reluctant planet,
However much or little that may be; and accordingly defended
At all times by the best. Just think, if I —
Who have much against it, and sleep badly —
Were to desert it, I would be like a fly
Ceasing to hold back a landslide. There and then
I would become a nothing and it would keep on going over me.
For otherwise everything would have to be overturned
And the architect's design fundamentally altered
To suit an utterly different, incredible, new valuation of man,
Which you people don't want any more than we do, for it
    would take effect
With neither us nor God, who would have no function left
And be dismissed accordingly. Therefore you really ought to
Collaborate with us, and even if you don't sacrifice
What we don't want of you anyhow, still sanction the
    sacrifices:
In a word, you really ought

To set God up once more —
The only salvation — and
Beat the drum for Him so that He may
Gain a foothold in the regions of misery and His
Voice may ring out among the slaughterhouses.
That would suffice.

Holding out the note to her.

Take what you get, but know the reason
Before you take it! Here's the voucher, this is four years' rent.

JOAN:

Mr. Mauler, I don't understand what you have been saying
And do not wish to either.

Rising.

I know I should be overjoyed to hear
That God is going to be helped, only
I belong to those for whom
This does not mean real help. And to whom
Nothing is offered.

MAULER:

If you take the money to the Black Straw Hats you can also
Stay in their house again: this living
On nothing is not good for you. Believe me,
They're out for money, and so they should be.

JOAN:

If the Black Straw Hats
Accept your money they are welcome to it,
But I will take my stand among the people waiting in the
    stockyards,
Until the factories open up again, and
Eat nothing but what they eat and if
They are offered snow, then snow,
And the work they do I will do also, for I have no money either
And no other way to get it — honorably, anyhow —
And if there is no more work, then let there be none
For me either, and
You, who live on poverty and
Cannot bear to see the poor and judge

Something you do not know and make arrangements
So as not to see what sits there being judged,
Abandoned in the slaughterhouses, disregarded,
If you want to see me again
Come to the stockyards.
Exit.

MAULER:

Tonight then, Mauler,
Get up every hour and look out of the window
To see if it's snowing, and if it is
It will be snowing on the girl you know.

9

JOAN'S THIRD DESCENT INTO THE DEPTHS: THE SNOWFALL

Stockyards district.

JOAN:

Listen to the dream I had one night
A week ago.
Before me in a little field, too small
To hold the shade of a middle-sized tree, hemmed in
By enormous houses, I saw a bunch
Of people: I could not make out how many, but
There were far more of them than all the sparrows
That could find room in such a tiny place —
A very thick bunch indeed, so that
The field began to buckle and rise in the middle
And the bunch was suspended on its edge, holding fast
A moment, quivering: then, stirred
By the intervention of a word — uttered somewhere or other,
Meaning nothing vital — it began to flow.
Then I saw processions, streets, familiar ones, Chicago! you!
I saw you marching, then I saw myself:
I, silent, saw myself striding at your head
With warlike step and bloodstains on my brow
And shouting words that sounded militant
In a tongue I did not know; and while many processions
Moved in many directions all at once
I strode in front of many processions in manifold shapes:
Young and old, sobbing and cursing,
Finally beside myself! Virtue and terror!
Changing whatever my foot touched,
Causing measureless destruction, visibly influencing
The courses of the stars, but also changing utterly

The neighborhood streets familiar to us all —
So the procession moved, and I along with it,
Veiled by snow from any hostile attack,
Transparent with hunger, no target,
Not to be hit anywhere, not being settled anywhere;
Not to be touched by any trouble, being accustomed
To all. And so it marches, abandoning the position
Which cannot be held: exchanging it for any other one.
That was my dream.
Today I see its meaning:
Before tomorrow morning we
Will start out from these yards
And reach their city, Chicago, in the gray of dawn,
Displaying the full range of our wretchedness in public places,
Appealing to whatever resembles a human being.
What will come after, I do not know.

Livestock Exchange.

MAULER (*to the* PACKERS):
My friends in New York have written me to say
That the tariff in the south
Was repealed today.

PACKERS:
This is awful, the tariff law gone and here we are
Without any meat to sell! It's been sold already
At a low price and now we are asked to buy meat when it's
    going up!

STOCKBREEDERS:
This is awful, the tariff law gone and here we are
Without any livestock to sell! It's already been sold
At a lower price!

SMALL SPECULATORS:
Awful! Eternally inscrutable
Are the eternal laws
Of human economy!
Without warning
The volcano erupts and lays the country waste!

Without an invitation
The profitable island rises from the barren seas!
No one is told, no one is in the picture! But the last in line
Is bitten by the dogs!

MAULER:
Well, seeing that livestock is being demanded
In cans at an acceptable price
I now request you to hand over quickly
The canned meat I am supposed to get from you
According to contract.

GRAHAM: At the old price?

MAULER:
As the contract specified, Graham.
Four hundred tons, if I remember correctly
A moment when I was not myself.

PACKERS:
How can we take livestock now, with prices rising?
Someone has made a corner in it,
Nobody knows who —
Release us from the contract, Mauler!

MAULER:
Unfortunately I must have those cans. But there is
Still livestock enough, a bit expensive, granted, but
Livestock enough. Buy it up!

PACKERS: Buy livestock now? The hell with it!

*A little tavern in the stockyards district. Men and women
workers,* JOAN *among them. — A group of Black Straw Hats
enter.* JOAN *rises and makes frantic gestures at them during
what follows.*

JACKSON (*after a hurried song*):
Brother, why won't you eat the bread that Jesus gives?
See how happy and glad are we.
It's because we have found the Lord Jesus, Lord of all our lives.
Hurry, come to Him heartily!
Hallelujah!

*One of the Black Straw Hat girls talks to the workers, making
side remarks to her comrades.*

BLACK STRAW HAT: (It's no use, is it?) Brothers and sisters, I too
used to stand sadly by the wayside, just as you are, and the
old Adam in me cared for nothing but meat and drink, but
then I found my Lord Jesus, and then it was so light and glad
inside me, but now (They aren't listening at all!) if I just think
real hard about my Lord Jesus, who redeemed us all by His
suffering in spite of our many wicked deeds, then I stop feeling hungry and thirsty, except for our Lord Jesus' word. (No
use.) Where the Lord Jesus is, there is not violence, but peace,
not hate but love. (It's quite hopeless!)

BLACK STRAW HATS: Hallelujah!

JACKSON *passes the box around. Nothing is put into it.*

Hallelujah!

JOAN:

If only they wouldn't stay here in the cold
Making all that nuisance and talking, talking!
Really, now I can hardly bear
To hear the words
That once were dear and pleasant to me! If only a voice,
Some remnant inside them, would say:
There's snow and wind here, be quiet here!

A WOMAN: Oh, let them be. They have to do this to get a bit of
warmth and food. I wish I was in their shoes.

MRS. LUCKERNIDDLE: That was nice music!

GLOOMB: Nice and short.

MRS. LUCKERNIDDLE: But they really are good people.

GLOOMB: Good and brief, short and sweet.

WOMAN WORKER: Why don't they give us a real talk, and convert us?

GLOOMB (*making a gesture of paying out money*): Can you keep the
pot boiling, Mrs. Swingurn?

WOMAN WORKER: The music is very pretty but I was expecting
them to give us a plate of soup, maybe, seeing they had brought
a pot along.

WORKER (*surprised at her*): No kidding, you thought that?

JOAN: Are there no people here with any enterprise?

A WORKER: Yes, the Communists.

JOAN: Aren't they people who incite to crime?

THE WORKER: No.

Livestock Exchange.

PACKERS:
> We're buying livestock! Yearlings!
> Feeders! Calves! Steers! Hogs!
> Offers, please!

STOCKBREEDERS: There isn't any! We've sold whatever was salable.

PACKERS: Isn't any? The depots are bursting with cattle.

STOCKBREEDERS: Sold.

PACKERS: To whom?

> *Enter* MAULER.

> *Milling around him:*

> Not a steer to be found in Chicago!
> You'll have to give us more time, Mauler.

MAULER: You'll deliver your meat as agreed. (*Going over to* SLIFT:) Squeeze 'em dry.

A STOCKBREEDER: Eight hundred Kentucky steers at 400.

PACKERS: Impossible. 400! Are you crazy?

SLIFT: I'll take them. At 400.

STOCKBREEDERS: Eight hundred steers sold to Sullivan Slift for 400.

PACKERS:
> It's Mauler! What did we say? He's the one!
> You crooked hound! He makes us deliver canned meat
> And buys up livestock! So we have to buy from him
> The meat we need to fill his cans!
> You filthy butcher! Here, take *our* flesh, hack yourself off a
> slice!

MAULER: If you're a dumb ox you shouldn't be surprised when people's appetites grow with looking at you.

GRAHAM (*makes as if to attack* MAULER): He's got it coming, I'll settle his hash!

MAULER:

All right, Graham, now I demand your cans.
You can stuff yourself into one of them.
I'll teach you the meat business, you
Traders! From now on I get paid, and well paid,
For every hoof, every calf from here to Illinois*
And so I'll offer five hundred steers at 56 to start with.
Dead silence.
And now, in view of the weak demand, seeing nobody here
Needs livestock,
I want 60! And don't forget my cans, either!

*Another part of the stockyards. Placards are inscribed: "Soli-
darity with Locked-out Stockyard Workers!" "All out for
General Strike!" In front of a shed two men from the union
local are speaking to a group of workers. Enter* JOAN.

JOAN: Are these the people who lead the movement of the unemployed? I can help them. I've learned to speak in streets and
meeting-halls, I have no fear of hecklers and I think I can explain a good thing well. Because, as I see it, something's got to
be done right away. I have some suggestions to make, too.

A LABOR LEADER: Listen, all. So far the meat gang hasn't shown the
least inclination to open up its factories. At first it seemed that
the exploiter Pierpont Mauler was all out for a reopening because he wants from the meat gang huge quantities of meat
that they owe him by contract. Then it became clear that the
meat they need for packing is in Mauler's own hands and he
won't even consider letting it go. Now we know that if things
are left up to the meat gang we workers will never all get back
into the slaughterhouses, and never at the old wages. With
things in this pass we've got to realize that nothing can help us
but the use of force. The city utilities have promised to join the
general strike by tomorrow morning at the latest. Now this
news must be spread in all parts of the stockyards; if it isn't,

* *Sic.* — F. J.

there's a danger that the masses will be excited by some rumor or other and leave the yards, and then be forced to yield to the meat gang's terms. So these letters, stating that the gasworks and waterworks and power stations are going to help us by going on strike, must be handed out to delegates who will be awaiting our password in different parts of the stockyards at ten o'clock tonight. Stick that under your vest, Jack, and wait for the delegates in front of Mother Schmitt's canteen.

A WORKER *takes the letter and leaves.*

SECOND WORKER: Give me the one for the Graham works, I know them.

LEADER: 26th Street, corner Michigan Park. (WORKER *takes letter and leaves.*) 13th Street by the Westinghouse Building. (*To* JOAN:) Well, and who may you be?

JOAN: I was fired from the job I had.

LEADER: What job?

JOAN: Selling magazines.

LEADER: Who were you working for?

JOAN: I'm a peddler.

A WORKER: Maybe she's a spy.

THE OTHER LEADER: Who can tell what she will do with the letter we give her?

FIRST LEADER: Nobody.

> *To* JOAN:
> A net with a torn mesh
> Is of no use:
> The fish swim through at that spot
> As though there were no net.
> Suddenly all its meshes
> Are useless.

JOAN: I used to sell papers on 44th Street. I'm no spy. I'm for your cause heart and soul.

SECOND LEADER: Our cause? Why, isn't it your cause?

JOAN: It certainly isn't in the public interest for the factory owners to leave all those people sitting in the streets just like that. Why, it makes you think the poverty of the poor is useful to the rich! You might say poverty is all their doing! (*The* WORKERS *laugh uproariously*.) It's inhuman, that's what it is! I even have people like Mauler in mind when I say that. (*Renewed laughter*.) Why do you laugh? I don't think you have any right to be malicious and to believe without proof that a man like Mauler can be inhuman.

SECOND LEADER: Not without proof! You can give the letter to her, all right.

FIRST LEADER: Go to Storehouse Five at the Graham plant. When you see three workers come up and look around them, ask if they are from the Cridle plant. This letter is for them.

Livestock Exchange.

SMALL SPECULATORS:

> Quotations going down! The packing plants in peril!
> What will become of us, the stockholders?
> The man with small savings who gave his last cent
> For the middle class, which is weakened anyway?
> A man like Graham ought to be
> Torn to shreds before he makes waste paper
> Out of the note with our share marked on it, the one
> We earned from his bloody cellars.
> Buy that livestock, buy it at any price!

> *Throughout this scene the names of firms suspending payment are being called out. "Suspending payment: Meyer & Co.," etc.*

PACKERS: We can do no more, the price is over 70.

WHOLESALERS: Mow 'em down, they won't buy, the high-hats.

PACKERS: Two thousand steers demanded at 70.

SLIFT (*to* MAULER, *beside a column*): Shove 'em up.

MAULER:

> I see that you have not stood by your part
> Of the contract I drew up with you that day
> In the wish to create employment. And now I hear
> They're still standing around out there in the yards. But

You're going to regret it: out with the canned meat
Which I have bought!

GRAHAM:

There's nothing we can do: meat has completely
Vanished from the market!
I'll take five hundred steers at 75.

SMALL SPECULATORS:

Buy them, you greedy hounds!
They won't buy! They'd rather hand over
The packing plants.

MAULER:

We shouldn't push it up any higher, Slift.
They're powerless now.
They are meant to bleed, but they mustn't perish;
If they go out we're goners too.

SLIFT:

There's life in them yet, put it up a notch.
Five hundred steers at 77.

SMALL SPECULATORS:

Did you hear that? Why
Didn't they buy at 75? Now
It's gone to 77 and still climbing.

PACKERS: We get 50 from Mauler for the cans and can't pay Mauler 80 for the livestock.

MAULER (*to a group of men*): Where are the people I sent to the stockyards?

A MAN: There's one.

MAULER: Well, let's have it.

The FIRST DETECTIVE *reports.*

FIRST DETECTIVE: Those crowds, Mr. Mauler, you can't see the end of them. If you called the name of Joan, ten or maybe a hundred would answer. The mob sits there and waits, without a face or a name. Besides, nobody can hear just one man's voice and there are far too many people running around asking after relatives they've lost. Serious unrest prevails in the sections where the unions are at work.

MAULER: Who's at work? The unions? And the police let them agitate? Damn it all! Go and call the police right away, mention my name, ask them what we're paying taxes for. Insist that the troublemakers get their heads cracked, speak plainly to them.

Exit FIRST DETECTIVE.

GRAHAM:
Oh, give us a thousand at 77, Mauler;
If it knocks us out, it's the end of us.

SLIFT: Five hundred to Graham at 77. All the rest at 80.

MAULER (*returning*):
Slift, this business no longer entertains me.
It might take us too far.
Go up to 80, then let it go at 80.
I'll hand it over and let them go.
Enough's enough. The town needs a breathing-spell.
And I have other worries.
Slift, this throat-squeezing isn't as much fun
As I thought it would be.

Seeing the SECOND DETECTIVE.

Did you find her?

SECOND DETECTIVE: No, I saw no woman in a Black Straw Hat uniform. There are a hundred thousand people standing around in the stockyards; besides, it's dark and that biting wind drowns your voice. Also, the police are clearing the yards and shots are being fired already.

MAULER:
Shots? At whom? Oh, yes, of course.
It seems strange — you can't hear a thing in this place.
So she's not to be found, and shots are being fired?
Go to the phone-booth, look for Jim and tell him
Not to call, or people will say again
That we demanded the shooting.

Exit SECOND DETECTIVE.

MEYERS: Fifteen hundred at 80!

SLIFT: Not more than five hundred at 80!

MEYERS: Five hundred at 80, you cutthroat!

MAULER (*returning to the column*): Slift, I feel unwell. Let up, will you?

SLIFT: I wouldn't think of it. There's life in them yet. And if you start to weaken, Mauler, I'll shove them up higher.

MAULER:
Slift, I need a breath of air. You carry on
The business. I can't. Carry it on
The way I would. I'd rather give it all away
Than have more things happen because of me!
Go no higher than 85! But manage it
The way I would. You know me.
Exit.

SLIFT: Five hundred steers at 90!

SMALL SPECULATORS:
We heard that Mauler was willing
To sell at 85. Slift has no authority.

SLIFT:
That's a lie! I'll teach you
To sell meat in cans and then
Not have any meat!
Five thousand steers for 95!
Uproar.

Stockyards. Many people waiting, JOAN *among them.*

PEOPLE: Why are you sitting here?

JOAN: I have to deliver a letter. Three men are supposed to come by here.

A group of REPORTERS *comes up, led by a* MAN.

MAN (*pointing to* JOAN): That's the one. (*To* JOAN:) These people are reporters.

REPORTERS: Hello, are you Joan Dark, the Black Straw Hat?

JOAN: No.

REPORTERS: We have heard from Mauler's office that you've sworn not to leave the stockyards before the plants open up. We have it, you can read it here, in big front-page headlines. (JOAN *turns away*.) Our Lady of the Stockyards Avers God Solidly Behind Stockyard Workers.

JOAN: I said no such thing.

REPORTERS: We can assure you, Miss Dark, that public opinion is on your side. All Chicago sympathizes with you, except a few unscrupulous speculators. Your Black Straw Hats will reap terrific success from all this.

JOAN: I'm not with the Black Straw Hats any more.

REPORTERS: That can't be. For us, you belong to the Black Straw Hats. But we don't want to disturb you, we'll keep well in the background.

JOAN: I would like you to go away.
They sit down some distance off.

WORKERS (*in the stockyards, rear*):
Before our need is at its worst
They will not open the factories.
When misery has mounted
They will open up.
But they must answer us.
Do not go before they answer.

COUNTER-CHORUS (*also rear*):
Wrong! Let misery mount,
They will not open up,
Not before profits mount.
If you wait for the answer
You will get the answer:
Out of cannon and machine guns
They will answer you.
And we advise you to wait
For this answer: do not go.

JOAN:
I see this system and on the surface
It has long been familiar to me, but not
In its inner meaning! Some, a few, sit up above
And many down below and the ones on top

Shout down: "Come on up, then we'll all
Be on top," but if you look closely you'll see
Something hidden between the ones on top and the ones below
That looks like a path but is not a path —
It's a plank and now you can see it quite clearly,
It is a seesaw, this whole system
Is a seesaw, with two ends that depend
On one another, and those on top
Sit up there only because the others sit below,
And only as long as they sit below;
They'd no longer be on top if the others came up,
Leaving their place, so that of course
They want the others to sit down there
For all eternity and never come up.
Besides, there have to be more below than above
Or else the seesaw wouldn't hold. A seesaw, that's what it is.

The REPORTERS *get up and move upstage, having received some
news.*

A WORKER (*to* JOAN): Say, what have you to do with those fellows?

JOAN: Nothing.

WORKER: But they were talking with you.

JOAN: They took me for someone else.

OLD MAN (*to* JOAN): You sure look frozen. Like a swig of whiskey?
   (JOAN *drinks.*) Stop! Stop! That's no mean shot you took!

A WOMAN: Scandalous!

JOAN: Did you say something?

WOMAN: I said, scandalous! Guzzling all the old man's whiskey!

JOAN: Shut your trap, you silly old thing. Hey, where's my shawl?
   They've gone and swiped it again. That's the last straw! Going
   and stealing my shawl, on top of everything else! Now who's
   got my shawl? Give it here pronto. (*She grabs a sack off the
   head of the woman standing next to her. The* WOMAN *resists.*)
   Oh, so it's you. No lies! Gimme that sack.

THE WOMAN: Help, she's killing me!

A MAN: Shut up!

Someone throws her a rag.

JOAN: For all you people care, I might be sitting around in this
draft nekkid.
It wasn't as cold as this in my dream.
When I came to this place with brave plans,
Fortified by dreams, I still never dreamed
That it could be so cold here. Now the only thing I miss
Of all I have is my nice warm shawl.
You may well be hungry, you have nothing to eat,
But they're waiting for me with a bowl of soup.
You may well freeze
But I can go into the warm hall any time,
Pick up the flag and beat the drum
And speak about HIM who lives in the clouds. After all,
What did you leave? What I left
Was no mere occupation, it was a calling,
A noble habit, but a decent job as well
And daily bread and a roof and a livelihood.
Yes, it seems almost like a play,
Something undignified, for me to stay in this place
Without extremely pressing need. And yet
I may not go, and still —
I'll be frank about it — fear tightens round my throat
At the thought of his not eating, not sleeping, not knowing
Where you are,
Habitual hunger, helpless cold and —
Worst of all — wanting to get away.

WORKER:
Stay here! Whatever happens,
Do not break ranks!
Only if you stand together
Can you help each other!
Realize that you have been betrayed
By all your public sponsors
And your unions, which are bought.
Listen to no one, believe nothing
But test every proposal
That leads to genuine change. And above all learn:

It will only work out by force
And only if you do it yourselves.

The REPORTERS *return.*

REPORTERS: Hey there, gal, you've had sensational success: we've just found out that the millionaire Pierpont Mauler, who has vast quantities of livestock in his hands now, is releasing it to the slaughterhouses in spite of rising prices. This being so, work will be resumed in the yards tomorrow.

JOAN:
Oh, what good news! The ice has thawed in their hearts. At least
The one just man among them
Has not failed us. Appealed to as a man,
He has answered as a man.
There *is* kindness in the world.

Machine guns rat-a-tat in the distance.

What's that noise?

REPORTER: Those are army machine guns. The army has orders to clear the stockyards because the agitators who are inciting to violence will have to be silenced now that the slaughterhouses are to be reopened.

A WORKER: You just take it easy and stay here. The stockyards are so big it'll take the army hours to get this far.

JOAN: How many people are there in them now, anyway?

REPORTER: There must be a hundred thousand.

JOAN:
So many?
Oh, what an unknown school, an unlawful space
Filled up with snow, where hunger is teacher and un-
preventably
Need speaks about necessity.
A hundred thousand pupils, what are you learning?

WORKERS (*rear*):
If you stay together
They will cut you to pieces.
We advise you to stay together!

If you fight
Their tanks will grind you to pulp.
We advise you to fight!
This battle will be lost
And maybe the next
Will also be lost.
But you are learning to fight
And realizing
That it will only work out by force
And only if you do it yourselves.

JOAN:

Stop: no more lessons
So coldly learned!
Do not use force
To fight disorder and confusion.
Certainly the temptation is tremendous!
Another night like this, another wordless
Oppression like this, and nobody
Will be able to keep quiet. And certainly
You have already stood together
On many a night in many a year and learned
To think coldly and terribly.
Certainly acts of violence and weakness
Are matching one another in the dark
And unsettled business is piling up.
But the meal that's cooking here — who
Will be the ones to eat it?
I'm leaving. What's done by force cannot be good. I don't belong with them. If hunger and the tread of misery had taught me violence as a child, I would belong to them and ask no questions. But as it is, I must leave.

She remains seated.

REPORTERS: Our advice to you is, leave the stockyards right now. You made a big hit, but that's over and done with.

Exeunt. Shouting, rear, spreading forward. The WORKERS *rise.*

A WORKER: They're bringing the men from the local. (*The two* LEADERS *of the workers are brought forward, handcuffed.*)

A WORKER (*to his handcuffed leader*): Never mind, William, it isn't evening every day.

ANOTHER (*shouting after the group*): Bloodhounds!

WORKERS: If they think they're stopping anything that way, they're on the wrong track. Our men have taken care of everything.

In a vision JOAN *sees herself as a criminal, outside the familiar world.*

JOAN:
The men who gave me the letter! Why are they
Handcuffed? What is in the letter?
I could do nothing
That would have to be done by force and
Would provoke force. A person like that would stand
Against his fellow man, full of malice
And beyond the range of any settlement
That human beings usually make.
Not belonging, he would lose his way
In a world no longer familiar to him. The stars
Would hurtle past his head breaking
The ancient rules. Words
Would change meaning for him. Innocence
Would abandon one who was constantly persecuted.
He can look at nothing without suspicion.
I could not be like that. So I'm leaving.
For three days Joan was seen
In Packingtown, in the stockyards swamps
Going down, downward from level to level
To clear the mud away, to manifest
To the lowest. Three days walking
Down the slope, growing weaker on the third
And finally swallowed by the swamp. Say:
"It was too cold."
She gets up and goes. Snow begins to fall.

A WORKER: I thought right away that she'd take off when the real snow came.

THREE WORKERS *come by, look around for someone, fail to find him, and leave.*

As it grows dark, a writing appears:
The snow is starting to fall,
Will anyone stay at all?
They'll stay today as they've stayed before —
Stony ground and folk that are poor.

PIERPONT MAULER CROSSES THE BOUNDARY OF POVERTY

A Chicago street corner.
MAULER (*to one of the detectives*):
No further, let's turn back now, what do you say?
Admit it: you laughed. I said, "Let's turn back now,"
And you laughed. They're shooting again.
Seems to be some resistance, eh? But this is what
I wanted to impress upon you: think nothing of it
If I turned back a couple of times
As we came nearer the stockyards. Thinking
Is nothing. I'm not paying you to think.
I probably have my reasons. I'm known down there.
Now you are thinking again. Seems I've taken
A couple of nitwits along. Anyway,
Let's turn back. I hope the person I was looking for
Has listened to the voice of sense and left that place
Where hell appears to be breaking loose.
A NEWSBOY goes by.
Aha! the papers! let's see how the livestock market is going!
He reads, and turns pale.
Well, something's happened here that changes things:
It's printed here, black on white, that livestock
Is down to 30 and not a slice is being sold,
That's what it says here, black on white, the packers
Are ruined and have left the livestock market.
And it also says that Mauler and Slift, his friend,
Are the worst hit of all. That's what it says and it means
That things have reached a point that certainly was not
    striven for,
But is greeted with sighs of relief. I can help them no further —

> I freely offered
> All my livestock for the use of any man that wanted it
> And nobody took it and so I am free now
> And without pretensions and hereby
> I dismiss you in order to cross
> The boundary of poverty, for I no longer require your services.
> Henceforth nobody will want to knock me down.

THE TWO DETECTIVES: Then we may go.

MAULER:

> You may indeed, and so may I, wherever I want.
> Even to the stockyards.
> And as for the thing made of sweat and money
> Which we have erected in these cities:
> It already seems as though a man
> Had made a building, the largest in the world and
> The most expensive and practical, but —
> By an oversight, and because it was cheap — he used dog-shit
> As its material, so that it would have been very difficult
> To live in and in the end his only glory was
> That he had made the biggest stink in the world.
> And anyone who gets out of a building like that
> Should be a cheerful man.

A DETECTIVE (*departing*): So, he's finished.

MAULER: Bad luck may crush the man of humble size;
> Me it must waft to spiritual skies.

A No-Man's-Land in the Stockyards. JOAN, *hurrying toward the city, overhears two passing workers.*

FIRST WORKER: First they let the rumor leak out that work would start up again, full blast, in the stockyards; but now that a part of the workers have left the yards to come back early tomorrow morning, they're suddenly saying that the slaughterhouses won't be opened at all, because Mauler has ruined them.

SECOND WORKER: The Communists were right. The masses shouldn't have broken ranks. All the more so because the Chicago utilities had all called a general strike for tomorrow.

FIRST WORKER: We didn't know that.

SECOND WORKER: That's bad. Some of the messengers must have failed us. A lot of people would have stayed put if they'd known about it. Even in the teeth of the cops' violence.

Wandering to and fro, JOAN *hears voices.*

A VOICE:
    He who does not arrive
    Can plead no excuse. The fallen man
    Is not excused by the stone.
    Let not even the one who does arrive
    Bore us with reports of difficulties
    But deliver in silence
    Himself or what is entrusted to him.

JOAN *has stood still and now runs in another direction.*

A VOICE (JOAN *stands still*):
    We gave you orders
    Our situation was critical
    We did not know who you were
    You might carry out our orders and you might
    Also betray us.
    Did you carry them out?

JOAN *runs farther and is halted by another voice.*

A VOICE: Where men are waiting, someone must arrive!

Looking around for an escape from the voices, JOAN *hears voices on all sides.*

VOICES:
    The net with a torn mesh
    Is of no use:
    The fish swim through it at that point
    As though there were no net.
    Suddenly all its meshes
    Are useless.

JOAN *falls to her knees.*

JOAN:
    Oh, truth, shining light! Darkened by a snowstorm in an evil hour!

Lost to sight from that moment! Oh, how violent are
   snowstorms!
Oh, weakness of the flesh! What would you let live, hunger?
Whatever outlasts you, frost of the night!

She runs back.

10

PIERPONT MAULER HUMBLES HIMSELF AND IS EXALTED

The Black Straw Hats' Mission.

MARTHA (*to another* BLACK STRAW HAT): Three days ago a messenger from Pierpont Mauler, the meat king, came to tell us that he wishes to pay our rent and join us in a big campaign for the poor.

MULBERRY: Mr. Snyder, it's Saturday evening. I'm asking you to pay your rent, which is very low, or get out of my building.

SNYDER: Mr. Mulberry, we expect Mr. Pierpont Mauler any minute now and he has promised us his support.

MULBERRY: Dick, old man, Albert, old man, put the furniture out in the street.

TWO MEN *begin to move the furniture out.*

BLACK STRAW HATS:
Oh! They're taking the prayer bench!
Their greedy grasp even threatens
Pipe organ and pulpit.
And louder still we cry:
Please, rich Mr. Mauler, come
And save us with your money!

SNYDER:
Seven days now the masses have been standing
In rusting stockyards, cut off from work at last.
Freed from every kind of shelter they stand
Under rain and snow again, sensing above them
The zenith of an unknown decision.
Oh, dear Mr. Mulberry, give us hot soup now
And a little music and they'll be ours. In my head I see
The Kingdom of Heaven ready and waiting.

234

> Just give us a band and some decent soup,
> Really nourishing, and God will settle things
> And all of Bolshevism, too,
> Will have breathed its last.

BLACK STRAW HATS:

> The dams of faith have burst
> In this Chicago of ours
> And the slimy flood of materialism surges
> Menacingly round the last of its houses.
> Look, it's tottering, look, it's sinking!
> Never mind — keep going — rich man Mauler's on the way!
> He's started out already with all his money!

A BLACK STRAW HAT: Where can we put the public now, Major?

Enter THREE POOR PEOPLE, MAULER *among them.*

SNYDER (*shouting at them*): Soup, that's all you want! No soup here! Just the Word of God! We'll get rid of them straight off when they hear that.

MAULER: Here are three men coming to their God.

SNYDER: Sit down over there and keep quiet.

The THREE *sit down. A* MAN *enters.*

MAN: Is Pierpont Mauler here?

SNYDER: No, but we're expecting him.

MAN: The packers want to speak to him and the stockbreeders are screaming for him.

Exit.

MAULER (*facing audience*):

> I hear they're looking for a man named Mauler.
> I knew him: a numskull. Now they're searching
> High and low, in heaven and in hell,
> For that man Mauler who was dumber all his life
> Than a dirty drink-sodden tramp.

Rises and goes over to BLACK STRAW HATS.

> I knew a man who once was asked
> For a hundred dollars. And he had about ten million.
> And he came along without the hundred but threw

The ten million away
And gave himself.

He takes two of the BLACK STRAW HATS *and kneels with them on the prayer bench.*

I wish to confess my sins.
No one who ever knelt here, friends,
Was as humble as I am.

BLACK STRAW HATS:

Don't lose confidence,
Don't be souls of little faith!
He's sure to come — already he's approaching
With all his money.

A BLACK STRAW HAT: Is he here yet?

MAULER:

A hymn, I pray you! For my heart
Feels heavy and light at once.

They intone a hymn. The BLACK STRAW HATS *join in abstractedly, eyes on the door.*

SNYDER (*bent over the account books*):

I won't tell how this comes out.
Quiet!
Bring me the housekeeping record and the unpaid bills. I've got to that stage.

MAULER:

I accuse myself of exploitation,
Misuse of power, expropriation of everybody
In the name of property. For seven days I held
The city of Chicago by the throat
Until it perished.

A BLACK STRAW HAT: That's Mauler!

MAULER:

But at the same time I plead that on the seventh day
I rid myself of everything, so that now
I stand before you without possessions.
Not guiltless, but repentant.

SNYDER: Are you Mauler?

MAULER: Yes, and torn to pieces by remorse.

SNYDER (*with a loud cry*): And without any money? (*To the* BLACK STRAW HATS:) Pack up the stuff, I hereby suspend all payments.

MUSICIANS:
> If that's the man you were waiting for
> To get the cash to pay us with
> Then we can go. Good night.
> *Exeunt.*

CHORUS OF BLACK STRAW HATS (*gazing after the departing musicians*):
> We were awaiting with prayers
> The wealthy Mauler, but into our house
> Came the man converted.
> His heart
> He brought to us, but not his money.
> Therefore our hearts are moved, but
> Our faces are long.
> *Confusedly the* BLACK STRAW HATS *sing their last hymns as they sit on their last chairs and benches.*

BLACK STRAW HATS:
> By the waters of Lake Michigan
> We sit down and weep.
> Take the proverbs off the walls
> Shove the songbooks into the cloth that wraps the defeated flag
> For we can pay our bills no more
> And against us rush the snowstorms
> Of approaching winter.
> *Then they sing "Go Into the Thick of the Fight."* MAULER *joins in, looking over a* BLACK STRAW HAT'S *shoulder.*

SNYDER:
> Quiet! Everybody out now — (*to* MAULER:) — especially you!
> Where is the forty months' rent from the unconverted
> Whom Joan expelled? Look what she's driven in instead! Oh, Joan,
> Give me my forty months' rent again!

MAULER:

I see you would like to build your house
In my shade. Well, for you a man
Is what can help you; likewise, for me
A man was only plunder. But even
If man were only what is helped,
There would be no difference. Then you'd need drowning
        men,
For then it would be your business
To be straws for them to clutch at. So all remains
Within the mighty orbit of wares, like that of the stars.
Such teaching, Snyder, leaves many souls embittered.
But I can see that as I am
I'm the wrong man for you.

MAULER *makes to go, but the meat kings stop him at the door;
they are all white as chalk.*

PACKERS:

Forgive us, noble Mauler, for seeking you out,
Disturbing you amid the involved emotions
Of your colossal head.
For we are ruined. Chaos is around us
And over us the zenith of an unknown intention.
What are you planning for us, Mauler?
What will your next step be? We're sensitive
To the blows you rain on our necks.

Enter the STOCKBREEDERS *in great commotion, equally pale.*

STOCKBREEDERS:

Damnable Mauler, is this where you've sneaked off to?
You pay for our livestock, instead of getting converted!
Your money, not your soul! You would not need
To lighten your conscience in a place like this
If you hadn't lightened our pockets! Pay for our livestock!

GRAHAM (*stepping forward*):

Permit us, Mauler, to give a brief account
Of the seven-hour battle which began this morning and ended
By plunging us all into the abyss.

MAULER:
    Oh, everlasting slaughter! Nowadays
    Things are no different from prehistoric times
    When they bloodied each other's heads with iron bars!

GRAHAM:
    Remember, Mauler, by our contract to deliver
    Meat to you, you forced us to buy meat
    In these of all times, and it had to be
    From you, as only you had meat to sell.
    Well, when you went away at noon, that Slift
    Pulled the rope even tighter around our necks.
    With harsh cries he kept on raising prices
    Until they stood at 95. But then
    A halt was called by the ancient National Bank.
    Bleating with responsibility, the old crone dumped
    Canadian yearlings on the chaotic market, and prices stood
      quivering.
    But Slift — that madman! — scarcely had he seen
    The handful of widely-travelled steers but he grabbed them
      at 95,
    As a drunkard who's already swilled an oceanful
    And still feels thirsty greedily laps up one
    Tiny drop more. The old crone shuddered at the sight.
    But some people leaped to the beldame's side to hold her up —
    Loew and Levi, Wallox and Brigham, the most reputable
      firms —
    And offered all their possessions down to the last eraser,
    As pledges that they would bring forth the last remaining steer
    From the Argentine and Canada within three days — they even
      promised
    To get hold of unborn ones, ruthlessly,
    Anything that was steerlike, calfly, hoggish!
    Slift yells: "Three days? No! Today, today!"
    And shoves the prices higher. And in floods of tears
    The banks threw themselves into the death-struggle,
    Because they had to deliver the goods and therefore buy.
    Sobbing, Levi himself punched one of Slift's brokers

In the belly, and Brigham tore his beard out
Screaming: NINETY-SIX! At that point
An elephant might have wandered in
And been crushed underfoot like a berry.
Even the pageboys, seized with despair, bit one another
Without saying a word, as horses in olden times
Would bite each others' flanks among their fighting riders!
Unsalaried clerks, famous for lack of interest in business,
Were heard gnashing their teeth that day.
And still we bought and bought; we had to buy.
Then Slift said: ONE HUNDRED! You could have heard
 a pin drop.
And as quietly as that the banks collapsed,
Like trampled sponges — formerly strong and firm,
Now suspending payment like respiration. Softly
Old Levi spoke, and all of us heard him: "Now
Take over the packing plants yourselves, we can no longer
Fulfill our contracts," and so,
Packer after packer, they sullenly laid
The shut-down, useless packing plants at your feet —
Yours and Slift's — and went away;
And the agents and salesmen snapped their brief cases shut.
And at that moment, with a sigh as of liberation —
Since no more contracts compelled its purchase —
Livestock settled into the bottomless pit.
For unto prices it was given
To fall from quotation to quotation
As water hurtles from crag to crag
Deep down into the infinite. They didn't stop before 30.
And so, Mauler, your contract became invalid.
Instead of gripping our throats you have strangled us.
What does it profit a man to grip the throat of a corpse?

MAULER:
So, Slift, that was how you managed the fight
I left on your hands!

SLIFT: Tear my head off.

MAULER:

    What good is your head?
    I'll take your hat, that's worth five cents!
    What is to become
    Of all that cattle no one has to buy?

THE STOCKBREEDERS:

    Without becoming excited
    We request you to tell us
    Whether, when and with what
    You wish to pay
    For the bought but unpaid-for cattle.

MAULER:

    At once. With that hat and this boot.
    Here is my hat for ten million, here
    My first shoe for five. I need the other.
    Are you satisfied?

THE STOCKBREEDERS:

    Alas, when moons ago
    We led the frisky calf
    And clean young steers,
    Carefully fattened, by ropes to the station in far-off Missouri
    The family yelled after us
    And even after the rolling trains,
    With voices broken by toil they yelled:
    "Don't drink the money away, fellows, and
    Let's hope prices will rise!"
    What'll we do now? How
    Can we go home? What
    Shall we tell them
    Showing the empty ropes
    And empty pockets?
    How can we go home in such a state, Mauler?

    MAN WHO WAS THERE BEFORE, *enters.*

MAN: Is Mauler here? There's a letter from New York for him.

MAULER. I *was* the Mauler to whom such letters were addressed.
    (*Opens it, reads it aside:*) "Recently, dear Pierpont, we wrote
    to tell you to buy meat. Today, however, we advise you to

arrive at a settlement with the stockbreeders and limit the
quantity of livestock, so as to give prices a chance to recover.
To this end we shall gladly be of service to you. More tomorrow, dear Pierpont. — Your friends in New York." No, no,
that won't work.

GRAHAM: What won't work?

MAULER: I have friends in New York who claim to know a way
out. It doesn't seem feasible to me. Judge for yourselves.
(*Gives them the letter.*)
How completely different
Everything seems now. Give up the chase, my friends.
Your property is gone: you must grasp that, it is lost.
But not because we are no longer blest with earthly
Goods — not everyone can be that —
Only because we have no feeling for higher things.
That's why we're poor!

MEYERS: Who are these friends of yours in New York?

MAULER: Horgan and Blackwell. Sell. . . .

GRAHAM: Would that be Wall Street?

Whispering spreads through the gathering.

MAULER: The inward man, so cruelly crushed within us. . . .

PACKERS AND STOCKBREEDERS:
Noble Mauler, consent to bring yourself
To descend to us from your lofty
Meditations! Think of the chaos
That would swoop on everything, and take up —
Since you are needed, Mauler —
The burden of responsibility again!

MAULER:
I don't like to do it.
And I won't do it alone, for the grumbling in the stockyards
And the rat-tat-tat of machine-guns
Still resound in my ears. It would only work
If it were sanctioned in a very grand style
And conceived as vital
To the public good.

Then it might work.
(*To* SNYDER:) Are there many Bible shops like this one?

SNYDER: Yes.

MAULER: How are they doing?

SNYDER: Badly.

MAULER:
Doing badly, but there are many of them.
If we promoted the cause of the Black Straw Hats
In a really big way — if you were equipped
With lots of soup and music
And suitable Bible quotations, even with shelter
In great emergencies — would you then speak
On our behalf, saying everywhere that we are good people?
Planning good things in bad times? For only
By taking extremest measures — measures that might seem harsh
Because they affect some people, quite a few really,
In short: most people, nearly everybody —
Can we preserve this system now, the system
Of buying and selling which is here to stay
And also has its seamy side.

SNYDER: For nearly everybody. I understand. We would.

MAULER (*to the* PACKERS):
I have merged your packing plants
As one ring and am taking over
Half of the stocks.

PACKERS: A great mind!

MAULER (*to the* STOCKBREEDERS):
My dear friends, listen!

They whisper.

The difficulty which oppressed us is lifting.
Misery, hunger, excesses, violence
Have one cause only and the cause is clear:
There was too much meat. The meat market was
All stuffed up this year and so the price of livestock
Sank to nothing. Now, to maintain it,

We, packers and stockbreeders, have formed a united front
To set some limits to this unbridled breeding:
To restrict the livestock coming into market
And eliminate excess from the current supply. This means
Burning one-third of the livestock total.

ALL: Simple solution!

SNYDER (*coming forward*):
Might it not be possible — if all that cattle
Is so worthless that it can be burned —
Just to give it to the many standing out there
Who could make such good use of it?

MAULER (*smiling*):
My dear Snyder, you have not grasped
The root of the situation. The many
Standing out there — *they are the buyers!*
To the others:
It's hardly credible.
All smile for a long time.
They may seem low, superfluous,
Indeed, burdensome sometimes, but it cannot elude
Profounder insight that *they* are the buyers!
Likewise — there are very many who do not understand this —
    it is essential
To lock out a third of the workers.
It is also work that has clogged our market and therefore
It must be limited.

ALL: The only way out!

MAULER: And wages lowered!

ALL: Columbus' egg!

MAULER:
All this is being done so that
In gloomy times of bloody confusion
Dehumanized humanity
When there is no end to the unrest in our cities
(For Chicago is again upset by talk of a general strike)
The brute strength of the short-sighted people

May not shatter its own tools and trample its own
  bread-baskets underfoot,
But peace and order may return. That is why we are willing
To facilitate by generous contributions
The work by which you Black Straw Hats encourage order.
It's true that there ought to be people among you again
Like that girl Joan, who inspires confidence
By her mere appearance.

A BROKER (*rushing in*): Glad tidings! The threatened strike has
been suppressed. They've jailed the criminals who impiously
troubled peace and order.

SLIFT:

Breathe freely now! The market's getting well!
Again the doldrums have been overcome.
The difficult task has once again been done
And once again a plan is finely spun
And the world resumes the way we like it run.

Organ.

MAULER:

And now, open wide your gates
Unto the weary and heavy laden and fill the pot with soup.
Tune up some music and we will sit
Upon your benches, in the very front row,
To be converted.

SNYDER: Open the doors!

The doors are flung wide open.

BLACK STRAW HATS (*singing, eyes on the door*):

Spread the net far out: they're bound to come!
They've just abandoned the last redoubt!
God's driving cold on them!
God's driving rain on them!
So they're bound to come! Spread the net far out!
Welcome! Welcome! Welcome!
Welcome to our humble home!

Bolt everything tight so that none will escape!
They're on their way down to us all right!

If they've no work to do
If they're deaf and blind too
Not one will escape! So bolt everything tight!
Welcome! Welcome! Welcome!
Welcome to our humble home!

Whatever may come, gather everything in!
Hat and head and shoe and leg and scamp and scum!
Its hat has gone sky-high
So it comes right in to cry!
Gather everything in, whatever may come!
Welcome! Welcome! Welcome!
Welcome to our humble home!

Here we stand! Watch them coming down!
Watch their misery drive them like animals to our hand!
Look, they're bound to come down!
Look, they're coming down!
They can't get away from this spot: here we stand!
Welcome! Welcome! Welcome!
Welcome to our humble home!

Stockyards. Environs of Graham's Warehouse. The yards are almost empty. Only a few groups of workers are still passing by.

JOAN (*coming up to ask*): Did three men go by here asking for a letter?

Shouting from rear, spreading toward front. Then enter FIVE MEN *escorted by* SOLDIERS: *the two from the union local and the three from the power stations. Suddenly one of the union men stands still and speaks to the soldiers.*

MAN: If you're taking us to jail now, there's something you ought to know. We did what we did because we are for you.

SOLDIER: Keep moving, if you're for us.

MAN: Wait a little!

SOLDIER: Getting scared, eh?

MAN: Yes, that too, but that's not what I'm talking about. I just want you to stand still a little so I can tell you why you have arrested us, because you don't know.

SOLDIERS (*laughing*): O.K., tell us why we arrested you.

MAN: Without property yourselves, you help men of property because you don't yet see any possibility of helping men without property.

SOLDIER: That's fine. Now let's move on.

MAN: Wait, I haven't finished the sentence: on the other hand, the working people in this town are starting to help the people without work. So the possibility is coming nearer. Now worry about that.

SOLDIER: I guess you want us to let you go, eh?

MAN: Didn't you understand me? We just want you to know that your time's coming soon too.

SOLDIERS: Can we go on now?

MAN: Yes, we can go on now.

> *They move on.*
> JOAN *stays where she is, watching the arrested men go. Then she hears two people talking beside her.*

FIRST MAN: Who are those people?

SECOND MAN:
Not one of them
Cared only for himself.
They ran without rest
To get bread for strangers.

FIRST MAN: Why without rest?

SECOND MAN: The unjust man may cross the street in the open, but the just man hides.

FIRST MAN: What's being done to them?

SECOND MAN:
Although they work for low wages and are useful to many
    men
Not one of them lives out the years of his life,
Eats his bread, dies contented
Or is honorably buried, but
They end before their time,
Struck down and trampled on and heaped with shame.

FIRST MAN: Why don't we ever hear about them?

SECOND MAN: If you read in the papers that certain criminals have been shot or thrown into prison, they're the ones.

FIRST MAN: Will it always be like that?

SECOND MAN: No.

As JOAN *turns to go, she is accosted by the* REPORTERS.

REPORTERS: Isn't this Our Lady of the Stockyards? Hi there! Things have gone wrong! The general strike was a flop. The stockyards are opening up again, but only for two-thirds of the personnel and only at two-thirds' pay. But meat prices are going up.

JOAN: Have the workers accepted this?

REPORTERS: Sure. Only a part of them knew the strike was being planned, and the cops drove that part out of the yards by force.

JOAN *falls to the ground.*

11

DEATH AND CANONIZATION OF ST. JOAN
OF THE STOCKYARDS

The BLACK STRAW HATS' *House is now richly furnished and decorated. Its doors are flung wide open; in ordered groups, the* BLACK STRAWS HATS *with new flags, packers, stockbreeders and wholesalers stand waiting for the Gloombs and Luckerniddles.*

SNYDER:
Thus our task meets happy ending:
God's foothold has been found again.
For the highest good contending,
We have faced the depths of pain.

Both our mounting and descending
Show what we can mean to you:
Lo, at last the happy ending!
Look, at last we've put it through!

Enter a group of poor people, with JOAN *at their head, supported by* TWO POLICEMEN.

POLICEMEN: Here's a homeless woman we picked up in the stockyards in a sick condition. Her last permanent residence was here, she says.

JOAN *holds her letter high as though still anxious to deliver it.*

JOAN:
The man who has perished will never
Take my letter from me.
Small enough service to a good cause, the only service
Demanded of me my whole life long! —
And I did not perform it.

While the poor people sit down on the benches to get their soup, SLIFT *consults with the packers and* SNYDER.

SLIFT: It's our own Joan. Why, her coming is like an answer to our prayers. Let's cover her with glory; by her philanthropic work in the stockyards, her championship of the poor, and even her speeches against us, she helped us over some really difficult weeks. She shall be our St. Joan of the Stockyards! We will cultivate her as a saint and refuse her no jot of respect. The fact that she is shown under our auspices will prove that we hold humaneness in high regard.

MAULER:
> May the pure and childlike soul
> Ever figure on our roll;
> May our humble choir delight
> In her singing clear and glad;
> May she damn whatever's bad
> And defend our every right.

SNYDER:
> Rise, Joan of the stockyards,
> Champion of the poor,
> Comforter of the lowest depths!

JOAN:
> What a wind in the depths! What is that shrieking
> The snow is trying to hush?
> Eat your soup, you!
> Don't spill your last bit of warmth, you
> Ragamuffins! If only I had lived
> As tranquilly as a cow,
> And yet delivered the letter that was entrusted to me!

BLACK STRAW HATS (*going up to her*):
> Sudden daylight makes her ache
> After nights of stupefaction!
> Only human was your action!
> Only human your mistake!

JOAN (*while the girls dress her in the Black Straw Hat uniform again*):
> The noise of transport is starting again, you can hear it.
> Another chance to stop it — wasted.
> Again the world runs

Its ancient course unaltered.
When it was possible to change it
I did not come; when it was necessary
That I, little person, should help,
I stayed on the sidelines.

MAULER:

Alas, that man cannot abide
In his distress the earthly bond,
But with swift and haughty stride
Rushes past the everyday
Which he thinks will turn him gray
Past his target and beyond
Into worlds outside his ken,
Endless worlds too high for men.

JOAN:

I spoke in every market place
And my dreams were numberless but
I did harm to the injured
And was useful to those who harmed them.

BLACK STRAW HATS:

Alas! All effort, sages write,
Achieves but patchwork, void of soul,
If matter make not spirit whole.

PACKERS:

And ever 'tis a glorious sight
When soul and business unite!

JOAN:

One thing I have learned and I know it in your stead,
Dying myself:
How can I say it — there's something inside you
And it won't come out! *What* do you know in your wisdom
That has no consequences?
I, for instance, did nothing.
Oh, let nothing be counted good, however helpful it may seem,
And nothing considered honorable except that
Which will change this world once for all: that's what it needs.
Like an answer to their prayers I came to the oppressors!

Oh, goodness without consequences! Intentions in the dark!
I have changed nothing.
Vanishing fruitless from this world
I say to you:
Take care that when you leave the world
You were not only good but are leaving
A good world!

GRAHAM: We'll have to see to it that her speeches only get through
if they are reasonable. We mustn't forget that she has been
in the stockyards.

JOAN:

For there is a gulf between top and bottom, wider
Than between Mount Himalaya and the sea
And what goes on above
Is not found out below
Or what happens below, above
And there are two languages, above and below
And two standards for measuring
And that which wears a human face
No longer knows itself.

PACKERS AND STOCKBREEDERS (*very loud, so as to shout* JOAN *down*):
Top and bottom must apply
For the building to be high
That's why everyone must stay
In the place where they belong
Day after day
Man must do what suits his stature
For if he forgets his nature
All our harmonies go wrong.
Underdogs have weight below,
The right man's right when up you go.
Woe to him who'd rouse that host —
Indispensable but
Demanding, not
To be done without
And aware of that —
Elements of the nethermost!

JOAN:

> But those who are down below are kept below
> So that the ones above may stay up there
> And the lowness of those above is measureless
> And even if they improve that would be
> No help, because the system they have made
> Is unique: exploitation
> And disorder, bestial and therefore
> Incomprehensible.

BLACK STRAW HATS (*to* JOAN): Be a good girl! Hold your tongue!

PACKERS:

> Those who float in boundless spaces
> Cannot rise to higher places,
> For to climb you need a rung,
> And to reach for things aloft
> You must make a downward tread!

MAULER:

> Action, alas, may break a head!

BLACK STRAW HATS:

> Though your shoe is stained with gore

PACKERS:

> Do not try to pull it off!
> You will need it more and more.

BLACK STRAW HATS:

> Keep conduct high and spirit young.
> But do not forget to rue it!

PACKERS:

> Do anything!

BLACK STRAW HATS:

> But always do it
> With a twinge of conscience, for —
> Being given to contemplation
> And to self-vituperation —
> Your conscience will be sore!
> Men of trade, be informed:
> You cannot afford

To forget the splendid
Quite indispensable
Word of the Lord
Which is never ended
And ever transformed!

JOAN:

Therefore, anyone down here who says there is a God
When none can be seen,
A God who can be invisible and yet help them,
Should have his head knocked on the pavement
Until he croaks.

SLIFT: Listen, people, you've got to say something to shut that girl up. You must speak — anything you like, but loud!

SNYDER: Joan Dark, twenty-five years old, stricken by pneumonia in the stockyards of Chicago, in the service of God: a fighter and a sacrifice!

JOAN:

And the ones that tell them they may be raised in spirit
And still be stuck in the mud, they should have their heads
Knocked on the pavement. No!
Only force helps where force rules,
And only men help where men are.

All sing the first verse of the chorale in order to stop JOAN'S *speeches from being heard.*

ALL:

Fill the full man's plate! Hosanna!
Greatness to the great! Hosanna!
To him that hath shall be given! Hosanna!
Give him city and state! Hosanna!
To the victor a sign from Heaven! Hosanna!

During these declamations loudspeakers begin to announce terrible news:

POUND CRASHES! BANK OF ENGLAND CLOSES FOR FIRST TIME IN 300 YEARS! EIGHT MILLION UNEMPLOYED IN U.S.A.! FIVE YEAR PLAN A SUCCESS! BRAZIL POURS A YEAR'S COFFEE HARVEST INTO OCEAN! SIX MILLION UNEMPLOYED IN GERMANY! THREE THOU-

SAND BANKS COLLAPSE IN U.S.A.! EXCHANGES AND BANKS CLOSED
DOWN BY GOVERNMENT IN GERMANY! BATTLE BETWEEN POLICE
AND UNEMPLOYED OUTSIDE FORD FACTORY IN DETROIT! MATCH
TRUST, BIGGEST IN EUROPE, CRASHES! FIVE YEAR PLAN IN FOUR
YEARS!

*Under the impression of this news those not engaged in decla-
mation scream abuse at one another, as:* "You slaughtered too
much livestock, you rotten butchers!" "You should have
raised more stock, you lousy stockbreeders!" "You crazy
money-grubbers, you should have employed more labor and
handed out more pay-checks! Who else will eat our meat?"
"It's the middleman that makes meat expensive!" "It's the
grain racket that raises livestock prices!" "The railroads' freight
rates are strangling us!" "The banks' interest rates are ruining
us!" "Who can pay those rents for stables and silos?" "Why
don't you start plowing under?" "We did, but you aren't!"
"The guilt is yours and yours alone!" "Things won't improve
until you're hanged!" "You should have been in jail years
ago!" "How come you're still at large?"

ALL (*sing second and third verses of chorale.* JOAN *is now inau-
dible*):
Pity the well-to-do! Hosanna!
Set them in Thy path! Hosanna!
Vouchsafe Thy grace, Hosanna!
And Thy help to him that hath! Hosanna!
Have mercy on the few! Hosanna!

ALL (JOAN's *talk is noticeably stopping*):
Aid Thy class, which in turn aids Thee, Hosanna!
With generous hand! Hosanna!
Stamp out hatred now! Hosanna!
Laugh with the laugher, allow, Hosanna!
His misdeeds a happy end! Hosanna!

*During this verse the girls have been trying to pour some soup
down* JOAN's *throat. Twice she has pushed the plate back; the
third time she seizes it, holds it high and then tips the contents
out. Then she collapses and is now lying in the girls' arms,*

mortally stricken, with no sign of life. SNYDER *and* MAULER *step toward her.*

MAULER: Give her the flag!

The flag is presented to her. It drops from her hands.

SNYDER: Joan Dark, twenty-five years of age, dead of pneumonia in the stockyards in the service of God, a fighter and a sacrifice!

MAULER:
Something pure
Without a flaw,
Uncorrupted, helpful, whole —
It thrills us common folk to awe!
Rouses in our breast a newer,
Better soul!

All stand in speechless emotion for a long time. At a sign from SNYDER, *all the flags are gently lowered over* JOAN *until she is entirely covered by them. A rosy glow illumines the picture.*

THE PACKERS AND STOCKBREEDERS:
The boast of man it that he owns
Immemorial desires
By which toward the higher zones
His spirit constantly aspires.
He sees the stars upon their thrones,
Senses a thousand ways to heaven,
Yet downward by the flesh is driven;
Then in shame his pride expires.

MAULER:
A twofold something cuts and tears
My sorely troubled inward state
Like a jagged, deep-thrust knife:
I'm drawn to what is truly great,
Free from self and the profit rate,
And yet impelled to business life
All unawares!

ALL:
Humanity! Two souls abide
Within thy breast!

Do not set either one aside:
To live with both is best!
Be torn apart with constant care!
Be two in one! Be here, be there!
Hold the low one, hold the high one —
Hold the straight one, hold the sly one —
Hold the pair!

MOTHER COURAGE

(1939)

English Version by
Eric Bentley

CHARACTERS

MOTHER COURAGE

EILIF

SWISS CHEESE } *her sons*

KATTRIN, *her daughter*

RECRUITING OFFICER

SERGEANT

COOK

COMMANDER

CHAPLAIN

ORDNANCE OFFICER

SERGEANT

YVETTE POTTIER

ONE EYE

SOLDIER

COLONEL

CLERK

OLDER SOLDIER

YOUNGER SOLDIER

FIRST SOLDIER

PEASANT

SECOND SOLDIER

PEASANT WOMAN

SOLDIER, *singing*

OLD WOMAN

YOUNG MAN

SOLDIER

LIEUTENANT

OLD PEASANT

FIRST SOLDIER

PEASANT WOMAN

SECOND SOLDIER

YOUNG PEASANT

THE TIME: 1624–1636

THE PLACE: *Sweden, Poland, Germany*

PROLOGUE: *THE SONG OF MOTHER COURAGE*

The wagon of a vivandière.

MOTHER COURAGE *sits on the wagon with her daughter* KATTRIN. *Her sons,* EILIF *and* SWISS CHEESE, *pull the wagon and join in the refrains of the song.* KATTRIN *plays a harmonica.*

Here's Mother Courage and her wagon!
 Hey, Captain, let them come and buy!
Beer by the keg! Wine by the flagon!
 Let your men drink before they die!
Sabers and swords are hard to swallow:
 First you must give them beer to drink.
Then they can face what is to follow —
 But let 'em swim before they sink!
  Christians, awake! The winter's gone!
  The snows depart, the dead sleep on.
  And though you may not long survive,
  Get out of bed and look alive!

Your men will march till they are dead, sir,
 But cannot fight unless they eat.
The blood they spill for you is red, sir,
 What fires that blood is my red meat.
For meat and soup and jam and jelly
 In this old cart of mine are found:
So fill the hole up in your belly
 Before you fill one underground.
  Christians, awake! The winter's gone!
  The snows depart, the dead sleep on.
  And though you may not long survive,
  Get out of bed and look alive!

1

Highway outside a town. A TOP SERGEANT *and a* RECRUITING
OFFICER *stand shivering.*

RECRUITING OFFICER: How the hell can you line up a squadron in
this place? You know what I keep thinking about, Sergeant?
Suicide. I'm supposed to slap four platoons together by the
twelfth — four platoons the Chief's asking for! And they're
so friendly around here, I'm scared to sleep nights. Suppose
I do get my hands on some character and squint at him so I
don't notice he's chicken-breasted and has varicose veins. I
get him drunk and relaxed, he signs on the dotted line. I pay
for the drinks, he steps outside for a minute. I get a hunch I
should follow him to the door, and am I right! Off he's shot
like a louse from a scratch. You can't take a man's word any
more, Sergeant. There's no loyalty left in the world, no trust,
no faith, no sense of honor. I'm losing my confidence in mankind, Sergeant.

SERGEANT: What they could use around here is a good war. What
else can you expect with peace running wild all over the
place? You know what the trouble with peace is? No organization. And when do you get organization? In a war. Peace is
one big waste of equipment. Anything goes, no one gives a
damn. See the way they eat? Cheese on rye, bacon on the
cheese? Disgusting! How many horses they got in this town?
How many young men? Nobody knows! They haven't
bothered to count 'em! That's peace for you!!! I been places
where they haven't had a war in seventy years and you know
what? The people can't remember their own names! They

262

don't know who they are! It takes a war to fix that. In a war, everyone registers, everyone's name's on a list. Their shoes are stacked, their corn's in the bag, you count it all up — cattle, men, *et cetera* — and you take it away! That's the story: no organization, no war!

RECRUITING OFFICER: It's the God's truth.

SERGEANT: Course, a war's like every real good deal: hard to get going. But when it's on the road, it's a pisser — everybody's scared off peace — like a crap-shooter that keeps fading to cover his loss. Course, *until* it gets going, they're just as scared off war — afraid to try anything new.

RECRUITING OFFICER: Look, a wagon! Two women and a couple of young punks. Stop 'em, Sergeant. And if there's nothing doing this time, you won't catch *me* freezing my ass in the April wind.

MOTHER COURAGE *enters on her wagon and with her children as in the prologue.*

MOTHER COURAGE: Good day to you, Sergeant.

SERGEANT *(barring the way)*: Good day! Who d'you think you are?

MOTHER COURAGE: Tradespeople.

(She prepares to go.)

SERGEANT: Halt! Where are you from, riffraff?

EILIF: Second Protestant Regiment!

SERGEANT: Where are your papers?

MOTHER COURAGE: Papers?

SWISS CHEESE: But this is Mother Courage!

SERGEANT: Never heard of her. Where'd she get a name like that?

MOTHER COURAGE: In Riga.

EILIF AND SWISS CHEESE *(reciting together)*: They call her Mother Courage because she drove through the bombardment of Riga with fifty loaves of bread in her wagon!

MOTHER COURAGE: They were going moldy, I couldn't help myself.

SERGEANT: No funny business! Where are your papers?

MOTHER COURAGE *rummages among papers in a tin box and clambers down from her wagon.*

MOTHER COURAGE: Here, Sergeant! Here's a whole Bible — I got it in Altötting to wrap my cucumbers in. Here's a map of Moravia — God knows if I'll ever get there. And here's a document saying my horse hasn't got hoof and mouth disease — too bad he died on us, he cost fifteen guilders, thank God I didn't pay it. Is that enough paper?

SERGEANT: Are you making a pass at me? Well, you got another guess coming. You must have a license and you know it.

MOTHER COURAGE: Show a little respect for a lady and don't go telling these grown children of mine I'm making a pass at you. What would I want with you? My license in the Second Protestant Regiment is an honest face — even if *you* wouldn't know how to read it.

RECRUITING OFFICER: Sergeant, we have a case of insubordination on our hands. (*To her:*) Do you know what we need in the army? (MOTHER COURAGE *starts to answer.*) Discipline!

MOTHER COURAGE: I was going to say sausages.

SERGEANT: Name?

MOTHER COURAGE: Anna Fierling.

SERGEANT: So you're all Fierlings.

MOTHER COURAGE: I was talking about me.

SERGEANT: And I was talking about your children.

MOTHER COURAGE: Must they all have the same name? This boy, for instance, I call him Eilif Noyocki — he got the name from his father who told me he was called Koyocki. Or was it Moyocki? Anyhow, the lad remembers him to this day. Only the man he remembers is someone else, a Frenchman with a pointed beard. But he certainly has his father's brains — that man could whip the pants off a farmer's behind before he could turn around. So we all have our own names.

SERGEANT: You're all called something different?

MOTHER COURAGE: Are you pretending you don't get it?

SERGEANT (*pointing at* SWISS CHEESE): He's a Chinese, I suppose.

MOTHER COURAGE: Wrong again. A Swiss.

SERGEANT: After the Frenchman?

MOTHER COURAGE: Frenchman? What Frenchman? Don't confuse the issue, Sergeant, or we'll be here all day. He's a Swiss, but he happens to be called Feyos, a name that has nothing to do with his father, who was called something else — a military engineer, if you please, and a drunkard.

SWISS CHEESE *nods, beaming; even* KATTRIN *smiles.*

SERGEANT: Then how come his name's Feyos?

MOTHER COURAGE: Oh, Sergeant, you have no imagination. *Of course* he's called Feyos: When he came, I was with a Hungarian. He didn't mind. He had a floating kidney, though he never touched a drop. He was a very *honest* man. The boy takes after him.

SERGEANT: But that wasn't his father!

MOTHER COURAGE: I said: he took after him. I call him Swiss Cheese. And that is my daughter Kattrin Haupt, she's half German.

SERGEANT: A nice family, I must say!

MOTHER COURAGE: And we've seen the whole wide world together — this wagon-load and me.

SERGEANT (*writing*): We'll need all that in writing.

RECRUITING OFFICER (*to* EILIF): So you two are the oxen for the wagon? Do they ever let you out of harness?

EILIF: Mother! May I smack him in the puss?

MOTHER COURAGE: You stay where you are. And now, gentlemen, how about a pair of pistols? Or a belt? Sergeant? Yours is worn clean through.

SERGEANT: It's something else *I'm* looking for. These lads of yours are straight as birch-trees. What are such fine specimens doing out of the army?

MOTHER COURAGE (*quickly*): The soldier's life is not for sons of mine!

RECRUITING OFFICER: Why not? It means money. It means fame. Peddling shoes is woman's work. (*To* EILIF:) Step this way and let's see if that's muscle or chicken fat.

MOTHER COURAGE: It's chicken fat. Give him a good hard look, and he'll fall right over.

RECRUITING OFFICER: Well, I hope he doesn't fall on me, that's all. (*He tries to hustle* EILIF *away.*)

MOTHER COURAGE: Let him alone! He's not for you!

RECRUITING OFFICER: He called my face a puss. That is an insult. The two of us will now go settle the affair on the field of honor.

EILIF: Don't worry, Mother, I can handle him.

MOTHER COURAGE: Stay here. You're never happy till you're in a fight. (*To the* OFFICER:) He has a knife in his boot and he knows how to use it.

RECRUITING OFFICER: I'll draw it out of him like a milk tooth. (*To* EILIF:) Come on, young fellow!

MOTHER COURAGE: Officer, I'll report you to the Colonel, and he'll throw you in jail. His lieutenant is courting my daughter.

SERGEANT (*to* OFFICER): Go easy. (*To* MOTHER COURAGE:) What have you got against the service, wasn't his own father a soldier? Didn't you say he died a soldier's death?

MOTHER COURAGE: He's dead all right. But this one's just a baby. You'll lead him like a lamb to the slaughter. I know you. You'll get five guilders for him.

RECRUITING OFFICER (*to* EILIF): First thing you know, you'll have a new cap and high boots, how about it?

EILIF: Not from you, thanks.

MOTHER COURAGE: "Let's you and me go fishing," said the angler to the worm. (*To* SWISS CHEESE:) Run and tell everybody they're trying to steal your brother! (*She draws a knife.*) Yes, just you try, and I'll cut you down like dogs! We sell cloth, we sell ham, we are peaceful people!

SERGEANT: You're peaceful all right: your knife proves that. Now tell me, how can we have a war without soldiers?

MOTHER COURAGE: Do they have to be mine?

SERGEANT: So that's the trouble! The war should swallow the pits and spit out the peach, huh? Tsk, tsk, tsk: call yourself Mother

Courage and then get scared of the war, your breadwinner? Your sons aren't scared, I know that much.

EILIF: No war can scare me.

SERGEANT: Of course not! Take me. The soldier's life hasn't done *me* any harm, has it? I enlisted at seventeen.

MOTHER COURAGE: You haven't reached seventy.

SERGEANT: I will, though.

MOTHER COURAGE: Above ground?

SERGEANT: Are you trying to rile me, telling me I'll die?

MOTHER COURAGE: Suppose it's the truth? Suppose I see it's your fate? Suppose I *know* you're just a corpse on furlough?

SWISS CHEESE: She can look into the future. Everyone says so.

RECRUITING OFFICER: Then by all means look into the Sergeant's future. It might amuse him.

SERGEANT: I don't believe in that stuff.

MOTHER COURAGE (*obeying the* OFFICER): Helmet! (SERGEANT *gives her his helmet.*)

SERGEANT: Anything for a laugh.

MOTHER COURAGE *takes a sheet of parchment and tears it in two.*

MOTHER COURAGE: Eilif, Swiss Cheese, Kattrin! So shall we all be torn asunder if we let ourselves get too deep into this war! (*To the* SERGEANT:) I'll give you the bargain rate, and do it for free. Watch! Death is black, so I draw a black cross.

SWISS CHEESE (*pointing to the second piece of parchment*): And the other she leaves blank, see?

MOTHER COURAGE: I fold them, put them in the helmet, and mix 'em up, the way we're all mixed up from our mother's womb on. Now draw!

RECRUITING OFFICER (*to* EILIF): I don't take just anybody. I'm choosy. And you've got guts, I like that.

SERGEANT (*after hesitating, fishes around in the helmet*): It's a lot of crap!

SWISS CHEESE (*watching over his shoulder*): The black cross! Oh, his number's up!

SERGEANT (*hoarsely*): You cheated me!

MOTHER COURAGE: You cheated yourself the day you enlisted. And now we must drive on. There isn't a war every day in the week.

SERGEANT: Hell, you're not getting away with this! We're taking that bastard of yours with *us!*

EILIF: I'd like that, mother.

MOTHER COURAGE: Quiet — you Finnish devil, you!

EILIF: And Swiss Cheese wants to be a soldier, too.

MOTHER COURAGE: That's news to me. I see I'll have to draw lots for all three of you. (*She goes to one side to do this.*)

RECRUITING OFFICER (*to* EILIF): People've been saying the Swedish soldier is religious. That kind of loose talk has hurt us a lot. One verse of a hymn every Sunday — and then only if you have a voice . . .

MOTHER COURAGE *returns with the slips and puts them in the* SERGEANT's *helmet.*

MOTHER COURAGE: So they'd desert their old mother, would they, the rascals? They take to war like a cat to cream! Well, there's yours, Eilif, my boy! (*As* EILIF *takes the slip, she snatches it and holds it up.*) See? A cross!

RECRUITING OFFICER (*to* EILIF): If you're going to wet your pants, I'll try your kid brother.

MOTHER COURAGE: Take yours, Swiss Cheese. You should be a better bet — you're my *good* boy. (SWISS CHEESE *draws.*) Don't tell me it's a cross? Is there no saving you either? Just look, Sergeant — a black cross!

SERGEANT: What I don't see is why *I* got one: I always stay well in the rear. (*To the* OFFICER:) It can't be a trick: it gets her own children.

MOTHER COURAGE (*to* KATTRIN): Now all I have left is you. You're a cross in yourself but you have a kind heart. (*She holds the helmet up but takes the slip herself.*) Oh dear, there must be some mistake! Don't be too kind, Kattrin, don't be too kind — there's a black cross in your path! So now you all know: be careful! Be very careful! (MOTHER COURAGE *climbs on her wagon, preparing to leave.*)

RECRUITING OFFICER (*to* SERGEANT): Do something!

SERGEANT: I don't feel too good.

RECRUITING OFFICER: Try doing business with her! (*In a loud voice:*) That belt, Sergeant, you could at least take a look at it! Hey, you, the Sergeant will take the belt!

MOTHER COURAGE: Half a guilder. Worth four times the price.

SERGEANT: It's not even a new one. But there's too much wind here. I'll go look at it behind the wagon.

MOTHER COURAGE: It doesn't seem windy to me.

SERGEANT: Maybe it's worth a half guilder at that. There's silver on it.

MOTHER COURAGE (*now following him eagerly behind the wagon*): A solid six ounces worth!

RECRUITING OFFICER (*to* EILIF): I can let you have some cash in advance, how about it?

EILIF *hesitates.* MOTHER COURAGE *is behind the wagon.*

MOTHER COURAGE: Half a guilder then. Quick.

SERGEANT: I still don't see why *I* had to draw a cross. As I told you, I always stay in the rear — it's the only place that's safe. You've ruined my afternoon, Mother Courage.

MOTHER COURAGE: You mustn't take on so. Here. Take a shot of brandy. (*He does.*) And go right on staying in the rear. Half a guilder.

The RECRUITING OFFICER *has taken* EILIF *by the arm and drawn him away.*

RECRUITING OFFICER: Ten guilders in advance, and you're a soldier of the king! The women'll be crazy about you, and you can smack me in the puss because I insulted you!

They leave. KATTRIN *makes harsh noises.*

MOTHER COURAGE: Coming, Kattrin, coming! The Sergeant's just paying his bill. (*She bites the half guilder.*) All money is suspect, Sergeant, but your half guilder is good. Let's go. Where's Eilif?

SWISS CHEESE: Gone with the recruiting officer.

Pause.

MOTHER COURAGE: Oh, you simpleton! (*To* KATTRIN:) You can't speak. You *couldn't* tell me.

SERGEANT: That's life, Mother Courage. Take a shot yourself.

MOTHER COURAGE: You must help your brother now, Kattrin.

Brother and sister get into harness together and pull the wagon. They all move off.

SERGEANT (*looking after them*):
    When a war gives you all you earn
    One day it may claim something in return!

2

IN THE YEARS 1625 AND 1626 MOTHER COURAGE JOURNEYS THROUGH
POLAND IN THE BAGGAGE TRAIN OF THE SWEDISH ARMY. SHE
MEETS HER BRAVE SON AGAIN BEFORE WALLHOF
CASTLE. OF THE SUCCESSFUL SALE OF A
CAPON AND GREAT DAYS FOR THE
BRAVE SON.

*The tent of the Swedish Commander, and the kitchen next
to it. Sound of cannon. In the kitchen:* MOTHER COURAGE *and
the* COOK. *The* COOK *has a Dutch accent.*

COOK: Sixty hellers — for that paltry piece of poultry?

MOTHER COURAGE: Paltry poultry? He's the fattest fowl you ever
saw. I could get sixty hellers for him — this Commander can
eat!

COOK: They're ten hellers a dozen on every street corner.

MOTHER COURAGE: A capon like that on every street corner? With
a siege going on and people all skin and bones? Maybe you
can find a field rat some place. I said maybe, because we're
all out of them too. All right, then, in a siege, my price for
this giant capon is fifty hellers.

COOK: *We're* doing the besieging, it's the other side that's "in a
siege"!

MOTHER COURAGE: A fat lot of difference that makes — we don't
have a thing to eat either. Look at the farmers round here.
They haven't a thing.

COOK: Sure they have. They hide it.

MOTHER COURAGE: They haven't a thing! They're ruined. They're
so hungry they dig up roots to eat. I could boil that leather
belt of yours and make their mouths water with it. And I'm
supposed to let a capon go for forty hellers?

COOK: Thirty. I said thirty hellers.

MOTHER COURAGE: I know *your* problem. If you don't find something to eat and quick, the Commander will cut your fat head off!

COOK: Look! Here's a piece of beef. I am about to roast it. I give you one more chance.

MOTHER COURAGE: Roast it. Go ahead. It's only twelve months old.

COOK: Twelve hours old! Why, only yesterday it was a cow — I saw it running around!

MOTHER COURAGE: Then it must have started stinking before it died.

COOK: I'll cook it five hours if I have to.

MOTHER COURAGE: Put plenty of pepper in.

THE SWEDISH COMMANDER, THE CHAPLAIN, *and* EILIF *enter the tent. The* COMMANDER *claps* EILIF *on the shoulder.*

COMMANDER: In your Commander's tent you go, Eilif, my son, sit at my right hand! Well done, good and faithful servant — you've played the hero in God's own war and you'll get a gold bracelet out of it yet if I have any say in the matter! We come to save their souls and what do they do, the filthy, irreligious sons of bitches? Try to hide their cattle from us — meanwhile stuffing beef into their priests at both ends! But you showed 'em — so here's a can of red wine for you. We'll drink together. (*They do so.*) The chaplain gets the dregs, he's so pious. And now, my hearty, what would you like for dinner?

EILIF: How about a slice of meat?

COOK: Nothing to eat — so he brings company to eat it.

MOTHER COURAGE: Sh!

COMMANDER: Cook! Meat!!

EILIF: Tires you out, skinning peasants. Gives you an appetite.

MOTHER COURAGE: Dear God, it's my Eilif!

COOK: Who?

MOTHER COURAGE: My eldest. It's two years since I saw him. He must be *high* in favor — the Commander inviting him to dinner! And what do you have to eat? Nothing. The Com-

mander's guest wants meat! Take my advice: buy the capon.
The price is one hundred hellers.

The COMMANDER *has sat down with* EILIF *and the* CHAPLAIN.

COMMANDER (*roaring*): Dinner, you pig! Or I'll have your head!

COOK: This is blackmail. Give me the damn thing!

MOTHER COURAGE: A paltry piece of poultry like this?

COOK: You were right. Give it here. It's highway robbery, fifty
hellers.

MOTHER COURAGE: One hundred hellers. No price is too high for
the Commander's guest of honor.

COOK: Well, you might at least pluck the wretched thing till I
have a fire going.

MOTHER COURAGE *sits down to pluck the capon.*

MOTHER COURAGE: I can't wait to see his face when he sees me.

COMMANDER: Another glass, my son! It's my favorite Falernian.
There's only one keg left but it's worth it to meet a soldier that
still believes in God! Our chaplain here only preaches. He
hasn't a clue how things get done. So now, Eilif my boy,
tell us how you fixed the peasants and grabbed the twenty
bullocks.

EILIF: It was like this. I found out the peasants had hidden the
oxen in a certain wood. The people from the town were to
pick them up there. So I let them go for their oxen in peace —
they should know better than me where they are, I said to
myself. Meanwhile I made my men crazy for meat. Their
rations were short already. I made sure they got shorter.
Finally, their mouths would water at the sound of *any* word
beginning with M — like mother.

COMMANDER: Smart kid!

EILIF: Not bad. The rest was a snap. Only the peasants had clubs —
and outnumbered us three to one. They made a murderous
attack on us. Four of them drove me into a clump of trees,
knocked my sword from my hand, and screamed: Surrender!
What now? I said to myself, they'll make mincemeat of me.

COMMANDER: So what did you do?

EILIF: I laughed.

COMMANDER: You what?

EILIF: I laughed. And so we got to talking. I came right down to business and said: "Twenty guilders an ox is too much, I bid fifteen." Like I wanted to buy. That foxed 'em. So while they were scratching their heads, I reached for my good sword and cut 'em to ribbons. Necessity knows no law, huh?

COMMANDER: What do *you* say, keeper of souls?

CHAPLAIN: Strictly speaking, that saying is not in the Bible. Our Lord made five hundred loaves out of five so that no necessity should arise. So when he told men to love their neighbors, their bellies were full. Things have changed since his day.

COMMANDER (*laughing*): Things have changed! Some wine for those wise words, you old Pharisee! Eilif my boy, you cut them to ribbons in a great cause! As for our fellows, "they were hungry and you gave them to eat!" You don't know how I value a brave soldier like you. (*He points to the map.*) Let's take a look at our position. It isn't all it might be, is it?

MOTHER COURAGE: He must be a very bad commander, this fellow.

COOK: Just a greedy one. Why bad?

MOTHER COURAGE: He says he needs *brave* soldiers. If his plan of campaign was any good, wouldn't plain ordinary soldiers do? Bravery! In a good country, such virtues wouldn't be needed. We could all be cowards and relax.

COMMANDER: I bet your father was a soldier.

EILIF: A very great soldier. My mother warned me about it. In a little song.

COMMANDER: Sing it! (*Roaring:*) Bring that meat!

EILIF: It's called The Fishwife and the Soldier.

THE FISHWIFE AND THE SOLDIER

To a soldier lad comes an old fishwife
 And this old fishwife, says she:
A gun will shoot, a knife will knife,
 You will drown if you fall in the sea.

Keep away from the ice if you want my advice,
   Says the old fishwife, says she.
The soldier laughs and loads his gun
Then grabs his knife and starts to run:
   It's the life of a hero for me!
From the north to the south I shall march through the land
With a knife at my side and a gun in my hand!
   Says the soldier lad, says he.

When the lad defies the fishwife's crics
   The old fishwife, says she:
The young are young, the old are wise,
   You will drown if you fall in the sea.
Don't ignore what I say or you'll rue it one day!
   Says the old fishwife, says she.
But gun in hand and knife at side
The soldier steps into the tide:
   It's the life of a hero for me!
When the new moon is shining on shingle roofs white
We are all coming back, go and pray for that night!
   Says the soldier lad, says he.

And the fishwife old does what she's told:
   Down upon her knees drops she.
When the smoke is gone, the air is cold,
   Your heroic deeds won't warm me!
See the smoke, how it goes! May God scatter his foes!
   Down upon her knees drops she.
But gun in hand and knife at side
The lad is swept out by the tide:
   He floats with the ice to the sea.
And the new moon is shining on shingle roofs white
But the lad and his laughter are lost in the night:
   He floats with the ice to the sea.

The third stanza has been sung by MOTHER COURAGE, *somewhat to the* COMMANDER'S *surprise.*

COMMANDER: What goes on in my kitchen? The liberties they take nowadays!

EILIF *has now left the tent for the kitchen. He embraces his mother.*

EILIF: You! Mother! Where are the others?

MOTHER COURAGE (*still in his arms*): Happy as ducks in a pond. Swiss Cheese is paymaster with the Second Protestant Regiment.

EILIF: Paymaster, eh?

MOTHER COURAGE: At least he isn't in the fighting.

EILIF: Your feet holding up?

MOTHER COURAGE: I have a bit of trouble getting my shoes on in the morning.

COMMANDER (*also in the kitchen by now*): So! You're his mother? I hope you have more sons for me like this young fellow?

EILIF: If I'm not the lucky one! To be the Commander's guest — while you sit listening in the kitchen!

MOTHER COURAGE: I heard you all right. (*She gives him a clout on the ear.*)

EILIF (*grinning*): Because I took the oxen?

MOTHER COURAGE: No. Because you didn't surrender when the four peasants tried to make mincemeat of you! Didn't I teach you to take care of yourself, you Finnish devil, you?

3

THREE YEARS PASS, AND MOTHER COURAGE, WITH PARTS OF A FINNISH
REGIMENT, IS TAKEN PRISONER. HER DAUGHTER IS SAVED, HER
WAGON LIKEWISE, BUT HER HONEST SON DIES.

A camp. The regimental flag is flying from a pole. Afternoon.
MOTHER COURAGE'S *clothes-line is tied to the wagon at one end,*
to a cannon at the other. She and KATTRIN *are folding the wash*
on the cannon. At the same time she is bargaining with an
ORDNANCE OFFICER *over a bag of bullets.* SWISS CHEESE, *wear-*
ing his Paymaster's uniform, looks on. YVETTE POTTIER, *a very*
good-looking young person, is sewing at a colored hat, a
glass of brandy before her. Her red boots are nearby; she is
in stocking feet.

ORDNANCE OFFICER: I'm letting you have the bullets for two guilders. Dirt cheap. 'Cause I need the money. The Colonel's been
drinking for three days and we're out of liquor.

MOTHER COURAGE: They're army property. If they find them here,
I'll be court-martialled. You sell your bullets, you bastards, and
send your men out to fight with nothing to shoot with.

ORDNANCE OFFICER: If you scratch my back, I'll scratch yours.

MOTHER COURAGE: I won't touch army stuff. Not at that price.

ORDNANCE OFFICER: You can resell 'em for five guilders, maybe
eight — to the Ordnance Officer of the 4th Regiment. All you
have to do is give him a receipt for twelve. He hasn't a bullet
left.

MOTHER COURAGE: Why don't you do it yourself?

ORDNANCE OFFICER: I don't trust him: we're friends.

MOTHER COURAGE (*taking the bag, to* KATTRIN): Take it round the
back and pay him a guilder and a half. (*As the* OFFICER *starts to*
protest:) A guilder and a half! (KATTRIN *drags the bag away,*
the OFFICER *follows. To* SWISS CHEESE:) Here's your under-

wear. Take care of it. It's October, autumn may come at any time. I don't say it must, but it may. Nothing *must* come, not even the seasons. Only your books *must* balance. Do your books balance, Mr. Paymaster?

SWISS CHEESE: Yes, Mother.

MOTHER COURAGE: Don't forget they made you paymaster because you're honest and so simple you'd never think of running off with the cash. Don't lose that underwear.

SWISS CHEESE: No, Mother. I'll put it under the mattress.

ORDNANCE OFFICER: I'll go with you, Paymaster.

MOTHER COURAGE: Don't teach him any finagling.

THE ORDNANCE OFFICER *and* SWISS CHEESE *leave.*

YVETTE (*waving to the* OFFICER): You might at least say good-bye!

MOTHER COURAGE (*to* YVETTE): I don't like that: he's no company for my Swiss Cheese. But the war's not making a bad start: if I look ahead and make no mistakes, business will be good. (*Noticing the brandy:*) Don't you know you shouldn't drink in the morning — with your sickness and all?

YVETTE: Who says I'm sick? That's a libel!

MOTHER COURAGE: They all say so.

YVETTE: Then they're all liars! I'm desperate, Mother Courage. They avoid me like a stinking fish. Because of those lies! So what am I fixing this hat for? (*She throws it down.*) That's why I drink in the morning. It gives you crow's feet, so what? The whole regiment knows me. I should have stayed home when my first was unfaithful. But pride isn't for the likes of us. You eat dirt or down you go.

MOTHER COURAGE: Don't start in again about your friend Peter Piper and How It All Happened — in front of my innocent daughter.

YVETTE: She's the one that *should* hear it. So she'll get hardened against love.

MOTHER COURAGE: That's something no one ever gets hardened against.

YVETTE: He was an army cook, blond, Dutch, and thin. Kattrin, beware of thin men! I didn't. I didn't even know he'd had another girl before me and she called him Peter Piper because he never took his pipe out of his mouth even in bed — it meant so little to him. (*She sings:*)

THE CAMP FOLLOWER'S SONG

Scarce seventeen was I when
  The foe came to our land
And laid aside his saber
  And took me by the hand.
    And we performed by day
    The sacred rite of May
    And we performed by night
    Another sacred rite.
    The regiment, well exercised,
    Presented arms, then stood at ease,
    Then took us off behind the trees
    Where we fraternized.

Each of us had her foe and
  A cook fell to my lot.
I hated him by daylight
  But in the dark did not.
    So we perform by day
    The sacred rite of May
    And we perform by night
    That other sacred rite.
    The regiment, well exercised,
    Presents its arms, then stands at ease,
    Then takes us off behind the trees
    Where we fraternize.

Ecstasy filled my heart, O
  My love seemed heaven-born!
Yet why were people saying
  It was not love but scorn?
    The springtime's soft amour
    Through summer may endure

But swiftly comes the fall
And winter ends it all.
December came. All of the men
Filed past the trees where once we hid
Then quickly marched away and did
Not come back again.

YVETTE: I made the mistake of running after him. I never found him. It's ten years ago now. (YVETTE *goes behind the wagon.*)

MOTHER COURAGE: You're leaving your hat.

YVETTE: For the birds.

MOTHER COURAGE: Let that be a lesson to you, Kattrin: never start anything with a soldier. Love does seem heaven-born, so watch out: they tell you they worship the ground under your feet — did you wash 'em yesterday, while we're on the subject? — then, if you don't look out, you're their slave for life.

THE CHAPLAIN *comes in with the* COOK.

CHAPLAIN: Mother Courage, I bring a message from your son Eilif. The cook came with me — you've made an impression on him.

COOK: Oh, I thought I'd get a little whiff of the breeze.

MOTHER COURAGE: You're welcome to it, but what does Eilif want? I don't have any money!

CHAPLAIN: My message is for his brother, the paymaster.

MOTHER COURAGE: He's not here. He's not anywhere. Look, he is not his brother's paymaster: I won't have him led into temptation! (*She takes money from a purse.*) Give him this. But it's a sin — he's speculating in mother love.

COOK: Maybe not for long. How d'you know he'll come back alive? You're hard, you women. A glass of brandy wouldn't cost you much. But no, you say, no — and six feet under goes your man.

CHAPLAIN: My dear Cook, you talk as if dying for one's beliefs were a misfortune — it is the highest privilege! This is not just any war, remember, it is a religious war, and therefore pleasing unto God.

COOK: I see that. In one sense it's a war because of all the cheating, plunder, rape, and so forth, but it's different from all other wars because it's a religious war and therefore pleasing unto God. At that it does make you thirsty.

CHAPLAIN (*to* MOTHER COURAGE): He says you've bewitched him. He says he dreams about you.

COOK (*lighting his pipe*): Innocent dreams! I dream of a fair lady dispensing brandy! Stop embarrassing me! The stories you were telling on the way over still have me blushing.

MOTHER COURAGE: I must get you two something to drink, or you'll be making improper advances out of sheer boredom.

CHAPLAIN: That is indeed a temptation — said the Court Chaplain, as he gave way to it. And who is this captivating young person?

MOTHER COURAGE (*looking at Kattrin*): That is not a captivating young person. That is a respectable young person. (*And she goes with* COOK *and* CHAPLAIN *behind the wagon.*)

MOTHER COURAGE: The trouble with Poland is the Poles. It's true our Swedish king moved in on them with his army — but instead of maintaining the peace the Poles would keep interfering. So their blood is on their own heads, *I* say.

CHAPLAIN: Anyway, since the German Kaiser had enslaved them, King Gustavus had no alternative but to liberate them!

COOK: Just what *I* always say. Your health, Mother Courage, your brandy is first-rate, I'm never mistaken in a face. This war is a religious war.

KATTRIN *watches them go behind the wagon, leaves the washing, picks up the hat, sits, takes up the red boots. The* COOK *sings:*

LUTHER'S HYMN

A mighty fortress is our God
A bulwark never failing.
Our helper He, amid the flood
Of mortal ills prevailing.
For still our ancient Foe
Doth seek to work us woe.
His craft and power are great
And armed with cruel hate
On earth is not his equal.

COOK: And King Gustavus liberated Poland from the Germans. Who could deny it? Then his appetite grew with eating, and he liberated *Germany* from the Germans. Made quite a profit on the deal, I'm told.

CHAPLAIN: That is a calumny! The Swedish king puts religion first!

MOTHER COURAGE: What's more, you eat his bread.

COOK: I don't eat his bread: I bake his bread.

MOTHER COURAGE: He'll never be conquered, that man, and you know why? We all back him up — the little fellows like you and me. Oh yes, to hear the big fellows talk, they're fighting for their beliefs and so on, but if you look into it, you find they're not that silly: they do want to make a profit on the deal. So you and I back them up!

COOK: Surely.

CHAPLAIN (*pointing to flag, to* COOK): And as a Dutchman you'd do well to look which flag is flying here!

MOTHER COURAGE: To our Protestant flag!

COOK: A toast!

And now KATTRIN *has begun to strut about with hat and boots on. Suddenly: cannon and shots. Drums.* MOTHER COURAGE, THE COOK, *and* THE CHAPLAIN *rush round to the front of the wagon, the two last with glasses in their hands. The* ORDNANCE OFFICER *and a* SOLDIER *come running for the cannon. They try to push it.*

MOTHER COURAGE: Hey, let me get my wash off that gun!

ORDNANCE OFFICER: Surprise attack! The Catholics! We don't know if we can get away! (*To the* SOLDIER:) Bring that gun! (*He runs off.*)

COOK: Good God! I must go to the commander. Mother Courage, I'll be back soon — for a short conversation. (*He rushes off.*)

MOTHER COURAGE: Hey, you're leaving your pipe!

COOK (*off*): Keep it for me, I 'll need it!

MOTHER COURAGE: This *would* happen just when we were making money.

CHAPLAIN: "Blessed are the peacemakers!" A good slogan for

wartime. Well, I must be going too. Yes, if the enemy's so close, it can be dangerous. I wish I had a cloak.

MOTHER COURAGE: I'm lending no cloaks. Not even to save a life. I've had experience in that line.

CHAPLAIN: But I'm in special danger — because of my religion!

MOTHER COURAGE (*bringing him a cloak*): It's against my better judgment. Now run!

CHAPLAIN: Thank you, you're very generous, but on second thought I better stay put. If I run, I might attract attention.

THE SOLDIER *is still struggling with the cannon.*

MOTHER COURAGE: Let it alone, you idiot, who's going to pay you for this? *You'll* pay — with your life. Let me keep it for you.

SOLDIER (*running off*): You're my witness: I tried!

MOTHER COURAGE: I'll swear to that. (*And now she sees* KATTRIN *with the hat and boots.*) Yvette's hat! Take it off this minute! Are you crazy — with the enemy coming? (*She tears it off her head.*) They'll make a whore of you when they see it! And she has the boots on, too, straight from Babylon, I'll soon fix that. (*She pulls at the boots.*) Chaplain, help me with these boots, I'll be right back. (*She runs to the wagon.*)

YVETTE *enters, powdering her face.*

YVETTE: What's this — the Catholics are coming? Where's my hat? Who's been trampling on it? I can't run around in that, what will they think of me? And I've no mirror. (*Coming very close to the* CHAPLAIN:) How do I look? Too much powder?

CHAPLAIN: No — er — just right.

YVETTE: And where are my red boots? (KATTRIN *is hiding her feet under her skirt.*) I left them here! Must I go barefoot? It's a scandal.

Exit YVETTE. SWISS CHEESE *comes running on with a cash-box. Enter* MOTHER COURAGE, *her hands smeared with ashes.*

MOTHER COURAGE (*to* SWISS CHEESE): What have you got there?

SWISS CHEESE: The regimental cash-box.

MOTHER COURAGE: Throw it away! Your paymastering days are over!

SWISS CHEESE: But they trusted me with it! (*He goes to one side.*)

MOTHER COURAGE (*to the* CHAPLAIN): Take your pastor's coat off, or they'll recognize you, cloak or no cloak. (*She is rubbing ashes into* KATTRIN's *face.*) Keep still! A little dirt, and you're safe. When a soldier sees a clean face, there's one more whore in the world. That does it. Now stop trembling. Nothing can happen now. (*To* SWISS CHEESE:) Where've you put that cash-box?

SWISS CHEESE: I thought I'd just leave it in the wagon.

MOTHER COURAGE: In my wagon?! Why, they'll hang all three of us!

SWISS CHEESE: Somewhere else then. Maybe I'll run away some place.

MOTHER COURAGE: It's too late for that.

CHAPLAIN (*still changing his clothes*): For Heaven's sake, that Protestant flag!

MOTHER COURAGE (*taking the flag down*): I've had it twenty-five years. I don't notice it any more.

The sound of cannon grows. Blackout. Three days later. Morning. The cannon is gone. MOTHER COURAGE, KATTRIN, THE CHAPLAIN, *and* SWISS CHEESE *sit eating anxiously.*

SWISS CHEESE: This is the third day I've sat doing nothing. The sergeant has always been patient with me, but by this time he must be asking himself: Now where is Swiss Cheese with that cash-box?

MOTHER COURAGE: Be glad they're not on the trail.

CHAPLAIN: What about me? I can't even hold service here. It is written: "Out of the abundance of the heart the tongue speaketh" — but woe is me if *my* tongue speaketh!

MOTHER COURAGE: So here you sit — one with his religion, the other with his cash-box! I don't know which is more dangerous.

CHAPLAIN: We're in God's hands now.

MOTHER COURAGE: Oh, I hope we're not as desperate as *that!* But it *is* hard to sleep at night. It'd be easier if you weren't here, Swiss Cheese. All the same I've not done badly.

CHAPLAIN: The milk is good. As for the quantity, we may have to reduce our Swedish appetites somewhat. We are defeated.

MOTHER COURAGE: Who's defeated? There've been cases where a defeat is a victory for the little fellows, it's only their honor that's lost, nothing serious. At that, either victory or defeat can be a costly business. The best thing, *I* say, is for politics to kind of get stuck in the mud. (*To* SWISS CHEESE:) Eat!

SWISS CHEESE: I don't like it. How will the sergeant pay the men?

MOTHER COURAGE: Soldiers in flight don't get paid.

SWISS CHEESE: Then they should refuse to flee! No pay, no flight!

MOTHER COURAGE: Swiss Cheese, I've brought you up honest because you're not very bright, but don't overdo it! And now I'm going with the Chaplain to buy a Catholic flag and some meat. (*She disappears into the wagon.*)

CHAPLAIN: She's worried about the cash-box.

SWISS CHEESE: I can get rid of it.

CHAPLAIN: You may be seen. They have spies everywhere. Yesterday one jumped out of the very hole I was relieving myself in. I was so scared I almost broke into a prayer — think how *that* would have given me away! He was a little brute with a patch over one eye.

MOTHER COURAGE *clambers out of the wagon with a basket.*

MOTHER COURAGE (*to* KATTRIN, *holding up the red boots*): You shameless little hussy! She went and snitched them — because you called her a captivating young person. (*She puts them in the basket. To* KATTRIN:) Stealing Yvette's boots! She at least gets paid for it, you just *enjoy* strutting like a peacock! Save your proud ways for peacetime!

CHAPLAIN: I don't find her proud.

MOTHER COURAGE: I like her when people say, I never even noticed her. I like her when she's a stone in Dalarna, where there's nothing but stones. (*To* SWISS CHEEESE:) Leave the cash-box where it is, and look after your sister, she needs it. You two are more trouble than a bag of fleas.

MOTHER COURAGE *and* THE CHAPLAIN *leave.* KATTRIN *clears the dishes away.*

SWISS CHEESE: Not many days more when you can sit in the sun in your shirtsleeves. (KATTRIN *points to a tree.*) Yes, the leaves are yellow already. (*With gestures,* KATTRIN *asks if he wants a drink.*) No, I'm not drinking, I'm thinking. (*Pause.*) Mother says she can't sleep, so I *should* take the cash-box away. I have a place for it: the mole-hole by the river. I can pick it up there — late tonight maybe — and take it to the sergeant. How far can they have fled in three days? The sergeant's eyes'll pop! "You've disappointed me most pleasantly, Swiss Cheese," he'll say, "*I* trust you with the cash-box, and *you* bring it back!" Yes, Kattrin, I *will* have a glass now.

When KATTRIN *gets behind the wagon, two men confront her. One is a* SERGEANT; *the other doffs his hat and flourishes it in a showy greeting; he has a patch over one eye.*

ONE EYE: Morning, young lady! Have you seen a staff officer from the Second Protestant Regiment?

KATTRIN *is terrified and runs away, spilling her brandy. The two men look at each other, see* SWISS CHEESE, *and withdraw.*

SWISS CHEESE (*starting up*): You're spilling it, can't you see where you're going? I don't understand you. Anyway, I must be leaving. That's what I've decided on. (*He stands up. She tries to make him understand the danger he is in. He pushes her away.*) I know you mean well, poor thing, you just can't get it out. And don't worry about the brandy. I'll live to drink so much brandy — what's one glass? (*He takes the cash-box out of the wagon and puts it under his coat.*) I'll be right back, but don't hold me up, or I'll have to scold you. Yes, I know you're trying to help!

He kisses her as she tries to hold him back, and pulls himself free. Exit SWISS CHEESE. KATTRIN *is now desperate. She runs up and down, making little sounds.* MOTHER COURAGE *and* THE CHAPLAIN *return.* KATTRIN *rushes at her mother.*

MOTHER COURAGE: What is it, what is it, control yourself! Have they done something to you? Where's Swiss Cheese? (*To the* CHAPLAIN:) And don't you stand around — get that Catholic flag up!

She takes the flag from her basket. THE CHAPLAIN *runs it up the pole.*

CHAPLAIN: God bless our Catholic flag!

MOTHER COURAGE: Now calm down, Kattrin, and tell me all about it. What? That little rascal has taken the cash-box away? Oh, he's going to get a good whipping! Now take your time, don't try to talk, use your hands. I don't like that howling — what will the Chaplain think? A man with one eye? Here?

CHAPLAIN: That fellow is an informer. They've captured Swiss Cheese?

KATTRIN *shakes her head, then shrugs her shoulders. Voices off.* ONE EYE *and the same* SERGEANT *bring in* SWISS CHEESE.

SWISS CHEESE: Let me go! I've nothing on me. You're breaking my shoulder. I am innocent!

SERGEANT: This is where he comes from. These are his friends.

MOTHER COURAGE: Us? Since when?

SWISS CHEESE: I was just getting my lunch here. I paid ten hellers for it. Maybe you saw me on that bench. The food was too salty.

MOTHER COURAGE: That's true. He got his lunch here. And it was too salty.

SERGEANT: Are you pretending you don't know him?

MOTHER COURAGE: I can't know all of them.

CHAPLAIN: He sat there like a law-abiding citizen and never opened his mouth except to eat. Which is necessary.

SERGEANT: Who d'you think you are?

MOTHER COURAGE: He's my bartender. And you must be thirsty. I'll bring you some brandy.

SERGEANT: No liquor while on duty. (*To* SWISS CHEESE:) You were carrying something. You must have hidden it. We saw the bulge in your shirt.

MOTHER COURAGE: Are you sure it was him?

SWISS CHEESE: I think you mean another fellow. There *was* a fellow with something under his shirt. I saw him.

MOTHER COURAGE: I think so too. It's a misunderstanding. Could happen to anyone. Oh, I know what people are like. I'm Mother Courage and I can tell you this: he looks honest.

SERGEANT: We want the regimental cash-box. And we know the looks of the fellow that's been taking care of it. It's you!

SWISS CHEESE: No! No, it's not!

SERGEANT: If you don't shell out, you're dead, see!

MOTHER COURAGE: Oh, he'd give it to you to save his life, he's not that stupid! Speak up, my boy, the sergeant's giving you one last chance!

SWISS CHEESE: What if I don't have it?

SERGEANT: We'll get it out of you.

ONE EYE *and the* SERGEANT *lead him off.*

MOTHER COURAGE (*shouting after them*): He'll tell you! He's not *that* stupid! And don't you break his shoulder!

She runs a little way after them. Blackout. The same evening. The CHAPLAIN *and* KATTRIN *are waiting.*

MOTHER COURAGE (*entering*): It's a matter of life and death. But the sergeant will still listen to us. Only he mustn't know it's our Swiss Cheese — or they'll say we helped him. It's just a matter of money. But where can *we* get money? Wasn't Yvette here? I just talked with her. She's picked up a Colonel, and she says he might buy her a canteen business.

CHAPLAIN: You'd sell the wagon, everything?

MOTHER COURAGE: Where else would I get the money for the sergeant?

CHAPLAIN: What are you going to live off?

MOTHER COURAGE: That's just it.

Enter YVETTE *with a hoary old* COLONEL. *She embraces* MOTHER COURAGE.

YVETTE: Dear Mrs. Fierling, we meet again! (*Whispering:*) He didn't say no. (*Loud:*) This is my friend, my . . . business adviser. I heard you might want to sell your wagon.

MOTHER COURAGE: I want to pawn it, not sell it. And nothing hasty. You don't find another wagon like this in a hurry.

YVETTE: In that case, I'm not sure I'd be interested. What do *you* think, my dear?

COLONEL: I agree with you, honey bun.

MOTHER COURAGE: It's only for pawn.

YVETTE: But I thought you *had* to have the money?

MOTHER COURAGE: I do have to. But I'd rather run my feet off looking for another offer than just sell. We live off that wagon.

COLONEL: Take it! Take it!

YVETTE: My friend thinks I might take it. (*Turning to him:*) But
you think we should buy it outright, don't you?

COLONEL: Oh, I do, bunny, I do!

MOTHER COURAGE: Then you must find one that's for sale.

YVETTE: Yes! We can travel around looking for one! I love going
around looking. Especially with you, Poldy!

COLONEL: Really? Do you?

YVETTE: Oh, I love it. I could take weeks of it!

COLONEL: Really? Could you?

YVETTE: If you get the money, when would you pay it back?

MOTHER COURAGE: In two weeks. Maybe one.

YVETTE: I can't make up my mind. Poldy, chéri, advise me! (*Aside
to him:*) She'll have to sell, don't worry. That lieutenant —
the blond one — remember? — he'll lend me the money. He's
crazy about me. He says I remind him of someone. What do
you advise?

COLONEL: Oh, I have to warn you against *him*: he's no good, he'll
only exploit the situation. I told you, bunny, I told you I'd
buy you something? Didn't I tell you that?

YVETTE: I can't let you.

COLONEL: Oh, please, please!

YVETTE: Well, if you think the lieutenant might exploit the
situation?

COLONEL: I do think so.

YVETTE: So you advise me to go ahead?

COLONEL: I do, bunny, I do!

YVETTE (*returning to* MOTHER COURAGE): My friend says all right:
two hundred guilders. And I need a receipt saying the wagon
would be mine in two weeks. With everything in it. I'll look
it all over right now. The two hundred can wait. (*To the*
COLONEL:) You go on ahead to the camp. I'll follow.

COLONEL (*helping her up the steps of the wagon*): I'll help you up. Come soon, honey bun. (*Exit* COLONEL.)

MOTHER COURAGE: Yvette, Yvette!

YVETTE: There aren't many shoes left.

MOTHER COURAGE: Yvette, this is no time for an inventory, yours or not yours. You promised to talk to the sergeant about Swiss Cheese. There isn't a minute to lose. He's up for court martial one hour from now.

YVETTE: I want to check through these shirts.

MOTHER COURAGE *drags her down the steps by the skirt.*

MOTHER COURAGE: You hyena! Swiss Cheese's life is at stake! And don't say where the money comes from. Pretend he's your sweetheart, or we'll all get it in the neck for helping him.

YVETTE: I arranged to meet One Eye in the bushes. He must be there by now.

CHAPLAIN: And don't give him the whole two hundred. A hundred and fifty should do the trick.

MOTHER COURAGE: You keep your nose out of this! I'm not doing you out of *your* porridge. Now run, and no haggling! Remember his life's at stake! (*She pushes* YVETTE *off.*)

CHAPLAIN: All I meant was: what are we going to live on?

MOTHER COURAGE: I'm counting on that cash-box. At the very least, Swiss Cheese'll get paid out of it.

CHAPLAIN: But d'you think Yvette can manage this?

MOTHER COURAGE: It's in her interest — if I don't pay their two hundred, she won't get the wagon. And she knows the score: she won't have this colonel on the string forever. Kattrin, go clean the knives! And don't you just stand around: wash those glasses: there'll be fifty cavalrymen here tonight . . . I think they'll let us have him. They're not wolves, they're human and after money. God is merciful and men are bribable — that's how His will is done on earth, I don't know about Heaven.

YVETTE (*entering*): They'll do it for two hundred if you make it snappy. He confessed he'd had the cash-box, they put the thumb screws on him, but he threw it in the river when he saw them coming at him. Shall I go get the money from my colonel?

MOTHER COURAGE: The cash-box in the river? How'll I ever get my two hundred back?

YVETTE: You were expecting to get it from the cash-box? I *would* have been sunk. Mother Courage, if you want your Swiss Cheese, you'll have to pay. Or shall I let the whole thing drop — so you can keep your wagon?

MOTHER COURAGE: Now I *can't* pay two hundred. I must hold on to something. Go say I'll pay one hundred twenty or the deal's off. Even at that I lose the wagon.

YVETTE: One Eye's in a hurry. Looks over his shoulder the whole time. Hadn't I better just give them the two hundred?

MOTHER COURAGE: I have her to think of. She's twenty-five and still no husband. I know what I'm doing. One hundred twenty or no deal.

YVETTE: You know best.

> YVETTE *runs off. After walking up and down abstractedly,* MOTHER COURAGE *sits down to help* KATTRIN *with the knives.*

MOTHER COURAGE: I *will* pay two hundred if I have to. With eighty guilders we could pack a hamper and begin over. It won't be the end of the world.

CHAPLAIN: The Bible says: the Lord will provide.

MOTHER COURAGE (*to* KATTRIN): You must rub them dry.

YVETTE (*re-enters*): They won't do it. I warned you. He said the drums would roll any second now — and that's the sign they've reached a verdict. I offered one hundred fifty. He didn't even shrug his shoulders.

MOTHER COURAGE: Tell him I'll pay two hundred. Run! (YVETTE *runs,* MOTHER COURAGE *sits,* THE CHAPLAIN *has finished the glasses.*) I believe — I haggled too long.

> *In the distance: a roll of drums. The* CHAPLAIN *stands up and walks away.* MOTHER COURAGE *remains seated. It grows dark; it gets light again.* MOTHER COURAGE *has not moved.*

YVETTE (*re-enters, pale*): You've done it — with your haggling. You can keep your wagon now. He got eleven bullets in him.

I don't know why I still bother about you, you don't deserve it, but I just happened to hear they don't think the cash-box is really in the river. They think it's here. And they think you were in with him. I think they're going to bring his body, to see if you give yourself away when you see him. You'd better not know him or we're in for it. And I should tell you straight: they're right behind me. Shall I keep Kattrin out of this? (MOTHER COURAGE *shakes her head.*) Does she know? Maybe she didn't hear the drums or didn't understand.

MOTHER COURAGE: She knows. Bring her.

YVETTE *brings* KATTRIN *who stands by her mother, who takes her hand. Two men come on with a stretcher. There is a sheet over it, and something underneath. Beside them, the* SERGEANT. *They put the stretcher down.*

SERGEANT: There's a man here we don't know the name of, but he has to be registered to keep the records straight. He bought a meal from you. Look at him. See if you know him. (*He draws back the sheet.*) You know him? (MOTHER COURAGE *shakes her head.*) What? You never saw him before he bought that meal? (MOTHER COURAGE *shakes her head.*) Lift him up. Throw him on the garbage dump. He has no one that knows him.

They carry him off.

4

Outside an officer's tent. MOTHER COURAGE *waits. A* REGIMENTAL
CLERK *looks out of the tent.*

REGIMENTAL CLERK: You want to speak to the captain? I know you.
You had a Protestant paymaster with you. He was hiding out.
Better make no complaint here.

MOTHER COURAGE: But I'm innocent and if I give up it'll look like
I have a bad conscience. They cut my wagon to ribbons with
their sabers, and then claimed a fine of five thalers — for nothing, for less than nothing!

REGIMENTAL CLERK (*quietly*): For your own good: keep your
mouth shut. We haven't many canteens, so we let you stay
in business, especially if you've a bad conscience and have to
pay a fine now and then.

MOTHER COURAGE: I'm going to lodge a complaint.

REGIMENTAL CLERK: As you wish. Wait here till the captain is free.

The CLERK *retires into the tent.* A YOUNG SOLDIER *comes storm-
ing in.*

YOUNG SOLDIER: Screw the captain! Where is the son of a bitch?
Grabbing my reward, spending it on brandy for his whores! I'll
rip his belly open!

OLDER SOLDIER (*following him*): Shut your hole, you'll only wind
up in the stocks!

YOUNG SOLDIER: I was the only one in the squad who swam the
river and *he* grabs the money. I can't even buy me a beer.
Come out, you thief, I'll make lamb chops out of you!

OLDER SOLDIER: Holy Christ, he'll destroy himself.

YOUNG SOLDIER (*pulling himself free of the older man*): Let me go
or I'll cut you down too!

OLDER SOLDIER: Saved the colonel's horse and didn't get the reward. He's young. He hasn't been at it long.

MOTHER COURAGE: Let him go. He doesn't have to be chained like a dog. Very reasonable to want a reward. Why else should he go to the trouble?

YOUNG SOLDIER: He's in there pouring it down. I done something special: I want the reward!

MOTHER COURAGE: Young man, don't scream at *me*, I have my own problems.

YOUNG SOLDIER: He's whoring on my money and I'm hungry! I'll murder him!

MOTHER COURAGE: You're hungry. You're angry. I understand.

YOUNG SOLDIER: Talking'll get you nowhere. I won't stand for injustice!

MOTHER COURAGE: How long? How long won't you stand for injustice? One hour? Or two? It's a misery to sit in the stocks: especially if you leave it till then to realize you do stand for injustice.

YOUNG SOLDIER: I don't know why I listen to you. Screw that captain!

MOTHER COURAGE: You listen because you know I'm right. Your rage has calmed down already. It was a short one, and you'd need a long one.

YOUNG SOLDIER: Are you trying to tell me I shouldn't ask for the money?

MOTHER COURAGE: Just the opposite. I only say your rage won't last, you'll get nowhere with it. If your rage was a long one, I'd say: go ahead, slice him up. But what's the use — if you don't slice him up? What's the use if you stand there with your tail between your legs?

OLDER SOLDIER: You're quite right: he's crazy.

YOUNG SOLDIER: All right, we'll see whether I slice him up or not. (*He draws his sword.*) When he comes out, I slice him up.

CLERK (*looking out again*): The captain will be right out. (*A military order:*) Be seated!

The YOUNG SOLDIER *sits.*

MOTHER COURAGE: What did I tell you? Oh, they know us inside
out. "Be seated!" And we sit. *I'm* no better. Let me tell you
about the great capitulation.

THE GREAT CAPITULATION

Long, long ago, a green beginner
   I thought myself a special case.
(None of your ordinary, run of the mill girls, with my looks
and my talent and my love of the Higher Things.)
I picked a hair out of my dinner
   And put the waiter in his place.
(All or nothing. Anyway, never the second best. I am the
master of my fate. I'll take no orders from no one.)
Then a little bird whispers!
     The bird says: "Wait a year or so
     And marching with the band you'll go
     Keeping in step, now fast, now slow,
     And piping out your little spiel.
     Then one day the battalions wheel!
     And you go down upon your knees
     To God Almighty if you please!"

My friend, before that year was over
   I'd learned to drink their cup of tea.
(Two children round your neck and the price of bread and
what all!)
When they were through with me, moreover,
   They had me where they wanted me.
(You must get in with people. If you scratch my back, I'll
scratch yours. Don't stick your neck out!)
Then a little bird whispers!
     The bird says: "Scarce a year or so
     And marching with the band she'd go
     Keeping in step, now fast, now slow,
     And piping out her little spiel.
     Then one day the battalions wheel!

> And she goes down upon her knees
> To God Almighty if you please!"

Our plans are big, our hopes colossal.
   We hitch our wagon to a star.
(Where there's a will, there's a way. You can't hold a good man down.)
"We can lift mountains," says the apostle.
   And yet: how heavy one cigar!
(You must cut your coat according to your cloth.)
That little bird whispers!
> The bird says: "Wait a year or so
> And marching with the band we go
> Keeping in step, now fast, now slow,
> And piping out our little spiel.
> Then one day the battalions wheel!
> And we go down upon our knees
> To God Almighty if you please!"

MOTHER COURAGE: So stay here with your sword drawn, if your anger is big enough. If it isn't, you'd better go.

YOUNG SOLDIER: Aw, shove it! (*He stumbles off, the* OLDER SOLDIER *following him.*)

REGIMENTAL CLERK (*again sticking his head out*): The captain is free now. You can lodge your complaint.

MOTHER COURAGE: I've thought better of it. I'm not complaining.

She leaves. The CLERK *looks after her, shaking his head.*

5

TWO YEARS HAVE PASSED. THE WAR COVERS WIDER AND WIDER TER-
RITORY. ALWAYS ON THE MOVE, THE LITTLE WAGON CROSSES
POLAND, MORAVIA, BAVARIA, ITALY, AND AGAIN
BAVARIA. 1631. GENERAL TILLY'S VICTORY
AT LEIPZIG COSTS MOTHER
COURAGE FOUR SHIRTS.

The wagon stands in a war-ruined village. Victory march in the distance. TWO SOLDIERS *are being served at a counter by* KATTRIN *and* MOTHER COURAGE. *One of them has a woman's fur coat about his shoulders.*

MOTHER COURAGE: What, you can't pay? No money, no schnapps! If they can play victory marches, they should pay their men.

FIRST SOLDIER: I want my schnapps! I arrived too late for plunder. The Chief allowed just one hour to plunder the town. He's not inhuman, he says — so I guess they bought him off.

CHAPLAIN (*staggering in*): There are people in the farmhouse. A whole family. Help me, someone! I need linen.

The SECOND SOLDIER *goes with him.* KATTRIN, *becoming excited, tries to get her mother to bring linen out of the wagon.*

MOTHER COURAGE: I have none. I sold all my bandages to the regiment. I'm not tearing up my officer's shirts for these people.

CHAPLAIN (*over his shoulder*): I said: I need linen!

MOTHER COURAGE *stops* KATTRIN *from entering the wagon.*

MOTHER COURAGE: Not on your life! They have nothing and they pay nothing.

The CHAPLAIN *carries in a* WOMAN.

CHAPLAIN: Why did you stay there — in the line of fire?

WOMAN (*faintly*): Our farm . . .

297

MOTHER COURAGE: Think they'd ever let go of anything? And now *I'm* supposed to pay. Well, I won't!

FIRST SOLDIER: They're Protestants. Why do they have to be Protestants?

MOTHER COURAGE: Protestant, Catholic, what do they care? It's their farm they're thinking of.

SECOND SOLDIER: Anyway, they're not Protestants. They're Catholics.

FIRST SOLDIER: I guess our cannon don't know the difference.

The CHAPLAIN *brings in a* PEASANT.

PEASANT: My arm's shot.

CHAPLAIN: Where's that linen?

MOTHER COURAGE: I can't give you any. With all I have to pay out in taxes, duties, bribes . . . (KATTRIN *picks up a board and threatens her mother with it, making gurgling sounds.*) Are you out of your mind? Put that board down this minute! I'm giving nothing! (*The* CHAPLAIN *lifts her bodily off the wagon steps, then brings the shirts from the wagon, and tears them in strips.*) My shirts! My officer's shirts!

From the house, the cry of a child in pain.

PEASANT: The child's still in the house.

KATTRIN *runs into the house.*

MOTHER COURAGE: Hey, grab Kattrin, the roof may fall in!

CHAPLAIN: I'm not going back in there.

MOTHER COURAGE: My officer's shirts, half a guilder apiece. I'm ruined! (KATTRIN *comes out with a baby in her arms. To her:*) Never happy till you're dragging babies around! Give it to its mother at once!

KATTRIN *is humming a lullaby to the child.*

CHAPLAIN (*bandaging*): The blood comes through.

MOTHER COURAGE: And, in all this, she's happy as a lark! Stop that music! I don't need music to tell me what victory's like. (*The* FIRST SOLDIER *tries to make off with the bottle he's been drinking from.*) Come back, you! If you want another victory, you'll have to pay for it.

FIRST SOLDIER: But I'm broke.

MOTHER COURAGE *tears the fur coat off his back.*

MOTHER COURAGE: Then leave this. It's stolen goods anyhow.

KATTRIN *rocks the child and raises it high above her head.*

6

*The interior of a canteen tent. The inside part of the counter
is seen at the rear. Funeral march in the distance. The* CHAPLAIN
and the REGIMENTAL CLERK *are playing checkers.* MOTHER
COURAGE *and* KATTRIN *are taking inventory.*

CHAPLAIN: The funeral procession is just starting out.

MOTHER COURAGE: Pity about the Chief — twenty-two pairs, socks
— getting killed that way. They say it was an accident. There
was a fog over the fields that morning, and the fog was to
blame. He'd been telling his men to fight to the death, and was
just riding back to safety when he lost his way in the fog,
went forward instead of back, found himself in the thick of
the battle, and ran right smack into a bullet. (*A whistle from
the counter. She goes over to attend to a soldier.*) It's a
disgrace — the way you're all skipping your Commander's
funeral.

REGIMENTAL CLERK: They shouldn't have handed out the money
before the funeral. Now the men are getting drunk instead
of going to it.

CHAPLAIN (*to the* REGIMENTAL CLERK): Don't you have to be there?

REGIMENTAL CLERK: I stayed away because of the rain.

MOTHER COURAGE: It's different for you. The rain might spoil your
uniform.

ANOTHER SOLDIER *comes to the counter. He sings:*

300

BATTLE HYMN

One schnapps, mine host, be quick, make haste!
A soldier's got no time to waste:
He must be shooting, shooting, shooting,
His Kaiser's enemies uprooting!

SOLDIER: A brandy.

Two breasts, my girl, be quick, make haste,
A soldier's got no time to waste:
He must be hating, hating, hating,
He cannot keep his Kaiser waiting!

SOLDIER: Make it a double, this is a holiday.

MOTHER COURAGE: Money first. No, you can't come inside, not with those boots on. Only officers are allowed in here, rain or no rain.

CHAPLAIN (*as the funeral music resumes*): Now they're filing past the body.

MOTHER COURAGE: I feel sorry for a commander like that — when maybe he had something big in mind, something they'd talk about in times to come, something they'd raise a statue to him for, the conquest of the whole world, for example — Lord, the worms have got into these biscuits! — he works his hands to the bone and then the common riffraff don't support him because all they care about is a jug of beer or a bit of company. Am I right?

CHAPLAIN: You're right, Mother Courage. Till you come to the riffraff. You underestimate them. Take those fellows outside right now, drinking their brandy in the rain, why, they'd fight for a hundred years, one war after another — if necessary, two at a time.

MOTHER COURAGE: Seventeen leather belts. — Then you don't think the war might end?

CHAPLAIN: Because a commander's dead? Don't be childish. Heroes are cheap. There are plenty of others where he came from.

MOTHER COURAGE: I wasn't asking just for the sake of argument. I was wondering if I should buy up a lot of supplies. They happen to be cheap right now. But if the war's going to end, I might just as well forget it.

CHAPLAIN: There are people who think the war's about to end, but I say: you can't be sure it will *ever* end. Oh, it may have to pause occasionally, for breath, as it were. It can even meet with an accident — nothing on this earth is perfect — one can't think of everything — a little oversight and a war may be in the hole and someone's got to pull it out again. That someone is the King or the Emperor or the Pope. But they're such friends in need, this war hasn't got much to worry about: it can look forward to a prosperous future.

MOTHER COURAGE: If I was sure you're right . . .

CHAPLAIN: Think it out for yourself. How *could* the war end?

REGIMENTAL CLERK: I'm from Bohemia. I'd like to get home once in a while. So I'm hoping for peace.

CHAPLAIN: Peace?

REGIMENTAL CLERK: Yes, peace! How can we live without it?

CHAPLAIN: We don't have to. There's peace even in war. War satisfies all needs — even those of peace. I know a song about that. (*He sings:*)

THE ARMY CHAPLAIN'S SONG

Does war, my friend, stop you from drinking?
  Does it not give you bread to chew?
To my old-fashioned way of thinking
  That much at least a war can do.

And even in the thick of slaughter
  A soldier feels the amorous itch
And many a buxom farmer's daughter
  Has lost her virtue in a ditch.

REGIMENTAL CLERK: Maybe. But when shall I get another good night's sleep?

CHAPLAIN: That also has been care of.

Somehow we find the bread and brandy
    And finding women is a snap.
And when there is a gutter handy
    We catch a twenty-minute nap.

As for the sleep that lasts forever
    Though it will come in any case
In war more Christian souls than ever
    Reach their eternal resting place.

REGIMENTAL CLERK: And when everyone's dead, the war won't stop even then, I suppose?

CHAPLAIN: Let me finish.

What won't a soldier do in wartime
    His savage lust to satisfy!
But after all, 'twas said aforetime:
    Be fruitful, lads, and multiply!

If you ignore this high injunction,
    The war will have to stop, my friend:
Perform your biologic function
    And then the war need never end!

REGIMENTAL CLERK: You admit the war *could* stop.

CHAPLAIN: Tsk, tsk, tsk. You don't know where God lives. Listen!

Peacemakers shall the earth inherit:
    We bless those men of simple worth.
Warmakers have still greater merit:
    They *have* inherited the earth.

I'll tell you, my good sir, what peace is:
    The hole when all the cheese is gone.
And what is war? This is my thesis:
    It's what the world is founded on.

War is like love: it'll always find a way. Why *should* it end?

MOTHER COURAGE: Then I *will* buy those supplies. I'll take your word for it. (KATTRIN, *who has been staring at the* CHAPLAIN, *suddenly bangs a basket of glasses down on the ground and runs out.* MOTHER COURAGE *laughs.*) She'll go right on waiting for peace. I promised her she'll get a husband when peace comes. (*She follows* KATTRIN.)

REGIMENTAL CLERK (*standing up*): You were singing. I win.

MOTHER COURAGE *brings* KATTRIN *back.*

MOTHER COURAGE: Be sensible, the war'll go on a bit longer, and we'll make a bit more money — then peace'll be all the nicer. Now you go into the town, it's not ten minutes' walk, and bring the things from the Golden Lion. Just the special things for your trousseau: the rest we can pick up later in the wagon. The Clerk will go with you, you'll be quite safe. Do a good job, and don't lose anything, think of your trousseau! (KATTRIN *ties a kerchief round her head and leaves with the* CLERK.) Now you can chop me a bit of firewood.

The CHAPLAIN *takes his coat off and prepares to chop wood.*

CHAPLAIN: Properly speaking, I am a pastor of souls, not a woodcutter.

MOTHER COURAGE: But I don't have a soul, and I do need wood.

CHAPLAIN: What's that little pipe you've got there?

MOTHER COURAGE: Just a pipe.

CHAPLAIN: I think it's a very particular pipe.

MOTHER COURAGE: Oh?

CHAPLAIN: The cook's pipe in fact. Our Swedish Commander's cook.

MOTHER COURAGE: If you know, why beat about the bush?

CHAPLAIN: I wondered if *you* knew. It was possible you just rummaged among your belongings and just lit on . . . some pipe.

MOTHER COURAGE: How d' you know that's not it?

CHAPLAIN: It isn't! You did know! (*He brings the axe down on the block.*)

MOTHER COURAGE: What if I did?

CHAPLAIN: Mother Courage, it is my duty to warn you. You are unlikely to see the gentleman again, but that's a blessing. Mother Courage, he did not strike me as trustworthy.

MOTHER COURAGE: Really? He was such a nice man.

CHAPLAIN: Well! So that's what you call a nice man! I do not. (*Again the axe falls.*) Far be it from me to wish him ill, but I cannot, cannot describe him as nice. No, he's a Don Juan, a cunning Don Juan. Just look at that pipe if you don't believe me — it tells all!

MOTHER COURAGE: I see nothing special about this pipe. It's been used, of course . . .

CHAPLAIN: It's been practically bitten through! Oho, he's a wild man! That is the pipe of a wild man! (*The axe falls more violently than ever.*)

MOTHER COURAGE: Now it's my chopping block that's bitten through!

CHAPLAIN: I told you the care of souls was my field. In physical labor my God-given talents find no adequate expression. You haven't heard me preach. Why, I can put such spirit into a regiment with a single sermon that the enemy's a mere flock of sheep to them and their own lives are no more than a smelly old pair of shoes to be instantly thrown away at the thought of final victory! God has given me the gift of tongues! I can preach you out of your senses!

MOTHER COURAGE: But I need my senses. What would I do without them?

CHAPLAIN: Mother Courage, I have often thought that — under a veil of blunt speech — you conceal a heart. You are human, you need warmth.

MOTHER COURAGE: The best way of warming this tent is to chop plenty of firewood.

CHAPLAIN: Seriously, my dear Courage, I sometimes ask myself how it would be if our relationship should be somewhat more firmly cemented. I mean: now the wild wind of war has whirled us so strangely together.

MOTHER COURAGE: The cement's pretty firm already. I cook your meals. And you lend a hand — at chopping firewood, for instance.

The CHAPLAIN *flourishes the axe as he approaches her.*

CHAPLAIN: Oh, you know what I mean by a closer relationship. Let your heart speak!

MOTHER COURAGE: Don't come at me like that with your axe! That'd be *too* close a relationship!

CHAPLAIN: This is no laughing matter. I have given it careful thought.

MOTHER COURAGE: My dear Chaplain, be sensible, I do like you. All I want is for me and mine to get by in this war. Now chop the firewood and we'll be warm in the evenings. What's that? (MOTHER COURAGE *stands up.* KATTRIN *enters with a nasty wound above her eye. She is letting everything fall, parcels, leather goods, a drum, etc.*) What happened? Were you attacked? On the way back? It's not serious, only a flesh wound. I'll bandage it up, and you'll be better within a week. Didn't the clerk walk you back? That's because you're a good girl, he thought they'd leave you alone. The wound isn't deep. It will never show. There! (*She has finished the bandage.*) Now I have a little present for you. (*She fishes Yvette's red boots out of a bag.*) See? You always wanted them — now you have them. Put them on before I change my mind. It will never show. Look, the boots have kept well, I cleaned them good before I put them away.

But KATTRIN *leaves the boots alone, and creeps into the wagon.*

CHAPLAIN: I hope she won't be disfigured.

MOTHER COURAGE: There'll be quite a scar. She needn't wait for peace now.

CHAPLAIN: She didn't let them get any of the things.

MOTHER COURAGE: I wish I knew what goes on inside her head. She stayed out all night once — once in all the years. I never did get out of her what happened. (*She picks up the things that* KATTRIN *spilled and angrily sorts them out.*) And this is war! A nice source of income, I must say!

Cannon.

CHAPLAIN: They're lowering the Commander in his grave. A historic moment!

MOTHER COURAGE: It's historic to me all right. She's finished. How would she ever get a husband now? And she's crazy for children. Even her dumbness comes from the war. A soldier stuck something in her mouth when she was little. I'll never see Swiss Cheese again, and where my Eilif is the Good Lord knows. Curse the war!

7

A highway. The CHAPLAIN *and* KATTRIN *are pulling the wagon. It is dirty and neglected, though new goods are hung around it.*

MOTHER COURAGE (*walking beside the wagon, a flask at her waist*): I won't have my war all spoiled for me! Destroys the weak, does it? Well, what does peace do for 'em? Huh? (*She sings The Song of Mother Courage:*)

So cheer up, boys, the rose is fading!
   When victory comes you may be dead!
A war is just the same as trading:
   But not with cheese — with steel and lead!
     Christians, awake! The winter's gone!
     The snows depart, the dead sleep on.
     And though you may not long survive
     Get out of bed and look alive!

8

IN THE SAME YEAR, THE PROTESTANT KING FELL IN THE BATTLE OF LÜTZEN. THE PEACE THREATENS MOTHER COURAGE WITH RUIN. HER BRAVE SON PERFORMS ONE HEROIC DEED TOO MANY AND COMES TO A SHAMEFUL END.

A camp. Summer morning. In front of the wagon, an OLD WOMAN *and her* SON. *The* SON *drags a large bag of bedding.* MOTHER COURAGE *is inside the wagon.*

MOTHER COURAGE: Must you come at the crack of dawn?

YOUNG MAN: We've been walking all night. Twenty miles. We have to get back today.

MOTHER COURAGE: What do I want with bed feathers? Take them to the town!

YOUNG MAN: At least wait till you see them.

OLD WOMAN: Nothing doing here either. Let's go.

YOUNG MAN: And let 'em sign away the roof over our heads for taxes? Maybe she'll pay three guilders if you throw in that bracelet. (*Bells start ringing.*) Hear that, Mother?

VOICE FROM A DISTANCE: It's peace! The King of Sweden got killed!

MOTHER COURAGE *sticks her head out of the wagon. She hasn't done her hair yet.*

MOTHER COURAGE: Bells? Bells in the middle of the week?

The CHAPLAIN *crawls out from under the wagon.*

CHAPLAIN: What's that they're shouting?

YOUNG MAN: It's peace.

CHAPLAIN: Peace?!

MOTHER COURAGE: Don't tell me peace has broken out — I've gone and bought all these supplies!

CHAPLAIN (*shouting*): Is it peace?

VOICE: Yes! The war stopped three weeks ago!

CHAPLAIN (*To* MOTHER COURAGE): Why else would they ring the bells?

VOICE: A big crowd of Lutherans just arrived — they brought the news.

YOUNG MAN: It's peace, Mother. (*The* OLD WOMAN *collapses.*) What's the matter?

MOTHER COURAGE (*back in the wagon*): Kattrin, it's peace! Put on your black dress, we're going to church, we owe it to Swiss Cheese.

YOUNG MAN: The war's over. (*The* OLD WOMAN *gets up, dazed.*) I'll get the harness shop going again now. Everything will be all right. Father will get his bed back. Can you walk? (*To the* CHAPLAIN:) It was the news. She didn't believe there'd ever be peace again. Father always said there would. We'll be going home.

They leave.

MOTHER COURAGE (*from the wagon*): Give them a schnapps!

CHAPLAIN: Too late: they've gone! And who may this be coming over from the camp? If it isn't our Swedish Commander's cook?!

The COOK *comes on, bedraggled, carrying a bundle.*

CHAPLAIN: Mother Courage, a visitor!

MOTHER COURAGE *clambers out of the wagon.*

COOK: I promised to come back, remember? For a short conversation? I didn't forget your brandy, Mrs. Fierling.

MOTHER COURAGE: The Commander's cook! After all these years! Where's Eilif?

COOK: Isn't he here yet? He went on ahead yesterday. He was on his way here.

CHAPLAIN: I'll be putting my pastor's clothes back on. (*He goes behind the wagon.*)

MOTHER COURAGE: Kattrin, Eilif's coming! Bring a glass of brandy for the cook! (*But* KATTRIN *doesn't.*) Oh, pull your hair over your face and forget it, the cook's no stranger! (*To him:*) She won't come out. Peace is nothing to her. It took too long to get here. Here's your schnapps. (*She has got it herself. They sit.*)

COOK: Dear old peace!

MOTHER COURAGE: Dear old peace has broken my neck. On the chaplain's advice I went and bought a lot of supplies. Now everybody's leaving, and I'm holding the baby.

COOK: How could you listen to a windbag like the chaplain? If I'd had the time I'd have warned you against him. But the Catholics were too quick for me. Since when did he become the big wheel around here?

MOTHER COURAGE: He's been doing the dishes and helping me with the wagon.

COOK: And telling you a few of his jokes? He has a most unhealthy attitude to women. He's completely unsound.

MOTHER COURAGE: And you're completely sound?

COOK: And I am completely sound. Your health!

MOTHER COURAGE: Sound! Only one person around here was ever sound, and I never had to slave as I did then. He sold the blankets off the children's beds in autumn. You aren't recommending yourself to me if you claim to be sound.

COOK: Ah well, here we sit, drinking your famous brandy while the bells of peace do ring!

MOTHER COURAGE: I don't see where they're going to find all this pay that's in arrears. Were you people paid?

COOK (*hesitating*): Not exactly. That's why we disbanded. Why stay? I said to myself. Why not look up a couple of friends? So here I am.

MOTHER COURAGE: In other words: you're broke.

COOK (*annoyed by the bells*): I wish they'd stop that racket! I'd like to set myself up in some business.

The CHAPLAIN *enters in his pastor's coat again.*

CHAPLAIN: Pretty good, eh? Just a few moth holes.

COOK: I have a bone to pick with you. You advised a lady to buy superfluous goods on the pretext that the war would never end.

CHAPLAIN: And what business is that of yours?

COOK: It's unprincipled behavior! How dare you interfere with the conduct of other people's businesses?

CHAPLAIN: Who's interfering now, I'd like to know? (*To* MOTHER COURAGE:) I was far from suspecting you had to account to *this* gentleman for everything!

MOTHER COURAGE: Now don't get excited. The cook's giving his personal opinion. You can hardly deny your war was a flop.

CHAPLAIN: You are a hyena of the battlefield! You are taking the name of peace in vain!

MOTHER COURAGE: I'm a what, did you say?

CHAPLAIN. A hyena!

COOK: Who insults my girl friend, insults me!

CHAPLAIN: *Your* intentions are only too transparent! (*To* MOTHER COURAGE:) But when I see *you* take peace between finger and thumb like a snotty old handkerchief, the humanity in me rebels! You want war, do you? Well, don't you forget the proverb: who sups with the devil must use a long spoon!

MOTHER COURAGE: Remember what one fox said to another that was caught in a trap? "If you stay there, you're just asking for trouble." I'm not in love with war, Mr. Army Chaplain, and when it comes to calling people hyenas, you and I part company!

CHAPLAIN: Then why all this grumbling about the peace? Is it just for the junk in your wagon?

MOTHER COURAGE: My goods are not junk. I live off them.

CHAPLAIN: You live off war. Exactly!

COOK: As a grown man, you should know better than to run around advising people. (*To* MOTHER COURAGE:) In your situation you should get rid of certain goods at once — before prices sink to zero.

MOTHER COURAGE: That's good advice. I think I'll take it. (*She climbs on to her wagon.*)

COOK: One up for me. Anyway, Chaplain, cockfights are unbecoming to your cloth!

CHAPLAIN: If you don't shut your mouth, I'll murder you, cloth or no cloth!

Enter YVETTE, *wearing black, leaning on a stick. She is much
older, fatter, and heavily powdered. Behind her, a* VALET.

YVETTE: Hullo everybody! Is this the Mother Courage establishment?

CHAPLAIN: Quite right. And with whom have we the pleasure?

YVETTE: I am Madam Colonel Starhemberg, good people. Where's
Mother Courage?

CHAPLAIN (*calling to the wagon*): Madam Colonel Starhemberg to
speak with you!

MOTHER COURAGE: Coming!

YVETTE (*calling*): It's me — Yvette!

MOTHER COURAGE: Yvette!

YVETTE: I've come to see how you're getting on! (*The* COOK *turns
round in horror.*) Peter!

COOK: Yvette!

YVETTE: Of all things. How did *you* get here?

COOK: On a cart.

CHAPLAIN: Well! You know each other? Intimately?

YVETTE: I'll say! You're fat.

COOK: For that matter, you're no beanpole.

YVETTE: It's good we've met. Now I can tell you what I think of
you, tramp.

CHAPLAIN: Do that. Tell him exactly what you think of him. But
wait till Mother Courage comes out.

COOK: Now don't make a scene.

MOTHER COURAGE *comes out, laden with goods.*

MOTHER COURAGE: Yvette! (*They embrace.*) But why are you in
mourning?

YVETTE: Doesn't it suit me? My husband, the colonel, died several
years ago.

MOTHER COURAGE: The old fellow that nearly bought my wagon?

YVETTE: Nah, not him. His older brother.

MOTHER COURAGE: Good to see one person that got somewhere in
this war.

CHAPLAIN: You promised to give us your opinion of this gentleman.

COOK: Now, Yvette, don't make a stink!

MOTHER COURAGE: He's a friend of mine, Yvette.

YVETTE: He's Peter Piper, that's what.

COOK: Cut the nicknames!

MOTHER COURAGE: Peter Piper? The one that turned the girls' heads? I'll have to sit down. And I've been keeping your pipe for you.

CHAPLAIN: And smoking it.

YVETTE: Lucky I can warn you against him. He's a bad lot. You won't find a worse on the whole coast of Flanders. He got more girls in trouble than . . .

COOK: That's a long time ago. It's not true any more.

YVETTE: Stand up when you talk to a lady! How I loved that man, and all the time he was having a little bowlegged brunette. He got her in trouble, too, of course.

COOK: I seem to have brought *you* luck.

YVETTE: Speak when you're spoken to, you hoary ruin! And take care, Mother Courage, this type is dangerous even in decay!

MOTHER COURAGE (*to* YVETTE): Come with me. I must get rid of this stuff before the prices fall.

YVETTE (*to* COOK): Miserable cur!

MOTHER COURAGE: Maybe you can help me at army headquarters — with your contacts.

YVETTE: Damnable whore hunter!

MOTHER COURAGE: Kattrin, church is all off, I'm going to market!

YVETTE: Inveterate seducer!

MOTHER COURAGE (*still to* KATTRIN): When Eilif comes, give him something to drink!

YVETTE: I've put an end to your tricks, Peter Piper, and one day, in a better life than this, the Lord God will reward me! (*She sniffs.*) Come, Mother Courage!

The two leave. Pause.

CHAPLAIN: As our text this morning, let us take the saying: the mills of God grind slowly. And you complain of my jokes!

COOK: I'll be frank with you: I was hoping for a good hot dinner. And now she'll be getting a wrong picture of me. I think I should leave before she comes back.

CHAPLAIN: I think so too.

COOK: Chaplain, peace makes me sick! It's the lot of mankind to perish by fire and sword! Oh, how I wish I was roasting a great fat capon for the Commander — with mustard sauce and those little yellow carrots . . .

CHAPLAIN: Red cabbage. With capon: red cabbage.

COOK: You're right. But he always wanted yellow carrots.

CHAPLAIN: He never understood anything.

COOK: You always put plenty away.

CHAPLAIN: Under protest.

COOK: Anyway, you must admit, those were the days.

CHAPLAIN: Yes, that I might admit.

COOK: And now you've called her a hyena, you haven't much future here either . . . What are you staring at?

CHAPLAIN: Why, it's Eilif! (EILIF *enters followed by two soldiers with halberds. His hands are fettered. He is white as chalk.*) What happened?

EILIF: Where's my mother?

CHAPLAIN: Gone to the town.

EILIF: They said she was here. I was allowed a last visit.

COOK (*to the soldiers*): Where are you taking him?

SOLDIER: For a ride.

The OTHER SOLDIER *makes the gesture of throat cutting.*

CHAPLAIN: What has he done?

SOLDIER: He broke in on a peasant. The wife is dead.

CHAPLAIN: Eilif, how could you?

EILIF: It's no different. It's what I did before.

COOK: That was in wartime.

EILIF: Shut your mouth. Can I sit down till she comes?

SOLDIER: No.

CHAPLAIN: It's true. In wartime they honored him for it. He sat at the Commander's right hand. It was bravery. Couldn't we speak with the provost?

SOLDIER: What's the use? Stealing cattle from a peasant, what's brave about that?

COOK: It was just dumb.

EILIF: If I'd been dumb, I'd have starved, smarty.

COOK: So you were bright — and paid for it.

CHAPLAIN: We must bring Kattrin out.

EILIF: Let her alone. Just give me some brandy.

SOLDIER: No.

CHAPLAIN: What shall we tell your mother?

EILIF: Tell her it was no different. Tell her it was the same. Aw, tell her nothing.

The soldiers lead him away.

CHAPLAIN: I'll come with you!

EILIF: I don't need any priest.

CHAPLAIN: You don't know — yet. (*He follows them.*)

COOK: I'll have to tell her, she'll expect to see him.

CHAPLAIN: Tell her he'll be back.

He leaves. The COOK *shakes his head, finally approaches the wagon.*

COOK: Hi! Won't you come out? I'm the cook! Have you got anything to eat in there? (*He looks in.*) She's got a blanket over her head.

Cannon. Re-enter MOTHER COURAGE, *breathless, still carrying her goods.*

MOTHER COURAGE: The peace is over! The war's on again — has been for three days! I didn't get rid of this stuff after all, thank God! The shooting has started in the town already. We must get away. Pack, Kattrin! What's on *your* mind?

COOK: Nothing.

MOTHER COURAGE: But there is. I see it in your face.

COOK: Eilif was here. Only he had to go away again.

MOTHER COURAGE: He was here? Then we'll see him on the march. I'll be with our side this time. How'd he look?

COOK: The same.

MOTHER COURAGE: He'll *never* change. And the war won't get *him*, he's bright. Help me with the packing. (*She starts it.*) Is Eilif in good with the captain? Did he tell you about his heroic deeds?

COOK: He's done one of them over again.

MOTHER COURAGE: Tell me about it later. (KATTRIN *appears.*) Kattrin, the peace is over. We're on the move again. (*To the* COOK:) What *is* eating you?

COOK: I'll enlist.

MOTHER COURAGE: Where's the Chaplain?

COOK: In the town. With Eilif.

MOTHER COURAGE: Stay with us a while, Cook, I need a bit of help.

COOK: This Yvette matter . . .

MOTHER COURAGE: Hasn't done you any harm in my eyes. Just the opposite. Where there's smoke, there's fire. You'll come?

COOK: I may as well.

MOTHER COURAGE: The twelfth regiment is under way. (THE COOK *gets into harness with* KATTRIN.) Maybe I'll see Eilif before the day is out! Let's go! (*She sings, and the* COOK *joins in the refrain,* The Song of Mother Courage:)

Up hill, down dale, past dome and steeple,
    My wagon always moves ahead.
The war can care for all its people
    So long as there is steel and lead.
Though steel and lead are stout supporters
    A war needs human beings too.
Report today to your headquarters!
    If it's to last, this war needs you!
        Christians, awake! The winter's gone!
        The snow departs, the dead sleep on.
        And though you may not long survive
        Get out of bed and look alive!

9

THE RELIGIOUS WAR HAS LASTED SIXTEEN YEARS, AND GERMANY HAS
LOST HALF ITS INHABITANTS. THOSE WHO ARE SPARED IN BATTLE DIE
BY PLAGUE. OVER ONCE-BLOOMING COUNTRYSIDE HUNGER RAGES.
TOWNS ARE BURNED DOWN. WOLVES PROWL THE EMPTY
STREETS. IN THE AUTUMN OF 1634 WE FIND MOTHER COURAGE
IN THE FICHTELGEBIRGE NOT FAR FROM THE ROAD THE
SWEDISH ARMY IS TAKING. WINTER HAS COME EARLY
AND IS SEVERE. BUSINESS IS BAD. ONLY BEGGING RE-
MAINS. THE COOK RECEIVES A LETTER FROM
UTRECHT AND IS SENT PACKING.

*In front of a half-ruined parsonage. Early winter. A grey
morning. Gusts of wind.* MOTHER COURAGE *and the* COOK *at
the wagon in rags.*

COOK: There are no lights. No one is up.

MOTHER COURAGE: But it's a parsonage. The parson'll have to leave
his feather bed to go ring the bells. Then he'll have himself
some hot soup.

COOK: Where'll he find it? The whole village is starving.

MOTHER COURAGE: Why don't we sing him something?

COOK: Anna, I've had enough. A letter came from Utrecht, did I
tell you? My mother died of cholera. The inn is mine. Look!
(*He hands her the letter. She glances through it.*)

MOTHER COURAGE: I'm tired of this wandering life. I feel like a
butcher's dog, taking meat to the customers and getting none
for myself.

COOK: The world's coming to an end.

MOTHER COURAGE: Sometimes I dream of driving through hell
with this wagon — and selling brimstone. Or I see myself
driving through heaven handing out supplies to wandering
souls! If only we could find a place where there's no shooting,
me and my children — what's left of 'em — we might rest
up a while.

318

COOK: Why don't we open this inn together? With you or without you, I'm leaving for Utrecht today. Think it over.

MOTHER COURAGE: I must tell Kattrin. Kattrin! (KATTRIN *comes out of the wagon*.) Listen. We're thinking of going to Utrecht, the cook and me. His mother's left him an inn. We'd be sure of our dinner. And you'd have a bed of your own. What about it?

COOK: Anna, I must speak to you alone.

MOTHER COURAGE: Go back in, Kattrin.

KATTRIN *does so*.

COOK: There's a misunderstanding. I hoped I wouldn't have to come right out with it — but if you're bringing her, it's all off.

KATTRIN *is listening — her head sticking out at the back of the wagon*.

MOTHER COURAGE: You want me to leave Kattrin behind?

COOK: There's no room. The inn isn't a place with three counters. If the two of us stand on our hind legs we can earn a living, but three's too many. Let Kattrin keep your wagon.

MOTHER COURAGE: I was thinking she might find a husband in Utrecht.

COOK: At her age? With that scar?

MOTHER COURAGE: Not so loud!

COOK: The customers wouldn't like it!

MOTHER COURAGE: Not so loud, I said!

COOK: There's a light in the parsonage. We'd better sing. Worthy Master Parson, and all within, we shall now sing the song of Solomon, Holy Saint Martin, and other good men who came to a bad end, so you can see we're good folk too, and have a hard time getting by, especially in winter. (*He sings*. MOTHER COURAGE *joins him in the refrains*.)

THE SONG OF THE WISE AND GOOD

You've heard of wise old Solomon
   You know his history.

He thought so little of this earth
He cursed the hour of his birth
   Declaring: all is vanity.
How very wise was Solomon!
   But ere night came and day did go
This fact was clear to everyone:
   It was his wisdom that had brought him low.
(Better for you if you have none.)

For the virtues are dangerous in this world, you're better off
without, you have a nice life — some good hot soup included.
We're told to be unselfish and share what we have, but what
if we have nothing? Unselfishness is a very rare virtue, it
simply doesn't pay.

Unselfish Martin could not bear
   His fellow creatures' woes.
   He met a beggar in the snows
And gave him half his cloak to wear:
   So both of them fell down and froze.
What an unselfish paragon!
   But ere night came and day did go
This fact was clear to everyone:
   It was unselfishness that brought him low.
(Better for you if you have none.)

That's how it is! We're good, we don't steal, we don't kill,
we don't burn the house down, and so, as the song says, we
sink lower and lower and there isn't a plate of soup going.

God's Ten Commandments we have kept
   And acted as we should.
   It has not done us any good.
O you who sit beside a fire
   Please help us now: our need is dire!
Strict godliness we've always shown.
   But ere night came and day did go
This fact was clear to everyone:

It was our godliness that brought us low.
(Better for you if you have none.)

VOICE (*from above*): You there! Come up! There's some hot soup
for you!

MOTHER COURAGE: I couldn't swallow a thing. Was that your last
word?

COOK: The inn isn't big enough. We better go up.

MOTHER COURAGE: I'll get Kattrin.

COOK: If there are three of us the parson won't like it. Stick something in your pocket for her.

The COOK *and* MOTHER COURAGE *enter the parsonage.* KATTRIN
*climbs out of the wagon with a bundle. Making sure the others
have gone, she lays out on a wagon wheel a skirt of her
mother's and a pair of the* COOK's *pants. She has just finished,
and picked her bundle up, when* MOTHER COURAGE *comes down
with soup for her.*

MOTHER COURAGE: Kattrin! Where do you think you're going?
(*She examines the bundle.*) Ah! So you were listening! I told
him: nothing doing — he can have his lousy inn. (*Now she
sees the skirt and pants.*) Oh, you stupid girl! Now what if
I'd seen that, and you'd been gone! (KATTRIN *tries to leave.
Her mother holds her.*) And don't imagine I sent him packing
on your account. It was the wagon. They can't part me from
my wagon. Now we'll put the cook's things here where he'll
find 'em, that silly man. You and I are leaving. (*She climbs up
on the wagon and throws the rest of the* COOK's *few things
down on to the pants.*) There! He's fired! The last man I'll
ever take into *this* business! Get into harness, Kattrin. This
winter will pass like all the others.

*The two women harness themselves to the wagon and start
out. A gust of wind. When they have disappeared, the* COOK
re-enters, still chewing. He sees his things.

10

On the highway. MOTHER COURAGE *and* KATTRIN *are pulling the wagon. They come to a prosperous farmhouse. Someone inside is singing.*

THE SONG OF SHELTER

In March a tree we planted
To make the garden gay.
In June we were enchanted:
A lovely rose was blooming
The balmy air perfuming!
Blest of the gods are they
Who have a garden gay!
In June we were enchanted.

When snow falls helter-skelter
And loudly blows the storm
Our farmhouse gives us shelter.
The winter's in a hurry
But we've no cause to worry.
Cosy are we and warm
Though loudly blows the storm:
Our farmhouse gives us shelter.

MOTHER COURAGE *and* KATTRIN *have stopped to listen. They start out again.*

11

JANUARY, 1636. CATHOLIC TROOPS THREATEN THE PROTESTANT TOWN
OF HALLE. THE STONES BEGIN TO TALK. MOTHER COURAGE
LOSES HER DAUGHTER AND JOURNEYS ONWARD
ALONE. THE WAR IS NOT YET NEAR ITS END.

*The wagon, very far gone now, stands near a farmhouse
with a straw roof. It is night. Out of the wood come a* LIEUTEN-
ANT *and* THREE SOLDIERS *in full armor.*

LIEUTENANT: And there mustn't be a sound. If anyone yells, cut
him down.

FIRST SOLDIER: But we'll have to knock — if we want a guide.

LIEUTENANT: Knocking's a natural noise, it's all right, could be a
cow hitting the wall of the cowshed.

The soldiers knock at the farmhouse door. An OLD PEASANT
WOMAN *opens. A hand is clapped over her mouth. Two soldiers
enter.*

PEASANT'S VOICE: What is it? (*The soldiers bring out an* OLD
PEASANT *and his* SON.)

LIEUTENANT (*pointing to the wagon on which* KATTRIN *has appeared*): There's another. (*A* SOLDIER *pulls her out.*) Is this
everybody?

OLD PEASANT: That's our son.

PEASANT WOMAN: And that's a girl that can't talk. Her mother's in
town buying up stocks because the shopkeepers are running
away and selling cheap.

OLD PEASANT: They're canteen people.

LIEUTENANT: I'm warning you. Keep quiet. One sound and you'll
have a sword in your ribs. I need someone to show us the path
to the town. (*Points to the* YOUNG PEASANT:) You! Come here!

YOUNG PEASANT: I don't know any path!

SECOND SOLDIER (*grinning*): He don't know any path!

323

YOUNG PEASANT: I don't help Catholics.

LIEUTENANT (*to* SECOND SOLDIER): Show him your sword.

YOUNG PEASANT (*forced to his knees, a sword at his throat*): I'd rather die!

SECOND SOLDIER (*again mimicking*): He'd rather die!

FIRST SOLDIER: We'll soon fix this. (*Walks over to the cowshed.*) Two cows and a bull. Listen, you. If you aren't going to be reasonable, I'll saber your cattle.

YOUNG PEASANT: Not the cattle!

PEASANT WOMAN (*weeping*): Spare the cattle, Captain, or we'll starve!

LIEUTENANT: If he must be stubborn.

FIRST SOLDIER: I think I'll start with the bull.

YOUNG PEASANT (*to his father*): Do I have to? (*The* OLD PEASANT *nods.*) I'll do it.

PEASANT WOMAN: Thank you, thank you, Captain, for sparing us, for ever and ever, Amen.

The OLD PEASANT *stops her going on thanking him.*

FIRST SOLDIER: I knew the bull came first all right!

Led by the YOUNG PEASANT, *the* LIEUTENANT *and the soldiers go on their way.*

OLD PEASANT: What goes on? Nothing good, I guess.

PEASANT WOMAN: Maybe they're just scouts. What are you doing?

OLD PEASANT (*setting a ladder against the roof and climbing up*): I'm seeing if they're alone. (*On the roof:*) Things are moving — all over. I can see armor. And a cannon. There must be more than a regiment. God have mercy on the town and its people!

PEASANT WOMAN: Are there lights in the town?

OLD PEASANT: No, they're all asleep. (*He climbs down.*) It's an attack. They'll all be slaughtered in their beds.

PEASANT WOMAN: The watchman'll give warning.

OLD PEASANT: They must have killed the watchman in the tower on the hill or he'd have sounded his horn before this.

PEASANT WOMAN: If there were more of us . . .

OLD PEASANT: But being that we're alone with that cripple . . .

PEASANT WOMAN: There's nothing we can do, is there?

OLD PEASANT: Nothing.

PEASANT WOMAN: We can't get to the town in the dark.

OLD PEASANT: The whole hillside's swarming with men.

PEASANT WOMAN: We could give a sign?

OLD PEASANT: And be cut down for it?

PEASANT WOMAN: No, there's nothing we can do. (*To* KATTRIN:) Pray, poor thing, pray! There's nothing we can do to stop this bloodshed, so even if you can't talk, at least pray! *He* hears, if no one else does. I'll help you. (*All kneel,* KATTRIN *behind.*) Our Father, which art in Heaven, hear our prayer, let not the town perish with all that lie therein asleep and fearing nothing. Wake them, that they rise and go to the walls and see the foe that comes with fire and sword in the night down the hill and across the fields. God protect our mother and make the watchman not sleep but wake ere it's too late. And save our son-in-law too, O God, he's there with his four children, let them not perish, they're innocent, they know nothing, one of them's not two years old, the eldest is seven. (KATTRIN *rises, troubled.*) Heavenly Father, hear us, only Thou canst help us or we die, for we are weak and have no sword nor nothing; we cannot trust our own strength but only Thine, O Lord; we are in Thy hands, our cattle, our farm, and the town too, we're all in Thy hands, and the foe is nigh unto the walls with all his power. (KATTRIN, *unperceived, has crept off to the wagon, has taken something out of it, put it under her skirt, and has climbed up the ladder to the roof.*) Be mindful of the children in danger, especially the little ones, be mindful of the old folk who cannot move, and of all Christian souls, O Lord.

OLD PEASANT: And forgive us our trespasses as we forgive them that trespass against us. Amen.

Sitting on the roof, KATTRIN *takes a drum from under her skirt, and starts to beat it.*

PEASANT WOMAN: Heavens, what's she doing?

OLD PEASANT: She's out of her mind!

PEASANT WOMAN: Get her down, quick! (*The* OLD PEASANT *runs to the ladder but* KATTRIN *pulls it up on the roof.*) She'll get us in trouble.

OLD PEASANT: Stop it this minute, you silly cripple!

PEASANT WOMAN: The soldiers'll come!

OLD PEASANT (*looking for stones*): I'll stone you!

PEASANT WOMAN: Have you no pity, don't you have a heart? We have relations there too, four grandchildren. If they find us now, it's the end, they'll stab us to death! (KATTRIN *is staring into the far distance, toward the town. She goes on drumming. To the* PEASANT:) I told you not to let that sort into the farm. What do *they* care if we lose our cattle?

LIEUTENANT (*running back with soldiers and* YOUNG PEASANT): I'll cut you all to bits!

PEASANT WOMAN: We're innocent, sir, we couldn't stop her!

LIEUTENANT: Where's the ladder?

OLD PEASANT: On the roof.

LIEUTENANT (*calling*): Throw down the drum. I order you! (*To peasants:*) You're all in this, but you won't live to tell the tale.

OLD PEASANT: They've been cutting down fir trees around here. If we get a good long trunk we can knock her off the roof . . .

FIRST SOLDIER (*to the* LIEUTENANT): May I make a suggestion? (*He whispers something to the* LIEUTENANT, *who nods. To* KATTRIN:) Listen, you! We'll do you a favor. Everyone in that town is gonna get killed. Come down, go with us to the town, show us your mother and we'll spare her.

KATTRIN *replies with more drumming.*

LIEUTENANT (*pushing him away*): She doesn't trust you, no wonder with your face. (*He calls up to* KATTRIN:) Hey, you! Suppose I give you my word? I'm an officer, my word's my bond! (KATTRIN *again replies with drumming — harder this time.*) Nothing is sacred to her.

FIRST SOLDIER: They'll sure as hell hear it in the town.

LIEUTENANT: We must make another noise. Louder than that drum. What can we make a noise with?

FIRST SOLDIER: We mustn't make a noise!

LIEUTENANT: A harmless noise, fool, a peacetime noise!

OLD PEASANT: I could start chopping wood.

LIEUTENANT: That's it! (*The* PEASANT *brings his axe and chops away.*) Chop! Chop harder! Chop for your life! It's not enough. (*To* FIRST SOLDIER:) You chop too!

OLD PEASANT: I've only one axe.

LIEUTENANT: We must set fire to the farm. Smoke her out.

OLD PEASANT: That's no good, Captain, when they see fire from the town, they'll know everything.

KATTRIN *is laughing now and drumming harder than ever.*

LIEUTENANT: Laughing at us, is she? I'll settle *her* hash if it's the last thing I do. Bring me a musket!

Two soldiers off.

PEASANT WOMAN: I have it, Captain. That's their wagon over there, Captain. If we smash that, she'll stop. It's all they have, Captain.

LIEUTENANT (*to the* YOUNG PEASANT): Smash it! (*Calling:*) If you don't stop that noise, we'll smash up your wagon!

The YOUNG PEASANT *deals the wagon a couple of feeble blows with a board.*

PEASANT WOMAN (*to* KATTRIN): Stop, you little beast!

KATTRIN *stares at the wagon and pauses. Noises of distress come out of her. She goes on drumming.*

LIEUTENANT: Where are those sonsofbitches with that gun?

FIRST SOLDIER: They can't have heard anything in the town or we'd hear their cannon.

LIEUTENANT (*calling*): They don't hear you. And now we're going to shoot. I'll give you one more chance: throw down that drum!

YOUNG PEASANT (*dropping the board, screaming to* KATTRIN): Don't stop now! Go on, go on, go on!

The soldier knocks him down and stabs him. KATTRIN *starts crying but goes on drumming.*

PEASANT WOMAN: You're killing him!

The soldiers arrive with the gun.

LIEUTENANT: Set it up! (*Calling while the gun is set up on forks:*) Once for all: stop that drumming! (*Still crying,* KATTRIN *is drumming as hard as she can.*) Fire!

The soldiers fire. KATTRIN *is hit. She gives the drum another feeble beat or two, then collapses.*

LIEUTENANT: So that ends the noise.

But the last beats of the drum are lost in the din of cannon from the town. Mingled with the thunder of cannon, alarm-bells are heard in the distance.

FIRST SOLDIER: She made it.

12

Toward morning. The drums and pipes of troops on the march, receding. In front of the wagon MOTHER COURAGE *sits by* KATTRIN'S *body. The* THREE PEASANTS *of the last scene are standing near.*

PEASANT WOMAN: The regiments have all left. No, there's still one to go.

OLD PEASANT (*to* MOTHER COURAGE): You must latch on to it. You'll never get by alone. Hurry!

MOTHER COURAGE: Maybe she's asleep. (*She sings:*)
Lullay, lullay, what's that in the hay?
The neighbor's kids cry but mine are gay.
The neighbor's kids are dressed in dirt:
Your silks were cut from an angel's skirt.
They are all starving: you have a cake;
If it's too stale, you need but speak.
Lullay, lullay, what's rustling there?
One lad fell in Poland. The other is — where?

MOTHER COURAGE: You shouldn't have told her about the children.

OLD PEASANT: If you hadn't gone off to get your cut, maybe it wouldn't have happened.

MOTHER COURAGE: I'm glad she can sleep.

PEASANT WOMAN: She's not asleep, it's time you realized, she's through.

OLD PEASANT: You must get away. There are wolves in these parts. And the bandits are worse.

MOTHER COURAGE (*stands up*): That's right.

OLD PEASANT: Have you no one left?

MOTHER COURAGE: Yes, my son Eilif.

OLD PEASANT: Find him then, leave *her* to us.

PEASANT WOMAN: We'll give her a proper burial, you needn't worry.

MOTHER COURAGE: Here's a little money for the expenses. (*She harnesses herself to the wagon.*) I hope I can pull the wagon by myself. Yes, I'll manage. There's not much in it now. (*The last regiment is heard passing.*) Hey! Take me with you!

The men are heard singing The Song of Mother Courage:

Dangers, surprises, devastations —
    The war takes hold and will not quit.
But though it last three generations
    We shall get nothing out of it.
Starvation, filth, and cold enslave us.
    The army robs us of our pay.
Only a miracle can save us
    And miracles have had their day.
        Christians, awake! The winter's gone!
        The snows depart, the dead sleep on.
        And though you may not long survive
        Get out of bed and look alive!

GALILEO

(1938–1939)

English Version by
Charles Laughton

It is my opinion that the earth is very noble and
admirable by reason of so many different alterations
and generations which are incessantly made therein.

— GALILEO GALILEI

CHARACTERS

GALILEO GALILEI

ANDREA SARTI (*two actors: boy and man*)

MRS. SARTI

LUDOVICO MARSILI

PRIULI, THE CURATOR

SAGREDO, *Galileo's friend*

VIRGINIA GALILEI

TWO SENATORS

MATTI, *an iron founder*

PHILOSOPHER (*later, Rector of the University*)

ELDERLY LADY

YOUNG LADY

FEDERZONI, *assistant to Galileo*

MATHEMATICIAN

LORD CHAMBERLAIN

FAT PRELATE

TWO SCHOLARS

TWO MONKS

INFURIATED MONK

OLD CARDINAL

ATTENDANT MONK

CHRISTOPHER CLAVIUS

LITTLE MONK

TWO SECRETARIES

CARDINAL BELLARMIN

CARDINAL BARBERINI

CARDINAL INQUISITOR

YOUNG GIRL

HER FRIEND

GIUSEPPE

STREET SINGER

HIS WIFE

REVELLER

A LOUD VOICE

INFORMER

TOWN CRIER
OFFICIAL
PEASANT
CUSTOMS OFFICER
BOY
SENATORS, OFFICIALS, PROFESSORS, LADIES, GUESTS, CHILDREN

There are two wordless roles: The DOGE *in Scene Two and* PRINCE COSIMO DE MEDICI *in Scene Four. The ballad of Scene Nine is filled out by a pantomime: among the individuals in the pantomimic crowd are three extras* (*including the* "KING OF HUNGARY"), COBBLER'S BOY, THREE CHILDREN, PEASANT WOMAN, MONK, RICH COUPLE, DWARF, BEGGAR, *and* GIRL.

1

*In the year sixteen hundred and nine
Science' light began to shine
At Padua City, in a modest house
Galileo Galilei set out to prove
The sun is still, the earth is on the move.*

GALILEO's *scantily furnished study. Morning.* GALILEO *is wash-ing himself. A barefoot boy,* ANDREA, *son of his housekeeper,* MRS. SARTI, *enters with a big astronomical model.*

GALILEO: Where did you get that thing?

ANDREA: The coachman brought it.

GALILEO: Who sent it?

ANDREA: It said "From the Court of Naples" on the box.

GALILEO: I don't want their stupid presents. Illuminated manu-scripts, a statue of Hercules the size of an elephant — they never send money.

ANDREA: But isn't this an astronomical instrument, Mr. Galilei?

GALILEO: That is an antique too. An expensive toy.

ANDREA: What's it for?

GALILEO: It's a map of the sky according to the wise men of ancient Greece. Bosh! We'll try and sell it to the university. They still teach it there.

ANDREA: How does it work, Mr. Galilei?

GALILEO: It's complicated.

ANDREA: I think I could understand it.

GALILEO (*interested*): Maybe. Let's begin at the beginning. Descrip-tion!

ANDREA: There are metal rings, a lot of them.

GALILEO: How many?

ANDREA: Eight.

GALILEO: Correct. And?

334

ANDREA: There are words painted on the bands.

GALILEO: What words?

ANDREA: The names of stars.

GALILEO: Such as?

ANDREA: Here is a band with the sun on it and on the inside band is the moon.

GALILEO: Those metal bands represent crystal globes, eight of them.

ANDREA: Crystal?

GALILEO: Like huge soap bubbles one inside the other and the stars are supposed to be tacked on to them. Spin the band with the sun on it. (ANDREA *does*.) You see the fixed ball in the middle?

ANDREA: Yes.

GALILEO: That's the earth. For two thousand years man has chosen to believe that the sun and all the host of stars revolve about him. Well. The Pope, the Cardinals, the princes, the scholars, captains, merchants, housewives, have pictured themselves squatting in the middle of an affair like that.

ANDREA: Locked up inside?

GALILEO (*triumphant*): Ah!

ANDREA: It's like a cage.

GALILEO: So you sensed that. (*Against the model:*) I like to think the ships began it.

ANDREA: Why?

GALILEO: They used to hug the coasts and then all of a sudden they left the coasts and spread over the oceans. A new age was coming. I was on to it years ago. I was a young man, in Siena. There was a group of masons arguing. They had to raise a block of granite. It was hot. To help matters, one of them wanted to try a new arrangement of ropes. After five minutes' discussion, out went a method which had been employed for a thousand years. The millennium of faith is ended, said I, this is the millennium of doubt. And we are pulling out of that contraption. The sayings of the wise men won't wash any more. Everybody, at last, is getting nosey. I predict that in our time astronomy will become the gossip of the market place and the sons of fishwives will pack the schools.

ANDREA: You're off again, Mr. Galilei. Give me the towel. (*He wipes some soap from* GALILEO's *back*.)

GALILEO: By that time, with any luck, they will be learning that the earth rolls round the sun, and that their mothers, the captains, the scholars, the princes and the Pope are rolling with it.

ANDREA: That turning-round-business is no good. I can see with my own eyes that the sun comes up in one place in the morning and goes down in a different place in the evening. It doesn't stand still, I can see it move.

GALILEO: You see nothing, all you do is gawk. Gawking is not seeing. (*He puts the iron washstand in the middle of the room*.) Now: that's the sun. Sit down. (ANDREA *sits on a chair*. GALILEO *stands behind him*.) Where is the sun, on your right or on your left?

ANDREA: Left.

GALILEO: And how will it get to the right?

ANDREA: By your putting it there, of course.

GALILEO: Of course? (*He picks* ANDREA *up, chair and all, and carries him round to the other side of the washstand*.) *Now* where is the sun?

ANDREA: On the right.

GALILEO: And did it move?

ANDREA: I did.

GALILEO: Wrong. Stupid! The chair moved.

ANDREA: But I was on it.

GALILEO: Of course. The chair is the earth, and you're sitting on it.

MRS. SARTI, *who has come in with a glass of milk and a roll, has been watching*.

MRS. SARTI: What are you doing with my son, Mr. Galilei?

ANDREA: Now, mother, you don't understand.

MRS. SARTI: You understand, don't you? Last night he tried to tell me that the earth goes round the sun. You'll soon have him saying that two times two is five.

GALILEO (*eating his breakfast*): Apparently we are on the threshold of a new era, Mrs. Sarti.

MRS. SARTI: Well, I hope we can pay the milkman in this new era. A young gentleman is here to take private lessons and he is well-dressed and don't you frighten him away like you did the others. Wasting your time with Andrea! (*To* ANDREA:) How many times have I told you not to wheedle free lessons out of Mr. Galilei? (MRS. SARTI *goes.*)

GALILEO: So you thought enough of the turning-round-business to tell your mother about it.

ANDREA: Just to surprise her.

GALILEO: Andrea, I wouldn't talk about our ideas outside.

ANDREA: Why not?

GALILEO: Certain of the authorities won't like it.

ANDREA: Why not, if it's the truth?

GALILEO (*laughs*): Because we are like the worms who are little and have dim eyes and can hardly see the stars at all, and the new astronomy is a framework of guesses or very little more — yet.

MRS. SARTI *shows in* LUDOVICO MARSILI, *a presentable young man.*

GALILEO: This house is like a marketplace. (*Pointing to the model:*) Move that out of the way! Put it down there!

LUDOVICO *does.*

LUDOVICO: Good morning, sir. My name is Ludovico Marsili.

GALILEO (*reading a letter of recommendation he has brought*): You came by way of Holland and your family lives in the Campagna? Private lessons, thirty scudi a month.

LUDOVICO: That's all right, of course, sir.

GALILEO: What is your subject?

LUDOVICO: Horses.

GALILEO: Aha.

LUDOVICO: I don't understand science, sir.

GALILEO: Aha.

LUDOVICO: They showed me an instrument like that in Amsterdam. You'll pardon me, sir, but it didn't make sense to me at all.

GALILEO: It's out of date now.

ANDREA *goes*.

LUDOCIVO: You'll have to be patient with me, sir. Nothing in science makes sense to me.

GALILEO: Aha.

LUDOVICO: I saw a brand new instrument in Amsterdam. A tube affair. "See things five times as large as life!" It had two lenses, one at each end, one lens bulged and the other was like that. (*Gesture*.) Any normal person would think that different lenses cancel each other out. They didn't! I just stood and looked a fool.

GALILEO: I don't quite follow you. What does one see enlarged?

LUDOVICO: Church steeples, pigeons, boats. Anything at a distance.

GALILEO: Did you yourself — see things enlarged?

LUDOVICO: Yes, sir.

GALILEO: And the tube had two lenses? Was it like this? (*He has been making a sketch*.)

LUDOVICO *nods*.

GALILEO: A recent invention?

LUDOVICO: It must be. They only started peddling it on the streets a few days before I left Holland.

GALILEO (*starts to scribble calculations on the sketch; almost friendly*): Why do you bother your head with science? Why don't you just breed horses?

Enter MRS. SARTI. GALILEO *doesn't see her. She listens to the following*.

LUDOVICO: My mother is set on the idea that science is necessary nowadays for conversation.

GALILEO: Aha. You'll find Latin or philosophy easier. (MRS. SARTI *catches his eye*.) I'll see you on Tuesday afternoon.

LUDOVICO: I shall look forward to it, sir.

GALILEO: Good morning. (*He goes to the window and shouts into the street:*) Andrea! Hey, Redhead, Redhead!

MRS. SARTI: The curator of the museum is here to see you.

GALILEO: Don't look at me like that. I took him, didn't I?

MRS. SARTI: I caught your eye in time.

GALILEO: Show the curator in.

She goes. He scribbles something on a new sheet of paper. THE CURATOR *comes in.*

CURATOR: Good morning, Mr. Galilei.

GALILEO: Lend me a scudo. (*He takes it and goes to the window, wrapping the coin in the paper on which he has been scribbling.*) Redhead, run to the spectacle-maker and bring me two lenses; here are the measurements. (*He throws the paper out of the window. During the following scene* GALILEO *studies his sketch of the lenses.*)

CURATOR: Mr. Galilei, I have come to return your petition for an honorarium. Unfortunately I am unable to recommend your request.

GALILEO: My good sir, how can I make ends meet on five hundred scudi?

CURATOR: What about your private students?

GALILEO: If I spend all my time with students, when am I to study? My particular science is on the theshold of important discoveries. (*He throws a manuscript on the table.*) Here are my findings on the laws of falling bodies. That should be worth 200 scudi.

CURATOR: I am sure that any paper of yours is of infinite worth, Mr. Galilei. . . .

GALILEO: I was limiting it to 200 scudi.

CURATOR (*cool*): Mr. Galilei, if you want money and leisure, go to Florence. I have no doubt Prince Cosimo de Medici will be glad to subsidize you, but eventually you will be forbidden to think — in the name of the Inquisition. (GALILEO *says nothing.*) Now let us not make a mountain out of a molehill. You are happy here in the Republic of Venice but you need money. Well, that's human. Mr. Galilei, may I suggest a simple solution? You remember that chart you made for the army to extract cube roots without any knowledge of mathematics? Now that was practical!

GALILEO: Bosh!

CURATOR: Don't say bosh about something that astounded the Chamber of Commerce. Our city elders are businessmen. Why don't you invent something useful that will bring them a little profit?

GALILEO (*playing with the sketch of the lenses; suddenly*): I see. Mr. Priuli, I may have something for you.

CURATOR: You don't say so.

GALILEO: It's not quite there yet, but . . .

CURATOR: You've never let me down yet, Galilei.

GALILEO: You are always an inspiration to me, Priuli.

CURATOR: You are a great man: a discontented man, but I've always said you are a great man.

GALILEO (*tartly*): My discontent, Priuli, is for the most part with myself. I am forty-six years of age and have achieved nothing which satisfies me.

CURATOR: I won't disturb you any further.

GALILEO: Thank you. Good morning.

CURATOR: Good morning. And thank you.

He goes. GALILEO *sighs.* ANDREA *returns, bringing lenses.*

ANDREA: One scudo was not enough. I had to leave my cap with him before he'd let me take them away.

GALILEO: We'll get it back some day. Give them to me. (*He takes the lenses over to the window, holding them in the relation they would have in a telescope.*)

ANDREA: What are those for?

GALILEO: Something for the senate. With any luck, they will rake in 200 scudi. Take a look!

ANDREA: My, things look close! I can read the copper letters on the bell in the Campanile. And the washerwomen by the river, I can see their washboards!

GALILEO: Get out of the way. (*Looking through the lenses himself:*) Aha!

2

No one's virtue is complete:
Great Galileo liked to eat.
You will not resent, we hope,
The truth about his telescope.

The great arsenal of Venice, overlooking the harbor full of ships. SENATORS *and* OFFICIALS *on one side,* GALILEO, *his daughter* VIRGINIA *and his friend* SAGREDO, *on the other side. They are dressed in formal, festive clothes.* VIRGINIA *is fourteen and charming. She carries a velvet cushion on which lies a brand new telescope. Behind* GALILEO *are some* ARTISANS *from the arsenal. There are onlookers,* LUDOVICO *amongst them.*

CURATOR *(announcing)*: Senators, Artisans of the Great Arsenal of Venice; Mr. Galileo Galilei, professor of mathematics at your University of Padua.

GALILEO *steps forward and starts to speak.*

GALILEO: Members of the High Senate! Gentlemen: I have great pleasure, as director of this institute, in presenting for your approval and acceptance an entirely new instrument originating from this our great arsenal of the Republic of Venice. As professor of mathematics at your University of Padua, your obedient servant has always counted it his privilege to offer you such discoveries and inventions as might prove lucrative to the manufacturers and merchants of our Venetian Republic. Thus, in all humility, I tender you this, my optical tube, or telescope, constructed, I assure you, on the most scientific and Christian principles, the product of seventeen years patient research at your University of Padua.

GALILEO *steps back. The* SENATORS *applaud.*

SAGREDO *(aside to* GALILEO*)*: Now you will be able to pay your bills.

GALILEO: Yes. It will make money for them. But you realize that it

is more than a money-making gadget? — I turned it on the
moon last night . . .

CURATOR (*in his best chamber-of-commerce manner*): Gentlemen:
Our Republic is to be congratulated not only because this
new acquisition will be one more feather in the cap of Venetian
culture . . . (*Polite applause.*) . . . not only because our
own Mr. Galilei has generously handed this fresh product
of his teeming brain entirely over to you, allowing you to
manufacture as many of these highly saleable articles as you
please . . . (*Considerable applause.*) . . . but, Gentlemen of
the Senate, has it occurred to you that — with the help of this
remarkable new instrument — the battlefleet of the enemy
will be visible to us a full two hours before we are visible to
him? (*Tremendous applause.*)

GALILEO (*aside to* SAGREDO): We have been held up three generations
for lack of a thing like this. I want to go home.

SAGREDO: What about the moon?

GALILEO: Well, for one thing, it doesn't give off its own light.

CURATOR (*continuing his oration*): And now, Your Excellency, and
Members of the Senate, Mr. Galilei entreats you to accept the
instrument from the hands of his charming daughter Virginia.
Polite applause. He beckons to VIRGINIA *who steps forward
and presents the telescope to the* DOGE.

CURATOR (*during this*): Mr. Galilei gives his invention entirely into
your hands, Gentlemen, enjoining you to construct as many of
these instruments as you may please.
More applause. The SENATORS *gather round the telescope, examining it, and looking through it.*

GALILEO (*aside to* SAGREDO): Do you know what the Milky Way
is made of?

SAGREDO: No.

GALILEO: I do.

CURATOR (*interrupting*): Congratulations, Mr. Galilei. Your extra
five hundred scudi a year are safe.

GALILEO: Pardon? What? Of course, the five hundred scudi! Yes!
A prosperous man is standing beside the CURATOR.

CURATOR: Mr. Galilei, Mr. Matti of Florence.

MATTI: You're opening new fields, Mr. Galilei. We could do with you at Florence.

CURATOR: Now, Mr. Matti, leave something to us poor Venetians.

MATTI: It is a pity that a great republic has to seek an excuse to pay its great men their right and proper dues.

CURATOR: Even a great man has to have an incentive. (*He joins the* SENATORS *at the telescope.*)

MATTI: I am an iron founder.

GALILEO: Iron founder!

MATTI: With factories at Pisa and Florence. I wanted to talk to you about a machine you designed for a friend of mine in Padua.

GALILEO: I'll put you on to someone to copy it for you, I am not going to have the time. — How are things in Florence?
They wander away.

FIRST SENATOR (*peering*): Extraordinary! They're having their lunch on that frigate. Lobsters! I'm hungry!
Laughter.

SECOND SENATOR: Oh, good heavens, look at her! I must tell my wife to stop bathing on the roof. When can I buy one of these things?

Laughter. VIRGINIA *has spotted* LUDOVICO *among the onlookers and drags him to* GALILEO.

VIRGINIA (*to* LUDOVICO): Did I do it nicely?

LUDOVICO: I thought so.

VIRGINIA: Here's Ludovico to congratulate you, father.

LUDOVICO (*embarrassed*): Congratulations, sir.

GALILEO: I improved it.

LUDOVICO: Yes, sir. I am beginning to understand science.
GALILEO *is surrounded.*

VIRGINIA: Isn't father a great man?

LUDOVICO: Yes.

VIRGINIA: Isn't that new thing father made pretty?

LUDOVICO: Yes, a pretty red. Where I saw it first it was covered in green.

VIRGINIA: What was?

LUDOVICO: Never mind. (*A short pause.*) Have you ever been to Holland?

They go. All Venice is congratulating GALILEO, *who wants to go home.*

3

January ten, sixteen ten:
Galileo Galilei abolishes heaven.

GALILEO'S *study at Padua. It is night.* GALILEO *and* SAGREDO *at a telescope.*

SAGREDO (*softly*): The edge of the crescent is jagged. All along the dark part, near the shiny crescent, bright particles of light keep coming up, one after the other and growing larger and merging with the bright crescent.

GALILEO: How do you explain those spots of light?

SAGREDO: It can't be true . . .

GALILEO: It *is* true: they are high mountains.

SAGREDO: On a star?

GALILEO: Yes. The shining particles are mountain peaks catching the first rays of the rising sun while the slopes of the mountains are still dark, and what you see is the sunlight moving down from the peaks into the valleys.

SAGREDO: But this gives the lie to all the astronomy that's been taught for the last two thousand years.

GALILEO: Yes. What you are seeing now has been seen by no other man beside myself.

SAGREDO: But the moon can't be an earth with mountains and valleys like our own any more than the earth can be a star.

GALILEO: The moon *is* an earth with mountains and valleys — and the earth *is* a star. As the moon appears to us, so we appear to the moon. From the moon, the earth looks something like a crescent, sometimes like a half-globe, sometimes a full-globe, and sometimes it is not visible at all.

SAGREDO: Galileo, this is frightening.

An urgent knocking on the door.

GALILEO: I've discovered something else, something even more astonishing.

346

More knocking. GALILEO *opens the door and the* CURATOR *comes in.*

CURATOR: There it is — your "miraculous optical tube." Do you know that this invention he so picturesquely termed "the fruit of seventeen years' research" will be on sale tomorrow for two scudi apiece at every street corner in Venice? A shipload of them has just arrived from Holland.

SAGREDO: Oh, dear!

GALILEO *turns his back and adjusts the telescope.*

CURATOR: When I think of the poor gentlemen of the senate who believed they were getting an invention they could monopolize for their own profit . . . why, when they took their first look through the glass, it was only by the merest chance that they didn't see a peddler, seven time enlarged, selling tubes exactly like it at the corner of the street.

SAGREDO: Mr. Priuli, with the help of this instrument, Mr. Galilei has made discoveries that will revolutionize our concept of the universe.

CURATOR: Mr. Galilei provided the city with a first rate water pump and the irrigation works he designed function splendidly. How was I to expect this?

GALILEO (*still at the telescope*): Not so fast, Priuli. I may be on the track of a very large gadget. Certain of the stars appear to have regular movements. If there were a clock in the sky, it could be seen from anywhere. That might be useful for your shipowners.

CURATOR: I won't listen to you. I listened to you before, and as a reward for my friendship you have made me the laughingstock of the town. You can laugh — you got your money. But let tell you this: you've destroyed my faith in a lot of things, Mr. Galilei. I'm disgusted with the world. That's all I have to say. (*He storms out.*)

GALILEO (*embarrassed*): Businessmen bore me, they suffer so. Did you see the frightened look in his eyes when he caught sight of a world not created solely for the purpose of doing business?

SAGREDO: Did you know that telescopes had been made in Holland?

GALILEO: I'd heard about it. But the one I made for the Senators was twice as good as any Dutchman's. Besides, I needed the money. How can I work, with the tax collector on the door-step? And my poor daughter will never acquire a husband unless she has a dowry, she's not too bright. And I like to buy books — all kinds of books. Why not? And what about my appetite? I don't think well unless I eat well. Can I help it if I get my best ideas over a good meal and a bottle of wine? They don't pay me as much as they pay the butcher's boy. If only I could have five years to do nothing but research! Come on. I am going to show you something else.

SAGREDO: I don't know that I want to look again.

GALILEO: This is one of the brighter nebulae of the Milky Way. What do you see?

SAGREDO: But it's made up of stars — countless stars.

GALILEO: Countless worlds.

SAGREDO (*hesitating*): What about the theory that the earth revolves round the sun? Have you run across anything about that?

GALILEO: No. But I noticed something on Tuesday that might prove a step towards even that. Where's Jupiter? There are four lesser stars near Jupiter. I happened on them on Monday but didn't take any particular note of their position. On Tuesday I looked again. I could have sworn they had moved. They have changed again. Tell me what you see.

SAGREDO: I only see three.

GALILEO: Where's the fourth? Let's get the charts and settle down to work.

They work and the lights dim. The lights go up again. It is near dawn.

GALILEO: The only place the fourth can be is round at the back of the larger star where we cannot see it. This means there are small stars revolving around a big star. Where are the crystal shells now that the stars are supposed to be fixed to?

SAGREDO: Jupiter can't be attached to anything: there are other stars revolving round it.

GALILEO: There is no support in the heavens. (SAGREDO *laughs awk-wardly*.) Don't stand there looking at me as if it weren't true.

SAGREDO: I suppose it is true. I'm afraid.

GALILEO: Why?

SAGREDO: What do you think is going to happen to you for saying that there is another sun around which other earths revolve? And that there are only stars and no difference between earth and heaven? Where is God then?

GALILEO: What do you mean?

SAGREDO: God? Where is God?

GALILEO (*angrily*): Not there! Any more than He'd be here — if creatures from the moon came down to look for Him!

SAGREDO: Then where is He?

GALILEO: I'm not a theologian. I'm a mathematician.

SAGREDO: You are a human being! (*Almost shouting:*) Where is God in your system of the universe?

GALILEO: Within ourselves. Or — nowhere.

SAGREDO: Ten years ago a man was burned at the stake for saying that.

GALILEO: Giordano Bruno was an idiot: he spoke too soon. He would never have been condemned if he could have backed up what he said with proof.

SAGREDO (*incredulously*): Do you really believe proof will make any difference?

GALILEO: I believe in the human race. The only people that can't be reasoned with are the dead. Human beings are intelligent.

SAGREDO: Intelligent — or merely shrewd?

GALILEO: I know they call a donkey a horse when they want to sell it, and a horse a donkey when they want to buy it. But is that the whole story? Aren't they susceptible to truth as well? (*He fishes a small pebble out of his pocket.*) If anybody were to drop a stone . . . (*Drops the pebble.*) . . . and tell them that it didn't fall, do you think they would keep quiet? The evidence of your own eyes is a very seductive thing. Sooner or later everybody must succumb to it.

SAGREDO: Galileo, I am helpless when you talk.

A church bell has been ringing for some time, calling people to mass. Enter VIRGINIA, *muffled up for mass, carrying a candle, protected from the wind by a globe.*

VIRGINIA: Oh, father, you promised to go to bed tonight, and it's five o'clock again.

GALILEO: Why are you up at this hour?

VIRGINIA: I'm going to mass with Mrs. Sarti. Ludovico is going too. How was the night, father?

GALILEO: Bright.

VIRGINIA: What did you find through the tube?

GALILEO: Only some little specks by the side of a star. I must draw attention to them somehow. I think I'll name them after the Prince of Florence. Why not call them the Medicean planets? By the way, we may move to Florence. I've written to His Highness, asking if he can use me as Court Mathematician.

VIRGINIA: Oh, father, we'll be at the court!

SAGREDO (*amazed*): Galileo!

GALILEO: My dear Sagredo, I must have leisure. My only worry is that His Highness after all may not take me. I'm not accustomed to writing formal letters to great personages. Here, do you think this is the right sort of thing?

SAGREDO (*reads and quotes*): "Whose sole desire is to reside in Your Highness' presence — the rising sun of our great age." Cosimo de Medici is a boy of nine.

GALILEO: The only way a man like me can land a good job is by crawling on his stomach. Your father, my dear, is going to take his share of the pleasures of life in exchange for all his hard work, and about time too. I have no patience, Sagredo, with a man who doesn't use his brains to fill his belly. Run along to mass now.

VIRGINIA *goes.*

SAGREDO: Galileo, do not go to Florence.

GALILEO: Why not?

SAGREDO: The monks are in power there.

GALILEO: Going to mass is a small price to pay for a full belly. And there are many famous scholars at the court of Florence.

SAGREDO: Court monkeys.

GALILEO: I shall enjoy taking them by the scruff of the neck and making them look through the telescope.

SAGREDO: Galileo, you are traveling the road to disaster. You are suspicious and skeptical in science, but in politics you are as naive as your daughter! How can people in power leave a man at large who tells the truth, even if it be the truth about the distant stars? Can you see the Pope scribbling a note in his diary: "Tenth of January, 1610, Heaven abolished"? A moment ago, when you were at the telescope, I saw you tied to the stake, and when you said you believed in proof, I smelt burning flesh!

GALILEO: I am going to Florence.

Before the next scene a curtain with the following legend on it is lowered:

"By setting the name of Medici in the sky, I am bestowing immortality upon the stars. I commend myself to you as your most faithful and devoted servant, whose sole desire is to reside in Your Highness' presence, the rising sun of our great age."

— GALILEO GALILEI

4

GALILEO's *house at Florence. Well-appointed.* GALILEO *is demonstrating his telescope to* PRINCE COSIMO DE MEDICI, *a boy of nine, accompanied by his* LORD CHAMBERLAIN, LADIES *and* GENTLEMEN *of the Court and an assortment of university* PROFESSORS. *With* GALILEO *are* ANDREA *and* FEDERZONI, *the new assistant (an older man).* MRS. SARTI *stands by. Before the scene opens the voice of the* PHILOSOPHER *can be heard.*

VOICE OF THE PHILOSOPHER: Quaedam miracula universi. Orbes mystice canorae, arcus crystallini, circulatio corporum coelestium. Cyclorum epicyclorumque intoxicatio, integritas tabulae chordarum et architectura elata globorum coelestium.

GALILEO: Shall we speak in everyday language? My colleague Mr. Federzoni does not understand.

PHILOSOPHER: Is it necessary that he should?

GALILEO: Yes.

PHILOSOPHER: Forgive me. I thought he was your mechanic.

ANDREA: Mr. Federzoni is a mechanic and a scholar.

PHILOSOPHER: Thank you, young man. If Mr. Federzoni insists . . .

GALILEO: I insist.

PHILOSOPHER: It will not be as clear, but it's your house. Your Highness . . . (THE PRINCE *is ineffectually trying to establish contact with* ANDREA.) I was about to recall to Mr. Galilei some of the wonders of the universe as they are set down for us in the Divine Classics. (THE LADIES *"ah."*) Remind him of the "mystically musical spheres, the crystal arches, the circulation of the heavenly bodies — "

ELDERLY LADY: Perfect poise!

PHILOSOPHER: " — the intoxication of the cycles and epicycles, the integrity of the tables of chords and the enraptured architecture of the celestial globes."

ELDERLY LADY: What diction!

PHILOSOPHER: May I pose the question: why should we go out of our way to look for things that can only strike a discord in this ineffable harmony?

The LADIES *applaud.*

FEDERZONI: Take a look through here — you'll be interested.

ANDREA: Sit down here, please.

The PROFESSORS *laugh.*

MATHEMATICIAN: Mr. Galilei, nobody doubts that your brain child — or is it your adopted brain child? — is brilliantly contrived.

GALILEO: Your Highness, one can see the four stars as large as life, you know.

The PRINCE *looks to the* ELDERLY LADY *for guidance.*

MATHEMATICIAN: Ah. But has it occurred to you that an eyeglass through which one sees such phenomena might not be a too reliable eyeglass?

GALILEO: How is that?

MATHEMATICIAN: If one could be sure you would keep your temper, Mr. Galilei, I could suggest that what one sees in the eyeglass and what is in the heavens are two entirely different things.

GALILEO (*quietly*): You are suggesting fraud?

MATHEMATICIAN: No! How could I, in the presence of His Highness?

ELDERLY LADY: The gentlemen are just wondering if Your Highness' stars are really, really there!

Pause.

YOUNG LADY (*trying to be helpful*): Can one see the claws on the Great Bear?

GALILEO: And everything on Taurus the Bull.

FEDERZONI: Are you going to look through it or not?

MATHEMATICIAN: With the greatest of pleasure.

Pause. Nobody goes near the telescope. All of a sudden the boy ANDREA *turns and marches pale and erect past them through the whole length of the room. The* GUESTS *follow with their eyes.*

MRS. SARTI (*as he passes her*): What is the matter with you?

ANDREA (*shocked*): They are wicked.

PHILOSOPHER: Your Highness, it is a delicate matter and I had no intention of bringing it up, but Mr. Galilei was about to demonstrate the impossible. His new stars would have broken the outer crystal sphere — which we know of on the authority of Aristotle. I am sorry.

MATHEMATICIAN: The last word.

FEDERZONI: He had no telescope.

MATHEMATICIAN: Quite.

GALILEO (*keeping his temper*): "Truth is the daughter of Time, not of Authority." Gentlemen, the sum of our knowledge is pitiful. It has been my singular good fortune to find a new instrument which brings a small patch of the universe a little bit closer. It is at your disposal.

PHILOSOPHER: Where is all this leading?

GALILEO: Are we, as scholars, concerned with where the truth might lead us?

PHILOSOPHER: Mr. Galilei, the truth might lead us anywhere!

GALILEO: I can only beg you to look through my eyeglass.

MATHEMATICIAN (*wild*): If I understand Mr. Galilei correctly, he is asking us to discard the teaching of two thousand years.

GALILEO: For two thousand years we have been looking at the sky and didn't see the four moons of Jupiter, and there they were all the time. Why defend shaken teachings? You should be doing the shaking. (*The* PRINCE *is sleepy*.) Your Highness! My work in the Great Arsenal of Venice brought me in daily contact with sailors, carpenters, and so on. These men are unread. They depend on the evidence of their senses. But they taught me many new ways of doing things. The question is whether these gentlemen here want to be found out as fools by men who might not have had the advantages of a classical education but who are not afraid to use their eyes. I tell you that our dockyards are stirring with that same high curiosity which was the true glory of Ancient Greece.

Pause.

PHILOSOPHER: I have no doubt Mr. Galilei's theories will arouse the enthusiasm of the dockyards.

CHAMBERLAIN: Your Highness, I find to my amazement that this highly informative discussion has exceeded the time we had allowed for it. May I remind Your Highness that the State Ball begins in three-quarters of an hour?

The COURT *bows low.*

ELDERLY LADY: We would really have liked to look through your eyeglass, Mr. Galilei, wouldn't we, Your Highness?

The PRINCE *bows politely and is led to the door.* GALILEO *follows the* PRINCE, CHAMBERLAIN *and* LADIES *towards the exit. The* PROFESSORS *remain at the telescope.*

GALILEO (*almost servile*): All anybody has to do is look through the telescope, Your Highness.

MRS. SARTI *takes a plate with candies to the* PRINCE *as he is walking out.*

MRS. SARTI: A piece of homemade candy, Your Highness?

ELDERLY LADY: Not now. Thank you. It is too soon before His Highness' supper.

PHILOSOPHER: Wouldn't I like to take that thing to pieces!

MATHEMATICIAN: Ingenious contraption. It must be quite difficult to keep clean. (*He rubs the lens with his handkerchief and looks at the handkerchief.*)

FEDERZONI: We did not paint the Medicean stars on the lens.

ELDERLY LADY (*to the* PRINCE, *who has whispered something to her*): No, no, no, there is nothing the matter with your stars!

CHAMBERLAIN (*across the stage to* GALILEO): His Highness will of course seek the opinion of the greatest living authority: Christopher Clavius, Chief Astronomer to the Papal College in Rome.

5

Things take indeed a wondrous turn
When learned men do stoop to learn.
Clavius, we are pleased to say,
Upheld Galileo Galilei.

A burst of laughter is heard and the curtains reveal a hall in the
Collegium Romanum. HIGH CHURCHMEN, MONKS *and* SCHOLARS
standing about talking and laughing. GALILEO *by himself in a*
corner.

FAT PRELATE (*shaking with laughter*): Hopeless! Hopeless! Will
you tell me something people won't believe?

A SCHOLAR: Yes, that you don't love your stomach!

FAT PRELATE: They'd believe that. They only do not believe what's
good for them. They doubt the devil, but fill them up with
some fiddle-de-dee about the earth rolling like a marble in the
gutter and they swallow it hook, line, and sinker. Sancta sim-
plicitas!

He laughs until the tears run down his cheeks. The others
laugh with him. A group has formed whose members boister-
ously begin to pretend they are standing on a rolling globe.

A MONK: It's rolling fast, I'm dizzy. May I hold on to you, Professor? (*He sways dizzily and clings to one of the scholars for*
support.)

THE SCHOLAR: Old Mother Earth's been at the bottle again. Whoa!

MONK: Hey! Hey! We're slipping off! Help!

SECOND SCHOLAR: Look! There's Venus! Hold me, lads. Whee!

SECOND MONK: Don't, don't hurl us off on to the moon. There are
nasty sharp mountain peaks on the moon, brethren!

VARIOUSLY: Hold tight! Hold tight! Don't look down! Hold tight!
It'll make you giddy!

FAT PRELATE: And we cannot have giddy people in Holy Rome.

They rock with laughter. An INFURIATED MONK *comes out from a large door at the rear holding a Bible in his hand and pointing out a page with his finger.*

INFURIATED MONK: What does the Bible say? — "Sun, stand thou still on Gideon and thou, moon, in the valley of Ajalon." Can the sun come to a standstill if it doesn't ever move? Does the Bible lie?

FAT PRELATE: How did Christopher Clavius, the greatest astronomer we have, get mixed up in an investigation of this kind?

INFURIATED MONK: He's in there with his eye glued to that diabolical instrument.

FAT PRELATE (*to* GALILEO, *who has been playing with his pebble and has dropped it*): Mr. Galilei, something dropped down.

GALILEO: Monsignor, are you sure it didn't drop up?

INFURIATED MONK: As astronomers we are aware that there are phenomena which are beyond us, but man can't expect to understand everything!

Enter a very old CARDINAL *leaning on a* MONK *for support. Others move aside.*

OLD CARDINAL: Aren't they out yet? Can't they reach a decision on that paltry matter? Christopher Clavius ought to know his astronomy after all these years. I am informed that Mr. Galilei transfers mankind from the center of the universe to somewhere on the outskirts. Mr. Galilei is therefore an enemy of mankind and must be dealt with as such. Is it conceivable that God would trust this most precious fruit of His labor to a minor frolicking star? Would He have sent His Son to such a place? How can there be people with such twisted minds that they believe what they're told by the slave of a multiplication table?

FAT PRELATE (*quietly to* CARDINAL): The gentlemen is over there.

OLD CARDINAL: So you are the man. You know my eyes are not what they were, but I can see you bear a striking resemblance to the man we burned. What was his name?

MONK: Your Eminence must avoid excitement, the doctor said . . .

OLD CARDINAL (*disregarding him*): So you have degraded the earth despite the fact that you live by her and receive everything from her. I won't have it! I won't have it! I won't be a nobody on an inconsequential star briefly twirling hither and thither. I tread the earth, and the earth is firm beneath my feet, and there is no motion to the earth, and the earth is the center of all things, and I am the center of the earth, and the eye of the creator is upon me. About me revolve, affixed to their crystal shells, the lesser lights of the stars and the great light of the sun, created to give light upon me that God might see me — Man, God's greatest effort, the center of creation. "In the image of God created He him." Immortal . . . (*His strength fails him and he catches the* MONK *for support.*)

MONK: You mustn't overtax your strength, Your Eminence.

At this moment the door at the rear opens and CHRISTOPHER CLAVIUS *enters followed by his* ASTRONOMERS. *He strides hastily across the hall, looking neither to right nor left. As he goes by we hear him say —*

CLAVIUS: He is right.

Deadly silence. All turn to GALILEO.

OLD CARDINAL: What is it? Have they reached a decision?

No one speaks.

MONK: It is time that Your Eminence went home.

The hall is emptying fast. One little MONK *who had entered with* CLAVIUS *speaks to* GALILEO.

LITTLE MONK: Mr. Galilei, I heard Father Clavius say: "Now it's for the theologians to set the heavens right again." You have won.

Before the next scene a curtain with the following legend on it is lowered:

"... *As these new astronomical charts enable us to determine longitudes at sea and so make it possible to reach the new continents by the shortest routes, we would beseech Your Excellency to aid us in reaching Mr. Galilei, mathematician to the Court of Florence, who is now in Rome. . . .*"

— FROM A LETTER WRITTEN BY A MEMBER
OF THE GENOA CHAMBER OF COMMERCE
AND NAVIGATION TO THE PAPAL LEGATION.

6

When Galileo was in Rome
A Cardinal asked him to his home
He wined and dined him as his guest
And only made one small request.

CARDINAL BELLARMIN'S *house in Rome. Music is heard and the chatter of many guests. Two* SECRETARIES *are at the rear of the stage at a desk.* GALILEO, *his daughter* VIRGINIA, *now twenty-one, and* LUDOVICO MARSILI, *who has become her fiancé, are just arriving. A few* GUESTS, *standing near the entrance with masks in their hands, nudge each other and are suddenly silent.* GALILEO *looks at them. They applaud him politely and bow.*

VIRGINIA: O father! I'm so happy. I won't dance with anyone but you, Ludovico.

GALILEO (*to a* SECRETARY): I was to wait here for His Eminence.

FIRST SECRETARY: His Eminence will be with you in a few minutes.

VIRGINIA: Do I look proper?

LUDOVICO: You are showing some lace.

GALILEO *puts his arms around their shoulders.*

GALILEO (*quoting mischievously*):
Fret not, daughter, if perchance
You attract a wanton glance.
The eyes that catch a trembling lace
Will guess the heartbeat's quickened pace.
Lovely woman still may be
Careless with felicity.

VIRGINIA (*to* GALILEO): Feel my heart.

GALILEO (*to* LUDOVICO): It's thumping.

VIRGINIA: I hope I always say the right thing.

LUDOVICO: She's afraid she's going to let us down.

VIRGINIA: Oh, I want to look beautiful.

GALILEO: You'd better. If you don't, they'll start saying all over again that the earth doesn't turn.

LUDOVICO (*laughing*): It *doesn't* turn, sir.

GALILEO *laughs.*

GALILEO: Go and enjoy yourselves. (*He speaks to one of the* SECRE-TARIES.) A large fête?

FIRST SECRETARY: Two hundred and fifty guests, Mr. Galilei. We have represented here this evening most of the great families of Italy, the Orsinis, the Villanis, the Nuccolis, the Soldanieris, the Canes, the Lecchis, the Estensis, the Colombinis, the . . .

VIRGINIA *comes running back.*

VIRGINIA: Oh father, I didn't tell you: you're famous.

GALILEO: Why?

VIRGINIA: The hairdresser in the Via Vittorio kept four other ladies waiting and took me first. (*Exit.*)

GALILEO (*at the stairway, leaning over the well*): Rome!

Enter CARDINAL BELLARMIN, *wearing the mask of a lamb, and* CARDINAL BARBERINI, *wearing the mask of a dove.*

SECRETARIES: Their Eminences, Cardinals Bellarmin and Barberini.

The CARDINALS *lower their masks.*

GALILEO (*to* BELLARMIN): Your Eminence.

BELLARMIN: Mr. Galilei, Cardinal Barberini.

GALILEO: Your Eminence.

BARBERINI: So you are the father of that lovely child!

BELLARMIN: Who is inordinately proud of being her father's daughter.

BARBARINI (*points his finger at* GALILEO): "The sun riseth and setteth and returneth to its place," saith the Bible. What saith Galilei?

GALILEO: Appearances are notoriously deceptive, Your Eminence. Once when I was so high, I was standing on a ship that was pulling away from the shore and I shouted, "The shore is moving!" I know now that it was the ship which was moving.

BARBERINI (*laughs*): You can't catch that man. I tell you, Bellarmin, his moons around Jupiter are hard nuts to crack. Unfortunately for me I happened to glance at a few papers on astronomy once. It is harder to get rid of than the itch.

BELLARMIN: Let's move with the times. If it makes navigation easier for sailors to use new charts based on a new hypothesis let them have them. We only have to scotch doctrines that contradict Holy Writ.

He leans over the balustrade of the well and acknowledges various GUESTS.

BARBERINI: But, Bellarmin, you haven't caught on to this fellow. The Scriptures don't satisfy him. Copernicus does.

GALILEO: Copernicus? "He that withholdeth corn the people shall curse him." Book of Proverbs.

BARBERINI: "A prudent man concealeth knowledge." Also Book of Proverbs.

GALILEO: "Where no oxen are, the stable is clean, but much increase is by the strength of the ox."

BARBERINI: "He that ruleth his spirit is better than he that taketh a city."

GALILEO: "But a broken spirit drieth up the bones." (*Pause.*) "Doth not wisdom cry?"

BARBERINI: "Can one walk on hot coals and his feet not be scorched?" — Welcome to Rome, Friend Galileo. You recall the legend of our city's origin? Two small boys found sustenance and refuge with a she-wolf and from that day we have paid the price for the she-wolf's milk. But the place is not bad. We have everything for your pleasure — from a scholarly dispute with Bellarmin to ladies of high degree. Look at that woman flaunting herself. No? He wants a weighty discussion! All right! (*To* GALILEO:) You people speak in terms of circles and ellipses and regular velocities — simple movements that the human mind can grasp — very convenient — but suppose Almighty God had taken it into His head to make the stars move like that . . . (*He describes an irregular motion with his fingers through the air.*) . . . then where would you be?

GALILEO: My good man — the Almighty would have endowed us with brains like that . . . (*Repeats the movement.*) . . . so that

we could grasp the movements . . . (*Repeats the movement.*)
. . . like that. I believe in the brain.

BARBERINI: I consider the brain inadequate. He doesn't answer. He
is too polite to tell me he considers *my* brain inadequate. What
is one to do with him? Butter wouldn't melt in his mouth. All
he wants to do is to prove that God made a few boners in
astronomy. God didn't study his astronomy hard enough before He composed Holy Writ. (*To the* SECRETARIES:) Don't
take anything down. This is a scientific discussion among
friends.

BELLARMIN (*to* GALILEO): Does it not appear more probable — even
to you — that the Creator knows more about His work than
the created?

GALILEO: In his blindness man is liable to misread not only the sky
but also the Bible.

BELLARMIN: The interpretation of the Bible is a matter for the min-
isters of God. (GALILEO *remains silent.*) At last you are quiet.
(*He gestures to the* SECRETARIES. *They start writing.*) Tonight
the Holy Office has decided that the theory according to
which the earth goes around the sun is foolish, absurd, and a
heresy. I am charged, Mr. Galilei, with cautioning you to
abandon these teachings. (*To the* FIRST SECRETARY:) Would
you repeat that?

FIRST SECRETARY (*reading*): "His Eminence, Cardinal Bellarmin, to
the aforesaid Galilei: The Holy Office has resolved that the
theory according to which the earth goes around the sun is
foolish, absurd, and a heresy. I am charged, Mr. Galilei, with
cautioning you to abandon these teachings."

GALILEO (*rocking on his base*): But the facts!

BARBERINI (*consoling*): Your findings have been ratified by the
Papal Observatory, Galilei. That should be most flattering to
you. . . .

BELLARMIN (*cutting in*): The Holy Office formulated the decree
without going into details.

GALILEO (*to* BARBERINI): Do you realize, the future of all scientific
research is . . .

BELLARMIN (*cutting in*): Completely assured, Mr. Galilei. It is not given to man to know the truth: it is granted to him to seek after the truth. Science is the legitimate and beloved daughter of the Church. She must have confidence in the Church.

GALILEO (*infuriated*): I would not try confidence by whistling her too often.

BARBERINI (*quickly*): Be careful what you're doing — you'll be throwing out the baby with the bath water, friend Galilei. (*Serious:*) We need you more than you need us.

BELLARMIN: Well, it is time we introduced our distinguished friend to our guests. The whole country talks of him!

BARBERINI: Let us replace our masks, Bellarmin. Poor Galilei hasn't got one.

He laughs. They take GALILEO *out.*

FIRST SECRETARY: Did you get his last sentence?

SECOND SECRETARY: Yes. Do you have what he said about believing in the brain?

Another cardinal — the INQUISITOR *— enters.*

INQUISITOR: Did the conference take place?

The FIRST SECRETARY *hands him the papers and the* INQUISITOR *dismisses the* SECRETARIES. *They go. The* INQUISITOR *sits down and starts to read the transcription. Two or three* YOUNG LADIES *skitter across the stage; they see the* INQUISITOR *and curtsy as they go.*

YOUNG GIRL: Who was that?

HER FRIEND: The Cardinal Inquisitor.

They giggle and go. Enter VIRGINIA. *She curtsies as she goes. The* INQUISITOR *stops her.*

INQUISITOR: Good evening, my child. Beautiful night. May I congratulate you on your betrothal? Your young man comes from a fine family. Are you staying with us here in Rome?

VIRGINIA: Not now, Your Eminence. I must go home to prepare for the wedding.

INQUISITOR: Ah. You are accompanying your father to Florence. That should please him. Science must be cold comfort in a

home. Your youth and warmth will keep him down to earth.
It is easy to get lost up there. (*He gestures to the sky.*)

VIRGINIA: He doesn't talk to me about the stars, Your Eminence.

INQUISITOR: No. (*He laughs.*) They don't eat fish in the fisherman's
house. I can tell you something about astronomy. My child,
it seems that God has blessed our modern astronomers with
imaginations. It is quite alarming! Do you know that the earth
— which we old fogies supposed to be so large — has shrunk
to something no bigger than a walnut, and the new universe
has grown so vast that prelates — and even cardinals — look
like ants? Why, God Almighty might lose sight of a Pope! I
wonder if I know your Father Confessor.

VIRGINIA: Father Christopherus, from Saint Ursula's at Florence,
Your Eminence.

INQUISITOR: My dear child, your father will need you. Not so much
now perhaps, but one of these days. You are pure, and there is
strength in purity. Greatness is sometimes, indeed often, too
heavy a burden for those to whom God has granted it. What
man is so great that he has no place in a prayer? But I am
keeping you, my dear. Your fiancé will be jealous of me, and
I am afraid your father will never forgive me for holding forth
on astronomy. Go to your dancing and remember me to
Father Christopherus.

VIRGINIA *kisses his ring and runs off. The* INQUISITOR *resumes
his reading.*

Galileo, feeling grim,
A young monk came to visit him.
The monk was born of common folk.
It was of science that they spoke.

Garden of the Florentine AMBASSADOR *in Rome. Distant hum of a great city.* GALILEO *and the* LITTLE MONK *of Scene Five are talking.*

GALILEO: Let's hear it. That robe you're wearing gives you the right to say whatever you want to say. Let's hear it.

LITTLE MONK: I have studied physics, Mr. Galilei.

GALILEO: That might help us if it enabled you to admit that two and two are four.

LITTLE MONK: Mr. Galilei, I have spent four sleepless nights trying to reconcile the decree that I have read with the moons of Jupiter that I have seen. This morning I decided to come to see you after I had said mass.

GALILEO: To tell me that Jupiter has no moons?

LITTLE MONK: No, I found out that I think the decree a wise decree. It has shocked me into realizing that free research has its dangers. I have had to decide to give up astronomy. However, I felt the impulse to confide in you some of the motives which have impelled even a passionate physicist to abandon his work.

GALILEO: Your motives are familiar to me.

LITTLE MONK: You mean, of course, the special powers invested in certain commissions of the Holy Office? But there is something else. I would like to talk to you about my family. I do not come from the great city. My parents are peasants in the Campagna, who know about the cultivation of the olive tree, and not much about anything else. Too often these days when I am trying to concentrate on tracking down the moons of Jupiter, I see my parents. I see them sitting by the fire with

my sister, eating their curded cheese. I see the beams of the
ceiling above them, which the smoke of centuries has black-
ened, and I can see the veins stand out on their toil-worn hands,
and the little spoons in their hands. They scrape a living, and
underlying their poverty there is a sort of order. There are
routines. The routine of scrubbing the floors, the routine of the
seasons in the olive orchard, the routine of paying taxes. The
troubles that come to them are recurrent troubles. My father
did not get his poor bent back all at once, but little by little, year
by year, in the olive orchard; just as year after year, with un-
failing regularity, childbirth has made my mother more and
more sexless. They draw the strength they need to sweat with
their loaded baskets up the stony paths, to bear children, even to
eat, from the sight of the trees greening each year anew, from
the reproachful face of the soil, which is never satisfied, and
from the little church and Bible texts they hear there on Sunday. They have been told that God relies upon them and that
the pageant of the world has been written around them that
they may be tested in the important or unimportant parts
handed out to them. How could they take it, were I to tell
them that they are on a lump of stone ceaselessly spinning in
empty space, circling around a second-rate star? What, then,
would be the use of their patience, their acceptance of misery?
What comfort, then, the Holy Scriptures, which have merci-
fully explained their crucifixion? The Holy Scriptures would
then be proved full of mistakes. No, I see them begin to look
frightened. I see them slowly put their spoons down on the
table. They would feel cheated. "There is no eye watching
over us, after all," they would say. "We have to start out on
our own, at our time of life. Nobody has planned a part for
us beyond this wretched one on a worthless star. There is no
meaning in our misery. Hunger is just not having eaten. It is
no test of strength. Effort is just stooping and carrying. It is
not a virtue." Can you understand that I read into the decree
of the Holy Office a noble motherly pity and a great goodness
of the soul?

GALILEO (*embarrassed*): Hm, well at least you have found out that
it is not a question of the satellites of Jupiter, but of the peas-

ants of the Campagna! And don't try to break me down by the halo of beauty that radiates from old age. How does a pearl develop in an oyster? A jagged grain of sand makes its way into the oyster's shell and makes its life unbearable. The oyster exudes slime to cover the grain of sand and the slime eventually hardens into a pearl. The oyster nearly dies in the process. To hell with the pearl, give me the healthy oyster! And virtues are not exclusive to misery. If your parents were prosperous and happy, they might develop the virtues of happiness and prosperity. Today the virtues of exhaustion are caused by the exhausted land. For that my new water pumps could work more wonders than their ridiculous superhuman efforts. Be fruitful and multiply: for war will cut down the population, and our fields are barren! (*A pause.*) Shall I lie to your people?

LITTLE MONK: We must be silent from the highest of motives: the inward peace of less fortunate souls.

GALILEO: My dear man, as a bonus for not meddling with your parents' peace, the authorities are tendering me, on a silver platter, persecution-free, my share of the fat sweated from your parents, who, as you know, were made in God's image. Should I condone this decree, my motives might not be disinterested: easy life, no persecution and so on.

LITTLE MONK: Mr. Galilei, I am a priest.

GALILEO: You are also a physicist. How can new machinery be evolved to domesticate the river water if we physicists are forbidden to study, discuss, and pool our findings about the greatest machinery of all, the machinery of the heavenly bodies? Can I reconcile my findings on the paths of falling bodies with the current belief in the tracks of witches on broom sticks? (*A pause.*) I am sorry — I shouldn't have said that.

LITTLE MONK: You don't think that the truth, if it is the truth, would make its way without us?

GALILEO: No! No! No! As much of the truth gets through as we push through. You talk about the Campagna peasants as if they were the moss on their huts. Naturally, if they don't get a move on and learn to think for themselves, the most efficient of irrigation systems cannot help them. I can see their divine patience, but where is their divine fury?

LITTLE MONK (*helpless*): They are old!

GALILEO *stands for a moment, beaten; he cannot meet the* LITTLE MONK's *eyes. He takes a manuscript from the table and throws it violently on the ground.*

LITTLE MONK: What is that?

GALILEO: Here is writ what draws the ocean when it ebbs and flows. Let it lie there. Thou shalt not read. (LITTLE MONK *has picked up the manuscript.*) Already! An apple of the tree of knowledge, he can't wait, he wolfs it down. He will rot in hell for all eternity. Look at him, where are his manners? — Sometimes I think I would let them imprison me in a place a thousand feet beneath the earth where no light could reach me, if in exchange I could find out what stuff that is: "Light." The bad thing is that, when I find something, I have to boast about it like a lover or a drunkard or a traitor. That is a hopeless vice and leads to the abyss. I wonder how long I shall be content to discuss it with my dog?

LITTLE MONK (*immersed in the manuscript*): I don't understand this sentence.

GALILEO: I'll explain it to you, I'll explain it to you.

They are sitting on the floor.

8

Eight long years with tongue in cheek
Of what ke knew he did not speak.
Then temptation grew too great
And Galileo challenged fate.

GALILEO's *house in Florence again.* GALILEO *is supervising his assistants* ANDREA, FEDERZONI, *and the* LITTLE MONK *who are about to prepare an experiment.* MRS. SARTI *and* VIRGINIA *are at a long table sewing bridal linen. There is a new telescope, larger than the old one. At the moment it is covered with a cloth.*

ANDREA (*looking up a schedule*): Thursday. Afternoon. Floating bodies again. Ice, bowl of water, scales, and it says here an iron needle. Aristotle.

VIRGINIA: Ludovico likes to entertain. We must take care to be neat. His mother notices every stitch. She doesn't approve of father's books.

MRS. SARTI: That's all a thing of the past. He hasn't published a book for years.

VIRGINIA: That's true. Oh Sarti, it's fun sewing a trousseau.

MRS. SARTI: Virginia, I want to talk to you. You are very young, and you have no mother, and your father is putting those pieces of ice in water, and marriage is too serious a business to go into blind. Now you should go to see a real astronomer from the university and have him cast your horoscope so you know where you stand. (VIRGINIA *giggles.*) What's the matter?

VIRGINIA: I've been already.

MRS. SARTI: Tell Sarti.

VIRGINIA: I have to be careful for three months now because the sun is in Capricorn, but after that I get a favorable ascendant, and I can undertake a journey if I am careful of Uranus, as I'm a Scorpion.

MRS. SARDI: What about Ludovico?

VIRGINIA: He's a Leo, the astronomer said. Leos are sensual. (*Giggles.*)

There is a knock at the door, it opens. Enter the RECTOR OF THE UNIVERSITY, *the philosopher of Scene Four, bringing a book.*

RECTOR (*to* VIRGINIA): This is about the burning issue of the moment. He may want to glance over it. My faculty would appreciate his comments. No, don't disturb him now, my dear. Every minute one takes of your father's time is stolen from Italy. (*He goes.*)

VIRGINIA: Federzoni! The rector of the university brought this.

FEDERZONI *takes it.*

GALILEO: What's it about?

FEDERZONI (*spelling*): DE MACULIS IN SOLE.

ANDREA: Oh, it's on the sun spots!

ANDREA *comes one side, and the* LITTLE MONK *the other, to look at the book.*

ANDREA: A new one!

FEDERZONI *resentfully puts the book into their hands and continues with the preparation of the experiment.*

ANDREA: Listen to this dedication. (*Quotes:*) "To the greatest living authority on physics, Galileo Galilei." — I read Fabricius' paper the other day. Fabricius says the spots are clusters of planets between us and the sun.

LITTLE MONK: Doubtful.

GALILEO (*noncommittal*): Yes?

ANDREA: Paris and Prague hold that they are vapors from the sun. Federzoni doubts that.

FEDERZONI: Me? You leave me out. I said "hm," that was all. And don't discuss new things before me. I can't read the material, it's in Latin. (*He drops the scales and stands trembling with fury.*) Tell me, can I doubt anything?

GALILEO *walks over and picks up the scales silently. Pause.*

LITTLE MONK: There is happiness in doubting, I wonder why.

ANDREA: Aren't we going to take this up?

GALILEO: At the moment we are investigating floating bodies.

ANDREA: Mother has baskets full of letters from all over Europe asking his opinion.

FEDERZONI: The question is whether you can afford to remain silent.

GALILEO: I cannot afford to be smoked on a wood fire like a ham.

ANDREA (*surprised*): Ah. You think the sun spots may have something to do with that again? (GALILEO *does not answer*.)

ANDREA: Well, we stick to fiddling about with bits of ice in water. That can't hurt you.

GALILEO: Correct. — Our thesis!

ANDREA: All things that are lighter than water float, and all things that are heavier sink.

GALILEO: Aristotle says —

LITTLE MONK (*reading out of a book, translating*): "A broad and flat disk of ice, although heavier than water, still floats, because it is unable to divide the water."

GALILEO: Well. Now I push the ice below the surface. I take away the pressure of my hands. What happens?
Pause.

LITTLE MONK: It rises to the surface.

GALILEO: Correct. It seems to be able to divide the water as it's coming up, doesn't it?

LITTLE MONK: Could it be lighter than water after all?

GALILEO: Aha!

ANDREA: Then all things that are lighter than water float, and all things that are heavier sink. Q.E.D.

GALILEO: Not at all. Hand me that iron needle. Heavier than water? (*They all nod.*) A piece of paper. (*He places the needle on a piece of paper and floats it on the surface of the water. Pause.*) Do not be hasty with your conclusion. (*Pause.*) What happens?

FEDERZONI: The paper has sunk, the needle is floating.

VIRGINIA: What's the matter?

MRS. SARTI: Every time I hear them laugh it sends shivers down my spine.

There is a knocking at the outer door.

MRS. SARTI: Who's that at the door?

Enter LUDOVICO. VIRGINIA *runs to him. They embrace.* LUDOVICO *is followed by a servant with baggage.*

MRS. SARTI: Well!

VIRGINIA: Oh! Why didn't you write that you were coming?

LUDOVICO: I decided on the spur of the moment. I was over inspecting our vineyards at Bucciole. I couldn't keep away.

GALILEO: Who's that?

LITTLE MONK: Miss Virginia's intended. What's the matter with your eyes?

GALILEO (*blinking*): Oh yes, it's Ludovico, so it is. Well! Sarti, get a jug of that Sicilian wine, the old kind. We celebrate.

Everybody sits down. MRS. SARTI *has left, followed by* LUDOVICO'S SERVANT.

GALILEO: Well, Ludovico, old man. How are the horses?

LUDOVICO: The horses are fine.

GALILEO: Fine.

LUDOVICO: But those vineyards need a firm hand. (*To* VIRGINIA:) You look pale. Country life will suit you. Mother's planning on September.

VIRGINIA: I suppose I oughtn't, but stay here, I've got something to show you.

LUDOVICO: What?

VIRGINIA: Never mind. I won't be ten minutes. (*She runs out.*)

LUDOVICO: How's life these days, sir?

GALILEO: Dull. — How was the journey?

LUDOVICO: Dull. — Before I forget, mother sends her congratulations on your admirable tact over the latest rumblings of science.

GALILEO: Thank her from me.

LUDOVICO: Christopher Clavius had all Rome on its ears. He said he was afraid that the turning-around-business might crop up again on account of these spots on the sun.

ANDREA: Clavius is on the same track! (*To* LUDOVICO:) My mother's baskets are full of letters from all over Europe asking Mr. Galilei's opinion.

GALILEO: I am engaged in investigating the habits of floating bodies. Any harm in that?

MRS. SARTI *re-enters, followed by the* SERVANT. *They bring wine and glasses on a tray.*

GALILEO (*hands out the wine*): What news from the Holy City, apart from the prospect of my sins?

LUDOVICO: The Holy Father is on his death bed. Hadn't you heard?

LITTLE MONK: My goodness! What about the succession?

LUDOVICO: All the talk is of Barberini.

GALILEO: Barberini?

ANDREA: Mr. Galilei knows Barberini.

LITTLE MONK: Cardinal Barberini is a mathematician.

FEDERZONI: A scientist in the chair of Peter!
    Pause.

GALILEO (*cheering up enormously*): This means change. We might live to see the day, Federzoni, when we don't have to whisper that two and two are four. (*To* LUDOVICO:) I like this wine. Don't you, Ludovico?

LUDOVICO: I like it.

GALILEO: I know the hill where it is grown. The slope is steep and stony, the grape almost blue. I am fond of this wine.

LUDOVICO: Yes, sir.

GALILEO: There are shadows in this wine. It is almost sweet but just stops short. — Andrea, clear that stuff away, ice, bowl and needle. — I cherish the consolations of the flesh. I have no patience with cowards who call them weaknesses. I say there is a certain achievement in enjoying things.

The PUPILS *get up and go to the experiment table.*

LITTLE MONK: What are we to do?

FEDERZONI: He is starting on the sun.

They begin with clearing up.

ANDREA (*singing in a low voice*):
    The Bible proves the earth stands still,

The Pope, he swears with tears:
The earth stands still. To prove it so
He takes it by the ears.

LUDOVICO: What's the excitement?

MRS. SARTI: You're not going to start those hellish goings-on again, Mr. Galilei?

ANDREA:
And gentlefolk, they say so too.
Each learned doctor proves
(If you grease his palm): The earth stands still.
And yet — and yet it moves.

GALILEO: Barberini is in the ascendant, so your mother is uneasy, and you're sent to investigate me. Correct me if I am wrong, Ludovico. Clavius is right: these spots on the sun interest me.

ANDREA: We might find out that the sun also revolves. How would you like that, Ludovico?

GALILEO: Do you like my wine, Ludovico?

LUDOVICO: I told you I did, sir.

GALILEO: You really like it?

LUDOVICO: I like it.

GALILEO: Tell me, Ludovico, would you consider going so far as to accept a man's wine or his daughter without insisting that he drop his profession? I have no wish to intrude, but have the moons of Jupiter affected Virginia's bottom?

MRS. SARTI: That isn't funny, it's just vulgar. I am going for Virginia.

LUDOVICO (keeps her back): Marriages in families such as mine are not arranged on a basis of sexual attraction alone.

GALILEO: Did they keep you back from marrying my daughter for eight years because I was on probation?

LUDOVICO: My future wife must take her place in the family pew.

GALILEO: You mean, if the daughter of a bad man sat in your family pew, your peasants might stop paying the rent?

LUDOVICO: In a sort of way.

GALILEO: When I was your age, the only person I allowed to rap me on the knuckles was my girl.

LUDOVICO: My mother was assured that you had undertaken not to get mixed up in this turning-around-business again, sir.

GALILEO: We had a conservative Pope then.

MRS. SARTI: Had! His Holiness is not dead yet!

GALILEO (*with relish*): Pretty nearly.

MRS. SARTI: That man will weigh a chip of ice fifty times, but when it comes to something that's convenient, he believes it blindly. "Is His Holiness dead?" — "Pretty nearly!"

LUDOVICO: You will find, sir, if His Holiness passes away, the new Pope, whoever he turns out to be, will respect the convictions held by the solid families of the country.

GALILEO (*to* ANDREA): That remains to be seen. — Andrea, get out the screen. We'll throw the image of the sun on our screen to save our eyes.

LITTLE MONK: I thought you'd been working at it. Do you know when I guessed it? When you didn't recognize Mr. Marsili.

MRS. SARTI: If my son has to go to hell for sticking to you, that's my affair, but you have no right to trample on your daughter's happiness.

LUDOVICO (*to his* SERVANT): Giuseppe, take my baggage back to the coach, will you?

MRS. SARTI: This will kill her. (*She runs out, still clutching the jug.*)

LUDOVICO (*politely*): Mr. Galilei, if we Marsilis were to countenance teachings frowned on by the church, it would unsettle our peasants. Bear in mind: these poor people in their brute state get everything upside down. They are nothing but animals. They will never comprehend the finer points of astronomy. Why, two months ago a rumor went around, an apple had been found on a pear tree, and they left their work in the fields to discuss it.

GALILEO (*interested*): Did they?

LUDOVICO: I have seen the day when my poor mother has had to have a dog whipped before their eyes to remind them to keep their place. Oh, you may have seen the waving corn from the window of your comfortable coach. You have, no doubt, nibbled our olives, and absentmindedly eaten our cheese, but you can have no idea how much responsibility that sort of thing entails.

GALILEO: Young man, I do not eat my cheese absentmindedly. (*To* ANDREA:) Are we ready?

ANDREA: Yes, sir.

GALILEO (*leaves* LUDOVICO *and adjusts the mirror*): You would not confine your whippings to dogs to remind your peasants to keep their places, would you, Marsili?

LUDOVICO (*after a pause*): Mr. Galilei, you have a wonderful brain, it's a pity.

LITTLE MONK (*astonished*): He threatened you.

GALILEO: Yes. And he threatened you too. We might unsettle his peasants. Your sister, Fulganzio, who works the lever of the olive press, might laugh out loud if she heard the sun is not a gilded coat of arms but a lever too. The earth turns because the sun turns it.

ANDREA: That could interest his steward too and even his money lender — and the seaport towns. . . .

FEDERZONI: None of them speak Latin.

GALILEO: I might write in plain language. The work we do is exacting. Who would go through the strain for less than the population at large!

LUDOVICO: I see you have made your decision. It was inevitable. You will always be a slave of your passions. Excuse me to Virginia, I think it's as well I don't see her now.

GALILEO: The dowry is at your disposal at any time.

LUDOVICO: Good afternoon. (*He goes, followed by the* SERVANT.)

ANDREA: Exit Ludovico. To hell with all Marsilis, Villanis, Orsinis, Canes, Nuccolis, Soldanieris. . . .

FEDERZONI: . . . who ordered the earth stand still because their castles might be shaken loose if it revolves . . .

LITTLE MONK: . . . and who only kiss the Pope's feet as long as he uses them to trample on the people. God made the physical world, God made the human brain. God will allow physics.

ANDREA: They will try to stop us.

GALILEO: Thus we enter the observation of these spots on the sun in which we are interested, at our own risk, not counting on protection from a problematical new Pope . . .

ANDREA: . . . but with great likelihood of dispelling Fabricius' vapors, and the shadows of Paris and Prague, and of establishing the rotation of the sun . . .

GALILEO: . . . and with *some* likelihood of establishing the rotation of the sun. My intention is not to prove that I was right but to find out *whether* I was right. "Abandon hope all ye who enter — an observation." Before assuming these phenomena are spots, which would suit us, let us first set about proving that they are not — fried fish. We crawl by inches. What we find today we will wipe from the blackboard tomorrow and reject it — unless it shows up again the day after tomorrow. And if we find anything which would suit us, that thing we will eye with particular distrust. In fact, we will approach this observing of the sun with the implacable determination to prove that the earth stands still and only if hopelessly defeated in this pious undertaking can we allow ourselves to wonder if we may not have been right all the time: the earth revolves. Take the cloth off the telescope and turn it on the sun.

Quietly they start work. When the corruscating image of the sun is focused on the screen, VIRGINIA *enters hurriedly, her wedding dress on, her hair disheveled,* MRS. SARTI *with her, carrying her wedding veil. The two women realize what has happened.* VIRGINIA *faints.* ANDREA, LITTLE MONK *and* GALILEO *rush to her.* FEDERZONI *continues working.*

9

On April Fools' Day, thirty two,
Of science there was much ado.
People had learned from Galilei:
They used his teaching in their way.

Around the corner from the market place a STREET SINGER *and
his* WIFE, *who is costumed to represent the earth in a skeleton
globe made of thin bands of brass, are holding the attention
of a sprinkling of representative citizens, some in masquerade
who were on their way to see the carnival procession. From
the market place the noise of an impatient crowd.*

BALLAD SINGER (*accompanied by his* WIFE *on the guitar*):
When the Almighty made the universe
He made the earth and then he made the sun.
Then round the earth he bade the sun to turn —
That's in the Bible, Genesis, Chapter One.
And from that time all beings here below
Were in obedient circles meant to go:
   Around the pope the cardinals
   Around the cardinals the bishops
   Around the bishops the secretaries
   Around the secretaries the aldermen
   Around the aldermen the craftsmen
   Around the craftsmen the servants
   Around the servants the dogs, the chickens, and the beggars.

A conspicuous reveller — henceforth called the SPINNER —
*has slowly caught on and is exhibiting his idea of spinning
around. He does not lose dignity, he faints with mock grace.*

BALLAD SINGER:
Up stood the learned Galileo
Glanced briefly at the sun
And said: "Almighty God was wrong
In Genesis, Chapter One!"

Now that was rash, my friends, it is no matter small
For heresy will spread today like foul diseases.
Change Holy Writ, forsooth? What will be left at all?
Why: each of us would say and do just what he pleases!

Three wretched EXTRAS, *employed by the Chamber of Commerce, enter. Two of them, in ragged costumes, moodily bear a litter with a mock throne. The third sits on the throne. He wears sacking, a false beard, a prop crown, he carries a prop orb and sceptre, and around his chest the inscription* "THE KING OF HUNGARY." *The litter has a card with* "No. 4" *written on it. The litter bearers dump him down and listen to the* BALLAD SINGER.

BALLAD SINGER:

Good people, what will come to pass
If Galileo's teachings spread?
No altar boy will serve the mass
No servant girl will make the bed.

Now that is grave, my friends, it is no matter small:
For independent spirit spreads like foul diseases!
(Yet life is sweet and man is weak and after all —
How nice it is, for a little change, to do just as one pleases!)

The BALLAD SINGER *takes over the guitar. His* WIFE *dances around him, illustrating the motion of the earth. A* COBBLER'S BOY *with a pair of resplendent lacquered boots hung over his shoulder has been jumping up and down in mock excitement. There are three more children, dressed as grownups among the spectators, two together and a single one with mother. The* COBBLER'S BOY *takes the three* CHILDREN *in hand, forms a chain and leads it, moving to the music, in and out among the spectators, "whipping" the chain so that the last child bumps into people. On the way past a* PEASANT WOMAN, *he steals an egg from her basket. She gestures to him to return it. As he passes her again he quietly breaks the egg over her head. The* KING OF HUNGARY *ceremoniously hands his orb to one of his bearers, marches down with mock dignity, and chastises the* COBBLER'S BOY. *The parents remove the three* CHILDREN. *The unseemliness subsides.*

BALLAD SINGER:

The carpenters take wood and build
Their houses — not the church's pews.
And members of the cobblers' guild
Now boldly walk the streets — in shoes.
The tenant kicks the noble lord
Quite off the land he owned — like that!
The milk his wife once gave the priest
Now makes (at last!) her children fat.

Ts, ts, ts, ts, my friends, this is no matter small
For independent spirit spreads like foul diseases
People must keep their place, some down and some on top!
(Though it is nice, for a little change, to do just as one
pleases!)

The COBBLER'S BOY *has put on the lacquered boots he was
carrying. He struts off. The* BALLAD SINGER *takes over the guitar
again. His* WIFE *dances around him in increased tempo. A*
MONK *has been standing near a rich* COUPLE, *who are in subdued
costly clothes, without masks: shocked at the song, he now
leaves. A* DWARF *in the costume of an astronomer turns his
telescope on the departing* MONK, *thus drawing attention to the
rich* COUPLE. *In imitation of the* COBBLER'S BOY, *the* SPINNER
*forms a chain of grownups. They move to the music, in and
out, and between the rich* COUPLE. *The* SPINNER *changes the*
GENTLEMAN'S *bonnet for the ragged hat of a* BEGGAR. *The*
GENTLEMAN *decides to take this in good part, and a* GIRL *is
emboldened to take his dagger. The* GENTLEMAN *is miffed,
throws the* BEGGAR'S *hat back. The* BEGGAR *discards the* GENTLE-
MAN'S *bonnet and drops it on the ground. The* KING OF HUNGARY
has walked from his throne, taken an egg from the PEASANT
WOMAN, *and paid for it. He now ceremoniously breaks it over
the* GENTLEMAN'S *head as he is bending down to pick up his
bonnet. The* GENTLEMAN *conducts the* LADY *away from the
scene. The* KING OF HUNGARY, *about to resume his throne, finds
one of the* CHILDREN *sitting on it. The* GENTLEMAN *returns to
retrieve his dagger. Merriment. The* BALLAD SINGER *wanders off.
This is part of his routine. His* WIFE *sings to the* SPINNER.

WIFE:

Now speaking for myself I feel
That I could also do with a change.
You know, for me . . . (*Turning to a reveller.*) . . . *you*
have appeal
Maybe tonight we could arrange . . .

The DWARF-ASTRONOMER *has been amusing the people by focusing his telescope on her legs. The* BALLAD SINGER *has returned.*

BALLAD SINGER:

No, no, no, no, no, stop, Galileo, stop!
For independent spirit spreads like foul diseases
People must keep their place, some down and some on top!
(Though it is nice, for a little change, to do just as one pleases!)

The SPECTATORS *stand embarrassed. A* GIRL *laughs loudly.*

BALLAD SINGER *and his* WIFE:

Good people who have trouble here below
In serving cruel lords and gentle Jesus
Who bids you turn the other cheek just so
With mimicry.

While they prepare to strike the second blow:
Obedience will never cure your woe
So each of you wake up and do just as he pleases!

The BALLAD SINGER *and his* WIFE *hurriedly start to try to sell pamphlets to the spectators.*

BALLAD SINGER: Read all about the earth going round the sun, two centesimi only. As proved by the great Galileo. Two centesimi only. Written by a local scholar. Understandable to one and all. Buy one for your friends, your children and your aunty Rosa, two centesimi only. Abbreviated but complete. Fully illustrated with pictures of the planets, including Venus, two centesimi only.

During the speech of the BALLAD SINGER *we hear the carnival procession approaching followed by laughter. A* REVELLER *rushes in.*

REVELLER: The procession!

The litter bearers speedily joggle out the KING OF HUNGARY. *The* SPECTATORS *turn and look at the first float of the procession, which now makes its appearance. It bears a gigantic figure of* GALILEO, *holding in one hand an open Bible with the pages crossed out. The other hand points to the Bible, and the head mechanically turns from side to side as if to say "No! No!"*

A LOUD VOICE: Galileo, the Bible killer!

The laughter from the market place becomes uproarious. The MONK *comes flying from the market place followed by delighted* CHILDREN.

10

The depths are hot, the heights are chill
The streets are loud, the court is still.

Antechamber and staircase in the Medicean palace in Florence.
GALILEO, *with a book under his arm, waits with his* DAUGHTER
to be admitted to the presence of the PRINCE.

VIRGINIA: They are a long time.

GALILEO: Yes.

VIRGINIA: Who is that funny looking man? (*She indicates the* IN-
FORMER *who has entered casually and seated himself in the
background, taking no apparent notice of* GALILEO.)

GALILEO: I don't know.

VIRGINIA: It's not the first time I have seen him around. He gives
me the creeps.

GALILEO: Nonsense. We're in Florence, not among robbers in the
mountains of Corsica.

VIRGINIA: Here comes the Rector.

The RECTOR *comes down the stairs.*

GALILEO: Gaffone is a bore. He attaches himself to you.

The RECTOR *passes, scarcely nodding.*

GALILEO: My eyes are bad today. Did he acknowledge us?

VIRGINIA: Barely. (*Pause.*) What's in your book? Will they say it's
heretical?

GALILEO: You hang around church too much. And getting up at
dawn and scurrying to mass is ruining your skin. You pray for
me, don't you?

A MAN *comes down the stairs.*

VIRGINIA: Here's Mr. Matti. You designed a machine for his iron
foundries.

MATTI: How were the squabs, Mr. Galilei? (*Low.*) My brother and I had a good laugh the other day. He picked up a racy pamphlet against the Bible somewhere. It quoted you.

GALILEO: The squabs, Matti, were wonderful, thank you again. Pamphlets I know nothing about. The Bible and Homer are my favorite reading.

MATTI: No necessity to be cautious with me, Mr. Galilei. I am on your side. I am not a man who knows about the motions of the stars, but you have championed the freedom to teach new things. Take that mechanical cultivator they have in Germany which you described to me. I can tell you, it will never be used in this country. The same circles that are hampering you now will forbid the physicians at Bologna to cut up corpses for research. Do you know, they have such things as money markets in Amsterdam and in London? Schools for business, too. Regular papers with news. Here we are not even free to make money. I have a stake in your career. They are against iron foundries because they say the gathering of so many workers in one place fosters immorality! If they ever try anything, Mr. Galilei, remember you have friends in all walks of life including an iron founder. Good luck to you. (*He goes.*)

GALILEO: Good man, but need he be so affectionate in public? His voice carries. They will always claim me as their spiritual leader particularly in places where it doesn't help me at all. I have written a book about the mechanics of the firmament, that is all. What they do or don't do with it is not my concern.

VIRGINIA (*loud*): If people only knew how you disagreed with those goings-on all over the country last All Fools' Day.

GALILEO: Yes. Offer honey to a bear, and lose your arm if the beast is hungry.

VIRGINIA (*low*): Did the prince ask you to come here today?

GALILEO: I sent word I was coming. He will want the book, he has paid for it. My health hasn't been any too good lately. I may accept Sagredo's invitation to stay with him in Padua for a few weeks.

VIRGINIA: You couldn't manage without your books.

GALILEO: Sagredo has an excellent library.

VIRGINIA: We haven't had this month's salary yet —

GALILEO: Yes. (*The* CARDINAL INQUISITOR *passes down the staircase. He bows deeply in answer to* GALILEO's *bow.*) What is he doing in Florence? If they try to do anything to me, the new Pope will meet them with an iron NO. And the Prince is my pupil, he would never have me extradited.

VIRGINIA: Psst. The Lord Chamberlain.

The LORD CHAMBERLAIN *comes down the stairs.*

LORD CHAMBERLAIN: His Highness had hoped to find time for you, Mr. Galilei. Unfortunately, he has to leave immediately to judge the parade at the Riding Academy. On what business did you wish to see His Highness?

GALILEO: I wanted to present my book to His Highness.

LORD CHAMBERLAIN: How are your eyes today?

GALILEO: So, so. With His Highness' permission, I am dedicating the book . . .

LORD CHAMBERLAIN: Your eyes are a matter of great concern to His Highness. Could it be that you have been looking too long and too often through your marvelous tube? (*He leaves without accepting the book.*)

VIRGINIA (*greatly agitated*): Father, I am afraid.

GALILEO: He didn't take the book, did he? (*Low and resolute:*) Keep a straight face. We are not going home, but to the house of the lens-grinder. There is a coach and horses in his backyard. Keep your eyes to the front, don't look back at that man.

They start. The LORD CHAMBERLAIN *comes back.*

LORD CHAMBERLAIN: Oh, Mr. Galilei, His Highness has just charged me to inform you that the Florentine Court is no longer in a position to oppose the request of the Holy Inquisition to interrogate you in Rome.

11

The Pope

A chamber in the Vatican. The POPE, URBAN VIII — *formerly* CARDINAL BARBERINI — *is giving audience to the* CARDINAL INQUISITOR. *The trampling and shuffling of many feet is heard throughout the scene from the adjoining corridors. During the scene the* POPE *is being robed for the conclave he is about to attend: at the beginning of the scene he is plainly* BARBERINI, *but as the scene proceeds he is more and more obscured by grandiose vestments.*

POPE: No! No! No!

INQUISITOR (*referring to the owners of the shuffling feet*): Doctors of all chairs from the universities, representatives of the special orders of the Church, representatives of the clergy as a whole who have come believing with child-like faith in the word of God as set forth in the Scriptures, who have come to hear Your Holiness confirm their faith: and Your Holiness is really going to tell them that the Bible can no longer be regarded as the alphabet of truth?

POPE: I will not set myself up against the multiplication table. No!

INQUISITOR: Ah, that is what these people say, that it is the multiplication table. Their cry is, "The figures compel us," but where do these figures come from? Plainly they come from doubt. These men doubt everything. Can society stand on doubt and not on faith? "Thou art my master, but I doubt whether it is for the best." "This is my neighbor's house and my neighbor's wife, but why shouldn't they belong to me?" After the plague, after the new war, after the unparalleled disaster of the Reformation, your dwindling flock look to their shepherd, and now the mathematicians turn their tubes on the sky and announce to the world that you have not the best advice about the heavens either — up to now your only uncontested sphere of influence. This Galilei started meddling

387

in machines at an early age. Now that men in ships are venturing on the great oceans — I am not against that of course — they are putting their faith in a brass-bowl they call a compass and not in Almighty God.

POPE: This man is the greatest physicist of our time. He is the light of Italy, and not just any muddlehead.

INQUISITOR: Would we have had to arrest him otherwise? This bad man knows what he is doing, not writing his books in Latin, but in the jargon of the market place.

POPE (*occupied with the shuffling feet*): That was not in the best of taste. (*A pause.*) These shuffling feet are making me nervous.

INQUISITOR: May they be more telling than my words, Your Holiness. Shall all these go from you with doubt in their hearts?

POPE: This man has friends. What about Versailles? What about the Viennese court? They will call Holy Church a cesspool for defunct ideas. Keep your hands off him.

INQUISITOR: In practice it will never get far. He is a man of the flesh. He would soften at once.

POPE: He has more enjoyment in him than any man I ever saw. He loves eating and drinking and thinking. To excess. He indulges in thinking-bouts! He cannot say no to an old wine or a new thought. (*Furious:*) I do not want a condemnation of physical facts. I do not want to hear battle cries: Church, church, church! Reason, reason, reason! (*Pause.*) These shuffling feet are intolerable. Has the whole world come to my door?

INQUISITOR: Not the whole world, Your Holiness. A select gathering of the faithful.

Pause.

POPE (*exhausted*): It is clearly understood: he is not to be tortured. (*Pause.*) At the very most, he may be shown the instruments.

INQUISITOR: That will be adequate, Your Holiness. Mr. Galilei understands machinery.

The eyes of BARBERINI *look helplessly at the* CARDINAL INQUISITOR *from under the completely assembled panoply of* POPE URBAN VIII.

12

June twenty second, sixteen thirty three,
A momentous date for you and me.
Of all the days that was the one
An age of reason could have begun.

Again the garden of the Florentine AMBASSADOR *at Rome,*
where GALILEO'S *assistants wait the news of the trial. The*
LITTLE MONK *and* FEDERZONI *are attempting to concentrate on*
a game of chess. VIRGINIA *kneels in a corner, praying and*
counting her beads.

LITTLE MONK: The Pope didn't even grant him an audience.

FEDERZONI: No more scientific discussions.

ANDREA: The "Discorsi" will never be finished. The sum of his
findings. They will kill him.

FEDERZONI (*stealing a glance at him*): Do you really thing so?

ANDREA: He will never recant.

Silence.

LITTLE MONK: You know when you lie awake at night how your
mind fastens on to something irrelevant. Last night I kept
thinking: if only they would let him take his little stone in with
him, the appeal-to-reason-pebble that he always carries in his
pocket.

FEDERZONI: In the room *they'll* take him to, he won't have a pocket.

ANDREA: But he will not recant.

LITTLE MONK: How can they beat the truth out of a man who gave
his sight in order to see?

FEDERZONI: Maybe they can't.

Silence.

ANDREA (*speaking about* VIRGINIA): She is praying that he will
recant.

FEDERZONI: Leave her alone. She doesn't know whether she's on her head or on her heels since they got hold of her. They brought her Father Confessor from Florence.

The INFORMER *of Scene Ten enters.*

INFORMER: Mr. Galilei will be here soon. He may need a bed.

FEDERZONI: Have they let him out?

INFORMER: Mr. Galilei is expected to recant at five o'clock. The big bell of Saint Marcus will be rung and the complete text of his recantation publicly announced.

ANDREA: I don't believe it.

INFORMER: Mr. Galilei will be brought to the garden gate at the back of the house, to avoid the crowds collecting in the streets. (*He goes.*)

Silence.

ANDREA: The moon is an earth because the light of the moon is not her own. Jupiter is a fixed star, and four moons turn around Jupiter, therefore we are not shut in by crystal shells. The sun is the pivot of our world, therefore the earth is not the center. The earth moves, spinning about the sun. And he showed us. You can't make a man unsee what he has seen.

Silence.

FEDERZONI: Five o'clock is one minute.

VIRGINIA *prays louder.*

ANDREA: Listen all of you, they are murdering the truth.

He stops up his ears with his fingers. The two other pupils do the same. FEDERZONI *goes over to the* LITTLE MONK, *and all of them stand absolutely still in cramped positions. Nothing happens. No bell sounds. After a silence, filled with the murmur of* VIRGINIA'S *prayers,* FEDERZONI *runs to the wall to look at the clock. He turns around, his expression changed. He shakes his head. They drop their hands.*

FEDERZONI: No. No bell. It is three minutes after.

LITTLE MONK: He hasn't.

ANDREA: He held true. It is all right, it is all right.

LITTLE MONK: He did not recant.

FEDERZONI: No.

They embrace each other, they are delirious with joy.

ANDREA: So force cannot accomplish everything. What has been seen can't be unseen. Man is constant in the face of death.

FEDERZONI: June 22, 1633: dawn of the age of reason. I wouldn't have wanted to go on living if he had recanted.

LITTLE MONK: I didn't say anything, but I was in agony. Oh, ye of little faith!

ANDREA: I was sure.

FEDERZONI: It would have turned our morning to night.

ANDREA: It would have been as if the mountain had turned to water.

LITTLE MONK (*kneeling down, crying*): Oh God, I thank Thee.

ANDREA: Beaten humanity can lift its head. A man has stood up and said "no."

At this moment the bell of Saint Marcus begins to toll. They stand like statues. VIRGINIA *stands up.*

VIRGINIA: The bell of Saint Marcus. He is not damned.

From the street one hears the TOWN CRIER *reading* GALILEO'S *recantation.*

TOWN CRIER: I, Galileo Galilei, Teacher of Mathematics and Physics, do hereby publicly renounce my teaching that the earth moves. I foreswear this teaching with a sincere heart and unfeigned faith and detest and curse this and all other errors and heresies repugnant to the Holy Scriptures.

The lights dim; when they come up again the bell of Saint Marcus is petering out. VIRGINIA *has gone but the* SCHOLARS *are still there waiting.*

ANDREA (*loud*): The mountain did turn to water.

GALILEO *has entered quietly and unnoticed. He is changed, almost unrecognizable. He has heard* ANDREA. *He waits some seconds by the door for somebody to greet him. Nobody does. They retreat from him. He goes slowly and, because of his bad sight, uncertainly, to the front of the stage where he finds a chair, and sits down.*

ANDREA: I can't look at him. Tell him to go away.

FEDERZONI: Steady.

ANDREA (*hysterically*): He saved his big gut.

FEDERZONI: Get him a glass of water.

The LITTLE MONK *fetches a glass of water for* ANDREA. *Nobody acknowledges the presence of* GALILEO, *who sits silently on his chair listening to the voice of the* TOWN CRIER, *now in another street.*

ANDREA: I can walk. Just help me a bit.

They help him to the door.

ANDREA (*in the door*): "Unhappy is the land that breeds no hero."

GALILEO: No, Andrea: "Unhappy is the land that needs a hero."

Before the next scene a curtain with the following legend on it is lowered:

"You can plainly see that if a horse were to fall from a height of three or four feet, it could break its bones, whereas a dog would not suffer injury. The same applies to a cat from a height of as much as eight or ten feet, to a grasshopper from the top of a tower, and to an ant falling down from the moon. Nature could not allow a horse to become as big as twenty horses nor a giant as big as ten men, unless she were to change the proportions of all its members, particularly the bones. Thus the common assumption that great and small structures are equally tough is obviously wrong."

— FROM THE "DISCORSI"

13

1633–1642.

*Galileo Galilei remains a prisoner
of the Inquisition until his death.*

A country house near Florence. A large room simply furnished. There is a huge table, a leather chair, a globe of the world on a stand, and a narrow bed. A portion of the adjoining anteroom is visible, and the front door which opens into it.

An OFFICIAL OF THE INQUISITION *sits on guard in the anteroom. In the large room,* GALILEO *is quietly experimenting with a bent wooden rail and a small ball of wood. He is still vigorous but almost blind.*

After a while there is a knocking at the outside door. The OFFICIAL *opens it to a* PEASANT *who brings a plucked goose.* VIRGINIA *comes from the kitchen. She is past forty.*

PEASANT (*handing the goose to* VIRGINIA): I was told to deliver this here.

VIRGINIA: I didn't order a goose.

PEASANT: I was told to say it's from someone who was passing through.

    VIRGINIA *takes the goose, surprised. The* OFFICIAL *takes it from her and examines it suspiciously. Then, reassured, he hands it back to her. The* PEASANT *goes.* VIRGINIA *brings the goose in to* GALILEO.

VIRGINIA: Somebody who was passing through sent you something.

GALILEO: What is it?

VIRGINIA: Can't you see it?

GALILEO: No. (*He walks over.*) A goose. Any name?

VIRGINIA: No.

GALILEO (*weighing the goose*): Solid.

VIRGINIA (*cautiously*): Will you eat the liver, if I have it cooked with a little apple?

GALILEO: I had my dinner. Are you under orders to finish me off with food?

VIRGINIA: It's not rich. And what is wrong with your eyes again? You should be able to see it.

GALILEO: You were standing in the light.

VIRGINIA: I was not. — You haven't been writing again?

GALILEO (*sneering*): What do you think?

> VIRGINIA *takes the goose out into the anteroom and speaks to the* OFFICIAL.

VIRGINIA: You had better ask Monsignor Carpula to send the doctor. Father couldn't see this goose across the room. — Don't look at me like that. He has not been writing. He dictates everything to me, as you know.

OFFICIAL: Yes?

VIRGINIA: He abides by the rules. My father's repentance is sincere. I keep an eye on him. (*She hands him the goose.*) Tell the cook to fry the liver with an apple and an onion. (*She goes back into the large room.*) And you have no business to be doing that with those eyes of yours, father.

GALILEO: You may read me some Horace.

VIRGINIA: We should go on with your weekly letter to the Archbishop. Monsignor Carpula to whom we owe so much was all smiles the other day because the Archbishop had expressed his pleasure at your collaboration.

GALILEO: Where were we?

VIRGINIA (*sits down to take his dictation*): Paragraph four.

GALILEO: Read what you have.

VIRGINIA: "The position of the Church in the matter of the unrest at Genoa. I agree with Cardinal Spoletti in the matter of the unrest among the Venetian ropemakers . . ."

GALILEO: Yes. (*Dictates:*) I agree with Cardinal Spoletti in the matter of the unrest among the Venetian ropemakers: it is better to distribute good nourishing food in the name of charity than to pay them more for their bellropes, it being surely better to strengthen their faith than to encourage their acquisitiveness. St. Paul says: Charity never faileth. — How is that?

VIRGINIA: It's beautiful, father.

GALILEO: It couldn't be taken as irony?

VIRGINIA: No. The Archbishop will like it. It's so practical.

GALILEO: I trust your judgment. Read it over slowly.

VIRGINIA: "The position of the Church in the matter of the unrest . . ."

There is a knocking at the outside door. VIRGINIA *goes into the anteroom. The* OFFICIAL *opens the door. It is* ANDREA.

ANDREA: Good evening. I am sorry to call so late, I'm on my way to Holland. I was asked to look him up. Can I go in?

VIRGINIA: I don't know whether he will see you. You never came.

ANDREA: Ask him.

GALILEO *recognizes the voice. He sits motionless.* VIRGINIA *comes in to* GALILEO.

GALILEO: Is that Andrea?

VIRGINIA: Yes. (*Pause.*) I will send him away.

GALILEO: Show him in.

VIRGINIA *shows* ANDREA *in.* VIRGINIA *sits,* ANDREA *remains standing.*

ANDREA (*cool*): Have you been keeping well, Mr. Galilei?

GALILEO: Sit down. What are you doing these days? What are you working on? I heard it was something about hydraulics in Milan.

ANDREA: As he knew I was passing through, Fabricius of Amsterdam asked me to visit you and inquire about your health.

Pause.

GALILEO: I am very well.

ANDREA (*formally*): I am glad I can report you are in good health.

GALILEO: Fabricius will be glad to hear it. And you might inform him that, on account of the depth of my repentance, I live in comparative comfort.

ANDREA: Yes, we understand that the church is more than pleased with you. Your complete cooperativeness has had its effect. Not one paper expounding a new thesis has made its appearance in Italy since your submission.

Pause.

GALILEO: Unfortunately there are countries not under the wing of the church. Would you not say the erroneous condemned theories are still taught — there?

ANDREA (*relentless*): Things are almost at a standstill.

GALILEO: Are they? (*Pause.*) Nothing from Descartes in Paris?

ANDREA: Yes. On receiving the news of your recantation, he shelved his treatise on the nature of light.

GALILEO: I sometimes worry about my assistants whom I led into error. Have they benefited by my example?

ANDREA: In order to work I have to go to Holland.

GALILEO: Yes.

ANDREA: Federzoni is grinding lenses again, back in some shop.

GALILEO: He can't read the books.

ANDREA: Fulganzio, our little monk, has abandoned research and is resting in peace in the church.

GALILEO: So. (*Pause.*) My superiors are looking forward to my spiritual recovery. I am progressing as well as can be expected.

VIRGINIA: You are doing well, father.

GALILEO: Virginia, leave the room.

VIRGINIA *rises uncertainly and goes out.*

VIRGINIA (*to the* OFFICIAL): He was his pupil, so now he is his enemy. — Help me in the kitchen.

She leaves the anteroom with the OFFICIAL.

ANDREA: May I go now, sir?

GALILEO: I do not know why you came, Sarti. To unsettle me? I have to be prudent.

ANDREA: I'll be on my way.

GALILEO: As it is, I have relapses. I completed the "Discorsi."

ANDREA: You completed what?

GALILEO: My "Discorsi."

ANDREA: How?

GALILEO: I am allowed pen and paper. My superiors are intelligent men. They know the habits of a lifetime cannot be broken abruptly. But they protect me from any unpleasant consequences: they lock my pages away as I dictate them. And I should know better than to risk my comfort. I wrote the "Discorsi" out again during the night. The manuscript is in the globe. My vanity has up to now prevented me from destroying it. If you consider taking it, you will shoulder the entire risk. You will say it was pirated from the original in the hands of the Holy Office.

ANDREA, *as in a trance, has gone to the globe. He lifts the upper half and gets the book. He turns the pages as if wanting to devour them. In the background the opening sentences of the "Discorsi" appear:*

MY PURPOSE IS TO SET FORTH A VERY NEW SCIENCE DEALING WITH A VERY ANCIENT SUBJECT — MOTION. AND I HAVE DISCOVERED BY EXPERIMENT SOME PROPERTIES OF IT WHICH ARE WORTH KNOWING. . . .

GALILEO: I had to employ my time somehow.

The text disappears.

ANDREA: Two new sciences! This will be the foundation stone of a new physics.

GALILEO: Yes. Put it under your coat.

ANDREA: And we thought you had deserted. (*In a low voice:*) Mr. Galilei, how can I begin to express my shame. Mine has been the loudest voice against you.

GALILEO: That would seem to have been proper. I taught you science and I decried the truth.

ANDREA: Did you? I think not. Everything is changed!

GALILEO: What is changed?

ANDREA: You shielded the truth from the oppressor. Now I see! In your dealings with the Inquisition you used the same superb common sense you brought to physics.

GALILEO: Oh!

ANDREA: We lost our heads. With the crowd at the street corners we said: "He will die, he will never surrender!" You came back: "I surrendered but I am alive." We cried: "Your hands are stained!" You say: "Better stained than empty."

GALILEO: "Better stained than empty." — It sounds realistic. Sounds like me.

ANDREA: And I of all people should have known. I was twelve when you sold another man's telescope to the Venetian Senate, and saw you put it to immortal use. Your friends were baffled when you bowed to the Prince of Florence: Science gained a wider audience. You always laughed at heroics. "People who suffer bore me," you said. "Misfortunes are due mainly to miscalculations." And: "If there are obstacles, the shortest line between two points may be the crooked line."

GALILEO: It makes a picture.

ANDREA: And when you stooped to recant in 1633, I should have understood that you were again about your business.

GALILEO: My business being?

ANDREA: Science. The study of the properties of motion, mother of the machines which will themselves change the ugly face of the earth.

GALILEO: Aha!

ANDREA: You gained time to write a book that only you could write. Had you burned at the stake in a blaze of glory they would have won.

GALILEO: They have won. And there is no such thing as a scientific work that only one man can write.

ANDREA: Then why did you recant, tell me that!

GALILEO: I recanted because I was afraid of physical pain.

ANDREA: No!

GALILEO: They showed me the instruments.

ANDREA: It was not a plan?

GALILEO: It was not.

Pause.

ANDREA: But you have contributed. Science has only one commandment: contribution. And you have contributed more than any man for a hundred years.

GALILEO: Have I? Then welcome to my gutter, dear colleague in science and brother in treason: I sold out, you are a buyer. The first sight of the book! His mouth watered and his scoldings were drowned. Blessed be our bargaining, whitewashing, death-fearing community!

ANDREA: The fear of death is human.

GALILEO: Even the church will teach you that to be weak is not human. It is just evil.

ANDREA: The church, yes! But science is not concerned with our weaknesses.

GALILEO: No? My dear Sarti, in spite of my present convictions, I may be able to give you a few pointers as to the concerns of your chosen profession. (*Enter* VIRGINIA *with a platter.*) In my spare time, I happen to have gone over this case. I have spare time. — Even a man who sells wool, however good he is at buying wool cheap and selling it dear, must be concerned with the standing of the wool trade. The practice of science would seem to call for valor. She trades in knowledge, which is the product of doubt. And this new art of doubt has enchanted the public. The plight of the multitude is old as the rocks, and is believed to be basic as the rocks. But now they have learned to doubt. They snatched the telescopes out of our hands and had them trained on their tormentors: prince, official, public moralist. The mechanism of the heavens was clearer, the mechanism of their courts was still murky. The battle to measure the heavens is won by doubt; by credulity the Roman housewife's battle for milk will always be lost. Word is passed down that this is of no concern to the scientist who is told he will only release such of his findings as do not disturb the peace, that is, the peace of mind of the well-to-do. Threats and bribes fill the air. Can the scientist hold out on the numbers? — For what reason do you labor? I take it the intent of science is to ease human existence. If you give way to coercion, science can be crippled, and your new machines may simply suggest new drudgeries. Should you then, in time, discover all there is to be discovered, your progress must then become a progress away from the bulk of humanity. The gulf might even grow so wide that the sound of your cheering at some new achievement would be echoed by a universal howl of horror. — As a scientist I had an almost unique opportunity. In my day astronomy emerged into the market place. At that particular time, had one man put up a fight, it could have had wide repercussions. I have come to believe that I was never in real danger; for some years I was as strong as the authorities, and I surrendered my knowledge to the powers that be, to use it, no, not *use* it, *abuse* it, as it suits their ends. I have betrayed my profession. Any man who does what I have done must not be tolerated in the ranks of science.

VIRGINIA, *who has stood motionless, puts the platter on the table.*

VIRGINIA: You are accepted in the ranks of the faithful, father.

GALILEO: (*sees her*): Correct. (*He goes over to the table.*) I have to eat now.

VIRGINIA: We lock up at eight.

ANDREA: I am glad I came. (*He extends his hand.* GALILEO *ignores it and goes over to his meal.*)

GALILEO (*examining the plate; to* ANDREA): Somebody who knows me sent me a goose. I still enjoy eating.

ANDREA: And your opinion is now that the "new age" was an illusion?

GALILEO: Well. — This age of ours turned out to be a whore, spattered with blood. Maybe, new ages look like blood-spattered whores. Take care of yourself.

ANDREA: Yes. (*Unable to go.*) With reference to your evaluation of the author in question — I do not know the answer. But I cannot think that your savage analysis is the last word.

GALILEO: Thank you, sir.

OFFICIAL *knocks at the door.*

VIRGINIA (*showing* ANDREA *out*): I don't like visitors from the past, they excite him.

She lets him out. The OFFICIAL *closes the iron door.* VIRGINIA *returns.*

GALILEO (*eating*): Did you try and think who sent the goose?

VIRGINIA: Not Andrea.

GALILEO: Maybe not. I gave Redhead his first lesson; when he held out his hand, I had to remind myself he is teaching now. — How is the sky tonight?

VIRGINIA (*at the window*): Bright.

GALILEO *continues eating.*

14

The great book o'er the border went
And, good folk, that was the end.
But we hope you'll keep in mind
You and I were left behind.

Before a little Italian customs house early in the morning.
ANDREA *sits upon one of his traveling trunks at the barrier and*
reads GALILEO'S *book. The window of a small house is still lit,*
and a big grotesque shadow, like an old witch and her caul-
dron, falls upon the house wall beyond. Barefoot CHILDREN *in*
rags see it and point to the little house.

CHILDREN (*singing*):
One, two, three, four, five, six,
Old Marina is a witch.
At night, on a broomstick she sits
And on the church steeple she spits.

CUSTOMS OFFICER (*to* ANDREA): Why are you making this journey?

ANDREA: I am a scholar.

CUSTOMS OFFICER (*to his* CLERK): Put down under "reason for leaving the country": Scholar. (*He points to the baggage.*) Books!
Anything dangerous in these books?

ANDREA: What is dangerous?

CUSTOMS OFFICER: Religion. Politics.

ANDREA: These are nothing but mathematical formulas.

CUSTOMS OFFICER: What's that?

ANDREA: Figures.

CUSTOMS OFFICER: Oh, figures. No harm in figures. Just wait a minute, sir, we will soon have your papers stamped. (*He exits*
with CLERK.)

Meanwhile, a little council of war among the CHILDREN *has*
taken place. ANDREA *quietly watches. One of the* BOYS, *pushed*
forward by the others, creeps up to the little house from

which the shadow comes, and takes the jug of milk on the doorstep.

ANDREA (*quietly*): What are you doing with that milk?

BOY (*stopping in mid-movement*): She is a witch.

The other CHILDREN *run away behind the Custom House. One of them shouts,* "Run, Paolo!"

ANDREA: Hmmm! — And because she is a witch she mustn't have milk. Is that the idea?

BOY: Yes.

ANDREA: And how do you know she is a witch?

BOY (*points to shadow on house wall*): Look!

ANDREA: Oh! I see.

BOY: And she rides on a broomstick at night — and she bewitches the coachman's horses. My cousin Luigi looked through the hole in the stable roof, that the snow storm made, and heard the horses coughing something terrible.

ANDREA: Oh! — How big was the hole in the stable roof?

BOY: Luigi didn't tell. Why?

ANDREA: I was asking because maybe the horses got sick because it was cold in the stable. You had better ask Luigi how big that hole is.

BOY: You are not going to say Old Marina isn't a witch, because you can't.

ANDREA: No, I can't say she isn't a witch. I haven't looked into it. A man can't know about a thing he hasn't looked into, or can he?

BOY: No! — But THAT! (*He points to the shadow.*) She is stirring hell-broth.

ANDREA: Let's see. Do you want to take a look? I can lift you up.

BOY: You lift me to the window, mister! (*He takes a sling shot out of his pocket.*) I can really bash her from there.

ANDREA: Hadn't we better make sure she is a witch before we shoot? I'll hold that.

The BOY *puts the milk jug down and follows him reluctantly to the window.* ANDREA *lifts the boy up so that he can look in.*

ANDREA: What do you see?

BOY (*slowly*): Just an old girl cooking porridge.

ANDREA: Oh! Nothing to it then. Now look at her shadow, Paolo.
The BOY *looks over his shoulder and back and compares the
reality and the shadow.*

BOY: The big thing is a soup ladle.

ANDREA: Ah! A ladle! You see, I would have taken it for a broomstick, but I haven't looked into the matter as you have, Paolo.
Here is your sling.

CUSTOMS OFFICER (*returning with the* CLERK *and handing* ANDREA
his papers): All present and correct. Good luck, sir.

ANDREA *goes, reading* GALILEO'S *book. The* CLERK *starts to
bring his baggage after him. The barrier rises.* ANDREA *passes
through, still reading the book. The* BOY *kicks over the milk
jug.*

BOY (*shouting after* ANDREA): She *is* a witch! She *is* a witch!

ANDREA: You saw with your own eyes: think it over!
The BOY *joins the others. They sing:*
One, two, three, four, five, six,
Old Marina is a witch.
At night on a broomstick she sits
And on the church steeple she spits.
The CUSTOMS OFFICERS *laugh.* ANDREA *goes.*

THE GOOD WOMAN
OF SETZUAN

(1938–1940)

English Version by
Eric Bentley

CHARACTERS

WONG, *a water seller*

THREE GODS

SHEN TE, *a prostitute, later a shopkeeper*

MRS. SHIN, *former owner of* SHEN TE'S *shop*

A FAMILY OF EIGHT (*husband, wife, brother, sister-in-law, grandfather, nephew, niece, boy*)

AN UNEMPLOYED MAN

A CARPENTER

MRS. MI TZU, SHEN TE'S *landlady*

YANG SUN, *an unemployed pilot, later a factory manager*

AN OLD WHORE

A POLICEMAN

AN OLD MAN

AN OLD WOMAN, *his wife*

MR. SHU FU, *a barber*

MRS. YANG, *mother of* YANG SUN

GENTLEMEN, VOICES, CHILDREN (*three*), etc.

PROLOGUE

At the gates of the half-Westernized city of Setzuan.* Evening. WONG *the Water Seller introduces himself to the audience.*

WONG: I sell water here in the city of Setzuan. It isn't easy. When water is scarce, I have long distances to go in search of it, and when it is plentiful, I have no income. But in our part of the world there is nothing unusual about poverty. Many people think only the gods can save the situation. And I hear from a cattle merchant — who travels a lot — that some of the highest gods are on their way here at this very moment. Informed sources have it that heaven is quite disturbed at all the complaining. I've been coming out here to the city gates for three days now to bid these gods welcome. I want to be the first to greet them. What about those fellows over there? No, no, they *work*. And that one there has ink on his fingers, he's no god, he must be a clerk from the cement factory. *Those* two are another story. They look as though they'd like to beat you. But gods don't need to beat you, do they? (THREE GODS *appear.*) What about those three? Old-fashioned clothes — dust on their feet — they *must* be gods! (*He throws himself at their feet.*) Do with me what you will, illustrious ones!

FIRST GOD (*with an ear trumpet*): Ah! (*He is pleased.*) So we were expected?

WONG (*giving them water*): Oh, yes. And I *knew* you'd come.

FIRST GOD: We need somewhere to stay the night. You know of a place?

WONG: The whole town is at your service, illustrious ones! What sort of a place would you like?

The GODS *eye each other.*

FIRST GOD: Just try the first house you come to, my son.

WONG: That would be Mr. Fo's place.

---

* Thus the first MS of the play. Brecht later learned that Setzuan (Szechwan) is not a city but a province, and changed the script accordingly. But, as often, the solecism seems more appropriate than the fact. E. B.

FIRST GOD: Mr. Fo.

WONG: One moment! (*He knocks at the first house.*)

VOICE FROM MR. FO'S: No!

WONG *returns a little nervously*.

WONG: It's too bad. Mr. Fo isn't in. And his servants don't dare do a thing without his consent. He'll have a fit when he finds out who they turned away, won't he?

FIRST GOD (*smiling*): He will, won't he?

WONG: One moment! The next house is Mr. Cheng's. Won't he be thrilled!

FIRST GOD: Mr. Cheng.

WONG *knocks*.

VOICE FROM MR. CHENG'S: Keep your gods. We have our own troubles!

WONG (*back with the* GODS): Mr. Cheng is very sorry, but he has a houseful of relations. I think some of them are a bad lot, and naturally, he wouldn't like you to see them.

THIRD GOD: Are we so terrible?

WONG: Well, only with bad people, of course. Everyone knows the province of Kwan is always having floods.

SECOND GOD: Really? How's that?

WONG: Why, because they're so irreligious.

SECOND GOD: Rubbish. It's because they neglected the dam.

FIRST GOD (*to* SECOND): Sh! (*To* WONG:) You're still in hopes, aren't you, my son?

WONG: Certainly. All Setzuan is competing for the honor! What happened up to now is pure coincidence. I'll be back. (*He walks away, but then stands undecided.*)

SECOND GOD: What did I tell you?

THIRD GOD: It *could* be pure coincidence.

SECOND GOD: The same coincidence in Shun, Kwan, and Setzuan? People just aren't religious any more, let's face the fact. Our mission has failed!

FIRST GOD: Oh come, we might run into a good person any minute.

THIRD GOD: How did the resolution read? (*Unrolling a scroll and reading from it:*) "The world can stay as it is if enough people are found (*at the word "found" he unrolls it a little more:*) living lives worthy of human beings." Good people, that is. Well, what about this Water Seller himself? *He's* good, or I'm very much mistaken.

SECOND GOD: You're very much mistaken. When he gave us a drink, I had the impression there was something odd about the cup. Well, look! (*He shows the cup to the* FIRST GOD.)

FIRST GOD: A false bottom!

SECOND GOD: The man is a swindler.

FIRST GOD: Very well, count *him* out. That's one man among millions. And as a matter of fact, we only need one on *our* side. These atheists are saying, "The world must be changed because no one can *be* good and *stay* good." No one, eh? I say: let us find one — just one — and we have those fellows where we want them!

THIRD GOD (*to* WONG): Water Seller, is it so hard to find a place to stay?

WONG: Nothing could be easier. It's just me. I don't go about it right.

THIRD GOD: Really?

He returns to the others. A GENTLEMAN *passes by.*

WONG: Oh dear, they're catching on. (*He accosts the* GENTLEMAN.) Excuse the intrusion, dear sir, but three gods have just turned up. Three of the very highest. They need a place for the night. Seize this rare opportunity — to have real gods as your guests!

GENTLEMAN (*laughing*): A new way of finding free rooms for a gang of crooks. (*Exit* GENTLEMAN.)

WONG (*shouting at him*): Godless rascal! Have you no religion, gentlemen of Setzuan? (*Pause.*) Patience, illustrious ones! (*Pause.*) There's only one person left. Shen Te, the prostitute. She *can't* say no. (*Calls up to a window:*) Shen Te!

SHEN TE *opens the shutters and looks out.*

WONG: Shen Te, it's Wong. *They're* here, and nobody wants them. Will you take them?

SHEN TE: Oh, no, Wong, I'm expecting a gentleman.

WONG: Can't you forget about him for tonight?

SHEN TE: The rent has to be paid by tomorrow or I'll be out on the street.

WONG: This is no time for calculation, Shen Te.

SHEN TE: Stomachs rumble even on the Emperor's birthday, Wong.

WONG: Setzuan is one big dung hill!

SHEN TE: Oh, very well! I'll hide till my gentleman has come and gone. Then I'll take them. (*She disappears.*)

WONG: They mustn't see her gentleman or they'll know what she is.

FIRST GOD (*who hasn't heard any of this*): I think it's hopeless.

> *They approach* WONG.

WONG (*jumping, as he finds them behind him*): A room has been found, illustrious ones! (*He wipes sweat off his brow.*)

SECOND GOD: Oh, good.

THIRD GOD: Let's see it.

WONG (*nervously*): Just a minute. It has to be tidied up a bit.

THIRD GOD: Then we'll sit down here and wait.

WONG (*still more nervous*): No, no! (*Holding himself back:*) Too much traffic, you know.

THIRD GOD (*with a smile*): Of course, if you *want* us to move.

> *They retire a little. They sit on a doorstep.* WONG *sits on the ground.*

WONG (*after a deep breath*): You'll be staying with a single girl — the finest human being in Setzuan!

THIRD GOD: That's nice.

WONG (*to the audience*): They gave me such a look when I picked up my cup just now.

THIRD GOD: You're worn out, Wong.

WONG: A little, maybe.

FIRST GOD: Do people here have a hard time of it?

WONG: The good ones do.

FIRST GOD: What about yourself?

WONG: You mean I'm not good. That's true. And I don't have an easy time either!

During this dialogue, a GENTLEMAN *has turned up in front of* SHEN TE'S *house, and has whistled several times. Each time* WONG *has given a start.*

THIRD GOD (*to* WONG, *softly*): Psst! I think he's gone now.

WONG (*confused and surprised*): Ye-e-es.

The GENTLEMAN *has left now, and* SHEN TE *has come down to the street.*

SHEN TE (*softly*): Wong!

Getting no answer, she goes off down the street. WONG *arrives just too late, forgetting his carrying pole.*

WONG (*softly*): Shen Te! Shen Te! (*To himself:*) So she's gone off to earn the rent. Oh dear, I can't go to the gods *again* with no room to offer them. Having failed in the service of the gods, I shall run to my den in the sewer pipe down by the river and hide from their sight!

He rushes off. SHEN TE *returns, looking for him, but finding the* GODS. *She stops in confusion.*

SHEN TE: You are the illustrious ones? My name is Shen Te. It would please me very much if my simple room could be of use to you.

THIRD GOD: Where is the Water Seller, Miss . . . Shen Te?

SHEN TE: I missed him, somehow.

FIRST GOD: Oh, he probably thought you weren't coming, and was afraid of telling us.

THIRD GOD (*picking up the carrying pole*): We'll leave this with you. He'll be needing it.

Led by SHEN TE, *they go into the house. It grows dark, then light. Dawn. Again escorted by* SHEN TE, *who leads them through the half-light with a little lamp, the* GODS *take their leave.*

FIRST GOD: Thank you, thank you, dear Shen Te, for your elegant hospitality! We shall not forget! And give our thanks to the Water Seller — he showed us a good human being.

SHEN TE: Oh, *I'm* not good. Let me tell you something: when Wong asked me to put you up, I hesitated.

FIRST GOD: It's all right to hesitate if you then go ahead! And in giving us that room you did much more than you knew. You proved that good people still exist, a point that has been disputed of late — even in heaven. Farewell!

SECOND GOD: Farewell!

THIRD GOD: Farewell!

SHEN TE: Stop, illustrious ones! I'm not sure you're right. I'd like to be good, it's true, but there's the rent to pay. And that's not all: I sell myself for a living. Even so I can't make ends meet, there's too much competition. I'd like to honor my father and mother and speak nothing but the truth and not covet my neighbor's house. I should love to stay with one man. But how? How is it done? Even breaking a few of your commandments, I can hardly manage.

FIRST GOD (*clearing his throat*): These thoughts are but, um, the misgivings of an unusually good woman!

THIRD GOD: Good-bye, Shen Te! Give our regards to the Water Seller!

SECOND GOD: And above all: be good! Farewell!

FIRST GOD: Farewell!

THIRD GOD: Farewell!

They start to wave good-bye.

SHEN TE: But everything is so expensive, I don't feel sure I can do it!

SECOND GOD: That's not in our sphere. We never meddle with economics.

THIRD GOD: One moment. (*They stop.*) Isn't it true she might do better if she had more money?

SECOND GOD: Come, come! How could we ever account for it Up Above?

FIRST GOD: Oh, there are ways. (*They put their heads together and confer in dumb show. To* SHEN TE, *with embarrassment:*) As you say you can't pay your rent, well, um, we're not paupers, so of course we *insist* on paying for our room. (*Awkwardly thrusting money into her hands:*) There! (*Quickly:*) But don't tell anyone! The incident is open to misinterpretation.

SECOND GOD: It certainly is!

FIRST GOD (*defensively*): But there's no law against it! It was never decreed that a god mustn't pay hotel bills!

The GODS *leave.*

1

A small tobacco shop. The shop is not as yet completely furnished and hasn't started doing business.

SHEN TE (*to the audience*): It's three days now since the gods left. When they said they wanted to pay for the room, I looked down at my hand, and there was more than a thousand silver dollars! I bought a tobacco shop with the money, and moved in yesterday. I don't own the building, of course, but I can pay the rent, and I hope to do a lot of good here. Beginning with Mrs. Shin, who's just coming across the square with her pot. She had the shop before me, and yesterday she dropped in to ask for rice for her children. (*Enter* MRS. SHIN. *Both women bow.*) How do you do, Mrs. Shin.

MRS. SHIN: How do you do, Miss Shen Te. You like your new home?

SHEN TE: Indeed, yes. Did your children have a good night?

MRS. SHIN: In that hovel? The youngest is coughing already.

SHEN TE: Oh, dear!

MRS. SHIN: You're going to learn a thing or two in these slums.

SHEN TE: Slums? That's not what you said when you sold me the shop!

MRS. SHIN: Now don't start nagging! Robbing me and my innocent children of their home and then calling it a slum! That's the limit! (*She weeps.*)

SHEN TE (*tactfully*): I'll get your rice.

MRS. SHIN: And a little cash while you're at it.

SHEN TE: I'm afraid I haven't sold anything yet.

MRS. SHIN (*screeching*): I've got to have it. Strip the clothes from my back and then cut my throat, will you? I know what I'll do: I'll dump my children on your doorstep! (*She snatches the pot out of* SHEN TE's *hands.*)

SHEN TE: Please don't be angry. You'll spill the rice.

414

Enter an elderly HUSBAND *and* WIFE *with their shabbily dressed* NEPHEW.

WIFE: Shen Te, dear! You've come into money, they tell me. And we haven't a roof over our heads! A tobacco shop. We had one too. But it's gone. Could we spend the night here, do you think?

NEPHEW (*appraising the shop*): Not bad!

WIFE: He's our nephew. We're inseparable!

MRS. SHIN: And who are these . . . ladies and gentlemen?

SHEN TE: They put me up when I first came in from the country. (*To the audience:*) Of course, when my small purse was empty, they put me out on the street, and they may be afraid I'll do the same to them. (*To the newcomers, kindly:*) Come in, and welcome, though I've only one little room for you — it's behind the shop.

HUSBAND: That'll do. Don't worry.

WIFE (*bringing* SHEN TE *some tea*): We'll stay over here, so we won't be in your way. Did you make it a tobacco shop in memory of your first real home? We can certainly give you a hint or two! That's one reason we came.

MRS. SHIN (*to* SHEN TE): Very nice! As long as you have a few customers too!

HUSBAND: Sh! A customer!

Enter an UNEMPLOYED MAN, *in rags.*

UNEMPLOYED MAN: Excuse me. I'm unemployed.

MRS. SHIN *laughs.*

SHEN TE: Can I help you?

UNEMPLOYED MAN: Have you any damaged cigarettes? I thought there might be some damage when you're unpacking.

WIFE: What nerve, begging for tobacco! (*Rhetorically:*) Why don't they ask for bread?

UNEMPLOYED MAN: Bread is expensive. One cigarette butt and I'll be a new man.

SHEN TE (*giving him cigarettes*): That's very important — to be a new man. You'll be my first customer and bring me luck.

The UNEMPLOYED MAN *quickly lights a cigarette, inhales, and goes off, coughing.*

WIFE: Was that right, Shen Te, dear?

MRS. SHIN: If this is the opening of a shop, you can hold the closing at the end of the week.

HUSBAND: I bet he had money on him.

SHEN TE: Oh, no, he said he hadn't!

NEPHEW: How d'you know he wasn't lying?

SHEN TE (*angrily*): How do you know he was?

WIFE (*wagging her head*): You're too good, Shen Te, dear. If you're going to keep this shop, you'll have to learn to say no.

HUSBAND: Tell them the place isn't yours to dispose of. Belongs to . . . some relative who insists on all accounts being strictly in order . . .

MRS. SHIN: That's right! What do you think you are — a philanthropist?

SHEN TE (*laughing*): Very well, suppose I ask you for my rice back, Mrs. Shin?

WIFE (*combatively, at* MRS. SHIN): So that's *her* rice?

Enter the CARPENTER, *a small man.*

MRS. SHIN (*who, at the sight of him, starts to hurry away*): See you tomorrow, Miss Shen Te! (*Exit* MRS. SHIN.)

CARPENTER: Mrs. Shin, it's you I want!

WIFE (*to* SHEN TE): Has she some claim on you?

SHEN TE: She's hungry. That's a claim.

CARPENTER: Are you the new tenant? And filling up the shelves already? Well, they're not yours till they're paid for, ma'am. I'm the carpenter, so I should know.

SHEN TE: I took the shop "furnishings included."

CARPENTER: You're in league with that Mrs. Shin, of course. All right. I demand my hundred silver dollars.

SHEN TE: I'm afraid I haven't got a hundred silver dollars.

CARPENTER: Then you'll find it. Or I'll have you arrested.

WIFE (*whispering to* SHEN TE): That relative: make it a cousin.

SHEN TE: Can't it wait till next month?

CARPENTER: No!

SHEN TE: Be a little patient, Mr. Carpenter, I can't settle all claims at once.

CARPENTER: Who's patient with me? (*He grabs a shelf from the wall.*) Pay up — or I take the shelves back!

WIFE: Shen Te! Dear! Why don't you let your . . . cousin settle this affair? (*To* CARPENTER:) Put your claim in writing. Shen Te's cousin will see you get paid.

CARPENTER (*derisively*): Cousin, eh?

HUSBAND: Cousin, yes.

CARPENTER: I know these cousins!

NEPHEW: Don't be silly. He's a personal friend of mine.

HUSBAND: What a man! Sharp as a razor!

CARPENTER: All right. I'll put my claim in writing. (*Puts shelf on floor, sits on it, writes out bill.*)

WIFE (*to* SHEN TE): He'd tear the dress off your back to get his shelves. Never recognize a claim! That's my motto.

SHEN TE: He's done a job, and wants something in return. It's shameful that I can't give it to him. What will the gods say?

HUSBAND: You did your bit when you took *us* in.

Enter the BROTHER, *limping, and the* SISTER-IN-LAW, *pregnant.*

BROTHER (*to* HUSBAND *and* WIFE): So this is where you're hiding out! There's family feeling for you! Leaving us on the corner!

WIFE (*embarrassed, to* SHEN TE): It's my brother and his wife. (*To them:*) Now stop grumbling, and sit quietly in that corner. (*To* SHEN TE:) It can't be helped. She's in her fifth month.

SHEN TE: Oh yes. Welcome!

WIFE (*to the couple*): Say thank you. (*They mutter something.*) The cups are there. (*To* SHEN TE:) Lucky you bought this shop when you did!

SHEN TE (*laughing and bringing tea*): Lucky indeed!

Enter MRS. MI TZU, *the landlady.*

MRS. MI TZU: Miss Shen Te? I am Mrs. Mi Tzu, your landlady. I hope our relationship will be a happy one. I like to think

I give my tenants modern, personalized service. Here is your lease. (*To the others, as* SHEN TE *reads the lease:*) There's nothing like the opening of a little shop, is there? A moment of true beauty! (*She is looking around.*) Not very much on the shelves, of course. But everything in the gods' good time! Where are your references, Miss Shen Te?

SHEN TE: Do I *have* to have references?

MRS. MI TZU: After all, I haven't a notion who you are!

HUSBAND: Oh, *we'd* be glad to vouch for Miss Shen Te! We'd go through fire for her!

MRS. MI TZU: And who may *you* be?

HUSBAND (*stammering*): Ma Fu, tobacco dealer.

MRS. MI TZU: Where is your shop, Mr. . . . Ma Fu?

HUSBAND: Well, um, I haven't got a shop — I've just sold it.

MRS. MI TZU: I see. (*To* SHEN TE:) Is there no one else that knows you?

WIFE (*whispering to* SHEN TE): Your cousin! Your cousin!

MRS. MI TZU: This is a respectable house, Miss Shen Te. I never sign a lease without certain assurances.

SHEN TE (*slowly, her eyes downcast*): I have . . . a cousin.

MRS. MI TZU: On the square? Let's go over and see him. What does he do?

SHEN TE (*as before*): He lives . . . in another city.

WIFE (*prompting*): Didn't you say he was in Shung?

SHEN TE: That's right. Shung.

HUSBAND (*prompting*): I had his name on the tip of my tongue. Mr. . . .

SHEN TE (*with an effort*): Mr. . . . Shui . . . Ta.

HUSBAND: That's it! Tall, skinny fellow!

SHEN TE: Shui Ta!

NEPHEW (to CARPENTER): *You* were in touch with him, weren't you? About the shelves?

CARPENTER (*surlily*): Give him this bill. (*He hands it over.*) I'll be back in the morning. (*Exit* CARPENTER.)

NEPHEW (*calling after him, but with his eyes on* MRS. MI TZU): Don't worry! Mr. Shui Ta pays on the nail!

MRS. MI TZU (*looking closely at* SHEN TE): I'll be happy to make his acquaintance, Miss Shen Te. (*Exit* MRS. MI TZU.)
Pause.

WIFE: By tomorrow morning she'll know more about you than you do yourself.

SISTER-IN-LAW (*to* NEPHEW): This thing isn't built to last.
Enter GRANDFATHER.

WIFE: It's Grandfather! (*To* SHEN TE:) Such a good old soul!
The BOY *enters.*

BOY (*over his shoulder*): Here they are!

WIFE: And the boy, how he's grown! But he always could eat enough for ten.
Enter the NIECE.

WIFE (*to* SHEN TE): Our little niece from the country. There are more of us now than in your time. The less we had, the more there were of us; the more there were of us, the less we had. Give me the key. We must protect ourselves from unwanted guests. (*She takes the key and locks the door.*) Just make yourself at home. I'll light the little lamp.

NEPHEW (*a big joke*): I hope her cousin doesn't drop in tonight! The strict Mr. Shui Ta!
SISTER-IN-LAW *laughs.*

BROTHER (*reaching for a cigarette*): One cigarette more or less . . .

HUSBAND: One cigarette more or less.
They pile into the cigarettes. The BROTHER *hands a jug of wine round.*

NEPHEW: Mr. Shui Ta'll pay for it!

GRANDFATHER (*gravely, to* SHEN TE): How do you do?
SHEN TE, *a little taken aback by the belatedness of the greeting, bows. She has the* CARPENTER'S *bill in one hand, the landlady's lease in the other.*

WIFE: How about a bit of a song? To keep Shen Te's spirits up?

NEPHEW: Good idea. Grandfather: you start!

SONG OF THE SMOKE

GRANDFATHER:

    I used to think (before old age beset me)
      That brains could fill the pantry of the poor.
    But where did all my cerebration get me?
      I'm just as hungry as I was before.
        So what's the use?
          See the smoke float free
        Into ever colder coldness!
          It's the same with me.

HUSBAND:

    The straight and narrow path leads to disaster
      And so the crooked path I tried to tread.
    That got me to disaster even faster
      (They say we shall be happy when we're dead.)
        So what's the use?
          See the smoke float free
        Into ever colder coldness!
          It's the same with me.

NIECE:

    You older people, full of expectation,
      At any moment now you'll walk the plank!
    The future's for the younger generation!
      Yes, even if that future is a blank.
        So what's the use?
          See the smoke float free
        Into ever colder coldness!
          It's the same with me.

NEPHEW (*to the* BROTHER): Where'd you get that wine?

SISTER-IN-LAW (*answering for the* BROTHER): He pawned the sack of tobacco.

HUSBAND (*stepping in*): What? That tobacco was all we had to fall back on! You pig!

BROTHER: *You'd* call a man a pig because your wife was frigid! Did you refuse to drink it?

    They fight. The shelves fall over.

SHEN TE (*imploringly*): Oh don't! Don't break everything! Take it, take it all, but don't destroy a gift from the gods!

WIFE (*disparagingly*): This shop isn't big enough. I should never have mentioned it to Uncle and the others. When *they* arrive, it's going to be disgustingly overcrowded.

SISTER-IN-LAW: And did you hear our gracious hostess? She cools off quick!

Voices outside. Knocking at the door.

UNCLE'S VOICE: Open the door!

WIFE: Uncle? Is that you, Uncle?

UNCLE'S VOICE: Certainly, it's me. Auntie says to tell you she'll have the children here in ten minutes.

WIFE (*to* SHEN TE): I'll have to let him in.

SHEN TE (*who scarcely hears her*):
The little lifeboat is swiftly sent down
Too many men too greedily
Hold on to it as they drown.

1a

WONG'S *den in a sewer pipe.*

WONG (*crouching there*): All quiet! It's four days now since I left the city. The gods passed this way on the second day. I heard their steps on the bridge over there. They must be a long way off by this time, so I'm safe. (*Breathing a sigh of relief, he curls up and goes to sleep. In his dream the pipe becomes transparent, and the* GODS *appear. Raising an arm, as if in self-defense:*) I know, I know, illustrious ones! I found no one to give you a room — not in all Setzuan! There, it's out. Please continue on your way!

FIRST GOD (*mildly*): But you did find someone. Someone who took us in for the night, watched over us in our sleep, and in the early morning lighted us down to the street with a lamp.

WONG: It was . . . Shen Te that took you in?

THIRD GOD: Who else?

WONG: And I ran away! "She isn't coming," I thought, "she just can't afford it."

GODS (*singing*):

O you feeble, well-intentioned, and yet feeble chap!
Where there's need the fellow thinks there is no goodness!
When there's danger he thinks courage starts to ebb away!
Some people only see the seamy side!
What hasty judgment! What premature desperation!

WONG: I'm *very* ashamed, illustrious ones.

FIRST GOD: Do us a favor, Water Seller. Go back to Setzuan. Find Shen Te, and give us a report on her. We hear that she's come into a little money. Show interest in her goodness — for no one can be good for long if goodness is not in demand. Meanwhile we shall continue the search, and find other good people. After which, the idle chatter about the impossibility of goodness will stop!

The GODS *vanish.*

2

A knocking.

WIFE: Shen Te! Someone at the door. Where is she anyway?

NEPHEW: She must be getting the breakfast. Mr. Shui Ta will pay for it.

The WIFE *laughs and shuffles to the door. Enter* MR. SHUI TA *and the* CARPENTER.

WIFE: Who is it?

SHUI TA: I am Miss Shen Te's cousin.

WIFE: What??

SHUI TA: My name is Shui Ta.

WIFE: Her cousin?

NEPHEW: Her cousin?

NIECE: But that was a joke. She hasn't got a cousin.

HUSBAND: So early in the morning?

BROTHER: What's all the noise?

SISTER-IN-LAW: This fellow says he's her cousin.

BROTHER: Tell him to prove it.

NEPHEW: Right. If you're Shen Te's cousin, prove it by getting the breakfast.

SHUI TA (*whose regime begins as he puts out the lamp to save oil; loudly, to all present, asleep or awake*): Would you all please get dressed! Customers will be coming! I wish to open my shop!

HUSBAND: *Your* shop? Doesn't it belong to our good friend Shen Te?

SHUI TA *shakes his head.*

SISTER-IN-LAW: So we've been cheated. Where *is* the little liar?

SHUI TA: Miss Shen Te has been delayed. She wishes me to tell you there will be nothing she can do — now I am here.

WIFE (*bowled over*): I thought she was good!

NEPHEW: Do you have to believe *him?*

HUSBAND: I don't.

NEPHEW: Then do something.

HUSBAND: Certainly! I'll send out a search party at once. You, you, you, and you, go out and look for Shen Te. (*As the* GRANDFATHER *rises and makes for the door:*) Not you, Grandfather, you and I will hold the fort.

SHUI TA: You won't find Miss Shen Te. She has suspended her hospitable activity for an unlimited period. There are too many of you. She asked me to say: this is a tobacco shop, not a gold mine.

HUSBAND: Shen Te never said a thing like that. Boy, food! There's a bakery on the corner. Stuff your shirt full when they're not looking!

SISTER-IN-LAW: Don't overlook the raspberry tarts.

HUSBAND: And don't let the policeman see you.

The BOY *leaves.*

SHUI TA: Don't you depend on this shop now? Then why give it a bad name by stealing from the bakery?

NEPHEW: Don't listen to him. Let's find Shen Te. She'll give him a piece of her mind.

SISTER-IN-LAW: Don't forget to leave us some breakfast.

BROTHER, SISTER-IN-LAW *and* NEPHEW *leave.*

SHUI TA (*to the* CARPENTER): You see, Mr. Carpenter, nothing has changed since the poet, eleven hundred years ago, penned these lines:
A governor was asked what was needed
To save the freezing people in the city.
He replied:
"A blanket ten thousand feet long
To cover the city and all its suburbs."
He starts to tidy up the shop.

CARPENTER: Your cousin owes me money. I've got witnesses. For the shelves.

SHUI TA: Yes, I have your bill. (*He takes it out of his pocket.*) Isn't a hundred silver dollars rather a lot?

CARPENTER: No deductions! I have a wife and children.

SHUI TA: How many children?

CARPENTER: Three.

SHUI TA: I'll make you an offer. Twenty silver dollars.

The HUSBAND *laughs.*

CARPENTER: You're crazy. Those shelves are real walnut.

SHUI TA: Very well. Take them away.

CARPENTER: What?

SHUI TA: They cost too much. Please take them away.

WIFE: Not bad! (*And she, too, is laughing.*)

CARPENTER (*a little bewildered*): Call Shen Te, someone! (*To* SHUI TA:) She's *good!*

SHUI TA: Certainly. She's ruined.

CARPENTER (*provoked into taking some of the shelves*): All right, you can keep your tobacco on the floor.

SHUI TA (*to the* HUSBAND): Help him with the shelves.

HUSBAND (*grins and carries one shelf over to the door where the* CARPENTER *now is*): Good-bye, shelves!

CARPENTER (*to the* HUSBAND): You dog! You want my family to starve?

SHUI TA: I repeat my offer. I have no desire to keep my tobacco on the floor. Twenty silver dollars.

CARPENTER (*with desperate aggressiveness*): One hundred!

SHUI TA *shows indifference, looks through the window. The* HUSBAND *picks up several shelves.*

CARPENTER (*to* HUSBAND): You needn't smash them against the doorpost, you idiot! (*To* SHUI TA:) These shelves were made to measure. They're no use anywhere else!

SHUI TA: Precisely.

The WIFE *squeals with pleasure.*

CARPENTER (*giving up, sullenly*): Take the shelves. Pay what you want to pay.

SHUI TA (*smoothly*): Twenty silver dollars.

He places two large coins on the table. The CARPENTER *picks them up.*

HUSBAND (*brings the shelves back in*): And quite enough too!

CARPENTER (*slinking off*): Quite enough to get drunk on.

HUSBAND (*happily*): Well, we got rid of *him!*

WIFE (*weeping with fun, gives a rendition of the dialogue just spoken*): "Real walnut," says he. "Very well, take them away," says his lordship. "I have three children," says he. "Twenty silver dollars," says his lordship. "They're no use anywhere else," says he. "Pre-cisely," said his lordship! (*She dissolves into shrieks of merriment.*)

SHUI TA: And now: go!

HUSBAND: What's that?

SHUI TA: You're thieves, parasites. I'm giving you this chance. Go!

HUSBAND (*summoning all his ancestral dignity*): That sort deserves no answer. Besides, one should never shout on an empty stomach.

WIFE: Where's that boy?

SHUI TA: Exactly. The boy. I want no stolen goods in this shop. (*Very loudly:*) I strongly advise you to leave! (*But they remain seated, noses in the air. Quietly:*) As you wish. (SHUI TA *goes to the door. A* POLICEMAN *appears.* SHUI TA *bows.*) I am addressing the officer in charge of this precinct?

POLICEMAN: That's right, Mr., um, what was the name, sir?

SHUI TA: Mr. Shui Ta.

POLICEMAN: Yes, of course, sir.

They exchange a smile.

SHUI TA: Nice weather we're having.

POLICEMAN: A little on the warm side, sir.

SHUI TA: Oh, a little on the warm side.

HUSBAND (*whispering to the* WIFE): If he keeps it up till the boy's back, we're done for. (*Tries to signal* SHUI TA.)

SHUI TA (*ignoring the signal*): Weather, of course, is one thing indoors, another out on the dusty street!

POLICEMAN: Oh, quite another, sir!

WIFE (*to the* HUSBAND): It's all right as long as he's standing in the doorway — the boy will see him.

SHUI TA: Step inside for a moment! It's quite cool indoors. My cousin and I have just opened the place. And we attach the greatest importance to being on good terms with the, um, authorities.

POLICEMAN (*entering*): Thank you, Mr. Shui Ta. It *is* cool!

HUSBAND (*whispering to the* WIFE): And now the boy *won't* see him.

SHUI TA (*showing* HUSBAND *and* WIFE *to the* POLICEMAN): Visitors, I think my cousin knows them. They were just leaving.

HUSBAND (*defeated*): Ye-e-es, we were . . . just leaving.

SHUI TA: I'll tell my cousin you couldn't wait.

Noise from the street. Shouts of "Stop, Thief!"

POLICEMAN: What's that?

The BOY *is in the doorway with cakes and buns and rolls spilling out of his shirt. The* WIFE *signals desperately to him to leave. He gets the idea.*

POLICEMAN: No, you don't! (*He grabs the* BOY *by the collar.*) Where's all this from?

BOY (*vaguely pointing*): Down the street.

POLICEMAN (*grimly*): So that's it. (*Prepares to arrest the* BOY.)

WIFE (*stepping in*): And *we* knew nothing about it. (*To the* BOY:) Nasty little thief!

POLICEMAN (*dryly*): Can you clarify the situation, Mr. Shui Ta?

SHUI TA *is silent.*

POLICEMAN (*who understands silence*): Aha. You're all coming with me — to the station.

SHUI TA: I can hardly say how sorry I am that *my* establishment . . .

THE WIFE: Oh, he saw the boy leave not ten minutes ago!

SHUI TA: And to conceal the theft asked a policeman in?

POLICEMAN: Don't listen to her, Mr. Shui Ta, I'll be happy to relieve you of their presence one and all! (*To all three:*) Out! (*He drives them before him.*)

GRANDFATHER (*leaving last, gravely*): Good morning!

POLICEMAN: Good morning!

SHUI TA, *left alone, continues to tidy up.* MRS. MI TZU *breezes in.*

MRS. MI TZU: *You're* her cousin, are you? Then have the goodness to explain what all this means — police dragging people from a respectable house! By what right does your Miss Shen Te turn my property into a house of assignation? — Well, as you see, I know all!

SHUI TA: Yes. My cousin has the worst possible reputation: that of being poor.

MRS. MI TZU: No sentimental rubbish, Mr. Shui Ta. Your cousin was a common. . . .

SHUI TA: Pauper. Let's use the uglier word.

MRS. MI TZU: I'm speaking of her conduct, not her earnings. But there must have *been* earnings, or how did she buy all this? Several elderly gentlemen took care of it, I suppose. I repeat: this is a respectable house! I have tenants who prefer not to live under the same roof with such a person.

SHUI TA (*quietly*): How much do you want?

MRS. MI TZU (*he is ahead of her now*): I beg your pardon.

SHUI TA: To reassure yourself. To reassure your tenants. How much will it cost?

MRS. MI TZU: You're a cool customer.

SHUI TA (*picking up the lease*): The rent is high. (*He reads on.*) I assume it's payable by the month?

MRS. MI TZU: Not in her case.

SHUI TA (*looking up*): What?

MRS. MI TZU: Six months rent payable in advance. Two hundred silver dollars.

SHUI TA: Six . . . ! Sheer usury! And where am I to find it?

MRS. MI TZU: You should have thought of that before.

SHUI TA: Have you no heart, Mrs. Mi Tzu? It's true Shen Te acted foolishly, being kind to all those people, but she'll improve with time. I'll see to it she does. She'll work her fingers to the bone to pay her rent, and all the time be as quiet as a mouse, as humble as a fly.

MRS. MI TZU: Her social background . . .

SHUI TA: Out of the depths! She came out of the depths! And before she'll go back there, she'll work, sacrifice, shrink from nothing. . . . Such a tenant is worth her weight in gold, Mrs. Mi Tzu.

MRS. MI TZU: It's silver we were talking about, Mr. Shui Ta. Two hundred silver dollars or . . .

Enter the POLICEMAN.

POLICEMAN: Am I intruding, Mr. Shui Ta?

MRS. MI TZU: This tobacco shop is well-known to the police, I see.

POLICEMAN: Mr. Shui Ta has done us a service, Mrs. Mi Tzu. I am here to present our official felicitations!

MRS. MI TZU: That means less than nothing to me, sir. Mr. Shui Ta, all I can say is: I hope your cousin will find my terms acceptable. Good day, gentlemen. (*Exit.*)

SHUI TA: Good day, ma'am.

Pause.

POLICEMAN: Mrs. Mi Tzu a bit of a stumbling block, sir?

SHUI TA: She wants six months' rent in advance.

POLICEMAN: And you haven't got it, eh? (SHUI TA *is silent.*) But surely you can get it, sir? A man like you?

SHUI TA: What about a woman like Shen Te?

POLICEMAN: You're not staying, sir?

SHUI TA: No, and I won't be back. Do you smoke?

POLICEMAN (*taking two cigars, and placing them both in his pocket*): Thank you, sir — I see your point. Miss Shen Te — let's mince no words — Miss Shen Te lived by selling herself. "What else could she have done?" you ask. "How else was she to pay the rent?" True. But the fact remains, Mr. Shui Ta, it is not respectable. Why not? A very deep question. But, in the first place, love — love isn't bought and sold like cigars, Mr. Shui Ta. In the second place, it isn't respectable to go waltzing off with someone that's paying his way, so to speak

— it must be for love! Thirdly and lastly, as the proverb has it: not for a handful of rice but for love! (*Pause. He is thinking hard.*) "Well," you may say, "and what good is all this wisdom if the milk's already spilt?" Miss Shen Te is what she is. Is *where* she is. We have to face the fact that if she doesn't get hold of six months' rent pronto, she'll be back on the streets. The question then as I see it — everything in this world is a matter of opinion — the question as I see it is: *how* is she to get hold of this rent? How? Mr. Shui Ta: I don't know. (*Pause.*) I take that back, sir. It's just come to me. A husband. We must find her a husband!

Enter a little OLD WOMAN.

OLD WOMAN: A good cheap cigar for my husband, we'll have been married forty years tomorrow and we're having a little celebration.

SHUI TA: Forty years? And you still want to celebrate?

OLD WOMAN: As much as we can afford to. We have the carpet shop across the square. We'll be good neighbors, I hope?

SHUI TA: I hope so too.

POLICEMAN (*who keeps making discoveries*): Mr. Shui Ta, you know what we need? We need capital. And how do we acquire capital? We get married.

SHUI TA (*to* OLD WOMAN): I'm afraid I've been pestering this gentleman with my personal worries.

POLICEMAN (*lyrically*): We can't pay six months' rent, so what do we do? We marry money.

SHUI TA: That might not be easy.

POLICEMAN: Oh, I don't know. She's a good match. Has a nice, growing business. (*To the* OLD WOMAN:) What do you think?

OLD WOMAN (*undecided*): Well —

POLICEMAN: Should she put an ad in the paper?

OLD WOMAN (*not eager to commit herself*): Well, if *she* agrees —

POLICEMAN: I'll write it for her. *You* lend us a hand, and *we* write an ad for you! (*He chuckles away to himself, takes out his notebook, wets the stump of a pencil between his lips, and writes away.*)

SHUI TA (*slowly*): Not a bad idea.

POLICEMAN: "What ... *respectable* ... man ... with small capital ... widower ... not excluded ... desires ... marriage ... into flourishing ... tobacco shop?" And now let's add: "Am ... pretty ..." No! ... "Prepossessing appearance."

SHUI TA: If you don't think that's an exaggeration?

OLD WOMAN: Oh, not a bit. I've seen her.

The POLICEMAN *tears the page out of his notebook, and hands it over to* SHUI TA.

SHUI TA (*with horror in his voice*): How much luck we need to keep our heads above water! How many ideas! How many friends! (*To the* POLICEMAN:) Thank you, sir. I think I see my way clear.

3

Evening in the municipal park. Noise of a plane overhead.
YANG SUN, *a young man in rags, is following the plane with
his eyes: one can tell that the machine is describing a curve
above the park.* YANG SUN *then takes a rope out of his pocket,
looking anxiously about him as he does so. He moves toward
a large willow. Enter two prostitutes, one old, the other the*
NIECE *whom we have already met.*

NIECE: Hello. Coming with me?

YANG SUN (*taken aback*): If you'd like to buy me a dinner.

OLD WHORE: Buy you a dinner! (*To the* NIECE:) Oh, we know him
— it's the unemployed pilot. Waste no time on him!

NIECE: But he's the only man left in the park. And it's going to
rain.

OLD WHORE: Oh, how do you know?

And they pass by. YANG SUN *again looks about him, again takes
his rope, and this time throws it round a branch of the willow
tree. Again he is interrupted. It is the two prostitutes returning
— and in such a hurry they don't notice him.*

NIECE: It's going to pour!

Enter SHEN TE.

OLD WHORE: There's that *gorgon* Shen Te! That *drove* your family
out into the cold!

NIECE: It wasn't her. It was that cousin of hers. She offered to
pay for the cakes. I've nothing against her.

OLD WHORE: I have, though. (*So that* SHEN TE *can hear:*) Now where
could the little lady be off to? She may be rich now but that
won't stop her snatching our young men, will it?

SHEN TE: I'm going to the tearoom by the pond.

NIECE: Is it true what they say? You're marrying a widower — with
three children?

432

SHEN TE: Yes. I'm just going to see him.

YANG SUN (*his patience at breaking point*): Move on there! This is a park, not a whorehouse!

OLD WHORE: Shut your mouth!

But the two prostitutes leave.

YANG SUN: Even in the farthest corner of the park, even when it's raining, you can't get rid of them! (*He spits.*)

SHEN TE (*overhearing this*): And what right have you to scold them? (*But at this point she sees the rope.*) Oh!

YANG SUN: Well, what are you staring at?

SHEN TE: That rope. What is it for?

YANG SUN: Think! Think! I haven't a penny. Even if I had, I wouldn't spend it on you. I'd buy a drink of water.

The rain starts.

SHEN TE (*still looking at the rope*): What is the rope for? You mustn't!

YANG SUN: What's it to you? Clear out!

SHEN TE (*irrelevantly*): It's raining.

YANG SUN: Well, don't try to come under this tree.

SHEN TE: Oh, no. (*She stays in the rain.*)

YANG SUN: Now go away. (*Pause.*) For one thing, I don't like your looks, you're bowlegged.

SHEN TE (*indignantly*): That's not true!

YANG SUN: Well, don't show 'em to me. Look, it's raining. You better come under this tree.

Slowly, she takes shelter under the tree.

SHEN TE: Why did you want to do it?

YANG SUN: You really want to know? (*Pause.*) To get rid of you! (*Pause.*) You know what a flyer is?

SHEN TE: Oh yes, I've met a lot of pilots. At the tearoom.

YANG SUN: You call *them* flyers? Think they know what a machine is? Just 'cause they have leather helmets? They gave the airfield director a bribe, that's the way *those* fellows got up in the air! Try one of them out sometime. "Go up to two thousand feet," tell him, "then let it fall, then pick it up again with a flick of the wrist at the last moment." Know what he'll say to that? "It's not in my contract." Then again, there's the landing problem. It's like landing on your own backside. It's no different, planes are human. Those fools don't understand. (*Pause.*) And I'm the biggest fool for reading the book on flying in the Peking school and skipping the page where it says: "We've got enough flyers and we don't need you." I'm a mail pilot with no mail. You understand that?

SHEN TE (*shyly*): Yes. I do.

YANG SUN: No, you don't. You'd never understand that.

SHEN TE: When we were little we had a crane with a broken wing. He made friends with us and was very good-natured about our jokes. He would strut along behind us and call out to stop us going too fast for him. But every spring and autumn when the cranes flew over the villages in great swarms, he got quite restless. (*Pause.*) I understand that. (*She bursts out crying.*)

YANG SUN: Don't!

SHEN TE (*quieting down*): No.

YANG SUN: It's bad for the complexion.

SHEN TE (*sniffing*): I've stopped.

She dries her tears on her big sleeve. Leaning against the tree, but not looking at her, he reaches for her face.

YANG SUN: You can't even wipe your own face. (*He is wiping it for her with his handkerchief. Pause.*)

SHEN TE (*still sobbing*): I don't know *anything!*

YANG SUN: You interrupted me! What for?

SHEN TE: It's such a rainy day. You only wanted to do . . . *that* because it's such a rainy day.

To the audience:

In our country
The evenings should never be somber
High bridges over rivers
The grey hour between night and morning
And the long, long winter:
Such things are dangerous

For, with all the misery,
A very little is enough
And men throw away an unbearable life.

Pause.

YANG SUN: Talk about yourself for a change.

SHEN TE: What about me? I have a shop.

YANG SUN (*incredulous*): You have a shop, have you? Never thought of walking the streets?

SHEN TE: I did walk the streets. Now I have a shop.

YANG SUN (*ironically*): A gift of the gods, I suppose!

SHEN TE: How did you know?

YANG SUN (*even more ironical*): One fine evening the gods turned up saying: here's some money!

SHEN TE (*quickly*): One fine morning.

YANG SUN (*fed up*): This isn't much of an entertainment.

Pause.

SHEN TE: I can play the zither a little. (*Pause.*) And I can mimic men. (*Pause.*) I got the shop, so the first thing I did was to give my zither away. I can be as stupid as a fish now, I said to myself, and it won't matter.
I'm rich now, I said
I walk alone, I sleep alone
For a whole year, I said
I'll have nothing to do with a man.

YANG SUN: And now you're marrying one! The one at the tearoom by the pond?

SHEN TE *is silent.*

YANG SUN: What do you know about love?

SHEN TE: Everything.

YANG SUN: Nothing. (*Pause.*) Or d'you just mean you enjoyed it?

SHEN TE: No.

YANG SUN (*again without turning to look at her, he strokes her cheek with his hand*): You like that?

SHEN TE: Yes.

YANG SUN (*breaking off*): You're easily satisfied, I must say. (*Pause.*) What a town!

SHEN TE: You have no friends?

YANG SUN (*defensively*): Yes, I have! (*Change of tone.*) But they don't want to hear I'm still unemployed. "What?" they ask. "Is there still water in the sea?" You have friends?

SHEN TE (*hesitating*): Just a . . . cousin.

YANG SUN: Watch him carefully.

SHEN TE: He only came once. Then he went away. He won't be back. (YANG SUN *is looking away.*) But to be without hope, they say, is to be without goodness!
Pause.

YANG SUN: Go on talking. A voice is a voice.

SHEN TE: Once, when I was a little girl, I fell, with a load of brushwood. An old man picked me up. He gave me a penny too. Isn't it funny how people who don't have very much like to give some of it away? They must like to show what they can do, and how could they show it better than by being kind? Being wicked is just like being clumsy. When we sing a song, or build a machine, or plant some rice, we're being kind. You're kind.

YANG SUN: You make it sound easy.

SHEN TE: Oh, no. (*Little pause.*) Oh! A drop of rain!

YANG SUN: Where'd you feel it?

SHEN TE: Between the eyes.

YANG SUN: Near the right eye? Or the left?

SHEN TE: Near the left eye.

YANG SUN: Oh, good. (*He is getting sleepy.*) So you're through with men, eh?

SHEN TE (*with a smile*): But I'm not bowlegged.

YANG SUN: Perhaps not.

SHEN TE: Definitely not.
Pause.

YANG SUN (*leaning wearily against the willow*): I haven't had a drop to drink all day, I haven't eaten anything for *two* days. I couldn't love you if I tried.

Pause.

SHEN TE: I like it in the rain.

Enter WONG *the Water Seller, singing.*

THE SONG OF THE WATER SELLER IN THE RAIN

"Buy my water," I am yelling
And my fury restraining
For no water I'm selling
'Cause it's raining, 'cause it's raining!
  I keep yelling: "Buy my water!"
  But no one's buying
  Athirst and dying
  And drinking and paying!
  Buy water!
  Buy water, you dogs!

Nice to dream of lovely weather!
Think of all the consternation
Were there no precipitation
Half a dozen years together!
  Can't you hear them shrieking: "Water!"
  Pretending they adore me?
  They all would go down on their knees before me!
  Down on your knees!
  Go down on your knees, you dogs!

What are lawns and hedges thinking?
What are fields and forests saying?
"At the cloud's breast we are drinking!
And we've no idea who's paying!"
  I keep yelling: "Buy my water!"
  But no one's buying
  Athirst and dying
  And drinking and paying!

Buy water!
Buy water, you dogs!

The rain has stopped now. SHEN TE *sees* WONG *and runs toward him.*

SHEN TE: Wong! You're back! Your carrying pole's at the shop.

WONG: Oh, thank you, Shen Te. And how is life treating *you?*

SHEN TE: I've just met a brave and clever man. And I want to buy him a cup of your water.

WONG (*bitterly*): Throw back your head and open your mouth and you'll have all the water you need —

SHEN TE (*tenderly*):

I want *your* water, Wong
The water that has tired you so
The water that you carried all this way
The water that is hard to sell because it's been raining.

I need it for the young man over there — he's a flyer!

A flyer is a bold man:
Braving the storms
In company with the clouds
He crosses the heavens
And brings to friends in far-away lands
The friendly mail!

She pays WONG, *and runs over to* YANG SUN *with the cup. But* YANG SUN *is fast asleep.*

SHEN TE (*calling to* WONG, *with a laugh*): He's fallen asleep! Despair and rain and I have worn him out!

3a

WONG's *den. The sewer pipe is transparent, and the* GODS *again appear to* WONG *in a dream.*

WONG (*radiant*): I've seen her, illustrious ones! And she hasn't changed!

FIRST GOD: That's good to hear.

WONG: She loves someone.

FIRST GOD: Let's hope the experience gives her the strength to stay good!

WONG: It does. She's doing good deeds all the time.

FIRST GOD: Ah? What sort? What sort of good deeds, Wong?

WONG: Well, she has a kind word for everybody.

FIRST GOD (*eagerly*): And then?

WONG: Hardly anyone leaves her shop without tobacco in his pocket — even if he can't pay for it.

FIRST GOD: Not bad at all. Next?

WONG: She's putting up a family of eight.

FIRST GOD (*gleefully, to the* SECOND GOD): Eight! (*To* WONG:) And that's not all, of course!

WONG: She bought a cup of water from me even though it was raining.

FIRST GOD: Yes, yes, yes, all these smaller good deeds!

WONG: Even they run into money. A little tobacco shop doesn't make so much.

FIRST GOD (*sententiously*): A prudent gardener works miracles on the smallest plot.

WONG: She hands out rice every morning. That eats up half her earnings.

FIRST GOD (*a little disappointed*): Well, as a beginning . . .

WONG: They call her the Angel of the Slums — whatever the Carpenter may say!

FIRST GOD: What's this? A carpenter speaks ill of her?

WONG: Oh, he only says her shelves weren't paid for in full.

SECOND GOD (*who has a bad cold and can't pronounce his n's and m's*): What's this? Not paying a carpenter? Why was **that**?

WONG: I suppose she didn't have the money.

SECOND GOD (*severely*): One pays what one owes, that's in **our** book of rules! First the letter of the law, then the spirit!

WONG: But it wasn't Shen Te, illustrious ones, it was her cousin. She called *him* in to help.

SECOND GOD: Then her cousin must never darken her threshold again!

WONG: Very well, illustrious ones! But in fairness to Shen Te, let me say that her cousin is a businessman.

FIRST GOD: Perhaps we should enquire what is customary? I find business quite unintelligible. But everybody's doing it. Business! Did the Seven Good Kings do business? Did Kung the Just sell fish?

SECOND GOD: In any case, such a thing must not occur again!

The GODS *start to leave.*

THIRD GOD: Forgive us for taking this tone with you, Wong, we haven't been getting enough sleep. The rich recommend us to the poor, and the poor tell us they haven't enough room.

SECOND GOD: Feeble, feeble, the best of them!

FIRST GOD: No great deeds! No heroic daring!

THIRD GOD: On such a *small* scale!

SECOND GOD: Sincere, yes, but what is actually *achieved?*

One can no longer hear them.

WONG (*calling after them*): I've thought of something, illustrious ones: Perhaps you shouldn't ask — too — much — all — at — once!

4

The square in front of SHEN TE's *tobacco shop. Besides* SHEN
TE's *place, two other shops are seen: the carpet shop and a bar-*
ber's. Morning. Outside SHEN TE's *the* GRANDFATHER, *the* SISTER-
IN-LAW, *the* UNEMPLOYED MAN, *and* MRS. SHIN *stand waiting.*

SISTER-IN-LAW: She's been out all night again.

MRS. SHIN: No sooner did we get rid of that crazy cousin of hers
than Shen Te herself starts carrying on! Maybe she does give
us an ounce of rice now and then, but can you depend on her?
Can you depend on her?
Loud voices from the Barber's.

VOICE OF SHU FU: What are you doing in my shop? Get out — at
once!

VOICE OF WONG: But sir. They all let me sell . . .

WONG *comes staggering out of the Barber's shop pursued by*
MR. SHU FU, *the Barber, a fat man carrying a heavy curling*
iron.

SHU FU: Get out, I said! Pestering my customers with your slimy
old water! Get out! Take your cup!

He holds out the cup. WONG *reaches out for it.* MR. SHU FU
strikes his hand with the curling iron, which is hot. WONG
howls.

SHU FU: You had it coming, my man!

Puffing, he returns to his shop. The UNEMPLOYED MAN *picks*
up the cup and gives it to WONG.

UNEMPLOYED MAN: You can report that to the police.

WONG: My hand! It's smashed up!

UNEMPLOYED MAN: Any bones broken?

WONG: I can't move my fingers.

UNEMPLOYED MAN: Sit down. I'll put some water on it.

WONG sits.

MRS. SHIN: The water won't cost you anything.

SISTER-IN-LAW: You might have got a bandage from Miss Shen Te till she took to staying out all night. It's a scandal.

MRS. SHIN (*despondently*): If you ask me, she's forgotten we ever existed!

Enter SHEN TE *down the street, with a dish of rice.*

SHEN TE (*to the audience*): How wonderful to see Setzuan in the early morning! I always used to stay in bed with my dirty blanket over my head afraid to wake up. This morning I saw the newspapers being delivered by little boys, the streets being washed by strong men, and fresh vegetables coming in from the country on ox carts. It's a long walk from where Yang Sun lives, but I feel lighter at every step. They say you walk on air when you're in love, but it's even better walking on the rough earth, on the hard cement. In the early morning, the old city looks like a great heap of rubbish! Nice, though, with all its little lights. And the sky, so pink, so transparent, before the dust comes and muddies it! What a lot you miss if you never see your city rising from its slumbers like an honest old craftsman pumping his lungs full of air and reaching for his tools, as the poet says! (*Cheerfully, to her waiting guests:*) Good morning, everyone, here's your rice! (*Distributing the rice, she comes upon* WONG:) Good morning, Wong, I'm quite lightheaded today. On my way over, I looked at myself in all the shop windows. I'd love to be beautiful.

She slips into the carpet shop. MR. SHU FU *has just emerged from his shop.*

SHU FU (*to the audience*): It surprises me how beautiful Miss Shen Te is looking today! I never gave her a passing thought before. But now I've been gazing upon her comely form for exactly three minutes! I begin to suspect I am in love with her. She is overpoweringly attractive! (*Crossly, to* WONG:) Be off with you, rascal!

He returns to his shop. SHEN TE *comes back out of the carpet shop with the* OLD MAN, *its proprietor, and his wife — whom we have already met — the* OLD WOMAN. SHEN TE *is wearing a shawl. The* OLD MAN *is holding up a looking glass for her.*

OLD WOMAN: Isn't it lovely? We'll give you a reduction because there's a little hole in it.

SHEN TE (*looking at another shawl on the* OLD WOMAN's *arm*): The other one's nice too.

OLD WOMAN (*smiling*): Too bad there's no hole in that!

SHEN TE: That's right. My shop doesn't make very much.

OLD WOMAN: And your good deeds eat it all up! Be more careful, my dear. . . .

SHEN TE (*trying on the shawl with the hole*): Just now, I'm light-headed! Does the color suit me?

OLD WOMAN: You'd better ask a man.

SHEN TE (*to the* OLD MAN): Does the color suit me?

OLD MAN: You'd better ask your young friend.

SHEN TE: I'd like to have your opinion.

OLD MAN: It suits you very well. But wear it this way: the dull side out.

SHEN TE *pays up.*

OLD WOMAN: If you decide you don't like it, you can exchange it. (*She pulls* SHEN TE *to one side.*) Has he got money?

SHEN TE (*with a laugh*): Yang Sun? Oh, no.

OLD WOMAN: Then how're you going to pay your rent?

SHEN TE: I'd forgotten about that.

OLD WOMAN: And next Monday is the first of the month! Miss Shen Te, I've got something to say to you. After we (*indicating her husband*) got to know you, we had our doubts about that marriage ad. We thought it would be better if you'd let *us* help you. Out of our savings. We reckon we could lend you two hundred silver dollars. We don't need anything in writing — you could pledge us your tobacco stock.

SHEN TE: You're prepared to lend money to a person like me?

OLD WOMAN: It's folks like you that need it. We'd think twice about lending anything to your cousin.

OLD MAN (*coming up*): All settled, my dear?

SHEN TE: I wish the gods could have heard what your wife was just saying, Mr. Ma. They're looking for good people who're happy — and helping me makes you happy because you know it was love that got me into difficulties!

The OLD COUPLE *smile knowingly at each other.*

OLD MAN: And here's the money, Miss Shen Te.

He hands her an envelope. SHEN TE *takes it. She bows. They bow back. They return to their shop.*

SHEN TE (*holding up her envelope*): Look, Wong, here's six months' rent! Don't you believe in miracles now? And how do you like my new shawl?

WONG: For the young fellow I saw you with in the park?

SHEN TE *nods.*

MRS. SHIN: Never mind all that. It's time you took a look at his hand!

SHEN TE: Have you hurt your hand?

MRS. SHIN: That barber smashed it with his hot curling iron. Right in front of our eyes.

SHEN TE (*shocked at herself*): And I never noticed! We must get you to a doctor this minute or who knows what will happen?

UNEMPLOYED MAN: It's not a doctor he should see, it's a judge. He can ask for compensation. The barber's filthy rich.

WONG: You think I have a chance?

MRS. SHIN (*with relish*): If it's really good and smashed. But is it?

WONG: I think so. It's very swollen. Could I get a pension?

MRS. SHIN: You'd need a witness.

WONG: Well, you all saw it. You could all testify.

He looks round. The UNEMPLOYED MAN, *the* GRANDFATHER, *and the* SISTER-IN-LAW *are all sitting against the wall of the shop eating rice. Their concentration on eating is complete.*

SHEN TE (*to* MRS. SHIN): You saw it yourself.

MRS. SHIN: I want nothing to do with the police. It's against my principles.

SHEN TE (*to* SISTER-IN-LAW): What about you?

SISTER-IN-LAW: Me? I wasn't looking.

SHEN TE (*to the* GRANDFATHER, *coaxingly*): Grandfather, *you'll* testify, won't you?

SISTER-IN-LAW: And a lot of good that will do. He's simple-minded.

SHEN TE (*to the* UNEMPLOYED MAN): You seem to be the only witness left.

UNEMPLOYED MAN: My testimony would only hurt him. I've been picked up twice for begging.

SHEN TE:
Your brother is assaulted, and you shut your eyes?
He is hit, cries out in pain, and you are silent?
The beast prowls, chooses and seizes his victim, and you say:
"Because we showed no displeasure, he has spared us."

If no one present will be a witness, I will. I'll say *I* saw it.

MRS. SHIN (*solemnly*): The name for that is perjury.

WONG: I don't know if I can accept that. Though maybe I'll have to. (*Looking at his hand:*) Is it swollen enough, do you think? The swelling's not going down?

UNEMPLOYED MAN: No, no, the swelling's holding up well.

WONG: Yes. It's *more* swollen if anything. Maybe my wrist is broken after all. I'd better see a judge at once.

Holding his hand very carefully, and fixing his eyes on it, he runs off. MRS. SHIN *goes quickly into the Barber's shop.*

UNEMPLOYED MAN (*seeing her*): She is getting on the right side of Mr. Shu Fu.

SISTER-IN-LAW: You and I can't change the world, Shen Te.

SHEN TE: Go away! Go away all of you!

The UNEMPLOYED MAN, *the* SISTER-IN-LAW, *and the* GRAND-FATHER *stalk off, eating and sulking.*
To the audience:

They've stopped answering
They stay put
They do as they're told
They don't care
Nothing can make them look up
But the smell of food.

Enter MRS. YANG, YANG SUN's *mother, out of breath.*

MRS. YANG: Miss. Shen Te. My son has told me everything. I am Mrs. Yang, Sun's mother. Just think. He's got an offer. Of a job as a pilot. A letter has just come. From the director of the airfield in Peking!

SHEN TE: So he can fly again? Isn't that wonderful!

MRS. YANG (*less breathlessly all the time*): They won't give him the job for nothing. They want five hundred silver dollars.

SHEN TE: We can't let money stand in his way, Mrs. Yang!

MRS. YANG: If only you could help him out!

SHEN TE: I have the shop. I can try! (*She embraces* MRS. YANG.) I happen to have two hundred with me now. Take it. (*She gives her the* OLD COUPLE's *money.*) It was a loan but they said I could repay it with my tobacco stock.

MRS. YANG: And they were calling Sun the Dead Pilot of Setzuan! A friend in need!

SHEN TE: We must find another three hundred.

MRS. YANG: How?

SHEN TE: Let me think. (*Slowly:*) I know someone who can help. I didn't want to call on his services again, he's hard and cunning. But a flyer must fly. And I'll make this the last time.

Distant sound of a plane.

MRS. YANG: If the man you mentioned can do it. . . . Oh, look, there's the morning mail plane, heading for Peking!

SHEN TE: The pilot can see us, let's wave!

They wave. The noise of the engine is louder.

MRS. YANG: You know that pilot up there?

SHEN TE: Wave, Mrs. Yang! I know the pilot who will be up there. He gave up hope. But he'll do it now. One man to raise himself above the misery, above us all.

To the audience:

Yang Sun, my lover:
Braving the storms
In company with the clouds

Crossing the heavens
And bringing to friends in far-away lands
The friendly mail!

4a

In front of the inner curtain. Enter SHEN TE, *carrying* SHUI TA'S *mask. She sings.*

THE SONG OF DEFENSELESSNESS

In our country
A useful man needs luck
Only if he finds strong backers
Can he prove himself useful.
The good can't defend themselves and
Even the gods are defenseless.

Oh, why don't the gods have their own ammunition
And launch against badness their own expedition
Enthroning the good and preventing sedition
And bringing the world to a peaceful condition?

Oh, why don't the gods do the buying and selling
Injustice forbidding, starvation dispelling
Give bread to each city and joy to each dwelling?
Oh, why don't the gods do the buying and selling?

She puts on SHUI TA'S *mask and sings in his voice.*

You can only help one of your luckless brothers
By trampling down a dozen others.

Why is it the gods do not feel indignation
And come down in fury to end exploitation
Defeat all defeat and forbid desperation
Refusing to tolerate such toleration?

Why is it?

448

5

SHEN TE's *tobacco shop. Behind the counter,* MR. SHUI TA, *reading the paper.* MRS. SHIN *is cleaning up. She talks and he takes no notice.*

MRS. SHIN: And when certain rumors get about, what *happens* to a little place like this? It goes to pot. *I* know. So, if you want my advice, Mr. Shui Ta, find out just what has been going on between Miss Shen Te and that Yang Sun from Yellow Street. And remember: a certain interest in Miss Shen Te has been expressed by the barber next door, a man with twelve houses and only one wife, who, for that matter, is likely to drop off at any time. A certain interest has been expressed. He was even enquiring about her means and, if *that* doesn't prove a man is getting serious, what would? (*Still getting no response, she leaves with her bucket.*)

YANG SUN's VOICE: Is that Miss Shen Te's tobacco shop?

MRS. SHIN's VOICE: Yes, it is, but it's Mr. Shui Ta who's here today.

SHUI TA *runs to the mirror with the short, light steps of* SHEN TE, *and is just about to start primping, when he realizes his mistake, and turns away, with a short laugh. Enter* YANG SUN. MRS. SHIN *enters behind him and slips into the back room to eavesdrop.*

YANG SUN: I am Yang Sun. (SHUI TA *bows.*) Is Shen Te in?

SHUI TA: No.

YANG SUN: I guess you know our relationship? (*He is inspecting the stock.*) Quite a place! And I thought she was just talking big. I'll be flying again, all right. (*He takes a cigar, solicits and receives a light from* SHUI TA.) You think we can squeeze the other three hundred out of the tobacco stock?

SHUI TA: May I ask if it is your intention to sell at once?

YANG SUN: It was decent of her to come out with the two hundred but they aren't much use with the other three hundred still missing.

SHUI TA: Shen Te was overhasty promising so much. She might have to sell the shop itself to raise it. Haste, they say, is the wind that blows the house down.

YANG SUN: Oh, she isn't a girl to keep a man waiting. For one thing or the other, if you take my meaning.

SHUI TA: I take your meaning.

YANG SUN (*leering*): Uh, huh.

SHUI TA: Would you explain what the five hundred silver dollars are for?

YANG SUN: Want to sound me out? Very well. The director of the Peking airfield is a friend of mine from flying school. I give him five hundred: he gets me the job.

SHUI TA: The price is high.

YANG SUN: Not as these things go. He'll have to fire one of the present pilots — for negligence. Only the man he has in mind isn't negligent. Not easy, you understand. You needn't mention that part of it to Shen Te.

SHUI TA (*looking intently at* YANG SUN): Mr. Yang Sun, you are asking my cousin to give up her possessions, leave her friends, and place her entire fate in your hands. I presume you intend to marry her?

YANG SUN: I'd be prepared to.

Slight pause.

SHUI TA: Those two hundred silver dollars would pay the rent here for six months. If you were Shen Te wouldn't you be tempted to continue in business?

YANG SUN: What? Can you imagine Yang Sun the Flyer behind a counter? (*In an oily voice:*) "A strong cigar or a mild one, worthy sir?" Not in this century!

SHUI TA: My cousin wishes to follow the promptings of her heart, and, from her own point of view, she may even have what is called the right to love. Accordingly, she has commissioned me to help you to this post. There is nothing here that I am not empowered to turn immediately into cash. Mrs. Mi Tzu, the landlady, will advise me about the sale.

Enter MRS. MI TZU.

MRS. MI TZU: Good morning, Mr. Shui Ta, you wish to see me about the rent? As you know it falls due the day after tomorrow.

SHUI TA: Circumstances have changed, Mrs. Mi Tzu: my cousin is getting married. Her future husband here, Mr. Yang Sun, will be taking her to Peking. I am interested in selling the tobacco stock.

MRS. MI TZU: How much are you asking, Mr. Shui Ta?

YANG SUN: Three hundred sil —

SHUI TA: Five hundred silver dollars.

MRS. MI TZU: How much did she pay for it, Mr. Shui Ta?

SHUI TA: A thousand. And very little has been sold.

MRS. MI TZU: She was robbed. But I'll make you a special offer if you'll promise to be out by the day after tomorrow. Three hundred silver dollars.

YANG SUN (*shrugging*): Take it, man, take it.

SHUI TA: It is not enough.

YANG SUN: Why not? Why not? Certainly, it's enough.

SHUI TA: Five hundred silver dollars.

YANG SUN: But why? We only need three!

SHUI TA (*to* MRS. MI TZU): Excuse me. (*Takes* YANG SUN *on one side.*) The tobacco stock is pledged to the old couple who gave my cousin the two hundred.

YANG SUN: Is it in writing?

SHUI TA: No.

YANG SUN (*to* MRS. MI TZU): Three hundred will do.

MRS. MI TZU: Of course, I need an assurance that Miss Shen Te is not in debt.

YANG SUN: Mr. Shui Ta?

SHUI TA: She is not in debt.

YANG SUN: When can you let us have the money?

MRS. MI TZU: The day after tomorrow. And remember: I'm doing this because I have a soft spot in my heart for young lovers! (*Exit.*)

YANG SUN (*calling after her*): Boxes, jars and sacks — three hundred for the lot and the pain's over! (*To* SHUI TA:) Where else can we raise money by the day after tomorrow?

SHUI TA: Nowhere. Haven't you enough for the trip and the first few weeks?

YANG SUN: Oh, certainly.

SHUI TA: How much, exactly.

YANG SUN: Oh, I'll dig it up, even if I have to steal it.

SHUI TA: I see.

YANG SUN: Well, don't fall off the roof. I'll get to Peking somehow.

SHUI TA: Two people can't travel for nothing.

YANG SUN (*not giving* SHUI TA *a chance to answer*): I'm leaving *her* behind. No millstones round *my* neck!

SHUI TA: Oh.

YANG SUN: Don't look at me like that!

SHUI TA: How precisely is my cousin to live?

YANG SUN: Oh, you'll think of something.

SHUI TA: A small request, Mr. Yang Sun. Leave the two hundred silver dollars here until you can show me two tickets for Peking.

YANG SUN: You learn to mind your own business, Mr. Shui Ta.

SHUI TA: I'm afraid Miss Shen Te may not wish to sell the shop when she discovers that . . .

YANG SUN: You don't know women. She'll want to. Even then.

SHUI TA (*a slight outburst*): She is a human being, sir! And not devoid of common sense!

YANG SUN: Shen Te is a woman: she *is* devoid of common sense. I only have to lay my hand on her shoulder, and church bells ring.

SHUI TA (*with difficulty*): Mr. Yang Sun!

YANG SUN: Mr. Shui Whatever-it-is!

SHUI TA: My cousin is devoted to you . . . because . . .

YANG SUN: Because I have my hands on her breasts. Give me a cigar. (*He takes one for himself, stuffs a few more in his pocket, then changes his mind and takes the whole box.*) Tell her I'll marry her, then bring me the three hundred. Or let her bring it. One or the other. (*Exit.*)

MRS. SHIN (*sticking her head out of the back room*): Well, he has your cousin under his thumb, and doesn't care if all Yellow Street knows it!

SHUI TA (*crying out*): I've lost my shop! And he doesn't love me! (*He runs berserk through the room, repeating these lines incoherently. Then stops suddenly, and addresses* MRS. SHIN:) Mrs. Shin, you grew up in the gutter, like me. Are we lacking in hardness? I doubt it. If you steal a penny from me, I'll take you by the throat till you spit it out! You'd do the same to me. The times are bad, this city is hell, but we're like ants, we keep coming, up and up the walls, however smooth! Till bad luck comes. Being in love, for instance. One weakness is enough, and love is the deadliest.

MRS. SHIN (*emerging from the back room*): You should have a little talk with Mr. Shu Fu the Barber. He's a real gentleman and just the thing for your cousin. (*She runs off.*)

SHUI TA:
A caress becomes a stranglehold
A sigh of love turns to a cry of fear
Why are there vultures circling in the air?
A girl is going to meet her lover.

SHUI TA *sits down and* MR. SHU FU *enters with* MRS. SHIN.

SHUI TA: Mr. Shu Fu?

SHU FU: Mr. Shui Ta.

They both bow.

SHUI TA: I am told that you have expressed a certain interest in my cousin Shen Te. Let me set aside all propriety and confess: she is at this moment in grave danger.

SHU FU: Oh, dear!

SHUI TA: She has lost her shop, Mr. Shu Fu.

SHU FU: The charm of Miss Shen Te, Mr. Shui Ta, derives from the goodness, not of her shop, but of her heart. Men call her the Angel of the Slums.

SHUI TA: Yet her goodness has cost her two hundred silver dollars in a single day: we must put a stop to it.

SHU FU: Permit me to differ, Mr. Shui Ta. Let us, rather, open wide the gates to such goodness! Every morning, with pleasure tinged by affection, I watch her charitable ministrations. For they are hungry, and she giveth them to eat! Four of them, to be precise. Why only four? I ask. Why not four hundred? I hear she has been seeking shelter for the homeless. What about my humble cabins behind the cattle run? They are at her disposal. And so forth. And so on. Mr. Shui Ta, do you think Miss Shen Te could be persuaded to listen to certain ideas of mine? Ideas like these?

SHUI TA: Mr. Shu Fu, she would be honored.

Enter WONG *and the* POLICEMAN. MR. SHU FU *turns abruptly away and studies the shelves.*

WONG: Is Miss Shen Te here?

SHUI TA: No.

WONG: I am Wong the Water Seller. You are Mr. Shui Ta?

SHUI TA: I am.

WONG: I am a friend of Shen Te's.

SHUI TA: An intimate friend, I hear.

WONG (*to the* POLICEMAN): You see? (*To* SHUI TA:) It's because of my hand.

POLICEMAN: He hurt his hand, sir, that's a fact.

SHUI TA (*quickly*): You need a sling, I see. (*He takes a shawl from the back room, and throws it to* WONG.)

WONG: But that's her new shawl!

SHUI TA: She has no more use for it.

WONG: But she bought it to please someone!

SHUI TA: It happens to be no longer necessary.

WONG (*making the sling*): She is my only witness.

POLICEMAN: Mr. Shui Ta, your cousin is supposed to have seen the Barber hit the Water Seller with a curling iron.

SHUI TA: I'm afraid my cousin was not present at the time.

WONG: But she was, sir! Just ask her! Isn't she in?

SHUI TA (*gravely*): Mr. Wong, my cousin has her own troubles. You wouldn't wish her to add to them by committing perjury?

WONG: But it was she that told me to go to the judge!

SHUI TA: Was the judge supposed to heal your hand?

MR. SHU FU *turns quickly around.* SHUI TA *bows to* SHU FU, *and vice versa.*

WONG (*taking the sling off, and putting it back*): I see how it is.

POLICEMAN: Well, I'll be on my way. (*To* WONG:) And you be careful. If Mr. Shu Fu wasn't a man who tempers justice with mercy, as the saying is, you'd be in jail for libel. Be off with you!

Exit WONG, *followed by* POLICEMAN.

SHUI TA: Profound apologies, Mr. Shu Fu.

SHU FU: Not at all, Mr. Shui Ta. (*Pointing to the shawl:*) The episode is over?

SHUI TA: It may take her time to recover. There are some fresh wounds.

SHU FU: We shall be discreet. Delicate. A short vacation could be arranged. . . .

SHUI TA: First of course, you and she would have to talk things over.

MR. SHU FU: At a small supper in a small, but high-class, restaurant.

SHUI TA: I'll go and find her. (*Exit into back room.*)

MRS. SHIN (*sticking her head in again*): Time for congratulations, Mr. Shu Fu?

SHU FU: Ah, Mrs. Shin! Please inform Miss Shen Te's guests they may take shelter in the cabins behind the cattle run!

MRS. SHIN *nods, grinning.*

SHU FU (*to the audience*): Well? What do you think of me, ladies and gentlemen? What could a man do more? Could he be less selfish? More farsighted? A small supper in a small but . . . Does that bring rather vulgar and clumsy thoughts into your mind? Ts, ts, ts. Nothing of the sort will occur. She won't even be touched. Not even accidentally while passing the salt.

An exchange of ideas only. Over the flowers on the table —
white chrysanthemums, by the way (*he writes down a note
of this*)— yes, over the white chrysanthemums, two young
souls will . . . shall I say "find each other"? We shall NOT
exploit the misfortune of others. Understanding? Yes. An
offer of assistance? Certainly. But quietly. Almost inaudibly.
Perhaps with single glance. A glance that could also — mean
more.

MRS. SHIN (*coming forward*): Everything under control, Mr. Shu
Fu?

SHU FU: Oh, Mrs. Shin, what do you know about this worthless
rascal Yang Sun?

MRS. SHIN: Why, he's the most worthless rascal . . .

SHU FU: Is he really? You're sure? (*As she opens her mouth:*) From
now on, he doesn't exist! Can't be found anywhere!
Enter YANG SUN.

YANG SUN: What's been going on here?

MRS. SHIN: Shall I call Mr. Shui Ta, Mr. Shu Fu? He wouldn't want
strangers in here!

SHU FU: Mr. Shui Ta is in conference with Miss Shen Te. Not to
be disturbed!

YANG SUN: Shen Te here? I didn't see her come in. What kind of
conference?

SHU FU (*not letting him enter the back room*): Patience, dear sir!
And if by chance I have an inkling who you are, pray take
note that Miss Shen Te and I are about to announce our engagement.

YANG SUN: What?

MRS. SHIN: You didn't expect that, did you?

YANG SUN *is trying to push past the barber into the back room
when* SHEN TE *comes out.*

SHU FU: My dear Shen Te, ten thousand apologies! Perhaps you . . .

YANG SUN: What is it, Shen Te? Have you gone crazy?

SHEN TE (*breathless*): My cousin and Mr. Shu Fu have come to an
understanding. They wish me to hear Mr. Shu Fu's plans for
helping the poor.

YANG SUN: Your cousin wants to part us.

SHEN TE: Yes.

YANG SUN: And you've agreed to it?

SHEN TE: Yes.

YANG SUN: They told you I was bad. (SHEN TE *is silent.*) And suppose I am. Does that make me need you less? I'm low, Shen Te, I have no money, I don't do the right thing but at least I put up a fight! (*He is near her now, and speaks in an undertone.*) Have you no eyes? Look at him. Have you forgotten already?

SHEN TE: No.

YANG SUN: How it was raining?

SHEN TE: No.

YANG SUN: How you cut me down from the willow tree? Bought me water? Promised me money to fly with?

SHEN TE (*shakily*): Yang Sun, what do you want?

YANG SUN: I want you to come with me.

SHEN TE (*in a small voice*): Forgive me, Mr. Shu Fu, I want to go with Mr. Yang Sun.

YANG SUN: We're lovers you know. Give me the key to the shop. (SHEN TE *takes the key from around her neck.* YANG SUN *puts it on the counter. To* MRS. SHIN:) Leave it under the mat when you're through. Let's go, Shen Te.

SHU FU: But this is rape! Mr. Shui Ta!!

YANG SUN (*to* SHEN TE): Tell him not to shout.

SHEN TE: Please don't shout for my cousin, Mr. Shu Fu. He doesn't agree with me, I know, but he's wrong.

To the audience:

I want to go with the man I love
I don't want to count the cost
I don't want to consider if it's wise
I don't want to know if he loves me
I want to go with the man I love.

YANG SUN: That's the spirit.

And the couple leave.

5a

In front of the inner curtain. SHEN TE *in her wedding clothes, on the way to her wedding.*

SHEN TE: Something terrible has happened. As I left the shop with Yang Sun, I found the old carpet dealer's wife waiting on the street, trembling all over. She told me her husband had taken to his bed — sick with all the worry and excitement over the two hundred silver dollars they lent me. She said it would be best if I gave it back now. Of course, I had to say I would. She said she couldn't quite trust my cousin Shui Ta or even my fiancé Yang Sun. There were tears in her eyes. With my emotions in an uproar, I threw myself into Yang Sun's arms, I couldn't resist him. The things he'd said to Shui Ta had taught Shen Te nothing. Sinking into his arms, I said to myself:

> To let no one perish, not even oneself
> To fill everyone with happiness, even oneself
> Is so good

How could I have forgotten those two old people? Yang Sun swept me away like a small hurricane. But he's not a bad man, and he loves me. He'd rather work in the cement factory than owe his flying to a crime. Though, of course, flying *is* a great passion with Sun. Now, on the way to my wedding, I waver between fear and joy.

6

The "private dining room" on the upper floor of a cheap restaurant in a poor section of town. With SHEN TE: *the* GRAND-FATHER, *the* SISTER-IN-LAW, *the* NIECE, MRS. SHIN, *the* UNEMPLOYED MAN. *In a corner, alone, a* PRIEST. *A* WAITER *pouring wine. Downstage,* YANG SUN *talking to his* MOTHER. *He wears a dinner jacket.*

YANG SUN: Bad news, Mamma. She came right out and told me she can't sell the shop for me. Some idiot is bringing a claim because he lent her the two hundred she gave you.

MRS. YANG: What did you say? Of course, you can't marry her now.

YANG SUN: It's no use saying anything to *her*. I've sent for her cousin, Mr. Shui Ta. He said there was nothing in writing.

MRS. YANG: Good idea. I'll go out and look for him. Keep an eye on things.

Exit MRS. YANG. SHEN TE *has been pouring wine.*

SHEN TE (*to the audience, pitcher in hand*): I wasn't mistaken in him. He's bearing up well. Though it must have been an awful blow — giving up flying. I do love him so. (*Calling across the room to him:*) Sun, you haven't drunk a toast with the bride!

YANG SUN: What do we drink to?

SHEN TE: Why, to the future!

YANG SUN: When the bridegroom's dinner jacket won't be a hired one!

SHEN TE: But when the bride's dress will still get rained on sometimes!

YANG SUN: To everything we ever wished for!

SHEN TE: May all our dreams come true!

They drink.

YANG SUN (*with loud conviviality*): And now, friends, before the wedding gets under way, I have to ask the bride a few questions. I've no idea what kind of a wife she'll make, and it worries me. (*Wheeling on* SHEN TE:) For example. Can you make five cups of tea with three tea leaves?

SHEN TE: No.

YANG SUN: So I won't be getting very much tea. Can you sleep on a straw mattress the size of that book? (*He points to the large volume the* PRIEST *is reading.*)

SHEN TE: The two of us?

YANG SUN: The one of you.

SHEN TE: In that case, no.

YANG SUN: What a wife! I'm shocked!

While the audience is laughing, his MOTHER *returns. With a shrug of her shoulders, she tells* SUN *the expected guest hasn't arrived. The* PRIEST *shuts the book with a bang, and makes for the door.*

MRS. YANG: Where are *you* off to? It's only a matter of minutes.

PRIEST (*watch in hand*): Time goes on, Mrs. Yang, and I've another wedding to attend to. Also a funeral.

MRS. YANG (*irately*): D'you think we planned it this way? I was hoping to manage with one pitcher of wine, and we've run through two already. (*Points to empty pitcher. Loudly:*) My dear Shen Te, I don't know where your cousin can be keeping himself!

SHEN TE: My cousin?!

MRS. YANG: Certainly. I'm old-fashioned enough to think such a close relative should attend the wedding.

SHEN TE: Oh, Sun, is it the three hundred silver dollars?

YANG SUN (*not looking her in the eye*): Are you deaf? Mother says she's old-fashioned. And I say I'm considerate. We'll wait another fifteen minutes.

HUSBAND: Another fifteen minutes.

MRS. YANG (*addressing the company*): Now you all know, don't you, that my son is getting a job as a mail pilot?

SISTER-IN-LAW: In Peking, too, isn't it?

MRS. YANG: In Peking, too! The two of us are moving to Peking!

SHEN TE: Sun, tell your mother Peking is out of the question now.

YANG SUN: Your cousin'll tell her. If he agrees. I don't agree.

SHEN TE (*amazed, and dismayed*): Sun!

YANG SUN: I hate this godforsaken Setzuan. What people! Know
what they look like when I half close my eyes? Horses!
Whinnying, fretting, stamping, screwing their necks up!
(*Loudly:*) And what is it the thunder says? They are su-per-
flu-ous! (*He hammers out the syllables.*) They've run their
last race! They can go trample themselves to death! (*Pause.*)
I've got to get out of here.

SHEN TE: But I've promised the money to the old couple.

YANG SUN: And since you always do the wrong thing, it's lucky
your cousin's coming. Have another drink.

SHEN TE (*quietly*): My cousin can't be coming.

YANG SUN: How d'you mean?

SHEN TE: My cousin can't be where I am.

YANG SUN: Quite a conundrum!

SHEN TE (*desperately*): Sun, I'm the one that loves you. Not my
cousin. He was thinking of the job in Peking when he promised
you the old couple's money —

YANG SUN: Right. And that's why he's bringing the three hundred
silver dollars. Here — to my wedding.

SHEN TE: He is not bringing the three hundred silver dollars.

YANG SUN: Huh? What makes you think that?

SHEN TE (*looking into his eyes*): He says you only bought one
ticket to Peking.

Short pause.

YANG SUN: That was yesterday. (*He pulls two tickets part way out
of his inside pocket, making her look under his coat.*) Two
tickets. I don't want Mother to know. She'll get left behind. I
sold her furniture to buy these tickets, so you see . . .

SHEN TE: But what's to become of the old couple?

YANG SUN: What's to become of me? Have another drink. Or do

you believe in moderation? If I drink, I fly again. And if you drink, you may learn to understand me.

SHEN TE: You want to fly. But I can't help you.

YANG SUN: "Here's a plane, my darling — but it's only got one wing!"

The WAITER *enters.*

WAITER: Mrs. Yang!

MRS. YANG: Yes?

WAITER: Another pitcher of wine, ma'am?

MRS. YANG: We have enough, thanks. Drinking makes me sweat.

WAITER: Would you mind paying, ma'am?

MRS. YANG (*to everyone*): Just be patient a few moments longer, everyone, Mr. Shui Ta is on his way over! (*To the* WAITER:) Don't be a spoilsport.

WAITER: I can't let you leave till you've paid your bill, ma'am.

MRS. YANG: But they know me here!

WAITER: That's just it.

PRIEST (*ponderously getting up*): I humbly take my leave. (*And he does.*)

MRS. YANG (*to the others, desperately*): Stay where you are, everybody! The priest says he'll be back in two minutes!

YANG SUN: It's no good, Mamma. Ladies and gentlemen, Mr. Shui Ta still hasn't arrived and the priest has gone home. We won't detain you any longer.

They are leaving now.

GRANDFATHER (*in the doorway, having forgotten to put his glass down*): To the bride! (*He drinks, puts down the glass, and follows the others.*)

Pause.

SHEN TE: Shall I go too?

YANG SUN: You? Aren't you the bride? Isn't this your wedding? (*He drags her across the room, tearing her wedding dress.*) If we can wait, you can wait. Mother calls me her falcon. She wants to see me in the clouds. But I think it may be St. Nevercome's Day before she'll go to the door and see my plane thunder by. (*Pause. He pretends the guests are still present.*) Why such a lull in the conversation, ladies and gentlemen? Don't you like it here? The ceremony is only slightly postponed — because an important guest is expected at any moment. Also because the bride doesn't know what love is. While we're waiting, the bridegroom will sing a little song. (*He does so:*)

THE SONG OF ST. NEVERCOME'S DAY

On a certain day, as is generally known,
   One and all will be shouting: Hooray, hooray!
For the beggar maid's son has a solid-gold throne
   And the day is St. Nevercome's Day
On St. Nevercome's, Nevercome's, Nevercome's Day
   He'll sit on his solid-gold throne

Oh, hooray, hooray! That day goodness will pay!
   That day badness will cost you your head!
And merit and money will smile and be funny
   While exchanging salt and bread
On St. Nevercome's, Nevercome's, Nevercome's Day
   While exchanging salt and bread

And the grass, oh, the grass will look down at the sky
   And the pebbles will roll up the stream
And all men will be good without batting an eye
   They will make of our earth a dream
On St. Nevercome's, Nevercome's, Nevercome's Day
   They will make of our earth a dream

And as for me, that's the day I shall be
   A flyer and one of the best
Unemployed man, you will have work to do
   Washerwoman, you'll get your rest
On St. Nevercome's, Nevercome's, Nevercome's Day
   Washerwoman, you'll get your rest

MRS. YANG: It looks like he's not coming.

The three of them sit looking at the door.

6a

WONG's den. The sewer pipe is again transparent and again the GODS appear to WONG in a dream.

WONG: I'm so glad you've come, illustrious ones. It's Shen Te. She's in great trouble from following the rule about loving thy neighbor. Perhaps she's *too* good for this world!

FIRST GOD: Nonsense! You are eaten up by lice and doubts!

WONG: Forgive me, illustrious one, I only meant you might deign to intervene.

FIRST GOD: Out of the question! My colleague here intervened in some squabble or other only yesterday. (*He points to the* THIRD GOD *who has a black eye.*) The results are before us!

WONG: She had to call on her cousin again. But not even he could help. I'm afraid the shop is done for.

THIRD GOD (*a little concerned*): Perhaps we should help after all?

FIRST GOD: The gods help those that help themselves.

WONG: What if we *can't* help ourselves, illustrious ones?
Slight pause.

SECOND GOD: Try, anyway! Suffering ennobles!

FIRST GOD: Our faith in Shen Te is unshaken!

THIRD GOD: We certainly haven't found any *other* good people. You can see where we spend our nights from the straw on our clothes.

WONG: You might help her find her way by —

FIRST GOD: The good man finds his own way here below!

SECOND GOD: The good woman too.

FIRST GOD: The heavier the burden, the greater her strength!

THIRD GOD: We're only onlookers, you know.

FIRST GOD: And everything will be all right in the end, O ye of little faith!
They are gradually disappearing through these last lines.

7

The yard behind SHEN TE's *shop. A few articles of furniture on a cart.* SHEN TE *and* MRS. SHIN *are taking the washing off the line.*

MRS. SHIN: If you ask me, you should fight tooth and nail to keep the shop.

SHEN TE: How can I? I have to sell the tobacco to pay back the two hundred silver dollars today.

MRS. SHIN: No husband, no tobacco, no house and home! What are you going to live on?

SHEN TE: I can work. I can sort tobacco.

MRS. SHIN: Hey, look, Mr. Shui Ta's trousers! He must have left here stark naked!

SHEN TE: Oh, he may have another pair, Mrs. Shin.

MRS. SHIN: But if he's gone for good as you say, why has he left his pants behind?

SHEN TE: Maybe he's thrown them away.

MRS. SHIN: Can I take them?

SHEN TE: Oh, no.

Enter MR. SHU FU, *running.*

SHU FU: Not a word! Total silence! I know all. You have sacrificed your own love and happiness so as not to hurt a dear old couple who had put their trust in you! Not in vain does this district —for all its malevolent tongues — call you the Angel of the Slums! That young man couldn't rise to your level, so you left him. And now, when I see you closing up the little shop, that veritable haven of rest for the multitude, well, I cannot, I cannot let it pass. Morning after morning I have stood watching in the doorway not unmoved — while you graciously handed out rice to the wretched. Is that never to happen again? Is the good woman of Setzuan to disappear? If only you would allow *me* to assist you! Now don't say anything! No assurances, no

exclamations of gratitude! (*He has taken out his check book.*)
Here! A blank check. (*He places it on the cart.*) Just my
signature. Fill it out as you wish. Any sum in the world. I
herewith retire from the scene, quietly, unobtrusively, making
no claims, on tiptoe, full of veneration, absolutely selflessly . . .
(*He has gone.*)

MRS. SHIN: Well! You're saved. There's always some idiot of a
man. . . . Now hurry! Put down a thousand silver dollars
and let me fly to the bank before he comes to his senses.

SHEN TE: I can pay you for the washing without any check.

MRS. SHIN: What? You're not going to cash it just because you
might have to marry him? Are you crazy? Men like him *want*
to be led by the nose! Are you still thinking of that flyer? All
Yellow Street knows how he treated you!

SHEN TE:

When I heard his cunning laugh, I was afraid
But when I saw the holes in his shoes, I loved him dearly.

MRS. SHIN: Defending that good-for-nothing after all that's happened!

SHEN TE (*staggering as she holds some of the washing*): Oh!

MRS. SHIN (*taking the washing from her, dryly*): So you feel
dizzy when you stretch and bend? There couldn't be a little
visitor on the way? If that's it, you can forget Mr. Shu Fu's
blank check: it wasn't meant for a christening present!

She goes to the back with a basket. SHEN TE's *eyes follow* MRS.
SHIN *for a moment. Then she looks down at her own body,
feels her stomach, and a great joy comes into her eyes.*

SHEN TE: O joy! A new human being is on the way. The world
awaits him. In the cities the people say: he's got to be reckoned
with, this new human being! (*She imagines a little boy to be
present, and introduces him to the audience.*) This is my son,
the well-known flyer!
Say: Welcome
To the conqueror of unknown mountains and unreachable
     regions
Who brings us our mail across the impassable deserts!

She leads him up and down by the hand.

Take a look at the world, my son. That's a tree. Tree, yes. Say: "Hello, tree!" And bow. Like this. (*She bows.*) Now you know each other. And, look, here comes the Water Seller. He's a friend, give him your hand. A cup of fresh water for my little son, please. Yes, it *is* a warm day. (*Handing the cup.*) Oh dear, a policeman, we'll have to make a circle round *him*. Perhaps we can pick a few cherries over there in the rich Mr. Pung's garden. But we mustn't be seen. You want cherries? Just like children with fathers. No, no, you can't go straight at them like that. Don't pull. We must learn to be reasonable. Well, have it your own way. (*She has let him make for the cherries.*) Can you reach? Where to put them? Your mouth is the best place. (*She tries one herself.*) Mmm, they're good. But the policeman, we must run! (*They run.*) Yes, back to the street. Calm now, so no one will notice us. (*Walking the street with her child, she sings:*)

Once a plum — 'twas in Japan —
Made a conquest of a man
But the man's turn soon did come
For he gobbled up the plum

Enter WONG, *with a* CHILD *by the hand. He coughs.*

SHEN TE: Wong!

WONG: It's about the Carpenter, Shen Te. He's lost his shop, and he's been drinking. His children are on the streets. This is one. Can you help?

SHEN TE (*to the* CHILD): Come here, little man. (*Takes him down to the footlights. To the audience:*)

You there! A man is asking you for shelter!
A man of tomorrow says: what about today?
His friend the conqueror, whom you know,
Is his advocate!

(*To* WONG:) He can live in Mr. Shu Fu's cabins. I may have to go there myself. I'm going to have a baby. That's a secret — don't tell Yang Sun — we'd only be in his way. Can you find the Carpenter for me?

WONG: I knew you'd think of something. (*To the* CHILD:) Goodbye, son, I'm going for your father.

SHEN TE: What about your hand, Wong? I wanted to help, but my cousin . . .

WONG: Oh, I can get along with one hand, don't worry. (*He shows how he can handle his pole with his left hand alone.*)

SHEN TE: But your right hand! Look, take this cart, sell everything that's on it, and go to the doctor with the money . . .

WONG: She's still good. But first I'll bring the Carpenter. I'll pick up the cart when I get back. (*Exit* WONG.)

SHEN TE (*To the* CHILD): Sit down over here, son, till your father comes.

The CHILD *sits crosslegged on the ground. Enter the* HUSBAND *and* WIFE, *each dragging a large, full sack.*

WIFE (*furtively*): You're alone, Shen Te, dear?

SHEN TE *nods.*

The WIFE *beckons to the* NEPHEW *off stage. He comes on with another sack.*

WIFE: Your cousin's away? (SHEN TE *nods.*) He's not coming back?

SHEN TE: No. I'm giving up the shop.

WIFE: That's why we're here. We want to know if we can leave these things in your new home. Will you do us this favor?

SHEN TE: Why, yes, I'd be glad to.

HUSBAND (*cryptically*): And if anyone asks about them, say they're yours.

SHEN TE: Would anyone ask?

WIFE (*with a glance back at her husband*): Oh, someone might. The police, for instance. They don't seem to like us. Where can we put it?

SHEN TE: Well, I'd rather not get in any more trouble . . .

WIFE: Listen to her! The good woman of Setzuan!

SHEN TE *is silent.*

HUSBAND: There's enough tobacco in those sacks to give us a new start in life. We could have our own tobacco factory!

SHEN TE (*slowly*): You'll have to put them in the back room.

The sacks are taken offstage, while the CHILD *is left alone. Shyly glancing about him, he goes to the garbage can, starts playing with the contents, and eating some of the scraps. The others return.*

WIFE: We're counting on you, Shen Te!

SHEN TE: Yes. (*She sees the* CHILD *and is shocked.*)

HUSBAND: We'll see you in Mr. Shu Fu's cabins.

NEPHEW: The day after tomorrow.

SHEN TE: Yes. Now, go. Go! I'm not feeling well.

Exeunt all three, virtually pushed off.

He is eating the refuse in the garbage can!
Only look at his little grey mouth!

Pause. Music.

As this is the world *my* son will enter
I will study to defend him.
To be good to you, my son,
I shall be a tigress to all others
If I have to.
And I shall have to.

She starts to go.

One more time, then. I hope really the last.

Exit SHEN TE, *taking* SHUI TA'S *trousers.* MRS. SHIN *enters and watches her with marked interest. Enter the* SISTER-IN-LAW *and the* GRANDFATHER.

SISTER-IN-LAW: So it's true, the shop has closed down. And the furniture's in the back yard. It's the end of the road!

MRS. SHIN (*pompously*): The fruit of high living, selfishness, and sensuality! Down the primrose path to Mr. Shu Fu's cabins — with you!

SISTER-IN-LAW: Cabins? Rat holes! He gave them to us because his soap supplies only went moldy there!

Enter the UNEMPLOYED MAN.

UNEMPLOYED MAN: Shen Te is moving?

SISTER-IN-LAW: Yes. She was sneaking away.

MRS. SHIN: She's ashamed of herself, and no wonder!

UNEMPLOYED MAN: Tell her to call Mr. Shui Ta or she's done for this time!

SISTER-IN-LAW: Tell her to call Mr. Shui Ta or *we're* done for this time!

Enter WONG *and* CARPENTER, *the latter with a* CHILD *on each hand.*

CARPENTER: So we'll have a roof over our heads for a change!

MRS. SHIN: Roof? Whose roof?

CARPENTER: Mr. Shu Fu's cabins. And we have little Feng to thank for it. (*Feng, we find, is the name of the child already there; his father now takes him. To the other two:*) Bow to your little brother, you two!

The CARPENTER *and the* TWO NEW ARRIVALS *bow to Feng. Enter* SHUI TA.

UNEMPLOYED MAN: Sst! Mr. Shui Ta!

Pause.

SHUI TA: And what is this crowd here for, may I ask?

WONG: How do you do, Mr. Shui Ta. This is the Carpenter. Miss Shen Te promised him space in Mr. Shu Fu's cabins.

SHUI TA: That will not be possible.

CARPENTER: We can't go there after all?

SHUI TA: All the space is needed for other purposes.

SISTER-IN-LAW: You mean we have to get out? But we've got nowhere to go.

SHUI TA: Miss Shen Te finds it possible to provide employment. If the proposition interests you, you may stay in the cabins.

SISTER-IN-LAW (*with distaste*): You mean *work?* Work for Miss Shen Te?

SHUI TA: Making tobacco, yes. There are three bales here already. Would you like to get them?

SISTER-IN-LAW (*trying to bluster*): We have our own tobacco! We were in the tobacco business before you were born!

SHUI TA (*to the* CARPENTER *and the* UNEMPLOYED MAN): You *don't* have your own tobacco. What about you?

The CARPENTER *and the* UNEMPLOYED MAN *get the point, and go for the sacks. Enter* MRS. MI TZU.

MRS. MI TZU: Mr. Shui Ta? I've brought you your three hundred silver dollars.

SHUI TA: I'll sign your lease instead. I've decided not to sell.

MRS. MI TZU: What? You don't need the money for that flyer?

SHUI TA: No.

MRS. MI TZU: And you can pay six months' rent?

SHUI TA (*takes the Barber's blank check from the cart and fills it out*): Here is a check for ten thousand silver dollars. On Mr. Shu Fu's account. Look! (*He shows her the signature on the check.*) Your six months' rent will be in your hands by seven this evening. And now, if you'll excuse me.

MRS. MI TZU: So it's Mr. Shu Fu now. The flyer has been given his walking papers. These modern girls! In my day they'd have said she was flighty. That poor, deserted Mr. Yang Sun!

Exit MRS. MI TZU. *The* CARPENTER *and the* UNEMPLOYED MAN *drag the three sacks back on the stage.*

CARPENTER (*to* SHUI TA): I don't know why I'm doing this for you.

SHUI TA: Perhaps your children want to eat, Mr. Carpenter.

SISTER-IN-LAW (*catching sight of the sacks*): Was my brother-in-law here?

MRS. SHIN: Yes, he was.

SISTER-IN-LAW: I thought as much. I know those sacks! That's our tobacco!

SHUI TA: Really? I thought it came from my back room! Shall we consult the police on the point?

SISTER-IN-LAW (*defeated*): No.

SHUI TA: Perhaps you will show me the way to Mr. Shu Fu's cabins?

Taking FENG *by the hand,* SHUI TA *goes off, followed by the* CARPENTER *and his* TWO OLDER CHILDREN, *the* SISTER-IN-LAW, *the* GRANDFATHER, *and the* UNEMPLOYED MAN. *Each of the last three drags a sack.*

Enter OLD MAN *and* OLD WOMAN.

MRS. SHIN: A pair of pants — missing from the clothes line one minute — and next minute on the honorable backside of Mr. Shui Ta.

OLD WOMAN: We thought Miss Shen Te was here.

MRS. SHIN (*preoccupied*): Well, she's not.

OLD MAN: There was something she was going to give us.

WONG: She was going to help me too. (*Looking at his hand:*) It'll be too late soon. But she'll be back. This cousin has never stayed long.

MRS. SHIN (*approaching a conclusion*): No, he hasn't, has he?

7a

The Sewer Pipe: WONG *asleep. In his dream, he tells the* GODS *his fears. The* GODS *seem tired from all their travels. They stop for a moment and look over their shoulders at the Water Seller.*

WONG: Illustrious ones. I've been having a bad dream. Our beloved Shen Te was in great distress in the rushes down by the river — the spot where the bodies of suicides are washed up. She kept staggering and holding her head down as if she was carrying something and it was dragging her down into the mud. When I called out to her, she said she had to take your Book of Rules to the other side, and not get it wet, or the ink would all come off. You had talked to her about the virtues, you know, the time she gave you shelter in Setzuan.

THIRD GOD: Well, but what do you suggest, my dear Wong?

WONG: Maybe a little relaxation of the rules, Benevolent One, in view of the bad times.

THIRD GOD: As for instance?

WONG: Well, um, good-will, for instance, might do instead of love?

THIRD GOD: I'm afraid that would create new problems.

WONG: Or, instead of justice, good sportsmanship?

THIRD GOD: That would only mean more work.

WONG: Instead of honor, outward propriety?

THIRD GOD: Still more work! No, no! The rules will have to stand, my dear Wong!

Wearily shaking their heads, all three journey on.

8

SHUI TA's *tobacco factory in* SHU FU's *cabins. Huddled to-gether behind bars, several families, mostly women and children. Among these people the* SISTER-IN-LAW, *the* GRAND-FATHER, *the* CARPENTER *and his* THREE CHILDREN. *Enter* MRS. YANG *followed by* YANG SUN.

MRS. YANG (*to the audience*): There's something I just *have* to tell you: strength and wisdom are wonderful things. The strong and wise Mr. Shui Ta has transformed my son from a dissipated good-for-nothing into a model citizen. As you may have heard, Mr. Shui Ta opened a small tobacco factory near the cattle runs. It flourished. Three months ago — I shall never forget it — I asked for an appointment, and Mr. Shui Ta agreed to see us — me and my son. I can see him now as he came through the door to meet us. . . .

Enter SHUI TA, *from a door.*

SHUI TA: What can I do for you, Mrs. Yang?

MRS. YANG: This morning the police came to the house. We find you've brought an action for breach of promise of marriage. In the name of Shen Te. You also claim that Sun came by two hundred silver dollars by improper means.

SHUI TA: That is correct.

MRS. YANG: Mr. Shui Ta, the money's all gone. When the Peking job didn't materialize, he ran through it all in three days. I know he's a good-for-nothing. He sold my furniture. He was moving to Peking without me. Miss Shen Te thought highly of him at one time.

SHUI TA: What do *you* say, Mr. Yang Sun?

YANG SUN: The money's gone.

SHUI TA (*to* MRS. YANG): Mrs. Yang, in consideration of my cousin's incomprehensible weakness for your son, I am prepared to give him another chance. He can have a job — here. The two hundred silver dollars will be taken out of his wages.

474

YANG SUN: So it's the factory or jail?

SHUI TA: Take your choice.

YANG SUN: May I speak with Shen Te?

SHUI TA: You may not.

Pause.

YANG SUN (*sullenly*): Show me where to go.

MRS. YANG: Mr. Shui Ta, you are kindness itself: the gods will reward you! (*To* YANG SUN:) And honest work will make a man of you, my boy. (YANG SUN *follows* SHUI TA *into the factory.* MRS. YANG *comes down again to the footlights.*) Actually, honest work didn't agree with him — at first. And he got no opportunity to distinguish himself till — in the third week — when the wages were being paid . . .

SHUI TA *has a bag of money. Standing next to his foreman — the former* UNEMPLOYED MAN — *he counts out the wages. It is* YANG SUN'S *turn.*

UNEMPLOYED MAN (*reading*): Carpenter, six silver dollars. Yang Sun, six silver dollars.

YANG SUN (*quietly*): Excuse me, sir. I don't think it can be more than five. May I see? (*He takes the foreman's list.*) It says six working days. But that's a mistake, sir. I took a day off for court business. And I won't take what I haven't earned, however miserable the pay is!

UNEMPLOYED MAN: Yang Sun. Five silver dollars. (*To* SHUI TA:) A rare case, Mr. Shui Ta!

SHUI TA: How is it the book says six when it should say five?

UNEMPLOYED MAN: I must've made a mistake, Mr. Shui Ta. (*With a look at* YANG SUN:) It won't happen again.

SHUI TA (*taking* YANG SUN *aside*): You don't hold back, do you? You give your all to the firm. You're even honest. Do the foreman's mistakes always favor the workers?

YANG SUN: He does have . . . friends.

SHUI TA: Thank you. May I offer you any little recompense?

YANG SUN: Give me a trial period of one week, and I'll prove my intelligence is worth more to you than my strength.

MRS. YANG (*still down at the footlights*): Fighting words, fighting words! That evening, I said to Sun: "If you're a flyer, then fly, my falcon! Rise in the world!" And he got to be foreman. Yes, in Mr. Shui Ta's tobacco factory, he worked real miracles. *We see* YANG SUN *with his legs apart standing behind the* WORKERS *who are handing along a basket of raw tobacco above their heads.*

YANG SUN: Faster! Faster! You, there, d'you think you can just stand around, now you're not foreman any more? It'll be your job to lead us in song. Sing!

UNEMPLOYED MAN *starts singing. The others join in the refrain.*

SONG OF THE EIGHTH ELEPHANT

Chang had seven elephants — all much the same —
  But then there was Little Brother
The seven, they were wild, Little Brother, he was tame
  And to guard them Chang chose Little Brother
    Run faster!
    Mr. Chang has a forest park
    Which must be cleared before tonight
    And already it's growing dark!

When the seven elephants cleared that forest park
  Mr. Chang rode high on Little Brother
While the seven toiled and moiled till dark
  On his big behind sat Little Brother
    Dig faster!
    Mr. Chang has a forest park
    Which must be cleared before tonight
    And already it's growing dark!

And the seven elephants worked many an hour
  Till none of them could work another
Old Chang, he looked sour, on the seven he did glower
  But gave a pound of rice to Little Brother
    What was that?

Mr. Chang has a forest park
Which must be cleared before tonight
And already it's growing dark!

And the seven elephants hadn't any tusks
   The one that had the tusks was Little Brother
Seven are no match for one, if the one has a gun!
   How old Chang did laugh at Little Brother!
      Keep on digging!
      Mr. Chang has a forest park
      Which must be cleared before tonight
      And already it's growing dark!

Smoking a cigar, SHUI TA *strolls by.* YANG SUN, *laughing, has joined in the refrain of the third stanza and speeded up the tempo of the last stanza by clapping his hands.*

MRS. YANG: And that's why I say: strength and wisdom are wonderful things. It took the strong and wise Mr. Shui Ta to bring out the best in Yang Sun. A real superior man is like a bell. If you ring it, it rings, and if you don't, it don't, as the saying is.

9

SHEN TE's shop, now an office with club chairs and fine carpets. It is raining. SHUI TA, *now fat, is just dismissing the* OLD MAN *and* OLD WOMAN. MRS. SHIN, *in obviously new clothes, looks on, smirking.*

SHUI TA: No! I can NOT tell you when we expect her back.

OLD WOMAN: The two hundred silver dollars came today. In an envelope. There was no letter, but it must be from Shen Te. We want to write and thank her. May we have her address?

SHUI TA: I'm afraid I haven't got it.

OLD MAN (*pulling* OLD WOMAN's *sleeve*): Let's be going.

OLD WOMAN: She's got to come back some time!

They move off, uncertainly, worried. SHUI TA *bows.*

MRS. SHIN: They lost the carpet shop because they couldn't pay their taxes. The money arrived too late.

SHUI TA: They could have come to me.

MRS. SHIN: People don't like coming to you.

SHUI TA (*sits suddenly, one hand to his head*): I'm dizzy.

MRS. SHIN: After all, you *are* in your seventh month. But old Mrs. Shin will be there in your hour of trial! (*She cackles feebly.*)

SHUI TA (*in a stifled voice*): Can I count on that?

MRS. SHIN: We all have our price, and mine won't be too high for the great Mr. Shui Ta! (*She opens* SHUI TA's *collar.*)

SHUI TA: It's for the child's sake. All of this.

MRS. SHIN: "All for the child," of course.

SHUI TA: I'm so fat. People must notice.

MRS. SHIN: Oh no, they think it's 'cause you're rich.

SHUI TA (*more feelingly*): What will happen to the child?

MRS. SHIN: You ask that nine times a day. Why, it'll have the best that money can buy!

SHUI TA: He must never see Shui Ta.

MRS. SHIN: Oh, no. Always Shen Te.

SHUI TA: What about the neighbors? There are rumors, aren't there?

MRS. SHIN: As long as Mr. Shu Fu doesn't find out, there's nothing to worry about. Drink this.

Enter YANG SUN *in a smart business suit, and carrying a businessman's briefcase.* SHUI TA *is more or less in* MRS. SHIN'S *arms.*

YANG SUN (*surprised*): I guess I'm in the way.

SHUI TA (*ignoring this, rises with an effort*): Till tomorrow, Mrs. Shin.

MRS. SHIN *leaves with a smile, putting her new gloves on.*

YANG SUN: Gloves now! She couldn't be fleecing you? And since when did *you* have a private life? (*Taking a paper from the briefcase:*) You haven't been at your best lately, and things are getting out of hand. The police want to close us down. They say that at the most they can only permit twice the lawful number of workers.

SHUI TA (*evasively*): The cabins are quite good enough.

YANG SUN: For the workers maybe, not for the tobacco. They're too damp. We must take over some of Mrs. Mi Tzu's buildings.

SHUI TA: Her price is double what I can pay.

YANG SUN: Not unconditionally. If she has me to stroke her knees she'll come down.

SHUI TA: I'll never agree to that.

YANG SUN: What's wrong? Is it the rain? You get so irritable whenever it rains.

SHUI TA: Never! I will never . . .

YANG SUN: Mrs. Mi Tzu'll be here in five minutes. *You* fix it. And Shu Fu will be with her. . . . What's all that noise?

During the above dialogue, WONG *is heard offstage, calling: "The good Shen Te, where is she? Which of you has seen Shen Te, good people? Where is Shen Te?" A knock. Enter* WONG.

WONG: Mr. Shui Ta, I've come to ask when Miss Shen Te will be back, it's six months now. . . . There are rumors. People say something's happened to her.

SHUI TA: I'm busy. Come back next week.

WONG (*excited*): In the morning there was always rice on her door-step — for the needy. It's been there again lately!

SHUI TA: And what do people conclude from this?

WONG: That Shen Te is still in Setzuan! She's been . . . (*He breaks off.*)

SHUI TA: She's been what? Mr. Wong, if you're Shen Te's friend, talk a little less about her, that's my advice to you.

WONG: I don't want your advice! Before she disappeared, Miss Shen Te told me something very important — she's pregnant!

YANG SUN: What? What was that?

SHUI TA (*quickly*): The man is lying.

WONG: A good woman isn't so easily forgotten, Mr. Shui Ta.

He leaves. SHUI TA *goes quickly into the back room.*

YANG SUN (*to the audience*): Shen Te pregnant? So that's why. Her cousin sent her away, so I wouldn't get wind of it. I have a son, a Yang appears on the scene, and what happens? Mother and child vanish into thin air! That scoundrel, that unspeakable . . . (*The sound of sobbing is heard from the back room.*) What was that? Someone sobbing? Who was it? Mr. Shui Ta the Tobacco King doesn't weep his heart out. And where does the rice come from that's on the doorstep in the morning? (SHUI TA *returns. He goes to the door and looks out into the rain.*) Where is she?

SHUI TA: Sh! It's nine o'clock. But the rain's so heavy, you can't hear a thing.

YANG SUN: What do you want to hear?

SHUI TA: The mail plane.

YANG SUN: What?!

SHUI TA: I've been told *you* wanted to fly at one time. Is that all forgotten?

YANG SUN: Flying mail is night work. I prefer the daytime. And the firm is very dear to me — after all it belongs to my ex-fiancée, even if she's not around. And she's not, is she?

SHUI TA: What do you mean by that?

YANG SUN: Oh, well, let's say I haven't altogether — lost interest.

SHUI TA: My cousin might like to know that.

YANG SUN: I might not be indifferent — if I found she was being kept under lock and key.

SHUI TA: By whom?

YANG SUN: By you.

SHUI TA: What could you do about it?

YANG SUN: I could submit for discussion — my position in the firm.

SHUI TA: You are now my Manager. In return for a more . . . appropriate position, you might agree to drop the enquiry into your ex-fiancée's whereabouts?

YANG SUN: I might.

SHUI TA: What position *would* be more appropriate?

YANG SUN: The one at the top.

SHUI TA: My own? (*Silence.*) And if I preferred to throw you out on your neck?

YANG SUN: I'd come back on my feet. With suitable escort.

SHUI TA: The police?

YANG SUN: The police.

SHUI TA: And when the police found no one?

YANG SUN: I might ask them not to overlook the back room. (*Ending the pretense:*) In short, Mr. Shui Ta, my interest in this young woman has not been officially terminated. I should like to see more of her. (*Into* SHUI TA's *face:*) Besides, she's pregnant and needs a friend. (*He moves to the door.*) I shall talk about it with the Water Seller.

Exit. SHUI TA *is rigid for a moment, then he quickly goes into the back room. He returns with* SHEN TE's *belongings: underwear, etc. He takes a long look at the shawl of the previous scene. He then wraps the things in a bundle, which upon hearing a noise, he hides under the table. Enter* MRS. MI TZU *and* MR. SHU FU. *They put away their umbrellas and galoshes.*

MRS. MI TZU: I thought your Manager was here, Mr. Shui Ta. He combines charm with business in a way that can only be to the advantage of all of us.

SHU FU: You sent for us, Mr. Shui Ta?

SHUI TA: The factory is in trouble.

SHU FU: It always is.

SHUI TA: The police are threatening to close us down unless I can show that the extension of our facilities is imminent.

SHU FU: Mr. Shui Ta, I'm sick and tired of your constantly expanding projects. I place cabins at your cousin's disposal; you make a factory of them. I hand your cousin a check; you present it. Your cousin disappears: you find the cabins too small and start talking of yet more —

SHUI TA: Mr. Shu Fu, I'm authorized to inform you that Miss Shen Te's return is now imminent.

SHU FU: Imminent? It's becoming his favorite word.

MRS. MI TZU: Yes, what does it mean?

SHUI TA: Mrs. Mi Tzu, I can pay you exactly half what you asked for your buildings. Are you ready to inform the police that I am taking them over?

MRS. MI TZU: Certainly, if I can take over your manager.

SHU FU: What?

MRS. MI TZU: He's so efficient.

SHUI TA: I'm afraid I need Mr. Yang Sun.

MRS. MI TZU: So do I.

SHUI TA: He will call on you tomorrow.

SHU FU: So much the better. With Shen Te likely to turn up at any moment, the presence of that young man is hardly in good taste.

SHUI TA: So we have reached a settlement. In what was once the good Shen Te's little shop we are laying the foundations for the great Mr. Shui Ta's twelve magnificent super tobacco markets. You will bear in mind that though they call me the Tobacco King of Setzuan, it is my cousin's interests that have been served . . .

VOICES (*off*): The police, the police! Going to the tobacco shop! Something must have happened!

Enter YANG SUN, WONG, *and the* POLICEMAN.

POLICEMAN: Quiet there, quiet, quiet! (*They quiet down.*) I'm sorry, Mr. Shui Ta, but there's a report that you've been depriving Miss Shen Te of her freedom. Not that I believe all I hear, but the whole city's in an uproar.

SHUI TA: That's a lie.

POLICEMAN: Mr. Yang Sun has testified that he heard someone sobbing in the back room.

SHU FU: Mrs. Mi Tzu and myself will testify that no one here has been sobbing.

MRS. MI TZU: We have been quietly smoking our cigars.

POLICEMAN: Mr. Shui Ta, I'm afraid I shall have to take a look at that room. (*He does so. The room is empty.*) No one there, of course, sir.

YANG SUN: But I heard sobbing. What's that? (*He finds the clothes.*)

WONG: Those are Shen Te's things. (*To crowd:*) Shen Te's clothes are here!

VOICES (*off, in sequence*):
Shen Te's clothes!
They've been found under the table!
Body of murdered girl still missing!
Tobacco King suspected!

POLICEMAN: Mr. Shui Ta, unless you can tell us where the girl is, I'll have to ask you to come along.

SHUI TA: I do not know.

POLICEMAN: I can't say how sorry I am, Mr. Shui Ta. (*He shows him the door.*)

MR. SHUI TA: Everything will be cleared up in no time. There are still judges in Setzuan.

YANG SUN: I heard sobbing!

9a

WONG'S den. For the last time, the GODS appear to the Water Seller in his dream. They have changed and show signs of a long journey, extreme fatigue, and plenty of mishaps. The FIRST no longer has a hat; the THIRD has lost a leg; all three are barefoot.

WONG: Illustrious ones, at last you're here. Shen Te's been gone for months and today her cousin's been arrested. They think he murdered her to get the shop. But I had a dream and in this dream Shen Te said her cousin was keeping her prisoner. You must find her for us, illustrious ones!

FIRST GOD: We've found very few good people anywhere, and even they didn't keep it up. Shen Te is still the only one that stayed good.

SECOND GOD: If she *has* stayed good.

WONG: Certainly she has. But she's vanished.

FIRST GOD: That's the last straw. All is lost!

SECOND GOD: A little moderation, dear colleague!

FIRST GOD (*plaintively*): What's the good of moderation now? If she can't be found, we'll have to resign! The world is a terrible place! Nothing but misery, vulgarity, and waste! Even the countryside isn't what it used to be. The trees are getting their heads chopped off by telephone wires, and there's such a noise from all the gunfire, and I can't stand those heavy clouds of smoke, and —

THIRD GOD: The place is absolutely unlivable! Good intentions bring people to the brink of the abyss, and good deeds push them over the edge. I'm afraid our book of rules is destined for the scrap heap —

SECOND GOD: It's people! They're a worthless lot!

THIRD GOD: The world is too cold!

SECOND GOD: It's people! They're too weak!

FIRST GOD: Dignity, dear colleagues, dignity! Never despair! As
for this world, didn't we agree that we only have to find one
human being who can stand the place? Well, we found her.
True, we lost her again. We must find her again, that's all!
And at once!

They disappear.

10

Courtroom. Groups: SHU FU *and* MRS. MI TZU; YANG SUN *and*
MRS. YANG; WONG, *the* CARPENTER, *the* GRANDFATHER, *the* NIECE,
the OLD MAN, *the* OLD WOMAN; MRS. SHIN, *the* POLICEMAN; *the*
UNEMPLOYED MAN, *the* SISTER-IN-LAW.

OLD MAN: So much power isn't good for one man.

UNEMPLOYED MAN: And he's going to open twelve super tobacco
markets!

WIFE: One of the judges is a friend of Mr. Shu Fu's.

SISTER-IN-LAW: Another one accepted a present from Mr. Shui Ta
only last night. A great fat goose.

OLD WOMAN (*to* WONG): And Shen Te is nowhere to be found.

WONG: Only the gods will ever know the truth.

POLICEMAN: Order in the court! My lords the judges!

Enter the THREE GODS *in judges' robes. We overhear their conversation as they pass along the footlights to their bench.*

THIRD GOD: We'll never get away with it, our certificates were so
badly forged.

SECOND GOD: My predecessor's "sudden indigestion" will certainly
cause comment.

FIRST GOD: But he *had* just eaten a whole goose.

UNEMPLOYED MAN: Look at that! *New* judges!

WONG: New judges. And what good ones!

The THIRD GOD *hears this, and turns to smile at* WONG. *The*
GODS *sit. The* FIRST GOD *beats on the bench with his gavel. The*
POLICEMAN *brings in* SHUI TA *who walks with lordly steps. He
is whistled at.*

POLICEMAN (*to* SHUI TA): Be prepared for a surprise. The judges
have been changed.

SHUI TA *turns quickly round, looks at them, and staggers.*

NIECE: What's the matter now?

WIFE: The great Tobacco King nearly fainted.

HUSBAND: Yes, as soon as he saw the new judges.

WONG: Does *he* know who they are?

SHUI TA *picks himself up, and the proceedings open.*

FIRST GOD: Defendant Shui Ta, you are accused of doing away with your cousin Shen Te in order to take possession of her business. Do you plead guilty or not guilty?

SHUI TA: Not guilty, my lord.

FIRST GOD (*thumbing through the documents of the case*): The first witness is the Policeman. I shall ask him to tell us something of the respective reputations of Miss Shen Te and Mr. Shui Ta.

POLICEMAN: Miss Shen Te was a young lady who aimed to please, my lord. She liked to live and let live, as the saying goes. Mr. Shui Ta, on the other hand, is a man of principle. Though the generosity of Miss Shen Te forced him at times to abandon half measures, unlike the girl he was always on the side of the law, my lord. One time, he even unmasked a gang of thieves to whom his too trustful cousin had given shelter. The evidence, in short, my lord, proves that Mr. Shui Ta was *incapable* of the crime of which he stands accused!

FIRST GOD: I see. And are there others who could testify along, shall we say, the same lines?

SHU FU *rises.*

POLICEMAN (*whispering to* GODS): Mr. Shu Fu — a very important person.

FIRST GOD (*inviting him to speak*): Mr. Shu Fu!

SHU FU: Mr. Shui Ta is a businessman, my lord. Need I say more?

FIRST GOD: Yes.

SHU FU: Very well, I will. He is Vice President of the Council of Commerce and is about to be elected a Justice of the Peace.

(*He returns to his seat.* MRS. MI TZU *rises.*)

WONG: Elected! *He* gave him the job!

With a gesture the FIRST GOD *asks who* MRS. MI TZU *is.*

POLICEMAN: Another very important person. Mrs. Mi Tzu.

FIRST GOD (*inviting her to speak*): Mrs. Mi Tzu!

MRS. MI TZU: My lord, as Chairman of the Committee on Social Work, I wish to call attention to just a couple of eloquent facts: Mr. Shui Ta not only has erected a model factory with model housing in our city, he is a regular contributor to our home for the disabled. (*She returns to her seat.*)

POLICEMAN (*whispering*): And she's a great friend of the judge that ate the goose!

FIRST GOD (*to the* POLICEMAN): Oh, thank you. What next? (*To the Court, genially:*) Oh, yes. We should find out if any of the evidence is less favorable to the defendant.

WONG, *the* CARPENTER, *the* OLD MAN, *the* OLD WOMAN, *the* UN-EMPLOYED MAN, *the* SISTER-IN-LAW, *and the* NIECE *come forward.*

POLICEMAN (*whispering*): Just the riffraff, my lord.

FIRST GOD (*addressing the "riffraff"*): Well, um, riffraff — do you know anything of the defendant, Mr. Shui Ta?

WONG: Too much, my lord.

UNEMPLOYED MAN: What don't we know, my lord.

CARPENTER: He ruined us.

SISTER-IN-LAW: He's a cheat.

NIECE: Liar.

WIFE: Thief.

BOY: Blackmailer.

BROTHER: Murderer.

FIRST GOD: Thank you. We should now let the defendant state his point of view.

SHUI TA: I only came on the scene when Shen Te was in danger of losing what I had understood was a gift from the gods. Because I did the filthy jobs which someone had to do, they hate me. My activities were restricted to the minimum, my lord.

SISTER-IN-LAW: He had us arrested!

SHUI TA: Certainly. You stole from the bakery!

SISTER-IN-LAW: Such concern for the bakery! You didn't want the shop for yourself, I suppose!

SHUI TA: I didn't want the shop overrun with parasites.

SISTER-IN-LAW: We had nowhere else to go.

SHUI TA: There were too many of you.

WONG: What about this old couple: Were *they* parasites?

OLD MAN: We lost our shop because of you!

SISTER-IN-LAW: And we gave your cousin money!

SHUI TA: My cousin's fiancé was a flyer. The money had to go to *him*.

WONG: Did you care whether he flew or not? Did you care whether she married him or not? You wanted her to marry someone else! (*He points at* SHU FU.)

SHUI TA: The flyer unexpectedly turned out to be a scoundrel.

YANG SUN (*jumping up*): Which was the reason you made him your Manager?

SHUI TA: Later on he improved.

WONG: And when he improved, you sold him to her? (*He points out* MRS. MI TZU.)

SHUI TA: She wouldn't let me have her premises unless she had him to stroke her knees!

MRS. MI TZU: What? The man's a pathological liar. (*To him:*) Don't mention my property to me as long as you live! Murderer! (*She rustles off, in high dudgeon.*)

YANG SUN (*pushing in*): My lord, I wish to speak for the defendant.

SISTER-IN-LAW: Naturally. He's your employer.

UNEMPLOYED MAN: And the worst slave driver in the country.

MRS. YANG: That's a lie! My lord, Mr. Shui Ta is a great man. He . . .

YANG SUN: He's this and he's that, but he is not a murderer, my lord. Just fifteen minutes before his arrest I heard Shen Te's voice in his own back room.

FIRST GOD: Oh? Tell us more!

YANG SUN: I heard sobbing, my lord!

FIRST GOD: But lots of women sob, we've been finding.

YANG SUN: Could I fail to recognize her voice?

SHU FU: No, you made her sob so often yourself, young man!

YANG SUN: Yes. But I also made her happy. Till he (*pointing at* SHUI TA) decided to sell her to you!

SHUI TA: Because you didn't love her.

WONG: Oh, no: it was for the money, my lord!

SHUI TA: And what was the money for, my lord? For the poor! And for Shen Te so she could go on being good!

WONG: For the poor? That he sent to his sweatshops? And why didn't you let Shen Te be good when you signed the big check?

SHUI TA: For the child's sake, my lord.

CARPENTER: What about *my* children? What did he do about them? SHUI TA *is silent*.

WONG: The shop was to be a fountain of goodness. That was the gods' idea. You came and spoiled it!

SHUI TA: If I hadn't, it would have run dry!

MRS. SHIN: There's a lot in that, my lord.

WONG: What have you done with the good Shen Te, bad man? She *was* good, my lords, she was, I swear it! (*He raises his hand in an oath.*)

THIRD GOD: What's happened to your hand, Water Seller?

WONG (*pointing to* SHUI TA): It's all his fault, my lord, *she* was going to send me to a doctor — (*To* SHUI TA:) You were her worst enemy!

SHUI TA: I was her only friend!

WONG: Where is she then? Tell us where your good friend is!

The excitement of this exchange has run through the whole crowd.

ALL: Yes, where is she? Where is Shen Te? (*Etc.*)

SHUI TA: Shen Te . . . had to go.

WONG: Where? Where to?

SHUI TA: I cannot tell you! I cannot tell you!

ALL: Why? Why did she have to go away? (*Etc.*)

WONG (*into the din with the first words, but talking on beyond the others*): Why not, why not? Why did she have to go away?

SHUI TA (*shouting*): Because you'd all have torn her to shreds, that's why! My lords, I have a request. Clear the court! When only the judges remain, I will make a confession.

ALL (*except* WONG, *who is silent, struck by the new turn of events*): So he's guilty? He's confessing! (*Etc.*)

FIRST GOD (*using the gavel*): Clear the court!

POLICEMAN: Clear the court!

WONG: Mr. Shui Ta has met his match this time.

MRS. SHIN (*with a gesture toward the judges*): You're in for a little surprise.

The court is cleared. Silence.

SHUI TA: Illustrious ones!

The GODS *look at each other, not quite believing their ears.*

SHUI TA: Yes, I recognize you!

SECOND GOD (*taking matters in hand, sternly*): What have you done with our good woman of Setzuan?

SHUI TA: I have a terrible confession to make: I am she! (*He takes off his mask, and tears away his clothes.* SHEN TE *stands there.*)

SECOND GOD: Shen Te!

SHEN TE: Shen Te, yes. Shui Ta *and* Shen Te. Both.
Your injunction
To be good and yet to live
Was a thunderbolt:
It has torn me in two
I can't tell how it was
But to be good to others
And myself at the same time
I could not do it
Your world is not an easy one, illustrious ones!
When we extend our hand to a beggar, he tears it off for us
When we help the lost, we are lost ourselves
And so
Since not to eat is to die
Who can long refuse to be bad?
As I lay prostrate beneath the weight of good intentions
Ruin stared me in the face
It was when I was unjust that I ate good meat

And hobnobbed with the mighty
Why?
Why are bad deeds rewarded?
Good ones punished?
I enjoyed giving
I truly wished to be the Angel of the Slums
But washed by a foster-mother in the water of the gutter
I developed a sharp eye
The time came when pity was a thorn in my side
And, later, when kind words turned to ashes in my mouth
And anger took over
I became a wolf
Find me guilty, then, illustrious ones,
But know:
All that I have done I did
To help my neighbor
To love my lover
And to keep my little one from want
For your great, godly deeds, I was too poor, too small.
Pause.

FIRST GOD (*shocked*): Don't go on making yourself miserable, Shen Te! We're overjoyed to have found you!

SHEN TE: I'm telling you I'm the bad man who committed all those crimes!

FIRST GOD (*using — or failing to use — his ear trumpet*): The good woman who did all those good deeds?

SHEN TE: Yes, but the bad man too!

FIRST GOD (*as if something had dawned*): Unfortunate coincidences! Heartless neighbors!

THIRD GOD (*shouting in his ear*): But how is she to continue?

FIRST GOD: Continue? Well, she's a strong, healthy girl . . .

SECOND GOD: You didn't hear what she said!

FIRST GOD: I heard every word! She is confused, that's all! (*He begins to bluster:*) And what about this book of rules — we can't renounce our rules, can we? (*More quietly:*) Should the world be changed? How? By whom? The world should

not be changed! (*At a sign from him, the lights turn pink, and music plays.*)
And now the hour of parting is at hand.
Dost thou behold, Shen Te, yon fleecy cloud?
It is our chariot. At a sign from me
'Twill come and take us back from whence we came
Above the azure vault and silver stars. . . .

SHEN TE: No! Don't go, illustrious ones!

FIRST GOD:

Our cloud has landed now in yonder field
From whence it will transport us back to heaven.
Farewell, Shen Te, let not thy courage fail thee. . . .
Exeunt GODS.

SHEN TE: What about the old couple? They've lost their shop! What about the Water Seller and his hand? And I've got to defend myself against the Barber, because I don't love him! And against Sun, because I do love him! How? How?

SHEN TE's *eyes follow the* GODS *as they are imagined to step into a cloud which rises and moves forward over the orchestra and up beyond the balcony.*

FIRST GOD (*from on high*): We have faith in you, Shen Te!

SHEN TE: There'll be a child. And he'll have to be fed. I can't stay here. Where shall I go?

FIRST GOD: Continue to be good, good woman of Setzuan!

SHEN TE: I need my bad cousin!

FIRST GOD: But not very often!

SHEN TE: Once a week at least!

FIRST GOD: Once a month will be quite enough!

SHEN TE (*shrieking*): No, no! Help!

But the cloud continues to recede as the GODS *sing:*

VALEDICTORY HYMN

What rapture, oh, it is to know
  A good thing when you see it

And having seen a good thing, oh,
    What rapture 'tis to flee it

Be good, sweet maid of Setzuan
    Let Shui Ta be clever
Departing, we forget the man
    Remember your endeavor

Because through all the length of days
    Her goodness faileth never
Sing hallelujah! Make Shen Te's
    Good name live on forever!

SHEN TE: Help!

THE CAUCASIAN CHALK CIRCLE

(1944–1945)

English Version by
Eric Bentley
and
Maja Apelman

This version was made from a manuscript
supplied by the author in 1946

CHARACTERS

OLD MAN *on the right*
PEASANT WOMAN *on the right*
YOUNG PEASANT
A VERY YOUNG WORKER
OLD MAN *on the left*
PEASANT WOMAN *on the left*
AGRICULTURIST KATO
GIRL TRACTORIST
WOUNDED SOLDIER
THE DELEGATE *from the capital*
THE STORY TELLER
GEORGI ABASHWILI, *the* GOVERNOR
NATELLA, *the* GOVERNOR'S WIFE
MICHAEL, *their son*
SHALVA, *an Adjutant*
ARSEN KAZBEKI, *a fat prince*
MESSENGER *from the capital*
NIKO MIKADZE *and* MIKA LOLADZE, *doctors*
SIMON SHASHAVA, *a soldier*
GRUSHA VASHNADZE, *a kitchen maid*
OLD PEASANT *with the milk*
CORPORAL *and* PRIVATE
PEASANT *and his wife*
LAVRENTI VASHNADZE, GRUSHA'S *brother*
ANIKO, *his wife*
PEASANT WOMAN, *for a while* GRUSHA'S *mother-in-law*
JUSSUP, *her son*
MONK
AZDAK, *village recorder*
SHAUWA, *a policeman*
GRAND DUKE
DOCTOR
INVALID

496

LIMPING MAN
BLACKMAILER
LUDOVICA
INNKEEPER, *her father-in-law*
STABLEBOY
POOR OLD PEASANT WOMAN
IRAKLI, *her brother-in-law, a bandit*
THREE WEALTHY FARMERS
ILLO SHUBOLADZE *and* SANDRO OBOLADZE, *lawyers*
OLD MARRIED COUPLE

SOLDIERS, SERVANTS, PEASANTS, BEGGARS, MUSICIANS,
MERCHANTS, NOBLES, ARCHITECTS

THE JUDGE: Officer, fetch a piece of chalk. You will trace below the bench a circle, in the center of which you will place the young child. Then you will order the two women to wait, each of them at opposite sides of the circle. When the real mother takes hold of him, it will be easy for the child to come outside the circle. But the pretended mother cannot lead him out.

The officer traces a circle with the chalk and motions the child to stand in the center of it. MRS. MA *takes the child's hand and leads him out of the circle.* HAI-TANG *fails to contend with her.*

THE JUDGE: It is evident that Hai-Tang is not the mother of the child, since she did not come forward to draw him out of the circle.

HAI-TANG: I supplicate you, Honored Sir, to calm your wrath. If I cannot obtain my son without dislocating his arm or bruising his baby flesh, I would rather perish under the blows than make the least effort to take him out of the circle.

THE JUDGE: A sage of old once said: What man can hide what he really is? Behold the power of the Chalk Circle! In order to seize an inheritance, Mrs. Ma has raised a young child that is not her own. But the Chalk Circle augustly brought out the truth and the falsehood. Mrs. Ma has an engaging exterior but her heart is corrupt. The true mother— Hai-Tang —is at last recognized.

From *The Chalk Circle,* an anonymous Chinese play of about 1300 A.D.

PROLOGUE

Among the ruins of a shattered Caucasian village the members of two Kolkhoz villages, mostly women and older men, are sitting in a circle, smoking and drinking wine. With them is a delegate of the State Reconstruction Commission from the capital.

PEASANT WOMAN, *left (pointing)*: In those hills over there we stopped three Nazi tanks, but the apple orchard was already destroyed.

OLD MAN, *right:* Our beautiful dairy farm, too: all in ruins.

GIRL TRACTORIST: I laid the fire, Comrade.

Pause.

THE DELEGATE: Now listen to the Report. Delegates of the goat-breeding Kolkhoz "Galinsk" have been to Nuka. When Hitler's armies approached, the Kolkhoz moved its goat-herds on orders from the authorities, further east. They are now thinking of returning. Their delegates have investigated the village and grounds and found a lot of it destroyed. (*Delegates on right nod.*) The neighboring fruit-culture Kolkhoz (*to the left:*) "Rosa Luxemburg" brings forward a motion to use the former grazing land of Kolkhoz "Galinsk," a valley with scanty growth of grass, for orchards and vineyards. As a delegate of the Reconstruction Commission, I request the two Kolkhoz villages to decide between themselves whether Kolkhoz "Galinsk" shall return here or not.

OLD MAN, *right:* First of all, I want to protest against the restriction of time for discussion. We of Kolkhoz "Galinsk" have spent three days and three nights getting here. And now discussion is limited to half a day.

WOUNDED SOLDIER, *left:* Comrade, we haven't as many villages as we used to have. We haven't as many hands. We haven't as much time.

GIRL TRACTORIST: All pleasures have to be rationed. Tobacco is rationed, and wine: and now discussion should be.

OLD MAN, *right* (*sighing*): Death to the fascists! But I will come to the point and explain to you why we want to have our valley back. There are a great many reasons, but I want to begin with one of the simplest. Makinä Abakidze, unpack the goat cheese. (*A peasant woman from right takes from a basket an enormous cheese wrapped in a cloth. Applause and laughter.*) Help yourselves, Comrades, start in!

OLD MAN, *left* (*suspiciously*): Is this a way of influencing us?

OLD MAN, *right* (*amid laughter*): How could it be a way of influencing you, Surab, you valley-thief? Everyone knows that you will take the cheese and the valley, too. (*Laughter.*) All I expect from you is an honest answer: Do you like the cheese?

OLD MAN, *left:* The answer is: yes.

OLD MAN, *right:* Really. (*Bitterly:*) I ought to have known you know nothing about cheese.

OLD MAN, *left:* Why not? When I tell you I like it.

OLD MAN, *right:* Because you can't like it. Because it's not what it was in the old days. And why not? Because our goats don't like the new grass as they used to like the old. Cheese is not cheese because grass is not grass, that's the thing. Please put that in your report.

OLD MAN, *left:* But your cheese is excellent.

OLD MAN, *right:* It isn't excellent. It's just passable. The new grazing land is no good, whatever the young people may say. One can't live there. It doesn't even smell of morning in the morning. (*Several people laugh.*)

THE DELEGATE: Don't mind their laughing: they understand you. Comrades, why does one love one's country? Because the bread tastes better there, the air smells better, voices sound stronger, the sky is higher, the ground is easier to walk on. Isn't that so?

OLD MAN, *right:* The valley has belonged to us from all eternity.

SOLDIER, *left:* What's that mean — from all eternity? Nothing belongs to anyone from all eternity. When you were young you didn't even belong to yourself, but to the Kazbeki princes.

OLD MAN, *right:* Doesn't it make a difference maybe what kind of trees stand next to the house you are born in? Or what kind of neighbor you have? Doesn't that make a difference? We want to go back just to have you near our Kolkhoz, you valley-thief. Now you can all laugh again.

OLD MAN, *left (laughing):* Then why don't you listen to what your neighbor, Kato Wachtang, our agriculturist, has to say about the valley?

PEASANT WOMAN, *right:* We've by no means said everything there is to be said about our valley. Not all the houses are destroyed. As for the dairy farm, at least the foundation wall is still standing.

DELEGATE: You can claim State support — here and there — you know that. I have suggestions here in my pocket.

PEASANT WOMAN, *right:* Comrade Specialist, we haven't come here to bargain. I can't take your cap and hand you another, and say: "This one's better." The other one might be better, but you like yours better.

GIRL TRACTORIST: A piece of land is not like a cap — not in our country, Comrade.

DELEGATE: Don't get angry. It's true that we have to consider a piece of land as a tool to produce something useful with, but it's also true that we must recognize the love for a particular piece of land. As far as I'm concerned, I'd like to find out more exactly what you (*to those on the left*) want to do with the valley.

OTHERS: Yes, let Kato speak.

DELEGATE: Comrade Agriculturist!

KATO (*rising; she's in military uniform*): Comrades, last winter, while we were fighting in these hills here as Partisans, we discussed how, after the expulsion of the Germans, we could build up our fruit culture to ten times its original size. I've prepared a plan for an irrigation project. By means of a coffer-dam on our mountain lake, 300 hectares of unfertile land can be irrigated. Our Kolkhoz could then not only cultivate more fruit, but also have vineyards. The project, however, would pay only if the disputed valley of Kolkhoz "Galinsk" were also included. Here are the calculations. (*She hands the delegate a briefcase.*)

OLD MAN, *right:* Write into the report that our Kolkhoz plans to start a new stud farm.

GIRL TRACTORIST: Comrades, the project was conceived during days and nights when we had to take cover in the mountains and were often without ammunition for our half-dozen rifles. Even to get a pencil was difficult. (*Applause from both sides.*)

OLD MAN, *right:* Our thanks to the Comrades of Kolkhoz "Rosa Luxemburg" and to all who have defended our country! (*They shake hands and embrace.*)

PEASANT WOMAN, *left:* In doing this our thought was that our soldiers — both your men and our men — should return to a still more productive homeland.

GIRL TRACTORIST: As the poet Mayakovski said: "The home of the Soviet people shall also be the home of Reason"! (*The delegates including the* OLD MAN *on right have got up, and with the delegate specified, proceed to study the agriculturist's drawings. Exclamations such as: "Why is the altitude of fall 22 meters?" — "This rock here must be blown up" — "Actually, all they need is cement and dynamite" — "They force the water to come down here, that's clever!"*)

A VERY YOUNG WORKER, *right* (*to* OLD MAN, *right*): They're going to irrigate all the fields between the hills, look at that, Aleko!

OLD MAN, *right:* I'm not going to look. I knew the project would be good. I won't have a revolver pointed at my chest.

DELEGATE: But they only want to point a pencil at your chest. (*Laughter.*)

OLD MAN, *right* (*gets up gloomily, and walks over to look at the drawings*): These valley-thieves know only too well that we can't resist machines and projects in this country.

PEASANT WOMAN, *right:* Aleko Bereshwili, you yourself are the worst one with new projects. That's well known.

DELEGATE: What about my report? May I write that you will support at your Kolkhoz the cession of your old valley for this project?

PEASANT WOMAN, *right:* I will support it. What about you, Aleko?

OLD MAN, *right* (*bent over drawings*): I suggest that you give us copies of the drawings to take along.

PEASANT WOMAN, *right:* Then we can sit down to eat. Once he has the drawings and is ready to discuss them, the affair is settled. I know him. And it will be the same with the rest of us.

Delegates laughingly embrace again.

OLD MAN, *left:* Comrades, in honor of the visit of the delegates from Kolkhoz "Galinsk," and of the Specialist, we have arranged, with the collaboration of the Story Teller Arkadi Tscheidse, to produce a play which has a bearing on our problem. (*Applause.* GIRL TRACTORIST *has gone off to bring* THE STORY TELLER.)

PEASANT WOMAN, *right:* Comrades, your play had better be good. We're going to pay for it with a valley.

PEASANT WOMAN, *left:* Arkadi Tscheidse knows 21,000 lines by heart.

OLD MAN, *left:* It's very difficult to get him. You and the Planning Commission should see to it that you get him to come North more often, Comrade.

DELEGATE: We are more concerned with economics.

OLD MAN, *left* (*smiling*): You arrange the redistribution of vines and tractors, why not of songs?

Enter THE STORY TELLER *Arkadi Tscheidse, led by* GIRL TRACTORIST. *He is a well-built man of simple manners, accompanied by four musicians with their instruments. The artists are greeted with applause.*

GIRL TRACTORIST: This is the Comrade Specialist, Arkadi.

THE STORY TELLER *greets them all.*

DELEGATE: I'm honored to make your acquaintance. I heard about your songs when I was a boy at school.

THE STORY TELLER: This time it's a play with songs, and nearly the whole Kolkhoz takes part. We've brought the old masks along

DELEGATE: Will it be one of the old legends?

THE STORY TELLER: A very old one. It's called the "Circle of Chalk" and comes from the Chinese. But we'll do it, of course, in a changed version. Jura, show them the masks.

OLD PEASANT, *right* (*recognizing one of the masks*): Ah! Prince Kazbeki!

THE STORY TELLER: Comrades, it's an honor for me to entertain you after a difficult debate. We hope you will find that the voice of the old poet also sounds well in the shadow of Soviet tractors. It may be a mistake to mix different wines, but old and new wisdom mix admirably. Now I hope we'll get something to eat before the performance begins. That surely helps.

VOICES: Certainly! Everyone into the Club House!

While everyone begins to move, the DELEGATE *turns to the* GIRL TRACTORIST.

DELEGATE: How long will the story take, Arkadi? I've got to get back to Tiflis tonight.

THE STORY TELLER (*casually*): It's actually two stories. A few hours.

GIRL TRACTORIST (*confidentially*): Couldn't you make it shorter?

THE STORY TELLER: No.

And they all go happily to eat.

PART ONE

1

THE NOBLE CHILD

As the lights go up, THE STORY TELLER *is seen sitting on the floor, a black sheepskin cloak round his shoulders, and a little, well-thumbed notebook in his hand. A small group of listeners — the chorus — sits with him. The manner of his recitation makes it clear that he has told this story over and over again. He mechanically fingers the pages, seldom looking at them. With appropriate gestures, he gives the signal for each scene to begin.*

THE STORY TELLER:

In olden times, in a bloody time,
There ruled in a Caucasian city —
Men called it the City of the Damned —
A governor.
His name was Georgi Abashwili.
He was rich as Croesus
He had a beautiful wife
He had a healthy child.
No other governor in Grusinia
Had so many horses in his stable
So many beggars on his doorstep
So many soldiers in his service
So many petitioners in his courtyard.

Georgi Abashwili — how shall I describe him?
He enjoyed his life.
On the morning of Easter Sunday
The Governor and his family went to church.

At the left a large doorway, at the right an even larger gateway. Beggars and petitioners pour from the gateway, holding up thin children, crutches, and petitions. They are followed by two IRONSHIRTS, *and then, expensively dressed,* THE GOVERNOR's *family.*

BEGGARS AND PETITIONERS: Mercy! Mercy, Your Grace! The taxes are way up, we can't pay!
— I lost my leg in the Persian War, where can I get . . .
— My brother is innocent, Your Grace, there's been a misunderstanding . . .
— The child is starving in my arms!
— Our petition is for our son's discharge from the army, our last remaining son!
— Please, Your Grace, the water inspector takes bribes.

One servant collects the petitions, another distributes coins from a purse. Soldiers push the crowd back, lashing at them with thick leather whips.

THE SOLDIER: Get back! Clear the church door!

Behind THE GOVERNOR, *his* WIFE, *and* THE ADJUTANT, THE GOVERNOR's CHILD *is brought through the gateway in an ornate carriage.*

THE CROWD: The child!
— I can't see it, don't shove so hard!
— God bless the child, Your Grace!

THE STORY TELLER (*while the crowd is driven back with whips*):
For the first time on that Easter Sunday, the people saw the Governor's heir.
Two doctors never moved from the noble child, apple of the Governor's eye.
Even the mighty Prince Kazbeki bows before it at the church door.

A FAT PRINCE *steps forward and greets the family.*

THE FAT PRINCE: Happy Easter, Natella Abashwili! A magnificent day! When it was raining in the night, I thought to myself: gloomy holidays! But this morning I said to myself: the sky is gay! I love a gay sky, a simple heart, Natella Abashwili. And little Michael is a governor from head to foot! Tititi! (*He tickles the child.*)

THE GOVERNOR'S WIFE: What do you think of this, Arsen? At last Georgi has decided to start building the wing on the east side. All those wretched slums are to be torn down to make room for a garden.

THE FAT PRINCE: That's good news after so much bad! What's the latest about the war, Brother Georgi? (THE GOVERNOR *indicates a lack of interest.*) A strategical retreat, I hear. Well, minor reverses are to be expected. Sometimes things go well, sometimes not. Such is war! What difference does it make?

THE GOVERNOR'S WIFE: He's coughing. Georgi, did you hear? (*She speaks sharply to the* DOCTORS, *two dignified men standing close to the little carriage.*) He's coughing!

THE FIRST DOCTOR (*to the second*): May I remind you, Niko Mikadze, that I was against the lukewarm bath? (*To* THE GOVERNOR'S WIFE:) There's been a little error over warming the bath water, Your Grace.

THE SECOND DOCTOR (*equally polite*): Mika Loladze, I can't possibly agree with you. The temperature of the bath water was the one prescribed by our great, beloved Mishiko Oboladze. It was more likely a slight draft during the night, Your Grace.

THE GOVERNOR'S WIFE: But do pay more attention to him. He looks feverish, Georgi.

THE FIRST DOCTOR (*bending over the child*): No cause for alarm, Your Grace. The bath water will be warmer. It won't occur again.

THE SECOND DOCTOR (*with a venomous glance at the first*): I won't forget that, my dear Mika Loladze. No cause for concern, Your Grace.

THE FAT PRINCE: Well, well, well! I always say: One pain in my liver and the doctor gets fifty strokes on the soles of his feet.

That's because we are living in a decadent age. In the old days one simply said: Off with his head!

THE GOVERNOR'S WIFE: Let's go into the church. Very likely it's the draft here.

The procession of family and servants turns into the doorway. THE FAT PRINCE follows, but THE GOVERNOR is kept back by THE ADJUTANT, a handsome young man. When the crowd of petitioners has been driven off, a young dust-stained rider, his arm in a sling, remains behind.

THE ADJUTANT (*pointing at the rider, who steps forward*): Won't you listen to the messenger from the capital, Your Excellency? He arrived this morning. With confidential papers.

THE GOVERNOR: Not before Service, Shalva. But did you hear Brother Kazbeki bid me a happy Easter? That's all very well, but so far as I know, it didn't rain here last night.

THE ADJUTANT (*nodding*): That will have to be gone into.

THE GOVERNOR: Yes, at once. Tomorrow.

They pass through the doorway. The rider, who has waited in vain for an audience, turns sharply round and, muttering a curse, goes off. Only one of the Palace Guards — SIMON SHASHAVA — remains at the door.

THE STORY TELLER:
On the church square, pigeons are strutting.
The city is still.
A soldier of the Palace Guard
Is joking with a kitchen maid
As she comes up from the river with a bundle.

A girl — GRUSHA VASHNADZE — comes through the gateway with a bundle made of large green leaves under her arm.

SIMON: What, the young lady is not in church? Shirking?

GRUSHA: I was dressed to go. But they needed another goose for the banquet. And they asked me to go and get it. I know a thing or two about geese.

SIMON: A goose? (*He feigns suspicion.*) I'd like to see that goose. (GRUSHA *does not understand.*) One has to be on one's guard with women. "I only went for a fish," they tell you, and then it turns out to be something else.

GRUSHA (*walking resolutely toward him and showing him the goose*): There! And if it isn't a fifteen-pound goose stuffed full of corn, I'll eat the feathers.

SIMON: A queen of a goose. The Governor himself will eat it. So the young lady has been down to the river again?

GRUSHA: Yes, at the poultry farm.

SIMON: Really? At the poultry farm, down by the river . . . not higher up maybe? Near those willows?

GRUSHA: I only go to the willows to wash the linen.

SIMON (*insinuatingly*): Exactly.

GRUSHA: Exactly what?

SIMON (*winking*): Exactly that.

GRUSHA: Why shouldn't I wash the linen by the willows?

SIMON (*with exaggerated laughter*): Why shouldn't I wash the linen by the willows! That's good, really good!

GRUSHA: I don't understand the soldier. What's so good about it?

SIMON (*slyly*): "If something *I* know someone learns, she'll grow hot and cold by turns!"

GRUSHA: I don't know what I *could* learn about those willows.

SIMON: Not even if there were a bush opposite? And everything could be seen from it? Everything that goes on there when a certain person is — er — "washing linen"?

GRUSHA: What *is* it that goes on? Won't the soldier say what he means and have done with it?

SIMON: Something goes on. And something can be seen.

GRUSHA: Could the soldier mean I put my toes in the water? When it was hot once in a while? There was nothing else.

SIMON: There were the toes. And more.

GRUSHA: More what? At most the foot?

SIMON: The foot. And a little more. (*He laughs heartily.*)

GRUSHA (*angrily*): Simon Shashava, you ought to be ashamed of

yourself! To sit in a bush on a hot day and wait till someone comes and dips her foot in the river! And I bet you bring
a friend along too! (*She runs off.*)

SIMON (*shouting after her*): I didn't bring any friend along!

As THE STORY TELLER *resumes his tale, the soldier steps into the
doorway as though to listen to the service.*

THE STORY TELLER:
The city lies still
But why are there armed men?
The Governor's palace is at peace
But why is it a fortress?
And the Governor returned to his palace
And the fortress was a trap
And the goose was plucked and roasted
But the goose was not eaten this time
And noon was no longer the time to eat
Noon was the time to die.

From the doorway at the left THE FAT PRINCE *quickly appears,
stands still, looks around. Before the gateway at the right two*
IRONSHIRTS *are squatting and playing dice.* THE FAT PRINCE
*sees them, walks slowly past, making a sign to them. They
rise: one goes through the gateway, the other goes off at the
right. Muffled voices are heard from various directions in the
rear:* "To your posts!" *The palace is surrounded.* THE FAT
PRINCE *quickly goes off. Church bells in the distance. Enter,
through the doorway,* THE GOVERNOR'S *family and procession,
returning from church.*

THE GOVERNOR'S WIFE (*passing* THE ADJUTANT): It's impossible to
live in this slum. But Georgi, of course, builds only for his little
Michael. Never for me. Michael is all! All for Michael!

The procession turns into the gateway. Again THE ADJUTANT
*lingers behind. He waits. Enter the wounded rider from the
doorway. Two* IRONSHIRTS *of the Palace Guard have taken up
positions by the gateway.*

THE ADJUTANT (*to the rider*): The Governor doesn't wish to receive military reports before dinner — particularly if they
are of a depressing nature, as I assume. In the afternoon His

Excellency will devote himself to conferences with prominent architects who are also invited to dinner. Here they are already. (*Enter three gentlemen through the doorway.*) Go to the kitchen and get yourself something to eat, friend. (*As the rider goes,* THE ADJUTANT *greets* THE ARCHITECTS.) Gentlemen, His Excellency expects you at dinner. All his time will be devoted to you. To your great new plans! Come, quickly!

ONE OF THE ARCHITECTS: We marvel that His Excellency intends to build. There are disquieting rumors abroad that the war in Persia has taken a bad turn.

THE ADJUTANT: All the more reason to build! That's nothing, you know. Persia is a long way off. The garrison here would let itself be hacked to bits for its Governor. (*Noise from the palace. The shrill scream of a woman. Someone is shouting orders. Dumbfounded,* THE ADJUTANT *moves toward the gateway. An* IRONSHIRT *steps out, points his lance at him.*) What's going on here? Put down that lance, you dog!

ONE OF THE ARCHITECTS: The Princes! Don't you realize that the Princes met last night in the capital? And that they are against the Grand Duke and his Governors? Gentlemen, we'd better make ourselves scarce. (*They rush off.* THE ADJUTANT *remains helplessly behind.*)

THE ADJUTANT (*furiously to the Palace Guard*): Lay down your arms. Don't you realize an attempt is being made on the Governor's life?

The IRONSHIRTS *of the Palace Guard refuse to obey. They stare coldly and indifferently at* THE ADJUTANT *and follow the next events without interest.*

THE STORY TELLER:
O blindness of great ones!
They wander like gods,
Great over bent backs,
Sure of hired fists,
Trusting in the power
Which has lasted so long.
But long is not forever.

O change from age to age!
Thou hope of the people!

Enter THE GOVERNOR, *through the gateway, between two soldiers fully armed. He is in chains. His face is gray.*

Up, great sir, deign to walk upright!
From your palace the eyes of many foes follow you!
You no longer need an architect, a carpenter will do!
You will not move into a new palace
But into a little hole in the ground.
Look about you once more, blind man!

The arrested man looks round.

Does all you had please you?
Between the Easter mass and the Easter meal
You are walking to the place whence no one returns.

THE GOVERNOR *is led off. A horn sounds an alarm. Noise behind
the gateway.*

When the house of a great one collapses
Many little ones are slain.
Those who had no share in the *good* fortunes of the mighty
Often have a share in their *mis*fortunes.
The plunging wagon
Drags the sweating beasts with it
Into the abyss.

THE SERVANTS *come rushing through the gateway in panic.*

THE SERVANTS (*among themselves*): The baskets!
— Take them all into the third courtyard! Food for five days!
— The mistress has fainted! Someone must carry her down.
She must get away.
— What about us? We'll be slaughtered like chickens, that's
how it always is.
— Goodness gracious, what'll happen? There's bloodshed al-
ready in the city, they say.
— Nonsense, the Governor has just been politely asked to
appear at a Princes' meeting. Everything'll be ironed out. I
heard this on the best authority . . .

THE TWO DOCTORS *rush into the courtyard.*

THE FIRST DOCTOR (*trying to restrain the other*): Niko Mikadze, it is your duty as a doctor to attend Natella Abashwili.

THE SECOND DOCTOR: My duty! It's yours!

THE FIRST DOCTOR: Whose turn is it to look after the child today, Niko Mikadze, yours or mine?

THE SECOND DOCTOR: Do you really think, Mika Loladze, I'm going to stay a minute longer in this blasted house on that little brat's account?

They start fighting. All one hears is: "You neglect your duty!" *and* "Duty, my foot!" *Then* THE SECOND DOCTOR *knocks* THE FIRST *down.*

THE SECOND DOCTOR: Oh, go to hell! (*Exit.*)

Enter the soldier, SIMON SHASHAVA. *He searches in the crowd for* GRUSHA.

THE SERVANTS: There's still time before tonight. The soldiers won't be drunk till then.
 — Does anyone know if the mutiny has begun?
 — The Palace Guard rode off.
 — Doesn't anybody know what's happened?

GRUSHA: Meliva the fisherman says a comet with a red tail has been seen in the sky over the capital. That means bad luck.

THE SERVANTS: Yesterday they were saying in the capital that the Persian War is lost.
 — The Princes have staged a big uprising.
 — There's a rumor that the Grand Duke has fled already.
 — All his governors are to be executed.
 — The little people will be left alone.
 — I have a brother with the Ironshirts.

THE ADJUTANT (*appearing in the doorway*): Everyone into the third courtyard! Everyone help with the packing.

He drives THE SERVANTS *away. At last* SIMON *finds* GRUSHA.

SIMON: Grusha! There you are at last! What are you going to do?

GRUSHA: Nothing. If the worst comes to the worst, I've a brother in the mountains. What about you?

SIMON: There is nothing to say about me. (*Formally again:*) Grusha Vashnadze, your desire to know my plans fills me with satisfaction. I have been ordered to accompany Madam Natella Abashwili as her guard.

GRUSHA: But hasn't the Palace Guard mutinied?

SIMON (*seriously*): That's a fact.

GRUSHA: But isn't it dangerous to accompany her?

SIMON: In Tiflis, they say: Is not the stabbing dangerous for the knife?

GRUSHA: You're not a knife. You're a man, Simon Shashava. What has that woman to do with you?

SIMON: That woman has nothing to do with me. I have my orders, and I go.

GRUSHA: The soldier is pigheaded: he gets himself into danger for nothing — nothing at all. Now I must go into the third courtyard. I'm in a hurry.

SIMON: Since we're in a hurry we shouldn't quarrel. You need time for a good quarrel. May I ask if the young lady still has parents?

GRUSHA: No, only a brother.

SIMON: As time is short — the second question is this: Is the young lady as healthy as a fish in water?

GRUSHA: Maybe once in a while I have a pain in the right shoulder. Otherwise I'm strong enough for my job. No one has complained. So far.

SIMON: Everyone knows that. Even if it's Easter Sunday, and there's a question who should run for the goose, she's the one. The third question is this: Is the young lady impatient? Does she want apples in winter?

GRUSHA: Impatient? No. But if a man goes to war without any reason and no message arrives — that's bad.

SIMON: A message will come. And now the final question . . .

GRUSHA: Simon Shashava, I must go to the third courtyard and quick. My answer is yes.

SIMON (*very embarrassed*): Haste, they say, is the name of the wind that blows down the scaffolding. But they also say: The rich don't know what haste is. I'm from . . .

GRUSHA: Kutsk . . .

SIMON: So the young lady has already inquired about me? I'm healthy, have no dependents, make ten piasters a month, as a paymaster twenty piasters and I'm asking — very sincerely — for your hand.

GRUSHA: Simon Shashava, it suits me well.

SIMON (*taking from his neck a thin chain with a little cross on it*): My mother gave me this cross, Grusha Vashnadze. The chain is silver. Please wear it.

GRUSHA: Many thanks, Simon. (*He hangs it round her neck.*)

SIMON: It would be better for the young lady to go to the third courtyard now. Or there will be difficulties. Anyway, I have to harness the horses. The young lady will understand.

GRUSHA: Yes, Simon.

They stand undecided.

SIMON: I'll only take the mistress to the troops that have remained loyal. When the war's over, I'll be back. In two weeks. Or three. I hope my intended won't get tired, waiting my return.

GRUSHA: Simon Shashava, I shall wait for you.
Go calmly into battle, soldier
The bloody battle, the bitter battle
From which not everyone returns:
When you return I shall be there.
I shall be waiting for you under the green elm
I shall be waiting for you under the bare elm
I shall wait until the last soldier has returned
And longer.
When you come back from the battle
No boots will lie before the door
The pillow beside mine will be empty
And my mouth will be unkissed.
When you return, when you return
You will be able to say: All is as it was.

SIMON: I thank you, Grusha Vashnadze. And goodbye!

He bows low before her. She does the same before him. Then she runs quickly off without looking round. Enter THE ADJUTANT *from the gateway.*

THE ADJUTANT (*harshly*): Harness the horses to the carriage! Don't stand there doing nothing, louse!

SIMON SHASHAVA *stands to attention and goes off. Two servants crawl from the gateway, bent low under huge trunks. Behind them, supported by her women, stumbles* NATELLA ABASHWILI. *She is followed by a woman carrying the child.*

THE GOVERNOR'S WIFE: I hardly know if my head's still on. Where's Michael? Don't hold him so clumsily. Pile the trunks onto the carriage. Shalva, is there any news from the city?

THE ADJUTANT: No. So far, all is quiet. But there's not a minute to lose. There's not enough room for the trunks in the carriage. Pick out what you need. (*Exit quickly.*)

THE GOVERNOR'S WIFE: Only essentials! Quick, open the trunks. I'll tell you what I've got to have. (*The trunks are lowered and opened. She points at some brocade dresses.*) The green one! And of course the one with the fur trimming. Where are Niko Mikadze and Mika Loladze? I've suddenly got the most terrible migraine again. It always starts in the temples. (*Enter* GRUSHA.) You're taking your time, eh? Go at once and get the hot water bottles. (GRUSHA *runs off, returns later with hot water bottles.* THE GOVERNOR'S WIFE *orders her about by signs.*) Don't tear the sleeves.

A YOUNG WOMAN: Pardon, madam, no harm has come to the dress.

THE GOVERNOR'S WIFE: Because I stopped you. I've been watching you for a long time. Nothing in your head but making eyes at Shalva Tzereteli. I'll kill you, you bitch! (*She beats the woman.*)

THE ADJUTANT (*appearing in the gateway*): Please make haste, Natella Abashwili. Firing has broken out in the city. (*Exit.*)

THE GOVERNOR'S WIFE (*letting go of the young woman*): Oh dear, do you think they'll do something to us? Why should they? Why? (*She herself begins to rummage in the trunks.*) How's Michael? Asleep?

THE WOMAN WITH THE CHILD: Yes, madam.

THE GOVERNOR'S WIFE: Then put him down a moment and get my little saffron-colored boots from the bedchamber. I need them for the green dress. (*The woman puts down the child and goes off.*) Just look how these things have been packed! No love! No understanding! If you don't give them every order yourself . . . At such moments you realize what kind of servants you have! They gorge themselves, and never a word of gratitude! I'll remember this.

THE ADJUTANT (*entering, very excited*): Natella, you must leave at once!

THE GOVERNOR'S WIFE: Why? I've got to take this silver dress — it cost a thousand piasters. And that one there, and where's the wine-colored one?

THE ADJUTANT (*trying to pull her away*): Riots have broken out! We must leave at once. Where's the child?

THE GOVERNOR'S WIFE (*calling to the young woman who was holding the child*): Maro, get the child ready! Where on earth are you?

THE ADJUTANT (*leaving*): We'll probably have to leave the carriage and go on horseback.

THE GOVERNOR'S WIFE *rummages again among her dresses, throws some onto the heap of chosen clothes, then takes them off again. Noises, drums are heard. The young woman who was beaten creeps away. The sky begins to grow red.*

THE GOVERNOR'S WIFE (*rummaging desperately*): I simply cannot find the wine-colored dress. Take the whole pile and carry it as it is to the carriage. Where's Asja? And why hasn't Maro come back? Have you all gone crazy?

THE ADJUTANT (*returning*): Quick! Quick!

THE GOVERNOR'S WIFE (*to the first woman*): Run! Just throw them into the carriage!

THE ADJUTANT: We are not going by carriage. Come on or I'll ride off on my own!

THE GOVERNOR'S WIFE (*as the first woman can't carry everything*): Where's that bitch Asja? (THE ADJUTANT *pulls her away.*) Maro, bring the child! (*To the first woman:*) Go and look for

Masha. No, first take the dresses to the carriage. Such nonsense, I wouldn't dream of going on horseback!

Turning round, she sees the the red sky, and starts back rigid. The fire burns. She is pulled out by THE ADJUTANT. *Shaking, the first woman follows with the dresses.*

MARO (*from the doorway with the boots*): Madam! (*She sees the trunks and dresses and runs toward the child, picks it up, and holds it a moment.*) They left it behind, the beasts. (*She hands it to* GRUSHA.) Hold it a moment. (*She runs off, following* THE GOVERNOR'S WIFE. *Enter servants from the gateway.*)

THE COOK: Well, they've actually gone. Without the food wagons, and not a minute too early. Now it's time to get out!

A GROOM: This'll be an unhealthy house for a while. (*To one of the women:*) Suliko, take a few blankets and wait for me in the foal stables.

GRUSHA: What have they done to the Governor?

THE GROOM (*gesturing throat cutting*): Ffffft.

A FAT WOMAN (*seeing the gesture and becoming hysterical*): Oh dear, oh dear, oh dear, oh dear! Our master Georgi Abashwili! A picture of health he was, at the Morning Mass — and now! Oh, take me away, we're all lost! We must die in sin! Like our master, Georgi Abashwili!

THE OTHER WOMAN (*soothing her*): Calm down, Nina! You'll be taken to safety. You've never done anyone any harm.

THE FAT WOMAN (*being led out*): Oh dear, oh dear, oh dear! Quick! Let's all get out before they come. Before they come!

A YOUNG WOMAN: Nina takes it more to heart than the mistress, that's a fact. *They* even have to have their weeping done for them.

THE COOK: We'd better get out, all of us.

ANOTHER WOMAN (*glancing back*): That must be the East Gate burning.

THE YOUNG WOMAN (*seeing the child in* GRUSHA'S *arms*): The child! What are *you* doing with it?

GRUSHA: It got left behind.

THE YOUNG WOMAN: She simply left it! Michael, who was kept out of all the drafts!

The servants gather round the child.

GRUSHA: He's waking up.

THE GROOM: Better put him down, I tell you. I'd rather not think what'd happen to anybody who's seen with that child.

THE COOK: That's right. Once they start, they'll kill each other off, whole families at a time. Let's go.

Exeunt all but GRUSHA, *with the child on her arm, and* TWO WOMEN.

THE TWO WOMEN: Didn't you hear? Better put him down.

GRUSHA: The nurse asked me to hold him a moment.

THE OLDER WOMAN: She'll never come back, you simpleton.

THE YOUNGER WOMAN: Keep your hands off it.

THE OLDER WOMAN (*amiably*): Grusha, you're a good soul, but you're not very bright and you know it. I tell you, if he had the plague it couldn't be worse.

GRUSHA (*stubbornly*): He hasn't got the plague. He looks at me! He's human!

THE OLDER WOMAN: Don't look at *him*. You are a fool — just the kind that always gets put upon. Someone says to you "Run for the salad, you have the longest legs," and you run. My husband has an ox cart — you can come with us if you hurry! Lord, by now the whole neighborhood must be in flames.

Both women leave, sighing. After some hesitation, GRUSHA *puts the sleeping child down, looks at it for a moment, then takes a brocade blanket from the heap of clothes and covers it. Then both women return, dragging bundles.* GRUSHA *starts guiltily away from the child and walks a few steps to one side.*

THE YOUNGER WOMAN: Haven't you packed anything yet? There isn't much time, you know. The Ironshirts will be here from the barracks.

GRUSHA: Coming.

She runs through the doorway. Both women go to the gateway and wait. The sound of horses is heard. They flee, screaming.

Enter THE FAT PRINCE *with drunken* IRONSHIRTS. *One of them carries* THE GOVERNOR's *head on a lance.*

THE FAT PRINCE: Here! In the middle! (*One soldier climbs onto the other's back, takes the head, holds it tentatively over the door.*) That's not the middle. Farther to the right. That's it. What I do, my friends, I do well. (*While, with hammer and nail, the soldier fastens the head to the wall by its hair:*) This morning at the church door I said to Georgi Abashwili: "I love a clear sky." Actually I prefer the lightning that comes out of a clear sky. Yes indeed. It's a pity they took the brat along, though. I need him. Urgently.

Exit with IRONSHIRTS *through the gateway. Trampling of horses again. Enter* GRUSHA *through the doorway looking cautiously about her. Clearly she has waited for the* IRONSHIRTS *to go. Carrying a bundle, she walks toward the gateway. At the last moment, she turns to see if the child is still there. Catching sight of the head over the doorway, she screams. Horrified, she picks up her bundle again, and is about to leave when* THE STORY TELLER *starts to speak. She stands rooted to the spot.*

THE STORY TELLER:
As she was standing between courtyard and gate,
She heard or she thought she heard a low voice calling;
The child called to her,
Not whining, but calling quite sensibly,
At least so it seemed to her.
"Woman," it said, "help me."
And it went on, not whining, but saying quite sensibly:
"Know, woman, he who hears not a cry for help
But passes by with troubled ears will never hear
The gentle call of a lover nor the blackbird at dawn
Nor the happy sigh of the exhausted grape-picker
        as the Angelus rings."

She walks a few steps toward the child and bends over it.

Hearing this she went back for one more look at the child.
Only to sit with him for a moment or two,

Only till someone should come,
Its mother, perhaps, or anyone else.

Leaning on a trunk, she sits facing the child.

Only till she would have to leave, for the danger was too great,
The city was full of flame and crying.

*The light grows dimmer, as though evening and night were
coming on.*

Terrible is the seductive power of goodness!

GRUSHA *now settles down to watch over the child through the
night. Once, she lights a small lamp to look at it. Once, she
tucks it in with a coat. From time to time she listens and looks
to see whether someone is coming.*

A long time she sat with the child
Till evening came, till night came, till dawn came.
Too long she sat, too long she saw
The soft breathing, the little fists,
Till toward morning the temptation grew too strong
And she rose, and bent down and, sighing, took the child
And carried it off.

She does what THE STORY TELLER *says as he describes it.*

Like plunder she took it to herself
Like a thief she crept away.

2

THE FLIGHT INTO THE NORTHERN MOUNTAINS

THE STORY TELLER:

As Grusha Vashnadze left the city
On the Grusinian highway
On the way to the Northern Mountains
She sang a song, she bought some milk.

THE CHORUS:

How will this human child escape
The bloodhounds, the trap-setters?
Into the deserted mountains she journeyed
Along the Grusinian highway she journeyed
She sang a song, she bought some milk.

GRUSHA VASHNADZE *walks on. On her back she carries the child in a sack, in one hand is a large stick, in the other a bundle. She sings.*

THE SONG OF THE FOUR GENERALS

Four generals
Set out for Baku.
The first no war had ever begun
The second fought but never won
For the third no weather was ever right
For the fourth the men would never fight
Four generals
And none got through.

Sosso Robakidse
Marched to Iran
A mighty war he'd soon begun
A mighty battle he'd soon won

For him the weather was always right
For him the men would always fight
Sosso Robakidse
Is our man!

A peasant's cottage appears.

GRUSHA (*to the child*): Noontime is eating time. Now we'll sit hopefully in the grass, while the good Grusha goes and buys a little pitcher of milk. (*She lays the child down and knocks at the cottage door. An* OLD MAN *opens it.*) Grandfather, could I have a litle pitcher of milk? And a corn cake, maybe?

THE OLD MAN: Milk? We haven't any milk. The soldiers from the city have our goats. Go to the soldiers if you want milk.

GRUSHA: But grandfather, you must have a little pitcher of milk for a child?

THE OLD MAN: And for a God-bless-you, eh?

GRUSHA: Who said anything about a God-bless-you? (*She shows her purse.*) We're going to pay like princes. "Head in the clouds, backside in the water." (*The peasant goes off, grumbling, for milk.*) How much for this little pitcher?

THE OLD MAN: Three piasters. Milk has gone up.

GRUSHA: Three piasters for that little drop? (*Without a word* THE OLD MAN *shuts the door in her face.*) Michael, did you hear that? Three piasters! We can't afford it! (*She goes back, sits down again, and gives the child her breast.*) Suck. Think of the three piasters. There's nothing there, but you *think* you're drinking, and that's something. (*Shaking her head, she sees that the child isn't sucking any more. She gets up, walks back to the door, and knocks again.*) Open, grandfather, we'll pay. (*Softly:*) May lightning strike you! (*When* THE OLD MAN *appears:*) I thought it would be half a piaster. But the child must have something. What about one piaster for that little drop?

THE OLD MAN: Two.

GRUSHA: Don't shut the door again. (*She fishes a long time in her bag.*) Here are two piasters. But the milk better be good. I still have two days' journey ahead of me. This is a murderous business and a sin too!

THE OLD MAN: Kill the soldiers if you want milk.

GRUSHA (*giving the child some milk*): This is an expensive joke. Take a sip, Michael, it's a week's pay. The people here think we earned our money just sitting around. Michael, Michael, you're a nice little load for anyone to take on! (*Uneasy, she gets up, puts the child on her back, and walks on.* THE OLD MAN, *grumbling, picks up the pitcher and looks after her unmoved.*)

THE STORY TELLER:

As Grusha Vashnadze went northward
The Princes' Ironshirts went after her.

THE CHORUS:

How will the barefoot girl escape the Ironshirts,
The bloodhounds, the trap-setters?
They are hunting even by night.
Pursuers never get tired.
Butchers sleep little.

TWO IRONSHIRTS *are trudging along the highway.*

THE CORPORAL: You'll never amount to anything, blockhead! Your heart's not in it. Your senior officer sees it in little things. Yesterday, when I made the fat gal, I admit you grabbed her husband as I commanded, and you *did* kick him in the stomach, but did you enjoy doing it like a loyal Private? Or were you just doing your duty? I've kept my eyes on you, blockhead. You're a hollow reed and a tinkling cymbal. You won't get promoted. (*They walk a while in silence.*) Don't imagine I don't remember how insubordinate you are in everything. I forbid you to limp! You only do it because I sold the horses, and I sold 'em because I couldn't have got that price again. You limp just to show me you don't like marching. I know you. It won't help. You wait. Sing!

THE TWO IRONSHIRTS (*singing*):

Off to the wars I went my way
Leaving my loved one at her door

My friends will keep her honor safe
Till from the wars I'm back once more.

THE CORPORAL: Louder!

THE TWO IRONSHIRTS (*singing*):
And when my heavenly rest is won
My love will at my grave declare:
"Here rest the feet that once to me would run
And here the hands that once caressed my hair!"

They begin to walk again in silence.

THE CORPORAL: A good soldier has his heart and soul in it. When he receives an order, he gets a hard on, and when he sends his lance into the enemy's guts, he comes. (*He shouts for joy.*) He lets himself be torn to pieces for his superior officer, and as he lies dying he takes note that his corporal is nodding approval. That's reward enough for him. That's all he wants. But *you* won't get a nod. Yet you'll croak all the same. Christ, how am I to get my hands on the Governor's bastard with a fool like you! (*They stay on stage behind.*)

THE STORY TELLER:
When Grusha Vashnadze came to the River Sirra
The flight grew too much for her, the helpless child too heavy.
In the cornfields the rosy dawn
Is cold to the sleepless one, only cold.
The gay clatter of the milk cans in the farmyard where the
      smoke rises
Is only a threat to the fugitive.
She who carries the child feels its weight and little more.

GRUSHA *stops in front of a farm. A fat* PEASANT WOMAN *is carrying a milk can through the door.* GRUSHA *waits until she has gone in, then approaches the house cautiously.*

GRUSHA (*to the child*): Now you've wet yourself again, and you know I've no linen. Michael, this is where we part company. This is far enough from the city. They wouldn't want you so much, little good-for-nothing, that they'd follow you all this way. The peasant woman is kind, and can't you just smell the milk? (*She bends down to lay the child on the threshold*.) So farewell, Michael, I will forget how you kicked me in the back all night to make me go faster. And you, forget the meager fare — it was meant well. I would like to have kept you — your nose is so tiny — but it cannot be. I would have shown you your first rabbit and how not to wet yourself, but I must turn back. My sweetheart the soldier might soon return. And suppose he didn't find me? You can't ask that.

She creeps up to the door and lays the child on the threshold. Then, hiding behind a tree, she waits until THE PEASANT WOMAN *opens the door and sees the bundle.*

THE PEASANT WOMAN: Good heavens, what's that? Husband!

THE PEASANT (*coming*): What's up? Let me get on with my soup.

THE PEASANT WOMAN (*to the child*): Where's your mother then? Haven't you got one? It's a boy. Fine linen — and a child. From a good family, you can see that. And they just leave him on our doorstep. Oh, these are times!

THE PEASANT: If they think we're going to feed it, they're mistaken. You can take it to the priest in the village. That's the best we can do.

THE PEASANT WOMAN: What will the priest do with it? It needs a mother. There, it's waking up. Don't you think we could keep it though?

THE PEASANT (*shouting*): No!

THE PEASANT WOMAN: I could lay it in the corner next to the armchair. I only need a crib for it. And I can take it into the fields with me. See how it's laughing? Husband, we have a roof over our heads and we can do it. Not another word!

She carries the child into the house. THE PEASANT *follows, protesting.* GRUSHA *steps out from behind the tree, laughs, and hurries off in the opposite direction.*

THE STORY TELLER: Why so cheerful, making for home?

THE CHORUS:
Because the child has won new parents with a laugh,
Because I'm rid of the little one, I'm cheerful.

THE STORY TELLER: And why so sad?

THE CHORUS:

Because I'm single and free, I'm sad.
Like one robbed, one newly poor.

She walks for a short while, then meets the TWO IRONSHIRTS, *who point their lances at her.*

THE CORPORAL: Lady, you are running into the Armed Forces. Where are you coming from? And when? Are you having illicit relations with the enemy? Where's he hanging out? What movements is he making in your rear? What about the hills? What about the valleys? How are your stockings fastened? (GRUSHA *stands there frightened.*) Don't be scared, we always stage a retreat, if necessary . . . what, blockhead? I always stage a retreat. In that respect, I can be relied on. Why are you staring like that at the lance? In the field no soldier ever drops his lance, that's a rule. Learn it by heart, blockhead. Now then, lady, where are you heading for?

GRUSHA: To meet my intended, one Simon Shashava, of the Palace Guard in Nuka.

THE CORPORAL: Simon Shashava? Sure, I know *him.* He gave me the key so I could look you up once in a while. Blockhead, we are getting to be unpopular. We must make her realize we have honorable intentions. Lady, behind apparent frivolity I conceal a serious nature. And so let me tell you officially: I want a child from you. (GRUSHA *utters a little scream.*) Blockhead, she understood. Uh-huh, isn't it a sweet shock? "Then first I must take the noodles out of the oven, Officer. Then first I must change my torn shirt, Colonel." But away with jokes, away with the lance! We are looking for a child in these parts. A child from a good family. Have you heard of such a child, from the city, dressed in fine linen, and suddenly turning up here?

GRUSHA: No, I haven't heard a thing. (*Suddenly she turns round and runs back, panic-stricken.* THE IRONSHIRTS *glance at each other, then follow her, cursing.*)

THE STORY TELLER:

Run, kind girl! The killers are coming!

Help the helpless child, helpless girl!
And so she runs!

THE CHORUS:

In the bloodiest times
There are kind people.

As GRUSHA *rushes into the cottage,* THE PEASANT WOMAN *is bending over the child's crib.*

GRUSHA: Hide it! Quick! The Ironshirts are coming! It was I who laid it on your doorstep. But it isn't mine. It's from a good family.

THE PEASANT WOMAN: Who's coming? What sort of Ironshirts?

GRUSHA: Don't ask questions. The Ironshirts that are looking for it.

THE PEASANT WOMAN: They've no business in my house. But I must have a little talk with *you,* it seems.

GRUSHA: Take off the fine linen. That will give us away.

THE PEASANT WOMAN: Linen, my foot! In this house *I* make the decisions. *You* can't vomit in *my* room! But why did you abandon it? That's a sin.

GRUSHA (*looking out of the window*): There, they're coming from behind the trees. I shouldn't have run away. That made them angry. Oh, what shall I do?

THE PEASANT WOMAN (*looking out of the window and suddenly starting with fear*): Good gracious! Ironshirts!

GRUSHA: They're after the child!

THE PEASANT WOMAN: But suppose they come in!

GRUSHA: You musn't give it to them. Say it's yours.

THE PEASANT WOMAN: Yes.

GRUSHA: They'll run it through if you hand it over.

THE PEASANT WOMAN: But suppose they ask for it? The silver for the harvest is in the house.

GRUSHA: If you let them have it, they'll run it through, here in your room! You've got to say it's yours!

THE PEASANT WOMAN: Yes. But what if they don't believe me?

GRUSHA: You must speak firmly.

THE PEASANT WOMAN: They'll burn the roof over our heads.

GRUSHA: That's why you've got to say it's yours. His name's Michael. I shouldn't have told you that. (THE PEASANT WOMAN *nods.*) Don't nod like that. And don't tremble — they'll notice.

THE PEASANT WOMAN: Yes.

GRUSHA: Stop saying yes, I can't stand it. (*She shakes the woman.*) Haven't *you* got a child?

THE PEASANT WOMAN (*muttering*): In the war.

GRUSHA: Then maybe he's an Ironshirt too? Do you want him to run children through with his lance? You'd bawl him out. "No fooling with a lance in *my* house!" you'd shout, "is that what I've reared you for? Wash your neck before you speak to your mother!"

THE PEASANT WOMAN: That's true, he couldn't get away with that around here!

GRUSHA: Promise me you'll say it's yours.

THE PEASANT WOMAN: Yes.

GRUSHA: There! They're coming now!

There is a knocking at the door. The women don't answer. Enter IRONSHIRTS. THE PEASANT WOMAN *bows low.*

THE CORPORAL: Well, there she is. What did I tell you? What a nose I have! I smell her. Lady, I have a question to ask you. Why did you run away? What did you think I would do to you? I'll bet it was something dirty. Confess!

GRUSHA (*while* THE PEASANT WOMAN *bows again and again*): I'd left some milk on the stove, and I suddenly remembered.

THE CORPORAL: Or maybe you imagined I'd looked at you in a dirty way? Like there could be something between us? A lewd look, know what I mean?

GRUSHA: I didn't see it.

THE CORPORAL: But it's possible, huh? You admit that. After all, I might be a swine. I'll be frank with you: I could think of all sorts of things if we were alone. (*To* THE PEASANT WOMAN:) Shouldn't you be busy in the yard? Feeding the hens?

THE PEASANT WOMAN (*falling suddenly to her knees*): Soldier, I didn't know a thing about it. Please don't burn the roof over our heads.

THE CORPORAL: What are you talking about?

THE PEASANT WOMAN: I had nothing to do with it. She left it on my doorstep, I swear!

THE CORPORAL (*suddenly seeing the child and whistling*): Ah, there's a little something in the crib! Blockhead, I smell a thousand piasters. Take the old girl out and hold on to her. It looks like I have a little cross-examining to do. (THE PEASANT WOMAN *lets herself be led out by the Private, without a word.*) Well, you've got that child I wanted from you. (*He walks toward the crib.*)

GRUSHA: Officer, it's mine. It's not the one you're after.

THE CORPORAL: I'll just take a look. (*He bends over the crib.* GRUSHA *looks round in despair.*)

GRUSHA: It's mine! It's mine!

THE CORPORAL: Fine linen!

GRUSHA *dashes at him to pull him away. He throws her off and again bends over the crib. Again looking round in despair, she sees a log of wood, seizes it, and hits* THE CORPORAL *over the head from behind.* THE CORPORAL *collapses. She quickly picks up the child and rushes off.*

THE STORY TELLER:
And in her flight from the Ironshirts
After twenty-two days of journeying
At the foot of the Janga-Tu glacier
Grusha Vashnadze decided to adopt the child.

THE CHORUS:
The helpless girl adopted the helpless child.

GRUSHA *squats over a half-frozen stream to get the child water in the hollow of her hand.*

GRUSHA:
Since no one else will take you, son,
I must take you now.
Since no one else will take you, son,

(O black day in a lean, lean year!)
You must take me.
I have carried you too long
My feet are tired and sore
And the milk cost much too much
I've grown fond of you:
I wouldn't be without you any more
I'll throw away your silken shirt
And wrap you in rags.
I'll wash you, son, and christen you
In glacier water.
You must see it through.

She has taken off the child's fine linen and wrapped it in a rag

THE STORY TELLER:
When Grusha Vashnadze
Pursued by the Ironshirts
Came to the bridge on the glacier
Leading to the villages of the Eastern Slope
She sang the Song of the Rotten Bridge
And risked two lives.

A wind has risen. The bridge on the glacier is visible in the dark. One rope is broken and half the bridge is hanging down the abyss. Merchants, two men and a woman, stand undecided before the bridge as GRUSHA *and the child arrive. One man is trying to catch the hanging rope with a stick.*

THE FIRST MAN: Take your time, young woman. You won't get over that pass anyway.

GRUSHA: But I simply have to get the little one over to the east side. To my brother.

THE MERCHANT WOMAN: Have to? What d'you mean by "have to"? I have to get there, too — because I have to buy two carpets in Atum — carpets a woman had to sell because her husband had to die. But can I do what I have to? Can she? For hours Andréi has been fishing for that rope. And I ask you, how are we to fasten it, even if he gets it up?

THE FIRST MAN (*listening*): Hush, I think I hear something.

GRUSHA: The bridge is not quite rotten. I think I'll try and make it.

THE MERCHANT WOMAN: I wouldn't try that if the devil himself were after me. Why, it's suicide.

THE FIRST MAN (*shouting*): Hi!

GRUSHA: Don't call! (*To* THE MERCHANT WOMAN:) Tell him not to call.

THE FIRST MAN: But there's someone down there calling. Maybe they've lost their way.

THE MERCHANT WOMAN: Why shouldn't he call? Is there something wrong about you? Are they after you?

GRUSHA: All right, I'll tell you. The Ironshirts are after me. I knocked one down.

THE SECOND MAN: Hide our merchandise!

The WOMAN *hides a sack behind a rock.*

THE FIRST MAN: Why didn't you tell us right away? (*To the others:*) If they catch her they'll make mincemeat out of her!

GRUSHA: Get out of my way. I've got to cross that bridge.

THE SECOND MAN: You can't. The precipice is two thousand feet deep.

THE FIRST MAN: Even with the rope it'd be no use. We could hold it with our hands, but then the Ironshirts could cross the same way.

GRUSHA: Go away.

There are calls from the distance: "Hi, up there!"

THE MERCHANT WOMAN: They're getting near. But you can't take the child across that bridge. It's sure to break. Just look down.

GRUSHA *looks down into the abyss. The* IRONSHIRTS *are heard calling again from below.*

THE SECOND MAN: Two thousand feet!

GRUSHA: But those men are worse.

THE FIRST MAN: You can't do it. There's the child. Risk *your* life but not the child's.

THE SECOND MAN: With the child she's all the heavier!

THE MERCHANT WOMAN: Maybe she's really got to get across. Give me the child. I'll hide it. You cross the bridge alone.

GRUSHA: I won't. We belong together. (*To the child:*) "Live together, die together." (*She sings.*)

THE SONG OF THE ROTTEN BRIDGE

Deep is the abyss, son,
I see the weak bridge sway
But it's not for us, son,
To choose the way.

The way I know
Is the one you must tread,
And all you will eat
Is my bit of bread.

Of every four pieces
You shall have three.
Would that I knew
How big they will be!
Get out of my way, I'll try it without the rope.

THE MERCHANT WOMAN: That's tempting God!

There are shouts from below.

GRUSHA: Please, throw that stick away, or they'll get the rope and follow me. (*Pressing the child to her, she steps onto the swaying bridge.* THE MERCHANT WOMAN *screams when it looks as though the bridge is about to collapse. But* GRUSHA *walks on and reaches the far side.*)

THE FIRST MAN: She's done it!

THE MERCHANT WOMAN (*who has fallen on her knees and begun to pray, angrily*): I still think it was a sin.

The IRONSHIRTS *appear;* THE CORPORAL's *head is bandaged.*

THE CORPORAL: Seen a woman with a child?

THE FIRST MAN (*while* THE SECOND MAN *throws the stick into the abyss*): Yes, there! But the bridge won't carry *you!*

THE CORPORAL: You'll pay for this, blockhead!

GRUSHA, *from the far bank, laughs and shows the child to the* IRONSHIRTS. *She walks on. The wind blows.*

GRUSHA (*turning to the child*): You mustn't fear the wind. He's just a poor thing too. He has to push the clouds along and he gets cold doing it. (*Snow starts falling.*) And the snow is not so bad, either, Michael. It covers the little fir trees so they won't die in winter. And now I'll sing you a little song. Listen! (*She sings.*)

THE SONG OF THE CHILD

Your father is a thief,
Your mother is a whore,
And all good people
Will kneel at your door.

The sons of the tiger
Are the horse's brothers,
The child of the snake
Brings milk to the mothers.

3

IN THE NORTHERN MOUNTAINS

THE STORY TELLER:

Seven days the sister, Grusha Vashnadze,
Journeyed across the glacier
And down the slopes she journeyed.
"When I enter my brother's house," she thought
"He will rise and embrace me."
"Is that you, sister?" he will say,
"I have been expecting you so long.
This is my dear wife.
And this is my farm, come to me by marriage,
With eleven horses and thirty-one cows. Sit down.
Sit down with your child at our table and eat."
The brother's house was in a lovely valley.
When the sister came to the brother,
She was ill from walking.
The brother rose from the table.

A fat peasant couple rise from the table. LAVRENTI VASHNADZE *still has a napkin round his neck, as* GRUSHA, *pale and supported by a servant, enters with the child.*

LAVRENTI: Where do you come from, Grusha?

GRUSHA (*feebly*): I've walked across the Janga-Tu Pass, Lavrenti.

THE SERVANT: I found her in front of the hay barn. She has a child with her.

THE SISTER-IN-LAW: Go and groom the mare. (*Exit* THE SERVANT.)

LAVRENTI: This is my wife. Aniko.

THE SISTER-IN-LAW: I thought you were in service in Nuka.

GRUSHA (*barely able to stand*): Yes, I was.

THE SISTER-IN-LAW: Wasn't it a good job? We were told it was.

GRUSHA: The Governor got killed.

LAVRENTI: Yes, we heard there were riots. Your aunt told us about it. Remember, Aniko?

THE SISTER-IN-LAW: Here, with us, it's very quiet. City people always want something going on. (*She walks toward the door, calling:*) Sosso, Sosso, don't take the cake out of the oven yet, d'you hear? Where on earth are you? (*Exit, calling.*)

LAVRENTI (*quietly, quickly*): Is there a father? (*As she shakes her head:*) I thought not. We must think up something. She's religious.

THE SISTER-IN-LAW (*returning*): Those servants! (*To* GRUSHA:) You have a child.

GRUSHA: It's mine. (*She collapses.* LAVRENTI *rushes to her assistance.*)

THE SISTER-IN-LAW: Good heavens, she's ill — what are we to do?

LAVRENTI (*escorting her to a bench near the stove*): Sit down, sit down. I think it's just weakness, Aniko.

THE SISTER-IN-LAW: As long as it's not scarlet fever!

LAVRENTI: Then she'd have spots. It's only weakness. Don't worry, Aniko. (*To* GRUSHA:) It's better sitting down?

THE SISTER-IN-LAW: Is the child hers?

GRUSHA: It's mine.

LAVRENTI: She's on her way to her husband.

THE SISTER-IN-LAW: I see. Your meat's getting cold. (LAVRENTI *sits down and begins to eat.*) Cold food's not good for you, the fat mustn't get cold, you know your stomach's your weak spot. *To* GRUSHA:) If your husband's not in the city, where is he?

LAVRENTI: She got married on the other side of the mountain, she says.

THE SISTER-IN-LAW: Oh, on the other side. (*She also sits down to eat.*)

GRUSHA: I think I should lie down somewhere, Lavrenti.

THE SISTER-IN-LAW: If it's consumption we'll all get it. (*She goes on cross-examining her.*) Has your husband got a farm?

GRUSHA: He's a soldier.

LAVRENTI: But he's coming into a farm — a small one from his father.

THE SISTER-IN-LAW: Isn't he in the war? Why not?

GRUSHA (*with effort*): Yes, he's in the war.

THE SISTER-IN-LAW: Then why d'you want to go to the farm?

LAVRENTI: When he comes back from the war, he'll return to his farm.

THE SISTER-IN-LAW: But you're going there now?

LAVRENTI: Yes, to wait for him.

THE SISTER-IN-LAW (*calling shrilly*): Sosso, the cake!

GRUSHA (*murmuring feverishly*): A farm — a soldier — waiting — sit down, eat.

THE SISTER-IN-LAW: It's scarlet fever.

GRUSHA (*starting up*): Yes, he's got a farm!

LAVRENTI: I think it's just weakness, Aniko. Wouldn't you like to go look after the cake yourself, dear?

THE SISTER-IN-LAW: But when will he come back if war's broken out again as people say? (*She waddles off, shouting:*) Sosso! Where on earth are you? Sosso!

LAVRENTI (*getting up quickly and going to* GRUSHA): You'll get a bed in a minute. She has a good heart. But wait till after supper.

GRUSHA (*holding out the child to him*): Take him.

LAVRENTI (*taking it and looking around*): But you can't stay here long with the child. She's religious, you see.

GRUSHA *collapses.* LAVRENTI *catches her.*

THE STORY TELLER:
The sister was so ill,
The cowardly brother had to give her shelter.
Summer departed, winter came.
The winter was long, the winter was short:
People mustn't know anything,
The rats mustn't bite,
The spring mustn't come.

GRUSHA *sits over the weaving loom in a workroom. She and the child, who is squatting on the floor, are wrapped in blankets. She sings.*

THE SONG OF THE CENTER

And the lover started to leave
And his betrothed ran pleading after him
Pleading and weeping, weeping and teaching:
"Dearest mine, Dearest mine
When you go to war as now you do
When you fight the foe as soon you will
Don't lead with the front line
And don't push with the rear line
At the front is red fire
In the rear is red smoke
Stay in the war's center
Stay near the standard bearer
The first always die
The last are also hit
Those in the center come home."

Michael, we must be clever. If we make ourselves as small as cockroaches, the sister-in-law will forget we are in the house. Then we can stay till the snow melts.

Enter LAVRENTI. *He sits down beside his sister.*

LAVRENTI: Why are you two sitting there muffled up like coachmen? Is it too cold in the room?

GRUSHA (*hastily removing one shawl*): It's not too cold, Lavrenti.

LAVRENTI: If it's too cold, you oughtn't to sit here with the child. Aniko would think herself to blame. (*Pause.*) I hope our priest didn't question you about the child?

GRUSHA: He did, but I didn't tell him anything.

LAVRENTI: That's good. I wanted to talk to you about Aniko. She has a good heart but she's very very sensitive. People have only to mention our farm and she's worried. She takes everything so hard, you see. One time our milkmaid went to church with a hole in her stocking. Ever since that day my Aniko has worn two pairs of stockings at church. It may seem hard to believe, but it's the old family in her. (*He listens.*) Are you sure there are no rats around? If there are, you couldn't live here. (*There are sounds as of dripping from the roof.*) What's that dripping?

GRUSHA: It must be a barrel leaking.

LAVRENTI: Yes, it must be a barrel. You've been here half a year now, haven't you? Was I talking about Aniko? (*They listen again to the snow melting.*) You can't imagine how worried she is about your soldier-husband. "Supposing he comes back and doesn't find her!" she says and lies awake. "He can't come before the spring," I tell her. The dear woman! (*The drops begin to fall faster.*) When d'you think he'll come? What do *you* think? (GRUSHA *is silent.*) Not before the spring, you think that too? (GRUSHA *is silent.*) So now you don't believe he'll come at all? (GRUSHA *is silent.*) But when the spring comes and the snow is melting here and on the passes, you can't stay any longer. They may come and look for you. People are already beginning to talk about an illegitimate child. (*The "glocken-spiel" of the falling drops has grown faster and steadier.*) Grusha, the snow is melting on the roof. And spring is here.

GRUSHA: Yes.

LAVRENTI (*eagerly*): Let me tell you what we'll do. You need a place to go, and because of the child (*he sighs*) you have to have a husband so people won't talk. Now I've made cautious inquiries to see if we can get a husband for you. Grusha, I've found one. I talked to a woman who has a son. Just the other side of the mountain, a small farm. She's willing.

GRUSHA: But I can't marry anyone! I must wait for Simon Sha-shava.

LAVRENTI: Of course. That's all been taken care of. You don't need a man in bed — you need a man on paper. And I've found you one. The son of this peasant woman is just going to die. Isn't it wonderful? He's at the last gasp. And every-thing's as we said it was. A husband from the other side the mountain. When you met him he was at the last gasp. And so you're a widow. What do you say?

GRUSHA: I could do with a document with stamps on it for Michael.

LAVRENTI: The stamps make all the difference. Without something in writing the Shah of Persia couldn't prove he's it. And you'll have a place to live.

GRUSHA: How much does the woman want?

LAVRENTI: Four hundred piasters.

GRUSHA: Where will you find the money?

LAVRENTI (*guiltily*): Aniko's milk money.

GRUSHA: No one would know us there. I'll do it.

LAVRENTI (*getting up*): I'll let the peasant woman know right away. (*Quick exit.*)

GRUSHA: Michael, you cause a lot of fuss. I came to you as the pear tree comes to the sparrows. And because a Christian bends down and picks up a crust of bread so nothing will go to waste. Michael, it would have been better had I walked quickly away on that Easter Sunday in Nuka in the second courtyard. Now I *am* a fool.

THE STORY TELLER:

The bridegroom was lying on his deathbed when the bride arrived.

The bridegroom's mother was waiting at the door, telling her to hurry.

The bride brought a child along.

The witness hid it during the wedding.

On one side the bed. Under the mosquito net lies a very sick man. GRUSHA *is pulled in at a run by her future mother-in-law. They are followed by* LAVRENTI *and the child.*

THE MOTHER-IN-LAW: Quick! Quick! Or he'll die on us before the wedding. (*To* LAVRENTI:) I was never told she had a child already.

LAVRENTI: What difference does it make? (*Pointing toward the dying man:*) It can't matter to him — in his condition.

THE MOTHER-IN-LAW: To him? But I'll never survive the shame. We are honest people. (*She begins to weep.*) My Jussup doesn't have to marry a girl with a child!

LAVRENTI: All right, I'll give you another two hundred piasters. You have it in writing that the farm will go to you. But she has the right to live here for two years.

THE MOTHER-IN-LAW (*drying her tears*): It'll hardly cover the funeral expenses. I hope she'll really lend me a hand with the work. And now what's happened to the monk? He must have crept out through the kitchen window. We'll have the whole village round our necks when they get wind that Jussup's end has come! Oh dear! I'll run and bring the monk. But he mustn't see the child.

LAVRENTI: I'll take care he doesn't see it. But why only a monk? Why not a priest?

THE MOTHER-IN-LAW: Oh, he's just as good. I only made one mistake: I paid half his fee in advance. Enough to go to the tavern with. I only hope . . . (*She runs off.*)

LAVRENTI: She saved on the priest, the wretch! Hired a cheap monk.

GRUSHA: Send Simon Shashava over to see me if he turns up after all.

LAVRENTI: Yes. (*Pointing at the sick man:*) Won't you have a look at him? (GRUSHA, *taking* MICHAEL *to her, shakes her head.*) He's not moving an eyelid. I hope we aren't too late.

They listen. On the opposite side enter neighbors who look around and take up positions against the walls, thus forming another wall near the bed, yet leaving an opening so that the bed can be seen. They start murmuring prayers. Enter THE MOTHER-IN-LAW *with a* MONK. *Showing some annoyance and surprise, she bows to the guests.*

THE MOTHER-IN-LAW: If you don't mind, please wait a few moments. My son's bride has just arrived from the city and an emergency wedding is about to take place. (*To the* MONK *in the bedroom:*) I might have known you couldn't keep your mouth shut. (*To* GRUSHA:) The wedding can take place immediately. Here's the license. I and the bride's brother (LAVRENTI *tries to hide in the background, after having quietly taken* MICHAEL *back from* GRUSHA. THE MOTHER-IN-LAW *waves him away*) who will appear at once, are the witnesses.

GRUSHA *has bowed to* THE MONK. *They go to the bed.* THE MOTHER-IN-LAW *lifts the mosquito net.* THE MONK *starts reeling off the marriage ceremony in Latin. Meanwhile,* THE MOTHER-IN-LAW *beckons to* LAVRENTI *to get rid of the child, but fearing*

that it will cry he draws its attention to the ceremony. GRUSHA
glances once at the child, and LAVRENTI *waves the child's hand
in a greeting.*

THE MONK: Are you prepared to be a faithful, obedient, and good
wife to this man, and to cleave to him until death you do part?

GRUSHA (*looking at the child*): I am.

THE MONK (*to the sick peasant*): And are you prepared to be a
good and loving husband to your wife until death you do
part? (*As the sick peasant does not answer,* THE MONK *looks in-
quiringly around.*)

THE MOTHER-IN-LAW: Of course he is! Didn't you hear him say yes?

THE MONK: All right. We declare the marriage contracted! Now
what about extreme unction?

THE MOTHER-IN-LAW: Nothing doing! The wedding was quite
expensive enough. Now I must take care of the mourners.
(*To* LAVRENTI:) Did we say seven hundred?

LAVRENTI: Six hundred. (*He pays.*) Now I don't want to sit
around getting to know people. So farewell, Grusha. And if
my widowed sister comes to visit me one day, she'll get a
welcome from my wife, or I'll show my teeth.

LAVRENTI *nods, gives the child to* GRUSHA, *and leaves. The
mourners glance after him without interest.*

THE MONK: And may one ask where this child comes from?

THE MOTHER-IN-LAW: Is there a child? I don't see a child. And
you don't see one either — you understand? Or else, I shall
have seen all kinds of things in the tavern! Now come on.
(*After* GRUSHA *has put the child down and told him to be quiet,
they move over left.* GRUSHA *is introduced to the neighbors.*)
This is my daughter-in-law. She arrived just in time to find
dear Jussup still alive.

ONE WOMAN: He's been ill now a whole year, hasn't he? When our
Vassili was drafted he was there to say goodbye.

ANOTHER WOMAN: Such things are terrible for a farm. The corn
all ripe and the farmer in bed! It'll really be a blessing if he
doesn't suffer too long, I say.

THE FIRST WOMAN (*confidentially*): At first we thought it was because of the draft he'd taken to his bed, you know. And now his end is coming!

THE MOTHER-IN-LAW: Sit yourselves down, please, and have some cakes.

She beckons to GRUSHA *and both women go into the bedroom, where they pick up the cake pans off the floor. The guests, among them* THE MONK, *sit on the floor and begin conversing in subdued voices.*

ONE PEASANT (*to whom* THE MONK *has handed the bottle which he has taken from his soutane*): There's a child, you say! How can that have happened to Jussup?

A WOMAN: She was certainly lucky to get herself hitched, with him so sick.

THE MOTHER-IN-LAW: They're gossiping already. And gorging on the funeral cakes at the same time! If he doesn't die today, I'll have to bake fresh ones tomorrow.

GRUSHA: I'll bake them.

THE MOTHER-IN-LAW: Yesterday some horsemen rode by, and I went out to see who it was. When I came in again he was lying there like a corpse! That's why I sent for you. It can't take much longer. (*She listens.*)

THE MONK: My dear wedding and funeral guests! Deeply touched, we stand before a bed of death and marriage. The bride gets the veil; the groom, a shroud: how varied, my children, are the fates of men! Alas! One man dies and has a roof over his head, and the other is married and the flesh turns to dust, from which it was made. Amen.

THE MOTHER-IN-LAW: He's taking his revenge. I shouldn't have hired such a cheap one. It's what you'd expect. A more expensive one would behave himself. In Sura there's one with a real air of sanctity about him, but of course he charges a fortune. A fifty-piaster monk like that has no dignity. And as for piety, just fifty piasters' worth and no more! When I came to get him in the tavern he had just made a speech and was shouting: "The war is over, beware of the peace!" We must go in.

GRUSHA (*giving* MICHAEL *a cake*): Eat this cake, and keep nice and still, Michael.

The two women offer cakes to THE GUESTS. *The dying man sits up in bed. He puts his head out from under the mosquito net, stares at the two women, then sinks back again.* THE MONK *takes two bottles from his soutane and offers them to* THE PEASANT *beside him. Enter* THREE MUSICIANS *who are greeted with a sly wink by* THE MONK.

THE MOTHER-IN-LAW (*to the* MUSICIANS): What are you doing here? With instruments?

ONE MUSICIAN: Brother Anastasius here (*pointing at* THE MONK) told us there was a wedding on.

THE MOTHER-IN-LAW: What? *You* brought them? Three more on my neck! Don't you know there's a dying man in the next room?

THE MONK: A very tempting assignment for a musician: something that could be either a subdued Wedding March or a spirited Funeral Dance!

THE MOTHER-IN-LAW: Well, you might as well play. Nobody can stop you eating in any case.

The musicians play a potpourri. The women serve cakes.

THE MONK: The trumpet sounds like a whining baby. And you, little drum, what have you got to tell the world?

THE DRUNKEN PEASANT (*beside* THE MONK, *sings*):
Miss Roundass took the old old man
And said that marriage was the thing
    To everyone who met 'er.
She later withdrew from the contract because
    Candles are better.

THE MOTHER-IN-LAW *throws* THE DRUNKEN PEASANT *out. The music stops.* THE GUESTS *are embarrassed.*

THE GUESTS (*loudly*): Have you heard? The Grand Duke is back! But the Princes are against him.
— Oh, the Shah of Persia, they say, has lent him a great army, to restore order in Grusinia. How is this possible? After all, the Shah of Persia is the enemy . . .

— Only the enemy of Grusinia, you donkey, not of the Grand Duke!

— In any case, the war's over, our soldiers are coming back.

GRUSHA *drops a cake pan.* GUESTS *help her pick up the cake.*

AN OLD WOMAN (*to* GRUSHA): Are you feeling bad? That's just excitement about dear Jussup. Sit down and rest awhile, my dear.

GRUSHA *staggers.*

THE GUESTS: Now everything will be the way it was. Only the taxes'll go up because we'll have to pay for the war.

GRUSHA (*weakly*): Did someone say the soldiers are back?

A MAN: I did.

GRUSHA: It can't be true.

THE FIRST MAN (*to a woman*): Show her the shawl. We bought it from a soldier. It's from Persia.

GRUSHA (*looking at the shawl*): They are here. (*She gets up, takes a step, kneels down in prayer, takes the silver cross and chain out of her blouse, and kisses it.*)

THE MOTHER-IN-LAW (*while the guests silently watch* GRUSHA): What's the matter with you? Won't you look after our guests? What's all this nonsense from the city got to do with us?

THE GUESTS (*resuming conversation while* GRUSHA *remains in prayer*): You can buy Persian saddles from the soldiers too. Though some exchange them for crutches.

— The big shots on one side can win a war, but the soldiers on both sides lose it.

— Anyway, the war's over now. It's something that they can't draft you any more. (*The dying man sits bolt upright in bed. He listens.*) What we need is two weeks of good weather.

— Our pear trees are hardly bearing a thing this year.

THE MOTHER-IN-LAW (*offering cakes*): Have some more cake and enjoy it. There are more. (THE MOTHER-IN-LAW *goes to the bedroom with the empty cake pans. Unaware of the dying man, she is bending down to pick up another tray when he begins to talk in a hoarse voice.*)

THE PEASANT: How many more cakes are you going to stuff down their throats? Does money grow on trees? (THE MOTHER-IN-

LAW *starts, stares at him aghast, while he climbs out from behind the mosquito net.*)

THE FIRST WOMAN (*talking kindly to* GRUSHA *in the next room*): Has the young wife someone at the front?

A MAN: That's good news, they're on their way home, huh?

THE PEASANT: Don't stare like that! Where's this wife you've hung round my neck?

Receiving no answer, he climbs out of bed and in his nightshirt staggers into the other room. Trembling, she follows him with the cake pan.

THE GUESTS (*seeing him and shrieking*): Good God! Jussup!

Everyone leaps up in alarm. The women rush to the door. GRUSHA, *still on her knees, turns round and stares at the man.*

THE PEASANT: The funeral supper! *That's* what you would like! Get out before I throw you out! (*As the guests stampede from the house, gloomily to* GRUSHA:) I've upset the apple cart, huh? (*Receiving no answer, he turns round and takes a cake from the pan which his mother is holding.*)

THE STORY TELLER:

O confusion! The wife discovers she has a husband.
By day there's the child, by night there's the husband.
The lover is on his way both day and night.
Husband and wife look at each other.
The bedroom is small.

Near the bed THE PEASANT *is sitting in a high wooden bathtub, naked.* THE MOTHER-IN-LAW *is pouring water from a pitcher. Opposite,* GRUSHA *cowers with* MICHAEL, *who is playing at mending straw mats.*

THE PEASANT (*to his* MOTHER): That's *her* work, not yours. Where's she hiding out now?

THE MOTHER-IN-LAW (*calling*): Grusha! The peasant wants you!

GRUSHA (*to* MICHAEL): There are still two holes to mend.

THE PEASANT (*when* GRUSHA *approaches*): Scrub my back!

GRUSHA: Can't the peasant do it himself?

THE PEASANT: "Can't the peasant do it himself?" Get the brush! To hell with you! Are you the wife here? Or are you a visitor? (*To* THE MOTHER-IN-LAW:) It's too cold!

THE MOTHER-IN-LAW: I'll run for hot water.

GRUSHA: Let me go.

THE PEASANT: You stay here. (THE MOTHER-IN-LAW *runs.*) Rub harder. And no finagling. You've seen a naked fellow before. That child didn't come out of thin air.

GRUSHA: The child was not conceived in joy, if that's what the peasant means.

THE PEASANT (*turning and grinning*): You don't look the type. (GRUSHA *stops scrubbing him, starts back. Enter* THE MOTHER-IN-LAW.) A nice thing you've hung around my neck! A simpleton for a wife!

THE MOTHER-IN-LAW: She just isn't cooperative.

THE PEASANT: Pour — but go easy! Ow! Go easy, I said. (*To* GRUSHA:) Maybe you did something wrong in the city . . . I wouldn't be surprised. Why else should you be here? But I won't talk about that. I've not said a word about the illegitimate object you brought into my house either. But my patience has limits! It's against nature. (*To* THE MOTHER-IN-LAW:) More! (*To* GRUSHA:) And even if your soldier does come back, you're married.

GRUSHA: Yes.

THE PEASANT: But your soldier won't return now. Don't you believe it.

GRUSHA: No.

THE PEASANT: You're cheating me. You're my wife and you're not my wife. Where you lie, nothing lies, and yet no other woman can lie there. When I go to work in the mornings I'm dead tired — when I lie down at night I'm awake as the devil. God has given you sex — and what d'you do? I don't have ten piasters to buy myself a woman in the city! Besides, it's a long way. Woman weeds the fields and opens up her legs, that's what our calendar says. D'you hear?

GRUSHA (*quietly*): Yes. I didn't mean to cheat you out of it.

THE PEASANT: She didn't mean to cheat me out of it! Pour some more water! (THE MOTHER-IN-LAW *pours*.) Ow!

THE STORY TELLER:
As she sat by the stream to wash the linen
She saw his image in the water
And his face grew dimmer with the passing moons.
As she raised herself to wring the linen
She heard his voice from the murmuring maple
And his voice grew fainter with the passing moons.
Evasions and sighs grew more numerous,
Tears and sweat flowed.
With the passing moons the child grew up.

GRUSHA *sits by a stream, dipping linen into the water. In the rear, a few children are standing.*

GRUSHA (*to* MICHAEL): You can play with them, Michael, but don't let them order you about just because you're the smallest. (MICHAEL *nods and joins the children. They start playing.*)

THE BIGGEST BOY: Today we're going to play Heads-Off. (*To a* FAT BOY:) You're the Prince and you must laugh. (*To* MICHAEL:) You're the Governor, and you laugh. (*To a* GIRL:) You're the Governor's wife and you cry when his head's chopped off. And I do the chopping. (*He shows his wooden sword.*) With this. First, the Governor is led into the yard. The Prince walks ahead. The Governor's wife comes last.

They form a procession. THE FAT BOY *goes ahead and laughs. Then comes* MICHAEL, *then* THE BIGGEST BOY, *and then* THE GIRL, *who weeps.*

MICHAEL (*standing still*): Me too chop head off.

THE BIGGEST BOY: That's my job. You're the smallest. The Governor's part is the easiest. All you have to do is kneel down and have your head chopped off — very simple.

MICHAEL: Me too have sword.

THE BIGGEST BOY: That's mine. (*He gives him a kick.*)

THE GIRL (*shouting to* GRUSHA): He doesn't want to play.

GRUSHA (*laughing*): Even the *little* duck can swim, they say.

THE BIGGEST BOY: You can play the Prince if you know how to laugh. (MICHAEL *shakes his head.*)

THE FAT BOY: I laugh best. Let him chop off a head just once. Then you do it, then me.

Reluctantly, THE BIGGEST BOY *hands* MICHAEL *the wooden sword and kneels down.* THE FAT BOY *sits down, beats his thigh, and laughs with all his might.* THE GIRL *weeps loudly.* MICHAEL *swings the big sword and "cuts off" the head. In doing so, he topples over.*

THE BIGGEST BOY: Ow! I'll show you how to hit the *right* way!

MICHAEL *runs away. The children run after him.* GRUSHA *laughs, following them with her eyes. On looking back, she sees* SIMON SHASHAVA *standing on the opposite bank. He wears a shabby uniform.*

GRUSHA: Simon!

SIMON: Is that Grusha Vashnadze?

GRUSHA: Simon!

SIMON (*formally*): A good morning to the young lady. I hope she is well.

GRUSHA (*getting up gaily and bowing low*): A good morning to the soldier. God be thanked he has returned in good health.

SIMON: They found better fish, so they didn't eat me, said the haddock.

GRUSHA: Courage, said the kitchen boy. Good luck, said the hero.

SIMON: And how are things here? Was the winter bearable? The neighbor considerate?

GRUSHA: The winter was a trifle rough, the neighbor as usual, Simon.

SIMON: May one ask if a certain person still dips her foot in the water when rinsing the linen?

GRUSHA: The answer is no. Because of the eyes in the bushes.

SIMON: The young lady is speaking of soldiers. Here stands a paymaster.

GRUSHA: A job worth twenty piasters?

SIMON: And lodgings.

GRUSHA (*with tears in her eyes*): Behind the barracks under the date trees.

SIMON: Yes, there. A certain person has kept her eyes open.

GRUSHA: She has, Simon.

SIMON: And has not forgotten? (GRUSHA *shakes her head.*) So the door is still on its hinges as they say? (GRUSHA *looks at him in silence and shakes her head again.*) What's this? Is something not as it should be?

GRUSHA: Simon Shashava, I can never return to Nuka. Something has happened.

SIMON: What can have happened?

GRUSHA: For one thing, I knocked an Ironshirt down.

SIMON: Grusha Vashnadze must have had her reasons for that.

GRUSHA: Simon Shashava, I am no longer called what I used to be called.

SIMON (*after a pause*): I do not understand.

GRUSHA: When do women change their names, Simon? Let me explain. Nothing stands between us. Everything is just as it was. You must believe me.

SIMON: Nothing stands between us and yet there *is* something?

GRUSHA: How can I explain it so fast and with the stream between us? Couldn't you cross the bridge there?

SIMON: Perhaps it's no longer necessary.

GRUSHA: It is very necessary. Come over on this side, Simon. Quick!

SIMON: Does the young lady wish to say that someone has come too late?

GRUSHA *looks up at him in despair, her face streaming with tears.* SIMON *stares before him. He picks up a piece of wood and starts cutting it.*

THE STORY TELLER:
So many words are said, so many left unsaid.
The soldier has come.
Where he comes from, he does not say.
Hear what he thought and did not say:
"The battle began gray at dawn, grew bloody at noon

The first fell before me, the second behind, the third at my side
On the first I stepped, the second I left, the third was run
    through by the captain
One of my brothers died by steel, the other by smoke
My neck was set aflame, my hands froze in my gloves, my toes
    in my socks
I fed on aspen buds, I drank maple juice, I slept on stone,
    in water."

SIMON: I see a cap in the grass. Is there a little one already?

GRUSHA: There is, Simon. How could I hide it? But please don't
worry, it is not mine.

SIMON: When the wind once begins to blow, they say, it blows
through every cranny. The wife need say no more.

    GRUSHA *looks into her lap and is silent.*

THE STORY TELLER:
There was yearning, but there was no waiting.
The oath is broken. No one could say why.
Hear what she thought but did not say:
"While you fought in the battle, soldier,
The bloody battle, the bitter battle
I found a child who was helpless
I had not the heart to destroy it
I had to care for what had gone astray
I had to bend down for bread crumbs on the floor
I had to rend myself for that which was not mine
That which was strange.
Someone must help.
For the little tree needs water
The lamb loses its way when the shepherd is asleep
And its cry is unheard!"

SIMON: Give me back the cross I gave you. Better still, throw it
into the stream. (*He turns to go.*)

GRUSHA (*getting up*): Simon Shashava, don't go away! It isn't
mine! It isn't mine! (*She hears the children calling.*) What is
the matter, children?

VOICES: Soldiers have come! They are taking Michael away!

GRUSHA *stands aghast as two* IRONSHIRTS, *with* MICHAEL *between them, come toward her.*

ONE OF THE IRONSHIRTS: Are you Grusha? (*She nods.*) Is this your child?

GRUSHA: Yes. (SIMON *goes.*) Simon!

THE IRONSHIRT: We have orders, in the name of the law, to take this child, found in your custody, back to the city. It is suspected that the child is Michael Abashwili, son and heir of the late Governor Georgi Abashwili, and his wife, Natella Abashwili. Here is the document and the seal. (*They lead the child away.*)

GRUSHA (*running after them, shouting*): Leave it here. Please! It's mine!

THE STORY TELLER:
The Ironshirts took the child, the beloved child.
The unhappy girl followed them to the city, the dreaded city.
She who had borne him demanded the child.
She who had raised him faced trial.
Who will decide the case?
To whom will the child be assigned?
Who will the judge be? A good judge? A bad?
The city was in flames.
In the judge's seat sat Azdak.*

* The name *Azdak* should be accented on the second syllable.

PART TWO

1

THE STORY OF THE JUDGE

THE STORY TELLER:

Hear the story of the judge

How he turned judge, how he passed judgment, what kind of
judge he was.

On that Easter Sunday of the great revolt, when the Grand
duke was overthrown

And his Governor Abashwili, father of our child, lost his head

The Village Recorder Azdak found in the woods a fugitive
and hid him in his hut.

AZDAK, *in rags and slightly drunk, is helping an old beggar into
his cottage.*

AZDAK: Stop snorting, you're not a horse. And it won't do you any
good with the police if you run like a snotty nose in April.
Stand still, I say. (*He catches* THE OLD MAN, *who has marched
into the cottage as if he'd like to go through the walls.*) Sit
down and feed. Here's a hunk of cheese. (*From under some
rags, in a chest, he fishes out some cheese, and* THE OLD MAN
greedily begins to eat.) Haven't eaten in a long time, huh?
(THE OLD MAN *growls.*) Why did you run like that, asshole?
The cop wouldn't even have seen you.

THE OLD MAN: I had to.

AZDAK: Blue funk? (THE OLD MAN *stares, uncomprehending.*) Cold
feet? Panic? Don't lick your chops like a Grand Duke. Or an

old sow. I can't stand it. We have to take respectable stinkers as God made them, but not you! I once heard of a senior judge who farted at a public dinner just to show an independent spirit! Watching you eat like that gives me the most awful ideas. Why don't you say something? (*Sharply:*) Show me your hand. Can't you hear? (THE OLD MAN *slowly puts out his hand.*) White! So you're not a beggar at all! A fraud, a walking swindle! And I'm hiding you from the cops as though you were a honest man! Why were you running like that if you're a landowner? For that's what you are. Don't deny it, I see it in your guilty face. (*He gets up.*) Get out! (THE OLD MAN *looks at him uncertainly.*) What are you waiting for, peasant-flogger?

THE OLD MAN: Pursued. Need undivided attention. Make proposition . . .

AZDAK: Make what? A proposition? Well, if that isn't the height of insolence. He's making me a proposition! The bitten man scratches his fingers bloody, and the leech that's biting him makes him a proposition! Get out, I tell you!

THE OLD MAN: Understand point of view. Persuasion! Pay hundred thousand piasters one night. Yes?

AZDAK: What, you think you can buy me? For a hundred thousand piasters? Let's say a hundred and fifty thousand. Where are they?

THE OLD MAN: Have not them here. Of course. Will be sent. Hope do not doubt.

AZDAK: Doubt very much. Get out!

THE OLD MAN *gets up, waddles to the door. A voice is heard off stage.*

A VOICE: Azdak!

THE OLD MAN *turns, waddles to the opposite corner, stands still.*

AZDAK (*calling out*): I'm not in! (*He walks to door.*) So you're sniffing around here again, Shauwa?

POLICEMAN SHAUWA (*reproachfully*): You've caught another rabbit, Azdak. You promised me it wouldn't happen again.

AZDAK (*severely*): Shauwa, don't talk about things you don't understand. The rabbit is a dangerous and destructive beast. It gorges itself on plants, especially on that species of plants known as weeds. It must therefore be exterminated.

SHAUWA: Azdak, don't be so hard on me. I'll lose my job if I don't arrest you. I know you have a good heart.

AZDAK: I do *not* have a good heart! How often must I tell you I'm a man of intellect?

SHAUWA (*slyly*): I know, Azdak. You're a superior person. You say so yourself. I'm just a Christian and an ignoramus. And so I ask you: When one of the Prince's rabbits is stolen and I'm a policeman, what am I to do with the offending party?

AZDAK: Shauwa, Shauwa, shame on you. There you stand asking me a question! What could be more tempting? Suppose you were a woman — let's say Nunowna, that bad girl — and you show me your thigh — Nunowna's thigh, that is — and ask me: What shall I do with my thigh, it itches? Is she as innocent as she pretends? No. I catch a rabbit, but you catch a man. Man is made in God's image. Not so a rabbit, you know that. I'm a rabbit-eater, but you're a man-eater, Shauwa. And God will pass judgment on you. Shauwa, go home and repent. No, stop, there's something . . . (*He looks at* THE OLD MAN *who stands trembling in the corner.*) No, it's nothing. Go home and repent. (*He slams the door behind* SHAUWA.) Now you're surprised, huh? Surprised I didn't hand you over? I couldn't bring myself to hand over a bedbug to that beast! It goes against the grain with me. Don't tremble because of a cop. So old and still so scared? Finish your cheese, but eat it like a poor man, or else they'll still catch you. Must I even tell you how a poor man behaves? (*He pushes him down, and then gives him back the cheese.*) The box is the table. Lay your elbows on the table. Now encircle the cheese on the plate as if it might be snatched away from you at any moment — what right have *you* to be safe, huh? Now hold the knife like an undersized sickle, and give your cheese a troubled look because, like all beautiful things, it's already fading away. (AZDAK *watches him.*) They're after you. That speaks in your favor. But how can we be sure they're not mistaken about

you? In Tiflis one time they hanged a landowner, a Turk, who
could prove he quartered his peasants instead of merely cutting them in half, as is the custom. And he squeezed twice the
usual amount of taxes out of them. His zeal was above suspicion. And yet they hanged him like a common criminal —
because he was a Turk — a thing he couldn't do much about.
An injustice! He got onto the gallows by a sheer fluke. In
short, I don't trust you.

THE STORY TELLER:
Thus Azdak gave the old beggar a bed,
And learned that old beggar was the old butcher, the Grand
      Duke himself,
And was ashamed.
He accused himself and ordered the policeman to take him to
      Nuka, to court, to be judged.

In the court of justice three IRONSHIRTS *sit drinking. From a
beam hangs a man in judge's robes. Enter* AZDAK, *in chains,
dragging* SHAUWA *behind him.*

AZDAK (*shouting*): I have helped the Grand Duke, the Grand Thief,
the Grand Butcher, to escape! In the name of justice I ask to
be severely judged in public trial!

THE FIRST IRONSHIRT: Who's this queer bird?

SHAUWA: That's our Recorder, Azdak.

AZDAK: I am despicable! treacherous! branded! Tell them, flat-
foot, how I insisted on being put in chains and brought to
the capital. Because I sheltered the Grand Duke, the Grand
Swindler by mistake. And how afterward I found out. Look,
a marked man is denouncing himself! Tell them how I forced
you to walk with me half the night to clear the whole thing up.

SHAUWA: And all by threats. That wasn't nice of you, Azdak.

AZDAK: Shut your mouth, Shauwa. You don't understand. A new
age has come. It'll go thundering over you. You're finished.
The police will be wiped out — pouf! Everything will be gone
into, everything brought into the open. A man will give himself up, and why? — because he couldn't escape the people in
any case. (*To* SHAUWA:) Tell them how I have been shouting
all along Shoemaker Street. (*With big gestures, looking at*

the IRONSHIRTS:) "In ignorance I let the Grand Swindler escape! Tear me to pieces, brothers!" To get it in first.

THE FIRST IRONSHIRT: And what was their answer?

SHAUWA: They comforted him in Butcher Street, and they laughed themselves sick in Shoemaker Street. That's all.

AZDAK: But here with you it's different, I know you're like iron. Brothers, where's the judge? I must be tried.

THE FIRST IRONSHIRT (*pointing at the hanged man*): Here's the judge. And please stop "brothering" us. That's rather a sore spot this evening.

AZDAK: "Here's the judge." That's an answer never heard in Grusinia before. Townsman, where's His Excellency the Governor? (*Pointing to the floor:*) Here's His Excellency, stranger. Where's the Chief Tax Collector? Where's the official Recruiting Officer? The Patriarch? The Chief of Police? Here, here, here — all here. Brothers, that's what I expected of you.

THE SECOND IRONSHIRT: Stop. What did you expect, funny man?

AZDAK: What happened in Persia, brother, what happened there?

THE SECOND IRONSHIRT: And what did happen in Persia?

AZDAK: Forty years ago. Everybody was hanged. Viziers, tax collectors. Everybody. My grandfather, a remarkable man by the way, saw it all. For three whole days. Everywhere.

THE SECOND IRONSHIRT: And who ruled when the Vizier was hanged?

AZDAK: A peasant.

THE SECOND IRONSHIRT: And who commanded the army?

AZDAK: A soldier, soldier.

THE SECOND IRONSHIRT: And who paid the wages?

AZDAK: A dyer. A dyer paid the wages.

THE SECOND IRONSHIRT: Wasn't it a weaver, maybe?

THE FIRST IRONSHIRT: And why did all this happen, Persian?

AZDAK: "Why did all this happen?" Must there be a special reason? Why do you scratch yourself, brother? War! Too long a war! And no justice! My grandfather brought back a song that tells how it was. I and my friend the policeman will sing it for you. (*To* SHAUWA:) And hold the rope tight. It's very suitable! (*He sings, with* SHAUWA *holding the rope tight around him.*)

THE SONG OF INJUSTICE IN PERSIA

Why don't our sons bleed any more? Why don't our daughters weep?
Why do only the slaughter-house calves have blood in their veins?
Why do only the willows shed tears on Lake Urmi?
The king must have a new province, the peasant must give up his savings.
That the roof of the world might be conquered, the roof of the cottage is torn down.
Our men are carried to the ends of the earth, so that great ones can eat at home.
The soldiers kill each other, the marshals salute each other.
They bite the widow's tax money to see if it's good, their swords break.
The battle was lost, the helmets were paid for.
(*refrain*) Is it so? Is it so?

SHAUWA (*refrain*): Yes, yes, yes, yes, yes it's so.

AZDAK: Do you want to hear the rest of it?

THE FIRST IRONSHIRT *nods.*

THE SECOND IRONSHIRT (*to* SHAUWA): Did he teach you that song?

SHAUWA: Yes, only my voice isn't very good.

THE SECOND IRONSHIRT: No. (*To* AZDAK:) Go on singing.

AZDAK: The second verse is about the peace. (*He sings.*)

The offices are packed, the streets overflow with officials.
The rivers jump their banks and ravage the fields.
Those who cannot let down their own trousers rule countries.
They can't count up to four, but they devour eight courses.
The corn farmers, looking round for buyers, see only the starving.

The weavers go home from their looms in rags.
(*refrain*) Is it so? Is it so?

SHAUWA (*refrain*): Yes, yes, yes, yes, yes it's so.

AZDAK:

That's why our sons don't bleed any more, that's why our daughters don't weep.

That's why only the slaughter-house calves have blood in their veins,

And only the willows shed tears by Lake Urmi toward morning.

THE FIRST IRONSHIRT: Are you going to sing that song here in town?

AZDAK: Sure. What's wrong with it?

THE FIRST IRONSHIRT: Do you see how the sky's getting red? (*Turning round,* AZDAK *sees the sky red with fire.*) That's in the suburbs. The carpet weavers have also caught the "Persian Sickness," and have asked if Prince Kazbeki isn't eating too many courses. And this morning they strung up the city judge. We have beaten them to pulp for one hundred piasters a man, you understand?

AZDAK (*after a pause*): I understand. (*He glances shyly round and, creeping away, sits down in a corner, his head in his hands.*)

THE IRONSHIRTS (*to each other*): If there ever was a trouble-maker it's him.

— He must've come to the capital to fish in the troubled waters.

SHAUWA: I don't think he's a really bad character, gentlemen. Steals a few chickens here and there. And maybe a rabbit.

THE SECOND IRONSHIRT (*approaching* AZDAK): Came to fish in the troubled waters, huh?

AZDAK (*looking up*): I don't know why I came.

THE SECOND IRONSHIRT: Are you maybe in with the carpet weavers?

AZDAK *shakes his head.*

THE SECOND IRONSHIRT: And what about that song?

AZDAK: From my grandfather. A silly and ignorant man.

THE SECOND IRONSHIRT: Right. And what about the dyer who paid the wages?

AZDAK (*muttering*): That was in Persia.

THE FIRST IRONSHIRT: And your denouncing yourself? For not having hanged the Grand Duke with your own hands?

AZDAK: Didn't I tell you I let him run? (*He creeps farther away and sits on the floor.*)

SHAUWA: I swear to that. He let him run.

THE IRONSHIRTS *burst out laughing and slap* SHAUWA *on the back.* AZDAK *laughs loudest. They slap* AZDAK *too, and unchain him. They all start drinking as* THE FAT PRINCE *enters with a young man.*

THE FIRST IRONSHIRT (*to* AZDAK, *pointing at* THE FAT PRINCE): There you have your new age! (*More laughter.*)

THE FAT PRINCE: Well, my friends, what have you got to laugh about? Permit me a serious word. Yesterday morning the Princes of Grusinia overthrew the war-mongering government of the Grand Duke and did away with his Governors. Unfortunately the Grand Duke himself escaped. In this fateful hour our carpet weavers, those eternal trouble-makers, had the effrontery to stir up a rebellion and hang the universally loved city judge, our dear Illo Orbeliani. Ts — ts — ts. My friends, we need peace, peace, peace in Grusinia! And justice! Here I bring you my dear nephew, Bizergan Kazbeki. He's to be the new judge. A very gifted fellow. What do you say? I want your opinion. I say: Let the people decide.

THE SECOND IRONSHIRT: Does this mean we elect the judge?

THE FAT PRINCE: Precisely. The people propose a very gifted fellow. Confer among yourselves, my friends. (THE IRONSHIRTS *confer.*) Don't worry, foxy. The job's yours. And the moment we catch the Grand Duke we'll not have to kiss this rabble's ass any more.

THE IRONSHIRTS (*between themselves*): That'll be fun.
— They have their pants full because they haven't caught the Grand Duke.
— When the outlook isn't so bright, they say: "My friends!" and "Let the people decide!" — Now he even wants justice for Grusinia! But fun is fun as long as it lasts! (*Pointing at*

AZDAK:) He knows all about justice. Hey, rascal, would you like to have the nephew be judge?

AZDAK: Are you asking me?

THE FIRST IRONSHIRT: Why not? Anything for a laugh!

AZDAK: I understand you want to test him to the marrow. Correct? Have you a criminal ready? An old hand? So the candidiate can show what he knows?

THE SECOND IRONSHIRT: Let me see, we've a couple of doctors downstairs. Let's use them.

AZDAK: Stop! That's no good. You can't take real criminals till we're sure of the judge being appointed. He may be dumb, but he must be appointed or else the law is violated. The law is a very sensitive creature. Like the spleen, it must never be assaulted or — it's all over. You can hang those two. Why not? You won't have violated the law, because the judge wasn't there. Judgment must always be pronounced with absolute gravity — why? Because it's such nonsense. Suppose, for instance, a judge jails a woman that's stolen a corncake for her child, and the judge isn't wearing his robes. Maybe he's scratching himself while passing sentence and nearly half his body is uncovered — a man must scratch his thigh once in a while — then the sentence he passes is a disgrace and the law is violated. It would be easier for a judge's robe and a judge's hat to pass judgment than for a mere man with no robe and no hat! If you don't watch out, the law just goes to pot. You don't try out a bottle of wine by offering it to a dog, and why not? Because you'd lose your wine.

THE FIRST IRONSHIRT: Then what do you suggest, hair-splitter?

AZDAK: I'll be the accused.

THE FIRST IRONSHIRT: You! (*He bursts out laughing.*)

THE FAT PRINCE: What have you decided?

THE FIRST IRONSHIRT: We've decided to stage a tryout. Our friend will be the accused, and here's the judge's seat for the candidate.

THE FAT PRINCE: It isn't customary, but why not? (*To* THE NEPHEW:) A mere formality, foxy. What have you learned? Who got there first? The slow runner or the fast?

THE NEPHEW: The silent runner, Uncle Arsen.

THE NEPHEW *takes the chair.* THE IRONSHIRTS *and* THE FAT PRINCE *sit on the steps. Enter* AZDAK, *mimicking the gait of* THE GRAND DUKE.

AZDAK: Is any here knows me? I am Grand Duke.

THE IRONSHIRTS: What is he?
— The Grand Duke. He really knows him.
— That's fine. Get on with the proceedings.

AZDAK: Listen! Am accused instigating war. Ridiculous! Am saying ridiculous! That enough? If not, have brought lawyers. Believe five hundred. (*He points behind him, pretending to be surrounded by lawyers.*) Requisition all available seats for lawyers!

THE IRONSHIRTS *laugh;* THE FAT PRINCE *joins in.*

THE NEPHEW (*to* THE IRONSHIRTS): Do you want me to try this case? I must admit I find it rather unusual. From the taste angle, I mean.

THE FIRST IRONSHIRT: Let's go!

THE FAT PRINCE (*smiling*): Let him have it, foxy!

THE NEPHEW: All right. People of Grusinia versus Grand Duke. Defendant, what have you to say!

AZDAK: Plenty. Naturally, have read war lost. Only started on the advice of patriots. Like Uncle Arsen Kazbeki. Demand Uncle Arsen as witness.

THE FAT PRINCE (*to* THE IRONSHIRTS, *delightedly*): What a screwball!

THE NEPHEW: Motion rejected. You cannot be accused of declaring a war, which every ruler has to do once in a while, but only of conducting it badly.

AZDAK: Rubbish! Did not conduct it at all! Had it conducted! Had it conducted by Princes! Naturally they messed it up.

THE NEPHEW: Do you by any chance deny having been commander-in-chief?

AZDAK: Not at all! Always was commander-in-chief. At birth shouted at wet nurse. Was trained to drop turds in toilet.

Grew accustomed to command. Always commanded officials rob my cash box. Officers flog soldiers only on command. Landowners sleep with peasants' wives only on strictest command. Uncle Arsen here grew his belly only by my command!

THE IRONSHIRTS (*clapping*): He's good! Long live the Grand Duke!

THE FAT PRINCE: Answer him, foxy! I'm with you.

THE NEPHEW: I shall answer him according to the dignity of the law. Defendant, preserve the dignity of the law!

AZDAK: Agreed. I command you to proceed with the trial!

THE NEPHEW: It's not your place to command me. So you claim that the Princes forced you to declare war. How can you claim then that they — er — "messed it up"?

AZDAK: Did not send enough people. Embezzled funds. Sent sick horses. During attack, drinking in whore house. Propose Uncle Arsen as witness.

THE NEPHEW: Are you trying to make the outrageous claim that the Princes of this country did not fight?

AZDAK: No. Princes fought. Fought for war contracts.

THE FAT PRINCE (*jumping up*): That's too much! This man talks like a carpet weaver!

AZDAK: Really? Nothing but the truth!

THE FAT PRINCE: Hang him! Hang him!

THE FIRST IRONSHIRT (*pulling the* PRINCE *down*): Keep quiet! Go on, Excellency!

THE NEPHEW: Quiet! I now render a verdict: You must be hanged! By the neck! Having lost war!

AZDAK: Young man, seriously advise not to fall publicly into jerky and clipped manner of speech. Cannot be employed as watchdog if howl like wolf. Got it? If people realize Princes talk same language as Grand Duke, may hang Grand Duke *and* Princes, huh? By the way, must overrule verdict. Reason? War lost, but not for Princes. Princes have won *their* war. Got themselves paid 3,863,000 piasters for horses not delivered, 8,240,000 piasters for food supplies not produced. Are therefore victors. War lost only for Grusinia, which is not present in this court.

THE FAT PRINCE: I think that's enough, my friends. (*To* AZDAK:) You can withdraw, funny man. (*To the* IRONSHIRTS:) I think you can now ratify the new judge's appointment, my friends.

THE FIRST IRONSHIRT: Yes, we can. Take down the judge's gown. (*One* IRONSHIRT *climbs on the back of the other, pulls the gown off the hanged man.*) And now (*to* THE NEPHEW:) you be off so the right ass can get on the right chair! (*To* AZDAK:) Step forward! Go to the judge's seat and sit up there, man. (AZDAK *steps up, bows, and sits down.*) The judge was always a rascal! Now the rascal shall be a judge! (*The judge's gown is placed round his shoulders, the hat on his head.*) And what a judge!

THE STORY TELLER:

And there was civil war in the land.

The ruler was unsafe.

And Azdak was made a judge by the Ironshirts.

And Azdak remained a judge for two years.

THE STORY TELLER AND CHORUS:

Conflagration's heat, and blood in every street,

And cockroach and bug in every town.

In the castle, fánatics. At the altar, heretics.

And Azdak wearing a judge's gown.

AZDAK *sits in the judge's chair, peeling an apple.* SHAUWA *is sweeping out the hall. On one side an* INVALID *in a wheelchair. Opposite, a young man accused of blackmail. An* IRONSHIRT *stands on guard, holding the Ironshirt's banner.*

AZDAK: In consideration of the large number of cases, the Court today will hear two cases at a time. Before I open the proceedings, a short announcement — I accept — (*He stretches out his hand.* THE BLACKMAILER *is the only one to produce any money. He hands it to* AZDAK.) — I reserve for myself the right to punish one of the parties here for contempt of court. (*He glances at* THE INVALID.) You (*to* THE DOCTOR:) are a doctor, and you (*to* THE INVALID:) are bringing a complaint against him. Is the doctor responsible for your condition?

THE INVALID: Yes. I had a stroke because of him.

AZDAK: That would be professional negligence.

THE INVALID: More than negligence. I gave this man money for his studies. So far, he hasn't paid me back a cent. And when I heard he was treating a patient free, I had a stroke.

AZDAK: Rightly. (*To a* LIMPING MAN:) And what do you want here?

THE LIMPING MAN: I'm the patient, your honor.

AZDAK: He treated your leg for nothing?

THE LIMPING MAN: The wrong leg! My rheumatism was in the left leg, and he operated on the right. That's why I limp now.

AZDAK: And you got it free?

THE INVALID: A five-hundred-piaster operation free! For nothing! For a God-bless-you! And I paid for this man's studies! (*To* THE DOCTOR:) Did they teach you to operate free?

THE DOCTOR: Your Honor, it is actually the custom to demand the fee before the operation, as the patient is more willing to pay before an operation than after. Which is only human. In the case in question I was convinced, when I started the operation, that my servant had already received the fee. In this I was mistaken.

THE INVALID: He was mistaken! A good doctor doesn't make mistakes! He examines before he operates.

AZDAK: That's right. (*To* SHAUWA:) Public Prosecutor, what's the other case about?

SHAUWA (*busily sweeping*): Blackmail.

THE BLACKMAILER: High Court of Justice, I'm innocent. I only wanted to find out from the landowner concerned if he really had raped his niece. He informed me very politely that this was not the case, and gave me the money only so I could pay for my uncle's studies.

AZDAK: Hm. (*To* THE DOCTOR:) You, on the other hand, can cite no extenuating circumstances for your offense, huh?

THE DOCTOR: Except that to err is human.

AZDAK: And you are perfectly well aware that in money matters a good doctor is conscious of his responsibility? I once heard of a doctor who made a thousand piasters out of one sprained finger: he discovered it had something to do with blood circula-

BERTOLT BRECHT

tion, which a less good doctor might have overlooked. On another occasion he made a real gold mine out of the careful treatment of a somewhat disordered gall bladder. You have no excuse, Doctor. The corn merchant, Uxu, had his son study medicine to get some knowledge of trade, our medical schools are so good. (*To the* BLACKMAILER:) What's the name of the landowner?

SHAUWA: He doesn't want it mentioned.

AZDAK: In that case I will pass judgment. The Court considers the blackmail proved. And you (*to* THE INVALID) are sentenced to a fine of one thousand piasters. If you have a second stroke, the doctor will have to treat you free. Even if he has to amputate. (*To* THE LIMPING MAN:) As compensation, you will receive a bottle of rubbing alcohol. (*To* THE BLACKMAILER:) You are sentenced to hand over half the proceeds of your deal to the Public Prosecutor to keep the landowner's name secret. You are advised, moreover, to study medicine — you seem well suited to that calling. (*To* THE DOCTOR:) You have perpetrated an unpardonable error in the practice of your profession: you are acquitted. Next cases!

THE STORY TELLER AND CHORUS:

> With a pound you're on firm ground (no one is willing for a
> shilling)
> And the law is a cat in a sack.
> But one whelp brings help to the many for a penny.
> The name of this rascal? Azdak.

Enter AZDAK *from the caravansary on the highroad, followed by an old bearded innkeeper. The judge's chair is carried by a stableman and* SHAUWA. *An* IRONSHIRT, *with a banner, takes up his position.*

AZDAK: Put it here. Then we'll get some air and maybe a good breeze from the lemon grove over there. It does justice good to be administered in the open: the wind blows her skirts up and you can see what she's got underneath. Shauwa, we've eaten too much. These official journeys are very exhausting. (*To* THE INNKEEPER:) It's a question of your daughter-in-law?

THE INNKEEPER: Your Worship, it's a question of the family honor.

I wish to bring an action on behalf of my son, who's on business on the other side of the mountain. This is the offending stableman, and here's my daughter-in-law.

Enter THE DAUGHTER-IN-LAW, *a voluptuous wench. She is veiled.*

AZDAK (*sitting down*): I accept . . . (*Sighing,* THE INNKEEPER *hands him some money.*) Good. Now the formalities are disposed of. This is a case of rape?

THE INNKEEPER: Your Honor, I caught the fellow in the act. Ludovica was already in the straw on the stable floor.

AZDAK: Quite right, the stable. Beautiful horses! I particularly liked the little roan.

THE INNKEEPER: The first thing I did, of course, was question Ludovica. On my son's behalf.

AZDAK (*seriously*): I said I particularly liked it.

THE INNKEEPER (*coldly*): Really? Ludovica confessed the stableman took her against her will.

AZDAK: Take your veil off, Ludovica. (*She does so.*) Ludovica, you please the Court. Tell us how it happened.

LUDOVICA (*well-schooled*): When I entered the stable to see the new foal the stableman said to me on his own accord: "It's hot today!" and laid his hand on my left breast. I said to him: "Don't do that!" But he continued to handle me indecently, which provoked my anger. Before I realized his sinful intentions, he had got much closer. It had already taken place when my father-in-law entered and accidentally trod on me.

THE INNKEEPER (*explaining*): On my son's behalf.

AZDAK (*to* THE STABLEMAN): Do you admit you started it?

THE STABLEMAN: Yes.

AZDAK: Ludovica, do you like to eat sweet things?

LUDOVICA: Yes, sunflower seeds!

AZDAK: Do you like to lie a long time in the bathtub?

LUDOVICA: Half an hour or so.

AZDAK: Public Prosecutor, drop your knife — there — on the floor.

(SHAUWA *does so.*) Ludovica, go and pick up the knife.
(LUDOVICA, *swaying her hips, does so.*) See that? (*He points at
her.*) The way it moves? The rape is now proven. By eating too
much — sweet things, especially — by lying too long in warm
water, by laziness and too soft a skin, you have raped that
unfortunate man. Do you imagine you can run around with a
behind like that and get away with it in court? This is a case
of intentional assault with a dangerous weapon! You are
sentenced to hand over to the Court the little roan which your
father liked to ride "on his son's behalf." And now, come
with me to the stables, so the Court may inspect the scene of
the crime, Ludovica.

THE STORY TELLER AND CHORUS:
All mankind should love each other but when visiting your
    brother
Take an ax along and hold it fast.
Not in theory but in practice miracles are wrought with axes
- And the age of miracles is not past.

AZDAK's *judge's chair is in a tavern. Three rich farmers stand
before* AZDAK. SHAUWA *brings him wine. In a corner stands an
old peasant woman. In the open doorway, and outside, stand
villagers looking on. An* IRONSHIRT *stands guard with a banner.*

AZDAK: The Public Prosecutor has the floor.

SHAUWA: It concerns a cow. For five weeks the defendant has
had a cow in her stable, the property of the farmer Suru. She
was also found to be in possession of a stolen ham, and a
number of cows belonging to Shutoff were killed after he had
asked the defendant to pay the rent on a piece of land.

THE FARMERS: It's a matter of my ham, Your Honor.
— It's a matter of my cow, Your Honor.
— It's a matter of my land, Your Honor.

AZDAK: Well, Granny, what have you got to say to all this?

THE OLD WOMAN: Your Honor, one night toward morning, five
weeks ago, there was a knock at my door, and outside stood
a bearded man with a cow, and said: "My dear woman, I am
the miracle-working Saint Banditus and because your son
has been killed in the war, I bring you this cow as a souvenir.
Take good care of it."

THE FARMERS: The robber, Irakli, Your Honor!
— Her brother-in-law, Your Honor!
— The cow-thief!
— The incendiary!
— He must be beheaded!
Outside, a woman screams. The crowd grows restless, retreats. Enter THE BANDIT IRAKLI *with a huge ax.*

THE BANDIT: A very good evening, dear friends! A glass of vodka!

THE FARMERS (*crossing themselves*): Irakli!

AZDAK: Public Prosecutor, a glass of vodka for our guest. And who are you?

THE BANDIT: I'm a wandering hermit, Your Honor. And thank you for the gracious gift. (*He empties the glass which* SHAUWA *has brought.*) Another!

AZDAK: I am Azdak. (*He gets up and bows.* THE BANDIT *also bows.*) The Court welcomes the foreign hermit. Go on with your story, Granny.

THE OLD WOMAN: Your Honor, that first night I didn't yet know that Saint Banditus could work miracles, it was only the cow. But one night, a few days later, the farmer's servants came to take the cow away again. Then they turned round in front of my door and went off without the cow. And on their heads sprouted bumps big as a fist. Then I knew that Saint Banditus had changed their hearts and turned them into friendly people.

THE BANDIT *roars with laughter.*

THE FIRST FARMER: I know what changed them.

AZDAK: That's fine. You can tell us later. Continue.

THE OLD WOMAN: Your Honor, the next one to become a good man was the farmer Shutoff — a devil, as everyone knows. But Saint Banditus has arranged it so that he let me off the rent on the little piece of land.

THE SECOND FARMER: Because my cows were killed in the field.

THE BANDIT *laughs.*

THE OLD WOMAN (*answering* AZDAK's *sign to continue*): And then one morning the ham came flying in at my window. It hit me in the small of the back. I'm still lame from it, see, Your Honor. (*She limps a few steps.* THE BANDIT *laughs.*) I ask Your Honor, was there ever a time when a poor old woman could get a ham without a miracle? (THE BANDIT *starts sobbing.*)

AZDAK (*rising from his chair*): Granny, that's a question that strikes straight at the Court's heart. Be so kind as to sit down here. (*Hesitating,* THE OLD WOMAN *sits in the judge's chair.* AZDAK *sits on the floor, glass in hand, reciting.*)
Granny, I almost called you Mother Grusinia the Woebegone,
The bereaved one, whose sons are at the war.
She is beaten with fists, but full of hope.
She weeps when she receives a cow.
She is surprised when she is *not* beaten.
May you render a merciful verdict on Us the Damned!
(*Bellowing at* THE FARMERS:) Admit that you don't believe in miracles, you atheists! Each of you is sentenced to pay five hundred piasters! For your godlessness! Get out! (THE FARMERS *slink out.*) And you Granny, and you (*to* THE BANDIT:) pious man, empty a pitcher of wine with the Public Prosecutor and Azdak!

THE STORY TELLER AND CHORUS:
Statute and rule he broke like a loaf to feed the folk.
On the wreck of the law he brought them to the shore,
Granted their shrill demands, took bribes from the empty hands
Of the simple and the poor.

Two years and more Azdak was a wolf to the wolf pack
And weighed with a false scale.
In the judge's seat he'd stay — the gallows not far away —
The law had a sting in its tail.

THE STORY TELLER:
But the era of disorder came to an end.
The Grand Duke returned.
The Governor's wife returned.
A trial was held.
Many people died.

The suburbs burned anew.
And fear seized Azdak.

AZDAK's *judge's chair stands again in the court of justice.*
AZDAK *sits on the floor, shaving and talking to* SHAUWA. *Noises
outside. In the rear* THE FAT PRINCE's *head is carried by on a
lance.*

AZDAK: Shauwa, the days of your slavery are numbered, maybe
even the minutes. For a long time I have held you in the iron
curb of reason, and it has torn your mouth till it bleeds. I
have lashed you with reasonable arguments and manhandled
you with logic. You are by nature a weak man, and if one
slyly throws an argument in your path, you have to snap it
up. You can't resist. By nature, you have to lick the hand of
a superior being, but superior beings can be of very different
kinds. And now with your liberation, you will soon be able
to follow your inclinations, which are low. You will be able to
follow your infallible instinct, which teaches you to plant your
fat heel on the faces of men. Gone is the era of confusion and
disorder, which I find described in the Song of Chaos. Let
us now sing that song together in memory of those terrible
days. Sit down and don't do violence to the music. Don't be
afraid. It sounds all right. And it has a fine refrain. (*He sings.*)

THE SONG OF CHAOS

Sister, hide your face! Brother, take your knife!
The times are out of joint!
Big men are full of complaints
And small men full of joy.
The city says:
"Let us drive the strong ones from our midst!"
Offices are raided. Lists of serfs are destroyed.
They have set Master's nose to the grindstone.
They who lived in the dark have seen the light.
The ebony poor box is broken.
Sesnem wood is sawed up for beds.

Who had no bread have barns full.
Who begged for alms of corn now mete it out.

SHAWA (*refrain*): Oh, oh, oh, oh.

AZDAK (*refrain*):
Where are you, General, where are you?
Please, please, please, restore order!

The nobleman's son can no longer be recognized;
The lady's child becomes the son of her slave.
The councilors meet in a shed.
Once, this man was barely allowed to sleep on the wall;
Now, he stretches his limbs in a bed.
Once, this man rowed a boat; now, he owns ships.
Their owner looks for them, but they're his no longer.
Five men are sent on a journey by their master.
"Go yourself," they say, "we have arrived."

SHAUWA (*refrain*): Oh, oh, oh, oh.

AZDAK (*refrain*):
Where are you, General, where are you?
Please, please, please, restore order!

Yes. So it might have been, had order been neglected much longer. But now the Grand Duke has returned to the capital, and the Persians have lent him an army to restore order with. The suburbs are already aflame. Go and get me the big book I always sit on. (SHAUWA *brings the big book from the judge's chair.* AZDAK *opens it.*) This is the Statute Book and I've always used it, as you can testify. Now I'd better look and see what they can do to me. I've let the down-and-outs get away with murder, and I'll have to pay for it. I helped poverty onto its skinny legs, so they'll hang me for drunkenness. I peeped into the rich man's pocket, which is bad taste. And I can't hide anywhere — everybody knows me because I have helped everybody.

SHAUWA: Someone's coming!

AZDAK (*in panic, he walks trembling to the chair*): The end! And now they'd enjoy seeing what a Great Man I am. I'll deprive them of that pleasure. I'll beg on my knees for mercy. Spittle will slobber down my chin. The fear of death is in me.

Enter NATELLA ABASHWILI, THE GOVERNOR'S WIFE, *followed by* THE ADJUTANT *and an* IRONSHIRT.

THE GOVERNOR'S WIFE: What sort of a creature is that, Shalva?

AZDAK: A willing one, Your Highness, a man ready to oblige.

THE ADJUTANT: Natella Abashwili, wife of the late Governor, has just returned and is looking for her two-year-old son, Michael. She has been informed that the child was carried off to the mountains by a former servant.

AZDAK: It will be brought back, Your Highness, at your service.

THE ADJUTANT: They say that the person in question is passing it off as her own child.

AZDAK: She will be beheaded, Your Highness, at your service.

THE ADJUTANT: That is all.

THE GOVERNOR'S WIFE (*leaving*): I don't like that man.

AZDAK (*following her to door, bowing*): At your service, Your Highness, it will all be arranged.

2

THE CHALK CIRCLE

THE STORY TELLER:

> Hear now the story of the trial
> Concerning Governor Abashwili's child
> And the establishing of the true mother
> By the famous test of the Chalk Circle.

The court of justice in Nuka. IRONSHIRTS *lead* MICHAEL *across stage and out at the back.* IRONSHIRTS *hold* GRUSHA *back with their lances under the gateway until the child has been led through. Then she is admitted. She is accompanied by the former Governor's* COOK. *Distant noises and a fire-red sky.*

GRUSHA (*trying to hide*): He's brave, he can wash himself already.

THE COOK: You're lucky. It's not a real judge. It's Azdak. Just a drunk who doesn't understand a thing. The biggest thieves have got by through him. Because he mixes everything up and the rich never offer him big enough bribes, the likes of us sometimes get off pretty well.

GRUSHA: Today I *need* luck.

THE COOK: Touch wood. (*She crosses herself.*) I'd better offer up another prayer that the judge may be drunk. (*She prays with motionless lips, while* GRUSHA *looks around, in vain, for the child.*)

THE COOK: What I can't understand is why you must hold on to it at any price if it isn't yours. In days like these.

GRUSHA: He's mine. I brought him up.

THE COOK: But have you never thought what'd happen when she came back?

GRUSHA: At first I thought I'd give him back to her. Then I thought she *wouldn't* come back.

THE COOK: And even a borrowed coat keeps a man warm, hm?

574

(GRUSHA *nods.*) I'll swear to anything for you. You're a decent girl. (*She sees the soldier* SIMON SHASHAVA *approaching.*) You have done a great wrong by Simon. I've talked with him. He can't understand it.

GRUSHA (*unaware of* SIMON'S *presence*): Just now I can't be bothered with him if he can't understand.

THE COOK: He has understood the child is not yours, but you married and not free until death you do part — he can't understand that.

GRUSHA *sees* SIMON *and greets him.*

SIMON (*gloomily*): I wanted to inform the lady I am ready to swear I am the father of the child.

GRUSHA (*low*): Thank you, Simon.

SIMON: At the same time I would like to inform the lady that I am not hereby bound to anything — nor she either.

THE COOK: That's unnecessary. She's married. You know that.

SIMON: That's her business and needs no rubbing in.

Enter an IRONSHIRT.

THE IRONSHIRT: Where's the judge? Has anyone seen the judge?

ANOTHER IRONSHIRT (*stepping forward*): The judge isn't here. There's nothing but a bed and a pitcher in the whole house. (*Exeunt* IRONSHIRTS.)

THE COOK: I hope nothing has happened to him. With any other judge you'd have about as much chance as a chicken has teeth.

GRUSHA (*who has turned away and covered her face*): Stand in front of me. I shouldn't have come to Nuka. If I run into the Ironshirt, the one I hit over head . . .

She screams. An IRONSHIRT *had stopped and, turning his back, had been listening to her. He now wheels around. It is* THE CORPORAL, *and he has a huge scar across his face.*

THE IRONSHIRT (*in the gateway*): What's the matter, Shotta? Do you know her?

THE CORPORAL (*after staring for some time*): No.

THE IRONSHIRT: She's the one who's supposed to have stolen the

Abashwili child. If you know anything about it you can make a pile of money, Shotta. (*Exit* THE CORPORAL, *cursing.*)

THE COOK: Was it him? (GRUSHA *nods.*) I think he'll keep his mouth shut, or he'd be admitting he was after the child.

GRUSHA: I'd almost forgotten I saved the child from them.

Enter THE GOVERNOR'S WIFE, *followed by* THE ADJUTANT *and two* LAWYERS.

THE GOVERNOR'S WIFE: At least there are no *common* people here, thank God. I can't stand their smell. It always gives me migraine.

THE FIRST LAWYER: Madam, I must ask you to be careful what you say until we have another judge.

THE GOVERNOR'S WIFE: But I didn't say anything, Illo Shuboladze. I *love* the people with their simple straightforward minds! It's only that their smell brings on my migraine.

THE SECOND LAWYER: There won't be many spectators. The population is sitting at home behind locked doors because of the riots in the suburbs.

THE GOVERNOR'S WIFE (*looking at* GRUSHA): Is that the creature?

THE FIRST LAWYER: Please, most gracious Natella Abashwili, I must ask you to abstain from all invective until it is absolutely certain that the Grand Duke has appointed a new judge, and we've got rid of the present one who is about the lowest fellow ever seen in a judge's gown. Things seem all set to move, you see.

Enter IRONSHIRTS *from the courtyard.*

THE COOK: Her Grace would pull your hair out on the spot if she didn't know Azdak is for the poor. He goes by the face.

IRONSHIRTS *begin fastening a rope to a beam.* AZDAK, *in chains, is led in, followed by* SHAUWA, *also in chains. The three farmers bring up the rear.*

AN IRONSHIRT: You were trying to run away, it seems. (*He strikes* AZDAK.)

ONE FARMER: Off with the judge's gown before we string him up.

IRONSHIRTS *and farmers tear off* AZDAK'S *gown. His torn underwear is visible. Then someone kicks him.*

AN IRONSHIRT (*pushing him into someone else*): If you want a heap of justice, here it is!

Accompanied by shouts of "You take it!" *and* "Let me have him, brother!" *they throw* AZDAK *back and forth until he collapses. Then he is lifted up and dragged under the noose.*

THE GOVERNOR'S WIFE (*who, during this "ball-game," has clapped her hands hysterically*): I disliked that man from the moment I first saw him.

AZDAK (*covered with blood, panting*): I can't see. Give me a rag.

AN IRONSHIRT: What is it you want to see?

AZDAK: You, you dogs! (*He wipes the blood out of his eyes with his shirt.*) Good morning, dogs! How goes it, dogs! How's the dog world? Does it smell good? Got another boot for me to lick? Are you back at each other's throats, dogs?

Accompanied by a CORPORAL, *a dust-covered* RIDER *enters. He takes some documents from a leather case, looks at them, then interrupts.*

THE RIDER: Stop! I bring a dispatch from the Grand Duke, containing the latest appointments.

THE CORPORAL (*bellowing*): Atten — shun!

THE RIDER: Of the new judge it says: "We appoint a man whom we have to thank for saving a life indispensable to the country's welfare — a certain Azdak of Nuka." Which is he?

SHAUWA (*pointing*): That's him, Your Excellency.

THE CORPORAL (*bellowing*): What's going on here?

AN IRONSHIRT: I beg to report that His Honor Azdak was already His Honor Azdak, but on these farmers' denunciation was pronounced the Grand Duke's enemy.

THE CORPORAL (*pointing at the farmers*): March them off! (*They are marched off. They bow all the time.*) See to it that His Honor Azdak is exposed to no more violence. (*Exeunt* RIDER *and* CORPORAL.)

THE COOK (*to* SHAUWA): She clapped her hands! I hope he saw it!

THE FIRST LAWYER: It's a catastrophe.

AZDAK *has fainted. Coming to, he is dressed again in judge's robes. He walks, swaying, toward the* IRONSHIRTS.

AN IRONSHIRT: What does Your Honor desire?

AZDAK: Nothing, fellow dogs, An occasional boot to lick. (*To* SHAUWA:) I pardon you. (*He is unchained.*) Get me some red wine, the sweet kind. (SHAUWA *stumbles off.*) Get out of here, I've got to judge a case. (*Exeunt* IRONSHIRTS. SHAUWA *returns with a pitcher of wine.* AZDAK *gulps it down.*) Something for my backside! (SHAUWA *brings the Statute Book, puts it on the judge's chair.* AZDAK *sits on it.*) I accept . . .

The prosecutors, among whom a worried council has been held, smile with relief. They whisper.

THE COOK: Oh dear!

SIMON: A well can't be filled with dew! they say.

THE LAWYERS (*approaching* AZDAK, *who stands up, expectantly*): A quite ridiculous case, Your Honor. The accused has abducted a child and refuses to hand it over.

AZDAK (*stretching out his hand, glancing at* GRUSHA): A most attractive person. (*He fingers the money, then sits down, satisfied.*) I open the proceedings and demand the absolute truth. (*To* GRUSHA:) Especially from you.

THE FIRST LAWYER: High Court of Justice! Blood, as the popular saying goes, is thicker than water. This old adage . . .

AZDAK (*interrupting*): The Court wants to know the lawyers' fee.

THE FIRST LAWYER (*surprised*): I beg your pardon? (AZDAK, *smiling, rubs his thumb and index finger.*) Oh, I see. Five hundred piasters, Your Honor, to answer the Court's somewhat unusual question.

AZDAK: Hear that? The question is unusual. I ask it because I listen in quite a different way when I know you are good.

THE FIRST LAWYER (*bowing*): Thank you, Your Honor. High Court of Justice, of all ties the ties of blood are strongest. Mother and child — is there a more intimate relationship? Can one tear a child from its mother? High Court of Justice, she has conceived it in the holy ecstasies of love. She has carried it in her womb. She has fed it with her blood. She has borne it with pain. High Court of Justice, it has been observed that even the wild tigress, robbed of her young, roams restless through the mountains, shrunk to a shadow. Nature herself . . .

AZDAK (*interrupting, to* GRUSHA): What's your answer to all this and anything else the lawyer might have to say?

GRUSHA: He's mine.

AZDAK: Is that all? I hope you can prove it. In any case, I wonder why you think I should assign the child to you.

GRUSHA: I brought him up like the priest says "according to my best knowledge and conscience." I always found him something to eat. Most of the time he had a roof over his head. And I went to such trouble for him. I had expenses too. I didn't look out for my own comfort. I brought the child up to be friendly with everyone, and from the beginning taught him to work as well as he could. He's still a very little thing.

THE FIRST LAWYER: Your Honor, it is significant that the girl herself doesn't claim any tie of blood between her and the child.

AZDAK: The Court takes note.

THE FIRST LAWYER: Thank you, Your Honor. Please permit a woman bowed in sorrow — who has already lost her husband and now has also to fear the loss of her child — to address a few words to you. The gracious Natella Abashwili is . . .

THE GOVERNOR'S WIFE (*quietly*): A most cruel fate, Sir, forces me to ask you to return my beloved child. It is not for me to describe to you the tortures of a bereaved mother's soul, the anxiety, the sleepless nights, the . . .

THE SECOND LAWYER (*bursting out*): It's outrageous the way this woman is being treated. She is not allowed to enter her husband's palace. The revenue of her estates is blocked. She is cold-bloodedly told that it's tied to the heir. She can't do anything without the child. She can't even pay her lawyers! (*To* THE FIRST LAWYER *who, desperate about this outburst, makes frantic gestures to keep him from speaking:*) Dear Illo Shuboladze, why shouldn't it be divulged now that it's the Abashwili estates that are at stake?

THE FIRST LAWYER: Please, Honored Sandro Oboladze! We had agreed . . . (*To* AZDAK:) Of course it is correct that the trial will also decide whether our noble client will obtain the right to dispose of the extensive Abashwili estates. I say "also" advisedly, for in the foreground stands the human tragedy of a mother, as Natella Abashwili rightly explained in the first words of her moving statement. Even if Michael Abashwili were *not* the heir of the estates, he would still be the dearly beloved child of my client.

AZDAK: Stop! The Court is touched by the mention of the estates. It's a proof of human feeling.

THE SECOND LAWYER: Thanks, Your Honor. Dear Illo Shuboladze, we can prove in any case that the woman who took the child is not the child's mother. Permit me to lay before the Court the bare facts. High Court of Justice, by an unfortunate chain of circumstances, the child Michael Abashwili was left behind while his mother was making her escape. Grusha, a palace kitchen maid, who was present on that Easter Sunday, was observed to be busy with the child . . .

THE COOK: All her mistress was thinking of was what kind of dresses she'd take along!

THE SECOND LAWYER (*unmoved*): Nearly a year later Grusha turned up in a mountain village with a child and there entered into the state of matrimony with . . .

AZDAK: How did you get to that mountain village?

GRUSHA: On foot, Your Honor. And he was mine.

SIMON: I am the father, Your Honor.

THE COOK: The child was in my care, Your Honor, for five piasters.

THE SECOND LAWYER: This man is engaged to Grusha, High Court of Justice, so his testimony is not trustworthy.

AZDAK: Are you the man she married in the mountain village?

SIMON: No, Your Honor, she married a peasant.

AZDAK (*to* GRUSHA): Why? (*Pointing at* SIMON:) Is he no good in bed? Tell the truth.

GRUSHA: We didn't get that far. I married because of the child. So he'd have a roof over his head. (*Pointing at* SIMON:) He was in the war, Your Honor.

AZDAK: And now he wants you again, huh?

SIMON: I wish to state in evidence . . .

GRUSHA (*angrily*): I am no longer free, Your Honor.

AZDAK: And the child, you claim, comes from whoring? (GRUSHA *doesn't answer.*) I'm going to ask you a question: What kind of a child is it? Is it a ragged little bastard or a child from a well-to-do family?

GRUSHA (*angrily*): He's just an ordinary child.

AZDAK: I mean — did he have refined features from the beginning?

GRUSHA: He had a nose on his face.

AZDAK: I consider that answer of yours important. It was said of me that once, before rendering a verdict, I went out and sniffed at a rosebush — tricks like that are needed nowadays. Well, I'll make it short, and not listen to any more lies. (*To* GRUSHA:) Especially not yours. (*To all the accused:*) I can imagine what you've cooked up to cheat me! I know you! You're swindlers.

GRUSHA (*suddenly*): I can quite understand your wanting to cut it short, now I've seen what you accepted!

AZDAK: Shut up! Did I accept anything from you?

GRUSHA (*while* THE COOK *tries to restrain her*): I haven't got anything.

AZDAK: That's true. Quite true. From starvelings I never get a thing. I might just as well starve, myself. You want justice, but do you want to pay for it? When you go to a butcher you know you have to pay, but you go to a judge as if you were off to a funeral supper.

SIMON (*loudly*): When the horse was shod, the horse-fly held out its leg, as the saying is.

AZDAK (*eagerly accepting the challenge*): Better a treasure in manure than a stone in a mountain stream.

SIMON: A fine day. Let's go fishing, said the angler to the worm.

AZDAK: I'm my own master, said the servant, and cut off his foot.

SIMON: I love you as a father, said the Czar to the peasants, and had the Czarevitch's head chopped off.

AZDAK: A fool's worst enemy is himself.

SIMON: However, a fart has no nose.

AZDAK: Fined ten piasters for indecent language in court! That'll teach you what justice is.

GRUSHA (*furiously*): A fine kind of justice! You play fast and loose with us because we don't talk as refined as that crowd with their lawyers!

AZDAK: That's so. You people are too dumb. It's only right you should get it in the neck.

GRUSHA: You want to hand the child over to her, and she wouldn't even know how to keep it dry, she's so "refined"! You know about as much about justice as I do!

AZDAK: There's something in that. I'm an ignorant man. I haven't even a decent pair of pants under my gown. See for yourself! With me, everything goes for food and drink — I was educated at a convent. Incidentally, I'll fine you ten piasters for contempt of court. And moreover you're a very silly girl, to turn me against you, instead of making eyes at me and wiggling your backside a little to keep me in a good temper. Twenty piasters!

GRUSHA: Even if it were thirty, I would tell you what I think of your justice, you drunken onion! (*Incoherently:*) How dare you talk to me like the cracked Isaiah on the church window? As if you *were* somebody? For you weren't born to this. You weren't born to rap your own mother on the knuckles if she snitches her little bowl of salt. Aren't you ashamed of yourself when you see how I tremble before you? You have made yourself their servant so no one will take their houses away, and they'd stolen them! Since when have houses belonged to the bedbugs? But you're on the watch, or they couldn't drag our men into their wars! You bribe-taker! (AZDAK *half gets up, starts beaming. With his little hammer he half-heartedly knocks on the table as if to get silence. As* GRUSHA's *scolding continues, he only beats time with his hammer.*) I've no respect for you. No more than for a thief or a robber with a knife! You can do what you want. You can take the child away from me, a hundred against one, but I tell you one thing: only extortioners should be chosen for a profession like yours, and men who rape children! As punishment! They should sit in judgment on their fellow creatures. Which is worse than to hang from gallows.

AZDAK (*sitting down*): Now it'll be thirty! And I won't go on squabbling with you as though we were in a tavern. What'd happen to my dignity as a judge? Anyway, I've lost interest in your case. Where's the couple who wanted a divorce? (*To* SHAUWA:) Bring 'em in. This case is adjourned for fifteen minutes.

THE FIRST LAWYER (*to* THE GOVERNOR'S WIFE): Even without using the rest of the evidence, Madam, we have the verdict in the bag.

THE COOK (*to* GRUSHA): You've gone and spoiled your chances with him. You won't get the child now.

THE GOVERNOR'S WIFE: Shalva, my smelling salts!

Enter a very old couple.

AZDAK: I accept . . . (*The old couple don't understand.*) I hear you want to be divorced. How long have you been living together?

THE OLD WOMAN: Forty years, Your Honor.

AZDAK: And why do you want a divorce?

THE OLD MAN: We don't like each other, Your Honor.

AZDAK: Since when?

THE OLD WOMAN: Oh, from the very beginning, Your Honor.

AZDAK: I'll think about your request and render my verdict when I'm through with the other case. (SHAUWA *leads them back.*) I need the child. (*He beckons* GRUSHA *to him, and bends not unkindly toward her.*) I've noticed you have a soft spot for justice. I don't believe he's your child, but if he were yours, woman, wouldn't you want him to be rich? You'd only have to say he isn't yours, and he'd have a palace and many horses in his stable and many beggars on his doorstep and many soldiers in his service and many petitioners in his courtyard, wouldn't he? What do you say — don't you want him to be rich?

GRUSHA *is silent.*

THE STORY TELLER: Hear now what the angry girl thought but did not say:

Had he golden shoes to wear
He'd be cruel as a bear.
Evil would his life disgrace.
He'd laugh in my face.

Carrying a heart of flint
Is too troublesome a stint.
Being powerful and bad
Is hard for a lad.

Then let hunger be his foe!
Hungry men and women, no.
Let him fear the darksome night
But not daylight!

AZDAK: I think I understand you, woman.

GRUSHA (*suddenly and loudly*): I won't give him up. I've raised him, and he knows me.

Enter SHAUWA *with the child.*

THE GOVERNOR'S WIFE: It's in rags!

GRUSHA: That's not true. I wasn't given time to put his good shirt on.

THE GOVERNOR'S WIFE: It must have been in a pigsty.

GRUSHA (*furiously*): I'm not a pig, but there are some who are! Where did you leave your child?

THE GOVERNOR'S WIFE: I'll show you, you vulgar creature! (*She is about to throw herself on* GRUSHA, *but is restrained by her* LAWYERS.) She's a criminal, she must be whipped. Immediately!

THE SECOND LAWYER (*holding his hand over her mouth*): Gracious Natella Abashwili, you promised . . . Your Honor, the plaintiff's nerves . . .

AZDAK: Plaintiff and defendant! The Court has listened to your case, and has come to no decision as to who the real mother is. I, as a judge, am obliged to choose a mother for the child. I'll make a test. Shauwa, get a piece of chalk and draw a circle on the floor. (SHAUWA *does so*.) Now place the child in the center. (SHAUWA *puts* MICHAEL, *who smiles at* GRUSHA, *in the center of the circle*.) Stand near the circle, both of you. (THE GOVERNOR'S WIFE *and* GRUSHA *step up to the circle*.) Now each of you take the child by one hand. (*They do so*.) The true mother is she who can pull the child out of the circle toward herself.

THE SECOND LAWYER (*quickly*): High Court of Justice, I object! The fate of the great Abashwili estates, which are bound to the child, as the heir, should not be made dependent on such a doubtful duel. In addition, my client does not command the strength of this person, who is accustomed to physical work.

AZDAK: She looks pretty well fed to me. Pull! (THE GOVERNOR'S WIFE *pulls the child out of the circle on her side.* GRUSHA *has let go and stands aghast*.) What's the matter with you? You didn't pull!

GRUSHA: I didn't hold on to him.

THE FIRST LAWYER (*congratulating* THE GOVERNOR'S WIFE): What did I say! The ties of blood!

GRUSHA (*running to* AZDAK): Your Honor, I take back everything I said against you. I ask your forgiveness. If only I could keep him till he can speak all the words. He knows a few.

AZDAK: Don't influence the Court. I bet you only know twenty yourself. All right, I'll do the test once more, to make certain. (*The two women take up their positions again.*) Pull! (*Again* GRUSHA *lets go of the child*.)

GRUSHA (*in despair*): I brought him up! Shall I tear him to pieces? I can't do it!

AZDAK (*rising*): And in this manner the Court has established the true mother. (*To* GRUSHA:) Take your child and be off. I advise you not to stay in the city with him. (*To* THE GOVERNOR'S WIFE:) And you disappear before I fine you for fraud. Your estates fall to the city. They'll be converted into a playground for the children. They need one, and I've decided it shall be called after me: Azdak's Garden. (THE GOVERNOR'S WIFE *has fainted and is carried out by the* LAWYERS *and* THE ADJUTANT. GRUSHA *stands motionless.* SHAUWA *leads the child toward her.*) Now I'll take off this judge's gown — it has grown too hot for me. I'm not cut out for a hero. In token of farewell I invite you all to a little dance outside on the meadow. Oh, I had almost forgotten something in my excitement . . . to sign the divorce decree.

Using the judge's chair as a table, he writes something on a piece of paper, and prepares to leave. Dance music has started.

SHAUWA (*having read what is on the paper*): But that's not right. You've not divorced the old people. You've divorced Grusha!

AZDAK: Have I divorced the wrong couple? What a pity! And I never retract! If I did, how could we keep order in our state? (*To the old couple:*) I'll invite you to my party instead. You don't mind dancing with each other, do you? (*To* GRUSHA *and* SIMON:) I've got forty piasters coming from *you.*

SIMON (*pulling out his purse*): Cheap at the price, Your Honor. And many thanks.

AZDAK (*pocketing the cash*): I'll need this.

GRUSHA (*to* MICHAEL): So we'd better leave the city tonight, Michael? (*To* SIMON:) You like him?

SIMON: With my respects, I like him.

GRUSHA: And now I'll tell you: I took him because on that Easter Sunday, I got engaged to you. And so he's a child of love. Michael, let's dance.

She dances with MICHAEL, SIMON *dances with* THE COOK, *the old couple with each other.* AZDAK *stands lost in thought. The dancers soon hide him from view. Occasionally he is seen, but less and less as more couples join the dance.*

THE STORY TELLER:

And after that evening Azdak disappeared and was not seen again.

The people of Grusinia did not forget him but long remembered

The period of his judging as a brief golden age
Almost an age of justice.

All the couples dance off. AZDAK *has disappeared.*

But you, you who have listened to the Story of the Chalk
  Circle,
Take note what men of old concluded:
That what there is shall go to those who are good for it,
Thus: the children to the motherly, that they prosper
The carts to good drivers, that they are driven well
And the valley to the waterers, that it bring forth fruit.